About the Author

Photo by Michael Harter.

John Renard received his doctorate in Islamic Studies from Harvard University's Department of Near Eastern Languages and Civilizations in 1978. Since then he has been teaching courses in Islam, Buddhism, and Hinduism, religion and the arts, and comparative theology in the Department of Theological Studies at Saint Louis University. Earlier publications include *All the King's Falcons: Rumi on Prophets and Revelation* (SUNY, 1994); *Seven Doors to Islam and Windows on the House of Islam* (California, 1996, 1998); and *Islam and the Heroic Image: Themes in Literature and the Visual Arts* (Mercer, 1999), as well as volumes on Islam, Buddhism, and Hinduism in Paulist Press's "101 Questions" series. His most recent books are *Friends of God: Islamic Images of Piety, Commitment, and Servanthood* (California, 2008), *Tales of God's Friends: Islamic Hagiography in Translation* (California, 2009), and *Islam and Christianity: Theological Themes in Comparative Perspective* (California, 2011).

Also from Visible Ink Press

THE
HANDY
RELIGION
ANSWER
BOOK

THE HANDY RELIGION ANSWER BOOK

Visible Ink Press®
43311 Joy Rd., #414
Canton, MI 48187–2075

Visible Ink Press is a registered trademark of Visible Ink Press LLC.

Most Visible Ink Press books are available at special quantity discounts when purchased in bulk by corporations, organizations, or groups. Customized printings, special imprints, messages, and excerpts can be produced to meet your needs. For more information, contact Special Markets Director, Visible Ink Press, www.visibleinkpress.com, or 734–667–3211.

Managing Editor: Kevin S. Hile
Art Director: Mary Claire Krzewinski
Typesetting: Marco Di Vita
Proofreaders: Sharon R. Gunton and Shoshana Hurwitz
Indexing: Shoshana Hurwitz

ISBN 978–1–57859–379–8

Library of Congress Cataloging-in-Publication Data

Renard, John, 1944-
  The handy religion answer book / by John Renard. — 2nd ed.
    p. cm.
  Includes bibliographical references (p.   ) index.
  ISBN 978-1-57859-379-8
  1. Religions — Miscellanea. I. Title.
  BL80.3.R47 2012
  200 — dc23
                                    2011050804

Printed in the United States of America

10 9 8 7 6 5 4 3 2 1

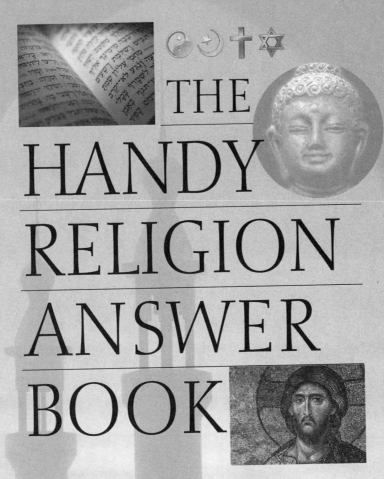

THE
HANDY
RELIGION
ANSWER
BOOK

SECOND EDITION

John Renard, Ph.D.

VISIBLE
INK
PRESS

Detroit

Contents

Religious Roles ... Holidays and Regular
Observances ... Customs and Rituals

SHINTO ... 411

History and Sources ... Religious Beliefs ...
Signs and Symbols ... Membership, Community, Diversity ... Leadership, Authority, and
Religious Roles ... Holidays and Regular
Observances ... Customs and Rituals

Acknowledgments

I am indebted to scholars too numerous to mention by name here, although the works listed in the "further reading" section offer some idea of the throng of dedicated specialists on whose work this volume relies on. Any errors of fact are, of course, my responsibility. My deepest gratitude goes, as always, to my spouse, Mary Pat, for her unfailing good humor through the project. Special thanks go to David Vila, then a graduate student at Saint Louis University, for his advice on an early draft, to Darius Makuja for his assistance early in the project, and to Elizabeth Staley Evans for her editorial and research assistance in preparing the final draft of the first edition. For their suggestions as to how to revise for the present edition, I thank graduate students in Comparative Theology courses in Fall 2009 and 2010: Alden Bass, Chih-Yin Chen, Jared Goff, Robert Munshaw, Alison Rose, Andrew Russell, and Caitlin Stevenson. To Alex Giltner and Jacob van Sickle, both of Saint Louis University, I am very grateful for their extensive assistance in various stages of the preparation and completion of this revised edition.

I thank also VIP publisher Roger Jänecke for requesting a revised edition, managing editor Kevin Hile, page and cover designer Mary Claire Krzewinski, typesetter Marco Di Vita, indexer Shoshana Hurwitz, and proofreader Sharon R. Gunton.

I am grateful also to Michael Harter, SJ, Beata Grant of Washington University, David Oughton of Saint Louis University, and the St. Louis Art Museum for kindly allowing me to use their photos. Unless otherwise credited, all photographs are by the author.

Photo Credits

Photos provided by Shutterstock, or by David Oughton, David Edwards, Beata Grant, and Michael Harter, S.J., where credited in the caption, except as indicated below.

Photos provided by **Dr. John Renard**: pp. 9, 10, 12, 15, 24, 25, 26, 27, 28, 39, 44, 60, 67, 81, 88, 90, 92, 93, 105, 110, 116, 117, 119, 129, 131, 134, 142, 150, 153, 157, 167, 175, 176, 178, 182, 241, 245, 251, 255, 261, 262, 263, 264, 267, 275, 285, 290,

300, 311, 313, 321, 323, 326, 336, 341, 344, 345, 346, 351, 354, 357, 363, 369, 371, 380, 381, 383, 384, 390, 401, 404, 408, 412, 422, 430, 431, 432, 434, 435, 437, 443, 444, 446, 452, 454, 458, 462, 463.

Photos provided by the **St. Louis Art Museum.** p. 124: purchase, 32:1948; p. 186: Vishnu statue, purchase, 2:1964; p. 186: Shiva statue, Friends Fund, 70:1962; p. 193: W. K. Bixby Oriental Art Purchase Fund, 26:1984; p. 208: statue of the goddess Parvati, funds given by Merrill Trust Foundation, 146:1966; p. 210: Shiva Nataraja, purchase 16:1978; p. 304: Daoist deity, purchase, 169:1919; p. 337: Daoist female Immortal He Xian'gu, gift of Dr. and Mrs. Frederick O. Schwartz, 207:1977; p. 379: "Pavilion in a Landscape," bequest of Leona J. Beckmann, 23:1985.

Wikimedia Commons: image of Imam Ghazali, p. 162, published in the US before 1923 and public domain in the US.

Introduction

Persistent predictions of the virtually certain demise of religion continue to run afoul of the facts. During the decade since the first edition of this volume appeared, religion and spirituality have only become more influential forces in the lives of hundreds of millions of people across the globe. Unfortunately, the perdurance and expansion of distinct faith communities has too often perpetuated age-old divisions rather than fostering unity within the larger human community. As a result, the need for adherents of the many and varied traditions and sub-communities of faith to pursue actively more accurate knowledge of the belief systems of others has risen dramatically.

New and ongoing regional and global geo-political realignments present increasingly daunting challenges. Our collective need for greater appreciation of the cultures of West, South and East Asia demands deeper understanding of the ancient systems of faith and values that remain integral to those cultures. Even in "officially" secularist societies, such as those of China and Russia, the pulse of historic religious energies still animates and motivates millions of people. The role of the signature wisdom at the heart of the faith traditions remains a key to understanding the shared humanity that unites us far more than our distinctive creeds divide us.

A word about the scope, orientation, and overall content of this book is in order here. Its title is both deceptively simple and outrageously presumptuous on the face of it. It purports to reduce an enormously complex, ancient and virtually universal human phenomenon to a set of brief packets of highly selective information, and implies that one can compare approaches to those discrete topics across a broad range of social, cultural, philosophical, and ethical contexts. And as for the choice of what qualifies here as "religious traditions," the reader will understandably ask why these specific traditions – Judaism, Christianity, Islam, Hinduism, Buddhism, Daoism, Confucianism, and Shinto? Indeed, are not Buddhism and Confucianism as often identified as "philosophies" rather than "religious faith" traditions? And why *only* these, to the exclusion of several other structurally similar traditions perhaps less widely known, but arguably of great significance in the history of human thought – such as

Zoroastrianism, Sikhism, Jainism, and Baha'i traditions? Why not include the "archa-ic" or "ancient" wellsprings of speculation on eternal verities such as the Mesopotami-an, Egyptian, and Graeco-Roman roots of religion, or the deeply rooted Wiccan, Druid and various "nature-oriented" systems? And what of the widespread but not so obvi-ously "organized" religious heritages of the "first nations" or "indigenous peoples," which have surely embraced huge numbers of people across the globe?

I have no truly satisfying answers to these and other questions, but here are the principles of selection operative here. Limitation of space in a "general interest" vol-ume such as this is a major concern. Second, the traditions to which I have been able to devote most attention over years of study are several of the more "structured" tradi-tions, still current and growing, and representative of major cultural, ethnic, and geo-political swaths of humankind. I would very much have liked to be able to give ade-quate attention to Native American traditions, for example, but they are in fact many and subtly varied and beyond my own academic scope. Perhaps the best example of a recent unified approach to an "indigenous" cluster of religious beliefs and practice that has in addition gained truly global reach is Stephen Prothero's chapter on "Yoru-ba Religion" in *God Is Not One: The Eight Rival Religions That Run the World—and Why Their Differences Matter* (HarperOne, 2010). He offers an intriguing description of how the originally Nigerian traditions have morphed into a significant component of popular traditions in a surprising array of current cultural contexts. Readers will also find a useful selection of "case studies" on a broader array of "indigenous" tradi-tions in Christopher Partridge (ed.), *Introduction to World Religions* (Fortress, 2005), part three.

One unfortunate development in perceptions of religion in our world since the original publication of *The Handy Religion Answer Book* is the increasing acceptance of the belief that "religious" justifications of violence somehow present a greater threat in the long term than do campaigns or ideologies of violence based on avowedly secular, ethnic, political or economic motives. In reality, however, it is not religion, or some gruesome distortion of it, that constitutes the most intractable problem in this regard. It is the fundamental human tendency to resort to violence long before we have tried other options adequately. We human beings have given evidence of abun-dantly poor judgment and impatience in millennia of bad behavior. In the process we have, sadly, shown not the slightest embarrassment about blaming our choices on our versions of supreme beings—deities who turn out to be every bit as petty and vindic-tive as we are. If "God" by any of dozens of names is what the great faith traditions claim God is, violence in God's name is unthinkable. Alas, our most prevalent images of "God" are degraded versions of the highest values manifest in the foundational insights of the great faith traditions.

Background and Methodological Considerations

However any of us feels personally about religion, it remains a powerful and perva-sive force in our world. To dismiss religion as so much superstition and delusional thinking is to brush aside one of the most important features of the human condition: what people believe, and why they believe it, profoundly influence the way they act. Religious beliefs and cultural assumptions are often so intimately intertwined that it is rarely, if ever, possible to disentangle them. It is possible, for the sake of clarity and to promote further discussion, to provide a general outline of major themes in history, belief, structure, and practice. But it is essential to keep in mind that any study of a phenomenon so complex and broad begins from a particular point of view, makes certain working assumptions, and must inevitably indulge in the luxury of sweeping generalizations.

A word about my own perspective on the practice and study of religion will be useful here. Raised in the Roman Catholic tradition, I began my professional study of religion after completing undergraduate work in Philosophy and Classical Languages. Graduate study toward an M.A. in Biblical Languages and Literature focused on the critical examination of the Hebrew and Christian scriptures. Since finishing a Ph.D. in Islamic Studies in 1978, I have been teaching courses on Islam and other non-Christian religious traditions to undergraduate and graduate students. I remain an adherent of Roman Catholicism, but I work from the conviction that it is my professional responsibility to ask hard critical questions about the nature and function of religion — beginning with my own. One might legitimately ask whether my Roman Catholic background might lead me to compare other traditions using my own as some sort of standard. My answer is that I have sought to set up categories of comparability that privilege no tradition in particular, drawing from a broad spectrum of religious studies concepts, and in no instance do I engage in the comparative evaluation of truth claims. Whether or not I have achieved an appropriate balance, others must decide.

Another personal conviction, based on over forty years of studying and teaching the history of religions, has had a particularly formative influence on my approach to the subject at hand. It is this: I am persuaded that, as the great traditions teach in so many ways, there is an "absolute truth" that is somehow accessible to human beings honestly in quest of it. But I am equally convinced that human beings are by definition incapable of possessing that truth either exhaustively, so that any person or group can claim to have it fully, or exclusively, so that the world divides itself neatly between the "we" who own the truth and the "they" who are simply out of luck. Any such view both inflates human capabilities and reduces transcendent realities to pocket-size trinkets. This does not mean that I am one of those intellectually indecisive people called "relativists," who believe either that all religious traditions are the same or that one is as good as another. I do believe, however, that God, or Ultimate Reality, is so much greater than any religious tradition, or all put together, can claim to master and dispense; and that each individual who seeks with a sincere heart the center and goal of his or her life will be led to it. Meanwhile, one of the noblest and most useful tasks we can commit ourselves to is a greater understanding of how and why other people believe as they do. I believe, perhaps naively but nonetheless firmly, that the world is richer for its religious pluralism, and that it would also be safer if the quest for mutual understanding of that diversity were a higher priority.

I begin with a number of assumptions about religion — that is, aspects of the subject that a book like this will not and could not, without expanding to many volumes, begin to address. In addition to the assertions with which I opened this introduction, here are several other "givens," naturally arguable and open to debate, on which this book builds. One is that it can be misleading to try to reduce any of the world's major religious traditions to a handful of questions and answers. But it can also be very helpful to do so occasionally, so long as one keeps in mind that these tidbits of information are offered as an invitation to dig deeper.

Another assumption is that because religion is so susceptible to misunderstanding and caricature, specialists in religious studies have a responsibility to devise balanced approaches to the subject. It is my hope that foregrounding my own biases and limitations will assist the reader in evaluating the approach in these pages. Misinformation about religious beliefs and practices, especially those of "other" people, abounds and has a way of perpetuating itself. This broad survey attempts to provide solid, basic information in the hope that readers will be encouraged to pursue particular aspects of this enormous subject and fill in for themselves the kind of historical context a book this size cannot provide.

This revised *The Handy Religion Answer Book* is organized in three parts. It first devotes a chapter each to the three traditions of Middle Eastern origin, namely, Judaism, Christianity, and Islam. Next to be covered are the two largest traditions of south Asian origin, Hinduism and Buddhism; the final chapters deal with three traditions of east Asian origin: China's Daoism and popular traditions, Confucianism together with imperial traditions, and Japan's Shinto. Each of the chapters organizes the material in seven subsections: origins and history; religious beliefs; signs and symbols; membership, community and diversity; leadership, authority, and organization; holidays and regular observances; and customs and rituals. In order to facilitate comparison, many of the questions are phrased generically rather than specifically, so that readers will hear echoes of questions posed in other sections. Other questions are concept-specific, especially where the issues at hand are already widely mentioned in popular media and thus readily recognizable.

Finally, these religious traditions all represent vast and complex developments over many centuries and in countless cultural contexts. Reducing them, as I have here, to fifty or sixty pages apiece means barely scratching the surface to offer the merest hint of their richness. This volume's modest goal is to provide the kind of solid, basic information upon which interested readers might build a broader and deeper understanding of these world-treasures through further investigation.

New in This Edition

First, at the suggestion of students and a number of readers, I have replaced the original general introduction to "Religion Studies" with a glossary of religious studies terminology for easy reference. Second, also as a result of reader suggestions, I have generally streamlined the coverage, by combining some questions on similar topics and making space for new material by removing questions on such matters of marginally "religious" import as religious education, conversion in traditions for which that is of little or no importance, creedal or doctrinal questions of minor significance in some traditions. Clearer organization also dictated that I move material from the former rather amorphous category "Powers and Personalities" into more appropriate places in other major categories. This streamlining and restructuring also makes for better flow and more logical order of individual topics.

Third, I have added questions on various topics, including religion and violence and important sub-organizations claiming affiliation with the major faith communities.

Fourth, a number of new sidebars and appendices include: glossaries of technical terms for each tradition; timelines for each tradition within the respective chapters as well as a global blended timeline in the back of this book (as in the first edition); summaries of major sub-groups and organizations, such as Buddhist lineages, for example; maps showing the general coverage areas for each of the major families of faith traditions.

Finally, a "For Further Reading" section provides a selection of some of the many fine publications that have appeared on the major traditions in the past decade or so.

A Note on Pronunciations: Basic Pronunciation Hints for Chinese Terms

The Handy Religion Answer Book makes use of the pinyin transliteration system, rather than the Wade-Giles, since the pinyin is rapidly replacing the older method. Consonants are generally pronounced as they appear, with several exceptions. An "x" sounds close to "sh"; "q" sounds like "ch" as in "cheek"; "z" is like a "dz"; "c" before a vowel is like a "tz."

Hints for Pronouncing Japanese Words

Consonants are pronounced very much as they appear. Vowels are always "long" (e.g., a = "ah," e = "ay," i = "ee," o = "oh," u = "oo.") Two items that are difficult for many people are these: the letters "ky" and "ry" followed by a vowel (kyo, ryu) are pronounced as a single syllable, so Tokyo is not To-kee-o, but To-kyo. When the letter "i" comes after "sh" and before "t" or "k," as in the company name Matsushita or the name of the Sumo champion Konishiki, the "i" is elided. So, Matsush'ta and Konish'ki. Similarly, a "u" between an "s" and another consonant (like "s," "t" or "k") is often elided, as in the name of the important Tokyo shrine, Yasukuni, pronounced Yas'kuni.

JUDAISM

HISTORY AND SOURCES

When and where did **Judaism begin**? Was it **founded** by an individual person?

Jewish tradition traces its beginnings back nearly four thousand years. Abraham is the key figure here, not as a founder but as the first "Hebrew" to receive a revelation from God. Genesis 11–25 contain the bulk of our scriptural information about Abraham. According to tradition, God told Abraham to leave his homeland in Mesopotamia (present-day Iraq). Trusting completely in God, the patriarch agreed to travel where God would lead him. As Abraham journeyed across the central Middle East from Mesopotamia to Egypt and back to what is now southern Israel, he and his son Isaac laid the foundations of a monotheistic tradition. Abraham's grandson Jacob sired the twelve sons who would bestow their names on the original twelve tribes. The second half of Genesis recounts their stories. But the appearance of Moses, beginning with the story of his being adopted by Pharaoh, marks another major turning point.

It is believed that Moses lived toward the end of the third quarter of the second millennium B.C.E. (about 1300 B.C.E.). His story occupies a larger portion of the Jewish scriptures than any other single figure, stretching from the beginning of Exodus to the end of Deuteronomy. From his inaugural revelation at the Burning Bush to leading the people called Israel (the name divinely given to the patriarch Jacob) on a journey that culminated at the banks of the Jordan River, Moses' story is that of the formation of a community of faith. At the center of that formative epoch is the pivotal revelation of the Law at Sinai which takes place at about the midpoint of that journey. Sources do not record use of the word "Jew" (from the Hebrew *yehudi*) until many centuries after Moses' time. Then the word referred to a member of the tribe of Judah, which in turn had given its name to the region called Judaea.

1

What are Judaism's **principal sacred writings**?

According to a traditional Jewish reckoning, the Hebrew Bible is a collection of twenty-four "books" divided into three main groupings: Torah, Prophets, and Writings. Jews, and Christians generally, identify the Torah as comprised of five texts: Genesis, Exodus, Leviticus, Numbers, and Deuteronomy. In the category of "Prophets" (*Nevi'im*), Jewish tradition includes eight books. The four "former" prophets are: Joshua, Judges (as individual books), I and II Samuel as one book, I and II Kings as another. Comprising the four "latter" prophets are: Isaiah, Jeremiah, Ezekiel, and the twelve "minor" prophets grouped as one. (*Trei Assar* in Aramaic, including Hosea, Joel, Amos, Obadiah, Jonah, Micah, Nahum, Habakkuk, Zephaniah, Haggai, Zechariah, and Malachi—called "minor" only because they are shorter texts.) Under the heading of Writings (*Ketuvim*) are a total of eleven books, because Ezra and Nehemiah are considered as one, as are I and II Chronicles. The "Five Scrolls" (*Megillot*) include the Song of Songs, Ruth, Lamentations, Ecclesiastes, and Esther; Psalms, Proverbs, Job and Daniel complete the "Writings." Taken together the *Torah, Nevi'im* and *Ketuvim* are designated by the acronym *TaNaKh*.

Torah Scrolls showing decorative finials (*rimonim*) and small hands (*yad* attached to cords) used to point to sacred text without touching it directly. Temple Shaare Emeth, St. Louis, Missouri. (Photo courtesy of David Oughton).

What is the **meaning of Torah**? Do Jews believe Moses wrote it all? What about "oral" Torah?

Torah is a Hebrew word generally translated as "teaching" or "instruction." In reference to the Hebrew scriptures, Torah means the first five books, Genesis through Deuteronomy. According to tradition, Moses himself composed the whole of the Torah under divine inspiration. This ancient attribution has the benefit of lending maximum authority to the earliest sacred texts by associating them with the man most identified with the divine revelation that shaped the faith community known as Judaism. Modern scholarship has demonstrated convincingly the historical improbability of the traditional attribution. In its most general sense, Torah means revealed or divine Law—all that God requires of Jews. But as the Jewish community has grown and spread, moving into new lands and cultural settings, interpreting the scriptural

Torah in practical terms has presented challenges. A highly stylized traditional reconstruction of sacred history suggests the following sequence of events.

When a group of Jews returned to Israel from exile in Babylon in the late sixth century B.C.E., many Jews no longer knew Hebrew. In the mid-fifth century B.C.E., Ezra "rediscovered" long-lost texts of scripture, but when he proposed to renew the community's knowledge of the sacred texts, he confronted a serious problem: he would have to design a way of interpreting the Hebrew sources into Aramaic. Ezra then commissioned scholars who could translate the Torah into Aramaic as it was being read aloud to the people. That translation, or paraphrase, was itself a kind of commentary on the sacred text. Thus began the phenomenon called "oral" Torah. From the fifth century B.C.E. on, classes of scholars would oversee its elaboration. One generation would pass oral tradition down to the next until it became so extensive that it had to be written down to be preserved. Then a new class of scholars would initiate commentary on the now written "oral" law, extending the process further, until once again the burgeoning oral tradition had to be committed to writing or be lost forever. Recent research suggests, however, that even during the Babylonian exile, scholars kept the study of Hebrew sources very much alive. It turns out that Ezra and Nehemiah played a less revolutionary role in the story, and the importance of the kind of Aramaic "translation" (*targum*) attributed to Ezra did not arise until much later.

How do Jews **interpret** their **scriptures**?

Biblical interpretation began within the Hebrew scriptures themselves, with later authors referring to the earlier texts and thus at least implicitly commenting on their meaning in new contexts. By the time the latest texts were written, new historical circumstances had inevitably led to interpretations of events long past that earlier authors could scarcely have imagined. According to tradition, one of the earliest rabbis to devise a systematic foundation for biblical exegesis was Hillel the Elder (c. 50 B.C.E.–30 C.E.). His "seven principles" (*middot*) of exegesis taught generations of scholars how to approach the sacred text rationally and consistently. One example of an important principle is called the "light and heavy" (*kal va-khomer*). According to this principle, if the scripture allows or prohibits a certain action in a minor matter, one is justified in assuming the same allowance or prohibition applies in a more serious case. If the Law allows you to rescue an animal from a ditch on the Sabbath, surely it will also permit alleviating a human being's suffering.

Later rabbinical scholars devised still more comprehensive and elaborate exegetical frameworks. Perhaps the most famous is summed up in the acronym *PaRDeS* (an ancient Persian term meaning "paradise"). Each of the uppercase consonants stands for a Hebrew term referring to one of the four principal levels or methods of exegesis. *Peshat* is the literal sense and the kind of interpretation prevalent in oral Torah; *remez* looks for the allegorical meaning; *derash* ("inquire") derives the homiletical or ethical significance; and *sod* ("mystery") unveils the mystical significance of a text.

3

Torah scroll being carried in family procession at Wailing Wall. (Photo courtesy of David Oughton.)

Jewish exegesis has devised highly sophisticated methods of drawing out the various meanings of the sacred text and has preserved the results in an enormous library known as rabbinical literature.

What's the difference between **prophetic** and **apocalyptic literature**?

It is not always possible to apply the distinction neatly to important texts in the Hebrew Bible, but it is useful to keep the following important differences in mind. First, prophets and apocalypticists have different missions. Prophets tend to be action-oriented, passing critical judgment on individual events as they unfold in the political and religious development of Israel, which is under both divine and Davidic sovereignty. Apocalyptic works are products of people dedicated to the written word as a vehicle for passing judgment on the whole of history, not just that of Israel and its monarchy. Second, the content of the biblical works they have produced differs markedly. Prophets describe specific examples of injustice seen in the context of an ethical struggle within Israel, which God's judgment over his people will resolve on the coming "Day of the Lord." Writers of apocalyptic works offer more generalized and highly symbolic visions of the reign of evil, visions that only a divinely commissioned "angel" can interpret. God's judgment will be manifest in a final cosmic cataclysm, a final battle (sometimes called Armageddon) between the forces of Good and Evil. Finally, prophetic texts generally claim authorship by name while apocalyptic texts typically use a pseudonym, either to add credibility to their visions of the "future" or to avoid retaliation from the authorities of their own day.

What are the Dead Sea Scrolls?

In the spring of 1947, a young Bedouin shepherd, Muhammad adh-Dhib, discovered eleven ancient leather scrolls in a cave located in the cliffs above the northeastern corner of the Dead Sea. The eleven so-called Dead Sea Scrolls comprise seven distinct manuscripts. Through the work of E. L. Sukenik and other authorities, the eleven scrolls have been authenticated as genuine documents of roughly the second century B.C.E. to the time of the unsuccessful Jewish revolt against Rome (66–70 C.E.). The manuscripts were written variously in Hebrew and Aramaic. They include portions of several of the books of the Old Testament, Apocrypha, prayers, hymns, commentaries, and rules; the most important set is "The Manual of Discipline."

Between 1949 and 1956, archaeological exploration of the area west of the Dead Sea was carried out by G. Lankester Harding and Father Roland De Vaux. The two men explored the original cave and more than two hundred others, finding numerous additional fragments of scrolls and other evidence of human occupancy. Most of these caves are located in the vicinity of Khirbet (Arabic for "ruin") Qumran—itself less than a mile south of the original cave—and in the ravine of Wadi Murabbaat some ten miles farther south. The manuscripts discovered at Wadi Murabbaat are very important in that, unlike those at Khirbet Qumran, they indicate that the Hebrew Bible had reached its final form by about 140 C.E. The older Khirbet Qumran biblical manuscripts reveal a scriptural text that was still evolving.

The discoveries of the Dead Sea Scrolls stand among the greatest finds in the history of modern archaeology. The scrolls shed much light on the religious and political life of the Jewish people in the centuries just before and after the time of Christ. In addition, the documents are of great importance for the understanding of early Christianity. The biblical scrolls antedate the earliest extant Hebrew text by about a thousand years. Fragments of the Isaiah text discovered at Wadi Murabbaat are in complete agreement with the current biblical text, thus confirming the authenticity of later Hebrew texts.

Did Jews develop any **post-biblical sacred texts**?

Jewish extrabiblical literature is vast and expansive. Two large bodies of literature are generally known as Talmud and Midrash. Talmud consists of the systematization of successive waves of originally oral commentary by religious scholars on sacred scripture. First, views of earlier generations of rabbis were codified in the Mishnah. Subsequent generations further commented on the Mishnaic material, and that was brought together in the Gemara. Then the Mishnah and Gemara were combined in the Talmud, which was produced in two versions, the Jerusalem or Palestinian Talmud and the considerably larger Babylonian Talmud.

The Shrine of the Book in Jerusalem is a museum housing priceless archaeological remains, most importantly the manuscripts discovered at the ancient Essene monastery of Qumran overlooking the Dead Sea.

Much of the content of the Talmud is described by the term *halakhah,* a word that means literally "proceeding, walking." It refers to the bulk of Talmud and more generally to the literature interpreting the specific rules and legislation found in the scripture. The plural of the term, *halakhot,* came to mean all the specific laws derived through exegesis, even if not explicitly mentioned in scripture. Halakhic literature peers into every conceivable nook and cranny of Jewish daily life, prescribing in minutest detail how the Torah should be used as a guide here and now. The term *midrash* means "study, commentary, amplification" and originally meant the method used by all scholars of sacred scripture. Hence, much Talmudic material is midrashic, for example. But eventually midrash came to be more popularly identified with the non-halakhic material in the Talmud and with another type of literature called *aggadah* (or *haggadah,* meaning "narrative"). Works of aggadic midrash, like halakhic works, primarily comment on scripture. But unlike *halakhah, aggadah* is more concerned with reading between the lines. Aggadic works tell the story behind the story and say little about specific legal implications. As such, *aggadah* is generally much more appealing and entertaining, offering interpretations that are frequently very moving, charming, and droll.

Were Jews ever **ruled** by a **monarchy**?

The thorny issue of monarchy arose during the later years of the Judges (c. 1200–1000 B.C.E.), who ruled Israel after Joshua had led the establishment of the people in the newly reached Promised Land of Canaan. Some argued that Israel should be like all the surrounding lands, each ruled by its own king. They saw no other solution to the lawlessness they believed had overcome their land. Others held on to the conviction that embracing the institution of monarchy would amount to a betrayal of God's sovereignty.

Saul was the first king (r. 1020–1000 B.C.E.). From his capital at Gilgal he succeeded in uniting the tribes against the common enemy, the Philistines. David (r. 1000–961 B.C.E.) established himself first at Hebron, but after taking Jerusalem from the Jebusites declared that city his capital. He sought to unify Jewish religious life and instituted the office of court prophet. David's son Solomon (r. 961–922 B.C.E.) further centralized Jewish ritual in his newly built Jerusalem Temple. But when Solomon died his sons divided the realm into the northern Kingdom of Israel (922–721 B.C.E.) and the southern Kingdom of Judah (922–586 B.C.E.). Two hundred years later the northern capital of Samaria fell to the Assyrians, never to be recovered. The southern kingdom carried on for over a century, with moments of greatness, and even major religious reform in the late seventh century B.C.E. Many of Israel's principal prophets lived and worked under the Kingdom of Judah. But Babylon was putting the squeeze on the small kingdom, and in 586 B.C.E. Jerusalem and its Temple fell to invading forces. Over a thousand years later, Jews founded the Khazar kingdom in the Caucasus, a small-scale experiment in monarchy that survived from about 700 to 1000 C.E.

What else is **important** about **David**?

David, second King of the Israelites (born c. 1013 B.C.E.), is one of the most vividly portrayed characters in the Hebrew Bible (Old Testament). He was a warrior, lawgiver, musician, and poet, loyal to his superiors, harsh in his judgments, ruthlessly cruel in war, but singled out by God for glory. He stands at the center of several crucial events in the history of the Israelites and has, accordingly, been a subject of exhaustive study among Jewish scholars for centuries. Christians have been almost equally fascinated with David, some seeing him as an Old Testament foreshadowing of Jesus, and others noting that Matthew's Gospel begins by tracing Jesus' lineage through the House of David. David is perhaps best remembered for his epic duel with the giant Goliath (begins I Samuel 17), a Philistine who was demoralizing the Hebrew army by offering single combat that no one dared accept. David, swearing that Yahweh would defend him, took up the challenge. He stepped forward, unarmed, and struck down the giant with a single stone from his slingshot. The Philistines panicked and fled, pursued and cut down by the Israelites. David is also known as the greatest of all Hebrew poets, having singlehandedly composed the biblical Book of Psalms.

What does the term **Babylonian Exile** (or Captivity) refer to?

The Kingdom of Judah had come under military and political pressure in the late 700s B.C.E., around the time of the fall of the northern kingdom. Some southern kings even paid tribute as vassals to Assyria. In the year 597 B.C.E. the Babylonians, successors to the

Assyrians as the major regional power, were closing in on Jerusalem. Though the city would hold out for another ten years, the invaders captured a number of leading Jews and deported them to Mesopotamia. In 587/6 B.C.E., the Babylonians laid final siege to Jerusalem, destroying the Temple. Along with other Middle Eastern powers, they had found it useful to take important Jews into exile, the better to demoralize the subject peoples and insure the success of the conquering regime. Exact numbers are impossible to reconstruct, but the total deportation seems to have uprooted as many as twenty thousand people. Since only the poorest and least educated were left behind, the Exile amounted to a virtually total elimination of Jewish presence in Jerusalem and its environs. The good news was that the community would realize the possibility of taking root in a new land. Prophets preached a message of encouragement and survival, devising a whole new "exilic" theology built around the hope of restoration and return. Enter the Achaemenid Persian empire stage left, exit Babylon stage right. Jewish fortunes changed under the new sovereigns of the central Middle East. In 539 B.C.E., Persian monarch Cyrus the Great decided to release the captives and allow them to return to Jerusalem.

How does Jewish tradition **interpret history**?

Large portions of the Hebrew scriptures include examples of the finest ancient historical writing. Authors of historical texts in the Bible do not merely catalogue events chronologically. They evaluate their data and pass judgment on the main characters from a particular perspective that views all happenings as part of a greater divine plan. They discern patterns in human behavior and in God's ways of dealing with people. So, for example, the author of the Book of Judges observes how, when the people do evil in the sight of God, God allows them to suffer the consequences. Once they've had enough chaos, they cry out to God for help. God then raises up a Judge to rule the people, and justice reigns for forty or eighty years. But when the strong ruler dies, the people again go astray, and the cycle starts again (Judges 2:16–23). History begins when God creates time and space, moves through many generations of human beings struggling with and for each other, and will come to an apocalyptic conclusion at a time known only to God. Above all, history is the arena in which God deals actively with humankind as a whole, but directs both attention and expectation to the Children of Israel.

What did the **Jerusalem Temple** look like?

Solomon built the first Temple around 950 B.C.E. After that was destroyed in 587/6 B.C.E., it was replaced by the Second Temple in about 516 B.C.E. That in turn was modified many times over the subsequent five centuries, most recently by King Herod. Though the Second Temple was destroyed in 70 C.E., parts of Herod's construction are still visible as the Western, so-called "Wailing," Wall. Biblical accounts offer detailed descriptions of various components of the Temple, filling in some of the information archaeology has yet to unearth. Solomon's Temple was in a way a permanent version of the Tabernacle described in the Torah. A rectangle about two hundred feet long by forty feet wide, the Temple consisted of three chambers. Up a few steps flanked by the two columns symbolic of the monarchs, Jachin and Boaz, and just through the east-facing main door was the vestibule. Beyond that was a large windowed room (the *heikhal*, "great hall") where most rituals occurred, and the dark Holy of Holies (*devir*, "shrine"), elevated five or six steps, which only the priestly staff could enter and where the Ark was kept. Surrounding the central building was a huge courtyard with three gates on each of its four sides. In the Second Temple the central building was larger and set in the grander context of a series of courtyards. Along the walls of the court immediately enclosing the Temple proper were chambers for the sacrificial materials. Directly in front of the Temple porch, in the Court of the Priests, was a large altar for burnt offerings and a small slaughterhouse. Directly east of that, through a gate and down six or eight steps, was the large Women's Court with corner chambers for lepers, Nazirites, oil, and wood. The Second Temple's shrine held no Ark of the Covenant. Surrounding the entire high platform was an immense wall, some of which remains today.

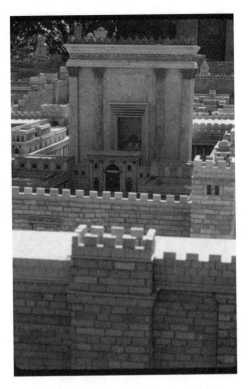

Model of the Second Temple, Herodian renovation, showing the forecourts and the main structure that contained the Holy of Holies.

How did other **Jewish communities develop** outside of Israel?

Small pockets of Jews had grown up in various places in the Middle East since at least the early days of the monarchy. Foreign alliances allowed Jewish kings to bargain for power and influence and opened economic doors. With the trade routes came traveling merchants, some of whom decided to relocate. The first major Jewish communities outside of Israel and Judah were the result of the various mass deportations. By the time Cyrus had made a return possible, Mesopotamian communities had been established for over two generations. With the threat of imminent persecution lifted by a tolerant ruler, many Jews simply stayed in Iraq. There they founded thriving cultural and religious institutions, including the academies that went on to produce some of Judaism's most important legal and theological works. Under successive political regimes with varying policies toward religious pluralism, Iraqi Jews experienced uneven fortunes, but on the whole did much better than merely survive. During the first several centuries of Islamic

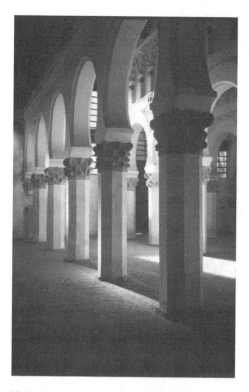

rule from the capital cities Damascus and Baghdad, Jews enjoyed considerable autonomy and even held high government offices. But after the invasion of the newly Islamized Saljuqid Turks from Central Asia, Jewish life in the Middle East changed dramatically. The Saljuqid Sultan effectively abolished the offices of Exilarchate and Gaonate, which had been the backbone of Jewish autonomy. Meanwhile Jewish communities had grown in Europe since Roman times and had begun to thrive in Germany under Charlemagne. Now many Middle Eastern Jews would look to Europe in hopes of another new start. From the eleventh century until at least the late nineteenth, the center of Judaism would shift from the eastern Mediterranean to central and eastern Europe.

Medieval synagogue of Joseph ibn Shushan (twelfth century), which was later turned into the church of Santa Maria La Blanca, Toledo, Spain (early 1400s). The "horseshoe" arches were typical of an architectural decorative style brought to Spain by Muslims of North Africa.

What was the genesis of rabbinical Judaism?

It may be helpful to think of rabbinical Judaism as evolving in a long history of classes of religious scholars. The earliest were the *Soferim,* or Scribes, scholars of the Second Temple period (400–200 B.C.E.) who emerged with Ezra's attempts to restore Torah to the center of Jewish life. From 200 B.C.E.–30 C.E., the period of the Five Pairs of Teachers (or *Zugot*) ended with Hillel and Shammai. A school called the *Tanna'im* ("Repeaters," 30–200) lay the foundations of the Mishnah. That would become the first major written systematization of oral Torah. They also initiated a branch of oral Torah commentary called the Tosefta ("additions"), collections of statements of *Tanna'im* not found in the Mishnah (called *beraitot,* meaning "outside") arranged according to Mishnaic order. From 200–500, the *Amora'im* ("spokesmen, interpreters") communicated lessons of the great rabbis to pupils and later scholars who taught in Babylon (Iraq) in rabbinical academies established after the Babylonian Exile. Their work eventually comprised the Gemara ("completion") of the Jerusalem Talmud, completed around 390. From 500 to about 589 a class called the *Savora'im* ("reflectors") completed the writing of the Babylonian Talmud but left no independent work.

The *Geonim* ("eminences," heads of the academies of Sura and Pumbedita in Iraq) dominated Jewish scholarship from about 589 to 1000, providing their answers to queries on the Torah from all over the diaspora in a body of literature called Responsa

What was the Holocaust?

The term "Holocaust" derives from a pair of Greek words that mean "whole burnt offering." The term originally referred to a kind of sacrifice performed in the Jewish Temple in Jerusalem. In more common contemporary usage, however, Holocaust refers to the suffering and death of as many as six million Jews during World War II as a result of Adolf Hitler's "Final Solution." Jews all over Europe were systematically targeted by Nazi propaganda and police action. The *Sho'ah,* as it is called in Hebrew, began in 1933 and escalated dramatically after a series of violent attacks on Jews called *Kristallnacht* ("the night of shattered glass," November 9–10, 1938). According to the Nazi view, only a return to Aryan racial purity could save the human race. With their Semitic blood, Jews were seen as a source of racial pollution and, therefore needed to be exterminated. Throughout the late 1930s and early 1940s, Hitler and his collaborators, led by the Gestapo (*Geheime Staats-polizei,* or state secret police) and the feared black-shirted S.S. (*Schutzstaffel*), rounded up hundreds of thousands of Jews and herded them into boxcars for transport to concentration camps scattered throughout central and eastern Europe. Many prisoners too small or too weak to work were immediately taken to the gas chambers—often disguised as showers—where they were killed with Zyklon-B gas. The Holocaust represents one of history's most extraordinary and horrifying examples of both genocide and scapegoating.

("responses"). From 1000 to 1400, the *Meforshim* and *Poseqim* elaborated on the practical implications of *halakhah* (rules and regulations); and the *Tosafists* ("those who added on") produced collections of comments on Talmud arranged according to the order of the Talmud's sections or tractates. They based their writings on comments of earlier authorities, especially the twelfth- to fourteenth-century school of Rashi in Germany and France. This ongoing layering of tradition turns out to be the complex and multifaceted foundation of what we know as Rabbinical Judaism.

Why do Jews, Christians, and Muslims all **claim** the same **Holy Land**?

Palestine, which covers an area of just over ten thousand square miles (roughly the size of the state of Maryland), lies in southwest Asia at the eastern end of the Mediterranean Sea. It is the Holy Land of Jews, since it was here that Moses led the Israelites after he brought them out of slavery in Egypt and it is the place where they subsequently established their homeland since it is where Jesus Christ was born, lived, and died. In the same way, the Christians feel that it is the seat of their faith since the Arab people conquered Palestine in the seventh century and, except for a brief period during the Crusades, it was ruled by various Muslim dynasties until 1516 (when it became part of the Ottoman Empire).

Upper floor of a sixteenth-century synagogue residential building in the old Jewish ghetto in Venice, Italy. The five windows symbolize the five books of the Torah, and the small dome-crowned apse at the right marks the place of the Ark inside, where the Torah scrolls were kept while the synagogue remained in use.

Palestine's capital, Jerusalem, is also claimed as a holy city by all three religions. Jews call it the City of David (or the City of the Great King) since it was made the capital of the ancient kingdom of Israel around 1000 B.C.E. Christians regard it as holy since Jesus traveled with his disciples to Jerusalem to observe the Passover. It is the site of the Last Supper, and just outside the city, at Golgotha, Jesus was crucified (c. 30 C.E.) Muslim Arabs captured the city in 638 C.E. (just after Muhammad's death), and, like the rest of Palestine, it has a long history of Muslim Arab rule. Jerusalem, which is now part of the modern State of Israel, is home to numerous synagogues, churches, and mosques. It also has been the site of numerous religious conflicts throughout history.

Major Dates in Jewish History

Date	Event
c. 2000–1400 B.C.E.	Patriarchal Age; Abraham, revered in Hebrew Bible as father of the Hebrew people, Isaac, Jacob, and Joseph
c. 1800 B.C.E.	God's Covenant with Abraham (Judaism)
c. 1250–1050 B.C.E.	Moses leads Exodus out of Egypt; conquest and subsequent settlement of Canaan; period of the Judges
c. 1020–587/6 B.C.E.	Kingdoms of Saul, David, Solomon, and divided (Northern and Southern) Kingdoms

835–587 B.C.E.	Age of the Pre-Exilic Prophets (Isaiah, Jeremiah, Hosea, Amos, etc.)
587/6 B.C.E.	Babylonian destruction of Temple, Jewish leaders into exile in Iraq
539 B.C.E.	Beginning of return from Babylonian Exile to Zion
515 B.C.E.	Jewish Temple rebuilt; emergence of classical Judaism
168–165 B.C.E.	Maccabean revolt, Temple defiled and restored
c. 50–135 C.E.	Martyr Rabbi Akiva
70 C.E.	Roman destruction of "Second Temple"; Rabbi Yochanan ben Zakkai founds first Rabbinical academy at Yavneh
c. 390 C.E.	Jerusalem Talmud completed in Northern Israel
c. 499 C.E.	Completion of Babylonian Talmud in Mesopotamia (Iraq)
762–c. 1000 C.E.	Karaite school of Jewish thought
1050 C.E.	Christian persecution and massacre of the Jews in the Rhineland
1134–1204 C.E.	Moses Maimonides, Jewish theologian (born Cordoba, Spain)
13th Century C.E.	Major developments in Jewish theology/spirituality in Spain
14th Century C.E.	Widespread persecution, expulsion of Jews from West/Central Europe
1516 C.E.	First Jewish "ghetto" opens in Venice
1728–1786 C.E.	Moses Mendelsohn promotes Enlightenment (*Haskalah*)
19th Century C.E.	Major European reform movements under Samuel Holdheim, Abraham Geiger
1873 C.E.	Union of American Hebrew Congregations founded
1881 C.E. to present	Revival of Jewish nationalism, Haim Weitzman founds movement later named Zionism
1917 C.E.	Balfour Declaration, early stirrings of State of Israel
1933 C.E.	The *Sho'ah* (Holocaust) begins in Central Europe
1948 C.E.	Founding of the State of Israel
20th Century C.E.	Major developments in Reform and Conservative Judaism

RELIGIOUS BELIEFS

Is there a Jewish **creed**?

Several important creedal formulations have appeared at different times in Jewish history, but a good starting point is the single sentence from Deuteronomy 6:4. It is called simply "the *Shema*." Devout Jews recite these few words more often than almost any other phrase. "Hear, O Israel: the Lord our God, the Lord is One" (or "the Lord our God is one Lord"). Two essential ingredients in Jewish belief are enshrined here in elegant simplicity: first, the notion that the people constitute a community of faith, and second, the affirmation of the absolute unity of God. In the next verse, Jews are enjoined to love the Lord with all their heart, soul, and strength.

13

Another very ancient text that functions like a creedal statement appears in Deuteronomy 26:5–10. In his final instruction to the people, Moses tells them that when they come into their newly God-given land they are to make an offering and recite a short historical summary of all that God has done for them. "A wandering Aramaean was my father," it begins, referring to Jacob, father of the twelve tribes. The text goes on to recount in brief how God rescued the people from slavery in Egypt and gave them a land in which to dwell. Apart from these two biblical texts, the anonymous fifteenth-century "I Believe" based on the "Thirteen Articles of Faith" of Maimonides (d. 1204) is the best-known creedal statement. Each of thirteen affirmations begins "I believe with an unwavering faith...." Articles one through five affirm that God is omnipotent and one, beyond all things material, master of time and space, and the sole object of prayer and devotion. Moses' prophetic authority (along with that of the other prophets as other prophets), scripture's authenticity and truth, and the finality of the divine Law are the subjects of articles six through nine. All of the remaining four articles speak of the ethical demands of adherence to the revealed law, of the final consequences of human choices in the form of reward or punishment, of the Messiah's eventual coming, and of the ultimate resurrection of the dead.

What are the **Thirteen Articles of Faith** traditionally attributed to Maimonides?

1. I believe with unwavering faith that the Creator, Blessed be His Name, is the Creator and Guide of everything that has been created; He alone has made, makes, and will make all things.

2. I believe with unwavering faith that the Creator, Blessed be His Name, is One, and that there is no unity in any manner like His, and that He alone is our God, who was, and is, and will be.

3. I believe with unwavering faith that the Creator, Blessed be His Name, has no body, that He is free from all the properties of matter, and that there can be no (physical) comparison to Him whatsoever.

4. I believe with unwavering faith that the Creator, Blessed be His Name, is the first and the last.

5. I believe with unwavering faith that to the Creator, Blessed be His Name, and to Him alone, it is right to pray, and that it is not right to pray to any being besides Him.

6. I believe with unwavering faith that all the words of the prophets are true.

7. I believe with unwavering faith that the prophecy of Moses our teacher, peace be upon him, was true, and that he was the chief of the prophets, both those who preceded him and those who followed him.

8. I believe with unwavering faith that the entire Torah that is now in our possession is the same that was given to Moses our teacher, peace be upon him.

9. I believe with unwavering faith that this Torah will not be exchanged, and that there will never be any other Torah from the Creator, Blessed be His Name.

10. I believe with unwavering faith that the Creator, Blessed be His Name, knows all the deeds of human beings and all their thoughts, as it is written, "Who fashioned the hearts of them all, Who comprehends all their actions" (Psalms 33:15).

11. I believe with unwavering faith that the Creator, Blessed be His Name, rewards those who keep His commandments and punishes those that transgress them.

12. I believe with unwavering faith in the coming of the Messiah; and even though he may tarry, nonetheless, I wait every day for his coming.

Statue of the great medieval Iberian rabbi Moses Maimonides (1135-1204) in the old Jewish quarter of his home town, Cordoba, Spain.

13. I believe with unwavering faith that there will be a revival of the dead at the time when it shall please the Creator, Blessed be His name, and His mention shall be exalted for ever and ever.

What do **Jews believe** about **God**?

God is both utterly transcendent and strikingly accessible, both awe-commanding and irresistible. As the ultimate majestic power, the merest hint of divine nearness brings all creation to its knees. This God is the Holy One of Israel, into whose presence only a fool would enter nonchalantly. Any person of sense knows instinctively that to approach God is to be filled with dread. That's what "holy" means—forbidden, off-limits, wholly other. Dread is not always a bad thing. Here it is clearly an appropriate response. This does not mean that God is cruel or despotic, although some scriptural accounts might seem to convey that impression. Recall the story of the men assigned to carry the Ark of the Covenant to its new abode. When their ox stumbled, one man lunged for the Ark to keep it from slipping from the cart and was instantly struck dead. The point of the story is that "God" means "danger." And when God claims allegiance, there is no room for the tentative. Abraham was ready to sacrifice his son Isaac. Israel's kings and military commanders were ordered to commit "total war," sparing nothing,

15

so jealous was God for complete dedication. At the same time, Jewish images of God convey a divine intimacy and immediacy. God creates all things by the unimaginable power of divine speech. Every divine word is immediately embodied in some undeniable event. God walks with Adam in the cool of the evening and delivers through the prophets a message of absolute tenderness. Most of all, the God of the Hebrew Bible is unfailingly devoted to his people. This God acts in all the events of human history.

Various important names of God appear throughout the Hebrew Bible. Torah uses the word *Elohim,* a kind of plural form related to the same Semitic root (*el*) from which the Islamic name for God, Allah, derives. But the word Yahweh is a still more central term. Sometimes translated as "He Who Is," in connection with God's identifying himself to Moses through the Burning Bush as "I Am Who I Am" or "I Will Be Who I Will Be" (*Ehyeh Asher Ehyeh*). Many Jews choose not to pronounce this most sacred name of God. When reading scripture they prefer to substitute the Hebrew *Hashem,* "the Name," every time the word Yahweh appears. Similarly, many Jewish publications in English print simply G-d in place of God, out of reverence for the sacred word. Another term, *Adonai* ("my Lord") is also significant here. Some people combine the vowels from *Adonai* with the consonants of *Yahweh* to get *Jehovah*. This linguistic compromise allows people to both say and not say the sacred name of God.

A sculpture of Moses by Renaissance artist Michelangelo.

How have **prophets** figured in **Jewish tradition**?

Even in the Torah we find references to Abraham and Moses as prophets, and Moses is told that his brother Aaron will be his "prophet" when they confront Pharaoh. In those texts the term appears to be a rather generic indicator of one who speaks for another rather than a reference to a figure of official or institutional status. Prophetic figures continue to appear during the days of the Judges. Deborah is a "prophetess," according to Judges 4:4; and Judges 6:8 says God sent an otherwise-unnamed prophet to the people of Israel with a divine message. Prophets as an institutional class rose to prominence in connection with the monarchy. Samuel, called as a youth to dedicated religious service, was both the last of the Judges and a prototype of the court prophet. He served as critic and spiritual guide to King

Who was Moses and why is he important in Jewish tradition?

Moses (born c. 1390 B.C.E.) was the son of a Hebrew from the tribe of Levi. His mother was named Jochebed. When Moses was just three months old, according to traditional accounts, his mother set him adrift in a basket on the Nile to save him from the pharaonic decree that all Hebrew male babies were to be slaughtered in their infancy. A daughter of Pharaoh found the infant Moses and raised him in her household. As a foster son of Pharaoh's daughter, Moses would have been well educated in political, religious, and military affairs, and he would have been given important responsibilities in government upon reaching maturity. Although he could have enjoyed prosperity, power, and respect in his adopted Egypt, he chose instead to associate himself with his downtrodden people. Moses led the people of Israel out of slavery in Egypt and through their desert wanderings, delivered to them their Law and liturgy—which remain to this day—and helped them form their nation. He supervised the construction of the Ark, a symbol of God's presence with Israel, and oversaw the construction of the tabernacle, a tent-shrine that was the focal point of the nation's worship. The celebration of Passover was begun in commemoration of the night God spared the lives of the Jewish firstborn sons and slew only the sons of the Egyptians.

Saul, as the prophet Nathan would be for David. Elijah and his successor Elisha are perhaps the most famous of the itinerant prophets of the early Monarchical years, best known for the wonders they worked. But it is the writing prophets, beginning with Amos, Hosea, Isaiah, and Jeremiah, who seem to exemplify the quintessence of Jewish prophetic office. They left amazing records of their experience of the prophetic vocation and the content of the message they believed God commissioned them to deliver. Prophets are, in short, a constant presence in the biblical record. Post-biblical Jewish tradition generally assumes that the age of prophecy is over for good.

What is a **Messiah** and how has belief in a coming Messiah played out in **Jewish history**?

Mashiach is a Hebrew word that means "anointed one" (*christos* is the Greek equivalent). Anointing is an ancient Jewish ritual first used to consecrate the priesthood and later to elevate Saul and David to kingly office. Expectation of the coming of a Messiah arose in Jewish tradition especially during and after the Babylonian Exile. Bereft of both Temple and monarchy, Jews longed for a restoration of their former estate under the guidance of a descendant of David. For the next several centuries various notions developed as to how one would recognize the Messiah when he appeared, but tradition did not arrive at a consensus. The Essene community evidently looked forward to two Messiahs, one with spiritual power and the other with political power.

Protracted Roman occupation of Israel two thousand years ago gave rise to renewed messianic expectation. One community of belief, now called Christianity, crystallized around Jesus, convinced that he had all the necessary qualifications. Even so, the New Testament gives evidence of mixed opinions as to how people would know with certainty that Jesus was the Messiah. For Jews, messianic expectation did not end with Jesus. A century later many Jews acclaimed Bar Kochba as Messiah and rallied in support of his revolt, but the Romans quelled the uprising in 135 when they laid siege to the famous Dead Sea stronghold called Masada. Several significant claimants to messiahship have appeared since then, especially under Muslim rule and in medieval Europe, including David Menachem Alroy (twelfth century Kurdistan), David Reuveni (d. c. 1538), Solomon Molcho (1500–1532), Shabbetai Zevi (1626–1676), and his successor in the movement, Jacob Frank (1726–1791). Some subcommunities of extremely Orthodox Jews have even more recently looked upon local leaders as Messiahs. For the majority of Jews today, messianic expectation remains a minor article of faith at most. Reform theology has spiritualized the concept, teaching that the advent of the Messiah is a purely personal event rather than one that will usher in a new age.

What is meant by the term "**covenant**"?

Covenant (*berith* in Hebrew) describes better than perhaps any other single notion the essential quality of God's relationship to humankind. Discussion of divine initiatives that result in the sealing of a covenantal bond appears early in the Torah and continues through the prophetic books. Covenants were a crucial social cement in many ancient Near Eastern societies, including Israel. Partners in a covenant need not be equal in status and power. Many covenants described between human partners in the Bible are between a lord or ruler and his vassals. A more or less common formula for these lord–vassal relationships evolved. This "covenant treaty" form typically began with a section in which the lord names himself in relation to the vassal or subject. A brief historical summary recalls all the good things the lord has provided. That is followed by a list of blessings that will accrue to the subject who is faithful, and the curses that will befall one who is lax or breaks the covenant. Some elements of the treaty form, as well as of the treaty "lawsuit" the lord might bring against one who violated the agreement, appear here and there in the Hebrew Bible.

Accounts of major covenants between God and his people include those with Noah (Genesis 6 and 9), marked by the appearance of the rainbow and the cessation of destruction by flood; Abraham (Genesis 15–17), sealed by the sign of circumcision; and Moses at Sinai (Exodus 19–24), embodied in the revealed Law. At various points in the historical and prophetic books we hear of covenant renewals. A leader, such as Joshua, calls the people to account for their past behavior and challenges them to reaffirm their allegiance to God, the sovereign. Joshua 24 is a fascinating example of how some elements of the ancient treaty formula apparently survived in the practice of Israel. King David's rule is also marked by a covenant renewal led by the court prophet Nathan (II Samuel 7). Prophets, such as Jeremiah, spiritualize the notion of covenant, saying that God wishes to inscribe the special relationship on the tablets of their hearts (Jeremiah 33).

What are the **Ten Commandments**?

Also known as the Decalogue, the so-called "Ten Commandments" are based on Exodus 20:1–17, in which God speaks to Moses at Mount Sinai and reveals his "Ten Words" on inscribed tablets. Various denominations of Jews and Christians alike have boiled down a relatively lengthy message into their own renderings of ten brief and direct statements. For the most part, they embody the following ten directives:

1. You shall have no other gods before me.
2. You shall not make unto yourself any graven image.
3. You shall not take the name of the Lord your God in vain.
4. Remember the Sabbath day, to keep it holy.
5. Honor your father and your mother.
6. You shall not kill.
7. You shall not commit adultery.
8. You shall not steal.
9. You shall not bear false witness against your neighbor.
10. You shall not covet anything that belongs to your neighbor.

The Decalogue is followed by scores of more specific regulations concerning every conceivable area of ordinary life that further interpret the details implied in the Ten Commandments. Thus the Ten function as a kind of minimum ethical standard. Following them carefully even in a general way is challenging enough, but to observe them in the full detail given in scripture is another matter altogether.

Do Jews believe in **angels**? What about the **devil**?

A number of important biblical narratives seem to describe encounters between divine emissaries or messengers and major religious figures. Three "visitors" tell Abraham that he and his barren wife will have a son in their old age (Genesis 18:1–15). Jacob dreams of a ladder to Heaven on which "messengers" ascend and descend (Genesis 28:10–22) and later wrestles with a mysterious "man" (Genesis 32:22–32). Tradition has often interpreted these and dozens of other texts in the Hebrew Bible as referring to angels. The texts are often quite ambiguous and do not describe the mysterious actors as winged beings of light or in ways that many people today would recognize as characteristic of angels. These figures are generally understood as messengers from God, and only much later did they acquire the features now commonly associated with angels. Demonic or diabolical presences also appear in the Hebrew scriptures. Tradition has sometimes identified the wily serpent in Genesis as Satan or the Devil, but not until the very latest books of the Bible, such as Job and Zechariah, do we find malevolent forces specifically called Satan. Post-biblical Jewish tradition often identifies Satan with the angel of death or with the innate human inclination to evil.

Do Jews believe in **miracles**?

Belief in miracles depends a great deal on what people think are the ordinary limits of nature, since a commonly accepted conception is that miracles presuppose some divine intervention in the order of nature. The Hebrew Bible tells of dozens of events, great and small, that appear to fit that broad definition. But what people took for the ordinary limits of nature were in all likelihood significantly narrower in biblical times than they are now. In fact, ancient Middle Eastern societies do not seem to have considered the natural world as a coherent, integral system. Virtually all unusual events were to some degree attributed directly to a divine power simply because by definition the deity had all power. In that world, secondary causes were practically negligible. Everything was cause for wonder.

Hebrew scripture calls important events several things signs: wonders or portents of the future, or simply prodigies or unexpected phenomena. The category of signs includes, for example, the plagues visited upon the Egyptians and the appearance of the rainbow as a sign of Noah's covenant with God. Wonders or portents include the unusual works of a false prophet. And such things as God's creative and redemptive deeds the scripture calls extraordinary events. On some curious happenings, such as the bodily "ascensions" of figures like Enoch (Genesis 5:24) and Elijah (II Kings 2:11), the scripture makes no evaluative comment, merely describing the occurrence briefly. Reference works on Judaism provide few entries on "miracles." But numerous religious figures in Jewish history and lore, particularly rabbis and mystics, are said to have occasioned or mediated marvels of all kinds.

What are the main Jewish notions of **afterlife**?

Surprisingly little detailed information on the afterlife is given in the Hebrew scriptures, and mostly in the very latest material at that. We find a few vague references to a nondescript region called Sheol, a gray, dreary warehouse of souls. Not a place of absolute suffering, Sheol is little more than a synonym for death itself. Toward the latter centuries of the first millennium B.C.E. more concrete notions of afterlife begin to emerge. Propelling the development were questions of justice such as those that the Book of Job raised. If a just man like Job suffers so much in this life, and so many wicked people seem to flourish, perhaps retribution for one's deeds will be deferred until after death. If not, how can one say that God is just?

Sheol becomes identified more as recompense for an evil life, but is gradually replaced by the concept of Gehenna. Just south of Jerusalem lies a small valley that

Gehenna Valley near Jerusalem.

may at one time have belonged to a man named Hinnom, hence *ge-hinnom,* the valley of Hinnom. It must have been a most unpleasant place. Long-standing tradition associates it with fiery punishment, possibly because it had been a place for incinerating refuse in ancient times. As a parallel to this abode of deserved misery there must surely be a place where the good are rewarded, perhaps near the dwelling of God himself. Generic notions of "the heavens" as a place above Earth appear very early in biblical thought. Gradual spiritualization of the idea of "Heaven" went along with the notion that there are multiple levels, a third of which is a paradise for the just. All of this is linked to the idea of resurrection of the body, taught by the Pharisees and accepted as a rule in post-biblical rabbinical tradition.

Is there a distinctively **Jewish ethic**?

Every major religious tradition has its equivalent of the "golden rule"—treat others as you would like them to treat you. One classic Jewish version says, "Do not do to others what you would not want others to do to you." As a humanistic guide, it is very important, and pretty obvious on the face of it. But no religious tradition has ever just left the matter there, hoping their members would work out the details. Most readers will be familiar with the expression "Judaeo-Christian ethic." Politicians and preachers alike are fond of using the phrase as a handy, if rather vague, summary of values espoused by large populations like those of the United States. The term does not suggest that there are no significant differences between Judaism and Christianity as communities of faith, but it clearly implies that Jews and Christians generally agree on basic ethical principles.

Most people would instinctively identify the "Ten Commandments" as that shared foundation of morals. But since for Christians as well as for Jews, the Decalogue functions as an ethical minimum, there is much more to both approaches to morality than one can squeeze into a handful of commands and prohibitions. This is where religious motivation enters the mix, making each tradition of religious ethics distinctive. Jews strive for a moral life because, in addition to the need for basic mutual respect (Golden Rule) and for broad guidelines meant to prevent social chaos (the Decalogue), the revealing God demands nothing less of believers. Some Jews also draw motivation from the prospect of reward or punishment in the next life. Many find it sufficient that God has given all good things and wants people to share them so that more people can enjoy the gift of life. Since life's gifts don't always simply fall into one's lap and take care of themselves, believers need to work toward worthy goals and use proper care of the gifts attained.

What does Jewish tradition teach about **religiously legitimate violence**?

Earlier books of the Hebrew Bible, especially the Torah and "historical books," are filled with texts about violence, both prescriptive and descriptive. God does not suffer enemies lightly, and many texts, such as Deuteronomy 32:40–42, pull no punches in their descriptions of the divine mind in this regard: "When I have whetted my flashing sword, when I have set my hand to judgment, then I shall punish my adversaries and wreak vengeance on my foes. I will make my arrows drunk with blood, my sword will devour flesh, blood of slain and captives, the heads of enemy princes." An important distinction here is that the Bible condemns violence when individuals engage in it for their own selfish purposes, but when violence is part of the larger picture of the divine purpose for Israel, it is presumed to be essential and positive.

Later texts, especially the Prophets and Wisdom literature, typically condemn human recourse to violence, insisting that vengeance is up to God alone. Rabbinic literature emphasizes, further, that peace is the original purpose of all creation, and that *shalom* (also meaning wholeness and health) is the ultimate blessing. According to the rabbis, forgiveness is always preferable to revenge; one must always choose the less destructive of two difficult options. They insist that only defensive war is acceptable, and indeed it is mandatory. They accept biblical wars of expansion as justifiable under the original circumstances, but no longer. And the rabbis discuss at length the complexities of such things as "preemptive" military action, acknowledging considerable moral ambiguity in deciding whether an enemy is likely to attack.

What are some important **Jewish religious terms**?

Amora'im—"speakers," early rabbinical scholars whose teachings eventually made up the Gemara.

El Shaddai—an ancient biblical name for God, sometimes rendered God of the Mountain.

Elohim—one of the earliest biblical names for God, especially important in Genesis and Exodus.

Gemara—learning or completion, result of reflection on the Mishnah ("repetition"), the core text of the Talmud.

Geonim—"Eminences" (singular *gaon*), a class of rabbinical scholars active from 589–c. 1000, especially in the academies of central Iraq.

(H)aggadah—"narrative," result of reflection on sacred sources especially as contained in the Talmud and Midrashic literature.

Halakhah—"way of walking," more explicitly legal texts that draw out juridical implications of sacred scripture.

Kabbalah—meaning "reception," most common name for Jewish mystical tradition.

Midrash—"study," reflective exegesis of scripture that can be either haggadic or halakhic.

Minyan—quorum needed for ritual service, ten males over age thirteen (women included in Reform and Conservative communities).

Mishnah—a compendium of originally oral tradition of biblical exegesis gathered by rabbis prior to 200 C.E.

Soferim—"people of the book," a classification of very early religious scholars considered responsible for the beginnings of oral interpretation of the Torah.

Talmud—two large compendia of Rabbinic scholarship and lore, the Jerusalem and the Babylonian, both structured as a commentary (Gemara) written in the margins of pages whose central text is the Mishnah.

Tanna'im—"Repeaters," scholars traditionally said to have laid the foundation of the written Mishnah (repetition).

Torah—the five "Books of Moses," the Pentateuch (Genesis, Exodus, Leviticus, Numbers, Deuteronomy), but by extension the whole of God's revealed teaching.

Yahweh—perhaps the most important biblical name of God, signified in Hebrew by the four-letter "tetragram" YHWH.

SIGNS AND SYMBOLS

What **signs or symbols** might **identify** an individual as **Jewish**?

One of the most common and easily visible signs of Jewishness is the small circular skullcap called the *yarmulke* or *kippah*. Worn by many Jewish men and boys as an ordinary item of clothing, the yarmulke is especially significant in ritual contexts. In some congregations, women rabbis now wear the head covering as well. Some Orthodox and most Hassidic males wear a plain black hat over the yarmulke. On Shabbat and holidays, some Hassidic men wear fur hats called shtreimels or spodiks. Orthodox men often dress all in black with long overcoats; some Sephardic groups wear white on Shabbat and holidays. Items of clothing for ritual purposes only include the larger woolen, cotton, or silk prayer shawl (*tallit*) with corner fringes (*tzitzit*) worn as an outer garment during morning prayer and all day on Yom Kippur. The *tallit katan* (smaller prayer garment) is a cotton undergarment, worn at all times, with fringes bearing 613 knots (the total number of commands [248] and prohibitions [365] in the Torah) that hang out at the belt line as stipulated in Numbers 15:37–38. Some Jewish men don phylacteries (*tefillin*) on the forehead and the non-dominant arm (that is, the left arm for right-handed people, and the right arm for left-handed people). These small leather boxes bound with leather thongs contain texts of scripture (Exodus 13:1–9, 11–16; Deuteronomy 6:4–9, 11:13–21) and are worn by Orthodox and some Conservative Jews for daily morning prayer both privately and in the synagogue. Another symbolic practice involving the body itself is the growth of sidelocks (*pe'ot*). Some Orthodox men and boys do not cut their forelocks in response to the biblical injunction of Leviticus 19:27, "You shall not trim the hair on your temples...." Smaller items often worn by both men and women, whatever their communal affiliation, include rings or necklaces with the six-pointed Star of David or the two Hebrew letters that spell out "*chai*" ("Living One").

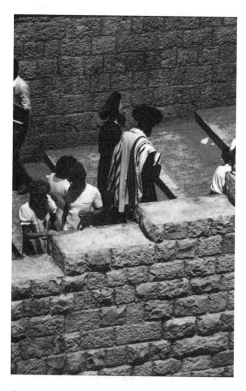

Hasidic Jews returning home after praying at the Western Wall in Jerusalem. One man wears the prayer shawl and both wear the decorative fur hat distinctive of Hasidic men's ritual fashions.

What is the meaning of the Star of David?

Known in Hebrew as *Magen David* ("Shield of David"), this important Jewish symbol is composed of two superimposed equilateral triangles forming a hexagram. The symbol was common in many ancient civilizations and cultures, where it served variously for decoration and for the practice of magic. The Star was not associated specifically with Judaism during biblical or Talmudic times. It appeared as early as the tenth century as a lucky sign in the *mezuzah*—a small container of scriptural texts from Deuteronomy 6:4–9 and 11:13–21 placed on traditional Jewish doorposts. Later—

around the seventeenth century—it began appearing on Jewish tombstones and as decoration in synagogues. In the nineteenth century, the appearance of the Star became widespread when it was adopted by central European Jews as a symbol to represent Judaism, much as the cross represents Christianity. The symbol spread quickly and was in use in most synagogues by the early years of the twentieth century. In 1897 the First Zionist Congress adopted the Star; later, it was utilized as the central image of the flag of the State of Israel. During the Nazi period, Jews in Europe were forced to wear a Magen David as an identifying badge.

Hasidic Jewish children in Jerusalem. Note the sidelocks and skullcaps.

What signs or symbols distinguish **ritual specialists** in Judaism?

Since the Temple was destroyed by the Romans in 70, there has been no formal Jewish priesthood. With the priesthood several other ranks of ritual specialists disappeared. What replaced the priesthood was a more egalitarian system of rabbinical leadership. Nowadays, when Jews worship together, the community leader is not nearly so visually distinctive as in days of old. Since the nature of post-Temple worship is radically different, leaders in worship are visually distinguishable largely by their being in front of the congregation, often on a raised stage. Temple priests once wore easily recognizable garb. In addition to the simpler vesture of the ordinary priests, with a full-length cloak and sash or girdle, the High Priest's cloak had a hem fringed with gold bells and woolen pomegranates. He also wore a tall miter with a blue band at the top and a gold headband. An elaborately decorated vestment called the ephod was worn over the cloak. Over that the High Priest wore the "breastplate" suspended from the shoulders like a large pendant on a necklace. This breastplate hung down the front from epaulette-like onyx stones, on each of which were written the names of six of the twelve tribes. Attached to the breastplate were twelve semiprecious stones symbolizing the tribes. And inside the breastplate pocket were the *urim* and *thummim,* mysterious devices used for divination.

What is a **menorah**?

Menorah means "an object that emits light," hence a candleholder. A seven-candle menorah was used in the ancient Temple and has continued to be perhaps the most widely known and used Jewish symbol. When the Romans despoiled the Jerusalem Temple in 70, they carted away all the temple's riches. They regarded the menorah as such an important emblem of their conquest that the Emperor Titus had it depicted

A twentieth-century monumental menorah engraved with low-relief biblical scenes, standing opposite the Israeli parliament, the Kenesset.

on his triumphal arch in the Roman Forum. Some scholars suggest the menorah is a variation on the symbolic "tree of life" that grew at the center of the original Paradise garden; versions of the tree of life are widely used in many cultures and religious traditions. A nine-branched candlestick, now also called a menorah, features prominently in the eight-day observance of Hanukkah.

What should I expect to see if I visit a synagogue?

In many parts of the world, Jewish places of worship have developed architecturally in the context of the local culture. The one architectural feature that sometimes distinguishes synagogues from nearby religious structures is that synagogues often have a central dome. A common decorative item that can mark synagogues externally is the twin tablets of the Law, a reminder of Moses' reception of the revelation at Sinai. A large Star of David often graces the facade or windows. Synagogues of more contemporary style often place a menorah in front. The menorah is usually of monumental scale, and sometimes even very abstract design.

Synagogues of the various different Jewish communities use their interior spaces in different ways, but the one thing you will invariably see is the Ark. Almost as soon as you enter your eye will be drawn to the back wall. There, a pair of small doors, or perhaps a beautifully embroidered or brocaded cloth, marks the place in which the Torah scrolls are kept. This is the post-Temple version of the Ark of the Covenant. Should you visit during worship ceremonies, you will also see the Torah scroll itself, often cloaked in a beautiful cloth (sometimes tooled silver). Some Torah scrolls are topped with a crown (*keter*) as a reminder of the kingly, royal status of the divine source. Inside the cloth a binder (*mappa*) might further protect the scrolls from damage. Many Ashkenazic synagogues in central and eastern Europe also adorn the scroll with a Torah shield (*tas*). Wealthier synagogues often possess many sets of Torah scrolls, used in rotation for different occasions. In order to keep track of the point in the text at which a given scroll was open, the elaborately tooled silver Torah shield might have interchangeable plates with the word "Sabbath" or the name of a particular holy day.

Many synagogues will have a *bimah* ("high place," also called *almemar*), a platform on which there is a desk to hold the Torah scrolls for reading. Traditional communities place the bimah, which symbolically replaces the Temple altar, in the center of the space facing the Ark. Reform synagogues move it nearer the Ark, elevated on a stage and facing the congregation. A sanctuary lamp is also symbolic of the sacred presence and is usually located near the Ark. One feature that often distinguishes Orthodox synagogues is the provision of separate sections for men and women, with men typically in front and women behind or to the side, either on the main floor or in a gallery above. Like many contemporary mosques, some synagogues separate genders with a partition running front to back down the center of the main floor.

Main synagogue of Florence, Italy (1882), showing the central dome that has historically been a feature of countless synagogues

Do Jews use **symbolism** in personal, private, or nonliturgical **rituals**?

In addition to the ritual articles mentioned earlier, Jews use a number of important symbols while praying at home or for occasions such as weddings. During the observance of Passover, the *Kiddush* (or blessing) cup is an important item. Some ritual sets designed for the *Seder* ("order," ritual of Passover) ceremony include an "Elijah cup" set aside for the guest, the prophet who may appear at any time. Some families are fortunate enough to own heirloom silver cups. Similar goblets are used in wedding ceremonies and in the ceremony called *havdalah* that marks the "separation" of holy Sabbath time from the rest of the week. Havdalah occurs Saturday evening at nightfall to mark the end of the twenty-five hour period begun Friday at sundown. (Jewish tradition measures all days this way.) Also used in the latter is a small symbol called the "spice tower" that recalls a reference in Song of Songs to the safekeeping of precious spices. Traditional Jewish communities have produced magnificent illuminated pages called *ketubbot* to recognize marriage vows. Typical decorations in these pages include allusions to the Temple and its implements in addition to scenes of domestic life. Amulets worn around the neck or suspended over an infant's cradle have been popular throughout Jewish history. Many are made of silver. A more elaborate and expensive amulet might include the tablets of the Law along with a number of symbols of the Temple, such as the menorah, incense burner, and ritual headdress of the High Priest. A stylized hand in outline, used as a pendant or on a keychain, symbolizes divine protection and functions as an amulet.

Are **number and letter symbolism** important in Jewish tradition?

Rabbinical interpreters of the sacred text have always loved to play with words. That is not so surprising in a tradition that teaches that words are so powerful that to speak a word is to bring its meaning into being as an event. Writers of *aggadah*—learned narrative intended to entertain as well as teach—analyzed words or clusters of words in the text at

27

Ritual objects for personal devotion and domestic worship displayed in a Jewish religious goods store, the Jewish ghetto of Venice. In addition to the Menorah and Star of David, there are miscellaneous small items such as the protective hand-shaped amulet.

hand, looking for hidden meanings. Every letter of the Hebrew alphabet has a numerical value, and the interpreters would, for example, count up the total numerical value of certain words in order to decide where to place their emphasis in interpreting a passage. This type of interpretation is based on a system called Gematria (from the Greek word for "geometry") and was especially associated with a kind of often arcane Jewish mysticism called *Kabbalah*. Other kinds of letter symbolism relates to the words with which the letter begins. A charming bit of lore called the Alphabet of Creation tells how the letters of the Hebrew alphabet debated among themselves which one should go first. They each made their case, responding to the others in turn, not hesitating to poke fun at some of the funnier-looking letters. In the end it was the humble letter *aleph* that God judged worthy of going first, because with *aleph* the name of God, *Elohim*, begins.

Do Jews use **statues** or other similar **imagery in worship**?

Along with Islam, Judaism has traditionally avoided three-dimensional figural art altogether in its ritual life. The prohibition against setting up any "graven images" that is mentioned in part of the Decalogue may have arisen as a way of establishing a clear distinction between Israel and its pagan neighbors, whose polytheistic beliefs were so vividly portrayed in the images they seemed to worship. The need to prevent believers from backsliding into pagan cultic practices was so strong that the prohibition of representational images in three dimensions was virtually absolute. There are minor exceptions. Some smaller ritual objects, such as Torah shields, depict human beings and animals in high relief. Surprisingly, some of these images even include sacred figures like Moses and Abraham, but these are extremely rare. A number of prominent sculptors have been Jewish, but they have typically not produced their work for explicitly ritual settings, even when the subject matter is expressly religious. Ancient mural and mosaic arts, as well as more recent (especially medieval) manuscript art, are another story. Illuminated texts, even some of the Bible, contain figural images of human beings and animals, but these are generally not done in very realistic fashion.

One of the ten panels created by fifteenth-century artist Lorenzo Ghiberti for the Baptistery of San Giovanni in Florence, Italy, depicts the Ark of the Covenant.

What is the **Ark of the Covenant**?

Part of the revelation Moses received at Sinai included specific instructions from God about how to prepare a holy place in which the people could come to be in the presence of God. First they were to fashion a special tent, called the tabernacle, then the Ark in which the tablets of the Law would be kept. The Ark was to be a gold-clad box of acacia wood of specific dimensions. It was to have two rings on either side to accommodate poles for carrying it, since the Ark had to be portable—the people were still on the move. On top there was to be a "mercy seat" made of gold in the shape of two cherubs facing each other, whose wings would spread over the mercy seat. Ironically, this feature of the most sacred of all ritual objects must have been one of the rare examples of three-dimensional figural art in the history of Judaism. The mercy seat was to be a symbol of the place to which God would descend to meet Moses. Inside the tabernacle a large veil was to separate the larger part of the space from a space called the Holy of Holies, in which the Ark would be kept. From then on, the Ark would travel with Israel, resting only temporarily in any given location, until Solomon built the first temple in Jerusalem. In the temple the Ark was to reside permanently in the innermost part, also called the Holy of Holies.

Have Jews used **symbolism** to **remind** them of the **Temple** since its destruction in 70 C.E.?

Many illuminated manuscripts of the Bible and other important Hebrew texts have included a one- or two-page spread depicting the various implements or ritual objects

29

once used in the Temple. These pages show all of the more portable items mentioned in the text of Exodus 25–30. They include, among other things, the tablets of the Law, the menorah, the table supporting the containers of the twelve loaves of sacred bread, a bronze "laver" used for ceremonial purification, the ram's horn (*shofar*), and the incense burner. Decorative panels or hangings, called *mizrach* (or "east" since they are hung on a home's eastern wall toward Jerusalem), also frequently depict a building meant to be the Jerusalem Temple. Sometimes these hangings show Temple implements rather than the building itself. The mizrach is a reminder not only of the ancient Temple, but of the holy city of Jerusalem, toward which Jews turn when they pray. Another ritual object that often uses imagery of the Temple is the Hanukkah lamp. Though some lamps look very much like the standard seven-branch menorah, many take the form of a small architectural design that can be either hung on the wall or set on a table. The architectural imagery sometimes depicts the back interior wall of a synagogue, with its Ark flanked by two pillars meant to recall the two pillars of the Temple representing Boaz and Jachin. Sometimes the Hanukkah lamp bears an elaborate architectural facade, the metalsmith's version of what the Temple looked like.

MEMBERSHIP, COMMUNITY, DIVERSITY

Where do **Jews live** and how large is the **global Jewish community**?

Communities of Jews have historically taken root in virtually every corner of the earth since over three thousand years ago. Naturally the State of Israel is a major population center (5.7 milion), barely edging out the USA (5.27 million) as the largest. Widely varying estimates as to the size of the global Jewish community make it difficult to land on a useful number, but 14.5 million seems a reasonable total.

What do the terms "**diaspora**" and "**aliyah**" mean?

Diaspora is Greek for scattering or dispersion. It refers to the growth of Jewish communities, at first throughout the Middle East, and eventually throughout the Mediterranean and the world at large. Some diaspora communities were the indirect result of the persecution and exile of Jews, not only from the eastern Mediterranean, but from numerous sites throughout the greater Mediterranean basin. In other words, Jews have experienced dispersion after dispersion. *Aliyah* means "going up" in Hebrew. Originally associated with travel to Jerusalem, which is a high point in the regional topography, the term eventually came to signify chiefly the modern-day return of Jews to Israel. It is thus the opposite of diaspora. But much of the impetus for aliyah continues to come from the very kind of intolerance and persecution that gave rise to many diaspora communities in the first place. In other words, global migration patterns in the history of Judaism have been cyclical.

What is a minyan?

When Jews gather for worship they need a minimum number in attendance, or quorum. Orthodox tradition excludes women from being counted toward the minimum of ten members over thirteen years of age. But both Reform and Conservative traditions have in recent times voted to count women in the minyan. The accommodation presupposes that women in the local community have passed their bat mitzvah. The notion of a religious quorum seems to rest on a fairly clear distinction between private and public worship. Since public or communal worship is of a different order than private worship, tradition draws a clear line between them. So when there are not enough people to form a minyan, everyone returns home or prays privately in the synagogue.

What is **Zionism**?

In general Zionism means the modern movement of Jewish return to the holy mountain of Zion in the hope of reclaiming it as the heart of the biblical Promised Land. Near the end of the nineteenth century, many Jews in eastern Europe began to view Israel as more than just a place for pilgrimages or for occasional settlement by strong believers. Encouraged by the rise of nationalism in Europe, certain Jews sought to return to the land of their ancestors and to make their homes there. This impulse gave rise to the political movement known as Zionism. (The expression comes from the word "Zion," which is a poetic term for the Holy Land.) Nathan Birnbaum coined the usage in 1890. In 1896 Theodor Herzl organized the political movement that has borne the name ever since. Herzl convened the first of many Zionist Congresses at Basel in 1897.

Chaim Weitzmann (1874–1952) was one of the most influential leaders of the movement. He was a powerful presence at the negotiation of the Balfour Declaration of 1917, a watershed document that ultimately made serious talk of a Jewish state possible, right through negotiations for Israeli statehood in 1948. Weitzmann also served as Israel's first president. Zionism has, to be sure, been a bone of contention because of the political and social implications of so dramatic a reshaping of what had formerly been called Palestine. Zionists see Jews as more than a loosely bound group of religious believers. Politically, Zionists argue that Jews are bound to the land—to Israel—and that they were chosen for a role that is inextricably connected with Abraham.

What is the story of the **formation** of the **State of Israel**?

In the 1930s the world's Jews could see that the survival of European Jews depended on mass immigration to Palestine and to friendly states. This humanitarian imperative, however, was rejected by Britain and by those countries, like the United States, where Jews might conceivably have found a home. Faced with Hitler's hatred on the one hand, and world indifference on the other, the world's Jews realized the absolute need for a Jewish homeland, a sovereign state where Judaism was not only a religion, but a nationality. With the Proclamation of an Independent Jewish State on May 14, 1948, for the first time since the destruction of the Temple and the dispersion of the Jews, Jewishness became a national as well as a religious identity. By the Law of Return every Jew had a right to Israeli citizenship. Thus the State of Israel had become a solution to the problem faced by the Jewish people, whose history since the dispersion had been one of trauma and tragedy. In medieval England the Jews had been expelled; in fifteenth-century Spain they had endured the same fate. In most cases, Jews could not achieve political equality in the lands where they settled, and they lacked a land they could call their own and to which they could return.

The proclamation of an independent Israel was the signal for a combined attack by the Arab states. After initial setbacks and mixed success, the Israelis were able to create a national army and to arm it, to an extent, with modern weapons. As a result of these efforts, the tide of battle gradually turned, and, by the end of 1948, Israeli forces led a campaign through southern Palestine and even into Egypt itself. In a later thrust, an Israeli column drove down to the Red Sea, securing the port of Eilat. During one of several ceasefires, Count Folke Bernadotte of Wisborg, the United Nations mediator, was assassinated by Zionist terrorists. Finally, by July, 1949, armistice agreements were signed with the Arab states.

What is a Jewish **ghetto**?

Some say that the word ghetto comes from the Italian word for "foundry" and that it came to mean a closed or restricted neighborhood because a Jewish community near a foundry in Venice was declared the only area open to Jews in 1516. The actual practice of restricting Jewish residences to a certain quarter of town is very ancient, even gaining official religious sanction, for example, from the Christian Third Lateran Council in 1179 in Rome. Jews have been forced to live in ghettos in many times and places. Most recently, Adolf Hitler used the practice fairly early in his career as a way of controlling Jewish residents. Nazis in effect turned these ghettos into urban concentration camps. The Yiddish term *shtetl* was the common European Jewish term for the local community, but it did not carry the often gruesome connotations now borne by the word ghetto.

Is there **internal religious diversity** within the global **Jewish community**?

Jews have formed a number of important subcommunities throughout their history, though there are generally fewer formally constituted denominations, sects, or other subgroups in Judaism than in most other major traditions. That is quite remarkable, considering the relatively small global population of Jews and the enormous diversity

Orthodox Jews praying at the Western ("Wailing") Wall, Jerusalem. Note the characteristic long black coat and circular hat, and the small wadded up paper notes stuffed into the chinks of the masonry, which are petitions and other prayers left by worshippers. (Photo courtesy of David Oughton.)

of cultures in which Jews now live. Major differences among Jewish communities appear most frequently in the relative strictness of ritual observance. Variations in theological views are also noteworthy in some cases, but they are less critical. Strictest in observance are Orthodox Jews, with Conservative communities somewhat less strict. Reform Judaism is further removed from the nearly all-inclusive adherence to biblical and traditional practices. And most flexible of all, both doctrinally and ritually, are the Reconstructionists.

What is distinctive about **Orthodox Judaism**?

Emphasis on the direct, verbatim revelation of the Torah to Moses is the foundation of Orthodox Jewish tradition. Rabbinical interpretation of Torah serves the purpose of drawing out the meanings of scripture so that every situation in life is anchored in divine revelation. If scripture does not address an issue directly, the rabbi employs traditional principles of exegesis to make what limited adaptations are deemed necessary. Strict observance of the 613 commands and prohibitions contained in the Torah is perhaps the most significant feature of Orthodoxy. As an increasingly distinctive approach, Orthodoxy began to emerge in eighteenth-century Europe in response to the perception that Jews were being assimilated too rapidly into society at large. Reform attempts to adapt ritual observance in early nineteenth-century Europe elicited a strong reaction on the part of those who refused to acknowledge a need for more

33

than the most minimal adaptation. Orthodox Jews consider their communities a last bastion of tradition in an increasingly secularized world. Just over one American Jew out of ten belongs to an Orthodox synagogue.

What problems did **Reform Judaism** attempt to solve?

Many German Jews of the early 1800s began to feel that the tradition-bound approach of Orthodox Judaism was losing touch with life in rapidly changing societies. Reform (alternatively called Liberal or Progressive) leaders began by seeking to adapt prayer and liturgy to the needs of people less able to follow them meaningfully in Hebrew. Ideas from the Enlightenment (*Haskalah*) that informed further developments were Moses Mendelsohn's (1728–1786) principles of rational religion: the existence of God, divine providence, and the immortality of the soul.

Reform was a grassroots movement initiated by laypeople and only later enjoying rabbinical support. A student of Mendelsohn, David Friedlander (1756–1834) launched the movement by replacing Hebrew prayers with German and replaced the Jews' plea for the restoration of Israel with hope for global renewal. Samuel Holdheim (1806–1860) took liturgical reforms further in Berlin, and, with Abraham Geiger (1810–1874), instituted dramatic changes. Sabbath worship moved to Sunday, with no gender separation, *kippah*, prayer shawl, or *shofar*. Their radical program of assimilation also rejected dietary laws and circumcision.

Geiger led a gathering of rabbis in 1837, arguing for a much-reduced authority for both Bible and Talmud. He believed Judaism was a world community rather than an ethnically based "nation." The World Union for Progressive Judaism is the movement's international umbrella organization. Several important developments have marked Reform Judaism in the United States. Reform theology regards scripture as divinely inspired (rather than directly revealed verbatim) and subject to the interpretation of each individual. In 1885 the Pittsburgh Platform altered ritual practice by doing away with strict dietary regulations and ancient codes of priestly purity. Reform Jews believe in the immortality of the soul, but not in bodily resurrection. Numbering about two million, they are the largest Jewish community in the United States, gathering in some nine hundred synagogues or temples.

How did **Conservative Judaism** get its name?

Many twentieth-century European and American Jews have agreed that Orthodoxy must adapt to changing times, but have found some modifications introduced by leaders of Reform Judaism too dramatic. Conservatives have thus become Judaism's midground. Responding to the Reform's Pittsburgh Platform of 1885, Sabato Morais (1823–97) joined other Reform rabbis to found the Jewish Theological Seminary of America as a way of promoting a middle path between Orthodoxy and Reform. They stressed the progressive nature of the faith while retaining traditional practices. Like the Reform, Conservatives allowed some English prayers as well as organ music, did not separate the sexes, and they taught immortality of the soul but not resurrection of the body. In 1924 the Rabbinical Assembly of America became Conservative Judaism's institutional anchor in this country. Conservatives retain the Orthodox emphasis on scripture as normative, along with the bulk of its traditional interpretation. They do, however, make allowances for adaptation to modern needs, such as driving to synagogue on the Sabbath. But while traditionalists among them insist that the revelation of Sinai was complete and definitive in itself, more liberal Conservatives lean toward the idea that divine revelation is an unfolding process. Conservatives make up the second-largest body of American Jews, numbering over one and a half million with about eight hundred synagogues. Zionism has had many staunch supporters among Conservative Jews.

What distinguishes **Reconstructionist Jews** from others?

Reconstructionists have sought to reorient Jewish belief from its generally otherworldly focus to greater attentiveness to the here and now. Mordecai Kaplan (1881–1983) led the movement and taught that Jews must understand themselves as a civilization in process. Jewish life depended on so much more than unchanging religious practice, and he introduced dramatic changes into the religious understanding of Judaism. He chose to refer to the "divinity" rather than to God, seeking to purge the object of prayer of its anthropomorphic overtones. Thus God is more of a cosmic process than a personal creator and sustainer of all that is. Kaplan was most influential in expanding the function of the typical synagogue to include much more than regular liturgical worship. Reconstructionism is by far the smallest of the subcommunities of Judaism, with only about a hundred thousand in the United States, since many Reform and Conservative Jews have come to accept much of what Kaplan taught. In general, Reconstructionist congregations retain more traditional practices, such as wearing the prayer shawl, than do the Reform.

What are **Hasidic Jews**?

Some of the biblical prophets emphasized the notion of God's unconditional, absolutely faithful love, *chesed* in Hebrew. They taught that God would continue to seek out sinners and bring them back. Out of that emphasis grew an important theme in Jewish spirituality, a focus on the transforming power of divine compassion. Learning and moral righteousness were still worthy goals, of course, but not to such a degree that they should raise divisions that amounted to religious class distinctions in the community. Most important was the quest for individual salvation sought within the community. A major movement organized around these emphases was begun in Eastern Europe by Israel ben Eliezer (c. 1700–1760), known as the Baal Shem Tov (Master of the Good Name, that is that of God). He was a highly charismatic man with a reputation for working wonders, especially healing. He de-emphasized Talmudic scholarship in favor of devotional intensity. After his death the Hasidic movement became more

Who were the Karaites?

Around the middle of the eighth century, Anan ben David (c. 762–767) was elected counterexilarch of the Jewish communities in Iraq. Tradition has it that he laid the foundations of a school of thought that would come to be called the Karaites (from the Hebrew "to read, recite scripture") because of their emphasis on scripture as the sole basis of Judaism. Like latter-day Sadducees, the Karaites rejected centuries of oral tradition as superfluous. Like the Maccabees of old, they proclaimed every individual his own rabbi, capable of interpreting scripture for himself. Benjamin of Nehavand (c. 850) is said to have further developed the thought of Anan during the ninth century. The principal systematizer of Karaite thought was Daniel ben Moshe (c. 900), who led a kind of proto-Zionist movement in Jerusalem. Karaite rejection of Talmudic learning gave rise to preaching a need to return to the Holy Land. Talmud and later oral tradition had, they argued, generally developed as a way of adapting the Law to Jewish communities in exile. Return to the Land would imply a return to the original sources and hence obviate the need for adaptive interpretation. Saadia (882–942), the most famous Gaon of the Iraqi communities, led a vigorous counterattack against the Karaite position, insisting on the need to combine tradition with revelation and reason for a balanced approach. Small groups of intellectual descendants of the original Karaites survived into the twentieth century, but they have had little influence in recent times.

formally organized as a closed society around a charismatic leader called a *tzaddik* (literally, "righteous one"). As the community grew, subgroups developed and carried the spirit of the tradition abroad, most notably to Israel and New York. The Chabad branch moved more toward scholarship and education while other groups stayed focused on emotional involvement in devotion. Hasidic groups have often been "excommunicated," even though none have formally broken away.

What is **Kabbalah**?

Kabbalah, or "received tradition," refers to an elaborate system of esoteric interpretation of certain texts of the Hebrew Bible that has formed the basis of Jewish mysticism. Visionary accounts in which the prophet Ezekiel, for example, describes seeing four wheels in the sky led to what is called *merkavah* (chariot or throne) mysticism. The Sefer Yetzirah (Book of Creation), an ancient cosmological treatise, eventually exercised great influence on mystical thinking. Traditional accounts trace the origins of mystical interpretation to twelfth-century Europe. There the originally Italian Kalonymus family, transplanted to the Rhine valley in Germany, became the nucleus of important developments. Samuel the Pious and son Judah began an important movement of

Hasidic spirituality at Speyer, as did Eleazar ben Judah (d. 1228) at Worms. These were contemporary with similar developments among Christian Rhenish mystics, and devised a style of spiritual canticle called the *Din Shamayim* ("Law of the Heavens") with a type of prayer, called "Jacob's Ladder," that symbolized spiritual ascent.

Further important developments occurred with a later generation of Iberian Jews. Abraham ben Samuel Abulafia (1240–1292) of Sarragossa wrote prolifically of the need to achieve spiritual freedom, liberating the soul through a combined discipline of contemplation, reflection on mystical meanings of Hebrew letters, and the cultivation of what was in effect a kind of Jewish "yoga." According to tradition, Abulafia's contemporary Moses ben Shem Tov of Leon (1240–1305) composed perhaps the single most influential mystical text, the *Zohar* (Book of Splendor). Based on a theory of emanation, the *Zohar* teaches that the divine presence becomes manifest in the material world through a series of ten *sefirot*, or spheres, that symbolize the increasingly tangible presence of divine energy (the *shekhinah*). As a movement, Jewish mysticism generally goes by the name Kabbalah ("reception"). It was revived in the sixteenth century in Israel by Solomon Alkabez (1505–1584) and Isaac Luria (1534–1573).

Who are the **Samaritans**?

After the northern kingdom's capital, Samaria, was overrun by the Assyrians in 721 B.C.E., many of the leading and best-educated Jewish citizens were deported. The invaders imported significant numbers of colonists who gradually infiltrated the people of Israel. They came to trace their ancestry to the tribes of Manasseh and Ephraim, thus identifying themselves as Jewish at least genealogically, and intermarried with Jews. The Samaritans established their own temple on Mt. Gerizim. As a result of a falling out with Nehemiah in the fifth century, the Samaritans split off from Judaism more or less definitively and came to think of themselves as a separate people. Now very few in numbers, the Samaritans still have their own version of the Torah and distinctive codes of religious law. At Passover they still sacrifice a lamb on Mt. Gerizim. Only a small community of Samaritans, well under a thousand, survive. Plagued by health problems as a result of inbreeding, most Samaritans live around the city of Nablus in the West Bank.

What's the difference between **Sephardic** and **Ashkenazic Jews**?

Prior to 1492 there were large Jewish communities on the Iberian peninsula, modern-day Spain and Portugal. During the final phases of the Catholic reconquest of Spain, Jews were given the option of converting or going into exile. Many of those who chose to leave migrated all over the Mediterranean basin, including North Africa and the Middle East, to found new communities. These descendants of Iberian Jewry are called Sephardic Jews. They comprise a small minority, perhaps twenty percent or less, of the global Jewish population. Sephardic Jews retain a number of distinctive ritual and legal interpretations, and in some places manage to preserve the Ladino language of their ancestral Iberia and maintain separate educational institutions. By far the majority of Jews are Ashkenazim. Their name derives from the medieval Hebrew designation of central Europe as Ashkenaz. Descendants of the early Jewish settlers in central and eastern Europe preserve Ashkenazic traditions all over the world. Most Jewish immigrants to the United States have been Ashkenazim, although the majority of the earliest, in colonial times, were Sephardim. In general, Jews in the Americas have not maintained a serious distinction between Sephardic and Ashkenazic customs and practices, and few synagogues nowadays restrict membership one way or the other.

Why is **Jerusalem** Judaism's **holiest city**? Are any others especially important?

Jerusalem was the last of several places that functioned as seats of power during the early years of Judaism's monarchy. Around the year 1000 B.C.E., King David captured the hilltop stronghold from a Canaanite tribe called the Jebusites. David's choice of location may well have been motivated by a desire to establish himself politically in a city that had few links to premonarchical Jewish factions. Jerusalem, also called the Hill of Zion, promised David a fresh start. Situated on the highest point in the region (some 2500 feet above sea level), and more or less in the center of tribal territories, the city already had great physical and topographical potential for acquiring symbolic power. But it would be Solomon's Temple, not David's royal headquarters, that would confer on Jerusalem the mantle of great holiness.

Within a few generations after David, the city had become the focal point not only of major Jewish ritual and pilgrimage, but the very throne of God. Messianic hopes and expectations came to be attached to Jerusalem. After the Babylonian Exile the prospect of restoring the city to its former glory gave rise to a new theological interpretation. No longer a mere earthly city, Jerusalem was also—and even more importantly—a heavenly reality mirrored in a terrestrial one.

For many centuries after the Romans destroyed the Second Temple in 70 C.E., Jerusalem was a source of longing for Jews scattered across the globe. As Jews began to return in significant numbers, especially after 1492, Jerusalem became concretely important to the people again. The proclamation of the State of Israel in 1948 raised hopes further, and with Israel's recapture of the city in the Six-Day War of 1967, many Jews revived plans for a full restoration of Jerusalem. For

The Tower of David in Jerusalem is believed to be located on the site of King David's palace.

some now that means plans to rebuild the Temple, but the political implications are so enormous as to make that a most unlikely eventuality. Virtually every square foot of the "Holy Land" bears some historic meaning. Places that had been especially holy in the days of the Patriarchs and Judges (prior to the monarchy) have retained only a shadow of their pristine sacredness. Nothing compares with Jerusalem in that regard.

Rolling stone door at the rock-cut burial place popularly known as the Tomb of Herod's Family (first century C.E.) just west of the Old City of Jerusalem.

What questions does the prospect of **interfaith marriage** raise for Jews?

Attitudes to interfaith marriages vary a great deal among Jews. It is probably fair to say that the preference of most Jews would be that their sons and daughters marry other Jews. But resistance to interfaith marriage is certainly stronger among Orthodox and Conservative Jews than among Reform. Virtually complete prohibition of interfaith marriages in some Jewish communities arises less out of concern for ethnic purity as such than out of a desire to prevent the faith tradition from being irreversibly diluted. Experience has shown that families in which the parents are not both Jewish are less likely to educate their children in the Jewish tradition. Tradition lost is extremely difficult to recover, especially in cultures and societies that seem to value the "new" much more highly than anything with deep historical roots. The musical *Fiddler on the Roof* goes a long way toward helping non-Jews to appreciate the beauty and centrality of "Tradition! Tradition!" for Jews. Families are the first line of defense against the permanent loss, not just of a collection of ritual deeds performed mechanically, but of the meaning of life itself as interpreted from a Jewish perspective.

What **gender-related issues** are important for religious Jews?

Concern for ritual purity has occupied a central place in much of Jewish tradition. Beginning with the Torah's laws of holiness and continuing in the observance of the stricter branches of Judaism, matters related to female fertility, menstruation, and childbearing, for example, have received a great deal of attention. According to scripture, menstruation renders a woman ritually unclean, as does the birth of a child (for seven days if a boy, fourteen if a girl). Gender has had significant implications in religious as well as social roles, especially in Orthodox and Conservative communities. In modern times the question of whether women should become rabbis has arisen. Reform and Reconstructionist communities do have increasing numbers of female

39

rabbis, and the Conservative Jewish Theological Seminary of America began accepting female candidates not long ago. In Orthodox communities, although women are afforded a position of respect and considered naturally more spiritually elevated than men, rabbis are still exclusively male.

Do Jewish communities practice **excommunication** or banishment for religious reasons?

Concern for purity led to the expulsion of lepers, those impure because of contact with the dead, and those "suffering from a discharge" of bodily fluids, from the camp of the Israelites as described in Book of Numbers 5:1–4. Lepers especially were considered not only unhealthy but ritually and ethically unclean, due to the prevalent belief that such an affliction implied some moral guilt on the part of either the individual or the leper's parents. Elsewhere in the Hebrew scripture we hear of the practice of *herem*, placing a "ban" on certain things, such as the spoils of war or the results of ritual sacrifice. In biblical usage, to ban an item was to dedicate it totally to the Lord. Later Jewish tradition used the term *herem* to apply to a kind of excommunication. When authenticated instances of heretical views came to the attention of rabbinical authorities, they could banish the culprit from the community. The philosopher Baruch Spinoza (1632–1677), for example, was excommunicated from the Sephardic community for his insistence on the primacy of reason and for views judged to be pantheistic. Earlier a Portuguese Jew named Uriel da Costa (1585–1640) underwent formal excommunication twice and endured public humiliation for his unacceptable views. Some interpret both Spinoza and da Costa as examples of a clash between Enlightenment views and traditional Jewish beliefs.

How do Jews view Judaism's **relationships to other traditions**?

Even the earliest biblical texts that describe the formative years of Judaism as a faith tradition show a vivid, if largely disapproving, awareness of the religious practices and beliefs of other peoples. Jews were to be a people of faith who would distinguish themselves by their faithful response to divine initiative. Biblical Judaism defined itself in the context of various Canaanite pagan cults, which often exercised an unholy fascination on Jews of wavering faith. Most Jews are, of course, keenly aware of their tradition's complex relationship to Christianity, which claims to be a fulfillment of an ancient messianic expectation. From the Jewish perspective, Christianity was just another of many false movements of its kind. Many have also been puzzled and hurt by ongoing Christian condemnations of Jews as "Christ-killers," a hateful epithet only recently repudiated by the pope.

Throughout medieval times in Europe, Jews often suffered cruelly as a result of severely prejudicial Christian decrees as to how Jews should live and even what they should wear in public. Most of all, many Jews simply do not understand why so many

Christians have harbored such a virulent animosity toward Jews. Judaism has also had an important connection to Islam over the centuries. Jews have generally fared better under Muslim regimes throughout the Middle East, North Africa, and Spain than under Christian authority. From a strictly religious perspective, however, Judaism is strikingly close to Islam in many respects, both in practice and belief: from an uncompromising monotheism to dietary concerns to an egalitarian style of worship and view of authority.

LEADERSHIP, AUTHORITY, AND RELIGIOUS ROLES

What are some of the main **varieties** of Jewish **religious officials** or specialists?

During biblical times the centralized cult of the Temple in Jerusalem required a large and elaborate system of specialists and functionaries. Emblematic roles were assigned to tribes, and to certain clans and families within the tribes. Destruction of the Second Temple in 70 C.E. brought dramatic change in its wake, including a great simplification in ritual practice. The shift to local synagogue worship naturally required the development of a local officialdom whose duties would include presiding over the much-smaller-scale ritual and, at the same time, looking after the more comprehensive spiritual needs of a local community for whom the synagogue was now the focus of religious life.

The *rabbi* (Hebrew for "my master") is the principal religious authority and community representative in contemporary Judaism, as well as the primary leader of synagogue worship. The latter function seems to be a relatively modern development, with emphasis in earlier post-biblical eras on the rabbi as scholar and teacher. In some regions, rabbinical conferences or other organizations may elect or appoint one of their members to serve as "chief" rabbi. Most synagogues and local communities divide duties among several other offices. One of the more important is that of the cantor (*hazzan*), often a person of considerable musical ability and training whose duty is to chant sacred text and to sing special prayers for the various religious observances. The position has been especially necessary in communities whose members generally do not read Hebrew. In Late

The rabbi is the principal religious authority and community representative in contemporary Judaism, as well as the primary leader of synagogue worship.

41

Antiquity the term *hazzan* referred to several community functions but later it was applied exclusively to the cantor (or *sheliach zibbur*, emissary of the congregation). Throughout Jewish history, many rabbis have served as cantors in their synagogues, but rabbi-cantors are now less common. In some congregations a layperson called the *gabbai* ("overseer," roughly) has the duty of commissioning Torah readers for each service.

How are Jewish **religious leaders chosen** and given authority?

In biblical times religious authorities and specialists came largely from hereditary lines within particular tribes that traced their sacred mandates back to the Mosaic revelation at Sinai. Post-biblical developments gradually moved away from hereditary models of religious leadership to a parallel model in which one leader passes on authority to a successor by laying on of hands (called *semikhah* in Hebrew). Thus did Moses "ordain" Joshua and the seventy elders (Numbers 11:16–25, 27:18–23). Members of the Sanhedrin were likewise ordained. But post-biblical communities in the Middle East eventually did away with formal ordination, preferring only to require that prospective rabbis were thoroughly versed in Talmudic and legal studies. A number of modern seminaries, (or rabbinical colleges as some are called), have broadened their curricula to include nontraditional studies to better equip future rabbis to engage more broadly educated congregations. The rich, age-old ritual of semikhah, imposing hands, survives largely in the practice of Orthodox rabbinical academies.

What is the **difference** between a **prophet** and a **sage**?

Biblical prophets and sages arose from similar backgrounds and cultural circumstances, but had different ways of describing the relationship between the human and the divine. First, their overall purpose—call it strategy if you like—differed in several ways. Prophets spoke for God, focused on divine justice, and were motivated by the divine Word and by a conviction of God's presence. Sages spoke for humankind, addressed human reason, and were moved by social conscience. The prophets' rhetoric was fiery and animated, idealistic, and meant to engage people's emotions, while that of the sages was cool and dispassionate, practical, and aimed at persuading listeners by the strength of the argument. Finally, prophets and sages directed their messages at different segments of the public. Prophets struggled urgently to make God known to the rich and powerful in the hope that they would modify their ways of ruling others. Sages sought through steady pedagogy to help ordinary people apply knowledge to their daily lives.

Do Jews **revere** any persons as **especially gifted** with **wisdom**?

Wisdom has always had a special place in Jewish tradition. King Solomon, for all his faults, has occupied the place of honor in this respect. In the biblical story of how two women came to him, both claiming a child as theirs, Solomon responds by decreeing that the child be cut in half. At that the child's true mother offered to save the baby's life by letting the other woman have the infant. Solomon then gave the child to its mother. Tradition says Solomon wrote a number of the "wisdom" books in the Hebrew Bible, as well as few extracanonical or apocryphal works. Since Solomon's time, the custodians of the tradition's treasures of wisdom have been known generically as sages. They have included largely religious scholars and rabbis, such as Hillel and the legendary Rabbi Akiva (c. 50–135 C.E.) and Yohannan ben Zakkai (c. 1–80 C.E.). According to legend, Moses went to Heaven for a preview of the Torah and asked God whether his works would prosper. God showed Moses a vision of a future disciple named Akiva. His lecture was so profound that even Moses could not understand it! The centrality of the sages in Jewish spirituality is indicative of the importance of practical wisdom in the tradition. Wisdom is the highest form of holiness.

Is there such a thing as a **Jewish saint**?

Jewish tradition tells of numerous individuals noted for their holiness and even for the ability to work marvels. But there has never been a formal process by which a man or woman was officially recognized as a paragon of sanctity. Embodiments of holiness fill the pages of the Bible, beginning with Abraham, Jacob, and Joseph and continuing with Moses and David. Numerous women of the Bible are revered for their virtues, including Sarah, Rebecca, Ruth, Esther, and Judith. But saintly figures are not lacking in post-biblical tradition. Some early rabbis, such as Simeon ben Yochai (c. 150), continue to fascinate, most notably in mystically oriented sects such as the Hasidim. Founders of certain sects have also been canonized by popular acclaim. The figure of the *tzaddik* has been especially important among mystically oriented groups, capable of performing wonders and possessed with esoteric knowledge. An important group of holy persons are the Jewish martyrs of various periods in history. When the Maccabeans revolted against the Seleucids, many of their number were martyred and acknowledged as heroes for the faith. During the Roman period, Jews were forbidden to teach Torah openly. According to much later traditional accounts a number of stalwart sages acted in defiance of the prohibition and were executed by Hadrian. They came to be called "The Ten Martyrs." One of the most famous of those killed by Hadrian was Rabbi Akiva (c. 50–135 C.E.), also celebrated for his profound wisdom.

Is there a central teaching or **legislative authority** for Jews?

During later biblical times, beginning around 200 B.C.E., a principal deliberative body of seventy-one members, called the Sanhedrin (Greek *synedrion*), handled all religious and secular matters of importance to Jewish life. Originally located in the Jerusalem Temple, the Sanhedrin remained active until around 425 C.E. Membership consisted of three groups (at least during New Testament times): the Elders, who represented the major tribal clans and families; the High Priests, including elders of the four priestly families as well as former High Priests; and the Scribes, religious legal scholars belonging mostly to the sect known as the Pharisees. The High Priest (or

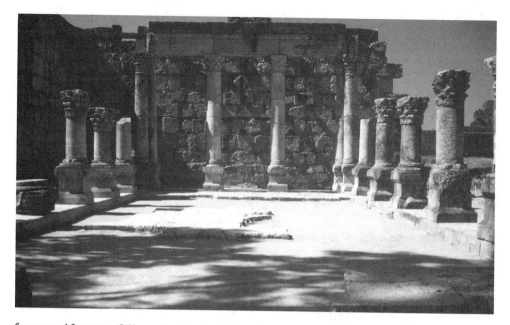

Synagogue of Capernaum, Galilee, northern Israel, c. 200 C.E., showing Hellenistic influence in its columns and plan.

nasi) was chosen from descendants of Moses' brother Aaron and governed the council. While the Sanhedrin did function as a court of law in exceptional cases, it was concerned mostly with larger administrative and juridical issues.

Meanwhile, the *Bet Din* (literally, "House of Judgment") generally adjudicated legal questions, including both religious and civil matters affecting the Jewish community exclusively. Roman law allowed for a large measure of internal rule among Jewish subjects. The Bet Din required at least three (male) judges but handled criminal cases with as many as twenty-three judges. The class of religious scholars known as the "Five Pairs of Teachers" bore responsibility for the two legal bodies. Hillel (nasi) and Shammai (*Av Bet Din,* Chief Justice of the Court) were the last of the Pairs. In this separation of civil and religious spheres, the High Priest generally retained final authority. The Sanhedrin temporarily ceased to exist during the long Exile, but will be renewed, according to tradition, with the arrival of the Messiah. Each Jewish community worldwide continues to have a Bet Din to arbitrate legal issues and disputes according to Jewish law.

During later Antiquity (c. 500–1000) the scholarly class called the Geonim ("Eminences") functioned as a major authority for Middle Eastern and European Jews by publishing their rulings in documents called Responsa. For Jewish communities in Iraq, land of the Exile, the position of Exilarch (*resh galuta,* "head of those in exile"), a position generally occupied by laymen, continued to wield some authority until about the mid-thirteenth century. For many generations, even up to early modern times, the *Qehillah,* or local Jewish community organization, was the principal decision-making body.

Do Jews have a system of religious law?

Jewish religious law is among the most highly developed and extensive systems ever devised. This is not surprising in a tradition whose scripture begins with a large section, the Torah, for which "law" is the chief synonym. Ever since the end of the monarchy, Jewish communities have struggled with the problem of how to observe their own religious ordinances within the context of a larger secular or civil regime. In some circumstances the civil authorities allowed Jews considerable autonomy in administering their religious law, with the understanding that none of its provisions would run afoul of secular statutes. Legal scholars in Late Antiquity and through the Middle Ages produced voluminous collections referred to generically as the "codes" of law. Ancient concern with ritual purity and precision persists in some branches of Judaism, especially among the Orthodox and many Conservatives. Rabbis function as legal scholars in those situations, interpreting the 613 specific commands and prohibitions of the Torah. For Jews less attentive to the minute details of practice, the rabbi's role is more broadly pastoral.

Who were the **Pharisees**?

During the Maccabean (or Hasmonean) revolt in 164 B.C.E. against the foreign rule of the Seleucids, a fascinating sect or school of thought called the Pharisees began to emerge from obscurity. They were called *Perushim* ("separatists, seceders, heretics") in Hebrew, but that may originally have been a pejorative term coined by their opponents, the Sadducees. At first the Pharisees supported the Maccabees, who initially packed their new Sanhedrin with members of the sect. But the Pharisees disapproved of the way ruler John Hyrcanus (135–104 B.C.E.) attempted to secure both religious and civil authority for himself and so they withdrew their support. In general the Pharisees enjoyed the favor of the masses for their stand on political issues.

Meanwhile the new Hasmonean ruler Alexander Yannai (103–76 B.C.E.) cultivated the support of the Sadducees, who tended to be aristocratic. When the Pharisees condemned Alexander's priestly conduct of sacred ritual as blasphemous, they paid with death or exile. But Alexander's wife, Alexandra, brought back the Pharisees after her husband's death, allowing them to restore both Sanhedrin and temple ritual. The Pharisees emphasized God's love for each person and taught the resurrection of the body. They stood against the priestly aristocracy in their teaching of the individual's personal relationship with God. After the Romans ended Hasmonean rule in 63 B.C.E., the Pharisees insisted that a separation of secular and sacred spheres would allow the Jewish people to tolerate foreign rule so long as the Romans left them their religious freedom. After 70 C.E., the Pharisees disappeared as a distinct sect or party, but much of their spirit lived on in the growth of rabbinical Judaism.

Who were the **Sadducees** and are they still around?

Around the time the Pharisees became important players in Jewish history, the Sadducees (*Tseduqim*) also emerged. They held that only the Torah was authentic revelation, repudiating the Pharisaic emphasis on the full Bible as well as all subsequent oral tradition. They also denied the Pharisees' teaching of the soul's immortality and bodily resurrection. As the Pharisees presented themselves as the heirs of Moses and of his authority as lawgiver, the Sadducees anchored their authority in that of Moses' priestly brother Aaron. More specifically, the Sadducees may have gotten their name because of their claim to be directly descended from Zadok, the High Priest in Solomon's temple. The Sadducees had struck a compromise with the Hasmoneans, agreeing to support the rulers if they would officially nullify the Pharisaic teaching on the validity of the Oral Law. In exchange, the Sadducees would tolerate the Hasmonean claim to priestly authority—a stunning accommodation indicative of the enmity between Pharisees and Sadducees. When the Pharisees were restored to favor under the ruler Alexandra (76–67 B.C.E.), they in turn struck a deal by which they would sanction the priesthood of the Sadducees in exchange for the Sadducees' acceptance of the binding force of Oral Torah. During the time of Jesus, the High Priest named Caiaphas was a Sadducee, but the sect disappeared along with the Temple, which was destroyed in 70 C.E.

What are some historically **important religio-ethnic groups**?

- Ashkenazic Jewry: Jews of Central European (esp. Rhineland) origin, many of whose descendants migrated to Eastern Europe.
- Conservative: nineteenth- to twentieth-century movement of largely American development, designed to allow more latitude for inculturation in practice while at least ostensibly not encouraging too much assimilation.
- Essenes: ascetic community living in the region of the Dead Sea at Qumran (150 B.C.E.–75 C.E.); like Pharisees, believed in immortality of soul and resurrection of the body.
- Hasidim: eighteenth-century European movement emphasizing prophetic message of divine unconditional love (*hesed*) and devotional fervor, known in the USA largely through the *Chabad* movement.
- Karaites: an early medieval "reform" movement that, in effect, revived basic theological principles more famously espoused by the Sadducees six hundred years previously.
- Orthodox: began to distinguish itself in early modern Europe, recommending strict observance of rabbinical law and avoidance of assimilation.
- Pharisees: a school of religious scholars (rabbis) active especially from the second century B.C.E. through the first century C.E., who believed in the resurrection, the fatherhood of God, and accepted as canonical the Prophets and Writings in addi-

tion to the Torah, and insisted on the need for oral tradition to understand the scripture in changing times.

- Reform: nineteenth-century European movement based on Enlightenment principles and designed to allow greater freedom both in theory and practice than "orthodox" traditions.

- Reconstructionist: twentieth-century adaptation more traditional in practice than Reform, but espousing a more generic theism than styles of Jewish theology.

- Sadducees: a school of religious scholars active from the second century B.C.E. through the first century C.E., who accepted Torah alone as sacred text, denied the legitimacy and need of oral tradition, and rejected belief in the resurrection.

- Sephardic Jewry: Jews of Iberian, and, by extension, North African or Middle Eastern origin.

HOLIDAYS AND
REGULAR OBSERVANCES

What kind of **religious calendar** do Jews observe?

The Jewish calendar is lunisolar—that is, it is regulated by the positions of both the moon and the sun. There are twelve alternating lunar months of twenty-nine and thirty days each. The year totals 353, 354, or 355 days. Leap years are introduced to conform to the solar year of 365.24 days. Leap years contain either 383, 384, or 385 days and occur seven times in every nineteen-year period. This is called the Metonic cycle. The first month of the year is that in which the Exodus began. But tradition dictates that certain feasts must occur during certain seasons, so the calendar has to be adjusted every so often to prevent the lunar months from straying too far from the agricultural, or solar, cycle. To make it work, an extra month, called *Adar Sheni* (Second Adar), is added during seven out of every nineteen years. Thus, the number of days in a given year is not fixed and may vary from 353 to 385 days, and the first day of the month can fall on any day of the week and will vary from year to year. The Jewish lunar months are called *Tishri* (September/October), *Cheshvan* (October/November), *Kislev* (November/December), *Tevet* (December/January), *Shevat* (January/February), *Adar* (February/March), *Adar Sheni* (Second Adar, inserted only in "leap years"), *Nisan* (March/April), *Iyyar* (April/May), *Sivan* (May/June), *Tammuz* (June/July), *Av* (July/August), and *Elul* (August/September). With the leap year provision, the lunar months slide back or forward but remain within the solar months indicated in parentheses.

The first and second days of Tishri during Rosh Hashanah are ushered in by blowing upon a ram's horn.

What are the **High Holy Days**?

The autumnal holy days begin with *Rosh Hashanah* ("Beginning of the Year") on the first and second days of Tishri, ushered in with the sound of the ram's horn (*shofar*) as a symbol of divine sovereignty over the universe. This begins a period in which people make an accounting of how they have cared for creation entrusted to them. On the third day of Tishri comes the "Fast of Gedaliah" (*Tzom Gedaliah*), on which Jews recall the end of the first Jewish commonwealth (II Kings 25:25). But the culmination of the period occurs on the tenth day of Tishri in a major fast observing the Day of Atonement (*Yom Kippur*). This day features five worship services and includes a communal confession. On the evening before, a cantor prays the very moving *Kol Nidrei* ("All the Vows") which annuls all rashly made promises of the previous year. Emphasis is on forgiveness of all wrongdoing. Regular morning prayer begins the next day, followed by additional prayers later in the morning focused specially on this feast. Afternoon prayer is followed by a service that recalls the closing of the Temple gate in olden days and includes the *Amidah,* a litany called "Our Father, Our King," the Shema, and a concluding sound of the ram's horn. The five services virtually flow from one to the next, making for a very full day of prayer.

How and when do Jews celebrate **Passover** (*Pesach*)?

Celebrated from the 15th to the 21st of Nisan (a day longer outside of Israel), Passover (*Pesach*) is a spring festival commemorating God's deliverance of Israel from Egypt. The rebirth of nature recalls the birth of Israel as a people. Specifically, its imagery derives from the belief that God instructed the Israelites to mark their doorposts with the blood of the sacrificial lamb. When God sent an angel to strike dead the first born of all the Egyptians, the angel would "pass over" the houses of the Israelites. The biblical account appears in Exodus 11–12.

During the observance of the Passover *Seder* ("order of service") participants recount the story in the *Haggadah Shel Pesach*. Celebrating with unleavened bread and wine, participants begin by blessing the wine and washing their hands. They then dip a vegetable into saltwater and eat it, recalling the Red Sea. They then break the second of three pieces of bread (*matzah*) and hide it for the children to search out later, in recollection of hunger and divine manna in the desert. After recounting the story of the Exodus, they drink a second cup of wine and wash their hands again. Blessing the bread, they eat the first piece and what remains of the second piece. They eat some bitter herbs, recalling the suffering of the slaves in Egypt, then dip some herbs into *charoset,* a paste of spices, wine, matzah, and fruit, symbolizing the mortar the former slaves made for Pharaoh. The main meal is followed by eating the hidden part of the second matzah, and by a final blessing and a third cup of wine. The celebration closes with psalms of praise and another cup of wine.

What are the other **great feasts of pilgrimage** and **remembrance**?

The feast of *Shavuot* ("Weeks") begins seven weeks after Passover. Originally coinciding with the wheat harvest, the Feast of Weeks recalls Israel's spiritual harvest of the divine Law at Sinai. The feast occurs on the 6th of Sivan (a day longer outside Israel), the fiftieth day (pentecost in Greek) after Passover, marking the end of the "days of the *omer*" ("sheaf") in reference to the ancient practice of bringing the first sheaves of barley as a Temple offering. The third of the great holidays is *Sukkot,* the Feast of Booths, or Tabernacles. Five days after the Day of Atonement, from the 15th to the 23rd of Tishri (a day longer outside Israel, except in Reform congregations) Jews celebrate this harvest festival marking the end of the vintage season. Many families construct small symbolic structures in the backyard, recalling as they take their meals there how God sheltered the people through the wilderness of the Exodus. Along with Passover and Shavuot, this was a pilgrimage feast before the destruction of the Temple, when many traveled to Jerusalem to celebrate. Families bless four plants as symbols of unity in diversity. Holding in the left hand a citrus called the *ethrog,* and in the right a bound cluster of one palm, two willow, and three myrtle branches (together called the *lulav*), they make gestures of blessing and sing *Hosanna,* "Save us."

What is the significance of **Hanukkah** and **Purim**?

An observance perhaps best known to non-Jews is the late autumn Feast of Dedication called Hanukkah, which begins on the 25th of Kislev and continues for eight days. The nine-branch candlestick (menorah) recalls how, during the Maccabean revolt against the Seleucid profanation of the Temple, a one-day supply of oil miraculously lasted all eight days of the rededication of the holy place, which occurred in 165 B.C.E. Each evening families light an additional candle from the central flame, sing devotional songs, and exchange small presents. Another remembrance of a similar Jewish victory against great odds is the feast of Purim. A month before Passover, after a daylong preparatory fast, the feast of "lots" on the 14th of Adar commemorates how the evil Persian Haman tried to wipe Israel out by casting lots. The Book of Esther (one of the five Megillot) tells the story of one of Judaism's most redoubtable heroines. The day before Purim recalls the Fast of

49

Western Wall of the Jewish Temple, popularly known as the "Wailing Wall" because of its association with annual lamentation on the 9th of Av over the destruction of the Temple. The lower courses of masonry are from Herod's time, identifiable as Herodian by the trimmed outer margin of each stone. (Photo courtesy of David Oughton.)

Esther (Ta'anit *Esther*), and the day after, called Shushan Purim, observes the memory of how Esther's deeds gave cause for joy among the Jews of Shushan. Purim has an almost carnival atmosphere, complete with costumes and the giving of gifts.

Are any **other regular observances** significant in the Jewish ritual year?

Three days of fasting and mourning, two in summer and one in winter, are connected to remembrance of the First and Second Temples. *Tisha b'Av* (the Ninth of Av) is a day of lamentation for the destruction of Solomon's Temple in 586 B.C.E. Israeli Jews and pilgrims gather at the Western Wall of the Herodian Temple to grieve over the loss. The short biblical book called Lamentations is a traditional reading for the occasion. Associated rituals have given the remains of the Temple the popular name the "Wailing Wall." Eight days after Hanukkah, on the 10th of Tevet, another fast commemorates the Babylonian king Nebuchadnezzar's initial siege of Jerusalem in 587 B.C.E. In more recent times the occasion has become associated with mourning for victims of the Holocaust. On the 17th of Tammuz, a less popular occasion, some Jews fast to recall the times when the armies of Nebuchadnezzar and Titus first broke through the walls of the Temple in 587/6 B.C.E. and 70 C.E., respectively. Finally, there are two other minor observances. One is the 15th of Shevat, the New Year for Trees (*Rosh ha-Shanah le-Ilanot*), a day of thanks to God for the bounty of the earth. The other is called *Simchat Torah* ("Rejoicing in the Torah"). The day after

Sukkot, Jews celebrate the end of the annual cycle of liturgical readings with processions in which the scrolls are carried around the synagogue with children leading the crowd.

Sacred and Notable Days of the Jewish Religious Year

Month, Day	Event
Tishri (September–October)	
1, 2	Rosh Hashana (New Year)
3	Tzom Gedaliah (Fast of Gedaliah)
10	Yom Kippur (Day of Atonement)
15–21	Sukkot (Tabernacles)
22	*Shemini Atzeret (Eighth Day of the Solemn Assembly)
23	*Simchat Torah (Rejoicing of the Law)
Cheshvan, or Marcheshvan (October–November)	
Kislev (November–December)	
25	Hanukkah (Feast of Dedication) begins
Tevet (December–January)	
2	Hanukkah ends
10	Asara be-Tevet (Fast of Tevet)
Shevat (January–February)	
15	Tu bi-Shevat (Fifteenth of Shevat: New Year for Trees)
Adar (February–March)	
13	Ta'anit Esther (Fast of Esther)
14, 15	Purim (Feast of Lots), Shushan Purim
Nisan (March–April)	
15–22	Pesach (Passover)
Iyyar (April–May)	
18	Lag ba-Omer (33d Day of the Omer Counting)
Sivan (May–June)	
6, 7	Shavuot (Feast of Weeks, or Pentecost)
Tammuz (June–July)	
17	Shiva Asar be-Tammuz (Fast of Tammuz)
Av (July–August)	
9	Tisha b'Av (Fast of Av)
Elul (August–September)	

*Note: In Israel and in Reform congregations, Shemini Atzeret and Simchat Torah are celebrated together on the 22nd.

Additionally, many Jewish calendars now list the 5th of Iyyar—Israel Independence Day—among the Jewish holidays.

CUSTOMS AND RITUALS

How do Jews observe the **Sabbath**?

Ritual observance of the Sabbath (Saturday) begins at sundown Friday and concludes twenty-five hours later at nightfall. In home ceremonies, families begin the day of rest by lighting two candles, one symbolizing resting from work and the other tranquility and joy, while many other families light the number of candles that equals the number of members in their family. Then after *Kiddush* (sanctification) prayers over a glass of wine, they celebrate with Sabbath dinner. The Friday night dinner is the first of three special meals, and at the end of the day on Saturday, the *havdalah* (separation) ceremony is performed, which marks the end of the sacred time of the Sabbath and transition back to "ordinary" time. Some celebrants include spices (and elaborately decorated spiceboxes) in that ceremony. Many Jews attend synagogue prayers on Friday evening, with typically larger numbers going to prayers together on Saturday. Refraining from labors on the Sabbath is variously interpreted, from Reform Judaism's definition of "work" as one's ordinary livelihood occupation, to Orthodox Judaism's meticulous attention to avoiding all of the thirty-nine varieties of work in Rabbinic tradition. For example, Orthodox Jews generally do not drive on the Sabbath, preferring to walk even considerable distances to synagogue services.

What kinds of **rituals** do Jews engage in **privately** or alone?

Home remains the principal place for Jewish prayer and religious observance. Traditional prayer includes the thrice-daily Amidah ("standing") prayer in the morning, afternoon, and evening. The morning and evening prayers begin with benedictions that praise God's love of Israel as manifested in the creation of light and in the ordering of day and night. The Shema follows, acknowledging God's unity and redemption of the people. At the center of all three prayers is the *Shimoneh Esreh,* or "Eighteen" blessings (which is actually made up of nineteen blessings, one being added later). Prayer ends with the *Aleinu,* "Upon us praise is encumbent...." Afternoon prayer usually adds Psalm 145. According to the Talmud, all Jews should pray a hundred benedictions (*berakhot*) every day, in recognition of all things enjoyable, to give thanks, and prior to all other religious duties, in addition to the blessings that are part of daily prayers.

How do Jews conduct their **regular communal liturgical worship**?

A feature of ritual practice common to all Jewish congregations is the reading of scripture. Ancient Palestinian custom used a cycle in which Sabbath readings completed the whole Torah in a three-year cycle. Some Reform and Conservative communities have reinstituted that practice in recent times. Orthodox and Reconstructionist congregations continue to use the ancient Babylonian custom of a one-year cycle of fifty-

A young woman lights two candles for the Sabbath. One candle represents resting from work, while the other represents tranquility and joy.

four *sedarim*. On Mondays, Thursdays, and Sabbath mornings and afternoons, as well as on new moons and religious festivals, Jews read the Torah in the synagogue. Regular Sabbath readings follow the Torah in order, continuously, from Genesis through Deuteronomy. Readings for the various feasts and fasts are chosen specially for the occasion and do not follow a continuous cycle.

In addition, texts from the Former and Latter Prophets (but not from the Writings) are selected as a kind of parallel or commentary on the day's Torah texts. These supplementary readings, used on Sabbaths, fasts, and feasts, are called the *Haftarah*. Some theorize that the practice of parallel readings originated during Seleucid times when persecution included a ban on Torah reading. Communal prayer adds to the regular prayers of the privately performed Amidah, the *Kedushah* ("Holy, Holy, Holy") at the end of the third benediction in the morning and afternoon, as well as the *Kaddish* ("Holy" in Aramaic) to mark the end of the various segments of the communal prayer and to bring it to a close. The standard prayerbook for synagogue worship is called the *Siddur* ("order"), which is based on the Psalter. The first formal edition dates back to about the ninth century C.E.

Do Jews practice **rituals of divination**?

In biblical times one of the roles of the Temple's High Priest was to serve as a medium for oracles. Part of the priestly paraphernalia was a mysterious pair of objects called the *Urim* and *Thummim,* which were a form of lots carried in a pocket called the "breastplate," which was suspended from the shoulders. The Urim and Thummim, a pair of flat stones, are mentioned a number of times in the Hebrew Bible, suggesting that this form of divination was of some importance, even though others forms were explicitly forbidden. Thummim may derive from a word that meant "perfect," hence of positive value. Scholars surmise that Urim probably carried a negative meaning. Thus, they may have been read as "yes" or "no," "guilty" or "innocent," for example, in determining the answer to a question. Even the word "Torah" apparently comes from a root that means to "cast lots" in order to obtain an oracle. The High Priest would toss the Urim and Thummim, one meaning "yes" and the other "no," in order to determine God's will in a given instance. King Saul was so chosen to rule Israel, as were priests in outlying areas selected to work in the Temple. Divination has found no significant place in post-biblical Jewish tradition.

Has **pilgrimage** ever figured prominently in **Jewish practice**?

In biblical times Jewish males were expected to make pilgrimages to Jerusalem for three occasions, the feasts of Passover, Booths, and Weeks. Specific ritual requirements attended each of the three pilgrimage feasts. But since all were tied to the existence of the Temple, pilgrimage as a specific religious duty lapsed during the Exile and again when the Second Temple was destroyed in 70 C.E. Throughout post-biblical Jewish history, Jews in the diaspora have continued to pray about Jerusalem and have longed to return to it. Since the Six-Day War of 1967, many have realized the dream of one day visiting the site of the Temple and praying at the Western Wall. Strictly speaking, modern-day Jewish pilgrims are not fulfilling a biblical injunction, since the Temple remains only a memory. But pilgrimage has in effect assumed a new form for many Jews. For most it is a journey of remembrance of a former dispensation and a chance to connect with deep roots. Some journey in the hope that they may live to see the glory of the Temple and its associated ritual practices restored.

What is the significance of **keeping kosher**?

Kashrut is the Hebrew term for the use of "ritually pure" (*kasher*) food. It refers to the way food is prepared as well as to certain types of food. With respect to manner of preparation, the opposite of kasher is *terefah,* "torn" by a predator, rather than properly butchered. The basic principle here is that an animal's death by predator constitutes a defect in the animal product. Proper butchering (called *shehitah*) involves using only perfectly smooth blades to slit the animal's throat and windpipe, draining the blood, and inspecting for blemishes. With respect to types of food, Jews make a number of major distinctions between what is clean and what is unclean. Clean animals include cattle, sheep, and other ruminants with fully cloven hooves (but not nonruminant mammals like pigs, or those with solid or only partly cloven hooves, such as dogs or horses). Clean birds include pigeons, doves, chickens, pheasant, and domestically raised geese and ducks (but not birds of prey, wild water fowl, or most other common wild birds). All reptiles and amphibians are unclean, but fish with scales and internal bones (as opposed to cartilage, as with shark) are acceptable.

In addition, expanding on the biblical prohibition of "cooking a kid in its mother's milk" (Exodus 34:26), dairy and meat products may not be combined in any way. Strict observers of kashrut keep separate sets of kitchen tools—some even totally separate kitchens—for meats and dairy products. Kosher practice is an excellent example of the distinction between custom and ritual. Observance of dietary laws often involves, or presupposes, precise ritual action, such as in the kosher method of slaughtering an animal or the care taken not to contaminate utensils. But in general it means simply a customary way of handling food that has religious implications.

In the ceremony of Kapporot, performed during Yom Kippur, sins are transferred to a chicken (or sometimes a bag of coins) and the chicken is ritually slaughtered. The meat is then given to the poor. (Dubova / Shutterstock.com.)

How do Jews **celebrate birth**?

When God made a covenant with Abraham (Genesis 17), the removal of the foreskin of the penis was to be the sign of its ratification. Circumcision of baby boys generally occurs on the eighth day, performed by a specialist called a *moyel,* who is often a rabbi, in the baby's home. After the surgical procedure and accompanying prayers are completed, participants bless a cup of wine. Parents then declare the child's name. Reform communities now have a parallel home ritual to welcome baby girls, including all but the surgery. Other congregations still generally perform the naming ritual for girls in the synagogue. Some still give children two names, one religious, in Hebrew or Yiddish, and one secular. In addition to these early rituals, a ritual of "redemption" of a firstborn son also occurs on the thirty-first day of his life. The practice arose from the biblical teaching that each firstborn son belongs to God but can be "bought back" (Numbers 18:15–16). In general the ritual is tied to the residual importance of the hereditary priesthood, for it requires a *kohen,* or descendant of the biblical priesthood, to perform it.

What does the ritual of **circumcision** entail?

Circumcision—the removal of the foreskin of the penis—is performed on all male Jewish children on the eighth day after their birth. It is also performed on male converts to Judaism. The operation is called for in Genesis 17 and is considered the strongest required sign of adherence to Judaism. It is also a powerful symbol of the Covenant of Abraham. As implied by the Talmudic tractate Nedarim 31b, circumcision was originally performed because the foreskin was considered to be a blemish. To attain a state of perfection, the foreskin had to be removed.

During ancient times, some Hellenistic Jews—especially those whose loins would be exposed in the course of athletics or public bathing—had an operation performed to conceal their circumcisions. Later, in order to prevent Jewish men from hiding their circumcisions, rabbis added the requirement that the entire foreskin—not just the end portion—be excised completely. This is known as *peri'ah*, the laying bare of the glans. At a later period an additional requirement was added, directing the circumciser to apply directing that the circumciser to apply his lips to the penis in order to draw the blood that flowed from the incision. For hygienic reasons, this practice was modified to allow the blood to be drawn through a glass tube.

For a baby boy, the circumcision must take place on the eighth day after birth, unless medical reasons prevent it. Only one exception is allowed to the universal requirement that Jewish infant boys be circumcised. If two previous sons have died as a result of the operation, thereby implying hereditary hemophilia, the third and all subsequent sons are exempted from circumcision. The day of circumcision for an infant boy is considered a time of celebration for the entire community. Customarily, the father of the boy hands his son to the circumciser, who recites appropriate prayers and typically invokes Elijah. The ceremony is often followed by a religious meal of celebration.

The coming of age ritual for young Jewish men is the bar mitzvah; for girls it is the bat mitzvah.

What are the principal **Jewish rites of passage**?

Circumcision, the naming ritual, and redemption of the firstborn son are important early rites. To welcome older youngsters into full membership in the community, the most prominent rites are puberty or coming-of-age rituals. At that time a young boy becomes a "Son of the Commandment" (*bar mitzvah*). In a similar ritual a young girl becomes a "Daughter of the Commandment" (*bat mitzvah*). "Confirmation" still often acknowledges an older teenager's full maturity. Jewish boys of thirteen and girls of twelve are formally recognized as religiously mature. They become sons and daughters of the commandment (bar or bat mitzvah) in rituals that acknowledge that they are now responsible for fulfilling the prescriptions of the divine Law.

Most communities, other than the Orthodox, celebrate this coming-of-age for both genders, but only the bar mitzvah is performed in a synagogue. A central feature of the ritual involves the initiate's reading from the Torah scroll in Hebrew. Other features can extend to a much broader participation in the service, including carrying the scroll to the reading table and reciting other prayers. In some communities, a joint confirmation ceremony for sixteen- or seventeen-year-old boys and girls occurs in conjunction with the Feast of Weeks, since that observance commemorates the original reception of the Torah at Sinai. Confirmation replaced the puberty rite in some European communities. Now some Reform, Conservative, and Reconstructionist congregations practice both confirmation and bar/bat mitzvah.

Is there a Jewish ritual of **marriage**?

Many readers will be familiar with the Jewish custom of having the groom, standing with the bride under a canopy (the *huppah*), shatter a wine glass with his foot at the conclusion of wedding ceremonies. The symbolic act is meant to help people keep in mind the seriousness of marriage, and perhaps recall the destruction of the Temple. The whole ceremony is called *kiddushin,* the sanctification. Taking place in almost any kind of public space, including a synagogue, it begins with a procession. The ritual is largely up to the couple and their families, along with the rabbi presiding, and is not dictated by traditional text or established rubrics. A reception typically follows, often with a blessing before and after the meal.

How do Jews deal **ritually** with **death**?

Most Jews do not observe the custom of the wake, either at the mortuary or in the private home, since embalming is not customary. Cremation is not ordinarily done. Family members prepare the body and burial ideally occurs within a day of death. Sitting *shivah* (literally, "seven") refers to a seven-day period of mourning for a family member. Friends and relatives visit the home of the deceased to extend their sympathy and pray with the family. Every period of seven days naturally includes a Sabbath, but on that day mourners refrain from manifesting their grief outwardly. Groups called the *hevra kaddisha* ("holy brotherhood") provide burial services. The custom of observing the anniversary or *yahrzeit* of a relative's death involves visiting the grave and reciting the Mourners' Kaddish, a prayer in praise of the Holy One whose dominion is everlasting.

CHRISTIANITY

HISTORY AND SOURCES

When and where did **Christianity begin?**

People who professed themselves to be followers of Jesus were first called "Christianoi" in the Syrian town of Antioch perhaps twenty or thirty years after the death of Jesus of Nazareth. But as with other traditions, it is difficult, if not impossible, to assign a precise date to the origins of Christianity. Reasonably sound historical information, however, supports a number of general conclusions about the matter. Most of the earliest followers of Jesus were Jews who believed that this man from Galilee, a northern sector of the Roman province known as Palestine and administered by the Herodian dynasty of Jewish kings, fulfilled enough of the traditional criteria to be proclaimed Messiah or, to use the Greek equivalent, "Christ."

Jesus seems to have formed a core community of supporters among Galileans and other Jews who, according to the Greek or New Testament, accepted his invitation to follow him on his itinerant mission to preach the coming of the Kingdom of God. During his lifetime, Jesus apparently sent out his seventy disciples, among whom were the twelve Apostles, to announce the Kingdom, to heal the sick, and to forgive sins. Jesus' death around 30 C.E. was a severe blow to his followers' sense of identity. But, reinvigorated by their belief that Jesus had risen from the dead, they regrouped and organized themselves as a missionary movement, some preaching to Jews and some to Gentiles (non-Jews). They fanned out over much of the eastern Mediterranean basin, and within a generation after Jesus' death, numerous small religious communities had begun to call themselves Christians. At first the Christians met in "house churches" under the local leadership of elders or "presbyters," later to be called priests. Deacons and deaconesses served the needs of the local community, and the communities in a given region looked to the leadership of "overseers" (from the Greek *episkopoi*) or "bishops."

59

Irish stained glass depiction of Jesus ascending into Heaven before Mary and the Apostles. Dublin, Ireland.

Did **Jesus "found" Christianity** as a distinct religious tradition?

Jesus and the Buddha had this in common: they were both primarily teachers who offered what were judged to be nontraditional interpretations of already ancient traditions. Neither seems to have set out deliberately to "found" a new religious community, though they both gathered about themselves the nucleus of what would eventually become distinct institutional structures. As such, Jesus and the Buddha were foundational figures rather than founders. Leaders among their immediate communities inherited the task of working out the organizational details. A number of able leaders emerged from the early followers of Jesus—in particular Peter, one of the original twelve Apostles, and Paul, a Pharisee from Asia Minor who had experienced a dramatic change of religious orientation. They and other members of the first-generation followers of Jesus disagreed about precisely what traditional Jewish practices they should retain and how they should set about establishing their own distinct religious identity: Should Christians keep the Mosaic Law? How much of it? Did that include circumcision? Should they continue to go to the Temple in Jerusalem?

Leaders convened a council or conference in Jerusalem around the year 48 C.E. to work out the most vexing of these problems (Acts of the Apostles 15). A group of Pharisees among them insisted on imposing Jewish Law and custom intact, but the majority opted to retain only basic dietary, ritual, and ethical constraints. A majority resolved to preach the Gospel to non-Jews, arguing that the Hebrew scriptures enjoin such universality. The "founding" of Christianity was far less the result of a clear one-time decision than the gradual evolution of a set of views and practices that the leaders representing the various local communities judged consistent with their emerging identity.

Do Christians consider the **Old Testament** identical to the **Hebrew scriptures**?

Christian communities identify and enumerate the canon of the "Old Testament" differently both from mainstream Jewish tradition and, in some instances, from each other. In theory, Christian churches agree in dividing the whole corpus into the Law, the Prophets, and the Writings, but they identify various groupings in the Hebrew scriptural canon as individual works and thus arriving at a total of thirty-nine books. But for pedagogical purposes, one could argue, Christian biblical studies distinguish the Pentateuch (the Jewish Torah), the Historical books, Prophets strictly so-called, and Wisdom literature.

The historical books include a group known to both Protestants and Jews also as the "former prophets" (Joshua, Judges, I and II Samuel, and I and II Kings); the books of Chronicles, Ezra and Nehemiah. Among the "Latter" Prophets, known to most Christians simply as the prophetic texts, are the three major prophetic books, Isaiah, Jeremiah, and Ezekiel; the twelve "minor" prophets counted as one in the Hebrew scriptures; and Daniel. Finally, among the category of texts collectively known to Jews as the Writings is a set of works some Christians call "wisdom literature," some traditionally attributed to David and his son Solomon, and the mini-anthology called the Five Scrolls (or *megillot*). Catholic versions of the Bible add seven works considered "apocryphal" in Protestant traditions, including the "historical" Books of Maccabees and the "wisdom" books Ecclesiasticus and Wisdom. Finally, both Protestants and Catholics call "apocryphal" three other short works, III and IV Esdras (Ezra) and the Prayer of Manasseh.

What are the **earliest Christian sacred writings**?

Two broad types of literature comprise the bulk of the Christian scripture. Among the earliest documents are the letters of Paul. Tradition attributes fourteen of the New Testament's twenty-seven "books" or epistles to Paul, but it seems likely that several were penned under a pseudonym. The largest and most important of the texts are addressed to local Christian communities collectively (Romans, I and II Corinthians, Galatians, Ephesians, Colossians, I and II Thessalonians). Four are addressed to individual Christian leaders who worked with Paul (I and II Timothy, Titus, Philemon). The addressees of the Letter to the Hebrews, almost certainly not written by Paul, are curiously diffuse and not as geographically identifiable as are the local churches. These epistles provide a great deal of information about the spread and organization of the early Church, and, to a lesser degree, about the personality of this man of prodigious energy called Paul, a man some regard as the true "founder" of Christianity. Seven other letters, two attributed to Peter, three to John, one to James, and one to Jude, afford small glimpses into the variety of theological and practical issues facing the Christian "*diaspora,*" the communities developing beyond the central Middle East.

At the heart of the Christian scriptures are four remarkable documents called "Gospels" ("good news"). Mark's Gospel, likely the earliest, is also the shortest of the four. Matthew's is addressed largely to those of Jewish background, and Luke's followed within the next twenty to thirty years. Luke's also has the distinction of being part of the only consciously crafted two-volume work in the New Testament, completed by Luke's account of the post-Jesus church in the Acts of the Apostles. Because of their similarity of perspective and emphases, the Gospels of Matthew, Mark, and Luke are called the "synoptic" Gospels. John's Gospel, often referred to as the most theological of the four, almost certainly came last, around the end of the first century C.E. Last but not least is the Book of Revelation, also called the Apocalypse. Tradition attributes the work to John the Evangelist, since the work seems to date from around the same time as the fourth Gospel.

How did the **early Christians** interpret the **Jewish scriptures**?

From the very beginning, the emergence of Christianity as a distinct tradition depended on the young community's exegesis of the Hebrew scriptures. Since the majority of the earliest Christians were Jewish by birth and education, they naturally regarded the Hebrew Bible as their own and as authoritative divine revelation. But the tradition of messianic expectation that had evolved especially in the later writings evoked continual scrutiny and reexamination among Jews everywhere: When would the Messiah come? And how was one to identify him? Largely on the basis of their reading of scripture, the early followers of Jesus found the answers in Jesus. By a process that would come to be known as "typological exegesis," early Christians saw in numerous Old Testament personages anticipations or "types" of Christ. Abraham, for example, was a type of God the Father in his willingness to sacrifice his only son, Isaac, who was in turn a type of Christ. Jonah, who emerged alive after three days in the belly of the whale, was a type of Christ's resurrection after three days in the grave. A variation on the theme of typology saw in Jesus the perfection of realities only adumbrated in the Hebrew scriptures. Aaron's priesthood, for example, was merely temporary (as evidenced by the destruction of the Temple), but that of Christ was eternal (Hebrews 7).

In addition to discerning these and other typological antecedents of Christ, interpreters saw in many prophetic writings veiled allusions to the Christ who was to come. In the so-called "suffering servant" texts of Second Isaiah, for example, early Christians detected such striking parallels to what they believed were the very essence of the life and death of Jesus that they felt the prophet could only have been referring to this Messiah. In the Greek Testament, Jesus suggests a parallel between the works he now performs and Isaiah's references to a Spirit-filled anointed one who preaches good news to the poor, frees the imprisoned, and heals the blind, and likens himself to Elijah and Elisha (Luke 4:16–30). These are only a few of the ways in which early Christians found legitimation for their views in Jewish tradition.

How do the Christian scriptures **describe Jesus**?

Weaving together historical fact, interpretation of pre-Christian sources, and an emerging understanding of the circumstances in which the earliest Christians found themselves, the Gospels provide insights of various kinds into the life and identity of Jesus. The four Gospels are not historical biography in the modern sense of that term. Behind each of the Gospels is a particular theological view about who Jesus is. A concrete example will make this clear. Matthew and Luke both include genealogies of Jesus. Not only are the figures mentioned not identical, but the two authors approach the matter quite differently. Matthew opens his Gospel with the genealogy, tracing Jesus from Abraham forward through David and the Babylonian Exile, emphasizing his Jewish lineage and explicitly calling him "the Christ," the Messiah (Matthew 1:1–17). Luke inserts his

genealogy just after John baptizes Jesus, a scene that ends with the voice of God declaring Jesus his "beloved son." Luke then traces the line backward through history all the way to Adam, "the son of God" (Luke 3:23–38), emphasizing the universality of Jesus in our shared humanity.

Taken together the Gospels give this general picture: Jesus was born in Bethlehem and raised in Galilee by devout Jewish parents. He was well educated—he quotes scripture liberally and reads in the synagogue—and his belief in immortality of the soul and resurrection of the body suggests that he had more in common theologically with the Pharisees than one might at first suspect. After perhaps thirty years of relative anonymity, Jesus' "public life" began with his baptism in the Jordan. After his initial desert experience, recalling the Exodus, he worked in Galilee, gathered followers, and turned toward Jerusalem for Passover (John says little about the Galilean period and has Jesus attending three Passovers in Jerusalem). After cleans-

Jewish King David by Michelangelo, sixteenth century, a copy of the original in the courtyard of the Palazzo Nazzionale in Florence. Jesus is a descendant of David.

63

Church of the Nativity, Bethlehem. (Courtesy of David Oughton.)

ing the Temple, driving away the merchants doing business in a holy place, Jesus gathers the Twelve for the "Last Supper," after which he is arrested, tried, executed, and rises from the dead. Luke's Acts of the Apostles picks up at that point and describes the post-resurrection appearances and Jesus' ascension into Heaven forty days later.

How do Christians interpret the **scriptures** they consider **uniquely theirs**?

Christians believe the sacred texts collectively called the New Testament are divinely inspired, but composed by the human authors to whom tradition attributes them. Some take that a step further, insisting that divine inspiration consisted of a literal transmission from God through the author who communicated the message unaltered. Early Christian exegesis of the Hebrew scriptures had already moved beyond merely literal interpretation.

Though the literal meaning of the sacred text naturally remained the bedrock of exegesis, typological understandings of Jewish tradition soon developed into more specific varieties of figurative exegesis to be applied to the Greek as well as the Hebrew scriptures. Within a few generations of the death of the last people who actually lived during the time of Jesus, Christian literature gives evidence of what would eventually develop into the "literal" and the "spiritual" senses, the latter then branching into three types. Taken together, the four senses are the literal meaning (*historia*); the symbolic or figurative meaning (*allegoria*); the moral or ethical implication (*tropologia*); and the eschatological parallels—that is, what the text suggests about the goal of human life (*anagogia*). A simple but useful rhyme helps keep the four levels of meaning straight: what our forebears did (history), where our faith is hid (allegory), rules for daily life (tropology), where we end our strife (anagogy).

A good example of how major early Christian interpreters applied the four senses might be the four rivers of Paradise mentioned in Genesis 2:10–14. Their literal meaning is simply that of historical identity—the Pishon, Gihon, Tigris, and Euphrates rivers. On the figurative level, the rivers might symbolize the four Gospels, the divine revelation fanning out to all the world's four directions. In addition, one might understand these four streams as the four cardinal virtues, prudence, justice, fortitude and temperance. And finally, the earthly rivers have their heavenly counterparts in the Paradise awaiting true believers.

Why, after Jesus Christ, is **Saint Paul** considered the **most influential** teacher in the history of Christianity?

Paul, whose original name was Saul or Sh'aul, was born in the town of Tarsus, Cilicia (in modern southeastern Turkey), of Jewish parents of the tribe of Benjamin. Both his parents were Roman citizens. It is safe to assume that Paul's earliest language was Koine Greek, the household language of all educated Roman citizens throughout the

empire. Paul was sent at an early age to Jerusalem to attend Bible school. Studying with a famous rabbi, Gamaliel, he learned to write in both Greek and Hebrew and became thoroughly versed in the law. It seems certain that Paul studied in Jerusalem during the three years of Jesus' public life and that he was present at the time that the Romans crucified Jesus. Paul may even have heard Jesus preach. He certainly must have heard of Jesus and his movement among the people. Apparently, Paul had gained an outstanding reputation as a young rabbinic student because he was authorized to seek out and prosecute members of a new sect who proclaimed that Jesus of Nazareth was the Messiah. Paul apparently made several trips throughout Palestine in search of Christians. On one such trip from Jerusalem to Damascus, in about the year 34 C.E., Paul underwent a conversion.

St. Paul's statue at St. Mark's Church, Florence, Italy.

Four accounts of Paul's conversion exist (Acts 9:3–19; 22:6–21; 26:12–18; and Galatians 1:12–16). According to the essential spirit of these sources, Paul underwent a supernatural experience in which he came to believe that Jesus was actually the Messiah of Israel and that God had called Paul to preach the message of Jesus to all people. The story adds that he was blinded and forced to fast for three days until a Christian named Ananias laid hands on him and restored his sight, after which he was baptized. The usual date assigned to this event is between 34 and 36 C.E.

During the next fifteen years Paul undertook three extensive journeys in the eastern Mediterranean region, preaching to the Gentiles particularly. Between the beginning of these missionary journeys and his marytrdom in Rome in 66 or 67 C.E., he wrote a number of letters that became part of the Christian New Testament. Paul's teaching rested on three main principles: Jesus is the Son of God and the Messiah foretold by the prophets of Israel; by his death, Jesus atoned for the sins of all and opened Heaven for humanity; the Mosaic law had, by the fact of Jesus' death and resurrection, been abrogated and replaced by the Law of Jesus. There was, therefore, no longer any distinction between Jew and Gentile. Paul frequently used texts from the Old Testament to argue his points, interpreting them according to the rabbinic method of exegesis that he had learned in Jerusalem.

As the first systematic theologian and writer of the Christian faith, Paul wielded great influence on such medieval theologians as St. Albertus Magnus, St. Anselm and St. Thomas Aquinas. Paul's writings also provided the sixteenth-century reformers with their basic ideas. These religious thinkers preferred to return to Paul's text rather than to adhere to the metaphysical speculations that had developed in Christianity throughout 1,500 years.

What does the term **"historical-critical method"** mean?

When Christians study their scriptures they can take any of a number of approaches, as already suggested. A common pastoral approach nowadays reads the scriptures almost entirely as if they are addressed to twentieth-century Christians and are thus in a way "timeless" and not subject to historical conditions. Another approach tries to get behind the words as much as possible to understand their meaning in their original context. This second approach by no means disregards the personal, pastoral, and deeply spiritual implications of the sacred text. But it begins with the assumption that one cannot know those deeper meanings without first understanding how and why the inspired authors wrote as they did.

Historical-critical scholarship looks, for example, at the differences in how even texts as generally concordant as the synoptic Gospels show divergences in vocabulary, major themes, order of events in the life of Jesus, and points of view tailored to different audiences. It notes how the inspired authors, as much editors as original writers, interwove Jesus' words and actions, telescoping time and space. As skilled literary communicators, the inspired writers also made use of stylized scenes that followed

St. Anselm's Abbey Church, St. Louis, Missouri, was designed in 1962.

predictable patterns in their description of the main actors, actions, and crowd responses. Combining analyses of the literary, linguistic, and historical elements, the historical-critical method seeks insight into how these documents, two millennia and many layers of culture removed from us, appear to speak in so many distinct voices about the same great spiritual reality.

Underlying it all, the method suggests, are the unique theological insights granted to each of the sacred authors. Each offers a characteristic reflection on the deeper meaning of the "good news" and of Jesus the Christ. For Mark, Jesus was most of all the Suffering Servant; for Matthew, the Messiah; for Luke, the Savior whose ongoing presence is the Holy Spirit; and for John, the Divine Son. These are not exclusive, but complementary insights. Unlike the predominantly spiritualized or pastoral method of interpretation, whose immediate concern is to deal with apparent inconsistencies among the sacred authors by "harmonizing" them into a seamless reconstruction, the historical-critical method seeks a unity of scriptural revelation through the uniqueness and diversity of the evidence.

What other **early texts** are especially **important** for Christians?

In addition to the twenty-seven books of the New Testament, early Christian authors produced a number of other important works. It is important to keep in mind that the formal canon of the New Testament was not finalized until around 198 C.E. Previous generations of Christians may well have been in general agreement about what constituted the core of their scripture, but until the late second century, some factions continued to claim the status of divine inspiration for a number of texts eventually judged to be apocryphal and thus not part of the Canon.

Most prominent among those apocryphal writings are a sizeable group calling themselves Gospels. Some (such as the Gospels of Thomas and Philip) were an attempt to support the views of tendentious or heretical factions, while others (such as Gospels of Nicodemus and of the Childhood of Jesus) purport to fill in the gaps of Canonical texts with legend and lore. Apocryphal works called "Acts" and identified with one or another of the Apostles generally, but not necessarily, reflect heretical views. Writings by a group of post-biblical authors known as the Apostolic Fathers, mostly of the late first or early to mid-second century, provide important information on the concerns and theological themes of bishops and their communities throughout the Mediterranean basin. A third significant corpus of writings dating from about 120 to 220 C.E. are those of authors known collectively as the Apologists. Major figures like Justin Martyr (c. 100–165), who founded a Christian school in Rome, and Tertullian (c. 160–220) of Carthage (in present-day Tunisia) and later Rome, wrote in defense of Christian views when outsiders mounted theoretical or political attacks against them.

Were early **Christians persecuted** by **Rome**? How long did that go on?

As Christianity became more clearly separated from its Jewish roots, Roman authorities all over the Mediterranean became more wary of Christianity's potential threat to Rome's authority. Many Christians refused to burn incense to the emperor and paid with their lives, but executions remained largely a matter of local jurisdiction until about the middle of the third century. Several Roman emperors, such as Nero and Marcus Aurelius, were known for their personal antipathy to Christians. But it was Decius who in 250 C.E. issued the first general order requiring all in the realm to worship the gods of Rome. Thousands of Christians were executed and many more renounced the faith, at least publicly. Diocletian (284–305 C.E.) began his reign with greater tolerance, but toward the end sanctioned the razing of churches, the burning of scriptures, and wholesale executions. The reign of terror continued until 311 C.E., when Emperor Galerius proclaimed a renewal of official toleration of Christians.

Why was the **Emperor Constantine** important in Christian history?

After learning the protocols of the Roman court by serving under Diocletian, Constantine (c. 274–337) consolidated his power in the eastern empire in around 312. Tradition says Constantine underwent a dramatic conversion to Christianity around that time. The following year he met with his western counterpart, Emperor Licinius, at Milan and the two concurred on a formula for what would become Christianity's political enfranchisement. In a dramatic about-face in the fortunes of its adherents all over the empire, Christianity now had power on its side. Thenceforth, whenever dissension within the ranks of Christians led to violence, the mainstream could enforce its views by appeal to the Emperor. Under Constantine, Sunday officially became a religious holiday for Christians. Constantine has the further considerable distinction of having convened the first of many "ecumenical councils," that of Nicea in 325.

A statue of Emperor Constantine stands outside York Minster in England.

Though he was as yet unbaptized, the Emperor presided over the debates concerning the damaging claims by the influential Arius (c. 250–336) that Jesus was a human creature, not eternal and divine, which were opposed by Bishop Athanasius (c. 296–373), who made the case for the orthodox response to Arius' heretical views. Five years later, Constantine tightened his grip on the empire, established his capital at Byzantium, newly renamed Constantinople ("City of Constantine"), and went on to become known among Orthodox Christians as the "thirteenth Apostle."

Who are the **Fathers of the Church** and why are they important?

Some of Christianity's most important religious and theological literature dates from the fourth to the eighth centuries C.E. During the Patristic Age, or "Late Antiquity," dozens of influential authors from North Africa, through the central Middle East and Anatolia (now called Turkey), to Rome and westward even to Spain, wrote major works in Latin, Greek, and Syriac. Patristic literature includes virtually every type, from extensive biblical commentaries to sermons to theological treatises.

Among the most important Latin Fathers is Augustine (354–430), Bishop of Hippo in North Africa and author of the monumental *City of God* and one of the best-known spiritual autobiographies, *The Confessions*. Tradition credits Augustine with a monastic rule that has influenced religious orders such as the Dominicans and Servites, as well as Ursuline and Visitation nuns. Major Greek Fathers include the three Cappadocians, so called because they lived and worked in the province of Cappadocia in Asia Minor (now in east-central Turkey). More famous were Basil (c. 330–379) and his brother Gregory of Nyssa (c. 330–395). Gregory of Nazianzus (329–389), like the other Gregory, was an outspoken bishop much involved in the theological controversies of the day. All three made critical contributions to the clarification of Christian doctrines about Christ and the Trinity. Less famous but very important in the early Christian history in the eastern Mediterranean are the Syriac Fathers. They wrote in a Semitic language related to the Aramaic commonly spoken in the time of Jesus. Ephrem of Syria (306–73) authored dozens of works, almost all in verse and including many hymns that are still sung in worship rituals.

An 1880 engraving depicting Saint Bernard of Clairvaux, a French abbot and reformer of the Cistercian order, leading the Second Crusade, a responsibility laid upon him by Pope Eugenius III.

Were there any **Mothers of the Church**?

There were many important "Church Mothers," women of great influence in the early Church. They have been less famous because they rarely wrote and published as did their male counterparts. Unfortunately, we know little of many of these women apart from often scanty or anonymous references in the writings of the Fathers and in early histories of Christianity. The historian Eusebius, for example, mentions some fifty-five women as making important contributions. Recent research has begun to give some of these outstanding women names and "faces." Some of the first well-known women were martyrs such as Blandina (d. 177), and Perpetua, and Felicitas, who both died in 203. Along with the so-called Desert Fathers credited with the beginnings of monasticism were a number of Desert Mothers. Macrina (c. 327–379), sister of Basil and Gregory of Nyssa, was also a prominent churchwoman. We know from the testimony of other authors that she was a respected theologian.

How did the term **"theology"** develop as a concept in the **third-century Mediterranean world**?

The term "theology" was generally used by the Greeks to describe the character of theogonies and to designate critical studies of Greek mythology. Plato in *The Republic,* Aristotle in his *Meteorology,* and Cicero in *The Nature of the Gods,* came to approximate the later historical use of the term. The Neoplatonists, however, seem to have been the first to consider theology as the science of God. The term is altogether missing in the

New Testament and in the apostolic Fathers. Early stirrings in the development of the concept of theology are to be found in the writings of Irenaeus of Lyons and Clement of Alexandria. The former was one of the first Christians to attempt to impose a rational economy upon God in his recapitulation theory, and the latter's *Stromata* was an early attempt to impose order upon divine revelation in general. The apologists, themselves educated as philosophers or lawyers, especially felt the need to present the educated pagan world with a philosophically coherent expression of faith. While Justin Martyr attempted judiciously to weave Platonism into the Christian scheme, Tertullian developed the technical terminology to be employed by subsequent theologians. Hippolytus, the first Christian to employ the word "theologian," was seriously concerned about launching an orderly investigation into the psychology and economy of God.

In the third century, Origen (c. 185-c. 254), molded in the concepts of Middle Platonism and to some extent of Stoicism, greatly influenced the emergence of theology as a sophisticated, philosophical pursuit. The Apostles, he felt, left the grounds of their statements to be examined by those who had the charismata of the Spirit: knowledge of the divine world, wisdom, skill in technical tools, and holiness of life. His express aim was to erect a clearly stated connected body of truth based on illustration and argumentation and arrived at by the "correct method." Even the title of his great work, *On First Principles*, betrays his intention to deal intelligently with God and heavenly beings and with men, the material world, and free will and its consequences. Origen was forced to rely heavily on the use of allegory to resolve contradictions, explain difficult passages, and correct misstatements purporting to be facts.

What were the **Crusades** and why are they important?

Beginning in 1096 and continuing intermittently for the next two centuries, the Crusades were wars fought over possession of the "Holy Land" and its chief sacred place, Jerusalem. Muslims had been in control of Jerusalem since around 636, but the Christian powers of central and eastern Europe mobilized only after a Turkish force vanquished a Byzantine army in eastern Asia Minor in 1071. The Byzantine emperor sought help from the pope in Rome and the first Crusade began twenty-five years later. From the Christian perspective the first was the only genuinely

Holy Sepulcher, Jerusalem, entry to tomb chamber. (Photo courtesy of David Oughton.)

successful Crusade, resulting in the establishment of the Latin Kingdom of Jerusalem. An ill-fated second Crusade was launched in 1147 in hopes of expanding Christian control.

From 1099 to 1187, Crusaders held the holy city and surrounding regions. Then, under the famous hero Saladin, Muslim armies brought the Latin Kingdom down and reclaimed Jerusalem, and in the following year Christians organized the third Crusade. The English king Richard I "The Lionhearted" managed a truce with Saladin in 1192, securing little more than a token visit to the Church of the Holy Sepulcher. One of the truly grim episodes in Crusading history occurred during the fourth Crusade. Western Christian troops overthrew the Byzantine emperor, vented their wrath on their Eastern Christian cousins, and never made it to the Middle East. Four more major Crusades and several minor ones followed during the thirteenth century. Only one was a qualified success, securing control over Jerusalem for fifteen years (1229–1244). Muslim authorities retained primary custody of the holy places for nearly the next seven centuries, finally yielding to the British mandate in the early 1900s. Christian sources often glorify the Crusades as examples of heroism, but in fact those who suffered most from their consequences were the Christian communities of the Middle East.

Key Dates in Christian History

Date	Event
c. 4 B.C.E.–29 C.E.	Life of Jesus of Nazareth; ministry (26–29); Crucifixion (29)
c. 65	Death of Apostle Paul
c. 120–220	Age of "Apologists" and "Apostolic Fathers," theologians; Roman persecutions
3rd–4th Centuries	Beginnings of monastic communities in Egypt
3rd–5th Centuries	Era of major Patristic (Church Fathers) writings in Greek, Latin, Syriac
337	Death of Emperor Constantine, who proclaimed Christianity the creed of the realm (313), thereafter largely protecting believers from persecution
354–430	Augustine of Hippo (North Africa), major Latin Father
4th–8th Centuries	Major early Ecumenical Councils (Nicea, Chalcedon, Constantinople)
800	Charlemagne crowned Holy Roman Emperor, Carolingian era begins
910	Cluniac Reform of European monasticism
1096–1187	First Crusade leads to Latin Kingdom of Jerusalem
12th–13th Centuries	Period of "High Scholasticism," major theological movement, along with founding of European universities and founding of major mendicant religious orders
1232	Establishment of Inquisition
1265–1321	Life of Dante Alighieri, author of *Divine Comedy*
1274	Deaths of Thomas Aquinas and Bonaventure, major theologians
1483–1546	Life of Martin Luther, major Protestant Reformer
c. 1491–1556	Life of Ignatius of Loyola, founder of Society of Jesus (Jesuits)
1545–1563	Council of Trent launches Catholic Reformation
1869–1870	Vatican Council I, first council in over three centuries

RELIGIOUS BELIEFS

Is there a **Christian creed**?

A number of New Testament texts suggest early forms of creedal statements. For example, the Letter to the Philippians 2:1–11 describes how Jesus "emptied himself" of all divine prerogatives, even to the point of becoming a slave and dying on the cross. The passage ends by saying that all should bend the knee at the name of Jesus and that "every tongue should confess that Jesus Christ is Lord, to the glory of the Father." The Gospel of Matthew 28:19 records Jesus sending his followers to baptize "In the name of the Father and of the Son and of the Holy Spirit," an early expression of the notion of the Holy Trinity. But the first important formal creedal statements did not gain wide currency until the early fourth century.

An important outcome of the Council of Nicea, in 325, was the Nicene Creed. As has so often been the case in the history of religion, Christians first formulated a comprehensive statement of "orthodox" or "right" belief in response to serious challenges that threatened to distort ancient traditional beliefs. In other words, the Nicene Creed does not represent the first expression of these beliefs, but rather the first comprehensive clarification of points that had come under attack by factions now considered "heretical." Christians all over the world now recite in their liturgies a later and somewhat longer version of the Nicene statement, with sections devoted to the Father, Son, and Holy Spirit, and concluding with affirmations of belief in the church, baptism, forgiveness, and the resurrection of the dead in the next life. The liturgical formula does not include the "anathemas" or condemnations of unacceptable views contained in the Council's original document. Subsequent Church councils have published other creedal statements, but the only other creed in common use (outside of the Eastern Christian churches) is the briefer so-called "Apostles' Creed," earlier versions of which seem to have come into common use around the fourth century.

What are the words of the **Nicene Creed**?

I believe in one God, the Father almighty, creator of Heaven and Earth, of all things visible and invisible.

And in one Lord Jesus Christ, Son of God, the only-begotten, born of the Father before all ages. Light from light, true God from true God, begotten, not made, of one substance with the Father through Whom all things were made.

Who for us and for our salvation, came down from Heaven, and was incarnate of the Holy Spirit and Mary the Virgin, and became man.

He was also crucified for us under Pontius Pilate, and suffered, and was buried.

He rose again on the third day according to the scriptures.

He ascended into Heaven, and sits at the right hand of the Father.

And He will come again with glory to judge the living and the dead, and of His kingdom there will be no end.

And in the Holy Spirit, the Lord and Giver of Life, who proceeds from the Father, Who together with the Father and the Son is worshipped and glorified, Who spoke through the prophets.

I believe in one, holy, catholic, and apostolic Church.

I profess one baptism for the remission of sins.

I expect the resurrection of the dead, and the life of the world to come. Amen.

Are **doctrine and dogma** important to Christians?

Clarity about the content of Christian beliefs has been a significant concern since at least the late first century C.E. Within a few generations after the death of Jesus, Christians had begun to debate doctrinal issues that went beyond the questions of ritual and practice that had preoccupied the earliest Christians. Emphasis shifted from the traditional Judaic orthopraxy to the gradual articulation of an increasingly distinctive body of Christian teaching about God, Jesus, and the ongoing divine presence called the Holy Spirit. Specific issues in the first of these categories included the concept of the Trinity and the relationship between divine grace and human initiative.

Christian teaching about Jesus sought to express the perfect blend of divinity and humanity in Christ and to understand how Christ is present in the sacrament or mystery called the Eucharist (where blessed bread and wine are partaken as a way of receiving Jesus). Doctrine concerning the Holy Spirit evoked questions as to the nature of revelation and of membership in the Christian community. The more these and other issues generated an increasing variety of views through the second and third centuries, the greater the need to set clear standards as to which were acceptable and which were potentially destructive. Beginning with the Council of Nicea in 325 C.E., mainstream Christian doctrine would take the shape of formal dogmatic expression. And since not all Christians would concur on a given formulation, differences of opinion on dogma would soon come to distinguish various churches from each other.

What do Christians **believe about God**?

God is first of all creator and sustainer of all that is. Lord of time as well as eternity, this Supreme Being is ceaselessly active in human history. Beginning with the divine labor of fashioning the universe, God has provided ongoing guidance and deliverance for all who believe in providence. Christians, like so many other religious people across the globe, sometimes have difficulty reconciling their belief in a God who is good and just with the undeniable evidence of cosmic evil and injustice. In general, Christians believe that God creates all possibilities, good and evil alike, but allows, rather than actively causes, evil actions. At the center of Christian theology is the doctrine of the Incarnation, according to which God the Son (Jesus Christ) came into the world, fully immersed in suffering and evil, in order to redeem humankind from sin by dying on the cross and rising from the dead. In the most vexing kind of paradox, the God-made-man Jesus Christ suffers and dies for human beings, who are in turn his murderers. According to Christian belief, God is "triune," three equal Persons in one deity—Father, Son, and Holy Spirit—and the Son is at once wholly human and wholly divine. The Holy Trinity represents perfect transcendence and perfect immanence. In other words, God is both infinitely beyond the realm of human experience and immediately accessible to all who seek divine aid.

What is the **central mystery** of the Christian faith?

The doctrine of the Trinity is the central Christian teaching about God. Christians believe that there is only one God, but in that one God are three distinct divine Persons—the Father, the Son (Jesus Christ), and the Holy Spirit—who possess equally and eternally the same divine nature. The early ecumenical councils took care to define the mystery of the Trinity with great preciseness because the mystery of God, obviously, is the most important of the mysteries of faith. During the early

centuries of the Church's life, many individuals denied elements of what Christians believed concerning the Trinity. Some claimed that Jesus was not really God; others rejected the divinity of the Holy Spirit; and some presented a very faulty understanding of God the Father. Belief in the Trinity is one main belief that distinguishes Christians from their Jewish and Muslim brethren.

What is **original sin**?

According to mainstream Christian tradition, the story Adam and Eve is critical to an understanding of the relationship between human beings and their Creator. According to Genesis 2:16–17 and 3:1–24, God commanded these first human beings not to eat of the Tree of the Knowledge of Good and Evil. A tempter tried to persuade them that God was merely attempting to prevent Adam and Eve from becoming like Himself. Once the primor-

A carving in a Vienna, Austria, church depicts the Holy Trinity.

75

A detail from the façade of Orvieto Cathedral, Umbria, Italy, depicts Adam and Eve being tempted by the serpent.

dial couple succumbed to the lure of such dangerous knowledge, they became aware of their potential for disobedience and lost their pristine innocence. Christian theologians have interpreted this critical moment in human history, known as the Fall, in various ways. From the time of the early Church Fathers on through the Middle Ages, theologians have discussed how the descendants of Adam and Eve inherited both their guilt and their inherent moral weakness. Protestant reformers stimulated further debate in the context of their discussion of faith and works. To what extent, they asked, can human beings remedy the situation by well-intentioned action?

And what is the **role of faith**, utter abandonment to divine grace, in remedying the situation?

Many interpreters associated the primal sin with sexuality and lust, but disagreed as to whether the descendants of Adam and Eve are merely deprived of original virtue or positively depraved and thus willfully wicked. More recently, exegetes and theologians have read the story of the Fall as a metaphor for the dawning of moral consciousness.

Why is the **Virgin Mary** important to Christians?

Mary, the mother of Jesus, occupies a preeminent position in the theology of the traditional Eastern and Western churches. Information about her life is extremely limited

(Matthew 1 and 2; Luke 1 and 2). It is clear that Matthew and Luke believed that Mary's conception of Jesus was miraculous, involving no human paternity, and that her son was the Messiah expected by Israel. Mary belonged to the house of David (Luke 1:26), was engaged to a man called Joseph (Matthew 1:18), and lived in Nazareth in lower Galilee (Luke 1:26). The Gospel of Luke relates that an angel of God announced that she, although a virgin, would conceive the son of the "Most High," to be named Jesus, and that he would found a new Davidic kingdom (Luke 1:31–33). Mary consented. When Joseph discovered that Mary was with child, he wished to dissolve the engagement quietly. In a dream, however, God's angel admonished him to marry Mary because the son she would bear was the result of divine intervention (Matthew 1:19–21).

A statue of the Virgin Mary and Jesus in St. Mark's Anglican Church in Florence, Italy.

The dates of Mary's life can only be surmised. Researchers place the birth of Jesus between 7 and 4 B.C.E. Granting Mary a minimal age of 16 to 18 years at the time of Jesus' birth, this would place her birth at sometime between 22–20 B.C.E. There is no precise information as to her death. At the Council of Ephesus in 431, Mary was proclaimed the *Theotokos* (Greek, God-bearer), or mother of God. Her position was further defined in the Roman Catholic Church, which in 1854 stated as an article of faith that Mary had been conceived without the original sin that affects all humanity. In 1950, Pius XII declared that at her death Mary's body had not corrupted in the grave but that God had taken both her body and soul into Heaven.

What do **salvation and redemption** mean for Christians?

All of the major religious traditions hold out the prospect that human beings can find a way out of the suffering, confusion, and alienation that are part of everyone's life. Some traditions emphasize that only steadfast adherence to a core of ethical doctrine can affect the ultimate transformation of the human condition. Others teach that even the strongest, best-motivated and most determined individuals need assistance from a greater-than-human power. "Grace" is a widely used term for that superhuman or divine aid, and it is the power of salvation.

77

Some traditions go so far as to say that grace alone, apart from any human action, has the power to save. Religious doctrine about the source, nature and function of such saving power is called soteriology (from the Greek *soter,* savior). Christianity and Buddhism, and to a slightly lesser extent, Hinduism, have developed the most elaborate soteriologies. For Christians generally, God's sending Jesus Christ to die and rise from the dead for humankind brings about salvation through victory over evil and death. But in addition to rescuing believers, Christ also redeems (from the Latin, meaning "to buy back") them from their former condition. According to some Christian thinkers this means a restoration to the condition of original innocence that human beings enjoyed prior to the Fall. Strictly speaking, Buddhist and Hindu notions of salvation are about release from the status quo and do not include this element of reinstatement. Christian soteriology is about both salvation and redemption.

Have **prophets and prophecy** figured prominently in Christian tradition?

Christianity grew at least initially out of Jewish tradition, in which the prophets of the Old Testament played a central role. A prophetess named Anna was in the Temple when Mary and Joseph presented their child there to fulfill the Law, and proclaimed Jesus the salvation of Jerusalem (Luke 2:36–38). Jesus himself was very much a part of that prophetic heritage. He and his contemporaries wondered about the spiritual identity of Jesus' cousin John (the Baptist). Many considered John a prophet (Mark 11:32), and Jesus told his followers that John was indeed a prophet, but even more, he was the very Elijah whose return had been foretold (Matthew 11:11–15). The Gospels report that many identified Jesus, too, as the expected prophet, and that Jesus even hinted that they were correct (see, e.g., Matthew 10:41, 13:57, 21:11). Paul's letters list prophets as belonging to a rank or office second only to that of Apostle, suggesting that prophecy continued to play an important role after Jesus' death (e.g., I Corinthians 12:28, Ephesians 4:11). It is not clear in those cases how these prophets functioned.

Long after the age of biblical prophecy, some Christians have identified modern "saints" as prophets who have raised their voices in opposition to oppression and injustice. Such courageous people are, therefore, spokespersons for God in our time, thus fulfilling the role of prophets of old. Some Christian (e.g. Charismatic) groups believe that prophecy continues today as a spiritual gift among their members.

Are **dreams and visions** important in Christian spirituality?

Some New Testament accounts describe dreams as a way God communicates warnings or courses of action to the dreamer. An angel tells Joseph to take Mary as his wife and to flee to Egypt (Matthew 1:20, 2:13). A dream warns the Magi not to return to Herod (Matthew 2:12), and as a result of a dream Pilate's wife counsels her husband to release Jesus (Matthew 27:19). The Acts of the Apostles records a number of instances in which visions supplied needed insights to Peter and Paul (Acts 11:5, 16:19, 18:5, 26:19).

Throughout Christian history individuals have reported privileged access to divine truth through both dreams and visions. Mystical insight is often described in visionary terms. The claim is not primarily one of optical vision, but of spiritual encounter. More prominent in recent times have been claims concerning apparitions, particularly of the Virgin Mary and Jesus. Individuals who claim to receive revelations typically communicate the need for peace or repentance and preparation for the coming apocalypse.

Do Christians believe in **miracles**?

Events that seem to defy scientific or commonsense explanation have been part of Christian tradition since biblical times. The Gospel of John refers to seven such marvels as signs of God's power and glory as manifested in Jesus. Beginning with his changing water into wine at the wedding feast at Cana (John 2:1–11) and ending with the raising of Lazarus from the dead (John 11), the fourth Gospel emphasizes the connection between faith and the recognition of signs. At the end of his work the evangelist refers to Jesus' post-resurrection appearances as signs as well, and says that Jesus worked many others not recorded in his Gospel, all so that people might believe in the name of Jesus Christ (John 20:30–31).

The other Gospels likewise use the language of signs so as to underscore two important aspects of miracles. First, miracles are in the mind of the believer. On numerous occasions Jesus performs a deed before large crowds. Some see the deed and believe; others see it and ask Jesus when he will work a "real" sign. Second, in the absence of faith on the part of those present, Jesus cannot or chooses not to effect his wondrous actions (Mark 6:5–6). In other words, miracles are not merely a gimmick for changing people's minds. Post-biblical Christian tradition has attributed numerous miraculous deeds to the mediation of holy persons as well as to direct divine intervention. Most common are reports of healings and apparitions, but accounts of paranormal events such as levitation or bleeding wounds on hands and feet (known as *stigmata*) are also well known.

What role do **angels** play in Christian belief?

Angels are spiritual beings with intuitive, though still partial, access to the ultimate truths. Roaming the universe at God's command, angels can make their presence known in countless ways. As messengers of the unseen world, angels represent God's ongoing communication with individuals on Earth. Tradition

A statue in Burggarten, Vienna, Austria, depicts cherubs.

79

divides angelic beings into three ranks or orders, each comprising three further "choirs." In descending order, the first rank includes the Seraphim, Cherubim, and Thrones. Second in rank are the Dominations, Principalities, and Powers. Virtues, Archangels, and Angels fill the lowest three orders.

Apart from Archangels and Angels, none of the angelic ranks descend to the human world, and the so-called guardian angels belong to the lowest rank. Michael, Raphael, and Gabriel are the only angels commonly named in Christian tradition. Many Christians consider themselves blessed and guarded by the presence of an angelic guardian, as the dramatic increase in colloquial American references to angels in recent times will attest. Even Christians whose traditions avoid talk of saints because their mediatorial role is deemed unnecessary now commonly talk of angelic intervention. Some perceive angels as kind strangers or as invisible forces that prevent accidents, for example.

How is the **devil** significant for Christians?

The English word "devil" comes from the Greek *diabolos,* meaning "one who throws something against"—in short, a disruptive power or presence. In the Gospels, Jesus deals with many such presences. Sometimes the presence is associated with a physical disease, sometimes with what seems to be a form of psychosis. There is a subtle distinction between a devil and an evil spirit, the latter being a soul gone awry under the influence of the former. According to tradition, the only difference between an angel and a devil is that a devil has made a choice that caused the loss of divine grace. Lucifer, "Bearer of Light," is the name of the angel who first separated himself definitively from God and got the name Satan or "adversary." Others are said to have followed his example and joined an army of malevolence under Satan's lead.

In one of the few remaining mythological elements in Christian tradition, Satan does battle against the forces of good represented by the Holy Spirit. At the end of time, Satan and his minions will suffer crushing defeat. Homage to the devil remains a feature of folk traditions among Christians in many parts of the world. In a mountainside cave in Guatemala overlooking Lake Atitlan, for example, locals still show interested visitors the remnants of chickens sacrificed to "the Prince of the World," represented oddly by a stone cross on the wall. This is not the same as Satanism or devil worship as such, but an acknowledgment of the continuing presence of evil in the world. Popular lore has cloaked the devil in red, given him horns, a pointed tail, and a pitchfork, but imagery of that sort does not have biblical roots.

What are the main Christian notions of **afterlife**?

Christian eschatology focuses on distinctive understandings of death, judgment, and consequential experiences called Purgatory, Heaven and Hell. First of all, death is not the end of life, but the beginning of a different mode of existence. Death is the doorway to a world beyond this. But since each person is responsible for his or her choices in

Hell is depicted in the form of a giant serpent, opening its jaws as demons eagerly stuff the damned into its gaping maw, in a portal sculpture on the Gothic-style Cathedral of Chartres, France, twelfth century.

life, there will be an accounting called Judgment. Immediately after death comes the Particular Judgment, of significance especially in Catholic theology. At that moment the individual becomes aware with utter clarity where he or she stands with God.

Depending on the situation, the state of the individual soul then changes to an experience of damnation, purification, or bliss. Individuals who have consistently chosen separation from God (a state called "mortal sin") will then be granted their wish permanently, in Hell. Those whose lifelong choices have been tainted with self-will and ill intent (called "venial sin") may need to experience a long but limited period of purification called Purgatory. Once cleansed of the last vestiges of self-absorption, these individuals will experience a change and be ready to enjoy the eternal presence of God. Those whom the Particular Judgment reveals to be in a "state of grace" are believed to move directly to the experience of the beatific vision, or Heaven, a state of eternal delight enveloped in divine love. All Christian theologies speak of a General Judgment, which will occur at the end of time at the Resurrection of the Dead. Then God will call all humanity to account and seal its fate for eternity.

Protestant reformers rejected both the notion of Particular Judgment and the intermediate state of Purgatory, teaching that only two possibilities, Heaven or Hell, awaited at the General Judgment. A further state known as "limbo" is reserved in some traditions for the unbaptized. Limbo is a rather neutral condition, lacking either suffering or supernal bliss, for all the righteous who lived before Christ, as well as for all infants who die without baptism.

What is meant by the phrase "**resurrection of the body**"?

Christians believe that all who have died will rise again when Jesus Christ comes in glory at the end of the world. Humanity's rising will be patterned on the resurrection of Jesus: "He who raised the Lord Jesus will raise us also with Jesus and bring us with you into His presence" (II Corinthians 4:14). Christians believe that human beings are called not to be simply souls or spirits, but to be fully alive, in body and in soul. Thus, the entire human person—body and soul—is destined to share eternal life with God in Heaven. Christians share this belief with religious/spiritual descendants of the Pharisees as well as with Muslims.

How does Christian tradition **interpret history**? What is **millennialism**?

Christian tradition, like the Jewish and Islamic traditions, views history generally as a linear process with a beginning, middle, and end. Christian and Islamic views are different from the Jewish in that both later traditions regard the ages of their central figures, Jesus and Muhammad, as the high points of history. Christians believe Jesus the Christ entered the world at the "fullness of time," establishing a new dispensation and initiating a sense of expectation of the eventual end of time. All that went before Jesus pointed to him and all that will happen since his life on Earth moves inexorably toward a final resolution over which Jesus Christ will preside. Christian expectation of the "end times" is an ancient theme with roots in Jewish tradition and in the New Testament. Just as the identification of Jesus as the Christ fulfilled the hopes of some Jews for a Messiah, Jesus' own preaching seems to have fueled further anticipation of history's grand finale. Many early Christians apparently thought the end was imminent, for we find important writers backtracking and suggesting that no one can know when the "Day of the Lord" will come (e.g. I Thessalonians 5:1–11). Eventually the idea emerged that Jesus would come again after a millennium, a thousand years, and rule for another thousand before bringing time to an end.

What is the **Parousia**?

According to the New Testament, Jesus promised his followers that he would come in glory at the end of the world as Lord and Judge. This coming of Christ in glory is called the "*Parousia*." The Greek word literally means presence or arrival. The ceremonial entry of a king or triumphant conqueror into a city was called a "parousia." In this final coming Christ will be recognized as Lord of all. Christians from the very start have looked forward with confident hope to the final coming of Christ in glory. The early Christians' prayer "Marana tha," Aramaic for "Our Lord, come!" (I Corinthians 16:22), was an expression of their eager desire to see the final triumph of Jesus' saving work.

Who is the **Antichrist**?

Antichrist is the generic title given to an individual, organization, or principle of evil believed to represent all that runs counter to the values of Jesus Christ. Only the two

Letters of John use the term, referring to people who refuse to believe in the Incarnation. Some early Christians labeled Roman emperors "Antichrists" because of their opposition to the faith. Some Protestant groups occasionally have dubbed the pope the Antichrist; similarily, some Muslims today characterize any external enemy as "The Great Satan." Christians throughout history have identified as the Antichrist the various evil forces of which the Book of Revelation speaks, including Rome and the "beasts" whose appearance will signal the apocalypse. Perhaps the most common and persistent view is that at the end of time, Jesus (in his "Second Coming") will confront and vanquish an impostor who claims to be Christ (i.e., the Antichrist), but not before the impostor has managed to lure many believers from the faith.

The word "Antichrist" has had a number of denotations and connotations over the centuries, but in modern times tends to refer to an individual who opposes the values of Jesus and leads humanity into Armageddon.

What is meant by the term "**the Rapture**"?

Some millenarian sects hold that at the Second Coming of Christ all believers will be taken up (rapt) into Heaven. Only those deemed to be "saved" will enjoy the benefit of the experience. Numbers of the saved and the criteria by which to determine one's own or others' membership in that group vary. Some churches adhere to a literal reading of the scriptural text, according to which one hundred and forty-four thousand, equal numbers from each of the twelve tribes of Israel, will be "sealed" on their foreheads (Revelation 7:1–8). Strict interpretations limit to that number those who will survive the "great tribulation" (Revelation 7:14) that will precede the Second Coming of Christ. Others allow that the number is symbolic, though the actual number of those saved will remain relatively small. Some (generally smaller) Christian groups continue to predict specific times when they are convinced the Rapture will occur.

What is Christian **fundamentalism**?

Christian fundamentalism as a specific movement began in the early 1900s, following the tragic events of World War I. Central to the movement's teaching are the notions of biblical inerrancy and verbatim divine revelation. Inerrancy means that any contradictions apparent in the Bible result from human misunderstanding alone. The so-called "Scopes Monkey Trial" of 1925 brought fundamentalist concerns great notoriety with its public debate over the question of evolution. The prosecution argued that science teacher J. T. Scopes was in violation of Tennessee law for exposing students to a doctrine clearly at odds with a type of biblical interpretation now widely known as "Creationism." According to that view, God created the universe in seven twenty-four-hour days—including a final day of rest—exactly as written in the Bible. Scopes was convicted, but the fundamentalist movement failed to make as much progress in purging American Christianity of traces of "modernism" as its leaders had anticipated.

A principal teaching is a type of biblical interpretation called Dispensationalism, which divides history into seven eras or dispensations that vary according to the quality of humanity's relationship with God. Believers await the seventh, the millennium, by cultivating a strict code of conduct designed to avoid contamination by such worldly behavior as smoking, dancing, gambling, and ostentatious dress. These and other beliefs and practices form the Fundamental Articles. Fundamentalists generally have avoided political involvement until recently.

What does Christian tradition teach about religiously **legitimate violence**?

Christians generally think of Jesus as a man of peace, though he is reported to have said once that he had come "not to bring peace but a sword." For their first three centuries, Christians as a group were largely on the receiving end of institutionalized violence in the form of Roman persecution, but that situation changed with the reign of Emperor Constantine. Saint Ambrose (c. 340-397), Saint Augustine's mentor, was one of the first to fashion a systematic philosophy of war based on the Old Testament. He interpreted war as an instrument of divine judgment on God's enemies, but insisted that Christians must interpret relevant texts of the New Testament in an inward or spiritual sense and seek peace in all their *personal* relationships.

Augustine (354-430) further developed the theme of *institutional* dimensions of violent means in his extensive reflections on criteria for a "just war." Religiously legitimate warfare must first be based on a just cause such as military aggression or violation of fair commerce. It must, secondly, be seen as a last resort after all peaceful means have been exhausted. Third, only a government with competent authority can declare war, and only, fourthly, with a realistic probability of success. Fifth, violence must be proportionate to the good results envisioned, and finally, combatants must have proper intention and may not target civilians directly.

Christians have continued to refine Augustine's theory over the centuries with very mixed results. Some would argue that the Crusades did not fulfill the criteria for a just war in Augustine's terms, but were closer to the use of secular power to suppress heresy. And in the "age of exploration," Christian armies engaged in violence on a large scale in many parts of the world, and by no means always in defense. In 1452, Pope Nicholas V charged the King of Portugal as follows: "In the name of our apostolic authority, we grant to you the full and entire faculty of invading, conquering, expelling and reigning over all the kingdoms, the duchies of the Saracens, of pagans and of all infidels, wherever they may be found; of reducing their inhabitants to perpetual slavery, of appropriating to yourself those kingdoms and all their possessions, for your own use and that of your successors." More recently, Christians have continued to debate the religious justification of violent means. Cardinal Ratzinger (who later became Pope Benedict XVI in 2005), for example, argued that the U.S. invasion of Iraq did not qualify as a just war, but his view has been widely disputed even among Catholics.

What are the "**beatitudes**"?

A beatitude is a blessing proclaimed by Jesus in the New Testament (Matthew 5:3–11; Luke 6:20–23), commending a characteristic of life that is most precious and dear to God. Jesus pronounced the beatitudes at the very beginning of his public ministry:

> Blessed are the poor in spirit, for theirs is the kingdom of Heaven.

> Blessed are those who mourn, for they shall be comforted.

> Blessed are the meek, for they shall inherit the land.

> Blessed are they who hunger and thirst for righteousness, for they shall be satisfied.

> Blessed are the merciful, for they shall obtain mercy.

> Blessed are the pure of heart, for they shall see God.

> Blessed are the peacemakers, for they shall be called children of God.

> Blessed are those persecuted for righteousness' sake, for theirs is the kingdom of Heaven.

What are some **key terms** in Christian traditions?

Anathema—Greek term for a ban or condemnation of incorrect belief, implying excommunication, separation from the community of faith.

Ecumenical Council—series of gathering of (Catholic) bishops and theologians, beginning at Nicea (Turkey) in 325c.e. and ending with Vatican II in 1965, to consider matters of faith.

Eucharist—Greek for "thanksgiving," primary term for communal liturgical ritual, also known as the Lord's Supper and the Mass.

Grace—divine aid made available to believers through faith and/or action ("works"), depending on denomination.

Incarnation—"enfleshment," concept of divine condescension to enter into human form for the sake of redemption.

Kerygma—Greek term for "proclamation" of the Gospel message of salvation through Christ.

Parousia—Greek term for "second coming" of Christ, fullness of salvation.

Purgatory—in some denominations, a state of being in the afterlife in which individuals who die without seeking forgiveness for sin experience purification before being allowed entry into Heaven.

Sacrament—"making sacred," referring to a set (from 2 to 7, depending on denomination) of ritual practices designed to facilitate divine–human connection.

Trinity—belief in a triune God, three equal persons in one deity: Father, Son, Holy Spirit.

SIGNS AND SYMBOLS

What signs or **symbols** might **identify an individual** as Christian?

Except in a few rare traditional societies in which ordinary garb can still distinguish members of different religious traditions, ordinary Christians typically display few obvious signs of their religious affiliations. The most common symbols are small items of

jewelry, such as rings or necklaces, displaying the symbol of the cross. Another decorative symbol is the stylized outline of a fish, with or without an enclosed text. Sometimes the fish has the word Jesus written within it, sometimes the Greek word for "fish" (*ichthus*). The symbolism of that Greek word derives from an ancient acronym meaning "Jesus Christ, Son of God, Savior" (*Iesous Christos Theou Uios Soter*). Fish symbols often take the form of metal automobile decorations or bumper stickers. Individuals wearing or displaying either the cross or the fish symbol might belong to any of a number of Christian denominations or communities. Angels have become extraordinarily popular in recent years among Christians of all persuasions and can be seen on such objects as lapel pins or dashboard magnets.

A cross with a fish symbol, as well as Alpha and Omega (left and right), bread of the Eucharist (above) with Greek letters "chi" and "rho" for first two letters of Christ, and grapes symbolizing wine below.

Other small identifying items are distinctively Roman Catholic. Various kinds of medals hung around the neck, or rings, might depict Jesus, his mother Mary, a patron saint, or an angel. Catholics sometimes use a variation on the more generic and plain Christian cross, called the crucifix, which depicts the body of the suffering Christ. In addition, Catholics and Orthodox Christians may make the "sign of the cross" in public, asking a blessing on the activity at hand.

What is the **Sign of the Cross**?

The sign of the cross is a simple and profound prayer. In part it is an action or gesture. A Christian marks himself with the cross to show faith in Christ's saving work. A cross is described on the body by the right hand moving from the forehead to the breast, and then from shoulder to shoulder. In the Eastern church the cross stroke is made from right to left; in the Western church from left to right. While tracing the sign of the cross, the Christian says: "In the name of the Father, and of the Son, and of the Holy Spirit." This formula, which recalls the words of Christ sending his Apostles to teach and baptize (see Matthew 28:19), expresses an act of the faith in the Trinity.

What signs or **symbols distinguish Christian ritual specialists** or religious officials?

A number of Christian communities expect their officials to wear distinctive clothing in public. Roman Catholics and Anglicans, especially, but increasingly clergy of other groups as well, wear dark or black suits with a clerical or "Roman" collar. A small square of white appears at the front-center of the shirt collar. Clerical shirts have become more colorful of late, so that one can expect to see clerical collars with white, gray, or any other shade of shirt. Many Protestant ministers prefer to dress in coat and tie. But when Christian officials lead their communities in worship they almost all wear distinctive garments or "vestments." Among the most elaborate are those of the Eastern churches—both Orthodox and Catholic—usually including richly brocaded copes and even regal crowns, especially for bishops and patriarchs. Roman and Anglo-Catholic liturgical garb ordinarily features a plain white undergarment called an alb, with a neck band, called the stole, hanging down in front, and perhaps an outer vestment, color-coordinated to the liturgical feast or season, called the chasuble. Ministers in some denominations wear an academic-style robe to preach and lead worship.

A Catholic priest wearing traditional dark clothing with a clerical or "Roman" collar.

Ethnically based Christian communities often supplement their ritual garb with distinctive colors or items of clothing, such as headgear or sashes.

Do Christians mark their **sacred spaces** with any **distinctive signs** and **symbols**?

Christian places of worship, generally called churches, almost always have one immediately identifiable feature—namely, a cross. Eastern churches often display a cross with distinctive short (sometimes slanted) bars above and below the main horizontal crossbar. Many also have one or more spires that have traditionally held the church's bells. Although the bells of most churches rarely mark all the hours of the day as they once did, some communities still mark the beginning of services by tolling them.

Church designs today are remarkably varied. Some employ medieval or classical models, some favor the simplicity of early American colonial models, and some represent the latest in avant-garde architecture. One symbolic feature of many traditional and contemporary designs alike is the arrangement of the interior space in the form of a cross. A metaphorical shape that has been fairly popular in modern churches is that of a ship, recalling ancient images of the church as "Peter's Barque." A feature of many churches is an antechamber or vestibule that marks a transition between outer and inner worlds, a brief passage that might allow worshippers to shift mental and spiritual gears.

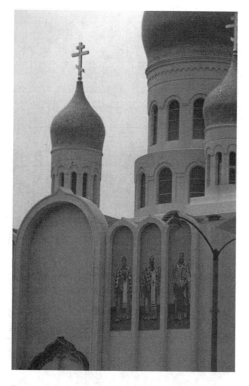

Russian Orthodox church in San Francisco, California. Note the additional upper and lower horizontal bars on the cross, and the distinctive "onion" dome and images of saints.

Interior features vary from one denomination to another. Catholic and Episcopalian churches, among others, typically have an altar table near the back wall. Almost all have one or more podiums, possibly well elevated. One of them will be called the pulpit, from which the preacher delivers the sermon or homily. Christian churches generally arrange their spaces for open visual communication between the sanctuary and the body or congregational area. Orthodox (such as Russian, Greek, Armenian, and Serbian) and some other Eastern churches often lack the benches or pews found in most other churches. They also typically have a high screen, called the "iconostasis," that hides the congregation's view of

actions that take place at the altar behind it, emphasizing the mysterious nature of the ritual.

Do Christians use **statues** or other similar imagery in **worship**?

Christian communities evidence a wide range of attitudes toward the use of visual imagery in the context of religious ritual or personal devotion. Some avoid it altogether, preferring all-white church decor and clear glass windows. At the other end of the spectrum are churches decorated with everything from stained glass to veritable galleries of statuary. Still others ornament their ritual spaces heavily, but use only two-dimensional images and no sculpture.

Some of the earliest evidence comes from the second- and third-century catacombs in which worshippers sought refuge from their Roman persecutors. Early Christians at first seemed to limit their sacred imagery, using human figures for sacred personages other than Christ. Perhaps they felt Christ was too sacred to depict directly or that representation violated the Jewish prohibition against graven images. In any case, they often used symbols such as the fish, or loaves of bread, or an empty cross.

By the Middle Ages Christians had developed extensive iconographic repertoires with which to depict an enormous array of holy personages. Elaborate programs in sculpture and stained glass depicted biblical figures, from patriarchs to kings to prophets, and saints, in addition to Jesus and Mary. Many sacred personages became associated with specific symbols as their identifying marks, such as St. Clement's anchor (he was martyred by drowning tied to one), the crutch of the ascetic hermit Anthony, and St. Ambrose's beehive (for his words were sweeter than honey). Some Protestant reformers vigorously opposed the use of images because of abuses associated with them (especially miracle-mongering), and as a result this imagery is generally less common in Protestant churches today.

What are **santos**?

Walk into virtually any small neighborhood or village church anywhere in Latin America and you will find *santos*. Santos (Spanish for "saints") are small carved, painted statues of holy persons specially revered because of their spiritual power and presence. You will generally see them lined up on shelves along the side walls of the church or occupying small side altars flanking the main altar. All who come to the church regularly are likely to have a particular favorite among the diminutive saints. Devotees are not shy about expressing their needs to their patrons and these little churches are often alive with voices communicating in loud whispers every conceivable physical and spiritual need. People often light candles, soften the wax on the bottoms so that they will stick to the floor, and proceed to harangue their santos with animated gestures, humbly demanding rain for the crops or asking why a sick child has not yet been healed. Santos are an important form of folk religious art that reveals a great deal about popular Christianity

Statues of patron saints, known popularly as "santos," lined up along a wall in the small Maya village church of Santiago Atitlan on the shores of Lake Atitlan in Guatemala. Devotees regularly visit, place candles, and engage in animated conversations with their patrons or saintly figures known for certain healing or other special powers.

in the Americas. Cathedrals and wealthier churches have their equivalent of santos in their multiple side altars and shrines, but there the conversations are quieter, the candles mounted on racks, and the saints often protected behind glass.

What is an **icon**?

"Icon" comes from the Greek word *eikon,* meaning image or likeness. From around the 400s on, the use of colorful two-dimensional images of Christ, Mary and the saints became an essential part of Byzantine liturgical and devotional prayer. Most icons depict the sacred figure frontally, often displaying a very stylized face that directs a striking gaze at the viewer. Some have described the devotional act of venerating an icon as a process of seeing and being seen, almost as if the image had a life of its own. Artists who create icons are called iconographers, people who "write with pictures." They undergo a long and very traditional course of training steeped in spiritual practices of prayer and asceticism. They employ only natural materials in their art and follow strict canons concerning characteristic ways of depicting certain figures and specific prescriptions about size and proportions of the sacred figure's form. Many icons use gold leaf for the sky around the holy figure, an immediate clue that the world into which the artist invites the viewer is not that of everyday life, but a spiritual realm beyond this. In Orthodox and other Eastern Catholic churches a screen called the *iconostasis* (place of the icons) stands between worshippers and the sacred action occurring on the altar beyond. In addition to individual icons placed on stands in various parts of the church, further mural-like images are displayed across the iconostasis.

What was the movement known as **Iconoclasm** and why was it important?

The Iconoclastic (from the Greek for "image-breaker") controversy arose in the early eighth century C.E. and lasted until 842 C.E. For centuries Byzantine Christianity had used sacred icons, but Emperor Leo III called the practice into question on the grounds that it prevented Muslims and Jews from converting. Leo's order that all icons be destroyed provoked turmoil throughout the church, both politically and theologically, with monks and their monasteries taking most of the punishment for refusing to submit. Sixty years after Leo began the controversy, the Second Council of Nicea in 787 reversed his decrees. But within less than thirty years another Leo (the Fifth) returned to his namesake's policies with a vengeance, severely persecuting iconodules (those who supported the use of icons). The theological sore point was the argument that people who venerated icons were ever on the brink of idolatry. Their counterargument was that icons were merely symbolic of the sacred realities beyond them. Though the controversy did considerable damage and cost a surprising number of lives and careers, the Eastern church recovered from it rapidly and has suffered no challenge of its kind since.

What is **holy water** and how do some Christians use it?

Roman and Anglo-Catholics especially are accustomed to blessing themselves when they enter church. They dip their right hand into a font filled with holy water and make the sign of the cross on themselves. Water is also a medium of blessing for a congregation. The celebrant takes a branch (or uses a small sprinkler with a handle) dipped in water and scatters a few drops over the crowd. Water from pilgrimage sites has long been a favorite religious souvenir, sometimes brought home to be given away as gifts or used for its healing properties. For many Christians, this is all an extension of the use of water for the rite of baptism, which in turn recalls how God brought the Israelites safely through the waters of the Red Sea and the Jordan River, and how Jesus was blessed by his cousin John the Baptist.

Have **relics** ever been **important** for Christians?

Since very early times, Christians have cultivated a sense of the sanctity of the remains and memorabilia of holy persons. Since Christians believed early on that Jesus had resurrected bodily from his tomb, they began to focus (by around the third or fourth century) on other reminders of Jesus' earthly life. People sought, and sometimes believed they had found, the cross on which Jesus was crucified, the nails that fastened him to it, or the crown of thorns he had worn. According to ancient tradition, St. Helena, mother of the Emperor Constantine, discovered the "true" cross of Christ during excavations for her son's new basilica of the Holy Sepulcher in Jerusalem. The resulting

Medieval reliquaries in the shape of the body part they were designed to contain. These hold arm and hand bones of holy persons.

devotional ritual of venerating the sacred relics there may have been among the first of its kind and the beginning of a much-expanded practice.

During late medieval times the Holy Shroud, thought to be the winding-cloth in which Christ had been buried, became a center of widespread devotion in Europe. A veil, said to be the one with which St. Veronica wiped Jesus' face during his march to Calvary, where he was crucified and to which an image of Jesus' face was transferred, was venerated at St. Peter's in Rome from the thirteenth century on. Far more numerous, of course, are the relics of martyrs and saints, some dating back to early Roman persecutions of Christians. Sacred remnants can be anything from entire bodies, skeletal remains, to intact or fragmentary bones and skulls, or items once owned or touched by the holy person. Claims to possession of certain sacred relics have often conflicted—there are several heads of John the Baptist, for example. Famous relics conferred a great deal more than religious prestige on the churches, monasteries, and shrines that owned them, for the more renowned and powerful the relic, the greater the traffic of pilgrims to the holy place. Relics generally have been more significant for Catholic and Orthodox Christians.

What is the **Tree of Jesse**?

According to ancient tradition, Jesus was a direct descendant of King David, who was the son of a successful farmer named Jesse. Beginning in the Middle Ages, the Tree of Jesse became a very widespread visual symbol displayed especially in the stained glass windows of Europe's great Gothic cathedrals and in illustrated manuscripts of the Bible. Depictions of the Tree typically show an aged Jesse sitting or lying down, with a large tree growing from his upper body or from the middle of his back. On the lower branches and trunk are shown the faces of David and Solomon and their royal descendants, along with other important figures in the genealogy of Jesus. An image of Mary holding the child Jesus typically appears at the apex of the tree. The symbolism emphasizes both Jesus' royal legitimacy and Mary's restitution for the evil originally caused by Eve eating from the Tree of Knowledge.

Medieval Gothic-style Cathedral of Notre Dame, Paris. The flying buttresses allow extensive wall space for stained glass, and the huge mandala-like "rose window" over the south transept is rich with biblical symbolism.

MEMBERSHIP, COMMUNITY, DIVERSITY

Have Christians traditionally sent out **missionaries** to **convert others**?

Christianity has historically been one of the three great missionary traditions, along with Islam and Buddhism. According to the Gospels, Jesus commissioned his followers to fan out into all the world and preach the Good News, baptizing as they went. Most famous among the early missionaries were Jesus' twelve Apostles. Tradition soon associated Christian communities all over the Middle East, and points farther flung, with individual Apostles. Along India's southwestern Malabar coast, for example, members of families that converted centuries ago still call themselves "Thomas Christians," in honor of Thomas the Apostle who is said to have brought the Gospel there shortly after the death of Jesus. Missionary activity on a global scale naturally increased dramatically with the Age of Discovery in the sixteenth and later centuries. Orders such as the Franciscans, Dominicans, and Jesuits sent their most talented people abroad, hoping to penetrate the exotic cultures of India, China, and the Middle East. In modern times Roman Catholic orders and Protestant organizations dedicated solely to missionary work have multiplied throughout the world. Still, contemporary Christians generally take a different approach to sharing their Good News with others, balancing missionary outreach with inter-religious dialogue.

93

Do Christians have a **holy city**?

Members of various individual churches have come to associate sanctity with a number of places uniquely important for their traditions. For Mormons, several sites along the church's difficult path from New York to Nevada are holy in retrospect, as well as nostalgically sad, because they represent places from which Mormons were expelled or where they were persecuted. Above all stands Salt Lake City, founded by Brigham Young, and seat of the church. Geneva remains a city with overtones of sanctity for Christians of Calvinist traditions. For Western Catholics, Rome is especially holy because of its place at the center of the church's entire history and because it is Catholicism's administrative home. But perhaps the majority of Christians consider Jerusalem the only genuinely holy city, and regard the surrounding territory as the Holy Land. Jerusalem, Bethlehem, Nazareth, and the hundreds of lesser sites associated with the life and death of Jesus remain for many a source of spiritual strength and hope.

Who are **Roman Catholics**?

As early as the fourth century, Christendom experienced political and religious tensions between Western (Latin) and Eastern (Greek) styles of theology and governance. These differences were magnified by the East-West division officially declared in 1054, with many Eastern communities (Orthodox or "right-believing" Christians) proclaiming themselves formally independent of Rome. But the use of the term "Roman Catholic" came into common use after the sixteenth-century Protestant Reformation. Papal authority, an often contested issue for at least a millennium, again became a critical question. The reformers protested against the Church's rigidly hierarchical structure, officially a kind of oligarchy but often in effect a monarchy in which the pope enjoyed greater power than the College of Cardinals.

The theological counterpart to the hierarchical system of internal governance were distinctively Roman teachings on the seven sacraments and on a vast multitiered celestial realm populated by saints and angels. Against these and other symbols of authority and mediated spiritual power, the reformers emphasized the priesthood of the faithful and the unmediated relationship of each believer to God. In response, Roman Catholicism further defined itself through the decrees of the Council of Trent (1545–1563) and the Catholic Reformation, spearheaded by the newly founded Society of Jesus or Jesuits (1540), among other emerging religious orders. Today Roman Catholics constitute about half the number of Christians worldwide.

What are some of the main **Protestant communities** that arose out of the **Reformation**?

As a result of the Reformation and associated movements in late medieval Christendom, four large families of Christian communities began to develop. Among the earliest were those identified with the reformer Martin Luther. Today a number of structurally distinct churches, all calling themselves Lutheran, have local branches all over Europe and the United States especially. Out of the reformist teachings of John Calvin have grown a variety of ecclesial bodies. Most notable are the half-dozen or more Presbyterian churches, which trace themselves directly to John Knox (c. 1513–1572), a Scottish reformer much influenced by Calvin's thought. The second group are known as the Reformed (including the Evangelical and Reformed) churches. A still more varied group of churches developed out of the so-called Radical Reform. From the Anabaptist wing of that movement came the numerous different Baptist churches as well as the Mennonites. From the Congregationalist wing arose the several Congregational churches, from which the United States organizations called the Unitarians and Jehovah's Witnesses split

A statue of Martin Luther, Wittenberg, Germany.

during the nineteenth century. While the reformers in Europe organized their various communities, King Henry VIII proclaimed himself head of the Church of England, no longer obedient to the Bishop of Rome. From that original movement, also known as Anglicanism, have emerged the Protestant Episcopal and Methodist churches, the latter beginning with the teaching of John Wesley (1703–1791).

Why are some **Eastern Christian groups** called **Orthodox** and others **Catholic**?

As early as the fifth century, Eastern Christians identified themselves as "orthodox" to distinguish themselves from the various heretical factions whose views the Council of Chalcedon had condemned in 451. When the Iconoclastic Controversy ended in 842, Eastern Christian authorities declared the first Feast of Orthodoxy. At that time, the term distinguished the "right belief" of all supporters of image veneration from all who opposed that essential part of liturgy and devotion. Since the definitive disconnection of several major Eastern churches from Papal authority, the term has generally distinguished them from the "Uniat," or Eastern Catholic communities that retained or renewed ties to Rome. Eastern Catholic churches include members of the Antiochene, Chaldean, Alexandrine, and Byzantine traditions. Individual bodies are the Ukrainian, Maronite, Armenian, Coptic, Ethiopian, Ruthenian, and Melkite, several of which also have their Orthodox counterparts.

How did so many different **Christian churches** come **into being**?

Three major points of division mark the history of Christianity, and nearly all of the tradition's diverse branches derive from those critical events. Intense controversy over the theological identity of Jesus culminated in the Council of Chalcedon (in present-day Turkey) in 451. Decrees of the Council taught definitively that Jesus was one person possessing both human and divine natures. In so doing, Chalcedon ruled against both the Nestorian heresy and the various Monophysite Christians. The former taught that Jesus was two distinct persons in one; modern-day Nestorians call themselves Assyrian Christians. According to the latter, Christ was not human at all. Today the many originally Monophysite churches include Coptic and Abyssinian groups in Egypt and Ethiopia, Syrian Jacobites, and the Armenian Orthodox Church.

Even though the majority of these groups eventually came to accept Chalcedon's formulation, the initial effect of the Council was to separate what have come to be the indigenous Middle Eastern churches from the rest of Mediterranean Christendom. A second point of division came officially in 1054, the culmination of centuries of disagreement, both theological and political, between the Rome-based Western church and the Constantinople-based Eastern church. Pope Leo IX (1049–1054) sent emissaries to excommunicate the Eastern patriarch on the basis of his refusal to accept changes in the language of the Nicene Creed. Finally, the largest of all the divisions was set in motion by several fourteenth-fifteenth century Christian reformers, including John Wycliffe (c. 1329–1384) and John Huss (c. 1369–1415), and culminating in the work of Martin Luther (1483–1546), John Calvin (1509–1564), and Henry VIII (1491–1547) of England.

The largest Mormon temple in the world is located in Salt Lake City, Utah.

Are **Mormons Christians**?

Members of the Church of Jesus Christ of Latter-day Saints consider the Bible a critical sacred text, and, as their official name suggests, consider themselves Christians. Anyone who visited the new Mormon Temple in St. Louis prior to its dedication in 1997 would have been impressed by the prominence of a huge statue of Jesus in the entrance tent. But one of Mormonism's central tenets presents a major problem for mainstream Christian tradition. That tenet is the belief in a prophet after Jesus, with its implication that the revelation of Jesus was not final and definitive.

Mormon tradition regards the work of founder and prophet Joseph Smith, Jr. (1805–1844) as a necessary corrective to centuries of corruption of the true Christian teaching of Jesus. Smith himself believed the scripture revealed to him, The Book of Mormon (origin of the popular name of the Church), did not replace the Bible but merely supplemented it. Today the majority of the growing global community of Mormons consider Salt Lake City, Utah, as their spiritual center, while members of a smaller branch called the Reorganized Church are headquartered in western Missouri. That some churches refuse to acknowledge Mormons as Christian is not unusual in itself; some Christians do not consider Catholics, or other groups, Christian either.

Are **Unitarians Christians**? How about **Jehovah's Witnesses**?

Unitarians, by definition, profess belief in a non-Trinitarian deity, denying the divinity of Jesus. Insistence on the "unipersonality" of God finds ancient echoes in teachings declared heretical by early church councils. Jesus' role is that of an important prophet, teacher and ethical model, but no more than an especially favored human being. Unitarianism began as an offshoot of Radical Reformation groups and in modern times was significantly reinterpreted by American thinkers William Ellery Channing (1780–1842) and Transcendentalist Ralph Waldo Emerson (1803–1882). Many Unitarians consider themselves part of the larger Christian community, but generally prefer the identity of an open community not defined by assent to a particular body of doctrine. Jehovah's Witnesses was founded in the United States by Charles Taze Russell (1852–1916). He emphasized Messianic expectation based on an Old Testament concept of theocracy. Jehovah's Witnesses publications have generally maintained a consistently critical attitude to mainstream Christian beliefs.

What **gender-related issues** are important for Christians?

According to the New Testament, women played important roles in the life of the early church, including that of deaconess, dedicated especially to ministering to women. Women in the categories of "virgins and widows" also occupied a special place in church society. The ordained office of deaconess was revived by the Church of England, and slightly later in Methodism, during the nineteenth century. Nowadays, opportunities for women to exercise leadership varies a great deal among Christian communities. Catholicism is well known for its refusal even to discuss the possibility that women might be ordained to the priesthood. But the Catholic Church is not alone in its stance on gender-exclusiveness for positions of official service and authority. Though many churches have never issued formal statements on the matter, the dominant social culture of the groups is such that an exclusively male officialdom is simply presumed. At the other end of the spectrum, Anglican churches in the United States have recently ordained women to the priesthood. Some Pentecostal and Holiness churches are entirely comfortable with women ministers and preachers, and in some cases have women as bishops.

What questions does the prospect of interfaith marriage raise for Christians?

Attitudes toward intermarriage vary from one church to another. It is safe to say that on the whole, Christian parents tend to prefer that their children marry other Christians, and that Christian pastors tend to offer similar advice. There are two large issues at stake here. One is that when both spouses worship together, they may have a better chance at a durable marriage. The other has to do with raising children. Without question, parents from two traditions often need to work much harder to arrive at a mutually satisfactory answer to the question, "What religious values, if any, do we want to inculcate in our children?"

Even when neither parent has been particularly active in any religious tradition, raising children often moves one or the other, or both, to reconsider the merits of some basic religious education. Some churches have historically done more than merely discourage interfaith unions. Catholics still cannot have their nuptials officially witnessed by a priest unless the Catholic spouse has agreed—and the non-Catholic spouse has not disagreed—to raise the children Catholic. Several other traditions have taken similar positions, and some have relaxed their position on intermarriage considerably in recent years.

Do Christian communities ever practice **excommunication** or banishment for religious reasons?

Various kinds of excommunication have played a role in a number of Christian organizations. In the Letter to the Galatians (1:8) Paul uses the word *anathema* (meaning literally "suspended or set above") in the sense of "cursed, cut off" in reference to individuals who preached an unacceptable interpretation of the Gospel. Early church councils as well as official documents from later times have often applied the term anathema to any beliefs deemed inadequate or simply mistaken as well as to those who held such beliefs. Until the sixth century, to be pronounced anathema was equivalent to excommunication, but thereafter Canon Law introduced an important distinction. Anathema meant total exclusion from the life of the church, while excommunication meant only an inability to participate in the full sacramental life of the community. These two degrees came to be known as Greater and Lesser Excommunication. In more recent times, the Roman Catholic practice has introduced the distinction between excommunicates who are "to be avoided entirely," a status now limited to persons who physically threaten the pope, and those who are "tolerated," allowed to attend certain services but not to receive communion.

Excommunication is one of three types of official "censure" in Canon Law, all of which are very rarely invoked nowadays. "Suspension" means that a cleric cannot perform certain ritual actions. "Interdict," denial of the right to celebrate some or all of the sacraments, can be imposed on individuals or groups, clergy or lay alike, in response to a cause for scandal. Roman and Anglo-Catholic traditions have by far the most elaborate juridical language, but many Christian churches have historically practiced varieties of excommunication. "Shunning," for example, forbids members in good standing to associate in any way with those under the ban, even if they are family members. The practice is rare except among Radical Reform groups such as the Mennonite and Amish.

How do Christians view Christianity's **relationship to other traditions**?

Three major issues are especially important here. First is the notion that Christianity completes, supersedes, or abrogates Judaism. Ancient Messianic expectation found its mark in Jesus, Christians believe, thereby rendering Judaism historically irrelevant. Second, Christians believe that in Jesus God has granted the final and definitive revelation. Any post-Christian claims to prophetic authority are therefore unacceptable and not to be believed. Islam is the most obvious example of a claim to prophetic revelation after Jesus, so it is not surprising that the history of Christian-Muslim relations has often been stormy. Third, personal assent to the divine revelation embodied in Jesus is essential to salvation, so that only those who so believe can hope to be rewarded in the hereafter.

For many Christians, it simply does not matter that most human beings through the course of history have never heard of Jesus. In this instance many Christians have in mind not only the 80 percent of humanity that are not Christian, but even some of their fellow Christians whose beliefs they consider flawed or incomplete. Such exclusive views are hardly unique to Christianity. But many Christian groups recently have begun to respond to the reality of the world as it is, with all its religious wealth, by understanding that very diversity as an essential ingredient in the divine plan. From this perspective it is no longer possible to assert simply and categorically that one segment of humanity is assured of salvation while another segment is lost virtually by an accident of birth.

How **many people** in the world identify themselves as **Christian** as of 2011, according to the Hartford Institute for Religion?

There were approximately 2.1 billion Christians in the world as of 2011. The table below lists the twenty-five largest Christian denominations in the United States as of 2011.

25 Largest Christian Denominations in the United States in 2011

Denomination	U.S. Population (in millions)
Roman Catholic Church	68.5
Southern Baptist Convention	16.16
United Methodist	7.8

Denomination	U.S. Population (in millions)
Latter-day Saints (Mormons)	6.1
Church of God in Christ	5.5
National Baptist Convention, U.S.A.	5
Evangelical Lutheran Church in America	4.54
National Baptist Convention of America	3.5
Assemblies of God	2.91
Presbyterian Church (U.S.A.)	2.77
African Methodist Episcopal Church	2.5
National Missionary Baptist Convention of America	2.5
Lutheran Church—Missouri Synod (LCMS)	2.31
Episcopal Church	2
Churches of Christ	1.64
Greek Orthodox Archdiocese of America	1.5
Pentecostal Assemblies of the World	1.5
African Methodist Episcopal Zion Church	1.4
American Baptist Churches in the U.S.A.	1.31
Jehovah's Witnesses	1.16
United Church of Christ	1.1
Church of God (Cleveland, Tennessee)	1.07
Christian Churches and Churches of Christ	1.07
Seventh-Day Adventist Church	1.04
Progressive National Baptist Convention	1.01

LEADERSHIP, AUTHORITY, AND RELIGIOUS ROLES

How are **Christian religious leaders** chosen, educated, and given authority?

Candidates for ministry and governance in most churches simply present themselves for admission to the appropriate educational branches of their organizations. Seminaries oversee the special ministerial training of church members. Many refer to the desire to enter the ministry as a "vocation" or a calling from God. In some cases members of many denominations take their ministerial theological education at non- or multidenominational seminaries or schools of divinity, generally emerging after three or four years with a Master of Divinity (M.Div.) degree or its equivalent. Some students may pursue further studies toward a Doctor of Ministry (D.Min.) degree or a Ph.D., hence the common appellation "Reverend Doctor." Protestant ministers more often than not obtain their pastoral appointments at local churches of their denominations through the mechanism of the "call," whereby a congregation interviews prospective pastors and then invites its first choice. Catholic bishops generally appoint priests of their dioceses to specific parishes without consulting the local congregations. Orthodox and other Eastern church administrators sometimes exercise a similar appointive authority.

What is a **bishop**? Do all Christian churches have them?

"Bishop" means "overseer" (from the Greek *episkopos*). Many churches use the episcopal system as their principal administrative structure. Among the churches for which episcopal succession represents an unbroken connection back to the Apostles, the first bishops, are the Catholic, the Orthodox, and the Anglican. Catholic bishops confer as a global body by sending representatives to occasional synods in Rome, and in many countries are organized into national conferences. Orthodox bishops also convene in synods, but usually on a nation-by-nation basis. Anglican bishops meet at the Lambeth Conference every ten years, but the results of their deliberations are not juridically binding. Many of the Methodist churches also have bishops, and there are Lutheran bishops as well. Some smaller churches, such as those in Holiness or Assembly of God traditions, sometimes refer to their founder as a bishop, but they are not linked with any larger episcopal governing body.

Alternative forms of governance are the presbyteral and the congregational. Presbyterian churches are governed by a body called the "session," elected by the congregation and consisting of ordained clerical and lay presbyters or elders. Local churches join together in a presbytery, and regional presbyteries (never fewer than three) in turn form a synod. Presbyteries also elect members of an overall body called the General Assembly. The congregational structure maintains the complete independence of each local community, but most churches that employ the structure nevertheless come together in national conventions or synods. Baptist churches and those forming the United Church of Christ use this general structure of governance.

A bishop rides horseback at the 2011 Pfingstritt religious procession in Bad Koetzting, Germany. (filmfoto / Shutterstock.com.)

What is a "hierarchy"?

"Hierarchy" comes from the Greek words for "sacred leadership." Church organizations vary from predominantly egalitarian and democratic to highly structured and institutionalized. Even the most egalitarian tend to feature some sort of division of labor within their leadership, but they typically choose leaders from among the rank and file members. Roman Catholicism is perhaps the most hierarchically structured of the churches. A leader, called the pope or Holy Father, has been elected, since the Middle Ages, by a body called the College of Cardinals. The pope is the ecclesiastical descendant of Peter and the custodian of apostolic tradition. Cardinals are specially appointed by the pope from among the bishops and archbishops. Another rank of clerics have the honorific title of monsignor, a designation until recently further divided into those called "right reverend" and a lower rank called "very reverend." The office of priest, from which the upper levels of the hierarchy are taken, consists of men responsible for the day-to-day life of the church in its thousands of parishes. Another office, that of deacon, is just below that of priest. Men studying for the priesthood are ordained as temporary deacons, but more recently the office of permanent deacon has been made up of laymen chosen and trained for the work of assisting parish priests. Several other churches retain a highly structured organization, but generally on a smaller scale. For example, many have archbishops and bishops as main administrators. Many of the Eastern Orthodox churches are governed by patriarchs, to whom archbishops (or metropolitans) and bishops report.

Is there a **central teaching authority** for Christians? What is a **pope**?

Not since very early in Christian history have all (or at least the vast majority of) Christians acknowledged a central temporal authority. The role of the papacy through

the centuries has been central to the story of pre-Reformation Christendom especially, and even churches that eventually repudiated papal authority indirectly acknowledged the importance of the institution. Roman Catholic tradition is structured around the institution of the papacy. Popes have exercised varying degrees of independence in their governance, depending on the will and vigor of the church's bishops in any given period. Eastern Orthodox churches have had their unique authority structures in the form of a federation of fourteen independent autocephalies (four of which are the patriarchates of early Christian times)

Pope Benedict XVI was elected to lead the Catholic Church in 2005.

each further divided into eparchies (or dioceses). Since the Reformation, proliferation of Christian churches and denominations has spurred the development of a variety of governance styles and systems. Within individual denominations (such as the Baptist) and even their subdenominations (such as the Southern Baptist Convention), governing bodies do not always exercise overall prescriptive control. Their central authority is in many cases largely advisory, since local church communities in many denominations enjoy considerable autonomy, both structurally and financially.

Do Christians have a system of **religious law**?

For over a millennium, Church law grew from the earliest ad hoc responses to particular problems of practice and discipline to an elaborate system called Canon Law. Early ecumenical councils promulgated their decisions in the form of "canons," or laws. Meanwhile, many major decrees from powerful bishops and formal opinions from important theologians added to the increasing body of legislation. Influenced by the codes of civil law of the Emperor Justinian and others, medieval authorities began to systematize the massive and still expanding body of legal tradition. Gratian (d. c. 1179) first began to impose order on the chaos and remained an important authority in Roman Catholicism until his work was thoroughly revised in 1917.

Meanwhile, the Protestant Reformation brought about major changes in the new church bodies. Nearly all of the larger church organizations have developed legal structures of some kind to serve the concerns of what is called "church polity." Often taking the form of articles, charters or conventions, the legal formulations of the various ecclesiastical bodies typically claim authority only within a particular family of churches. For example, the Southern Baptist, Northern Baptist, and National Baptist Conventions have all developed distinctive legislative and procedural frameworks within which to handle matters of policy and discipline. In this respect, Christians who follow Canon Law are similar to Jews who abide by rabbinical law and Muslims who follow Shari'a in their personal lives—the religious legal systems rarely if ever intrude into the civil law of the nation state in which the believers live.

Are there **characteristically Christian views** about religion and political power?

Views about church–state relations have varied over the centuries among Christian groups. Bearing in mind that the following is an oversimplification of a very complicated issue, it is possible to characterize four principal positions on this issue. At some times and in some places, Christians have thought of the state as virtually synonymous with the church. The early years of the Church of England as proclaimed by Henry VIII and the Byzantine church under Constantine are examples. Some traditions have accorded the state enormous power over the church, as with early Lutheranism in northern Europe. Reversing the situation, the church has sometimes dominated the **103** state, as during the heyday of Calvinism in Switzerland. Finally, certain communities of the "radical reformation" proclaimed a total separation of church and state, insisting on their right to reject some aspects of ordinary corrupt society altogether. Some descendants of those communities continue to practice conscientious objection with respect to compulsory military service, for example. Throughout history prior to the Reformation, popes often had stormy relationships with the monarchs of the Mediterranean world. The result was a variety of official church positions ranging from supremacy over temporal power, to an attempt at equal balance between the spiritual and the temporal, to de facto admission that the civil authority held supremacy.

Has **monasticism** played a significant role in Christianity?

Since about the third century, small numbers of Christian men and women have sought ways of dedicating themselves entirely to an intensified spiritual quest. At first that quest typically took the form of a highly ascetic withdrawal from society. One of the earliest, and eventually most influential, of these hermits was St. Antony of Egypt (c. 250–350). Early in the fourth century he decided to organize a community of fellow hermits. Later monastic founders also developed rules of common life. Pachomius (c. 290–346), also of Egypt, is known as the true founder of communal or cenobitic monasticism. During his lifetime, there were nine male and two female monasteries. Other important developments were the work of Benedict of Nursia (c. 480–550), whose Rule became the basis of the worldwide order called the Benedictines, now including a number of women's orders as well as monks. Benedict himself was not an ordained priest, although nowadays the majority of Benedictine monks study for the priesthood.

Other important monastic orders have been founded since, especially in medieval times. Major orders are the Franciscans, founded by Francis of Assisi (1181–1226), with various sub-branches, and the Dominicans, founded by Dominic (1170–1221). They are known as "mendicant" orders, since they were historically dependent on alms for monetary support. The Church of England also still sponsors several small monastic orders, such as the Monks of St. John the Divine, and distinctive monastic communities, such as the Order of St. Basil the Great, continue to make important contributions to several of the Eastern churches.

What kinds of **smaller religious organizations** do some Christians belong to?

In addition to the various monastic orders that are still an integral part of religious life in the Anglo and Roman Catholic as well as Eastern communities, a number of non-monastic religious and lay organizations have also made significant contributions. There are several types of organizations for men and women fully committed to various kinds of religious life. Members of those formally known as "orders" (such as the Society of Jesus, or the Jesuits) take solemn vows of perpetual poverty, chastity, and obedience. Members of "congregations" take simple vows that can be either per-

An Orthodox Christian monastery clings to the side of a cliff overlooking ancient Jericho, the West Bank, Palestine. Its placement in the Judaean wilderness reflects longstanding tradition of preference for austere environs for monastic asceticism.

petual or renewable at set intervals. Most religious organizations belong in this category. "Lay institutes" are like congregations, except that most or all members of the former are not ordained to the priesthood, as with the Daughters of Charity or Christian Brothers. In addition, a number of the "orders" strictly so-called (such as the Dominicans and Franciscans) have "second" orders (for female members) and "third" orders (also called Tertiaries) for lay affiliates. Although the Roman Catholic tradition is more structured in this respect than most others, almost all Christian churches provide multiple organizational opportunities designed to allow members fuller participation in the life of the community. These groups typically revolve around some specific socioreligious focus, such as church maintenance, social outreach, or the interface of religion and politics.

What role **do saints** play in Christian tradition?

Paragons of holiness and virtue have always played an important role in Christian tradition. The Old and New Testaments describe hundreds of outstanding models of the life of faith. Different churches have had various ways of acknowledging sanctity in historical individuals. Roman Catholic, Orthodox, and other Eastern traditions have placed the greatest emphasis on the role of saints in piety and devotion. All share a reverence for the great Greek Fathers of the Church, for example. All mention the names of saints as part of their liturgical prayer, and Eastern Christians venerate icons of saints much as Catholics incorporate various types of saints' images in their devotional life. Holy persons are especially important as mediators, embodiments of holiness popularly thought to be immediately accessible to ordinary people. Saints hear the needs and aspirations of those who beseech them, and present these prayers to God.

Protestant tradition has generally denied any such mediatorial role, as well as the human mediation implied in priesthood. Many Protestant reformers regarded devotion to the saints as an unacceptable dilution of Christian piety, an unnecessary detour on a direct road to God. Catholics and Orthodox continue to identify extraordinary individuals as worthy of sainthood, and the Catholic Church particularly maintains an elaborate mechanism for assessing the merits of individual claims. Advocates for a potential saint present the case to the local bishop, perhaps including claims of miracles and authentication of relics. The bishop may then forward the case to the Sacred Congregation for the Causes of Saints. A church official known popularly as a "devil's advocate" raises objections to the cause so as to expose any weaknesses in the argument. Once sufficient evidence of two authentic miracles has been advanced, the pope may declare the person "blessed" in what is called a "beatification" ceremony. Before the final declaration of sainthood, or "canonization," proof of two further miracles is required.

Have there been important **Christian mystics**?

Since Late Antiquity many Christian men and women have been known for their profound experiential insight into the divine mystery. Some of these mystics have been theologians, authors of important treatises on various aspects of the Christian faith. But more importantly, theirs is a legacy of wonder and even bewilderment at the ways God relates to attentive human beings. Some of the best-known Christian women have been mystics.

Accounts of Christian mysticism typically begin with the sixth-century Dionysius the Pseudo-Areopagite, whose Greek writings laid the foundations of mystical thinking and provided a lexicon that subsequent authors would use for many centuries. Most of the great mystics lived during the high and late Middle Ages, though a number lived during Renaissance and early modern times as well. Hugh (c. 1096–1141) and Richard (d. 1173) of St. Victor, leaders of the Victorine School of Paris, believed that creation manifested the mind of God and was thus the beginning of a path to contemplation. Hildegard of Bingen (1098–1179) was a visionary Benedictine nun whose extensive writings and musical compositions have enjoyed remarkable popularity of late, thanks to fine new translations and CD recordings. Mechtild of Magdeburg (c. 1210–80), a member of a lay sisterhood called the Beguines, recorded her revelatory visions of the Sacred Heart of Jesus, as did her younger contemporary Gertrude (1256–1302). Meister Eckhart (c. 1260–1327) was a German Dominican whose teaching on divine–human intimacy evoked accusations of pantheism and heresy. His spiritual descendants Henry Suso (c. 1295–1366) and Johann Tauler (c. 1300–61) sought to clarify Eckhart by connecting him to the officially acceptable thought of Thomas Aquinas (c. 1225-1274). Other famous mystics, far too numerous to mention individually even briefly, included Catherine of Siena (c. 1340–80), Jan van

Ruysbroeck (1293–1381), Juliana of Norwich (c. 1342–1413), Ignatius Loyola (1491–1556), Teresa of Avila (1515–82), and John of the Cross (1542–91).

Have **martyrs** been accorded any **special status** in Christian history?

According to Christian tradition, Stephen was the first person to die for his commitment to faith in Jesus Christ (Acts 6–7). Paul, one of those among the crowd that stoned Stephen to death, would later become a martyr himself, as would Peter and many others among the earliest Christians. In Christian prayer, martyrs have enjoyed an honor above that of all other saints. Most of the martyrs whose stories are told in a literary form called "martyrology" lived during the first three centuries, the time of direst persecution by Roman authorities. But martyrs more recently have also been celebrated for their witness to the faith as missionaries in far-flung lands. The high age of missionary martyrs coincided roughly with the opening of new maritime routes around the globe. Even more recently a young woman shot to death in a Colorado school massacre has been hailed as a martyr, for when her assailant asked her if she believed in God, she bravely said "Yes," and died moments later. Martyrs are those who witness to their faith regardless of the threat of dire consequences to themselves.

What is a **Doctor of the Church**?

Since the Middle Ages, the Catholic Church has recognized individuals known for their theological learning and spiritual wisdom with the formal title "Doctor of the Church." At first the title applied only to four of the Latin Fathers of the Church, Jerome, Ambrose, Augustine, and Gregory the Great. Before long, to balance things off, four Greek Fathers were named: Athanasius, Basil, Gregory of Nazianzus, and Gregory of Nyssa. But since the mid-sixteenth century, another two dozen have had the title officially conferred upon them. These include, for example, Church Fathers (Venerable Bede, Cyril of Alexandria, John of Damascus, and Ephrem of Syria); medieval theologians (Anselm of Canterbury, Albert the Great, Thomas Aquinas, and Bonaventure); and mystics (John of the Cross, Francis de Sales, and the only two female Doctors, Catherine of Siena and Teresa of Avila).

What is a **patron saint**?

Patron saints function in some Christian communities as a human counterpart to guardian angels. There are two general types of patron saint. It was once common for some Christians to name their children after holy men and women, thus attaching the youngsters to "patrons" who would look after their spiritual needs. More often, saints are identified with groups of people, such as members of a profession (carpenters, musicians, mariners), or those with difficult circumstances, such as affliction with a particular illness or challenge. People pray to St. Jude, patron of lost causes, for relief from apparently incurable diseases. Some beseech St. Anthony for help in finding what has been lost.

HOLIDAYS AND
REGULAR OBSERVANCES

What kind of **religious calendar** do Christians observe?

Most of the world's Christians mark time on the solar Gregorian calendar, a late medieval correction of the much-older Julian calendar. Julius Caesar had initiated the calendar named after him in 46 B.C.E., but it was based on some miscalculations. In 1582, Pope Gregory XIII shortened the Julian year by ten days and added a day to February every fourth or "leap" year. Some Eastern Christian churches still use the Julian calendar, so that their major feasts fall just less than two weeks later than those of the Western churches. Until the Gregorian reform, Christians considered March 25 the beginning of the year, since that was judged to be the day on which Gabriel announced to Mary that she would give birth to Jesus. March 25, which had in ancient times been mistakenly calculated as the spring equinox, the first day of spring, remains the Feast of the Annunciation.

For centuries Christians continued to observe the timing of traditional Jewish feasts, which were movable within limits of specific agricultural seasons (such as planting and harvest times). Using the Jewish seven-day week, Christians gradually added fixed feasts, such as those of saints and martyrs. The custom of designating Sunday as a day of religious observance began during the first generation after Jesus' death and Emperor Constantine decreed it a day of rest in 321. Wednesdays and Fridays had anciently been days of fasting, a practice now surviving largely on the first day of Lent, Good Friday, and other Fridays during Lent. For most Christians the year consists of three liturgical seasons: Advent and Christmastide, Lent and an Eastertide that ends with Pentecost Sunday, and "Ordinary" time until the first Sunday of the following Advent. Some Christians in Egypt and Ethiopia still use the solar Coptic calendar, based on the ancient Egyptian reckoning. Recent recalculations suggest that Jesus was actually born closer to 4 B.C.E. than to the year 1.

A Good Friday procession held in Luqa, Malta, in 2009. (William Attard McCarthy / Shutterstock.com.)

What is the season of **Advent**? Why is **Christmas** so important for Christians?

The Western Christian liturgical year begins with the first Sunday of Advent. Western churches set that Sunday as the one closest to the feast of St. Andrew (November 30), while Eastern Christians begin a period of fast in preparation for Christmas on the feast of St. Philip (November 14). For most Christians, four Sundays mark this season of waiting and expectation of the birth of Christ. Christmas, the celebration of Jesus' birth, was originally fixed on December 25 around the year 336. That was the date then calculated as the winter solstice on the Roman calendar, with its symbolic celebration of the rebirth of the sun after the year's darkest day. In the practice of the liturgical churches, purple vestments still recall the originally penitential spirit of the season, with its overtones of apocalyptic expectation of Christ's second coming. But on the third Sunday, called Gaudete ("Rejoice") Sunday, rose vestments introduce a note of relief. Christmas represents for all Christians the pivotal event in human history called the Incarnation, in which God took on human flesh and assumed all aspects of the human condition except sinfulness.

What is the meaning of the season of **Lent or the Great Fast**?

For at least three centuries, early Christians observed a two- or three-day fast in preparation for Easter. Canons of the Council of Nicea in 325 represent the first reference to the later observance of a forty-day fast recalling symbolically similar practices by Moses and Jesus. Lent now begins for Western Christians on Ash Wednesday, while Eastern Christians typically begin the "Great Fast" two days earlier. Until the seventh century, the season began on a Sunday, but since Sunday was exempted from fasting, the beginning was advanced so as to include a full forty days' fast. Ashes applied to the head are a reminder of human sinfulness and mortality and recall an earlier practice in which penitents appeared in public wearing sackcloth and ashes. For centuries Christians fasted for a significant portion of each Lenten day, Monday through Saturday, and generally abstained entirely from meat. Contemporary practice has generally limited a modified form of fasting and abstinence to the first day of Lent and Good Friday. For example, Catholic practice recommends taking smaller meals at breakfast and lunch, together equaling less than one takes at the main meal, with no food in between. That is a far cry from serious fasting, but still at least a reminder of the purpose of the season—namely, a heightened awareness of the need for spiritual conversion and dependence on God.

What do Christians commemorate on **Holy (Maundy) Thursday, Good Friday, and Holy Saturday**?

The Easter Triduum (three-day period) begins with the commemoration of the evening on which Jesus gathered his Apostles for the Last Supper. Maundy (from the Latin word *mandatum,* the new "commandment" of service Jesus gave his disciples then) or Holy Thursday is marked in several churches by rituals that include a symbolic "washing of

Christian pilgrims carrying the Cross in procession through the streets of Jerusalem en route to the Church of the Holy Sepulcher, recalling the last hours of Jesus' life.

the feet" of several attendees by the priest or bishop. Good Friday recalls the crucifixion and death of Jesus. What could be "good" about such a day?

It represents the ultimate sacrifice by which God redeemed the world through the offering of the only Son. For Christians, this is at the heart of the mystery of salvation. Rituals acknowledge the sanctity and somber nature of the occasion. Some churches feature an extended reading of one of the Gospel accounts of the Passion and Death of Jesus, while some perform classic music; others commemorate the events of the day with a ritual called the Stations of the Cross, the "Three Hours" ritual recalling the time Jesus spent on the cross, or by reenacting Christ's deposition from the cross and burial. Pilgrims to Jerusalem on this day participate in a lengthy procession through the streets of the old city, retracing (at least in part) the steps of Jesus toward Calvary or Golgotha, the hill of the crucifixion. In liturgical Western churches, the day ends with the stripping of the altar, leaving a bare table and an empty tabernacle (where the consecrated bread is ordinarily kept) as symbols of mourning. Holy Saturday memorializes the day of waiting and uncertainty experienced by Jesus' followers, who hoped his predictions of a victory over death would prove true. Some churches celebrate a ritual on Saturday at midnight or earlier in the evening in anticipation of Easter.

What is the Christian feast of **Easter** about?

Christ chose to suffer death on the cross to save humanity from its sin, and Christ's victory over death fulfilled the promise of redemption. As the name suggests, Easter celebrates the rising of the sun of life from the dark night of the grave. Christian tradition teaches that when a group of myrrh-bearing women and then the Apostles went to Jesus' tomb on the third day after the crucifixion, they found the grave empty. Enemies of the early Christians argued that Jesus' followers had taken his body away to give credence to his predictions that he would rise from the dead. New Testament accounts in the Gospels and Acts of the Apostles narrate a number of post-resurrection appearances in which Jesus visited his disciples and spoke with them. The Eastern Christian year is organized entirely around Easter in three segments: ten weeks prior to Easter, fifty days after Easter, and a more generic "remainder of the year." Western churches generally accord the Christmas season a liturgical and spiritual importance equal to that of Easter.

Why do Christians **celebrate** the **Ascension and Pentecost**?

Christ's Ascension into Heaven is commemorated on a Thursday forty days after Easter. Tradition places the event on the Mount of Olives, to the east of Jerusalem. It was the culmination of a period of post-resurrection appearances in which Jesus is said to have visited with his disciples. Christians have been observing the day since at least the end of the fourth century. Now, on the site traditionally connected with the event stands not a church but a small mosque. Ten days after the Ascension, the feast of Pentecost ("Fifty") recalls how Jesus promised his disciples he would soon send a "paraclete," or advocate, to continue guiding the young community in his stead. Tradition identifies the paraclete as the Holy Spirit. The Acts of the Apostles recounts how the disciples were gathered in an upper room when something like a storm enveloped them,

An Easter procession of Nazarenes in Malaga, Spain. (Pabkov / Shutterstock.com.)

and they experienced the power of the Spirit descending upon them in "tongues as of fire." Many Christians refer to this event as the birthday of the Church, since it gave the disciples the courage to emerge from hiding to preach the Gospel far and wide.

What are some of the **other religious days** Christians observe annually?

Numerous fixed feast days recall the lives of important saints as well as significant moments in the lives of Jesus and his mother Mary. Two significant events in the life of Jesus include the day his parents presented the infant in the Temple (February 2, The Presentation) and the Transfiguration in which he appeared in divine glory to several Apostles (August 6). Jesus' baptism by his cousin John is, in the western liturgical tradition, a movable feast that always occurs within the first two weeks of January. Feasts honoring Mary include those commemorating her being conceived without sin (Immaculate Conception, December 8); her birth (September 8); her presentation in the Temple (November 21); Elizabeth's visitation with Mary (May 31); and her bodily ascension into Heaven (Dormition/Assumption, August 15). In some churches well over half the days of the year are associated with holy persons, often commemorating the death date. A major saint such as John the Baptist might even merit an observance of both his birth (June 24) and his death (August 29).

111

CUSTOMS AND RITUALS

What **rituals** do Christians **practice in church**?

Primary Christian communal rituals are as nearly varied as the communities that perform them. A broad distinction between liturgical and nonliturgical churches is useful here. Liturgical churches feature a carefully regulated set of rituals, often of great antiquity. Only a handful of specialists, typically garbed in traditional vestments and sometimes using ancient liturgical languages for all or part of the ritual, may participate. In liturgical churches this spectator model emphasizes the performance of a sacred action with relatively limited participation by the congregation. In the middle of the spectrum, some churches follow what is called an "order of service," with the emphasis on preaching rather than on the sacred action of liturgical ritual as such. Leaders here often wear an academic-style robe and lead from a pulpit within a separate space called the sanctuary. Activities in entirely nonliturgical churches often tend to be more like a town meeting. Worship leaders sometimes wear a robe, but more often ordinary semi-formal street clothes. Services emphasize more inclusive participation during virtually all phases of the gathering, but preaching by the leader, and sometimes by one or more others as well, remains a centerpiece.

What is a **sacrament**?

"Sacrament" comes from a Latin root that originally referred to an oath by which soldiers swore their loyalty (Eastern Christians typically call a sacrament a holy "mystery"). Traditional Christian sources from a variety of churches generally define a sacrament as a visible sign of divine grace bequeathed by Christ himself. Since the Middle Ages, Catholics and Eastern Orthodox Christians have held that there are seven sacraments of equal spiritual significance: Baptism, Confirmation or Chrismation, the Eucharist, Penance, Holy Orders, Matrimony, and Final Anointing. Most Protestant communities have accorded a central place to baptism and the Eucharist, usually called the Lord's Supper, regarding the other five as of lesser importance, but some churches have recently begun to pay greater attention to those five as well. Almost all Christian communities practice baptism frequently, though in very different ways. As for the Eucharist or the Lord's Supper, frequency varies a great deal. Catholic and Orthodox churches, for example, give "holy communion" as part of nearly every liturgical worship service. In most Protestant communities, the Lord's Supper is much more occasional and a ritual set apart from the usual Sunday worship. The Society of Friends (Quakers) and the Salvation Army are the only larger groups that have no sacramental rituals at all.

What kinds of **ritual objects** figure in Christian **worship and prayer**?

In addition to the cross or crucifix Christians use a variety of ritual objects, more commonly in liturgical communities than in non-liturgical ones. The more elaborate the

What is the difference between a sermon and a homily?

In general, sermons tend to be longer and organized around a doctrinal or moral theme. Homilies may be lengthy, but they are generally situated in the context of a larger liturgical service, whereas sermons as often as not are the main focus of a worship gathering. Sermons frequently take as their subject a line or somewhat longer passage from scripture. The homily form seeks to comment on and elucidate a pair or set of scriptural texts precisely as scripture and not so much as a springboard for an ethical discourse. The preacher typically chooses the sermon's signature passage because of its theme, rather than because the text has come up in due course as part of a prearranged cycle of readings. Homilies are more often a way of helping the congregation appreciate how the selected readings fit together and comment on each other, and how they fit in the larger scheme of the liturgical cycle for the season at hand (such as Advent/Christmas, Lent/Easter, Ordinary time).

liturgical practice, in general, the more kinds of symbolic and practical implements are required. Most Christian churches have an altar on a raised platform in front of, or in the midst of, the congregation. Exceptions are Pentecostal and similar groups whose primary rituals revolve entirely around preaching, singing, and the ongoing interaction of the leaders with the congregation.

Churches such as the Roman and Anglo-Catholic, most Eastern churches and some Lutheran groups, feature a ritual that includes some reenactment of the Eucharistic prayer. Their ritual leader typically wears vestments and handles the sacred vessels. A large cup called the chalice, traditionally either made of or lined with precious metal, holds the wine (grape juice in some churches). A still larger vessel called the *ciborium* (Latin for "food container"), kept covered except during the prayers of consecration, holds the altar bread either in the form of small unleavened wafers (called hosts) or leavened cubes that can be dipped into the wine before dispensing to communicants.

Another common implement used in more elaborate liturgies is the thurible or incense burner, a small spherical container with a lighted charcoal for igniting grains of incense, which is swung from a chain in gestures of benediction. Less common but worth mentioning if only because of its artistic beauty is the *ostensorium* or monstrance, a large ornate device shaped like a spectacular sunburst or a small Gothic cathedral used for displaying the consecrated host during processions or for Western congregational adoration.

Are **music and dance** important in Christian religious ritual?

Almost all Christian churches make music an important element in worship, and a few engage in various forms of prayer-related movement. In some non-liturgical **113** churches, singing and dancing form the majority of congregational worship, even to the point of having music accompany the preaching. Individual hymns, some lasting ten to fifteen minutes or more, are the largest feature in those cases, punctuated by prayer and testimony from the assembled worshippers. In other words, songs and preaching make up most of the "order of service." Liturgical traditions use the hymn form, but also sing set pieces of the liturgical ritual itself. For example, the "Holy, Holy, Holy" announces the beginning of the Eucharistic Prayer, and the "Lamb of God" is sung just before communion in the Western liturgical tradition.

Since the liturgical traditions strive for an atmosphere of greater solemnity, they tend to incorporate dancing less often, and then only of a rather restrained kind. In many nonliturgical churches the expression of feeling is a major component, so that one can expect to find much more animated movement in such settings. More staid and stately liturgical traditions have historically preferred the majestic sonorities of the pipe organ, occasionally joined by brass, woodwinds, or classical strings. In other traditions, piano is the primary instrument, and even small congregations may feature bands with electric guitar and other keyboards, bass, and full drum kit. In most Eastern Christian traditions, however, liturgical services are chanted without any musical accompaniment. Christian communities all over the world naturally make use of distinctive ethnic and local musical styles and instruments.

What is **The Lord's Prayer**?

The Lord's Prayer, or the "Our Father," is found in the gospels of Matthew (6:9–13) and Luke (11:2–4). Both gospels position the Lord's prayer as Jesus' response to his disciples' request to teach them how to pray. Based on linguistic studies, most biblical scholars today agree that this prayer likely came from Jesus' own lips, and virtually all Christians acknowledge it as a prime example of prayer:

> Our Father, who art in Heaven,
> hallowed be Thy name;
> Thy kingdom come;
> Thy will be done on Earth as it is in Heaven.
> Give us this day our daily bread;
> and forgive us our trespasses
> as we forgive those who trespass against us;
> and lead us not into temptation,
> but deliver us from evil. Amen.

What is **the Rosary** and what Christians consider it an **important ritual prayer**?

The Rosary is a popular form of Roman Catholic prayer that combines meditation on the mysteries of faith with the recitation of vocal prayers. A "decade" of the Rosary corresponds to each of the fifteen mysteries commemorated in the Rosary. Ten Hail

Marys are said for each decade; they are preceded by an Our Father and followed by a Glory Be to the Father. While reciting a decade of the Rosary, one is to meditate on the particular mystery for that decade and on its meaning for life. The entire Rosary was for many years divided into three chaplets: the joyful, the sorrowful, and the glorious mysteries. To "say a Rosary" commonly means to pray one such chaplet of five mysteries. Commonly a chaplet is preceded by the recitation of the Apostles' Creed and of an Our Father and three Hail Marys. The Roman Catholic Church has long recommended this form of prayer as a convenient and effective way of meditating on the Christian mysteries of salvation.

Prayer beads are often used as a way of keeping track of the number of repetitions of a Rosary prayer.

The Joyful Mysteries

1. The Annunciation
2. The Visitation of Mary to her cousin Elizabeth
3. The Birth of Jesus Christ
4. The Presentation of Jesus in the Temple in Jerusalem
5. The Finding of the child Jesus in the Temple in Jerusalem

The Sorrowful Mysteries

1. The Agony of Jesus in the Garden of Gethsemane
2. The Scourging of Jesus at the Pillar
3. The Crowning with Thorns
4. The Carrying of the Cross
5. The Crucifixion

The Glorious Mysteries

1. The Resurrection of Jesus from the Dead
2. The Ascension of Jesus into Heaven
3. The Descent of the Holy Spirit upon the Apostles
4. The Assumption of Mary into Heaven
5. The Coronation of Mary as Queen of Heaven

More recently, the Luminous Mysteries were added, along with various other ways of praying the Rosary, called "chaplets." The Luminous mysteries are:

1. The Baptism in the Jordan
2. The Wedding at Cana
3. The Proclamation of the Kingdom
4. The Transfiguration
5. The Institution of the Eucharist

Do Christians engage in **exorcism**?

Irish stained glass depiction of Holy Spirit descending as tongues of fire on Jesus' Disciples. Dublin, Ireland.

Many readers will be at least vaguely familiar with a novel called *The Exorcist,* or with the movie based on it. The author, William Peter Blatty, based his story loosely on a now legendary series of events said to have taken place in St. Louis, Missouri some fifty years ago. Exorcism has long been available to Roman Catholics as a ritual designed to free individuals thought to be possessed and tormented by evil spirits. Church authorities have very rarely given permission to perform exorcisms and only after extensive psychiatric and medical consultation. The local bishop appoints a priest known for his sanctity, sanity, and personal strength to act as the principal ritual specialist. That exorcist then prepares to use a set ritual and to subject himself to whatever spiritual discipline may be necessary to withstand the rigors of the experience. Peculiar and frightening occurrences are said to accompany exorcisms. Father William Bowdern, the Jesuit priest who performed the St. Louis exorcism, refused ever to speak of the experience in public, except to affirm that he did indeed believe in the existence of the devil.

According to the New Testament, Jesus and his Apostles performed a number of exorcisms, a practice not altogether rare among Jews and pagans of the time. His actions are the ultimate sanction for the practice in Roman Catholicism. During medieval and even into early modern times, some people were executed as witches because they proved impervious to exorcism. Until about thirty years ago, Roman Catholic practice continued to confer on candidates to the priesthood the "minor order" or office of exorcist. Exorcism remains relatively common among some Christian denominations, especially Pentecostal or Charismatic groups. Leaders of worship might perform an exorcism as one among many manifestations of the Spirit, by prayer and touch intended to free the one possessed. Here exorcism is generally a very brief part of the larger ritual. A much-simplified form of exorcism remains a brief preliminary part of the ritual of baptism in many churches.

Votive offerings left by pilgrims in search of healings and other blessings at the shrine Sanctuary of Chimayo, New Mexico. Just to the right rear is the small outer room where pilgrims scoop sacred dust from the dirt floor as religious mementoes.

Is **pilgrimage** an important part of Christian tradition?

By about the fourth century, pilgrimage to Jerusalem had become common enough that significant examples of a type of literature called the pilgrimage narrative have survived. Pilgrims talk of their burning desire to visit sites mentioned in the Old Testament as well as those associated with key events in the life of Christ. Emperor Constantine's renovation of many of the holy places also made the practice more popular. After the Muslim conquest of Jerusalem and surrounding lands in 638, Christian access diminished somewhat, then improved for a while under the Crusaders' Latin Kingdom. But during the Middle Ages, other sacred sites associated with famous saints gradually replaced Jerusalem as the goal of choice for countless European pilgrims. The shrine of Santiago de Compostela in northwestern Spain was a major site, said to be built around the remains of St. James the Apostle. Compostela came to symbolize Christian efforts against the infidel Muslims in the Holy Land. In more recent times the practice of pilgrimage to Jerusalem and associated holy places has revived with increased ease of travel. Some Christians also flock to lesser shrines associated with saints or apparitions of the Virgin Mary. Pilgrimage was once occasionally prescribed for individuals as penance for sins, but it has never been a central requirement for Christians as it has for Muslims.

How do Christians mark **formal initiation** into their various faith communities?

Along with the Lord's Supper, baptism is one of the two rituals the vast majority of Christians recognize as a sacrament. Its symbolism recalls the cleansing waters of the **117**

Flood and the crossing of the Red Sea and Jordan. Essential elements in baptism are flowing water and the formula "I baptize you (or "The servant of God is baptized") in the name of the Father, and of the Son, and of the Holy Spirit." Infant baptism was the norm until the Reformation. Catholic, Orthodox, Lutheran, Methodist, Presbyterian, and Congregational churches still baptize infants, while some churches defer the ritual until the candidate is a teenager or older. Baptism can be administered by total or partial immersion, with the candidate descending into a pool or with the officiant lowering the infant into a font, or by affusion, in which the officiant pours water over the candidate's head only.

Do Christians practice any **other forms of initiation ceremony**?

Confirmation, or Chrismation as it is called in the Eastern churches, has historically been closely linked with baptism, in some cases even conferred immediately afterward. But in some churches confirmation represents the remnant of an ancient puberty rite, in which the baptized Christian is strengthened by the Holy Spirit. To the baptismal use of water symbolism, confirmation adds anointing and laying on of hands as symbols of further sealing the candidate's full membership in the Christian community. In some Western churches a bishop administers confirmation, but priests can do so under some circumstances as well.

Are there Christian **rituals of marriage**?

Most Christian communities have developed some form of ritual, however brief or simple, to acknowledge and bless the union of two people in matrimony. Marriage ceremonies can occur in church, in the home, or in some place chosen for its beauty or romantic appeal, such as a garden. By custom, representatives of the church community who preside over the ceremonies typically function as the primary witnesses of the union and sign the marriage license, which is then filed as a legal record of the marriage. In that capacity, ministers and priests are acting as representatives of the civil authorities as well, but the ceremony emphasizes the religious context and divine sanction of loving union. Religious weddings often include readings from scripture—perennial favorites are Genesis 2:18–25 on Adam and Eve and Paul's splendid description of true love in I Corinthians 13—as well as brief homiletical reflections and exhortation to the new spouses. Catholics, and Eastern churches that call the ceremony the "Crowning," generally situate weddings in the context of the Eucharistic liturgy. Christians generally believe that the couple themselves effect the marriage and that the officials and assembled community are there to witness and support their union.

What do Christians believe about **divorce and remarriage**?

Whether or not the witnessing community regards matrimony as a sacrament, Christian groups universally teach that marriage is a permanent commitment. Unfortunately, there is often a large gap between ideals and realities. However common it has become in some societies, most Christian communities consider divorce a solution of last resort. Many churches train their ministers and priests in marriage and family counseling so that they can assist their members when they find their relationships threatened for whatever reason. In the hope of obviating the eventual need for divorce, some churches recommend or even require premarital counseling and education, designed to impress on the couple the nature of the commitment they envision. Some churches do not recognize divorce as a religiously acceptable choice, teaching that marriage is an indissoluble bond. But those churches also acknowledge that in some cases the parties in a marriage may not have made the commitment with sufficient maturity, proper intent, or full consent. In those instances the marriage can be annulled, allowing both parties to seek legal divorce and remarry if they choose.

How do Christians deal **ritually** with **death and mourning**?

Death signals the final rite of passage, and most Christian communities have rituals designed specially to help mourners understand their loss from a religious perspective. A more or less formal period of mourning generally follows for a day or two. A few Christian groups do not permit embalming, preferring to bury the body on the day of death or shortly thereafter. American Christians generally prefer to have a "wake," usually at a mortuary but sometimes in a church or even in the home, during which mourners offer their condolences to the dead person's family. Wakes can last from several hours to several days. Some groups prefer a memorial service in the mortuary chapel following the

wake. Many churches offer funeral rites in church, either as part of a variation on the regular liturgical prayer (as with the Roman and Anglo-Catholic Mass) or as a distinct ceremony. Generally the body of the deceased is present in the casket, which is sometimes open for a final viewing and generally closed during the funeral ritual itself. When the deceased has willed his or her body to a medical school, or when an immediate cremation is judged necessary, a memorial service is held without the body. In the United States burial is still the most common means of dealing with human remains, but cremation is gaining acceptance even in churches traditionally opposed to the practice.

Catholic cemetery outside of New Orleans, Louisiana, where the dead are buried in mausolea above ground because of the area's susceptibility to flooding.

ISLAM

HISTORY AND SOURCES

When did **Islam begin**?

Five hundred years after the Roman destruction of the Temple in Jerusalem dramatically altered the history of Judaism, an equally momentous event occurred in the Arabian Peninsula. According to tradition, Muhammad was born around 570 C.E. in the trading town of Mecca. When he was about twenty-five, Muhammad married a businesswoman named Khadija, who was fifteen years his senior. Muhammad developed the habit of seeking prayerful solitude in the hills and caves surrounding Mecca. One day around the year 610, he began to undergo some troubling auditory and visual experiences. Encouraged by Khadija not to dismiss the experiences, Muhammad came to understand them as divine revelations that he was meant to communicate to his fellow Meccans. He was to be a messenger of God, a prophet charged with delivering a message that would set straight misinterpretations of earlier revelations given through the prophets God had sent to the Jews and Christians.

What and where is **Arabia**?

The Arabian Peninsula is an enormous land mass that makes up the south-central portion of western Asia, also known as the Middle East. It is now home to the nations of Saudi Arabia, Yemen, Oman, and United Arab Emirates, and several other small so-called Gulf States. Arabia is bordered on the west by the Red Sea, on the south by the Arabian Sea, and on the east by the Persian Gulf. Mostly desert, the peninsula is larger than Iran and Iraq combined, twice the size of Egypt, and about 10 percent larger than Alaska. The total population today is just over twenty million. Riyadh is the capital of Saudi Arabia, the peninsula's largest nation state. Jidda is the Red Sea port that serves

Pilgrims circumambulate the Ka'aba at Masjidil Haram in Mecca. Mecca is the birthplace of Muhammad and Islam's most holy city. (Ahmad Faizal Yahya / Shutterstock.com.)

the holy city of Mecca, Muhammad's home town. Medina, the second holy city, is about two hundred miles north of Mecca.

Why is **Mecca** a **holy city** for Muslims?

Mecca, in western Saudi Arabia, is the birthplace of the prophet Muhammad (c. 570) and was his home until the year 622, when those who opposed him forced him to flee to Medina (a city about two hundred miles north of Mecca). Muhammad later returned to Mecca on his farewell pilgrimage in 632. Mecca is also the site of the Great Mosque, which is situated in the heart of the city. The outside of the mosque is an arcade, made up of a series of arches enclosing a courtyard. In that courtyard is the most sacred shrine of Islam, the Ka'aba, a small stone building that contains the Black Stone, which Muslims believe was sent from Heaven by Allah (God). When Muslims pray (five times a day, according to the Five Pillars of Faith), they face the Ka'aba. It is also the destination of the *Hajj*, or pilgrimage.

What were some **critical events** in Islam's earliest years?

Over the next twenty-three years or so after the initial revelations in 610, Muhammad continued to preach the word God had spoken directly to him. At the heart of the message was the notion of "surrender" (the root meaning of the Arabic word *islam*, pronounced isLAAM) to the one true God. His early preaching called for social justice and equality and condemned oppression of the poor by the wealthy and powerful. Muhammad belonged to a powerful tribe called the Quraysh, who exercised considerable control over the lives of the Meccans generally. But Muhammad's family and the clan of which they were a part were among the poorer and less influential within the tribe. Muhammad's preaching did not endear him to the Quraysh, who made life difficult for the small community of Muslims. In 622, Muhammad and his followers made the crucial decision to move north to the city of Yathrib, whose representatives had offered the young community sanctuary. This "emigration" or Hijra marked the official beginning of the Muslim calendar. Muhammad the prophet became a statesman as well, and Yathrib became known as Madinat an-Nabi, the City of the Prophet, or Medina for short. The Muslim community grew rapidly, doing battle with the Meccans and eventually regaining access to Mecca in 630.

What place does **Muhammad occupy** in **Islamic tradition**?

Muslims consider Muhammad the last in a line of prophets commissioned to act as God's spokesmen to humankind. Beginning with Adam and continuing down through Jesus, the pre-Islamic prophets preached the same fundamental message of belief in one sovereign transcendent God. But because successive generations invariably found the message difficult and inconvenient, people sometimes corrupted or diluted the revelation. Hence, God chose upright individuals to reassert the original revelation. Muhammad was a man singled out for his natural virtue and integrity to fulfill the role of final and definitive intermediary of the divine communication. As a human being, Muhammad naturally had his faults. But Muslims regard him as the finest our species has yet produced, the ideal family man and leader of humanity.

Muhammad himself never claimed to be a wonder-worker. His sole miracle was the Qur'an (pronounced koRAAN and hereafter transliterated as Qur'an), the Muslim sacred scripture. Popular tradition has nevertheless sometimes idealized Muhammad, expanding his powers and prerogatives to include various kinds of marvels. One dual experience, called the Night Journey and Ascension, stands out. According to tradition, God conveyed Muhammad by night from Mecca to Jerusalem, and from there through the various levels of Heaven and Hell. Popular lore has attributed other wonders to Muhammad, but what is most important is to appreciate the enormous affection and reverence Muslims universally feel for their Prophet.

What is the **principal Muslim sacred text**?

In about the year 610, Muhammad began to deliver orally the messages he believed were of divine origin. His "recitation" (qur'an) of the revelation was initially held in memory by his followers, and, according to traditional accounts, was not produced in full written form until some years after Muhammad's death in 632. What began as "an Arabic recitation" retained that name even after it was written down, and the resulting book is still known as "The Recitation" or Qur'an.

123

A page from the Qur'an, eighth-ninth century, Middle East. The Saint Louis Art Museum.

How **big** is the **Qur'an** and how is it **organized**?

The sacred scripture contains about 6,200 verses, roughly equivalent in length to the New Testament, arranged in 114 sections called *suras* (pronounced SUrah). Muhammad's earliest revelations tend to be short, rhetorically potent utterances in an ancient form of rhymed prose used by pre-Islamic seers and soothsayers. Later *suras* tend to be lengthier and more prosaic, and often take up more practical concerns. *Suras* are arranged in more or less descending order of length, so that many of the earlier sections are actually in the latter part of the book now. The heading of each *sura* contains the title, number of verses, and an indication as to whether it was revealed at Mecca or Medina. Interpreters consider it very important to place each text historically, for the "circumstances of the revelation" are critical in unwrapping its original meaning. Tradition has identified the *suras*, or portions of them where it is clear that a single *sura* is actually a composite—as early, middle, or late Meccan (610–622) or Medinan (622–632). Muslims believe the Qur'an is the direct, literal word of God unmodified in any way by the Prophet who uttered them at God's bidding.

What was **pre-Islamic religion** like and did Islam retain any of its features?

Pre-Islamic Arabian tribes believed that the universe was animated by innumerable spirits, each inhabiting its own distinctive elements and natural features. They called each of these minor deities an *ilah*, "god," but tribespeople in many regions singled out one particular local power as the chief spiritual force. That power they called the

What is the Ka'aba and why is it important?

According to tradition, Abraham and his son Ishmael built (or perhaps rebuilt) a simple cubelike structure in what came to be the center of the city of Mecca. During Muhammad's time the Ka'aba was a relatively small structure, about fifteen feet tall, with a black stone, the size of a bowling ball, of (perhaps) meteoric origin built into one of its corners. Rebuilt several times since Muhammad's day, the Ka'aba now stands about forty-three feet high, with irregular sides ranging from thirty-six to forty-three feet. During Muhammad's lifetime, the building is said to have housed some 360 idols. In 630, Muhammad cleansed the Ka'aba, and it has since remained empty except for some lamps. Its holiness as a symbol of divine presence derives largely from its associations with the lives of Abraham and Muhammad.

god *al-ilah* or *allah* (pronounced al-LAAH). Mecca was one of several major cultic sites over which such a chief deity ruled. There, a peculiar cubic-shaped structure called the Ka'aba stood for perhaps centuries at the center of pilgrimage traffic associated with a lively caravan trade. Pre-Islamic beliefs also acknowledged the existence of numerous troublesome beings called *jinns*, as well as downright diabolical spiritual forces. Muhammad's ancestors emphasized the importance of following the moral code of tribal custom unquestioningly and did not believe in an afterlife. In his early preaching the Prophet focused on the need to behave morally and justly in light of the coming judgment. He taught that a divine will was more important than tribal custom, however ancient, and gradually increased his condemnation of the cult of many spiritual powers (called polydaemonism). The Ka'aba remained an important symbol, as did the practice of pilgrimage, but Muhammad appropriated those aspects of tradition by underscoring their association with Abraham and Ishmael especially.

Are there any important **links** between the **Qur'an and the Bible**?

Since the Islamic interpretation of history overlaps in significant ways with those of Judaism and Christianity, one should not be surprised to find that some material in the Qur'an parallels some biblical material. Some narrative treatments of various biblical patriarchs and kings, whom the Qur'an identifies as prophets and messengers, immediately recall aspects of biblical accounts. But there are also interesting variations in the stories. Adam and Eve's fall, for example, is connected with eating from a forbidden tree (or an ear of wheat in one version). Sprinkled throughout the scripture are references to Abraham's near-sacrifice of his son (whom Islamic tradition takes to be Ishmael rather than Isaac), and to Moses' mission to Pharaoh, David's musical gifts, Solomon's royal grandeur, and others. Perhaps the single most important parallel is the story of Joseph of the many-colored coat, son of Jacob and father of two tribes of Israel. Sura 12 of the Qur'an retells the tale found in Genesis 39–50 with its own distinctive flavor and variations in detail. Only Joseph's story is told in its entirety, and all in a single *sura* dedicated entirely to it.

Though many Jewish and Christian readers often conclude that Muhammad "borrowed" from the Bible, that is not necessarily the case. The way the Qur'an tells the stories, mostly in short excerpts and allusions, suggests that Muhammad's listeners must have been already familiar with at least the general drift of the narratives. There are also some accounts of non-biblical prophetic figures, called Hud, Salih, and Shuayb, in some ways unique to the Arabian peninsula. It is important to note that Muslim tradition has discerned in both the Old and New Testaments references to the coming of Islam's prophet. God promised to raise up for Israel a prophet like Moses (Deuteronomy 18:18)—Muhammad. The prophet Isaiah sees two riders approaching, one on a donkey and the other on a camel: Jesus and Muhammad. Jesus promised to send a *parakletos* ("advocate," John 14:16), but Muslim commentators argue that with the correct vowels, the Greek word is *periklutos,* meaning "highly praised," the exact meaning of *muhammad* in Arabic.

What **other early texts** are especially important for Muslims?

Second only to the Qur'an in both authority and antiquity is the large body of works containing sayings attributed to Muhammad, along with hundreds of anecdotes about him. This material is known collectively as Hadith (sayings or traditions, pronounced haDEETH). When Muhammad died, neither the scripture nor the Prophet's words and deeds had been formally committed to writing. And even long after the Qur'an had been carefully edited, Muslims hesitated to produce written versions of Muhammad's sayings. Custodians of these Prophetic Traditions kept them by heart, much as the earliest followers preserved the Qur'anic revelations.

Not until over two centuries after Muhammad died did his community deem it necessary to gather and edit the Hadith. The impetus to do so came in part from legal scholars, who believed that the only way to interpret the spirit of the Qur'an faithfully in cases not explicitly treated in the scripture was to have a sound testimony of the Prophet's own views. Through much of the ninth century, Muslim religious scholars undertook the massive task of traveling widely and gathering and recording thousands of Hadiths from countless individuals known for their reliable memories. These scholars, often working independently and at some distance in time and space, then sifted through what they had gathered. Since the very existence of this treasure trove depended on its oral transmission from one generation to another, scholars looked first at the chains of transmission to see whether all individuals listed were trustworthy. If not, one likely could dismiss the Hadith itself as not entirely reliable. By the end of the ninth century half a dozen authoritative collections of Hadith were available, and many lesser ones as well, complete with scholarly evaluation as to the relative soundness of each saying and anecdote. Muslims traditionally consider the content of the Hadith to be divinely inspired, only expressed in Muhammad's own words, unlike the Qur'an, which is in God's own diction.

How do Muslims **interpret** their **sacred texts**?

Discussion of the Qur'an is a regular activity in most mosques, usually in connection with the Friday congregational prayer (and in the United States also held on Sundays). One or more discussion leaders might present a text and then open the floor to comments and questions. The first concern is generally to establish the "circumstances of the revelation." What was the specific occasion on which this particular text was revealed to Muhammad? Was it revealed in connection with any unusual or momentous event? Was it a direct response to some question or predicament that had arisen in the early Muslim community?

Contemporary Muslims can dip into an enormous reservoir of traditional scholarship for help in interpreting the Qur'an. Exegetes began compiling detailed and extensive commentaries on the sacred scripture as early as the eighth century. They refined the tools of a specialty called *tafsir* (pronounced tafSEER, "explanation, elaboration"). Dozens of multivolume works in Arabic (plus countless more in various other languages) of great antiquity and authority are still widely available from publishers of Islamic books, and many are now being translated into Western languages. Classical commentators and modern-day interpreters alike look first to the Hadith for help on obscure passages of the Qur'an, for Muhammad himself often responded to questions about specific texts. Careful study of Arabic grammar and a wide knowledge of other works of Arabic literature for purposes of comparison are also essential background for professional exegetes. In addition to elucidating the basic or literal meanings of a sacred text, Qur'an commentary can also probe into further levels of meaning. Muslim mystics especially have written allegorical or symbolic interpretations (called *ta'wil,* pronounced ta'WEEL) to uncover the deeper spiritual implications of the scripture.

What was **happening** in and around Arabia **when Islam began**?

In pre-Islamic times the Arabian Peninsula had rarely been at the center of Middle Eastern events. An immense coastline made the land accessible to and from the Red Sea on the west, the Persian Gulf on the east, and the Indian Ocean on the south, but the real estate of that vast, inhospitable ocean of sand held little strategic interest for the regional powers. Local kingdoms had ruled to the north, in Syria, and to the southwest, in the Yemen. Although the Greeks and Romans knew about the place and liked its incense, they never set their sights on the territory.

When Muhammad was growing up, an important trade route ran up and down the western coastal region, a highway for exchange from Abyssinia (Ethiopia) and the Yemen, to Syria and points north by way of Mecca. To the northwest of the peninsula, the Christian Byzantine empire ruled. To the northeast, in Persia, the Zoroastrian Sasanian empire had displaced the Parthians, a client state of Rome, in 226 C.E. These two "confessional" (i.e., religiously connected) empires had been engaged in a protracted tug-of-war over the Fertile Crescent with its enormous river systems. Two Arab tribes in adjacent states did much of their fighting for them, namely the Monophysite Christian Ghassanids for Byzantium and the unchurched Lakhmids for Persia. As it turned out, their ongoing struggle would pave the way for the early expansion of Islam. By the time Muhammad died, Byzantium and Persia had all but spent themselves into bankruptcy and had so worn each other down that neither would mount serious resistance when the Muslim tribes advanced out of Arabia in a conquering mood.

Who were the **Companions of the Prophet** and why are they important?

Muslims have long known their tradition's earliest stalwart and exemplary figures as the Companions (*sahaba*) of the Prophet. The Companions included, naturally, the elect cadre of first converts to Islam, but eventually embraced a much broader variety of people. Beneath the retrospective listing of Companions that began to take shape some seventy to eighty years after Muhammad's death (632) lies a skein of inter-related criteria that characterize an authentic Companion. In addition to having "seen" the Prophet, Companions were ranked first in terms of chronological order in conversion (the earliest known as the *sabiqun,* predecessors). Other criteria included, for example, accompanying Muhammad in the Hijra to Medina (622), fighting in the Battle of Badr (624), participation in the Treaty of Hudaybiya (628), or presence among the early converts in Medina known as the Prophet's "Helpers" (*Ansar*). A host of other qualifications, mostly related to pinpointing date of conversion, include participation in the battles of Uhud and the Ditch, for example, and relatively late conversion to Islam during Muhammad's visit to Mecca after the Muslims reclaimed it in 630. These were such signal events in the life of Muhammad and the early community that participation in them became roughly analogous to the presence of leading first-generation Christians at major moments in Christ's life.

How did **Islam spread** under **Mohammad's** immediate **successors**?

Muhammad's immediate successors, called *caliphs* (pronounced KAYliff), inherited an expanding but loose-knit social fabric. The Prophet had united the Bedouin tribes under the banner of Islam, but tribal loyalties cooled quickly when the leader died. When Muslim elders in Medina chose Muhammad's father-in-law Abu Bakr as the first *caliph*, the initial challenge was to regather the tribes already reverting to their pre-Islamic ways. Umar (634–644), the second *caliph*, then mobilized tribal forces to move northward into Syria and Mesopotamia (Iraq), westward into Egypt, and eastward into Persia. Next, Umar instituted important policies in the conquered lands, allowing the subjected peoples to retain their religion and law, and levied taxes often lower than what had been paid previously to Byzantium and Persia. Muslim armies remained apart in garrisons that eventually became cities in their own right. Umar's successors, Uthman (644–656) and Ali (656–661), compassed the downfall of the last Sasanian emperor, but had to deal with disastrous internal strife as well.

What were the **first great Muslim dynasties**?

Relatives of Uthman, called the Umayyads, brought Ali down for his complicity in the murder of Uthman. They established a new seat of power in the ancient city of Damascus (Syria), thus inaugurating the first of a series of Muslim dynasties. Under the Umayyads the map of Islamdom expanded dramatically. By the year 711, Muslim armies had claimed ground across North Africa to Spain, and as far east as the Indus River in present-day Pakistan. Consolidation and some further expansion continued under the Abbasid dynasty, which ruled from its newly founded capital, Baghdad, after supplanting the Umayyads in 750. But the early

Mosaic decoration on the main dome of the Great Mosque of Cordoba, Spain, tenth century, over the *mihrab*, the niche indicating the direction of Mecca toward which Muslims face during ritual prayer.

plan for a single unified Islamic domain soon began to unravel. Increasingly aware that Baghdad could not continue to hold its far-flung empire together, regional governors and princes at the fringes began to declare independence. Although the Abbasid caliph would continue to claim nominal allegiance until 1258, the future belonged to countless successor states, from Spain to Central and South Asia.

What were the most important **early Islamic sectarian movements**?

Immediately upon Muhammad's death Muslims had to face the question of succession to leadership of the community. One faction claimed that the Prophet had designated his cousin and son-in-law, Ali, as his successor. They were to become known as the Party or Faction (*Shi'a*) of Ali, and today their various subcommunities are called Shi'a Muslims or Shi'ites. But a majority held that Muhammad had made no such appointment and that it was up to the elders to choose from among themselves. They considered their course of action to be both in keeping with the example of Muhammad (called his *Sunna,* SUNnah) and in the spirit of the needs of the whole community (*jama'a,* jaMAA'ah) of Muslims. This majority group came to be known as the People of the Sunnah and the Assembly (*Ahl as-sunna wa-l'jama'ah*), or Sunni Muslims for short.

Were there any **other early sectarian developments**?

Several other sects made their views known early on. When Ali was doing battle with the Umayyads to claim his rights to the caliphate, a number of his troops seceded on

129

the grounds that Ali was too lax in his appeal to religious principles in the conduct of battle. They judged Ali a serious sinner who was no longer worthy of the name Muslim. That group became known as the Kharijites (or *Khawarij*, "those who secede"), and a small remnant of their several factions live today largely in Oman on the Persian Gulf. Several other groups also expressed their opinions as to how far one might go in judging another person's suitability for true membership in the Muslim community. One of the more influential believed that only God could judge a person's soul, and that it was therefore best to postpone judgment on the matter. They were known as the Murji'ites or "Postponers."

Was Islam especially important in **medieval Spain**?

Not long after Arab troops began to occupy the Iberian peninsula, Muslim princes (called *amirs,* literally commanders; pronounced aMEER) established themselves in major cities. In 750 the Abbasids sought to put an end to their Umayyad rivals by assassinating all of the family's princes. One managed to escape and take refuge in Spain. This Abd ar-Rahman proclaimed himself Amir of Cordoba, still holding aloft the Umayyad standard. His successors eventually broke with Baghdad definitively by proclaiming the Umayyad Caliphate of Cordoba. A major step up from an Amirate, the Caliphate laid claim to the universal allegiance of all Muslims. For several centuries Cordoba would be a marvel of cultural splendor and inter-religious harmony. On the whole, Cordoba was an outstanding example of how Jews, Christians, and Muslims could live together in peace under Muslim rule.

Islam's presence was highly visible in other Spanish cities as well. Seville became an important political and cultural center as Cordoba receded in importance in the mid-eleventh century. Christian reconquest of Spain gradually retook ground from Muslim rule, from Toledo to Cordoba to Seville. Granada would remain the last stronghold of Islam until the armies of Catholic monarchs Ferdinand and Isabella took the legendary Alhambra in 1492. Nearly eight centuries of Islamic presence in Spain left a rich religious and cultural heritage. Five hundred years after the fall of Granada, small communities of Muslims are once again taking root in Spain.

How did Muslim history unfold **after** the age of the **first great Caliphal dynasties**?

Among the numerous dynasties and political regimes that ruled throughout the Mediterranean and Central and South Asia, several stand out. In Egypt, the Mamluk dynasty (1250–1517) presided over two and a half centuries of relative peace and prosperity throughout the central Middle East. They were patrons of the arts and architecture on a grand scale under whom Cairo especially grew into a worthy rival of any great Mediterranean city. The Ottoman Turks (1300–1921) supplanted the Mamluks as they expanded to conquer most of the former Byzantine empire and more. To the east, the Safavid dynasty (1501–1722) replaced the descendants of Genghis Khan, who had ruled Iraq and Iran for 250 years. Establishing Twelver Shi'a Islam the official creed of the realm, the Safavids created splendid art and architecture in cities such as Isfahan.

How did Islam become important in **South Asia**?

Further east than Iraq and Iran, the Mughal dynasty (1502–1757) established Islamic rule over much of South Asia, from Afghanistan across at least the northern two-thirds of India. Great monarchs such as Akbar, Jahangir, and Shah Jahan

The Taj Mahal, a seventeenth century tomb constructed by Mughal Muslim ruler Shah Jahan as a burial place of his favorite wife. It is located in Agra in north-central India.

turned cities like Delhi and Agra into architectural showpieces with works like the Taj Mahal. After about the mid-eighteenth century, European colonialism began to make inroads into lands formerly under Islamic regimes. Not until the mid-twentieth century did major colonial powers begin to withdraw, ceding political control back to indigenous populations. One dramatic example of that relatively recent change is the independence of India from Britain and the partition of India that created the Muslim state of Pakistan (1948), itself divided in 1971 into Pakistan and Bangladesh.

Timeline of Major Events, Developments, and Figures

Year	Event
570	Birth of Muhammad
595	Muhammad's marriage to Khadija, mother of Fatima
610	Initial revelation of Qur'an to Muhammad through the angel Gabriel
622	Hijra, emigration of Muslim community from Mecca to Medina
632	Muhammad's death in Medina
632–661	Period of the "Rightly Guided Caliphs," first successors to Muhammad
661–750	Period of the Umayyad Dynasty, capital at Damascus, major expansion as far as Spain and India; gradual development of Shi'a Islam following death of Ali
750–1258	Period of the Abbasid Dynasty, capital at Baghdad, gradual breakdown into regional political entities from Spain to India
750–900	Formation of the four major Sunni schools of religious law, major developments in Qur'anic exegetical sciences, canonization of the Hadith literature
700–765	Ja'far as-Sadiq, generally acclaimed as Sixth Imam by all Shi'a Muslims
857–922	Hallaj, acknowledged by Sufis as first martyr-mystic

Timeline of Major Events, Developments, and Figures (continued)

Year	Event
873–935	Ash'ari, systematic theologian responsible for crucial religious studies synthesis
980–1037	Ibn Sina, a.k.a. Avicenna, major Central Asian philosopher (from Uzbekistan)
1088–1166	'Abd al-Qadir al-Jilani, early influence on institutionalization of Sufi communal life
1099–1189	First Crusade resulting in Latin Kingdom of Jerusalem, ended by Saladin
1189–1290	Muslim responses to subsequent major Crusades leave Muslims in control of most of the central Middle East
1100–1400	Growth and spread of major Sufi brotherhoods from Iberia to Indonesia
1059–1111	Abu Hamid al-Ghazali, influential religious thinker and author
1126–1198	Ibn Rushd (Averroes), famed Iberian-born philosopher (from Cordoba)
1210–1526	Delhi Sultanates, powerful Muslim presence in India
1250–1517	Mamluk dynasty in Egypt and central Middle East
1258	Mongols destroy Baghdad, ending the Abbasid Dynasty
1207–1273	Jalal ad-Din Rumi, major Sufi poet, originator of "Whirling Dervishes" (Sufi order known officially as the Mawlawiya)
1300–1921	Ottoman Dynasty rules Turkey and much of the eastern Mediterranean
1263–1328	Ibn Taymiya, major religious scholar of the Hanbali law school
1453	Fall of Byzantine capital at Constantinople to Ottoman Turks
1492	Fall of the Nasrid Dynasty in Granada, last major Muslim presence in Spain
1414–1492	Jami, major Sufi mystical poet
1470–1506	Behzad, influential miniature painter from Timurid Herat (Afghanistan)
1526–1757	Mughal Dynasty rules much of India
1489–1578	Sinan, chief architect of Sulayman the Magnificent, one of the Muslim world's greatest designers of religious space
1791	Death of Muhammad ibn Abd al-Wahhab, founder of Wahhabi movement in Arabian Peninsula
1849–1905	Muhammad Abduh, proponent of reason as source of knowledge
1865–1935	Rashid Rida, founder of Egyptian Salafi movement calling for retrival of pristine days of the Prophet
1922–1924	Mustafa Kemal Ataturk secularizes Turkish state
1906–1949	Hasan al-Banna, whose Muslim Brotherhood (1929) gains strength with failure of liberal Muslim governments and proclamation of the State of Israel
1909–1966	Sayyid Qutb, influential theorist of Muslim Brotherhood movement
1947	Partition of India creates Muslim state of Pakistan (East and West)
1971	Separation of East Pakistan as the nation of Bangladesh
1979	Islamic Republic of Iran proclaimed after overthrow of second and last Pahlavi Shah
2010	Global Muslim population reaches 1.57 billion

RELIGIOUS BELIEFS

Is there an **Islamic creed**?

One short, two-part statement sums up the essentials of Muslim belief. "I confess that there is no deity but God, and that Muhammad is the messenger of God." In this "testimony" called the *shahada* ("confession or witnessing," pronounced shaHAAda), Muslims affirm the two foundational elements from which all other beliefs and practices flow. First, they assert that only the one, transcendent, supreme being called Allah in Arabic can claim the full allegiance of humankind. Allah means literally "the deity," or what ordinary English usage calls God "with a capital G." Allah is therefore not a distinct name for God as such, but the primary designation for the Absolute, the deity above all other powers both spiritual and worldly. Affirming God's absolute oneness is called *tawhid* (pronounced tawHEED).

Second, Muslims attest that human beings know of this Supreme Being through the agency of prophets, the last of whom was Muhammad. This profession of faith is the first of the "five pillars" of Islam (along with almsgiving, daily ritual prayer, fasting during Ramadan—pronounced RamaDAAN—and pilgrimage to Mecca, all of which will be discussed later in detail). Muslim religious scholars between about 750 and 950 formulated a number of other, more detailed creedal statements, but none has been as widely known as the Nicene Creed among Christians or the "Thirteen Articles" among Jews. Those later Islamic creeds developed largely as correctives to theological positions that arose during Islam's early centuries, views that the creeds formally repudiated as unacceptable.

What are the **"Five Pillars"** of Muslim faith?

Muslims practice adherence to the Five Pillars of Faith: 1) profession (*shahada*) of belief in Allah as the only God and Muhammad as his prophet; 2) ritual prayer (*salat,* pronounced saLAAT) five times daily—at dawn, at noon, in the afternoon, in the evening, and at nightfall; 3) giving alms to the poor (*zakat,* pronounced zaKAAT); 4) fasting from dawn until dusk during the holy month of Ramadan (*sawm*) ; and 5) making the pilgrimage (*Hajj*) to the holy city of Mecca at least once during their lifetime.

What do Muslims **believe about God**?

God is one, transcendent, and wholly unlike anything in ordinary human experience. But such a barebones description of ultimate reality leaves little for the human heart to grasp. Muslim tradition speaks of God most of all through the "Ninety-Nine Beautiful Names." "Compassionate" and "Merciful" are by far the most important of these. They occur in the phrase "In the name of God, the Compassionate, the Merciful," with which all but one of the suras of the Qur'an begin. Whatever devout Muslims do, they

A plaque at the Mosque of Lady Khadija, Kusadasi, Turkey, indicates the times for the five regular daily prayers plus one devotional time.

dedicate with that phrase. God's names include about equally those that suggest divine power and majesty (*jalal*, pronounced jaLAAL) and those that speak of his beauty and infinite attractiveness (*jamal*, pronounced jaMAAL). God creates life and causes death, gives freely and calls all creation to account.

Non-Muslims often have the mistaken impression that the Islamic God is most of all a fearsome, even despotic, power before whom all must cower and cringe. To the contrary, while Muslims are ever aware of God's uncontested sovereignty and dominion over all things, they believe as well that, as the Qur'an teaches, God is closer to individual persons than even their jugular vein. Muslim tradition reminds believers that, in the end, God's mercy outweighs his anger. Scores of Hadiths describe this God of mercy in such beautiful and moving terms that any outsider who studies them can readily understand why so many Muslims find devotion to such a deity so compelling.

What does the term **"revelation" mean** in Islamic tradition?

Islam's scripture, the Qur'an, consistently refers to itself as the word that God has "sent down" (*tanzil*, pronounced tanZEEL) to humankind through Muhammad. That which is "sent down" represents a manifestation of truths that have existed from all eternity in the heavenly archetype of the Qur'an known as the "Mother of the Book." God reveals by communicating in a language understandable to the intended audience. Both the Qur'an and subsequent Muslim tradition describe the actual process of revelation by a technical term (*wahy*) that distinguishes prophetic revelation from the kinds of "inspiration" that animate holy persons and artists, for example. The prophet-ic intermediary "hears" the message, not with physical ears but with the ears of the spirit and heart. Some descriptions of revelation suggest a visionary dimension as well, as when the angel Gabriel or another mysterious unnamed presence appears.

According to both Qur'an and Hadith, Muhammad received revelations in a wide variety of circumstances. In some cases revelation is given in response to a particular question asked of the Prophet. In others, Muhammad is described as praying, preaching, eating, or even bathing. Muhammad is said to have experienced a variety of actual sensa-tions when he received a revelation. He spoke of a sound like bees humming around his face, or a loud bell, the sound of which was physically painful. Sometimes he broke into a cold sweat or showed signs like those of a trance or seizure. All of the prophets are said to have experienced similar forms of revelation. What is most significant here is Muhammad's overwhelming sense of the divine presence at these moments.

Is there an **Islamic fundamentalism**?

Unfortunately, the term "fundamentalist" has become virtually synonymous with "Mus-lim" in contemporary American usage. This is unfortunate because, when applied to Muslims, "fundamentalist" has been simultaneously linked to terrorism. It is fair to say that most devout Muslims interpret their scriptures conservatively and quite literally, as do the vast majority of devout adherents to many traditions. Islamic fundamentalism is not inherently more likely to be expressed in extreme behavior than any other brand of fundamentalism. One can of course point to examples of such behavior in virtually every tradition—including the assassination of abortion providers by American Chris-tians and the burning of Christian villagers by angry Hindu mobs in India.

Extreme and violent behavior that claims religious justification invariably has a great deal to do with predominant political and social climates in particular places and times. Non-Muslims often apply the epithet "fundamentalist" indiscriminately to widely diverse situations. For example, so-called militant fundamentalists in Algeria attempt to justify their activism on very different grounds than do, say, Shi'a factions in southern Lebanon, the Palestinian organization called Hamas, the Taliban of Afghanistan and Pakistan, and the revolutionary government of Iran. On the other hand, Muslim-led states whose leaders are avowedly secularist in orientation are responsible for at least as much violence against their own people than avowedly "Islamist" states. In other words, while the term fundamentalism has value in describ-ing some religious phenomena, it has become so imprecise as to be virtually useless as a way of describing Muslims.

What's the difference between a **prophet** and a **messenger**?

Central to Islamic tradition is the belief that God communicates ultimate truths through specially chosen persons called prophets. Without prophetic revelation, human

135

beings would be forced to rely on intellect alone and thus could not arrive at the knowledge necessary to attain their final purpose. Every prophet (*nabi,* pronounced NAbee) passes along the divine word to a particular people and inevitably meets with tremendous resistance, at least initially. Some of these prophets receive the further designation of "messenger" or "apostle" (*rasul,* pronounced raSOOL), "one who is sent." God sends but one messenger to a given people. Prophets specified as messengers include Noah, Lot, Ishmael, Moses, Shuayb, Hud, Salih, Jesus, and of course Muhammad. Prophets preach and warn their people, but messengers are also commissioned to lead a community of faith called an *umma.* Post-Qur'anic tradition also teaches that messengers function as lawgivers, whereas the other prophets do not. In short, one might say that all messengers are prophets, but not all prophets are messengers.

Why are **Jesus and Mary important** to Muslims?

Muslims revere Jesus (Arabic: 'Isa, pronounced EEsa) as the second-to-last in a long line of prophets that culminated in Muhammad. They thus consider Jesus a man of lofty spiritual estate, but no more than a human being. Born of the Virgin Mary, 'Isa was a specially chosen instrument of divine revelation, but he was not the Son of God. Muslim texts call Jesus the *masih,* but the term does not carry the sense of expectation connoted by its nearest English equivalent, Messiah. He is "God's word," but not in the sense that Christians understand the term *logos.* Mary is mentioned more often by name in the Qur'an than in the Bible.

The purely human nature of Jesus is not the only major issue on which Islamic tradition disagrees dramatically with the Christian view. Qur'an 4:157 states that though the Jews boasted they had killed 'Isa, they did not in fact do so. It was, rather, one who looked like Jesus who hung on the cross. Muslim tradition holds, nevertheless, that God did raise Jesus bodily into Heaven in the Ascension. Since 'Isa did not die an earthly death, he did not experience resurrection. 'Isa has a significant place in the Qur'an. According to the Islamic sacred text, Mary became pregnant with 'Isa when the angel Gabriel appeared to her in human form to announce the news. Joseph plays no part in the Muslim story of Jesus. After the child was born, Mary brought him to her people. When even they expressed doubt as to Mary's integrity, the infant spoke in her defense and lifted her opprobrium. One of the Qur'anic stories not found in the canonical Gospels is that the boy 'Isa formed a bird of clay in his hands, and when he breathed on it, it took flight—a story also told in a Christian apocryphal. Principal Qur'anic texts on 'Isa (and Mary) are: 3:37–48; 4:169–70; 5:76–79 and 109–117; 19:1–36; 21:91–92; 43:57–65; 57:26–27.

Hagiographical texts known collectively as *Tales of the Prophets* expand further a number of important themes. The *Tales* embellish the accounts of 'Isa's infancy and youth. They feature 'Isa as a wandering ascetic with the power to give and restore life. They also add to the number of his miracles and emphasize his sinlessness and the significance of his Ascension and second coming. Islam's mystical authors develop the figure of

'Isa in particularly colorful and imaginative ways. 'Isa is for many mystics the image of the near-perfect Sufi—near-perfect because he once carried a needle with him during his desert wanderings, thus falling short of absolute trust in God. But even when storms threatened, 'Isa refrained from seeking shelter, for he epitomized the homeless pilgrim. Still the Sufis celebrated 'Isa as the prophet who laughed heartily and often, by contrast with Yahya (John the Baptist) who had a penchant for weeping. Sufi poets delight in tales of 'Isa's ability to restore life through the incantation of a powerful name only a select few may utter. Though the Qur'an does not mention Lazarus ('Azar) by name, from popular hagiography Sufi writers picked up the story of 'Isa raising 'Azar from the dead. Finally, Sufis love to describe how Jesus embodies their focus on mystical knowledge through his mastery of the the body, which they compare to the "donkey," a symbol of ignorance.

Islam is called one of the "Abrahamic" faiths—so why is **Abraham important to Muslims**?

Islam's sacred scripture, the Qur'an, makes numerous references to both biblical and extra-biblical stories about Abraham, whose Arabic name is Ibrahim. For Muslims, Ibrahim's status is that of a Prophet, a recipient of God's direct revelation. That he does not function as a Patriarch in Islamic tradition is significant, for Ibrahim's primary theological role is not that of the father of a chosen nation, but that of the first *"muslim"*— the first human being to whom God revealed explicitly the call to be a seeker after divine unity and, therefore, the first to "surrender." The Arabic term *muslim* means "one who surrenders" to God and who thereby enacts the full meaning of the term *islam*.

Fundamental to this aspect of Ibrahim's Islamic role is the tradition that the prophet's father, 'Azar according to the Qur'an, made his living by carving idols. Though he grew up in an environment of idol worship, Ibrahim nevertheless had the spiritual gift of seeking after the one true God. He was thus the first *hanif* (haNEEF)— a term that was also used to describe Muhammad himself as a man driven by a spiritual quest. A lovely account (Qur'an 6:74–82) tells how God revealed his oneness to Ibrahim. One evening Ibrahim came out and beheld a star, and he said "This is my Lord." But when the star disappeared, he said, "I love not things that set." And when the moon rose, he took that for his Lord; but when it, too, sank from view, he sought divine protection from error. And when the sun rose, he thought this must surely be his

The Sacred Fish Pool in Sanliurfa, Turkey, is where it is said Abraham was thrown into a lake of fire by King Nimrod. For Muslims, Abaraham (Ibrahim) was the first person to "surrender to God."

Lord, for it was greater by far. Then even the sun set. And Ibrahim said to God, "I have surrendered" (become a muslim). Other related texts are Qur'an 19:42–49, 21:52–70, 26:69–104, 29:15–24, and 37:81–96.

Perhaps the most peculiar of all the biblical Abrahamic (Genesis 15:8–18) texts occurs in an intriguingly different version in Qur'an 2:260. In Genesis, Abraham asks God for a sign that he will indeed possess the land promised. God tells him to bring a heifer, a she-goat, a ram, a turtle dove and a pigeon. Abraham then cut the animals—all but the birds—in two and separated the pieces. In the Qur'an, the prophet wants a sign that God has the power of life. Ibrahim is instructed to take four birds, cut them into pieces and put a portion on various hills. He must then call to them and they will fly together as proof of God's power.

Unlike the Bible, the Qur'an connects Abraham with Nimrod, whom Genesis mentions only briefly and much earlier than Abraham (Genesis 10:8–10). In Islamic lore, Nimrod functions as the Prophet's nemesis. Qur'an 21:68–70 alludes, without naming the evil king explicitly, to Ibrahim's conflict with the unbeliever. According to the important Islamic religious genre *The Tales of the Prophets*, Nimrod was to the child Ibrahim what Pharaoh would be to Moses and Herod to Jesus—a mortal enemy bent on the infant's destruction. Failing in his earlier attempts, Nimrod managed to capture Ibrahim and catapult him into a bonfire. But there in the flames, Gabriel appeared to transform them into a pleasant garden for the prophet.

Another distinctively Islamic take on the Abraham story has to do with interpreting the tradition that God commanded the prophet to sacrifice his "firstborn son." By Islamic reckoning, Ishmael (Isma'il in Arabic) merits that distinction, since he was indeed born before Isaac. The Qur'an does not specifically name the boy whom Ibrahim is prepared to sacrifice, but the tradition presumes, by this logic, that it was Isma'il. Jewish and Christian tradition discount the son of Hagar as illegitimate and therefore not truly Abraham's son. *The Tales of the Prophets* devote considerably more attention than the Qur'an (11:72–78, 37:100–113, 51:24–34) to the individual birth stories of the two sons.

Finally, Islam's mystical poets delight in transforming the Prophet into a paragon of mystical love. Ibrahim was a "sighful" man (*awwah*—the Persian expression for "sigh" is "heart-smoke") whose heart bubbled over when he thought of God. They say you could hear his heart "bubble" for miles, so intense was his longing.

Why do Jews, Christians, and Muslims all claim parts of **Israel/Palestine** as **Holy Land**?

Palestine lies in southwest Asia at the eastern end of the Mediterranean Sea. It is the Holy Land of Jews, since it was here that Moses led the Israelites after he led them out of slavery in Egypt and where they subsequently established their homeland; of Christians, since it is where Jesus Christ was born, lived, and died; and of Muslims, since the Arab people conquered Palestine in the seventh century and, except for a brief period during the Crusades, it was ruled by various Muslim dynasties until 1516 (when it became part of the Ottoman Empire). Palestine, which covers an area of just over ten thousand square miles, is roughly the size of Maryland.

Palestine's capital, Jerusalem, is also claimed as a holy city by all three religions. Jews call it the City of David (or the City of the Great King) since it was made the capital of the ancient kingdom of Israel around 1000 B.C.E. Christians regard it as holy since Jesus traveled with his disciples to Jerusalem to observe the Passover. It is the site of the Last Supper, and just outside the city, at Golgotha, Jesus was crucified (c. 30). Muslim Arabs captured the city in 638 (just after Muhammad's death), and, like the rest of Palestine, it has a long history of Muslim Arab rule. Jerusalem, which is now part of the modern State of Israel, is home to numerous synagogues, churches, and mosques. It also has been the site of numerous religious conflicts throughout history.

Do Muslims believe in **angels**?

Angels function in Islamic tradition much the way they do in Christian tradition. They are beings of light and great intelligence who enjoy the presence of God and do the divine bidding throughout creation. Several angels stand above the rest. The four archangels include Gabriel, who brings revelation to the prophets; Michael, arch-nemesis of Satan; Israfil, who will sound the final trumpet; and the angel of death, Azrael. In some important respects human beings stand above the angels. When God has Gabriel guide Muhammad through the seven Heavens, Gabriel must part company with the Prophet as they approach the Throne of God, lest he be burnt to a crisp. Even the first human being, Adam, knew something the angels did not: the divinely ordained names of all things created. God assigns two guardian angels to each human being. Two especially businesslike angels called Munkar and Nakir have the unpleasant but necessary task of visiting each deceased person in the grave and administering a "final exam" about the content of the individual's beliefs. Numerous Hadiths and charming traditional stories tell of the solicitous presence of countless angelic spirits, who are ready to attend the devout at every important moment and squire them through life's most trying challenges.

Do Muslims believe in the **devil**?

Within the larger category of jinn are many beings who were once angels. The principal diabolical figure is called Iblis (pronounced ibLEES, from the Greek *diabolos*). God ordered him to do homage to the newly created body of Adam, but Iblis refused, arguing that a creature of fire need not bow to one made of clay. God banished Iblis from Paradise and he became the personification of the choice for evil over good. It was Iblis who tempted Adam and Eve (Qur'an 2:35–39, 7:19–25, 20:120–121). Tradition also names the devil Shaytan (shayTAAN) and often refers to many Satans, the lesser

139

What is a jinni?

You've probably heard stories about the magical powers of genies who appear when someone rubs a magic lamp just right. The word "genie" comes from the Arabic word *jinni/jinn*, which refers to creatures of smokeless fire who inhabit a mysterious realm somewhere between the human and the divine. According to popular lore in Muhammad's time, the *jinns* would eavesdrop on the heavenly councils and offer to divulge their secrets to a soothsayer (called a *kahin*, pronounced KAAhin) who uttered the proper formula. Some of Muhammad's early critics charged that he was not a prophet but just another *majnun* (pronounced majNOON), one possessed by a *jinn*. To call someone *majnun* is to question the person's credibility as well as sanity. Countless *jinns* inhabit the world, some mischievous and some helpful and benevolent. King Solomon had the gift of "taming" the *jinn* and enlisting them for the construction of his majestic temple. Particularly troublesome are the frighteningly ugly jinns called *ghuls* (from which we get the word "ghoul"). For those who do not know how to handle them, *jinns* can make life unpleasant, but their powers are limited.

minions of Iblis who fan out to beset humanity with temptations of every kind. Some of Islam's mystics have focused on the story of Iblis' fall as an occasion for discussing the infinite mercy of God. As evil as the devil is, they argue, even Iblis still has hope of enjoying the transforming power of divine forgiveness at the end of time. The mystics are not suggesting that the devil is soft on sheer nastiness, only that no power in the universe can compare with God's mercy.

Is there such a thing as **heresy** in Islamic tradition?

Muslim tradition recognizes varying degrees of deviation from pure faith or *iman* (eeMAAN). Certain forms of departure from strict Qur'anic teaching and practices clearly identified as deriving from the Sunna of the Prophet have been labeled "innovation" (*bid'a*, BID'ah). Some things once considered innovations, such as attaching minarets to mosques, have long since become widely accepted. All but today's most traditionally minded Muslims give little consideration to this category. A daily danger for all human beings, one that Muslims seek to combat constantly, is called shirk, or associating partners with God. Any undue attention or attachment to that which is not God is thus a form of shirk, but while it is a natural tendency, it is not necessarily a permanent condition unless one chooses to make it so. A more serious problem, known technically as "deviation" (*ilhad*, pronounced ilHAAD), comes closer to what many understand by the term heresy. A *mulhid* is someone who deliberately strays from the broadly accepted tenets of the faith, introducing innovations to the extent that one can no longer readily recognize basic Islamic teachings in the new formulation. Farthest from adherence to true belief is the category of *kufr,* the kind of willful unbelief that leads to outright blasphemy.

Do Muslims believe in **miracles**?

Muhammad's early critics in Mecca sometimes taunted him for being so much like an ordinary human being: If he were really a prophet of God, surely he would entertain them with some sort of heavenly pyrotechnics. Muhammad regarded the Qur'an itself as his only miracle, a marvel of eloquence uttered by a man considered technically "unlettered." But the scripture does refer often to spectacular "signs" God brought about to vindicate earlier prophets. For example, Moses' staff became a dragon that devoured Pharaoh's magicians, and Moses' hand turned white with leprosy and was then restored to health (Qur'an 7:107–108).

Within a generation or two of Muhammad's death, tradition had begun to attribute to the Prophet a number of extraordinary occurrences. He could fast for inordinately long periods, could see people behind him, heal various ailments, supply water where there was none, and stretch limited food sources as needed. Trees and stones saluted Muhammad, a pillar in his house mourned that the Prophet no longer leaned on it when he preached, and the Prophet split the moon in two to confound his critics.

Throughout the history of Islam holy persons called "Friends of God" have been famous for the ability to perform wondrous deeds. Many Muslims today regard accounts of such legend and lore of secondary importance. Classical Muslim theologians devised technical terms to distinguish between two levels of miracle. They called the works God did as proof of his prophets' truthfulness "evidentiary miracles" (*mu'jizat,* pronounced mu'jiZAAT), and those effected by Friends of God "marvels" (*karamat,* pronounced karaaMAAT). Theologians further called attention to key differences between works of sorcery and wonders performed authentically under divine power.

What are the main Islamic notions of the **afterlife**?

Muslim eschatology has much in common with most Christian and some Jewish traditions about the afterlife. Death is not the end of life, but a transition to another level of existence. Muslims believe human beings are accountable for all of their free moral decisions. People are not held similarly responsible for actions with negative consequences but done under duress or in the absence of intent to do evil. Numerous texts of the Qur'an warn of the coming Day of Judgment, the Day of Resurrection, the Hour in which the true quality of everyone's deeds will be revealed. On the basis of that accounting, individuals will go across a narrow passage of no return called the *barzakh* (pronounced BARzakh) to one of several destinations. Paradise is called the Garden (*janna,* pronounced JANnah), a verdant place of repose and delight, an oasis for the just. Heaven is not so much literally a place as a state of being whose principal feature is the vision of God. Qur'anic texts refer to several different levels or degrees of heavenly reward.

141

Visitors to the tomb-shrine of Shaykh Salim Chishti (sixteenth century), the spiritual director of the Mughal Emperor Akbar, Fatehpur Sikri, India.

Hell, known as the Fire or Gehenna (*jahannam,* pronounced jaHANnam), represents the state of refusal to acknowledge God's sovereignty. Some Muslim theologians have taught that Hell is not necessarily a permanent state, since God can always forgive any sin except unrelenting denial of God's existence. Hell can thus function in a way similar to that of the state of Purgatory in Christian tradition, though Islamic tradition does not have a separate term for that state of purification. Muslim tradition also hints at something like an intermediate state, perhaps similar to the Christian idea of limbo.

Do Muslims believe in **predestination** or fatalism?

A common misperception of Islamic tradition is that God exercises such minute and perfect control over all things that human actions have no bearing on the individual's ultimate destiny. When Muslims use the expression "God willing," they do not mean to suggest that human beings are mere marionettes dancing at the whim of the divine puppeteer. They are simply reminding themselves that God is ultimately in charge of everything, regardless of individual human preferences. True, the Qur'an often describes how God both guides and leads astray "whomever he chooses." But that does not suggest that God is capricious or spiteful, only that God is God and that lesser beings ought not to take God's sovereignty for granted even for a second. Equally often, the Qur'an reminds believers how God lays out his "signs" in creation and in the individual heart, adding "perhaps you will understand."

142

Muslims believe in God's justice. The Qur'an insists that each person will be held accountable for his or her actions at judgment. But since God is just, Muslims conclude that human beings exercise a significant freedom of choice—otherwise accountability at the judgment would be a sham, a cruel hoax to which God hardly needs to resort. All in all, Muslim tradition seeks to maintain the delicate balance between belief in God's absolute power, and a limited, but more than adequate, human freedom to choose either good or evil.

Does anything like **millennialism** have a place in Islamic thinking?

Yes, so long as one understands "millennialism" broadly rather than as a precise reference to measures of a thousand years. Numerous Hadith, called Traditions of Discord, talk of various general features that mark a decidedly downward trend in human life. Honesty will be hard to find, fewer and fewer people will observe the religious law, and violence will rise. According to other ancient traditions, various explicit signs will herald the end of time itself. A resurgence of chaos symbolized by Gog and Magog will mark a radical turn for the worse, the beginning of the final chapter in the unraveling of history. A figure resembling the Prophet, called the *Mahdi* (Guided One), will usher in a temporary age of justice. Numerous individuals throughout the history of Islam have sought to gain political power by claiming to be the Mahdi, most recently in 1979, when armed bandits seized control of the sanctuary of the Ka'ba in Mecca. A one-eyed Antichrist figure (called the *Dajjal,* pronounced dajJAAL) will supplant the *Mahdi,* luring people away through magic masquerading as miracle. Jesus will eventually return to battle the Antichrist, overthrowing that false prophet and paving the way for the Day of Judgment.

Shi'a tradition features its own distinctive type of millenialism. According to the Shi'a interpretation of history, Muhammad's spiritual authority was passed along through a series of descendants called Imams. In the view of the "Twelvers"—by far the majority of Shi'ites—the twelfth and last of these Imams (also called the *Mahdi*) went into "greater concealment" in 940. This Hidden Imam did not die but has remained in a mysterious state from which he will return to establish full justice. In the meantime, the Imam hears prayers and intercedes for believers. Although both the Qur'an and Hadith warn against attempting to calculate precisely the arrival of the "Hour" at which the world will come to an end, small groups of Muslims have tried to do just that through history.

What is **jihad**?

Jihad (pronounced jiHAAD) comes from an Arabic verb that means "to struggle or exert oneself." In recent years both Muslims and non-Muslims alike have bandied the term about so loosely that one has to do some digging to retrieve an accurate understanding of it. According to news reports, everyone from the scarcely devout Saddam Hussein to Usama bin Ladin and the Taliban has called for a *jihad* against somebody,

143

For most Muslims, "jihad" does not refer to a fight against others but, rather, is an inner spiritual struggle against evil and injustice.

usually "the West." Hence the virtually automatic translation of *jihad* as "holy war"—at best a misleading, and at worst a highly inflammatory, interpretation. *Jihad* does have a range of precisely defined meanings in Islamic tradition. Under prescribed circumstances *jihad* can include offensive military action against any place where the free practice of Islam is under threat of constraint. Many scholars in recent times have held that one cannot justify an offensive *jihad* unless Muslims are being persecuted religiously. Even then, therefore, we are talking about a type of defensive action.

Military *jihad* has always been subject to strict criteria and is in many ways parallel to the Christian notion of "just war." Criteria in classical sources include the following: warriors must be believers (though some jurists disagree, and Muhammad was flexible), adult, and male (except in surprise attack or indirect support roles); they must be of sound mind and body, free, economically independent, and acting with parental support and good intentions. *Jihad* must be declared by an authoritative leader following an offer of terms of peace. Warriors must spare noncombatants unless they are clearly helping enemy cause. Very few, if any, recent calls for *jihad* have actually satisfied the necessary criteria.

Muslims also speak of various nonviolent forms of *jihad*. One can battle injustice and evil through *jihad* of the pen or the tongue, for example. When someone asked Muhammad what the greatest *jihad* was, the Prophet replied that it was to speak a word of truth in the ear of a tyrant. An important theme in Islamic spirituality has been called the "Greater *Jihad*," as distinct from all the various forms of exterior, lesser *jihads*. Warriors of the spirit must take up the sword of self-knowledge against the fiercest enemy of all, their own inner tendencies to evil and idolatry.

How do contemporary Islamic **religious and legal scholars** deal with the realities of **terrorism** perpetrated by people who call themselves Muslims?

Since immediately after the horrors of 9/11/2001, Muslim religious scholars have been publishing legal advisories known as *fatwas* denouncing the actions of Al-Qaeda and

What is the source of the apparent claim that every person who dies a "martyr" in *jihad* will have seventy-two virgins awaiting in Paradise?

The Qur'an itself mentions nothing of the sort, referring only to the presence of *houris* (dark-eyed maidens, perhaps) in the "gardens" of reward, and with no reference to martyrdom in that context. Only two *hadiths* (sayings of Muhammad), each found in only one of the "six" authoritative collections of *hadiths* (those of Tirmidhi and Ibn Majah), seem to refer to this claim. One of the traditions places seventy-two *houris* among the "eighty thousand servants" (not seventy-two for each) residing on the "lowest Heaven" and makes no mention of martyrs there (Ibn Majah); and martyrs are typically said to reside in a loftier Heaven. In the version most quoted we find: "The martyr has six distinctions in the view of God: he will be forgiven from the start, be shown his resting place in Paradise, be protected from the torment of the tomb, be secured from the greatest terror, have a crown of dignity put on his head, of which one ruby will be better than the world and all that is in it, be married to seventy-two wives among the *houris* and be given to intercede for seventy of his relatives" (Tirmidhi). Note that this *hadith* says nothing about precisely what constitutes "martyrdom," while equally ancient and much better-attested traditions condemn all forms of suicide unequivocally.

Both traditions are attested by only one transmitting source, and are thereby judged by most scholars to be well below the maximum level of authenticity and credibility. Attestation of a saying by so few authoritative sources, and its correspondingly low authenticity rating, are among the criteria that undercut the credibility of a saying attributed to Muhammad. In other words, the text almost automatically cited in news reports as clear motivation is not only flimsily attested, according the well-known judgments of ancient Muslim scholars, but does not in fact say precisely, let alone clearly, what popular reporting (both Muslim as well as non-Muslim) claims it says.

other organizations that claim religious legitimacy for their use of the tactics of indiscriminate mass violence. Such public denunciations have, for a variety of reasons, almost never been reported in European or American news media. But here are some principles by which one of the more recent, and most detailed, *fatwas* distinguishes between legitimate *jihad* and religiously indefensible uses of violence.

London-based Pakistani Shaykh Tahir al-Qadri argues, first, that Islamic teaching forbids the indiscriminate torturing or killing of Muslims or non-Muslims, even in the conduct of legitimate warfare. He then assembles extensive evidence from Islamic history and major sources condemning the forcing of Islamic beliefs on non-Muslims, the destruction of non-Muslim places of worship, and rebellion by Muslims against legitimate Muslim government administration. In considerable detail, the *shaykh* addresses forthrightly the historical reality that people identifying themselves as Muslims have indeed rationalized numerous violations of all of these explicit prohibitions. He identifies the seventh-century Khawarij (seceeders) as the earliest such movement: they rebelled against Ali (the fourth Rightly-Guided Caliph) and condemned Ali and all who continued to support him as infidels and proclaimed that all such people should be eliminated. The *shaykh* describes in detail how the Khawarij, and other groups like them through history, have portrayed themselves as the champions of "true" Islam and attempted to persuade the public of the religious righteousness of their cause and methods, all the while distorting the tradition to arrive at their conclusions; and they have recruited and brainwashed adolescents to do their dirty work. Qadri concludes with evidence of Muhammad's own condemnation of such people as "the dogs of Hell," and calls on the global Muslim community to fulfill their historical obligation of struggling (i.e., engaging in *jihad*) to eliminate the scourge of the modern-day Khawarij.

What is the most widely accepted belief about **suicide**? How is suicide different from "**self-selected martyrdom**"? Have all "**suicide bombers**" identified themselves as Muslims?

Classic sources universally condemn all manner of deliberately ending one's own life, for whatever reason. Most of those sources make it crystal clear that individuals who choose suicide as a way out will be punished severely in the next life. Unfortunately, terrorist methods over the past couple of decades have increasingly resorted to the use of "suicide bombers" to take vengeance on people identified by the perpetrators as enemies of Islam. Most such perpetrators have chosen to distort the ancient and unambiguous prohibition of suicide by relabeling such self-destructive behavior "self-selected martyrdom," arguing that God not only forgives such conduct but indeed rewards it for its unselfish defense of Islam against infidels. An investigation of forty-one earliest such Middle Eastern incidents occurring between 1982 and 1986 in Lebanon identified and traced thirty-eight of the perpetrators in detail. Twenty-eight of them were avowedly secularist and most belonged to communist or other leftist Arab organizations; three were Christian, including a young woman who was a primary school teacher; only seven of the thirty-eight were known to have espoused a distinctly religious ideology. These figures apply explicitly only to Lebanon during a four-year period that saw no other such action elsewhere in the Middle East, and they hint at the enormous complexity of the issue and the multiple motivations behind the tactic. In an environment in which the vast majority of Americans assume with certainty that *all* such actions are purely "religious," data like this require a closer look across the board.

Glossary of Key Islamic Religious Terms

Āya(t)—a "verse" of the Qur'an; a "sign" of God in the created world.

Dhikr (reminder, recollection)—A prayer service for Sufis that can include recitation of the Qur'an, chanting and dancing; reminding oneself of God.

Du'ā'—(appeal, invocation) Private, "free" devotional prayer.

Faqīh—jurist, someone who studies and interprets fiqh.

Fatwā—legal advisory, determining whether a course of action is forbidden, discouraged, legal neutral, recommended, or required.

Fiqh (deep understanding)—by extension, study of positive law.

Hadīth—"tradition, sayings" of Muhammad, second in authority only to the Qur'an.

Hajj (Major)—pilgrimage to Mecca during the pilgrimage month, twelfth of the lunar year.

Hijra—muhammad's "emigration" from Mecca to Medina in 622 C.E. marking the beginning of Islamic history.

Ijmā'—"consensus" of the community with regard to the application of the revealed law.

Ijtihād—exerting oneself (struggling) in the interpretation of Islamic legal sources, independent investigation.

Jihād—"striving, struggle" in the way of God, including religiously sanctioned warfare.

Madhhab—a school of Islamic jurisprudence or legal methodology.

Minaret—a tall, slender tower attached to a mosque from which the call to prayer emanates.

Mi'rj—"ascension" of Muhammad into Heaven; metaphor for spiritual journey.

Muftī—legal specialist with the authority to issue *fatwās*.

Mujtahid—legal scholar with the authority to exercise independent investigation (*ijtihād*).

Mujāhidīn—persons who partake in *jihād,* whether physical or spiritual.

Qibla—the "direction" of Mecca, toward which one turns in prayer and spiritual readiness.

Salāt—the technical term for the ritual prayer offered five times daily.

Shahāda—profession of faith: There is no god but God, Muhammad is the messenger of God.

Sharī'a—"main road" along which Muslims walk as a community; hence, all of divinely revealed Law.

Shirk—setting up partners or associates with God; idolatry.

Sunna—"way of life," normative example of Muhammad transmitted largely in the Hadith.

Tawhīd—the acknowledgment and assertion of the oneness and transcendence of God.

'Ulamā'—class of persons who are "learned" in religious matters, religious scholars.

Umma—the global community of Muslims.

'Umra (Lesser)—pilgrimage to Mecca, often performed outside of formal Pilgrimage month.

SIGNS AND SYMBOLS

Are there any **signs or symbols** that might **identify** an **individual** as a Muslim?

Muslim men and women sometimes wear items or styles of clothing that clearly set them apart from non-Muslims. Stop by the local mosque on Friday afternoon and you will invariably find men arriving for the congregational prayer wearing long flowing gowns and small knit or other fabric caps that cover most of the head, in honor of Muhammad's practice of covering his head during prayer. Men of southern Asian origin (India, Pakistan, Bangladesh) sometimes wear a kind of boat-shaped cap commonly worn back home. In some parts of the world men who have made the *Hajj* signify their status as *hajjis* by wearing a burgundy *fez* wrapped in a white cloth. The rimless fez became popular because it was practical for use during prostration in prayer, allowing easy contact of the forehead with the ground. More than likely the women attending a mosque will be wearing some form of head covering and an ankle-length dress or tunic with slacks.

In many instances the choice of distinctive garb is related to an individual's personal devotion and desire to symbolize his or her commitment to Islamic religious and social values. Most items of clothing are best understood as traditional rather than inherently religious, since they carry no explicit and uniquely Islamic symbolism. However, many Muslim women and men wear various items of jewelry bearing Islamic symbols. Most common are rings, pendants, and bracelets containing religious words or phrases in Arabic. Some show a star within a crescent moon, a symbol some interpret as a reference to the astronomical signs that mark the onset of the month of Ramadan. Favorite texts include the word Allah, phrases such as *In sha'a 'Llah* (God Willing), the *Shahada,* names of Muhammad and the four Rightly Guided Caliphs (Abu Bakr, Umar, Uthman, and Ali). Muslim designers produce a wide range of religious adornment and market them through an increasing number of suppliers and boutiques that advertise in Muslim publications worldwide.

What does the **crescent moon and star** symbol mean?

A crescent moon embracing a single star adorns the flags of a number of modern nation-states with majority Muslim populations. The sign is almost certainly not of Arab origin, and the Ottoman Turks may have appropriated the symbolism from Byzantium. At first, the symbol appeared on the flags of lands formerly under Ottoman rule, but other states with no historical connection to the Ottoman empire have also adopted the imagery.

Popular understanding of the symbol usually identifies the crescent moon as the essential indicator of the beginning of Ramadan, the ninth lunar month. More generally still, the symbol reminds some of the lunar cycles that regulate Islam's religious calendar. Appearing frequently at the top of domes and minarets, the symbol has become a generic reminder of Islam, much the way the cross has for Christianity and the six-pointed star for Judaism.

Are Muslim **women** required to **veil their faces**?

Use of the veil depends a great deal on cultural custom. The Qur'an does not explicit-

A crescent moon symbol tops the Malaysia Mosque in Singapore, Masjid Sultan. the crescent moon has been adopted by Arabic cultures, most likely from ancient Byzantium.

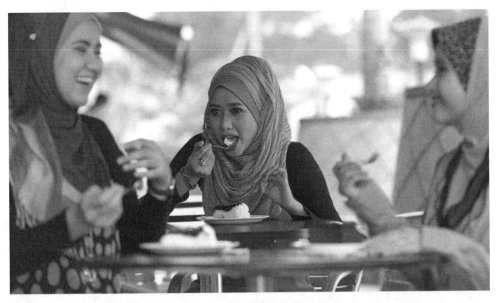

Muslim women are not required to wear veils. The Qur'an only states that they should dress modestly.

ly require that women cover their faces. It calls for modest dress, but some have interpreted one ambiguous text—"they should draw their veils over their bosoms...." (Qur'an 24:31)—to mean that the head covering should continue down over the upper body. In some cultures, Muslim women wear various forms of facial covering, whether drawn across the lower face from side to side or covering the head completely like a small tent. Those coverings also vary in texture from a fine gauze to a fairly heavy weave with slits cut at eye level. The majority of women who wear some form of distinctive clothing, technically known as *hijab* (pronouned hiJAAB, veiling or covering), opt for a head scarf down to the mid-forehead so that it covers all the hair. Some wear a flowing gown (*jilbab,* pronounced jilBAAB) that extends to the ankles; some a face veil (*niqab*) that leaves only the eyes exposed; still others the *burqa,* a tentlike garment that covers all but the feet.

Note that the emphasis is on modesty rather than on some specific style of covering. Muslim immigrants to Europe or the United States from the Middle East or southern Asia might choose to continue wearing styles common in their homelands. Where prevailing social norms allow greater latitude in choice of dress, Muslim women often report that they opt for fuller covering for two reasons: They seek an explicit symbolic connection with Islamic practice and they choose to make a statement of personal freedom from the general exploitation of women that they often experience in society at large.

What **signs or symbols** distinguish Muslim **ritual or religious specialists**?

There is no ordained Muslim clergy as such, but a category of specialists, known as religious scholars, sometimes wear distinctive garb. Style and color generally depend **149**

Expanded facilities of the Islamic Foundation of St. Louis, Missouri. The minaret symbolizes the call to prayer, but in this suburban neighborhood the call to prayer does not actually emanate from the tower; and the five windows on the front and left sides symbolize the Five Pillars of Islam. The small houselike feature protruding from the front marks the place of the niche (*mihrab*) that indicates the direction of Mecca. Joined to the mosque at right is a recently added expansion of the K-8 school formerly housed in the lower level of the original structure.

on variant traditions in the country of origin. Many religious scholars from many lands prefer the *fez* wrapped in the white cloth (signifying that the wearer has made Hajj). Some, from the Sudan for example, wear a white turban. Shi'a *mullahs* and higher-ranking scholars in Iran and Iraq often wear a black turban that identifies them as *Sayyids,* descendants of Muhammad through his daughter Fatima and her husband, Ali. Size, color, number of turns, and so forth, allow a practiced eye to distinguish national and sectarian connections. Members of Sufi orders often wear special clothing, particularly during their prayer gatherings. Various organizations have unique headgear, sometimes using colors or varied ways of wrapping the basic cap with windings to indicate rank or status within the order.

Do Muslims mark their **sacred spaces** with any distinctive **signs and symbols**?

Drive by the mosque nearest you—there is probably one not very far away—and you are likely to notice two distinctive features. Attached to, or alongside, the building you will see one or perhaps two slender towers called minarets. Originally designed to provide maximum broadcast of the call to prayer, the minaret eventually became a visual symbol of Islamic presence. Most structures designed as mosques feature a dome of some sort, typically spanning the central interior space called the prayer hall. Many synagogues and Eastern Christian churches also use central domes, but generally do

The Prophet's mosque in Medina. The large dark (green) dome at right marks the grave of the Prophet.

not have towers that one might mistake for minarets. Atop some minarets and domes you will find a finial in the shape of a crescent moon encircling a single star.

Some communities choose to have their mosques reflect architecturally a particular national or regional heritage. They might hire, for example, an Egyptian architect to design in a neo-classical Egyptian style, as with the national mosque in Washington, D.C. Or they might choose to incorporate some visual allusion to a particularly important mosque, the way the new Islamic Center of Cleveland aligns a large central and a smaller secondary dome, recalling the Dome of the Rock and Al-Aqsa mosque in Jerusalem.

Interior decorations typically feature elegant calligraphic texts, either painted or carved in marble or other stone, of the names Allah and Muhammad, and of the Shahada and Basmallah ("In the name of God ..."), and possibly of any number of the "Ninety-Nine Beautiful Names" of God. Calligraphic decoration often appears around the drum of the dome and around the niche on the wall facing Mecca. Prayer rugs or carpeting sometimes show designs of niches like that of the *mihrab* (pronounced mihRAAB, niche). And somewhere in the mosque there will more than likely be a large picture of the sanctuary of the Ka'ba in Mecca, and possibly also of the Prophet's mosque in Medina.

Is it true that Muslims **never depict human** or **animal figures**?

Browse the pages of virtually any publication designed for Muslim readers and you may be surprised at the number of illustrations featuring human and animal figures. **151**

Shelves of mosque bookstores are filled with books, especially those designed for children, similarly illustrated. Still, the notion persists, among Muslims and non-Muslims alike, that "Muslims don't do pictures." What most people popularly perceive as a blanket prohibition of images actually applies only to ritual settings. In other words, you will not find figural or representational imagery in a mosque. Islamic and Jewish tradition share the concern that inherent in representational visual imagery, especially of the three-dimensional sort (sculpture), is the risk of idolatry.

Muslim artists throughout the ages and across the globe have produced a great deal of figural art, even including images of prophets and other holy persons. But their images are so clearly abstract and unrealistic that they can scarcely be taken as the artist's attempt to usurp God's creative power. For purposes of education and entertainment, two-dimensional images generally have been perfectly acceptable. In fact, even the prohibition on three-dimensional imagery is far from absolute, except in the context of worship. For example, Muslim children play with dolls. Devout Muslims express a preference for educationally suitable imagery that exemplifies virtue and ethical values. Under the heading "Move Over Barbie!" one company markets a doll called Razanne, dressed in a white head-and-shoulder covering (the *hijab*) and green full-length gown (*jilbab*). The hijab is removable so that little girls can learn about donning the proper covering. Razanne's clothes are decoratively trimmed, but she wears no makeup.

What is the meaning of the **hand symbol**?

Silhouettes of a five-fingered open hand appear often as a motif in jewelry and on staffs that function as standards in some Shi'a religious rituals. Called "the five," the symbol reminds devotees of the five principal members of the Prophet's family: Muhammad, Fatima, Ali, Hasan, and Husayn. Many Shi'a mosques display the hand as a finial on both domes and minarets in mosques of classical design. Sometimes the hand was hoisted atop a staff as a battle standard, emblazoned with prayers to Ali on the fingers and the names of all twelve Imams encircling the palm. As a symbol used by Muslims in various parts of the world, the hand functions as a talismanic magical device, a symbol of control or power associated with Muhammad's daughter Fatima.

Have **relics** ever been **important** for Muslims?

Popular Islamic spirituality in many parts of the world has included devotional practices associated with the tombs of holy persons. People visit the shrines of the Friends of God in hopes of gaining blessings and other favors as a result of saintly intercession. Many of these shrines hold items the saint is believed to have owned, such as headgear, a symbolic frock called the *khirqa*, walking staff, begging bowl, prayer beads, or symbolic weapon. Devotees who come to the shrines sometimes receive an object, such as a simple head wrapping or other token, that has been in contact with the holy person's tomb. Only one object has been similarly associated with Muhammad.

The Dome of the Rock in Jerusalem is traditionally believed to be on the site of Solomon's temple, built over a large rock formation from which Muhammad is said to have experienced his Mi'raj, or Ascension heavenward.

Since the thirteenth century, Turkish Muslims believed they owned the so-called mantle of the Prophet, a green robe now in the possession of the Topkapi Museum in Istanbul. People there and in many other countries still recite a traditional poem called the Burda (mantle poem) during the observance of Muhammad's birthday, but the mantle itself has never been the focus of devotional practice as have the relics of many Friends of God. As in many other traditions, sacred footprints function like relics in Islamic tradition. Pilgrims to Mecca pray at the "Station of Abraham" just opposite the door of the Ka'ba—a small glass and gold-colored cupola covers a small stone said to contain footprints God caused Abraham to leave in the softened stone as a proof of his prophethood. Tradition says that as Muhammad rose heavenward on his Ascension, he left still-visible prints in the large stone beneath the Dome of the Rock. Muhammad's footprints became the inspiration for several types of visual symbolism still popular in North Africa, for example. Footprints of Ali have likewise been at the devotional center of a number of shrines.

Are **dreams** and **visions** particularly **important** in Islamic tradition?

In the Qur'anic story of Joseph (Sura 12) Muslims find the paradigm of religious insight as represented by the ability to interpret dreams. Traditional Islamic sources further describe a wide range of religious and spiritual experiences, beginning of course with Muhammad's role in the unfolding revelation of the Qur'an. The Prophet "sees" mysterious visions as part of the divine communication. Later religious figures,

153

especially noted spiritual guides and Friends of God, have left numerous personal accounts of their dreams and interpretations of them. Muhammad himself is one of the presences they report meeting most often in dreams and visionary experiences. These reports tell of encountering various holy persons in addition to the Prophet, especially those who had in life been of particular significance to the dreamer or visionary. Sufis sometimes tell of meeting the mysterious Khizr, a figure included in many lists of prophets, who appears for the purpose of initiating the dreamer into the Sufi path through investiture with the "patched frock" (khirqa). Though the accounts sound as if they are reporting events as "real" as having breakfast, most are clearly talking about spiritual experiences that are well beyond the ordinary and thus are not subject to ordinary scrutiny.

MEMBERSHIP, COMMUNITY, DIVERSITY

Where does the **word Muslim** come from? Is it the same as Moslem?

Arabic is a Semitic language, as is its distant cousin Hebrew. Both languages are based on roots made up of three consonants. For example, many words can be derived from the root S-L-M (Sh-L-M in Hebrew). Keep your eye on the uppercase letters to follow the root. A basic verb from that root, *SaLiMa,* means to be safe or whole. A related Arabic noun is salaam, meaning "peace" (like the Hebrew *ShaLoM*), which is part of a standard greeting among Muslims. When Arabic speakers want to build further meanings on a particular root, they do so by modifying the root with either prefixes, infixes (modifying interior letters), or suffixes. For example, to convey the notion of "causing someone to be safe or at peace," one modifies the root *SaLiMa* so that it becomes *aSLaMa*.

In religious terms, to bring about a state of safety, peace, and wholeness, one has to get one's relationship to God in perfect order. That means letting God be God, and giving up all pretense at trying to do what only God can do—in short, surrendering to the supreme power. That state of surrender is called *iSLaaM,* and a person who acts in such a way as to cause that state is called a *muSLiM*. One of the first major non-Semitic languages early Muslim conquerors encountered was Persian, in which the u was pronounced as an o, and the i as an e. Hence the variation so common today, Moslem. Both mean exactly the same thing; the variations are entirely due to differences in pronunciation.

Who are **Sunni Muslims**?

About 85 to 90 percent of the world's Muslims consider themselves Sunni. Their historic patrimony derives directly from the Prophet himself as institutionalized in the caliphate. Sunni tradition has been embodied in most of the regimes that have held political power from Morocco to Indonesia, since the early Middle Ages until early modern times. The ideal of the *caliph*, legitimate successor to Muhammad, as the spiritual as well as temporal ruler of all Muslims, has survived largely as a distant dream since the Mongols destroyed Baghdad in 1258. And since the last Ottoman sultan fell from power in the 1920s, virtually no Muslim ruler has been even nominally regarded as a universal ruler. Some Muslims still entertain the possibility of a resurgence of the caliphate, but that is definitely a minority view.

Who are **Shi'ai Muslims**?

Various Shi'a communities have been identifiable since at least the eighth century. Among the principal features that distinguish Shi'a from Sunni tradition is the belief that a legitimate successor to leadership, called *imam* (pronounced eeMAAM), must be designated by his predecessor and belong to the family of the Prophet. According to ancient Shi'a belief, Muhammad did designate his cousin Ali, but Abu Bakr, Umar and Uthman managed to usurp power and prevent Ali from assuming his rightful place. Around the middle of the eighth century a split developed over who would be the seventh Imam. One group continued to pledge their loyalty to a man named Isma'il, who

had just died, even though Isma'il's father, the seventh Imam Ja'far, appointed a replacement when Isma'il died. The faction that stayed with Isma'il came to be called the Isma'ilis, or Seveners, since their line of Imams ended then. There are now at least two major branches of Seveners, one of which looks to the Aga Khan as its spiritual leader. The larger group of Shi'ites in the eighth century believed the legitimate line of Imams extended to a twelfth, and ended when that Imam went into concealment until his expected return at the end of time. Twelver Shi'ites are by far the majority community, constituting nearly all of Iran's and more than half of Iraq's people.

Who are the **Black Muslims** and the **Nation of Islam**?

In 1930s Detroit, W. D. Fard began teaching that the ancestors of black Americans had been Muslims. Young Elijah Poole became a devoted follower, and Fard declared Poole his successor and prophet.

Many African Americans in the United States have joined the ranks of the Muslim faithful. The movement toward Islam was sparked in the 1930s by W. D. Fard, who taught that the ancestors of African Americans had originally been Muslims.

Elijah took the last name Muhammad and continued to develop a community called the Nation of Islam, or the Black Muslims. Two prominent young followers of Elijah Muhammad were Malcolm X and Louis Farrakhan. Malcolm X tells in his autobiography how he discovered during his pilgrimage to Mecca that Elijah Muhammad's teachings of a kind of reverse racism were a lie. All human beings were brothers and sisters under God, and Malcolm returned to try to counter-teach Muhammad's misinterpretations of Islam. Malcolm was assassinated in 1965, but ten years later, when Muhammad died, Elijah's son Wallace took over and continued to pursue the reform movement Malcolm X had begun. Wallace sought to bring the Nation of Islam, newly named the World Community of Islam in the West, in line with mainstream Muslim teachings. Louis Farrakhan, on the other hand, chose to continue the separatist doctrines of Elijah Muhammad and, with his approximately fifty thousand followers, retained the name Nation of Islam.

What is the **Muslim Brotherhood** we hear of often in news reports these days?

Hasan al-Banna (1906–49), generally acknowledged as the founder of the Muslim Brotherhood (1927), was a well-educated man from a religiously conservative Egyptian family who believed that Muslims should be more active in promoting the broader societal implications of the Islamic faith. His theoretical works on "politicizing" Islam have been widely influential in the growth of a wide variety of contemporary activist Muslim organizations, especially in the Middle East and North Africa. Political activist organizations related to the Brotherhood include, for example, Hamas.

Though the Brotherhood began and developed largely in Egypt, it has gained political footing in other Middle East nations by running for office and having members elected to national assemblies. In countries such as Jordan, independent branches of the Brotherhood have arisen. More recently, the Brotherhood has exerted considerable influence in the aftermath of early 2011 "revolutionary" events that resulted in the ouster of long-time dictator Husni Mubarak. Banna himself did not advocate violent means, and his contemporary disciples generally strive to bring about their goal of integrating society under religious values—acknowledging religious pluralism and rights of non-Muslims—through political activism and reform. Some other organizations indirectly influenced by Brotherhood values have, however, embraced the use of violence as necessary for overthrowing non-Islamic rule. This includes such groups as Al-Qaeda and its spinoffs, the Taliban, and a host of Islamic "jihadist" organizations based in various states from North Africa through the Middle East and into Central and South Asia.

Do **Sunni** and **Shi'a Muslims** worship in **separate mosques**?

That depends on a host of other social and political circumstances. In many places where Muslims are a small minority of the regional population, there are very few mosques. Most of them serve Muslims from all over the world without inquiring as to whether new members are Sunni or Shi'ite. Shi'a Muslims who attend a predominantly Sunni mosque may discover that some themes they were accustomed to hearing in sermons, for example, are no longer so prominent. In some areas of countries like the United States, where there are growing numbers of immigrant and indigenous Muslims—people with ties to Iran or Iraq, for example—there might be sufficient numbers to begin plans for a Shi'a mosque. The motivation for doing so more than likely will have a great deal to do with ties to a country of origin as well as a desire for a kind of spirituality more in keeping with distinctively Shi'a interpretations of history and emphasis on the redemptive suffering of the Imams.

Where do Muslims live today? What are their estimated numbers?

Islam is now a truly global religious tradition. Approximately 1.57 billion Muslims live worldwide, on every continent and in most countries. In very general terms, about a third of the total live in the Middle East and North Africa. Several major ethno-linguistic groups are represented there, including Arabs, Turks, Persians, and Berbers. Many people associate Islam with Arabs even though they are now a relatively small minority of the global population. Another third live in central and southern Asia, including the southern republics of the former Soviet Union, Western China, India, Pakistan, and Bangladesh. Pakistan is the most important modern example of a nation-state established as a Muslim land. Another third are in sub-Saharan Africa, Indonesia, and in smaller concentrations in several dozen other countries. Indonesia boasts the single largest national population of Muslims, approaching two hundred million. At over a hundred million, India is home to the world's largest minority Muslim population. Muslims number from six to eight million in the United States.

It may also be helpful to think in terms of religio-cultural spheres, defined by key language groups, in which Islam has been a particularly important influence. The Arabicate sphere, for example, includes all those areas in which Arabic has been the dominant vehicle of Islamic expression, namely, the central Middle East, north Africa, and east Africa. The Persianate sphere consists of Iran, Afghanistan, and all of southern Asia. Within the Malayo-Polynesian sphere are Malaysia, Indonesia, and the Philippines. Central Asia, including western China, and present-day Turkey and the Balkans comprise the Turkic sphere. Last but not least is the sub-Saharan sphere, in which Nigeria and other west African nations are most significant.

Sultan's mosque in the city of Shah Alam, Malaysia, near the capital city of Kuala Lumpur. One of the world's largest mosques, its minarets are nearly 450 feet tall.

Have Muslims traditionally sent out **missionaries** to convert others?

Islam has been a missionary tradition since its earliest days. Muhammad's preaching eventually gathered a community of Meccans which in turn grew dramatically after migrating to Medina in the Hijra. Muslims believe in spreading the word whenever possible. Proselytizing is called "inviting" (*da'wa*, pronounced DA'wah) others to join the community of Islam. Many regard it as a basic religious duty, second only to their fulfillment of the five pillars. Despite perceptions to the contrary, Islam has spread far more often through peaceful means than through the sword. Among the earliest dedicated missionaries were Sufis who traveled with Muslim merchants along the trade routes to establish communities all over Asia and Africa. Some larger mission-oriented organizations have developed and moved into new territory with local or governmental sponsorship in a home country, but Muslim missionary societies are generally fewer and smaller than their Christian counterparts.

Is **Mecca** the **only** Islamic **holy city**?

As the birthplace of Muhammad and the site of the Ka'ba, Mecca (and its immediate environs), is naturally the holiest place on Earth for Muslims. According to tradition, other prophets and important holy people passed through Mecca as well. Abraham nearly sacrificed his son Ishmael at Arafat (the valley just outside Mecca) and built the Ka'ba. God rescued Abraham's consort, Hagar, and their son Ishmael from dying of thirst in the desert by causing the well of Zamzam to bubble forth. In 622 Muhammad traveled with his young community to Medina and there established Islam as an all-encompassing social entity. From Medina, the Prophet secured access to Mecca for Muslims and in Medina he died. Muhammad's house and earliest mosque remain a regular stop for most pilgrims who make *Hajj* and *Umra*. For these reasons and more, Medina ranks as second-holiest city for Muslims.

But Muhammad and a number of the other prophets also have important connections to Jerusalem. Muslim tradition has it that God carried Muhammad from Mecca to Jerusalem, to the "farther mosque," where he met and led the other major prophets in prayer. From a spot nearby Muhammad began his Ascension or *Mi'raj* (pronounced mi'RAAJ). For a time the young Muslim community in Medina faced Jerusalem when they prayed, but the orientation for prayer changed to Mecca in connection with a falling-out with the local Jewish tribes. Nevertheless, Jerusalem has retained a lofty place in Muslim piety and remains politically sensitive real estate.

How does the practice of **almsgiving** express Muslims' sense of community?

Zakat (pronounced zaKAAT), almsgiving, is one of the five pillars. It requires all financially stable Muslims to contribute varying amounts, depending on the type of goods being taxed. For example, it comes to 10 percent of agricultural produce in general, but 2.5 percent of a person's savings or profits over and above what one needs to live. There are many ways of calculating the matter these days. What is most important to understand about religious almsgiving is that for Muslims it is an institutionalized form of social concern. Muslim authorities see to the distribution of the funds among the neediest, both at home and abroad. The United Arab Emirates, for example, might earmark charitable funds for building an airstrip for the delivery of desperately needed supplies to the Albanian Muslim refugees from Kosovo. Devout Muslims are encouraged to give far beyond the minimum *zakat* as well. At the end of the month-long fast of Ramadan, many give generously to the *zakat al-fitr,* or alms for the breaking of the fast. Those and all other voluntary charitable donations are called *sadaqa* (pronounced SAdakah, "righteousness, uprightness"), for through these signs of social concern individual Muslims gain blessing and forgiveness. A related practice among Shi'a Muslims is the *khums* or "fifth." The tax was originally the custom of providing the Prophet a portion of the military spoils, but some Shi'a religious authorities have collected it from their constituencies up to modern times as an offering for the Twelfth Imam expected to return at the end of time.

What **gender-related issues** are important for Muslims?

Muslim tradition places great emphasis on understanding and facilitating social relations according to gender-appropriate roles and religiously acceptable behavior. In some societies, women are excluded from certain occupations, but in most instances those are cultural rather than explicitly religious norms. For example, American Muslim women participate in a wider range of professions than do their sisters in some other countries. Non-Muslim American professional women may experience the same kinds of occupational limitations as their Muslim counterparts. All societies and cultures have their gender biases, and religious sanction and justification often becomes inextricably intertwined with them, largely because religious argument can be a useful element in social control. Gender-related restrictions by which many devout Muslims abide are largely family matters arising from the belief that God has ordained certain tasks to men and certain others to women. Gender and sex differences are real, they observe, and part of a larger plan. Traditional family life calls for a division of labor and a clear understanding of individual and collective priorities. Non-Muslims sometimes conclude that Muslim women who choose to observe a dress code are oppressed. Talk to the Muslim women, many of whom are successful physicians, lawyers, and engineers, and you get a different perspective.

What does one do to **convert to Islam**?

Converting to Islam is a relatively simple matter. Interested individuals have typically already done some basic study of the tradition, but no prescribed course of religious education is required or expected. Naturally most Muslims believe that the more converts know about the tradition and its history, the more likely they can make an informed decision. Before entering into the brief ceremony that renders a candidate officially Muslim, the convert performs the major purification ritual called *ghusl*. Formal assent to the tenets of Islam entails a simple repetition of the Shahada before any two adult male witnesses.

How do Muslims view Islam's **relationship** to **other religious traditions**?

According to the Qur'an, the revelation delivered through Muhammad is not new, but a continuation and reaffirmation of the divine message given to all the earlier prophets acknowledged in the Jewish and Christian traditions. If prior generations of Jews and Christians had not misinterpreted or even willfully corrupted the message, subsequent corrective revelations would have been unnecessary. In other words, Muslims regard Islam's relationship to the earlier Abrahamic faiths somewhat the way Christians regard their tradition's relationship to Judaism. The later revelation completes, fulfills, corrects or abrogates the earlier one. Islamic tradition regards the "Peoples of the Book" as especially close kin. The Qur'an suggests that Muslims should consider Christians perhaps somewhat closer than Jews, even though there are far larger theological differences between Islam and Christianity than between Islam and Judaism. The concept of "Peoples of the Book" also came to include other minority religious communities of the Middle East, such as the Zoroastrians. In general, Muslims are inclined to regard members of other traditions, such as Hindus and Buddhists, for example, as considerably further removed from the possibility of salvation. But views of that sort naturally vary somewhat from region to region, as for example, in India, where Muslims and Hindus often live side by side.

LEADERSHIP, AUTHORITY, AND RELIGIOUS ROLES

What is an **imam**?

In Arabic, the word *imam* means "one who is in front." Three distinct meanings are attached to the term. First, and most commonly, *imam* refers to the individual who leads the ritual prayer in the local mosque. Any mature adult can fulfill the role, and members of local communities frequently share this responsibility. Women may lead prayer and preach to groups of women only. Once local communities become large enough to have the necessary funds, they typically hire a religious scholar to serve as full-time spiritual leader with the more official title of *Imam* (with a capital I). An *Imam*'s overall function is roughly similar to that of the pastor of a parish church. He counsels, visits the sick, performs funeral services, and generally administers the affairs of the mosque. To assist him in his work, the community often hires secretaries, directors of education and other services, and teachers, if the mosque sponsors a school. Second, important spiritual and intellectual leaders throughout Islamic history have gained the title *Imam* in recognition of their prominence and accomplishments. In those instances the title is honorary rather than functional. Finally, the term *imam* refers to the individuals whom the various Shi'a communities regard as spiritual descendants of Muhammad. This narrowest of the three meanings is applied and interpreted in different ways by the major Shi'a groups (Twelvers, Seveners, and Fivers). Most recently Twelver Shi'ites of Iran and Iraq bestowed the title on the Ayatollah Khomeini in a way that suggested a blend of the second and third meanings explained here.

An imam reads from the Qur'an at the Hassan II Mausoleum in Rabat, Morocco. (posztos [colorlab.hu] / Shutterstock.com.)

What are some of the main **varieties** of Islamic **religious officials or specialists**?

Islamic religious specialists are a large general class of people called *'ulama* (oolaMAA) meaning "those who possess knowledge" (*'ilm*). An *'alim* (pronounced AAlim, commonly used singular of 'ulama) is an individual who has done extensive study of the Qur'an, *tafsir* (exegetical commentary), and Hadith, for starters. Some become specialists in Qur'an recitation. One who memorizes the entire text and learns to "recite" it in an elaborate and demanding style called *tajwid* (pronounced tajWEED, "embellished, excellent") is called a *qari* (pronounced KAAHree, "Professional Qur'an reciter"). Some religious scholars further specialize in religious jurisprudence (*fiqh*, "understanding"). Such a scholar is called a *faqih* (pronounced faKEEH), "one who understands deeply," because he applies his intellect to plumb the depths of the fundamental religious sources in an effort to apply their principles to daily life. Some religious scholars routinely engage in the categorization of various acts according to their relative legal and moral acceptability. In that capacity the scholar is called a *mufti* (pronounced MUFtee), "one who issues a legal advisory called a *fatwa*" (pronounced FATwah). Specialists in the religious sciences often carry the honorific title of *shaykh*, "elder," a term that was reserved for tribal leaders during pre-Islamic times. Spiritual guides of the various Sufi organizations called "orders" or "paths" (*tariqa,* pronounced taREEkah) also generally bear the title of shaykh or its Persian equivalent, *pir* (pronounced peer).

What is an **Ayatollah**?

Ayatollah is Arabic for "Sign of God," an honorific title conferred on leading Shi'a religious scholars, especially in Iran and Iraq. In traditional Shi'a circles, accomplished scholars can attain the rank of *Ayatollah* by popular acclaim and through the acknowledgment of their peers. Among those of that rank, some are also further distinguished by the title "Grand *Ayatollah*." Of those, in turn, a group of seven have traditionally been singled out as "Sources of Imitation" and are thereby acknowledged as the most influential teachers among Shi'a Muslims.

Who would be a good example of a **major Muslim theologian**?

Abū Hāmid al-Ghazālī (d. 1111) was a major religious scholar who spent much of his adult life teaching and writing in Baghdad. His works covered a wide range of theological, philosophical, and spiritual themes. Some have compared him to Christianity's Augustine, citing rough similarities between Augustine's *Confessions* and Ghazali's intriguing quasi-autobiographical account of his personal spiritual quest. One could also argue that Ghazali's influence on Islamic tradition Ghazali equaled that of Thomas Aquinas on Christian thought.

Ghazali produced one of the most influential and perhaps also the most systematic treatment of the spiritual quest. He organized his multivolume *Revitalization of the Religious Disciplines* into four large sections consisting of ten "books" each. Structuring the whole work along the lines of a juridical treatise, he begins with the fundamentals required of those just embarking on the journey, external comportment in relation to God. Part Two treats external obligations in relation to other people. After ending the

second section with a book on the Prophet as ultimate human exemplar, Ghazālī moves from action to virtue and addresses the more difficult task of inward disposition required for the reformation of character. Finally, drawing on such earlier masters as Muhāsibī and Abū Tālib, he leads the traveler up the steep slope to the pinnacle of mystical experience, ecstatic love of God. Ghazālī's work integrates mystical theology into the larger framework of pastoral theology, embracing the spiritual needs of the broadest possible spectrum of Muslim faithful.

Do Muslims have a **system of religious law**?

As the young community grew and established itself in Medina, it became increasingly necessary for Muhammad to address countless questions of order and acceptable practice. Some of the later texts of the Qur'an deal with specific issues, such as how to pray, what foods and activities to avoid, and how to observe basic social relationships. After Muhammad died and the Arab armies expanded into new territories and encountered new cultures and religious communities, the Muslims had to confront countless problems previously unknown: How would they deal with issues that neither the Qur'an nor the Hadith addressed?

Local Muslim leaders often had to improvise, exercising their best personal judgment and acting as they believed Muhammad would have done. They strove to perpetuate the Prophet's example, his *sunna*. But authorities and leading scholars in Medina, and later in other cities, looked for ways to standardize the procedure of extending the application of the Qur'an and Hadith to changing circumstances. They gradually agreed that one could solve problems not treated directly in the Qur'an and Hadith by appealing to the "actual practice" of the local community or to the "consensus" (*ijma'*, pronounced ijMAA) of legal scholars. But since some questions were too new for any consensus to have developed, scholars agreed that one could apply a form of "reasoning by analogy" (*qiyas*, pronounced keeYAAS) that followed strict rules so as to keep the process as free of personal whim as possible. Leading legal scholars in different cities devised slightly different formulas for using the four "roots" of the law (Qur'an, Hadith, Consensus, and Analogical Reasoning), some allowing greater latitude in appealing to the third and fourth roots. Four legal methodologies dominant among Sunni Muslims came to be called the "schools" (*madhhabs*), while several other distinctively Shi'a schools eventually developed as well.

How does this **system of religious law work** in practice?

Some legal specialists rise to greater prominence because of their erudition, earning the title *mujtahid* (pronounced MUJtahid, "one who exercises independent investigation" of the sacred sources). In Sunni tradition, the "door of independent investigation" closed by the year 900, making further bold scholarship of this level unnecessary. According to that classical view, the founders of the four major Sunni schools of legal theory were the last *mujtahids*. But in Shi'a tradition, the highest ranking *ayatollahs* continue to exercise the authority of mujtahids.

In both traditions, it is up to scholars to offer rulings on controversial or contemporary issues. If a new ethical and legal question arises—a question of artificial life support or some other thorny biomedical matter, for example—a legal scholar would search the relevant sources to determine whether the Qur'an or Hadith might shed light on the precise issue at hand. If the scholar found only vague parallels that offer insufficient evidence to make a firm ruling on the new problem, he would then study further to see whether in the actual practice of Muslim communities there was an approach that might solve the problem. If the problem is too new to have any kind of useful history, the scholar might appeal to reasoning by analogy, looking for a "link" between ancient sources and practice and the new problem. Ancient sources may say nothing about artificial life support, but they have much to say about the nature of human life and about human authority to intervene.

On the basis of his research, the scholar might then issue a legal advisory called a *fatwa*. In that statement he would indicate to which of five ethico-legal categories the proposed course of action belonged: forbidden, discouraged, neutral, recommended, or required. Acting upon the advisory, the parties to the case might then choose to bring the matter before a religious judge called a *qadi* (pronounced KAAdee), himself authorized as a mufti. to adjudicate the matter. The outcome of all this study and interpretation is called *Shari'a* (pronounced shaREE'ah), the divinely revealed law or way of life prescribed for all Muslims.

Is there a **central teaching authority** for Muslims?

No single individual or institution has universal authority over the global Islamic community. For Sunni Muslims the nearest approximation to centralized teaching authorities are religiously affiliated educational institutions in Egypt and Saudi Arabia, venerable and influential for very different reasons. Cairo's Al-Azhar, founded in 972 by the Isma'ili (Sevener Shi'ite) Fatimid dynasty, has worn the mantle of religious prestige and authoritative conservatism since it was converted by Saladin and his dynasty (after 1171) for the task of defending the cause of Sunni Islam. In Saudi Arabia, educational institutions of Mecca and Medina have come to share in Al-Azhar's prestige in modern times. Young men seeking careers in religious studies come from all over the world, looking forward to returning home with credentials from these institutions.

Nowadays, a senior jurist somewhere might on very rare occasions issue a legal advisory (*fatwa*) claiming universal force, so that every Muslim ought to abide by it. The Ayatollah Khomeini, for example, delivered an order that Salman Rushdie was liable to the death penalty for blasphemy, and Usama bin Ladin has called for a *jihad* against the United States. But rare claims of that sort do not have the binding authority of a centralized institution like the papacy. In various parts of the world, religious scholars join together for consultative purposes. In the United States, for example, a Council of Imams holds regular gatherings to discuss practical and pastoral problems that arise in local communities. Elsewhere, *muftis* in a given region sometimes submit their decisions to the further judgment of a "grand *mufti*," who exercises jurisdiction in religious matters.

Have there been any important **Muslim religious reformers**?

According to a Hadith, Muslims believe that at the beginning of each Islamic century God will raise up for the community a *mujaddid* (muJADdid), a "renewer" who calls people to a fresh awareness of their faith. Muslim tradition has identified a succession of important historical renewers. In modern times, too, a number of major reformers have taken on the daunting task of inciting their fellow religionists to adapt their

164

ancient faith heritage to changing circumstances. Like reformers in any tradition, these Muslim pioneers have often met with resistance to the changes they proposed. Muhammad Abduh (1849–1905), for example, worked to promote reason as nearly equal with revelation as a source of knowledge. His suggestion that some elements of the Qur'an were not of divine origin caused considerable stir. Abduh, nevertheless, served as Grand Mufti of Egypt and was a leading influence at the al-Azhar University, a flagship institution of Islamic traditionalism.

Are there religious **hierarchical structures** in any branch of Islam?

Sunni Muslims constitute the vast majority of Islam's global membership. Since the generation that succeeded Muhammad, the dominant ideal of governance has been that a leader should be first among equals. Centuries of caliphal splendor might persuade a student of history that a type of monarchy was the preferred form of Islamic governance. In practice many of the most powerful Muslim rulers over the centuries have at least tried to call the shots religiously as well as politically. Nevertheless, Sunni Islam has never evolved quite the kind of hierarchical structure found, for example, in Roman Catholicism. Muslim authority structures in various countries and regions often take the form of councils of religious or legal scholars or of imams. In practice, jurisdiction in matters of religious law and discipline is limited generally to the confines of modern nation-states.

Following a very different model, the largest branch of Shi'a Islam, Twelver or Imami Shi'ism, has evolved a much more centralized authority structure. As a result of the Iranian revolution of 1979, the Ayatollah Khomeini and his followers sought to replace a monarchy with a theocracy. They established a pyramidal hierarchy of religious authority with Khomeini at the top. He was the most influential of a number of leading Ayatollahs (Sign of God) and won the title *Imam* by virtue of his dominance. Below him was a cluster of "grand *ayatollahs*" and a larger group of lesser *ayatollahs*. Just beneath them were two ranks of religious scholars with the title *Hujjatolislam* (Proof of Islam), and finally

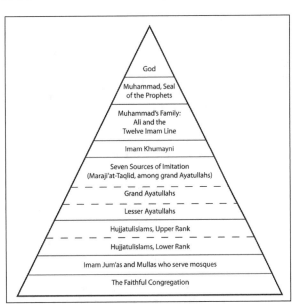

The hierarchical structure of Shi'a Islamic Republic of Iran.

165

the several thousand *Mullahs* (from a word that means roughly "master, reverend") who staffed the country's mosques.

Are there **characteristically Muslim views** about how **religion** and **political power** come together?

Muslims often describe their tradition as a "total way of life," a comprehensive approach that goes far beyond mere ritual observance or showing up at the mosque once a week. Some believe that such an all-encompassing teaching must ultimately be expressed in political terms, referring to early Muslim community life under the Prophet's leadership in Medina as the ideal. Throughout history Muslims have experimented with various models for balancing or integrating religious and civil authority. Some have worked well enough, allowing for freedom of religious practice and expression among members of religious minorities under Muslim rule. In fact, the historical record suggests that Muslims have been at least as successful as any other group at administering religiously sponsored regimes fairly and evenhandedly. Muslims in various parts of the world today continue to believe that an Islamic government represents the best hope of justice in a troubled world. But in a world where religious pluralism is increasingly evident, dividing humankind along religious lines seems a less than desirable option. The challenge now, as in the past, is to live by the Qur'anic dictum "There is no compulsion in religion."

What is a **Sufi**?

The word Sufi seems to derive from the Arabic word for "wool" (*suf*, pronounced soof). Among the first generations of Muslims Sufis were ascetics, spiritual athletes who strove to detach themselves from whatever distracted them from worshipping God. Garments of rough wool symbolized their desire for a simple life. Some of these early ascetics gained a reputation, often much to their personal consternation, for holiness. But some early seekers of deeper spirituality found ascetical discipline and self-denial an unsatisfactory path. A woman of Baghdad named Rabi'a (d. 801, pronounced RAAbi'ah) gave expression to a fierce longing for God in bold, shocking love poetry. How dare a mere mortal talk of a loving relationship with the infinite God! Rabi'a was the first true mystic, an inspiration to many who would risk all to communicate the unspeakable. Some, like Hallaj (d. 922), would die for their presumptuousness, accused of blasphemy and fatally misinterpreted, thus sharing the fate of mystics in many traditions. People everywhere sought out these spiritual beacons for guidance and blessing. Communities gathered around some prominent Sufis and eventually developed into formal organizations called *Tariqas* (pronounced taREEkah, meaning "path").

Over the centuries dozens of major Sufi men and women have left a legacy of poetry, arresting insight, and leadership. Jalal ad-Din Rumi (d. 1273), the original "whirling dervish," is one of the more famous classical Sufis, translations of his poetry

A gathering of Sufis and their families in a fourteenth century *madrasa* (theological college) during a religious festival in Cairo, Egypt.

now ranking among the best sellers in the United States. In some parts of the world, such as the Central Asian republics that made up the southern tier of the former Soviet Union, Sufi orders have been responsible in large part for the very survival of Islam through very difficult times. Many international Sufi organizations now maintain Web sites. Some teach that one does not need to be a Muslim to be a Sufi, but it is nevertheless important to keep in mind that Sufism is a genuinely Islamic phenomenon.

Is there such a thing as a **Muslim saint**?

In addition to sages and prophets, widespread Muslim tradition holds in high regard other individuals singled out for particularly intimate relationships with God. They are called Friends of God (*awliya,* pronounced awleeYAH: singular *wali*) and are generally analogous to what Christians and others mean when they refer to "saints." A major difference is that Friends of God are popularly acclaimed as such rather than formally declared by an institutional procedure. Muslims from Muhammad's own generation are among the earliest individuals called Friends of God, some so designated because of their devotion to the Prophet. Subsequent generations of Muslims have acclaimed Friends of God virtually everywhere right on down to modern times, with the notable exception of Saudi Arabia and other Gulf states. There and in a few other places, modern reformers have sought to purge Islamic practice of devotional customs judged to be inauthentic expressions of Islam and distortions of core teachings. They have argued that beseeching Friends of God for miracles is simply unnecessary, since no human being can mediate between the individual believer and his or her God. Virtually everywhere else, from Morocco's *marabouts* to Indonesia's distinctive *wali*

167

songo (Nine Friends of God), devotion to holy persons has been an important element in the spiritual life of hundreds of millions.

Who are the most **important martyrs** in Islamic history?

The Arabic word *shahid* (shaHEED) means "one who testifies or witnesses," and is thus more or less equivalent to the word martyr. Since earliest times Muslim sources have referred to those who gave their lives for the cause of Islam as martyrs. Shi'a tradition has held martyrs in especially high regard. Beginning with Muhammad's grandson Husayn, killed with his small band of fighters resisting the tyranny of the Umayyads in 680 C.E., the *Imams* have been the focus of a central belief in redemptive suffering. In this case the blood of the martyr not only assures the martyr's place in Heaven but becomes a source of grace for all believers. When the Ayatollah Khomeini returned to Iran from his exile in France in 1979, he made his first major address in a cemetery called the Paradise of Martyrs, associating the revolutionary struggle of twentieth century Shi'a Iranians with that of the proto-martyr Husayn. Placing such value on martyrdom does not imply that Shi'ites or other Muslims are eager to die. It means that some Muslims, like believers in several other traditions, value their faith and are willing to give their lives for it.

Do Muslims **revere** any persons as **especially gifted** with wisdom?

In Islamic tradition, as in Jewish and Christian, King Solomon (Sulayman) is the paradigm of wisdom. Solomon's sagacity enabled him to communicate with creatures of every kind, so that his sovereignty encompassed all of creation. Another figure from pre-Islamic history known for his wisdom is Luqman. Some traditions include him among the ranks of the prophets, but he is best understood as a prince among Muslim sages. According to the Qur'an, one chapter of which bears his name, Luqman was a teacher and coiner of proverbs. "Walk at a moderate pace and speak in measured tones," he advises, "for the most annoying of voices is that of the jackass" (Qur'an 31:19). Islamic lore describes Luqman in ways that recall the Greek sage Aesop.

Wisdom did not cease with the passing of the ancients. Muslims have continued to discern in teachers, scholars, and spiritual guides the embodiment of a practical insight that goes far beyond mere intellectual understanding. God has entrusted certain individuals with the gift of wisdom, the ability to penetrate the veils of life's mystery and to untangle the snarl of daily experience. Perhaps the most unusual personality in this general category is Khidr. The name means "Green One," suggesting that this character originated as a generic mythic or folkloric fertility figure. Some scholars connect Khidr with the Gilgamesh epic's sage Utnapishtim, who had survived the Flood. Gilgamesh searches for Utnapishtim in hopes that the sage will guide him to a plant that will provide him with the secret of immortality. Islamic lore attributes to Khidr arcane knowledge of the whereabouts of the Fountain of Life. Some accounts of his discovery of the Fountain pair him with Ilyas, since Elijah is another of the few who (along with Jesus and Idris) have attained immortality. Even as Jews often leave a chair and a glass for Elijah on ritual occasions, some Muslims greet the unseen Khidr because they know he is there somewhere.

Khidr's mysteriousness is deepened by the fact that he is one of only three significant figures not specifically identified in the Qur'an to whom later tradition has attached names. The others are Alexander the Great, associated with the Qur'anic Dhu 'l-Qarnayn—"The One with Two Horns"—and Joshua, who is said to be the anonymous servant of Moses in the Qur'anic story now connected with Khidr.

HOLIDAYS AND REGULAR OBSERVANCES

What kind of **religious calendar** do Muslims observe?

Muslims follow a lunar calendar whose twelve months add up to 354 days. In a cycle of thirty lunar years, eleven are leap years, with one day added to the last month. During Muhammad's time the lunar months were associated with seasons (*Ramadan* means "extreme heat," *Rabi'* "rainy season," and *Jumada* "dry season," for example). As in the Jewish calendar, the pre-Islamic year maintained its connection with agricultural cycles and seasons by the intercalation of a whole month in certain years. Since the practice of intercalation ended around Muhammad's time, the Islamic lunar year rotates backward eleven days each year in relation to the Gregorian solar year. If Ramadan, for example, begins on January 12 this year, next year it will begin on January 1, and so on. Certain practical results of this backward rotation are worth noting because of the way timing can affect religious practice. When Ramadan (the ninth month) occurs in the dead of winter, when days are shortest, the fast from sunrise to sunset is less arduous than when Ramadan falls during the height of summer. Pilgrimage to Mecca can also be more strenuous when the season of *Hajj* (in the twelfth month) occurs during the hottest season. Muslims the world over therefore must learn to work with two different systems of marking special times. Muslims begin their count of years with the Hijra of 622. Approximately every thirty-three years the beginnings of the Islamic lunar and Gregorian solar years roughly coincide.

Major Muslim Observances, with names of the Islamic Lunar Months

Date	Event
1 Muharram	Islamic New Year
10 Muharram	Day of 'Ashura (i.e., "tenth" day) For Sunni Muslims, day of recommended fast (parallel to Jewish Day of Atonement originally). For Shia Muslims, the martyrdom of Husayn ibn Ali, the grandson of Muhammad, and his followers in 680 C.E.
12 Rabi al-Awal	Birthday of the Prophet observed by many Sunni Muslims

Date	Event
17 Rabi al-Awal	Birthday of the Prophet observed by Twelver Shia Muslims
13 Rajab	Birthday of Ali ibn Abi Talib
27 Rajab	Muhammad's Night Journey and Ascension
15 Sha'ban	Middle of Sha'ban, or Night of Forgiveness, and the birthday of Muhammad al-Mahdi, Twelfth Shia Imam
1 Ramadan	Beginning of month-long fast
21 Ramadan	Martyrdom of Ali ibn Abi Talib
27 Ramadan	Initial "descent/revelation of the Qur'an," (observed on the 17th of Ramadan in Indonesia and Malaysia; also known as the "Night of Power")
1 Shawwal	Feast of the Breaking of the Fast, closing Ramadan—one of the two greatest festal days
8–13 Dhu al-Hijjah	Season of official *Hajj* to Mecca
10 Dhu al-Hijjah	Feast of Sacrifice during *Hajj* season, recalling God's command that Abraham sacrifice his son (Isma'il)—second of the two greatest festal days
18 Dhu al-Hijjah	Feast of Ghadir Khumm, Shia observance of the Prophet's designation of Ali as his "*caliph*"

What is the importance of the month of **Ramadan**?

During pre-Islamic times the month called Ramadan ("high summer") was religiously significant as a time during which the Arab tribes observed a truce from all hostilities. Of all the months the Qur'an mentions only Ramadan by name, identifying it as the month during which the scripture was revealed. Scripture suggests that the initial

divine revelation is the reason for the practice of fasting throughout the month. Ramadan begins with the sighting of the new moon on the last night of the eighth month. Each day, from dawn until sunset, Muslims are enjoined to fast from all food and liquid, as well as from sexual activity and other forms of sensual pleasure. Fasting also means refraining from negative attitudes and complaining, and developing a sense of solidarity with those who suffer from want all year long. After Muslims break the fast with some water and dates, they eat a meal before retiring. Before dawn they may have another meal, but limit other forms of

Celebrants during the last day of Ramadan, Milan, Italy. (Eugenio Marongiu / Shutterstock.com.)

celebration during the entire month. Special prayers are scheduled in mosques, along with the recitation of one of thirty "sections" of the Qur'an, completing the entire sacred text over the thirty nights.

A number of important dates fall during Ramadan. Most important is the "Night of Power," one of the odd-numbered nights among the last ten, usually observed on the twenty-seventh. Muslims believe that God's initial revelation to Muhammad makes this the holiest time of the entire year. Other important times during Ramadan include the birthday of the martyr Husayn (6th), death of Muhammad's first wife, Khadija (10th), the Battle of Badr (a key event in 625, the 17th), the retaking of Mecca in 630 (19th), the deaths of Ali and of the eighth Shi'a Imam, Ali Reza (21st), and Ali's birthday (22nd). Where Muslims are in the majority or a very sizable minority, the rhythm of life slows dramatically during Ramadan. At the sighting of the next new moon, all rejoice in the Feast of Fastbreaking, 'Id al-Fitr.

When do Muslims make **pilgrimage to Mecca** and what do they do there?

Formal season for the greater pilgrimage, called the *Hajj*, occurs between the eighth and thirteenth day of the twelfth lunar month. The journey is required of all Muslims with sufficient health and financial resources, assuming also that making the Hajj would not require them to shirk serious family responsibilities at home. As pilgrims enter a "forbidden zone" that encircles Mecca (called the *haram*), they put on the plain white wraps called the *ihram* (pronounced ihRAAM). The garb marks a transition to sacred space and time and reminds pilgrims of their simple equality before God.

Though precise ritual activities depend on both variations within the four Sunni law schools as well as on whether or not pilgrims intend to combine *Hajj* with *'Umra* (lesser pilgrimage), the following offers an idea of the major elements of *Hajj*. On the first day (the 8th of the month) they usually circumambulate the Ka'ba seven times, pray at the Station of Abraham, pray two cycles of prostrations, and drink from the spring of Zamzam. Heading for Mina outside of Mecca, most pilgrims will stay overnight

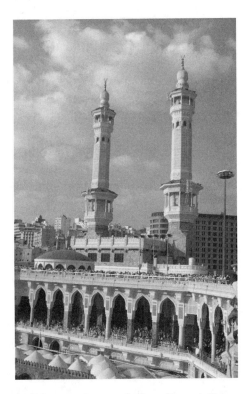

Two of the nine minarets at the Haram Mosque in Mecca. (Ahmad Faizal Yahya / Shutterstock.com.)

171

there before moving on to the plain of Arafat. They stand before the Mount of Mercy, recalling the deeds of Muhammad and Abraham there long ago. That evening they go a short distance back toward Mecca, to Muzdalifa, where on the third day they celebrate the Feast of Sacrifice ('Id al-Adha). Moving back to Mina later that day, pilgrims cast seven stones at one of three pillars, a symbolic repudiation of the temptations of Satan. After a symbolic clipping or shaving of hair, pilgrims remove the ihram and return to Mecca to circumambulate the Ka'ba and run seven times between the hills Safa and Marwa to commemorate Hagar's frantic search for water. During the eleventh through thirteenth days, pilgrims remain at Mina, casting the remainder of forty-nine stones collected earlier at all three of the pillars. Those who did not participate in the sacrifice on the tenth day may do so now. To end the whole event, most will again circumambulate the Ka'ba seven times. In recent years the Saudi government has expanded their pilgrimage facilities dramatically in order to accommodate annual crowds now numbering two million or more.

Are any **occasions** associated with Muhammad **especially important**?

Since medieval times Muslims in many countries have celebrated Muhammad's birthday, *Mawlid an-Nabi,* on the 12th of Rabi'. Street parties and grand banquets often provide opportunity for prayers and speeches. A very popular part of the festivities is the recitation of a poem by the thirteenth-century Egyptian poet Busiri, the *Burda* ("mantle," pronounced BURdah). Translated into Swahili and a number of other languages, the poem sings the Prophet's praises in truly cosmic terms, attributing to his birth all manner of marvels and blessings. In some places, where festivities are minimized or forbidden altogether, even the Prophet's birthday is a kind of national holiday. On the 27th of Rajab, Muslims recall the Night Journey and Ascension (*Laylat al-Isra wa-'l-Mi'raj*). According to traditional accounts, the Prophet experienced this timeless mystical moment sometime during the years just before the Hijra. A major feature of the celebrations is the retelling of any of several narratives that follow Gabriel and Muhammad through the heavens, including descriptions of his meetings and conversations with the other major prophets, each associated with one of the seven celestial levels. During the course of his journey Muhammad received instructions about instituting the five daily ritual prayers.

Do Muslims **celebrate events** in connection with any **other religious figures**?

Popular practice in many places still includes annual commemorations of birthdays and death anniversaries of various important holy persons and Friends of God. Birthday celebrations of members of the Prophet's family, such as Sayyida Zaynab, remain popular in places like Egypt. Lasting for up to seven days, the festivities are like sprawling street parties. Crowds grow daily, as does the intensity of the celebration. Vendors sell food and souvenirs and Qur'an reciters fill the air with sacred sounds from their booths up and down the streets. Mosques within the central area of celebration can be packed to overflowing. Birthdays of famous Friends of God frequently include recitation of classic poems extolling the saints' spiritual achievements and glorious intimacy with God. Anniversaries of the death of God's friends are also important in many regions, especially those further to the east. Since holy persons are fully united with God at death, the occasions are sometimes referred to as the saint's Wedding Day (*'Urs,* pronounced OORS). On the 6th of Rajab many Indian Muslims (and members of other faiths as well) observe the 'Urs of Mu'in ad-Din Chishti, founder of a famous Sufi order, at his tomb in the city of Ajmer.

What are some of the **other religious days** Muslims observe?

On the 15th of Sha'ban many Muslims, especially in South Asia, observe the Night of Forgiveness (*Laylat al-Bara'a,* pronounced baRAA'ah). Popular belief says that the names of all persons are written on the leaves of a great cosmic tree. On the evening of the 14th, the tree shakes and loses some of its leaves. Those whose leaves fall are destined to die during the coming year. According to a Hadith, God comes down to the lowest Heaven that night and asks if anyone seeks forgiveness. That is the moment for

all to wipe the slate clean, since no one knows whether his or her leaf has fallen. Celebrations of many holy persons, often centering around the individual's tomb, vary according to region. In addition to birthday (*mawlid*) and death anniversary (*'urs*) celebrations, Muslims in various places observe seasonal times (*mawsim*) with festivities connected to agricultural or other natural cycles. One such celebration is that of Nabi Musa (Prophet Moses), observed around his alleged tomb-shrine near Jericho. Its timing coincides roughly with the Orthodox Christian Holy Week, featuring elaborate processions that begin in Jerusalem.

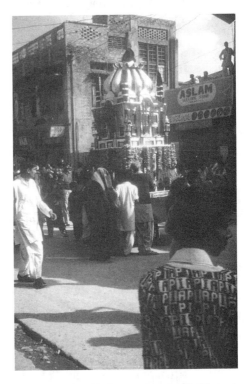

Does the **beginning** of the **Muslim year** have any particular significance?

During the first ten days of the month of Muharram, Muslims reflect on a variety of spiritual themes. During Muhammad's time the community observed a one-day fast on the 10th of the month (*'Ashura,* pronounced aaSHOOrah), possibly paral-

Procession of Shi'a Muslims carrying a model of the tomb of the proto-martyr Husayn in commemoration of his death, as they observe 'Ashura (the tenth day of the first lunar month) in Rawalpindi, Pakistan. (Courtesy of David Edwards.)

leling the Jewish practice of fasting on the 10th of Tishri, generally known as *Yom Kippur.* Though the major fast was formally shifted to Ramadan, Muslims still observe this day, some with fasting and prayer. Like many holy days, 'Ashura has become associated with ancient events of great significance. This day marks the day on which Noah left the ark. Visitors to Mecca can enter the Ka'ba itself (not just the sanctuary around it) on this day alone.

But the first ten days of the year are still more important for Shi'a Muslims. Some readers may recall the day in 1979 when Iranian students took over the U.S. embassy in Tehran. It occurred on the 1st of Muharram in the year 1400 after the Hijra, the beginning of the traditional period of mourning for the proto-martyr Husayn, who died at the hands of a tyrannical ruler in the year 680 C.E. Observance of the sad event gains in intensity until the actual day of martyrdom, some observing a fast on the 9th day. On 'Ashura itself, some Shi'ites make pilgrimages to Karbala in Iraq, site of the martyrdom, or to the tombs of other Imams in Iran and Iraq. In more traditional Shi'a villages, people still gather to reenact the events in a "passion play" called the *Ta'ziya* (pronounced ta'ZEEyah). Looking at the bigger picture, a Hadith says that at the beginning of each new century (on the lunar Islamic calendar) God will raise up for the Muslim community a "renewer" who will call all believers to a fuller participation in the faith.

CUSTOMS AND RITUALS

What **activities** do Muslims typically do in and around the **mosque**?

Throughout history and in many parts of the world mosques have stood at the center of an enormous range of activities. In Egypt, Turkey, Iran, and India, for example, mosque complexes have combined educational facilities of various levels, libraries, medical schools and hospitals, social service facilities, funerary facilities, and religious residences. Many of the monumental complexes depended on the sort of equally monumental royal patronage that is rare these days. But plans for somewhat less ambitious projects are afoot now in various parts of the United States. As local communities grow, mosque complexes will become increasingly visible. Meeting and social spaces are just the first of many needs beyond the basic requirement of a place for communal ritual prayer.

Is there a **standard** Islamic group **liturgical worship**?

Islamic ritual prayer, performed five times daily, is called *salat* (from a root that means to make holy). Whenever Muslims gather they perform the ritual prayer together. That applies not only to the prescribed Friday midday congregational prayer but to any of the set times at which two or more Muslims come together any day of the week, whether in the mosque or elsewhere. As with all Muslim ritual practice, worshippers preface this prayer with the clearly stated intention (*niyya*, pronounced NEEyah), saying "I intend to pray the dawn (for example) salat." From two to four cycles of standing, bowing to place hands on knees (*ruku'*, pronounced ruKOO), sitting on the heels (*jalsa*, pronounced JALsah), stretching forward toward prostration (*sajda*, pronounced SAJdah) to place hands flat on the floor at shoulder width, and touching the forehead to the floor, make up the fundamental salat ritual. The number of cycles (*rak'a*, pronounced RAK'ah) depends on which prescribed prayer one is performing.

Do Muslims engage in any specific **purification rituals**?

Prior to each act of ritual prayer Muslims perform a brief purification called *wudu'* (pronounced wuDOO). Worshippers perform each of the following cleansing motions three times: rinse hands and wrists, rinse out the mouth, then the nostrils likewise, rinse the whole face, arms up to the elbows, whole head and neck, and finally toes and feet up to the ankles. Mosques today typically provide separate facilities in which men and women can perform the ablution. Older mosques often have fountains or taps running along an exterior wall, with small benches or stools for worshippers to sit on. They usually use tap water, but under peculiar circumstances even sand or earth is acceptable, in which case it is called *tayammum* (pronounced taYAMmum). Clearly the idea is to prepare oneself symbolically to enter a state of mindfulness. In addition to this cleansing, Muslims also regard a more thorough bathing (called *ghusl*) essential to restore the state of ritual purity after sexual intercourse, seminal discharge, or the menstrual cycle. *Ghusl* includes the motions of the ablution just described, but encompasses the entire body as well. The intent of these rituals is to put the individual in a state of maximum attentiveness to and spiritual worthiness for entering into the presence of God.

Do Muslims ever **visit** their **holy cities outside** of the **formal pilgrimage season**?

Hajj, or major pilgrimage, fulfills a religious duty only in connection with the formal season. But travelers to the holy city can perform the *Umra* or lesser pilgrimage any time of year. *Umra* is a strictly devotional activity, optional but highly recommended. Rituals include a much scaled-down version of important *Hajj* activities. To be more precise, *Umra* is actually a component of *Hajj* that can be performed separately. Pilgrims enter

Ablution taps used for ritual cleansing. Edirne, Turkey.

into the state of ritual consecration by donning the same seamless white cloth worn for *Hajj* before entering the sacred zone surrounding Mecca. They proceed to the Ka'ba, circumambulate it seven times, perform two cycles of ritual prayer, take a drink from the well of Zamzam, and walk rapidly seven times between the small hillocks called Marwa and Safa. They conclude the lesser pilgrimage by clipping a lock of hair or shaving the head, symbolizing the spiritual change desired as a result of the pilgrimage. As at *Hajj* time, many pilgrims add a visit to the Prophet's Mosque in Medina, but that is a separate devotional activity.

Are there any **other forms** of **religious pilgrimage**?

Ziyara (pronounced zeeYAArah, meaning "visitation") is a form of minor pilgrimage still popular all over the world, with a few regional exceptions such as the Arabian peninsula. Devout Muslims travel to the tombs of holy persons to receive *baraka* (blessing/power, pronounced BAraka) by association with the saint's power and holiness. Elaborate shrine complexes have grown up around some of these sacred sites. Since the nineteenth century especially, Muslim authorities in Saudi Arabia have sought to stamp out the practice because they have deemed the veneration of miracle-working saints a threat to pure monotheism. Ironically, Saudi Arabia remains the home of the prime example of *ziyara*. Each year millions of pilgrims to Mecca make a trip north to Medina to visit the mosque in which Muhammad, his daughter Fatima, and the first *caliph*, Abu Bakr, are buried. Sunni Muslims from Morocco to Malaysia continue to visit secondary holy places, most of which are graves of Sufi shaykhs. Shi'a Muslims also visit sites connected with similar Friends of God, but their devotional travel revolves more around a number of distinctively Shi'a holy places. They are the tombs of the *Imams*, spiritual and biological descendants of Muhammad through his daughter Fatima. Most of the *Imams'* shrines are in Iran, with its overwhelmingly Shi'a population, and southern Iraq, where most of that country's slight majority of Shi'ites live.

176 Faithful entering a mosque in Tangier, Morocco.

What are **Muslim sermons** like?

An address called the *khutba* (pronounced KHUTbah) is a standard feature of every Friday congregational prayer service. Members of the congregation sit on the floor while the preacher stands near the niche (*mihrab*) or ascends a few steps of a pulpit called the *minbar* (pronounced MINbar). In larger, more established mosques, the Imam generally delivers the sermon on Fridays at the early afternoon congregational prayer. But either the

Imam or some other adult might also offer some reflections at other times when smaller groups gather for *salat*. Speakers have a wide range of appropriate topics from which to choose. High on the list are ethical concerns such as social responsibility, the need for parents to take an active part in their children's education, and speaking out in public venues about problems that need attention from concerned citizens. Speakers might also choose any of scores of devotional themes, such as cultivating one's relationship with God, or the need to set aside time for personal reading and reflection on the Qur'an. Preachers often tailor their sermons to a specific religious season, especially during Ramadan and pilgrimage season. Encouragement during the month-long fast is always helpful and welcome. Scripture naturally plays a major part in sermons, and preachers generally cite Hadiths along with Qur'anic texts to illustrate their themes. Sermons vary in length from five or ten minutes to perhaps a half hour for special occasions.

Do Muslims use **ritual sacrifice**?

Muslims mark the high point of the annual season of *Hajj*, which runs from the eighth to the thirteenth day of the ninth lunar month, with the Feast of the Sacrifice. Also called "The Great Feast," the rituals on the tenth of the month include the slaughtering of an animal in memory of God providing a ram for Abraham to sacrifice in lieu of his son Ishmael. Sheep, goats, oxen or cows, and camels are traditional sacrificial animals. The person performing the sacrifice dedicates the animals to God and mentions the names of those partaking of the fruits of the sacrifice. Muslims all over the world observe the Feast of Sacrifice with prescribed activities. Food ritually sacrificed is usually prepared in large quantities, so that as those present for the festivities share in the feast, the abundance can be distributed to those in need. Animals ritually slaughtered during *Hajj* season are not sold for profit. In some parts of the world, Muslims still sacrifice a sheep in connection with an optional birth ritual. When a child is seven days old, some families shave the baby's head, a practice dating to Muhammad's time.

Do Muslims follow specific **dietary customs** or rituals?

Muslim dietary practice is similar in many ways to Jewish traditions known as *kashrut,* or keeping kosher. Certain foods are forbidden altogether, except in direst need. These include intoxicating beverages, pork, blood, foods prepared or cooked with pork fat (some would include, for example, doughnuts and other fried breads), and animals that eat mainly carrion (i.e., scavengers). If non-Muslims invite Muslim friends for a celebration with a meal, it is important that they give due consideration to what they will serve. Muslims do not require the separation of meats from dairy products as do Orthodox Jews, but hosts should avoid pork of any kind if at all possible.

Meat of certain animals is acceptable only when the animal has been ritually slaughtered. As in every Muslim ritual, one begins by declaring the "intention" to perform the action religiously. After pronouncing the first part of the *basmallah* (In the name of **177**

God—leaving off the names Compassionate and Merciful) and the *takbir* (*Allahu akbar,* God is supreme), the butcher severs the jugular and windpipe with a single blade stroke. The idea is to drain as much of the blood as possible, for it symbolizes the life force. By custom, Muslims in various places consider certain foods traditional for festal occasions, such as the meal that breaks the daily fast of Ramadan and the celebration that marks the end of that month. Many of these customs are inspired by Muhammad's own practice. For example, he is said to have broken his daily fast with a glass of water and a few dates before taking a meal, so Muslims generally try to do likewise.

Do Muslims practice **polygamy**?

Long before the beginnings of Islam plural marriage was a fairly common practice. A number of the biblical patriarchs and kings had several wives. Wealthier men of the pre-Islamic Arab tribes apparently engaged in polygamy, marrying as many wives as their wealth would allow. A major concern seems to have been that, in the inhospitable environs of that desert world, women not attached to families had little hope of survival. As cities like Mecca developed, the practice survived in somewhat modified form. But according to a text of the Qur'an, polygamy in the early Muslim community was to be limited. A man could marry up to four women, provided he could treat all of his wives with complete equity, both materially and emotionally. In modern times a number of national governments in the Middle East have outlawed the practice, arguing that modern social and economic conditions have made perfectly fair treatment all but impossible. Even where local laws allow polygamy, relatively few men marry more than one woman, and those who marry four are a very small minority.

What kinds of **ritual objects** figure in Muslim **worship and prayer**?

By far the most important ritual object is the Qur'an. Since Muslims regard the sacred book as the very word of God, they try to treat the physical object with the greatest respect. Some mosques own ancient and beautifully wrought Qur'ans, often in multiple volumes, that are used only for special occasions. The more ancient the mosque, the more likely it will also have specially crafted podiums

Islamic ritual and devotional objects in a mosque shop, Turkey.

on which to place the Qur'an, and possibly also storage containers. Both stand and box often feature carefully chosen inscriptions from the Qur'an and Hadith that remind devotees of the divine origin and power of the sacred word. One of the most important among the relatively few other items that have been a regular part of Muslim devotions is the classic prayer rug. Displaying a central shape that recalls the *mihrab* on the Mecca-facing wall of the mosque, high-quality prayer rugs often use geometric and floral designs inspired by the Qur'an's "Verse of Light": "God is the light of the heavens and the earth. His light is like a niche in which is a lamp within a glass like a shining star kindled from a sacred olive tree neither of east nor west whose oil would nearly glow even if no fire touched it" (Qur'an 24:35). Inspired by the same verse, beautifully enameled glass lamps were once raised to a fine art and hung by the dozens in the great mosques of the Middle East. The shimmering light cast through their multicolored Qur'anic inscriptions and arabesque designs would have been similar to that cast through Europe's stained-glass windows.

Are **music and dance** important in Islamic **religious ritual**?

Muslims do not incorporate either music or dance into their primary religious rituals, and they use no musical instruments as part of communal worship. Though Muslims do not as a group sing hymns or other types of vocal prayer set to music, a type of tonal recitation is very much a part of Islamic religious life. A "call to prayer" (*adhan*) broadcast from the minaret (at least in areas where Muslims are the majority population) announces each of the five daily times for *salat*. The *muezzin* (pronounced muEZzin) makes the call using a form of chanting that can strike the ear as very musical, even though it has no melody such as we generally associate with songs. Formal "recitation" of the Qur'an is perhaps the closest approximation to music in Muslim ritual. Specially trained reciters, who typically have memorized the entire Qur'an, chant texts of the scripture using either of two styles of presentation. The simpler form is called "measured" and is sung with a recurring pattern of only four or five notes. A more ornate form, called "embellished," uses a much wider tonal range, proceeds much more slowly, and punctuates the text with dramatic silences. Such recitation can be part of any religious observance in any venue. Outside of primary ritual contexts, Muslims all over the world have set religious themes and sentiments to music in countless local and regional styles and languages. Muslim musicians and singers across the globe are now producing devotional music for mass-market consumption. From Morocco to Indonesia, tapes and CDs filled with contemporary musical interpretations of classical texts and prayers are becoming increasingly popular. Dancing often accompanies popular musical performances, especially those associated with the feasts of local holy persons.

Do Muslims **pray** in any **particular language**?

Arabic is the liturgical language of Islam. All formal prayers and Qur'an recitation are in Arabic. Most non-Arabic speaking Muslims learn at least some texts of the scripture **179** by heart in Arabic, along with a dozen or so other short texts that are recited regularly during ritual prayer as well as in personal devotions. Scriptural texts include, for example, Sura 1, called The Opening, a lovely prayer reminiscent of the Christian Lord's Prayer, and Sura 112, an affirmation of God's absolute oneness. In addition to the *shahada,* shorter phrases used during ritual prayer include *Allahu akbar* (God is Supreme), *Al-hamdu li-'llahi* (Praise be to God), and *Sami'a 'llahu li-man yusabbihhu* (God listens to one who praises him). Other Arabic phrases in common use all over the world include *In sha'a 'Llah* (God willing), *Wa 'Llahu a'lam* (God knows best), and *La hawla wa la quwwata illa bi 'Llah* (In God alone is power and strength). During the midday congregational prayer on Friday, the prayer leader gives an address, sometimes called a sermon. The preacher often prefaces the sermon with a series of divine praises in Arabic, and then delivers the address in the local vernacular. Preachers occasionally deliver the entire address in Arabic and then provide a translation. Arabic is so important because it is the language of the Qur'an and of the Prophet, whose very sound carries great symbolic associations even for Muslims who do not speak it.

What kinds of **rituals** do Muslims engage in **privately**?

Since one can perform the five daily ritual prayers anywhere, most Muslims generally pray the *salat* alone or in small groups. In mosques everywhere you can find individual Muslims praying privately outside the regular ritual prayer times as well. But Muslims also engage in a variety of other private devotions. Some are associated with local or regional custom, others practiced across the globe. Private recitation of the sacred scripture is foremost among the universal customs. Muslims who read Arabic but who are not formally trained in the refinements of performative recitation often sit alone and recite in a low voice. Meditative reading of the text in any language can nourish the spiritual life. Another popular devotion involves a prayerful consideration of the "Ninety-Nine Beautiful Names" of God. Many Muslims use the *tasbiha,* a set of either thirty-three or ninety-nine beads, to keep count. (These are the so-called "worry beads" people all over the world like to fidget with even when not praying.) Islamic traditions of spirituality also offer a vast array of devotional literature, from hagiography (lives of prophets and holy persons) to prayers recommended for daily use and refined religious poetry suitable for praying.

How do Muslims **celebrate birth**?

A recommended but optional ceremony called the *'Aqiqa* (aKEEkah) occurs when a baby is seven days old. In the home or in a part of the mosque outside the prayer hall, parents name their child and clip a lock of hair. Tradition suggests that parents give at least the hair's weight in silver as a charitable donation. In some places it remains customary to perform ritual animal sacrifice and distribute food to the needy. Parents can formally name their child at this time, often choosing from among the names of religiously important men and women. Sometimes the baby's father will whisper the call to prayer (*adhan,* pronounced aTHAAN) in the infant's right ear and the invitation to begin the prayer (*iqama,* pronounced iQAAmah) in the left. Some Muslims choose to practice a rite of circumcision on infant boys, though some prefer to postpone the practice until puberty. Depending on circumstances, some kind of reception may follow the rituals.

Are there distinctive forms of Islamic **initiation ritual**?

Teenagers can be welcomed formally into the adult community of believers with a simple ceremony during which the young man or woman pronounces the *shahada* before two male or eight female witnesses. Sometimes the occasion is combined with a regular congregational prayer service on Friday afternoon, but the ritual can also take place in the home. The young Muslims so initiated may also recite various prayers in Arabic as part of the ceremony. There is ordinarily no reception following the ritual. As a rite of passage, the ritual itself is roughly parallel to the Jewish *bar* and *bat mitzvah.*

What are the Islamic rituals of **marriage**? Do Muslims favor **arranged marriages**?

In the United States, Muslim nuptials (called *nikah* in Arabic) can occur in the prayer hall of the local mosque in a separate ceremony not connected with the regular ritual prayer. In other places, weddings typically occur in homes or in the presence of a Muslim judge (*qadi*). The imam of the mosque, or the judge, presides over the ceremony and may offer religious reflections on the sacredness of the marriage contract. In some countries elaborate processions and house-warming ceremonies are part of the festivities. As in many other traditions, two witnesses attest to the agreement. Written documentation includes both mosque records and the usual license required by civil law. A reception called a *walima* (pronounced waLEEmah) follows weddings nearly everywhere. In some countries the bridal dowry remains an essential item in the social contract between families. Many Muslim families continue to prefer marriages in which the parents do the initial negotiating. They present their favored prospect to their son or daughter, but in most situations the young people have the option of declining. Many Muslims regard open dating as undesirable and believe the arranged relationship is healthier and more acceptable morally. Some parents will even take out ads, especially on behalf of a daughter, in the "personal" sections of Muslim publications, seeking interested parties who are well educated and religiously committed.

How do Muslims deal ritually with **death and mourning**?

In most places Muslims retain the ancient custom of burying the unembalmed body before sundown on the day of death. Family members generally prepare the body with

A Muslim cemetery in Kusadasi, Turkey, showing both head and foot-stones, trees painted white several feet up from the ground, and stone replicas of the headgear once worn by the deceased person, indicating that person's rank in traditional Ottoman society.

purification rituals similar to those used prior to prayer or to remove some ritual impurity. Sometimes mourners will say special prayers in the mosque after the regular ritual prayer, with or without the body. Basic prayers include the *takbir* (saying *"Allahu akbar"*) spoken four times, interspersed with longer devotional prayers calling down blessings on the deceased and on all present. In the United States, Muslim obsequies often occur in funeral homes, always with a closed casket. There the *imam* of the mosque leads mourners in prayer and may also deliver a brief eulogy. American funerals often do not occur immediately after death as in some other countries. At the cemetery, mourners gather around the grave and offer burial prayers called *janaza* (jaNAAzah). Muslims do not practice cremation. Bodies are buried in such a way that if turned onto their right side, they would be facing Mecca. Following burial, mourners generally gather to express condolences either at the family home or in a space set aside specially for the purpose. Some families arrange to have a Qur'an reciter present or else play recorded recitation for silent reflection.

HINDUISM

HISTORY AND SOURCES

What is **India** and what is its **importance** in terms of religion?

India is a large diamond-shaped land mass bounded to the north by the Himalaya mountains, to the west by the Arabian Sea, and to the east by the Bay of Bengal. To the northwest is the vast plain of the Indus river system, and to the northeast that of the Ganges and its tributaries. Prior to 1947 India included what is now the nation-state of Pakistan and covered some 1.7 million square miles, roughly half the size of the United States of America. Today India's population is 1.2 billion, with the populations of Pakistan and Bangladesh (which split from Pakistan in 1971) totaling another third of a billion. India is the original home of both Buddhism and Hinduism, as well as of the smaller Jain and Sikh religious traditions. In addition, Islam has had enormous influence on the history of the Indian subcontinent ever since the first Muslim armies made incursions as far east as the Indus River by the early eighth century. During subsequent centuries, various Muslim dynasties ruled from eastern Afghanistan/western Pakistan to the east across much of northern India. The Mughal Muslim dynasty also began in Afghanistan around 1500 and quickly established control over Pakistan and northern India, remaining a major power ruling from Delhi until the mid-eighteenth century. An important result of the long history of Muslim rule in the subcontinent was the "Partition" of 1947 in which large segments of Indian Muslim communities were compartmentalized in what became Pakistan and Bangladesh.

What does the **term "Hinduism"** mean?

As a standard term in religious studies, Hinduism refers to a whole family of religious traditions deeply rooted in the Indian subcontinent. "Hinduism" derives from an **183** ancient linguistic root that means "to flow," and rivers have been a central feature in the religious life of nearly a billion Indians. A bit of river imagery here will help to explain how many diverse traditions have come together to form the "greater Hinduism" of our day. Imagine an extensive network of rivers of belief stretching across the whole of the Indian subcontinent beginning perhaps six thousand years ago. One major river flows from the northwest down toward the Indian heartland. Another originates in the south. Each grows as dozens of tributaries flow into it along its course. In the center of the subcontinent the two broad streams come together into one vast waterway. As it nears the sea, the great river opens again into a broad delta. The northern river, representing the Aryan ethnic and cultural elements, carries a system of religious beliefs that came together from tributaries to the northwest of India as long as five or six millennia ago (even longer according to some scholars).

Deities of the Aryan tradition seem to have much in common with those of the classical Greek and Roman pantheons with their lords of wind, weather, and sky. A river of Dravidian ethnic and cultural elements to the south represents ancient indigenous traditions surrounding the forces that rule earth and fertility, mountain and valley, powers of life and death. This vast "river system" of religious families, commonly referred to as "Hinduism" is in reality not a single "religion" but a complex blend of many diverse religious traditions.

Did Hinduism have a **historical founder** as Christianity and Islam did?

All but two of the major religious traditions trace their origins to a specific individual teacher or foundational figure. Only Hinduism and Shinto do not—keeping in mind that the individual founders of other religious traditions may be impossible to pin down historically. Some people regard historical concreteness and detail as an essential feature of a religious tradition's credibility. From the Hindu perspective, it is the very uncertainty as to the tradition's origins that enhances its attractiveness. The eternal truth that Hindus call *sanatana dharma* emerges from the mists of antiquity in an aura of perfect mystery, as befits a truth of divine origin.

What are the principal historical stages in the **evolution of "greater Hinduism"**?

A stage known as the Vedic period began as early as 4000 B.C.E. (Some Indian scholars push the origins back as much as three or four thousand years before that.) Archaeological evidence from Harappa and Mohenjo Daro point to a highly developed civilization in the Indus river valley from around 2700 to 1500 B.C.E. Early texts suggest a religious culture centered on worship of numerous deities associated with forces of nature. Around 2000 B.C.E., there may have been a major population shift from the northwest of India to the Ganges plain as a result of the drying up of the Sarasvati river, once a prominent feature of the Indus valley. The Vedic period comes to a close around the time of that shift. The period of the Upanishadic scriptures and the Epic age, from 1500 to 500 B.C.E., witnessed dramatic changes and the evolution of major new forms of religious expression. During these centuries, the Upanishads developed the speculative approach now known generically as Vedanta, the "culmination of the Vedas." For the next millennium or so (500 B.C.E.–500 C.E.), sometimes referred to as the Classical Period), new post-Vedantic sacred texts, called Sutras, Shastras, Agamas, and the earliest Puranas, formed the bases of a number of important schools of thought. From this period, too, came the written Epics, the Ramayana and Mahabharata. Between around 500 and 1800 C.E., the so-called Medieval Period, popular devotional theism—based largely on mythic narrative texts called the Puranas—spread across most of India. Beginning with the arrival of the British in the mid-eighteenth century, the Modern Period extends into the mid-twentieth century, the declaration of India's Independence, and the partition that created East and West Pakistan as separate Muslim states.

What were the **earliest Hindu sacred texts**?

A set of sacred scriptures, called the Vedas, consists of four distinct collections of texts, each with its own distinctive purpose. The name Veda comes from a Sanskrit root meaning "wisdom" or "vision," the same root that gives us English words like *video*." According to tradition, "seers," called *rishis,* composed the texts and communicated them orally. The *rishis* were able to see the truths revealed to them because they were also "hearers" of the sacred word. In fact, Hindu tradition groups the most sacred of its scriptures in the category of "that which is heard" (*shruti*), to distinguish them from a secondary level of revelation called "that which is remembered" (*smriti*). The Vedas evolved over a period of centuries, and religious specialists eventually wrote them down in an ancient form of Sanskrit. The earliest and most important of the four scriptures is called the Rig Veda, an anthology of more than a thousand hymns to various deities. A second collection, called the Sama Veda, includes material from the Rig, edited for ease of ritual use according to melodies and poetic meters. In the Yajur Veda, the early priesthood gathered the most important sacred mantras. A final collection of ritual incantations makes up the Atharva Veda. Many of the Vedic hymns are especially beautiful and offer a unique insight into how the early ritual specialists who made up the priesthood sought to understand and affect their world through contact with forces beyond human control.

How did the **Vedic scriptures describe** the **ultimate spiritual powers**?

Vedic cosmology divided the universe into three regions: sky, lower atmosphere, and Earth. Eleven of the thirty-three chief deities held sway over each of the cosmic realms. A deity much like the Greek Zeus ruled the sky, but he was not the head of a divine—if often unruly—family as Zeus was. Members of the Vedic pantheon seem to have risen to prominence at different times, as reflected by the numbers of hymns devoted to several individual gods. An atmospheric wind deity called Vayu and the celestial Surya, the sun, played important but still not central roles. The celestial

The god Vishnu, Chola Period, eleventh century, South India, bronze. Note discus in upper right hand, conch shell in upper left. Lower left once held a mace, while the lower right gestures "do not fear." (Courtesy of the St. Louis Art Museum.)

Shiva as "Man-woman Lord" (Ardhanarishwara) standing in the "triple-bend" posture, with his mount, the bull Nandi, behind him. Chola period, twelfth century. (The Saint Louis Art Museum. Friends Fund.)

Varuna had once headed the pantheon and oversaw cosmic order. His main competition was the atmospheric Indra, lord of inclement weather. At some point Indra eclipsed Varuna, perhaps because Indra represented a more fearsome power and imminent danger. Only the terrestrial Agni, god of fire and thus essential to Vedic sacrifice, merited more hymns than Indra. But before long even Indra bowed to two upcoming powers, the celestial Vishnu ("all-pervading") and the atmospheric Rudra ("the howler"). Rudra eventually came to be associated with the formidable Shiva. Together, Vishnu and Shiva symbolized the global forces of sustenance and dissolution—powers that most engaged the Hindu religious imagination.

What **other early scriptures** are especially important for Hindus?

Over a span of perhaps two thousand years (c. 3000–1000 B.C.E., according to some Indian scholars), Hindu ritual specialists produced a substantial body of sacred literature by way of commentary and reflection on the Vedas. The earliest of these works were manuals for priests, or Brahmanas, each attached to one of the four Vedas. These

Brahmanas elaborated on the mythic stories to which the Vedic hymns often had made only passing allusions, expanding on the tradition much as the early Jewish rabbis had developed the oral Torah. The Brahmanas served the practical purpose of recording for posterity precise directions for correct ritual performance. Still another layer of scriptural development gave rise to a series of works called Aranyakas, "Forest Treatises." Composed by and for hermits, these texts offered further commentary on the Vedas meant to foster the contemplative life. Aranyakas were connected with the Brahmanas much as the Brahmanas were linked to the various Vedas. With their emphasis on inward reflection, the Aranyakas signal an important turn away from the ancient Vedic and Brahmanical reliance on external ritual. Another type of sacred text called the Upanishads evolved from about 1500 to 500 B.C.E. The name *upa-ni-shad* means, loosely, "sitting at the feet of" a mentor. These remarkable documents, many in the form of a dialogue between teacher and student, reflect deeply on the nature of the divine and of the self. Life's true meaning rests not primarily in dealing with forces beyond human control, but in understanding both the ultimate causes of all things and the relationship of the self to those causes. The Upanishads represent major developments known collectively as Vedanta, the "end or culmination of the Vedas."

Major Hindu Scriptures

Shruti ("heard")

Four Vedas: Rig, Sama, Yajur, and Atharva

Brahmanas (ritual manuals)

Aranyakas (forest treatises)

Upanishads (theological and philosophical reflections on the Vedas)

Smriti ("remembered")

Epics: huge, poetic compositions still reenacted, including Ramayana (story of Rama's quest to recover his wife Sita, abducted by the demon Ravana); Mahabharata (India's national epic); and Bhagavad Gita (now part of the Mahabharata and sometimes called the Fifth Veda)

Puranas: mythic narratives of the principal deities

Sutras: commentary on earlier scriptures

Shastras: treatises of religious law

Agamas: Shaivite (tantras) and Vaishnavite (samhitas) sectarian texts

How did **Hinduism** become a **religion of the masses**?

For as long as several millennia, earlier forms of the greater Hinduism apparently limited direct involvement in religious ritual to a kind of religious elite. Full participation was open for many centuries only to the various ranks of priestly ritual specialists. Even after the climate began to change in the Upanishadic period, religion remained

A performance of "Nakrathundi," which is based on the Puranas and other ancient literature. Jayantha, son of the deity Indra, is depicted at left. (Zzvet / Shutterstock.com.)

the province of professionally religious types who wrote the Upanishads, as well as independent-minded seekers who founded the early ascetic and philosophical movements. With the growth of mythic religious texts, called the Puranas, came parallel developments in a type of devotional theism called *bhakti* that no longer regarded the ultimate spiritual forces as fearsome and impersonal. Nor was spiritual realization reserved only for the few who had access to the lofty speculation of the Upanishads and the teachers. The Puranas talked of divine involvement in human affairs in ways that appealed to the imagination of ordinary people. Eighteen major Puranas, six dedicated to each of the three principal popular names and forms of God (Shiva, Vishnu, and the Goddess or *Shakti*), opened up a world in which the humblest person could approach God and be assured of acceptance. Out of that broader movement have grown the many denominations and sects that comprise popular Hinduism today. Major sub-communities are named for the principal deities they worship: devotees of Shiva are called Shaivas; devotees of Vishnu, Vaishnavas; and devotees of the female deities, Shaktas.

What **sacred source**s do the various **denominations rely on**?

During the so-called Classical Period (500 B.C.E.–500 C.E.) especially, various denominations developed their own distinctive sacred texts called *sutras* ("threads, aphorisms"), *shastras* ("treatise, rule"), and *agamas* ("what has come down"). *Sutras* often take the form of commentary on earlier major texts and are major sources for the six philosophical schools called the *darshanas*. Some philosophical texts are called *shastras,* but this category is best known as a vehicle for treatments of religious law. *Agamas* belonging to the various sects often include various types of material ranging from the mythic to the epic to the philosophical. Shaivites generally use the term *agama* to describe their twenty-eight canonical works, while Vaishnavite communities often call their unique scriptures *samhitas* ("collections") and *Shakta* groups prefer the term *Tantra*.

Was Hinduism ever **identified** with any **political regimes**?

Several important royal dynasties that identified themselves with Hindu tradition ruled various parts of India and southeast Asia over a span of about two thousand years. In some cases the dynasties bolstered their claims to political legitimacy by appealing to the concept of divine kingship. A series of fairly short-lived early Hindu dynasties, the Nanda (362–322 B.C.E.), Maurya (322–185 B.C.E.), and Shunga (185–73 B.C.E.), evidently faltered as a result of their failure to keep priestly members of the royal court happy with the balance of power. The Gupta dynasty (320–647 C.E.) was the first major success story, taking control over the northern two-thirds of India. Promoting devotion to Vishnu especially, the Guptas oversaw what some call a renaissance of Hindu culture. After the fall of the Guptas, several Hindu dynasties ruled various segments of central and southern India. Among the most important were the Tamil kingdoms of the south—especially the Pallavas (c. 250–750 C.E.), Chalukyas (450–1189 C.E.), and the Cholas (minor power from 100 C.E., expanded 800–1300 C.E.)—all of which were major patrons of religious art and architecture.

Were there ever **Hindu kingdoms outside** of **India**?

Hindu kingdoms, mostly Shaivite in orientation, had significant influence on parts of southeast Asia, giving rise to the names Indo-China and Indonesia. The kingdom of Champa held sway over most of Vietnam from 150 to 1471 C.E., while several other dynasties arose in Cambodia in the second century and expanded their control over Laos and Thailand from 800 to 1200 C.E. During that same period, Hindu monarchies took root in Java and Sumatra, the principal islands of Indonesia, as well as in Malaysia. For nearly two centuries, Hinduism was a major influence throughout Indonesia, until its political patrons succumbed to Muslim invasions in the early sixteenth century.

Champa kingdom ruins in Vietnam showing linga-yoni in foreground, indicating that the complex was dedicated to Shiva.

189

The remnants of the southeast Asian Hindu kingdoms took refuge on the island of Bali, where many still practice Hinduism.

Timeline of Hindu/Indian History

Date	Event
5500–2500 B.C.E.	Growth of civilization in the Indus Valley
1700–1100 B.C.E.	Composition of the Vedic Samhitas
900–500 B.C.E.	Composition of later parts of the Samhitas, of the Brahmanas and early Upanishads
500–200 B.C.E.	Epic poems: Mahabharata (Bhagavad Gita), Ramayana
327–325 B.C.E.	Alexander the Great invades India
322 B.C.E.	Chandragupta founds Mauryan Empire
100–100 C.E.	Rise of *bhakti* literature
300–600 C.E.	Composition of some Puranas in their present form
647 C.E.	Fall of Gupta Empire
680 C.E.	Flourishing of Tamil *bhakti* movement
788–820 C.E.	Shankara, theology of non-duality (*advaita*)
1017–1138 C.E.	Ramanuja, theology of qualified non-duality (*vishisht-advaita*)
1175 C.E.	First Muslim empire in India
1486–1533 C.E.	Chaitanya, saint of Krishna-*bhakti*
1498 C.E.	Vasco da Gama visits India
1526 C.E.	Rise of Muslim Mughal Dynasty
1653 C.E.	Taj Mahal completed by Mughal Shah Jahan
1657 C.E.	Muslim Dara Shikoh translates Upanishads into Persian
1690 C.E.	British found Calcutta, East India Company
1707 C.E.	Mughal power into decline
1836–1886 C.E.	Ramakrishna, "All religions can lead to God" realization
1857 C.E.	British put down rebellion, inaugurate British Raj
1869–1948 C.E.	Mohandas Karmachand "Mahatma" Gandhi
1885 C.E.	Indian National Congress
1947 C.E.	Indian Independence, partition of West and East Pakistan
1971 C.E.	Separation of Bangladesh from Pakistan, both Muslim states

Have there ever been any **reform movements** within Hinduism?

Since the early nineteenth century, various important reform movements have addressed the need to reinterpret ancient tradition for modern times. The *Brahmo Samaj* (Society of God) denounced the practice of widow suicide (sati) and promoted a monotheistic understanding of Hindu faith. Its successor organization, the *Sadharan Brahmo Samaj* (Universal Society of God), took aim at the caste system and looked for ways to update the tradition without having to resort to European ways of thinking. Some reformers, such as Ramakrishna (1836–86) and his disciple Vivekandanda (1863–1902), offered fresh interpretations of both *bhakti* and Vedanta that they hoped would appeal to the world beyond India. Twentieth-century successors to those pioneering reformers included Shri Aurobindo (1872–1950) and Mahatma Gandhi (1869–1948). Both studied in England and returned with distinctive views on how modern Hindus might revitalize their traditions. Shri Aurobindo proposed a form of "modernist" interpretation incorporating elements of European philosophy, and Gandhi emphasized simplicity of life and taught nonviolent means of political protest. Both men founded *ashrams*, quiet places in which spiritual seekers could find spiritual refuge.

RELIGIOUS BELIEFS

Is there a **Hindu creed**? What are the most **basic Hindu beliefs**?

Hindu tradition has not historically developed the kinds of creedal formulations so important in some other communities of faith. But a number of important themes run like brightly colored threads through the fabric of the greater Hinduism. Bear in mind that some of the various denominations and smaller sects interpret these themes in different ways. Material and spiritual existence unfolds in a series of unimaginably long cycles governed by a cosmic Law called *dharma* (from a root that means "to hold together"). That Law manifests itself on the level of individual beings as a potentially endless succession or cycle of birth and rebirth. The human predicament consists in getting stuck in that cycle, which is called *samsara*, "cosmic flow, endless wandering." Each being's earthly existence or lifespan comes to an end at death or dissolution, but the state of each one's soul at that moment determines whether that being remains caught in the cycle. All action (*karma*) has spiritual consequences. To break the cycle, human beings must gradually purify all actions of ego-centeredness, seeking to act only in accord with their personal *dharma*. According to the law of cause and effect, or *karma*, all deeds done out of inappropriate motivation chain the individual to the wheel of *samsara*.

Hindu tradition offers various ways of ridding one's actions of all ulterior motive and progressing toward the ultimate goal of liberation (*moksha*) from the endless cycle of rebirths. Those methods or paths include the classical mode of ritual action, the quest for knowledge and full realization of the ultimate truths of existence, and personal devotion to a manifestation of God. Beginning with the earliest scriptures, the Vedas, and extending through subsequent unfoldings of ever-new sources of divine truth as explained by generations of teachers, Hindu tradition offers access to knowledge of God and hence to the hope of salvation.

Are **doctrine and dogma** important to Hindus?

Over the centuries many important Hindu philosophers and theologians have devised elaborate and sophisticated systems of thought. Those systems are an attempt to structure essential elements of ancient tradition so as to show their internal logic and

191

consistency. Their teachings have had the force of doctrine for those who subscribe to the various schools of thought, but they do not constitute a body of authoritative dogma as such. The vast majority of Hindus grow up hearing about the basic themes described above. Their parents and teachers pass along the traditional stories about the forces of good and evil. But few devout Hindus think of religious belief in terms of formal assent to a body of officially defined truths. Most Hindus have a sense of great flexibility with respect to the content of the faith.

Do Hindus really believe in and **worship many gods**?

Hindu tradition uses language and symbolism that seems at first glance to suggest what is called polytheism, worship of many deities. Most Hindus, however, will tell you they believe in God, one transcendent spiritual reality. Since human beings are incapable of grasping the fullness of divine truth in anything like a comprehensive and definitive way, believers are left with a basic choice: Either they keep quiet about matters of faith and belief altogether, since the realities will forever elude ordinary language and symbolism, or they indulge in ordinary forms of expression, ever aware that those forms will never be adequate.

Hindu tradition has become a monument to the second option and the world of religious belief is all the richer for that. But why not opt for mute adoration? Why choose to complicate matters by multiplying hopelessly inadequate attempts at capturing divinity? Because that is an important part of being human. People need to talk about the sources of greatest wonderment as well as about their hopes and fears and suffering. At the risk of being accused of idolatry, a charge non-Hindus often level at them, Hindus acknowledge a fundamental need for imagery. All religious traditions finally do something similar. Even the traditions that sound the loudest alarm about the dangers of idolatry, Judaism and Islam, for example, use extensive and vivid verbal imagery to say the ineffable. Most Hindus, like certain Christian and Buddhist communities, for example, include a wide array of visual expression side by side with the verbal. Words can become idols, too.

What do Hindus believe about **ultimate spiritual reality** or **God**?

Hindu conceptions about God are among the most expansive and arresting in the history of religion. Scores of "names and forms" (*nama/rupa*) make up the enormous Hindu theological lexicon. Some names and forms emphasize divine majesty and power, others divine beauty and attractiveness. For Hindus generally, the purpose of religious belief and devotion is to cultivate a relationship with the Holy, the source of benevolence and blessing as well as of death and difficulty. Most of all, God is a mystery that is willing to be unveiled. Hindu theologians define two broad ways of talking about the God, Ultimate Reality, called Brahman in Sanskrit. God is beyond all imagining and impossible to shoehorn into humanly devised words and concepts. But believers can still refer to the Ultimate Reality in a roundabout way, hinting at what God is by saying explicitly what God is not. From this perspective, theologians call

God "Brahman without Qualities" (*Nir-guna Brahman*). But the "negative way" of thinking about God can be very abstract and difficult. Human beings generally need something more concrete, something that engages the feelings and imagination as well as the logic-bound mind. Hindu tradition therefore acknowledges that one can approach the truth by considering God as "Brahman with Qualities" (*Sa-guna Brahman*). In this approach, one always has to keep in mind that those qualities are remote approximations at best, and ultimately just a concession to the human need to imagine the unimaginable.

How did the overall structure of the **Hindu pantheon evolve**?

First, divine personalities that would eventually become major deities (especially Vishnu and Shiva) emerged from among the Vedic pantheon. Ancient lore from all over India contributed to the gradual "fleshing out" of stories of the major deities. Meanwhile stories of other "names and forms" of lesser divine beings continued to develop a life of their own in various regions of India. As major communities of belief formed around stories of Vishnu, Shiva, and their various female counterparts, larger mythic frameworks evolved to integrate narratives of lesser deities into those of the greater

deities. For example, Vaishnavite tradition developed the structure of Vishnu's "Ten Avatars" or "descents." That mythic framework brought together an astonishing assortment of descriptions of God's involvement in human affairs.

The first three avatars are nonhuman divine interventions in the birth of the cosmos: Matsya (the fish), Kurma (the tortoise), and Varaha (the boar). Three avatars represent divine confrontation with evil and demonic forces: Nara-simha (the man-lion), Vamana (the dwarf), and Parashurama (Rama with the Axe). The two most popular avatars are those of Rama and Krishna, heroes both on and off the field of combat, whose consorts Sita and Radha are of nearly equal importance. As a statement of its even greater inclusiveness, the list includes the Buddha himself. Avatar number ten is the dark and mysterious Kalki, the only avatar yet to come, whose task is to bring an apocalyptic end to the present age.

Krishna visiting Radha, awaiting word from her maiden, Kangra school painting, India, c. 1820–1825. (Photo courtesy of the St. Louis Art Museum. W. K. Bixby Oriental Art Purchase Fund.)

193

Integrating Shaiva imagery is the concept of Shiva's "holy family." Both Vishnu and Shiva have their consorts (Lakshmi or Bhu, and Parvati, Durga, or Kali respectively). Unlike Vishnu, Shiva has children. Stories of Ganesha and Skanda brought these formerly local or regional deities into the larger structure of the divine family. Finally, a concept known as the "triple form" (*tri-murti*) unites the whole complex of images by identifying a "trinity" of divine roles. Brahma, never an object of great popular devotion, creates. Vishnu sustains. And Shiva destroys, paving the way for renewal of the endless cosmic process.

What are some of the **principal "names and forms" of God**?

One of the first questions non-Hindus ask about the imagery of Hinduism's deities is: "Why the multiple limbs and nonhuman features?" Hindu tradition answers: "Why not?" Since no one can know definitively and in detail what God looks like or how God operates, God sees fit to allow human beings to describe the indescribable. God is by definition beyond anything in human experience, so Hindu tradition often depicts the deity in clearly nonhuman form.

Names of the deities always have some symbolic meaning. For example, Vishnu comes from a root that means "to pervade," alluding to the divine omnipresence. Shiva means "auspicious." Traditional sources often pun on the name, suggesting that without the "i" in Shakti (Shiva's feminine side) Shiva would be *Shava*, "corpse." Ganesha's name is a compound meaning "Lord of the [attendant Vedic deities called] *ganas*." Shiva's terrifying feminine side is called Kali, "Dark."

As for their multiple forms, Hindu images of deity remind believers of the infinite variety that makes God God. As a reminder of the perfect balance of energies, most male deities have a female counterpart. A popular image of Shiva in both painting and sculpture depicts the deity as "half-woman lord," one side of the body male and the other displaying the features of Shiva's consort Parvati. As a reminder of God's complete dominion over all forces and conditions, including those most of us would rather not have to deal with, Hindu deities appear in shocking and even terrible forms as well as in attractive and approachable aspects. There is a hierarchy among divine beings, a ranking that naturally develops within each denomination or sect. Among Shaivas, Shiva is the supreme deity to whom all the others defer. For Vaishnavas, Vishnu or one of the Avatars heads the list.

Major Hindu Deities

Principal Vedic Gods

Agni, god of fire and sacrifice
Indra, god of sky and war
Varuna, upholder of cosmic order

Surya, the sun

Vishnu, consorts and avatars

Principal consorts: Lakshmi, Shri, Bhu

Ten Avatars: Matsya (the fish), Kurma (the tortoise), Varaha (the boar), Nara-simha (the man-lion), Vamana (the dwarf), Parashurama (Rama who wields the axe), Rama (with his consort Sita), Krishna (with his consort Radha), Buddha, Kalki (the dark horse who brings on the end of the age)

Shiva, consorts and offspring

Principal consorts: Parvati and Uma (gracious manifestations), Kali and Durga (fearsome manifestations)

Children of Shiva: Ganesha (elephant-headed deity, lord of life's transitions), Skanda (also known as Karttikeya and Murugan)

Do Hindus believe in **miracles**?

A distinctive quality of Hindu belief generally is that all things, whether spiritual or material, result from the divine play or *lila*. God brings all things into being, sustains them for a time, then withdraws them from the realm of human experience, not by laboring, but as a kind of divine entertainment. That does not mean that God is cynical or cruel, dangling his creatures like so many marionettes. It means only that what we know as our "world" is the product of God's delight. Hindu tradition teaches that human beings are the beneficiaries of that delight. We are, in other words, invited to the party. The concept of miracle presupposes that human beings already know the limits of ordinary causality. From the Hindu perspective, that assumption is the height of arrogance because it suggests that human beings have things pretty well figured out—such as the causes and cures of disease, the roots of evil, and the wellsprings of good. One of the many aspects of the Hindu tradition's genius, and one of its major contributions to humanity, is that it refuses to close the door on surprise. All things, not merely the odd event that appears to defy the laws of nature, are cause for wonder. There is but one great miracle: God has chosen eternally to pour out the divine essence in its countless forms—and enjoys doing so. What a gift of the ultimate perspective on life, to see it all as part of one great marvel and learn not to take oneself so seriously.

Are there **mythic elements** in Hindu tradition?

Hinduism's sacred texts comprise one of the world's greatest treasure troves of myth. Non-Hindus, especially "westerners" who find themselves inclined to discount Hindu tradition as "just a collection of stories," are shutting the door to that watershed of insight called the imagination. All religious traditions build on a master story composed of accounts about how the world came to be, what human beings are all about, and the relationship between humankind and the greater Being or Power responsible for the shape of things. Some traditions, such as the Abrahamic faiths, wrap themselves around narratives they call their sacred history. Other traditions, such as Hinduism and Buddhism, for example, consider human history much too small a stage for any drama under the direction of the Ultimate Reality. History begins, stretches out, and comes to a definitive end. But the view that history is all about what "actually happened" while myth is purely "imaginary" is seriously flawed.

History and myth are two very different ways to answer the big questions about human life. Sacred history tells how God has worked in the world by identifying certain events as the result of divine intervention. Mythic narrative tells the story of the otherness of Ultimate Reality by stretching the limits of the imagination. History works from the ground up, so to speak, and turns around the power of memory, while myth starts with mystery and cultivates the human capacity for wonder. What non-Hindus may be tempted to criticize as a weakness in Hindu tradition, Hindus regard as their tradition's great strength. Both approaches yield important forms of narrative theology. Far from being simply contradictory, myth and history complement each other.

Early Hinduism and Early Buddhism Compared

	Hinduism	Buddhism
Scriptures	Divinely inspired	Words of Buddha
Deity	Nearly ultimate power	No immediate consequence
Society	Caste	Not stratified, *Sangha*
Individual	Eternal *Atman* (self/soul)	*Anatta* (no indestructible self)
Karma/Action	Without thought of results	Unattached, compassionate
Dharma/Law	Cosmic/individual rule	Teaching of Buddha
Samsara/World	Cycle of transmigration	Rebirth of consciousness
Sacred Ritual	God-oriented sacrifice/devotion	Meditation/Buddha as teacher
Proximate Goal	Improve one's station	Reduce attachment/suffering
Ultimate Goal	*Moksha*, end of rebirth	*Nirvana*, end of suffering

Do Hindus believe in **angels**?

Nothing in Hindu lore corresponds exactly to the spiritual beings known in some traditions as angels. But a host of lesser deities (called *devatas*) and spirits make up the entourages of many of the major deities. These versatile beings are often grouped in families whose mission is to do their deity's every bidding. Like the angels in some traditions, lesser deities fill the spiritual air around the major deities. In popular spirituality devotees often consider the need to render an account to these divine vanguards nearly equal to their duties to the central deity, for the lesser deities preside over essential areas of life such as fertility, childbirth, and disease. Those that wield more positive energies have their darker counterparts that need to be appeased in order to hold evil at bay. Among the more common beings of this rank are the "door guardians" (*dvarapalas*) who keep undesirable elements out of temples and away from the shrines of the deities to whom they are assigned. Door guardians are often depicted with iconographic clues very similar to those of their major deities. So, for example, guardians in a Vaishnavite temple typically have four arms and are equipped with Vishnu's conch shell, discus, and mace.

Do Hindus believe in **devils**?

No single personification of evil functions in Hindu tradition quite like the Satan of other traditions. Multiple embodiments of malice, perversity, and general negativity are called *asuras,* or demons. Ancient myths tell of the ongoing struggle between the *devas,* deities, and the demons for control of the cosmos. Originally the demons were not necessarily considered altogether evil. Even their generic names are ambiguous:

Stone devatas in Angkor Wat, Cambodia.

deva is from the same root as "devil," while *asura* shows up in the name of the main Iranian deity, Ahura mazda. Both deities and demons descended from Prajapati, Lord of Living Things. Demons were at first ethically on a par with the gods. But the gods generally managed to win more battles than their siblings. Eventually the deities came to be known as more clever and more truthful. Finally, the gods achieved immortality while preventing the demons from winning that prize. Demons retained the ability to assume virtually any form in their attempts to disrupt cosmic affairs. Powerful people intent on evil could enlist the aid of demons to carry out their wicked deeds. Some demons came to represent impersonal negative qualities, such as ignorance. Lesser but still troublesome forces known as *bhutas* remain important in the lives of many villagers. *Bhutas* are the spirits of those who died violently, or too young, or after betrothal but before marriage, for example. Resentful and frustrated, they wander about harassing the living unless appeased by proper rituals. Hindus believe that ultimately the divine power will overcome all demonic forces.

How does Hindu tradition talk about the **origins of the universe**?

Early Vedic hymns as well as later sources reflect deeply and evocatively on the marvels of the world. They propose tentative possibilities as to how it came to be. Perhaps

Dreams and visions are often described as the means by which particularly holy individuals receive special knowledge or responsibilities. Spiritually advanced members of different denominations describe experiences in which their particular "chosen deity" appears and manifests his or her divine form. The deity's desires for the founding of a temple in a particular place are often communicated in dreams or visions. Traditional Hindu psychology considers dreaming one of the four ordinary states of consciousness. Founders of various denominations and sects often report dreams or visions as the impetus for a personal conversion or for proclaiming a new teaching.

it all began as an embryo or fertile egg, out of which all the divine powers emerged from potentiality into action, separating the gold of Heaven from the silver of Earth. From the egg's outer membrane arose the mountains, from the inner membranes the clouds, and from its veins the rivers. Perhaps there was once, before time began, an ocean of milk on which the serpent of eternity floated in infinite silence. And as Lord Vishnu ("Pervasive") rested undisturbed in the serpent's coils, from the divine body emerged a great fecund lotus flower, unfolding to release the creative power (called Brahma). Looking in all four directions Brahma created the world, thereafter to close again with the lotus blossom, and reopen in a new cycle.

Perhaps the world came to be when the gods offered sacrifice to the Ultimate Reality. From the sacred body of the Primal Person offered in sacrifice came all the elements of the universe. From his eyes the heavenly lights, from his nostrils the winds, from his mouth the priestly caste, from his arms the soldier, until all things originated from the divine body. Or perhaps the creative power was unleashed when the deity entered into ascetic meditation. Focusing the divine energy inward, he generated such spiritual fire that it could no longer be contained and burst forth in creation. But an even greater mystery than the "how" of creation is the "why." Ultimately one can only stand in awe, admitting that the mystery may forever elude the human capacity to know.

What **solutions** to the **human predicament** does Hindu tradition propose?

Hindus seek the ultimate spiritual goal of liberation through any of four traditional ways or paths called *margas,* "methods of seeking" or *yogas,* "joining by means of discipline." The most ancient and slowest method is that of ritual action, *karma.* Originally associated with scrupulous fulfillment of the prescriptions of Vedic ritual practice, *karma* is kept within reach of contemporary Hindus by interpreting it as "unselfish service." In that sense the way of action recommends itself to all, even in the absence of a vital tradition of ritual sacrifice.

The second path begins with the conviction that ignorance causes suffering. Intuitive experiential knowledge (*jñana*) is available through various intellectual and meditative disciplines associated with a variety of philosophical approaches called *darshanas* ("views"). Most of all, the way of knowledge seeks the full realization of the perfect oneness of all reality and the illusory nature of our instinctive conviction that individuality of persons and multiplicity of all things is the substance of life. It is a difficult and abstract method attractive to relatively few people. Its best-known form is that of Shankara's Advaita Vedanta school.

Closely associated with the way of knowledge is a path that uses the formal disciplines popularly known as "*yoga.*" Proceeding from the conviction that suffering is the result of physical and mental distraction, meditational yoga combines various physical practices (*hatha yoga*) designed to control one's physiological states, with belief in divine assistance toward higher contemplative states (*raja yoga*). Far more popular and accessible is the way of devotion or *bhakti* ("participation"). Whereas the way of knowledge seeks realization of a union that already exists in an impersonal Ultimate Reality, the way of devotion seeks to cultivate the union of the two distinct parties to the divine–human relationship. *Bhakti* (from a root meaning "to participate") connotes dedication to a personal God whose love, mercy, and grace elicit a response of complete faith and surrender. It proceeds from the conviction that suffering arises out of separation from one's divine source and goal. The devotee approaches God in full confidence of divine protection and the hope of salvation.

Do Hindus believe in the concept of **salvation**?

Most Hindus prefer the way of devotion because it is so concrete and personal. *Bhakti* offers the assurance of divine aid in all of life's difficulties, as well as cause for rejoicing in better times. Seekers who choose any of the classical spiritual paths are aware that human beings are ever in need of help from sources beyond themselves. But the notion of salvation assisted by divine grace is especially strong in popular theistic or devotional Hinduism. Even in the denominations that teach a modified form of predestination, such as those of Madhva and Vallabha, grace is a central feature of *bhakti*. Since the human soul is, so to speak, naturally divine, grace is the power that refreshes and renews the soul in its original state. Hindus, like members of various other major traditions, have held differing views as to how divine grace works. A particularly vivid pair of images characterizes one view as that of the "Cat School," another that of the "Monkey School." According to the Cat School, divine grace is all sufficient and does not depend at all on human action. Mother cats carry their kittens around by picking them up with their teeth. According to the Monkey School, human beings must cooperate in the saving action of divine grace. Mother monkeys rescue their babies from danger, but the baby first climbs aboard and holds tight. The two schools therefore represent different views as to the relationship between divine power and human action.

What are Hinduism's **Principal Spiritual Paths**?

Ancient tradition distinguishes among several key spiritual paths or *margas*. First and most fundamental is that of *karma,* action: proper ritual and ethical action as a means to spiritual progress, including purification of one's deeds through detachment from the fruits of one's actions. More demanding is the path of *jñana* or knowledge: attainment of intuitive or mystical understanding of the essential unity of all reality, resulting from a meditative approach to the scriptures and wisdom traditions. But perhaps the most broadly pursued as a mode of popular spirituality is the way of devotion or *bhakti*: "participation" in the divine life through devotion to a chosen manifestation of the deity, complete emotional attachment to the chosen deity, and unselfish service to God.

What are some basic Hindu **ethical considerations**?

Hindu tradition describes a range of morally and religiously acceptable goals or motives for action. What matters most is not the substance of the particular type of goal, but the quality of one's intentions. All good things in life are gifts of God. One has only to learn how best to use and value them. In the greater scheme of things, three of the four major goals are means rather than ends in themselves. Even so, a devout Hindu can pursue them with vigor and determination, as long as the pursuit is balanced and not obsessive. Most fundamental is the goal of *dharma,* the quest for one's own individual ethical calling in accord with the cosmic Law that holds all things together. Personal justice and righteousness are the cardinal virtues. But wealth, material success, power, and social status (*artha*) are also worthy goals, so long as one keeps them in perspective. People who use their worldly success in ethically laudable ways are exercising responsible stewardship and can make wonderful things happen for the benefit of many.

In addition, a devout Hindu can enjoy to the full all of life's legitimate pleasures (*kama*) associated with culture, the arts, sexuality, and family life. This traditional teaching undercuts the common stereotype of Hinduism as world-rejecting and self-denying asceticism. On the other hand, the opposite stereotype that identifies Hinduism as the kind of wild-eyed lust sometimes associated with the Kama Sutra is equally inappropriate. Ultimately, Hindu tradition teaches, the sincere seeker will find that none of the first three goals offers permanent satisfaction. What remains is the quest for final liberation from the enslavement that goes with even well-moderated attachments. *Moksha,* meaning "release," is the only goal worthy of being considered an end in itself. Most people will spend many lifetimes striving for it.

What **other ideals** does the Hindu tradition **recommend**?

A classical formulation of the ideal life cycle is called the "four stages of life." It applies almost exclusively to males, but the implications for women are fairly clear. The traditional system is called *varnashramadharma,* the "law (*dharma*) of caste (*varna*) and

View of the seventeenth-century Temple of Minakshi, Madurai, south India. Massive royal gateways define the inner (mostly covered) courtyards, and the two spires protruding through the roof stand over the main "womb chambers." (Photo courtesy of Michael Harter, S.J.)

life stage (*ashrama*)." Upper-caste Hindu males begin the cycle as students, in a stage between the ages of twelve and twenty-four. Under the tutelage of a guru young men learn the basic sacred traditions, rituals, and sacred texts. From ages twenty-four to forty-eight they become "householders," marrying and raising a family according to conventional norms. During these first two stages, men seek religious fulfillment by turning outward and engaging their world with extroverted energy and drive. At forty-eight a man enters into the stage of a "forest-dweller" or "senior mentor" to younger men. Some actually move toward a life of greater solitude during this stage, even if they do not head for a hermitage in the forest. Some men past the age of seventy-two enter the stage of the renunciant, or *sannyasi*. They formally set aside as many ordinary ties to their former lives as possible, leaving behind wealth as well as material responsibility in quest of self-realization. Both of the latter two stages call for increasing introspection and time for personal prayer and devotion. Though fewer individuals follow the four stages formally now than in the past, the cycle remains a traditional ideal and a useful map of spiritual progress for those who choose to pursue it.

What do Hindus believe about **life after death**?

At the heart of Hindu belief about the nature of human life is a notion called metempsychosis, also called reincarnation or transmigration of soul. Life is an infinite continuum punctuated by episodes of embodiment. Death is therefore the opposite of birth, not of life. One can escape the cycle of birth and death by liberating the soul, freeing the self from all attachments. According to the law of karma, human beings always get what they wish for—in spades: If my every effort in this life is the selfish acquisition of wealth or power or pleasure, chances are I will die wanting more. Unsatisfied desire is a form of energy so potent that it keeps the self ensnared in the bonds of attachment that ensure the soul will experience yet another embodiment in some form or another. Hindus call this potentially endless cycle of rebirths *samsara*.

Does that mean Hindus **do not believe in Heaven or Hell**?

Traditional Hindu cosmologies speak of three realms of existence or *lokas*. One scheme describes an "in-between realm" (*antarloka*), where individual souls abide both during sleep and between incarnations. This reflects the persistence of important features of ancient Vedic views of the cosmos. A version of Hell called *naraka* (literally, "referring to humankind") is a thoroughly unpleasant lower part of the *antarloka* that functions rather like a Purgatory. In any of its seven (or even as many as twenty-one) levels souls can overcome through suffering some of the effects of bad *karma*. A multilevelled region called *anandloka* ("realm of bliss"), also called *svarga* ("region of light"), is roughly equivalent to a paradise or Heaven. It is a temporary abode in which people who have died approaching liberation acquire knowledge that can assist them toward greater spiritual progress in their next life. Hindu cosmology includes multiple levels, both in this in-between realm and in the uppermost realms beyond that reserved for those who have achieved *moksha*. Most Hindus regard the intermediate equivalents of Heaven and Hell as temporary, although some smaller sects teach the existence of more or less permanent abodes of punishment in the next life.

What do Hindus think about **history and time**?

Imagine a bird flying past the Himalayas every hundred years, brushing the mountain peaks with the silk scarf it holds in its beak. What we call history is the time it would take that bird to wear the mountains flat. And that would be only an infinitesimal fraction of divine time. History is an infinite cycle made up of smaller, measurable cycles of creation and destruction, but even the smaller cycles are unimaginably long. Hindu myth says that God, manifested as Brahma the creator, unfolds the material world over and over. Each lifetime of Brahma lasts a hundred divine years. Each day in the life of the creator deity is called a *kalpa,* lasting 4,320,000,000 years. Each *kalpa,* or great age (*mahayuga*), in turn is made up of four ages or aeons called *yugas*. The present cycle of human history began with the first *yuga,* a time of order and peace when the cosmic law (*dharma*) kept evil in check. During the second age disorder entered history. *Dharma* diminished, as did the span of human life. There followed a third age, when evil gained still greater strength and dharma weakened. Social fragmentation gave rise to the caste system and attempts to gain power through ritual sacrifice. We are now in the fourth and bleakest age, a time of darkness and lawlessness destined to end in four hundred thousand years. Then, after a period of quiescence, all will begin again, another day in the life of Brahma.

Are there Hindu **fundamentalists**?

If fundamentalism may be defined as an aggressive and intolerant religious exclusivism, there are several manifestations of it in the history of Hinduism. A nineteenth-century reformist movement called the Arya Samaj (Society of Aryans) sought to cleanse modern Hindu thought and practice of unnecessary clutter that had contaminated the tradition over the centuries. The Society condemned not only Muslims and Christians but members of various Hindu denominations as well. To its great credit, the Arya Samaj attempted to make Hindu practice more egalitarian, giving women and socially marginal groups equal access. Another fundamentalist-style force in recent times has been the political faction called Bharatiya Janata or BJP. In 1992 the party supported agitation by the militant Vishva Hindu Parishad (Universal Hindu Assembly) to destroy a sixteenth-century mosque in Ayodhya. They wanted to replace the mosque with a temple to Rama and to rededicate the site as Rama's birthplace, which Muslims had desecrated centuries before. The VHP throws its considerable weight behind political candidates who promise to do whatever is necessary to keep power in the hands of Hindus.

What does Hindu tradition teach about **religion and violence**?

In most religious traditions, theology and associated images of deity are always about conceptions of ultimate power. In many traditions, power in turn invariably has something to do with how a deity deals with evil, and an important ingredient in Hinduism's various theologies is related to violence. Every deity's iconography includes some sort of "weapon," with which he or she dispatches demons and humans of ill intent. Such imagery has made its way more recently even into the Indian government's ways of describing devices clearly associated with at least potential violence. India's first military missile capable of delivering a nuclear warhead was named "Agni," after the Vedic god of fire. And its earliest nuclear reactor was explicitly designed to resemble the religious symbol of the mysterious power of the god Shiva and his female consort, the "linga/yoni."

On the other hand, many people have the general impression that Hinduism is perhaps as close to a nonviolent tradition

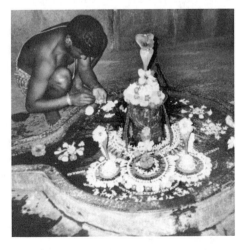

Hindu boy placing garlands around a *linga,* the principal aniconic symbol of Shiva. (Photo courtesy of Beata Grant.)

203

as one can imagine. Readers familiar with Dr. Martin Luther King, Jr., for example, may recall that he spoke of being especially influenced by Mahatma Gandhi's teachings on nonviolent resistance. Concern for *ahimsa* ("noninjury"), including respect for all forms of life, did indeed become an important theme in Hindu tradition following the rise of Buddhism and Jainism in the sixth and fifth centuries B.C.E. *Ahimsa* ranks first among a list of ten spiritual qualities, called *yamas* or "restraints," in the classical system of yoga attributed to Patañjali. Avoidance of all injury in word and deed began with the rejection of Vedic sacrifice—and as a central practice of small groups of ascetics—and grew to include the practice of vegetarianism.

However, alongside that nonviolent tradition, frank acknowledgment of the need for violent solutions to some problems has long been institutionalized in Hindu culture and has been a significant theme in some sacred texts. The second-highest rung in the traditional caste system is that of the Warrior class (*Kshatriya*). And the entire plot of the Bhagavad Gita revolves around a dilemma concerning the use of violence: a member of the *Kshatriya* caste hesitates when faced with joining battle with an army of his own relatives. His charioteer counsels him that he *must* fulfill his warrior duty (*dharma*) without sentimentality or concern for the "fruits of his action." That charioteer gradually reveals himself to be the god Krishna and counsels the warrior to devote himself entirely to Krishna and proceed with his duty—a truly shocking scenario from a religious perspective. When J. Robert Oppenheimer, known as "father of the atom bomb," observed the horrific power of the first nuclear weapon, he quoted Krishna in the Gita: "I am become death, destroyer of worlds."

Many important Hindu religious figures have struggled with how to interpret this sacred text. Perhaps most influential of all advocates of nonviolence, Mahatma Gandhi, insisted that the Gita was his favorite scripture. But in order to find meaning in it, he had to argue that the Gita's apparent mandate of violence must be understood metaphorically, using physical warfare as image for the internal struggle we all face, the imagery functioning merely to make the story more engaging. In this respect, Gandhi reflects the problem faced by major religious figures from many traditions—how to get around the obvious bias toward violence that one finds in so many sacred scriptures.

Select Glossary of Hindu Sanskrit Technical Terms

Ananda—"bliss, delight," a characteristic of ultimate reality and the liberated soul.

Artha—worldly success, wealth, influence; second of the four laudable goals of life.

Asana—a seated "posture" assumed as part of spiritual practice, as in yoga, and in sculpture.

Ashram(a)—a place of spiritual retreat; term for the four "stages of life."

Atman—the "indivisible" and indestructible spiritual center of each being, and the ultimate "Self" underlying all reality.

Avatar(a)—"crossing-over-downward," a deity's (especially Vishnu's) descent into the world of human experience.

Bhakti—"participation," devotional relationship to one's chosen deity, a major "path" to liberation.

Brahman—Ultimate Reality enveloping all appearances of multiplicity.

Brahmin—member of the priestly class.

Chit—spiritual "consciousness," a characteristic of ultimate reality and the liberated soul.

Darshan(a)—"seeing, being seen by" the deity, goal of devotional practice; philosophical school.

Dharma—that which holds all things together, the cosmic "law"; religio-social propriety, one's individual religious duty, and one of the four acceptable goals of life.

Dhyana—concentration, meditation, one of the eight "limbs" of yogic practice.

Guna—"strand," an attribute or quality according to one classic tripartite Hindu analysis of phenomenal reality into passion, goodness, darkness.

Guru—from a root meaning "grave, heavy," a spiritual guide or teacher.

Jati—"birth status," one of the distinguishing features in social stratification, often called "caste."

Jñana—"knowledge," insight into the spiritual meaning of things, one of the principal "paths" to liberation.

Kama—"pleasure," one of the four legitimate goals of life.

Karma—"action," ritual or ethical conduct and the consequences thereof, one of the traditional "paths" to liberation.

Marga—path, way, method of spiritual progress toward liberation.

Moksha—liberation from the round of rebirth, ultimate goal of Hindu spiritual practice.

Namarupa—"name form," a reference to the appearances under which the deity condescends to be known, out of deference to human need.

Puja—ritual worship of one's chosen deity, either at home or in a temple or other shrine.

Sadhu—"accomplished one," an individual who has achieved liberation in this life.

Samsara—"journeying," the endless round of rebirth from which Hindus seek to be free.

Sannyasi—renunciant, the fourth of the traditional life stages or *ashramas*.

Sat—"being," along with consciousness (*chit*) and bliss (*ananda*), one of the characteristics of Ultimate Reality.

Shakti—"feminine energy," generic name of female divine consorts.

Shruti—"heard," referring to the authoritative status of the earliest categories of sacred scriptures, the Vedas and Upanishads.

Smriti—"remembered," the later scriptures, including the epics and puranas, for example.

Varna—"color," referring to one of the four major traditional socio-religious distinctions: priest, warrior, merchant, peasant, popularly but erroneously understood as "caste."

Vedanta—"end of the Veda," originally referring to the Upanishads; a school of thought dedicated to the path of knowledge.

Yoga—"joining, harnessing," system of physical and spiritual disciplines practiced by a *yogi*.

SIGNS AND SYMBOLS

Are there any **signs or symbols** that might **identify an individual** as a Hindu?

A small dot on the forehead (called a *bindu* or *bindi*) is perhaps the most common individual symbol in Hinduism. Many Indian women wear a small round red dot in the middle of the forehead to indicate that they are married, and some wear a black dot to ward off evil prior to marriage. Some regard the red dot as a generic symbol of one's Hindu faith, as worn by both men and women. Hindus in Europe and the United States sometimes have difficulty deciding whether to wear the dot in public or whether to confine its use to worship. As with so many personal religious symbols, it has become associated with issues of religious distinctiveness and cultural assimilation. Some believe the dot alludes to Shiva's third eye, a symbol of wisdom and divine power. Shaivites often wear three parallel horizontal lines on the forehead, and often on the upper arms and chest as well. The marks are sometimes made with paint and sometimes with ash to symbolize cremation. Vaishnavites wear what appears to be a large *V* or double *V* on the forehead and sometimes on the upper arm.

What signs or symbols **distinguish Hindu religious specialists?**

Priests in most Hindu temples, whatever the denomination, generally wear a simple body wrap that covers one or both shoulders. Sometimes they will remove the upper wrap altogether. Priests may wear a white thread across the left shoulder, a symbol of initiation into the sacred scriptures. Some priests wear a set of beads (called a *mala,* or "rosary"), used to count in the repetition of sacred words or syllables, around the neck or wrist. Members of various monastic orders often wear a saffron or salmon-colored robe that is the "habit" or distinctive garb of the organization. Shaivite Sadhus sometimes carry the trident, a symbol sacred to Shiva.

Do Hindus mark their **sacred spaces** with any distinctive **signs and symbols?**

Shikhara ("mountain peak") over the womb chamber of Shiva, Temple of Minakshi, Madurai, southern India. (Photo courtesy of Michael Harter, S.J.)

Hindu temples are often very easily identified, especially if the sacred place has been built as such from the start, rather than occupying a structure originally designed for some other purpose. Two major architectural styles developed in India. The "Southern" style features three-tiered pyramidal spires (called *shikhara*) atop each of the temple's interior shrines or "womb chambers" (*garbha griha*). A monumental trapezoidal facade called a "royal gateway" (*raja gopuram*) typically rises thirty to fifty feet above the main roofline. Both the spires and the facade are nowadays generally finished in white, with small gold finials on top. Southern temples often house several shrines under a single flat roof, with the individual spires of the shrines protruding through the roof and visible to all who approach. The classic "Northern" style historically had a large outer unroofed enclosure, within which stood a series of separate ritual spaces arranged additively along a single east-west axis.

As in the southern style, the center of northern temples is always the shrine or womb chamber, typically a small dark room with only one door and a tall multitiered spire above. Attached to the shrine by a narrow passageway toward the east one might find a larger room for devotees to gather, and sometimes another, still larger, east of that dedicated to other ritual needs, such as ritual dancing. In other words, the various ritual functions the southern style puts together under one roof, the northern style arranges in more or less distinct spaces that look like small separate structures. Most of the Hindu temples built recently in the United States are in the southern style. The overall design is more convenient in multiseasonal climates and allows for a variety of shrines, so that one temple can serve the needs of members of various denominations.

Two sculpture-covered "royal gateways" at the Temple of Minakshi, Madurai. (Photo courtesy of Michael Harter, S.J.)

What sort of **symbols and signs** will I see in a **Hindu temple**?

First you will remove your shoes as a sign of respect for a holy place, and to help keep it clean, since worshippers often sit on the floor. Very near the door you will see an image or statue of the elephant-headed deity called Ganesha. One of Shiva's two sons, Ganesha is the guardian of openings, beginnings, and travelers, and he generally bestows blessings on worshippers as they enter. Even Vaishnavite temples usually have a Ganesha at the door. Along the side walls you may see smaller shrines containing images of deities important in one or another denomination but secondary to this particular temple's devotional focus. Straight ahead you will see the central shrine, perhaps flanked by a pair of subordinate shrines holding images of deities directly related to the one in the central shrine. For example, if the temple is primarily dedicated to a manifestation of Vishnu called Shri Venkateshvara (as are temples in Pittsburgh and St. Louis), flanking shrines might house Krishna and Radha on one side and Rama with wife Sita, brother Lakshmana, and the monkey assistant Hanuman on the other.

207

An eleventh century bronze of the goddess Parvati, consort and divine energy (*Shakti*) of Shiva, Chola period (c. 900–1200), Tanjore district, India. (The Saint Louis Art Museum.)

The subordinate shrines may have prominent spires somewhat shorter than that of the central shrine. If the temple serves a large and diverse community, other side rooms may be devoted to other deities. Vishnu's consort, Lakshmi, goddess of wealth and success, often has her own shrine, sometimes with a *shikhara,* whose external elevation is slightly lower than those of the central shrine and its flanking shrines. Another room might house one large and several smaller shrines dedicated to Shiva and his "holy family." In the main Shiva shrine you will see an abstract symbol of power and blessing called the *linga-yoni,* the principal aniconic symbol of Shiva. Alongside, smaller shrines will display images of Parvati, Shiva's wife, and their two sons, Ganesha and Skanda (also known as Karttikeya and Murugan). Many, if not all, images will be elaborately clothed and festooned with floral garlands. Decorative themes on the shrines might include images of guardian figures called "door-keepers" and other protective symbols that look like small lion faces.

How do Hindus use **statues** and other similar **visual imagery** in **worship**?

Sacred sculpture plays a central role in the overall symbolism of Hindu devotional ritual. Individual images (called *vigraha,* "something one can grasp") of each of the major deities are generally of granite or marble, though some are made of other materials. Sculptors follow principles laid down in medieval texts that stipulate in detail the proportions and features essential for each deity. Some regard dark stone as the ideal medium because it suggests infinite power and mystery. Images are not themselves deities, but merely specific places in which the deity condescends to dwell for the benefit of devotees. When devotees lavish ritual attention on the images, they acknowledge the sacred symbolized there, rather than any power inherent in the material image. Each major temple image resides in a cavelike shrine called the "womb chamber" (*garbha griha*) that offers an essential clue to the metaphorical purpose of sacred sculpture: Images represent the dark mystery of divine fecundity from which all things emerge. Central to image-based ritual is the notion of *darshan,* seeing and being seen by the deity. In a manner analogous to Eastern Christian use of icons, Hindu practice interprets the eyes as the central visual symbol in the relationship between the devotee and the ultimate object of devotion. God sees the individual as surely as the devotee sees God. It is neither magic nor simple idolatry, but an acknowledgment of the fundamental human need to pray with all the senses. Images offer devotees something to hold on to, a way of understanding.

What sort of **symbolism** is important in Hindu **religious sculpture and painting**?

Images of the deities convey their distinctive meanings through a combination of iconographic clues or themes. Here are some of the most important categories or types of imagery. Unusual physical features naturally strike the viewer immediately. They may include nonhuman appendages, multiple arms or faces, and stylized or highly exaggerated male or female characteristics. Features like these function as reminders of the "otherness" and mystery of the deity. Smaller distinctive bodily marks (the diamond on Vishnu's chest), along with items of clothing or ornament, are part of the standard repertoire. Posture and gesture are very important. Some deities are shown in a rigidly upright posture, but many popular images adopt the "triple bend" or S-curve posture that suggests warmth, attractiveness, and accessibility. Artists can choose from a wide range of hand gestures, but certain specific gestures are by convention associated with certain deities. They can communicate anything from reassurance to the wrath that awaits evildoers. The same is true of the various implements or devices symbolic of each deity's prerogatives. Weapons and musical instruments are the most common items of this type. Weapons remind devotees of the deity's protective power; musical instruments, of the divine power of enchantment. Deities often appear with their consorts, or female counterparts (Shiva with Parvati, Vishnu with Lakshmi, Krishna with Radha, Rama with Sita), and with their offspring (Shiva's Ganesha and Skanda), or assistants (Rama with Hanuman, and any number of deities with guardian figures). Finally, each of the major deities has his or her vehicle or mode of conveyance (Vishnu's eagle Garuda, for example), and these often appear in images.

What **vehicles do the gods use** to get around?

The principal "vehicles" (*vahana*) of the principal deities are as follows:

- Shiva: the bull Nandi
- Parvati: lion
- Durga: lion, tiger, or parrot
- Ganesha: mouse or rat
- Skanda: peacock
- Brahma: goose or swan
- Vishnu: the eagle Garuda or the serpent Ananta
- Lakshmi: owl

What are some **basic clues** about the **iconography** of the major deities?

Shiva Nataraja ("Dance King"), Chola Period, twelfth century, South India, bronze. His upper right hand holds the drum of creation, his upper left the fire of destruction. With his lower right hand he makes a gesture of reassurance, while his lower left points to the earth, where his left foot tramples on the demon of ignorance. The circle of flame recalls the world in flux. (Courtesy of the St. Louis Art.)

Walk through the Asian galleries of your local museum, or visit a Hindu temple, and chances are good that you will spot some of the following images. Shiva's main symbol is the short pillar-like object called the *linga* which, together with the female yoni, represents divine creative power. But you may also find Shiva Nataraja ("Dance King") surrounded by a ring of fire (cosmic flux) and trouncing the demon of ignorance. His upper right hand holds the drum whose sound is that of creation, his upper left the fire of destruction. His lower left points to the earth, the lower right raised in a gesture of reassurance. From his head flows the Ganges, whose fall to Earth Shiva breaks with his matted locks. You may find his beloved mount, the bull Nandi, nearby. Shiva may also appear seated with his very voluptuous wife, Parvati, and their very human-looking son Skanda. There Shiva will hold an axe and a deer as symbols of his lordship over nature. You may also see the combined male and female Shiva-Parvati called "Half-woman Lord." Their other son, Ganesha, is the one with the elephant head and pot belly. He holds a bowl of sweets in one hand, and in the other one of his own tusks, which he is about to hurl at the demon who made fun of him. His vehicle is a mouse or rat, an obvious dash of humor. Vishnu may appear alone or with his wife, Lakshmi. He typically carries the conch shell (capable of making a world-shuddering sound), the discus (a weapon for cutting enemies off at the knees), and the mace, while raising a fourth hand in reassurance. Vishnu's most popular avatar, Krishna, frequently plays his world-charming flute, with his legs crossed jauntily in a dance step. His beloved Radha often appears with him. Rama is the second most important avatar, recognizable by his bow when standing alone, but usually seen in company of his wife Sita, his brother Lakshmana, and their faithful monkey assistant Hanuman.

Have **relics** ever been part of Hindu practice?

Concern over the sacred remnants of human embodiments of holiness—often called relics—does not play as important a role in Hindu tradition as in, say, Christianity or Buddhism. One reason is that Hindu myth describes the whole Earth as sacred. All of creation is itself the body of God. With that kind of pervasive sense of holiness, reminders of the holiness of individual human beings are hardly necessary. Even so,

Hindu popular devotional practice displays an ample array of concrete symbols that function much the way relics do in other traditions. One fine example is the use of sacred footprints called *padukas*. Footprints of Vishnu often appear in paintings, small items of jewelry, and metal stamps with which devotees can apply inked impressions of the deity's two feet. Especially sacred are the feet and sandals of one's guru. Devotees sometimes gather to collect the water and other materials used to bathe either the holy one's feet, or, in his absence, an image of his feet called the *shri paduka*. Devotees often convey the *padukas* of famous saints on wagons in procession as they sing of their desire to be at sacred feet of the holy one.

What does the symbol called the swastika have to do with Hinduism?

The name *"swastika"* comes from a Sanskrit term that means "all is well." It is a

Ganesha, the half-elephant god, is the son of Parvati and Shiva.

symbol of auspiciousness and good fortune. The symbol may derive from a four-spoked wheel, possibly connected with the crossed firebrands of ancient Vedic sacrifice. Originally a solar symbol, the *swastika* was anciently associated with Vishnu, but eventually became important in Buddhism as well. Even though Shiva has been particularly connected with lunar symbolism, the *swastika* has become common in the iconographic repertoire of Shaivites too. *Swastikas* can appear to be spinning either to the right or to the left, and have accordingly been associated with either the so-called right- or left-handed sects of Shaktism and Tantrism. The female symbolism of the left-handed *swastika* was generally considered inauspicious. Nazi Germany adopted the right-handed *swastika* because they associated it with Aryan ethnicity and thus with their pretensions to ancient racial purity. Hindus and Buddhists continue to use the symbol in many contexts.

Why are cows considered sacred in India?

Hindu tradition teaches that all living beings are sacred and inherently deserving of respect. Within that framework of reverence for nature, cows have a special place for several reasons. As far back as Vedic times, the "Mother Cow" was both source of food and material goods, and bulls and non-milking cows were the preferred sacrificial offering. When the rise of Jainism and Buddhism brought concern for non-injury to the fore,

Hindu tradition began to repudiate sacrificial ritual and recommended protection for all living things. Cows still provide much in the way of food and fuel, and remind many of the all-sustaining Mother deity. Some Hindus, especially Vaishnavites, attach further meanings, since Lord Krishna was the *Gopala,* the Lord of Cows, whose dalliance with the *Gopis* (cowherd maidens) became a metaphor for the divine–human relationship. Cows are humble and ordinary and so numerous now that one wonders how people could consider them as special in any way. Perhaps it is those very qualities that so endear them to India's Hindus, for they are ever-present reminders of the divine bounty.

MEMBERSHIP, COMMUNITY, DIVERSITY

Where do **Hindus live today**? Any estimates of **numbers** available?

India is home to the vast majority (about 95%, over 950 million) of the world's nearly one billion Hindus. Other significant minority populations have Hindu communities in more than half a dozen other lands. Almost twenty-four million Hindus are Nepalese. As many as eighteen million live in Bangladesh, some three million in Pakistan, nearly five million in Indonesia, perhaps 1.2 million in the United States, approaching a million and a half in each Malaysia, and a shade over half a million in South Africa and England. Virtually every nation on Earth now has representatives of Hinduism among its citizenry. Hindus are about 600 million fewer than Muslims, half the total global population of Christians, and somewhere between two and three times that of Buddhism.

Are there any Hindu **holy cities**?

Hinduism's sacred cities far outnumber those of any other major religious tradition. All the earth is of divine origin and India stands at the center of that divinity. According to one model there are seven sacred cities, each associated with a divine event. Banaras or Kashi (City of Light) is the home of Shiva. In Ayodhya, Rama set the capital of his realm. Krishna was born in Mathura, and from Hardvar the Ganges begins its journey to the south. These (along with Kanchi, Ujjain, and Dvaraka) form the basic grid of a vast network of sacred geography in which countless other places are sacred for innumerable reasons. All important sacred places are called *tirthas*, places at which one can cross a river. Four cities function as directional tirthas at the four cardinal points: Badrinath in the north, Rameshwara in the south, Puri in the east, and Dvaraka in the west. According to one mythic narrative, 108 places became sacred by association with the body of Shiva's wife Sati. After she threw herself on the funeral pyre, a grieving Shiva carried her remains across India, and every place bits of her fell to Earth became a "seat" of the goddess. Every denomination and sect has its favored sacred city. Perhaps the single most important city, one that most Hindus acknowledge as sacred, is Banaras. Though it is particularly holy for Shaivites, Banaras's spiritual magnetism works on all devout Hindus.

Located on the banks of the Ganges, the holy city of Banaras is the home of Shiva. (Jeremy Richards / Shutterstock.com.)

Are there anything like **denominations or sects** within greater Hinduism?

Mark Twain once observed that compared to India, other lands and cultures were paupers in religion. He was referring to the large number of major religious traditions that have been born in India or had a significant impact in Indian history. (Recall, for example, the river imagery used earlier.) Hindu tradition alone accounts for an astounding diversity. Most Hindus belong to one of two major denominations (called *sampradaya* in Sanskrit, "handing down, tradition"). Devotees of Vishnu and his various manifestations or avatars are called Vaishnavites (or Vaishnavas). Shaivites (or Shaivas) are those for whom Shiva and the various names and forms of divinity associated with him offer the path to salvation.

Two other smaller groups within the greater Hinduism are also important. Hindus who focus on the feminine manifestations of Shiva's divine power (*shakti*) are called Shaktas. Shaktism is also sometimes called Tantrism because of its connection with a category of esoteric scriptures called Tantras. So-called "right-handed" *Shaktas* espouse practices very much like the other *bhakti* traditions, emphasizing worship of the goddess. Sects described as "left-handed" tend to be more secretive and esoteric. Finally, the term Smarta, as it is commonly used, now refers to Hindus for whom the path of knowledge (*jñana yoga*) represents the greatest hope of spiritual realization. Some Smartas adhere to the *advaita* or monistic philosophical teaching of Shankara. Others are devotionally and ritually eclectic, focusing on one of five names and forms of God (Vishnu, Shiva, Durga, Ganesha, and Surya) as their chosen deity. These four

213

designations are still very broad groupings, each of which is made up of a number of sub-denominations or sects.

Who are the **Vaishnavites**?

About half the world's Hindus belong to the various sub-denominations of Vaishnavism. In general, northern Vaishnavas understand Vishnu as a form of Krishna, while most southerners think of either Rama or Krishna as forms of Vishnu. Five major Vaishnava schools trace their origins to famous founders who lived between about 1000 and 1500 C.E. Different ways of describing the divine–human relationship mark the principal distinctions among the five denominations and the various sectarian divisions that have arisen from them. Ramanuja (1017–1137) was a major figure in a predominantly southern school called Shrivaishnavism, so called because of the centrality of Vishnu's consort Shri. Ramanuja taught a modified form of non-dualism (called *Vishisht-advaita*) according to which individual souls are aspects of the divine, part of God, but retain their individuality and do not lose their identity in their union with the divine.

Madhva (1197–1278) disagreed, insisting on a fuller distinction between the human and the divine. His teaching is a type of pure theism in which God freely chooses to reach with love and grace across an infinite and otherwise unbridgeable chasm. Madhva's dualist (*Dvaita*) branch is also primarily a southern tradition, while the remaining three are more popular in the north. Nimbarka (1125–1162) focused on the role of the guru as the central means of grace in his Minandi school. Vallabha (1475–1530) taught a form of "pure non-dualism," also called "panentheism" (God in all things). His commentaries on the *Bhagavata Purana* detail his mystical interpretation of the so-called "Love Games of Krishna," in which the Lord's romance with the *gopis* becomes a model of the human quest for the divine beloved—and vice versa. Chaitanya (1485–1534) preached devotion to Krishna and Radha through communal dance and song. Of the several contemporary subsects of his Gaudiya Vaishnava group perhaps the best known is the International Society for Krishna Consciousness.

Who are the **Shaivites**?

At least six sub-denominations make up Shaiva Hinduism. As with Vaishnavism, their views on the nature of the divine–human relationship set them apart. A major sect in south and southeast Indian region called Tamilnadu is known as Shaiva Siddhanta ("Truth about Shiva"). Tracing its roots to Rishi Turmular (c. 200 C.E.), the group's central teaching is a blend of theism and monism: individual souls seek God, and devotees and worshippers in this life ultimately will merge totally with Shiva. Pashupata Shaivism, founded by Lakulisha (c. 200) and popular in far northeast, north, and western-central India, holds a variation on that teaching. Souls finally merge with God but maintain individuality somewhat, just as stars still shine, but are lost as discrete bodies in the infinite night sky. Also found in the northern state of Kashmir is a distinctive Shaiva sect founded by Vasugupta (c. 800 C.E.). The Kashmiri school is monistic, teaching the complete and perfect oneness of all reality in Shiva. A major sect in northeast India is called Siddha Siddhanta, with roots in the teaching of Rishi Gorakshanatha (c. 950 C.E.). Blending theism and monism, this school says all individual things are eventually reabsorbed into Shiva as bubbles arise in water. A minor group still influential in southern India is called Shiva Advaita. Its first teacher, Shrikantha (c. 1050), preferred a qualified theism in which the worshipper participates in divinity without losing identity. Finally, a major sect in southwest India is known as Virashaivism. Members are sometimes referred to as Lingayats because many carry with them in a small case a miniature Shiva-linga. A major poet called Basavanna (1105–1167) remains an influential source of the sect's teaching of qualified theism, according to which God is like the sun, souls its rays.

Have Hindus traditionally sent out **missionaries** to convert others?

Hinduism has generally not produced the kind of missionary activity characteristic of traditions like Christianity, Islam, and Buddhism. Significant traces of Hindu tradition and culture are very much in evidence all over southeast Asia, especially in parts of Indonesia. Throughout Late Antiquity (fourth through eighth centuries) and the Middle Ages (ninth through fifteenth centuries), important Hindu dynasties ruled portions of present-day Cambodia, Laos, and Vietnam. Major archaeological research attests to their splendor and power. But their trappings of Hindu symbol and ritual were less a matter of missionary zeal than of a desire to cloak themselves with the prestige of the great Indian dynasties. In addition, they sought to enhance their political legitimacy through the concept of divine kingship by identifying their monarchs as descendants of the gods. In modern times, however, a number of missionary organizations have grown from Hindu roots. In addition to the International Society for Krishna Consciousness, Vivekananda's (1863–1902) Ramakrishna Mission has made important contributions in this regard. Although its gains have been modest in terms of numbers, the Mission's members have become known for various kinds of social outreach as well as for offering lectures and spiritual guidance. In many major United States cities, branches of an organization called the Vedanta Society appeal to a well-educated public by emphasizing the traditional Way of Knowledge, rather than the Way of Devotion preferred by both Vivekananda and his teacher Ramakrishna (1834–86).

Are the **Hare Krishna** people Hindus?

Members of an organization known officially as the International Society for Krishna Consciousness are Vaishnavites and devotees of Krishna and his consort Radha. They are followers of the teaching of the Bengali saint Chaitanya. A former pharmaceutical salesman named A. C. Bhaktivedanta (1896–1977) was initiated by a Vaishnava guru and eventually became a sannyasi in 1959. He founded the organization in 1965 in the United States, establishing a number of temples. Membership includes both married householders and celibate members of monastic communities attached to the temples. Bhaktivedanta instilled in the organization a sense of missionary zeal, and in 1970 decided to take the movement back to India. There he established denominational temples in Vrindavan and Mayapur, the birthplaces of Krishna and Chaitanya respectively. ISKCON maintains a number of temples across North America, some supporting themselves through vegetarian restaurants attached to them. Devotees in the United States came to be popularly known as the "Hare Krishna" people because they often gathered in public to celebrate their joyous praise of God by chanting "Hare Krishna, Hare Krishna, Hare Rama, Hare Hare."

Members of the International Society for Krishna Consciousness are Vaishnavites—popularly known in the United States as Hare Krishnas—follow the teachings of the Hindu saint Chaitanya. (joyfull / Shutterstock.com.)

How do Hindus view Hinduism's **relationships to other traditions**?

For many centuries the greater Hindu tradition has shown enormous flexibility in adapting to religious pluralism. It came to be the "greater" Hinduism, in part at least, because of that quality of expansiveness. Many Hindus regard their religious heritage as a kind of spiritual umbrella capable of sheltering all who seek refuge beneath it. Historically, different denominations have drawn once-separate traditions into their embrace. For example, Vaishnavite tradition came to incorporate Buddhism by installing the Buddha as the ninth of Vishnu's ten avatars—a hospitable gesture, perhaps, but one that Buddhists do not recognize. Some Hindus have suggested that Jesus and other foundational figures also find a place in the greater Hindu scheme of things. A major early modern movement that began as an attempt to soften the animosity between Hindus and Muslims in northwestern India especially is now known as Sikhism. The Sikh community has become largely identified with a region called the Punjab, which straddles the India-Pakistan border. Sikh separatists have continued to assert their desire for a homeland.

LEADERSHIP, AUTHORITY, AND RELIGIOUS ROLES

How are Hindu **religious leaders chosen** and given authority?

Priesthood is generally a hereditary office, with families often tracing their sacerdotal lineages back many generations. Priests who serve in local temples are not typically members of the Brahmin caste, but their religious roles are likewise hereditary. Spiritual guides and teachers called gurus are those who rise to local or wider prominence as a result of their proficiency in various facets of religious knowledge and practical wisdom. In this instance the classical system of training provides the equivalent of a license or seal of approval. But many famous teachers achieve wider notoriety as a result of popular acclaim. They set up shop initially, so to speak, with official sanction as products of the system, but their spiritual prowess spreads by word of mouth. Other religious figures gain prominence outside the system. An individual's reputation for holiness begins when they are found to have extraordinary powers or qualities, and this reputation grows as seekers gather in hopes of sharing in the wisdom and sanctity.

Who are the main Hindu **religious officials** or specialists?

Traditional Hindu vocabulary includes dozens of technical terms to designate virtually every imaginable variety of religious function or specialized qualification. Essential to every Hindu temple is its priestly staff. Larger temples often have many priests, sometimes called *pujaris*—those who engage in the daily worship called *puja*—on the staff, one of whom generally serves as chief or senior priest. People generally address priests as *Shri*, the equivalent of "Reverend." Frequently but not exclusively of the Brahmin caste nowadays, temple priests marry and have families. At temples that have become important pilgrimage centers, specialists called *pandas* serve as pilgrim guides and keep records of the families who make up the regular membership of the temple. Ritual specialists called *purohitas* ("those who lead") are generally Brahmins of the Smarta denominations who do mostly home ceremonies for Brahmin families. *Gurus*, who are generally learned Brahmins, still almost exclusively perform the various *samskaras,* or rites of passage, and tutor upper-caste children in the ancient traditions.

Are there religious **hierarchical structures** in any branch of Hinduism?

None of Hinduism's various denominations has ever developed a formal institutional hierarchy parallel to those of, for example, Roman Catholicism or Shi'a Islam. But there have been de facto social rankings in which some representatives of the tradition have very definite priority. In Vedic times, there were at least seven (and perhaps as many as sixteen) different types of priests, distinguished according to specific function in the Vedic sacrifice. Among them were the Brahmins, the one category of priests that has retained its influence over the centuries. Hindu religious hierarchy has generally ranked its specialists according to learning, with teachers and guardians of tradition (such as *gurus, acharyas,* and *pandits*) ranking high on the list. Historically, figures called *purohita* served as high priests at the courts of Hindu monarchs. That individual's role was to protect his royal patron through ritual and teaching, as well as by his spiritually potent presence. In modern times the *purohita* has become the family priest charged with keeping caste and ritual practices intact. Temple priesthood staffs typically have chief priests who supervise the overall running of the temple rituals.

Is there a **central teaching authority** for Hindus?

Since Hindu tradition is a complex of many denominations and sub-traditions, there is no central institutional structure that functions as a central teaching authority. Many of the individual denominations and sects maintain systems of checks on the integrity of the tradition in the form of teaching lineages. Instruction has historically been based on oral transmission of the basic sources, along with extensive commentary, both oral and written, on those sources. Perhaps the closest thing to centralized authority is the living master to whom disciples give their uncontested allegiance. That living master embodies both the authority of an unbroken succession of teachers and his or her personal authority as one spiritually connected to the ancient wellsprings of wisdom. Even the Vedas and the associated primary sacred texts grouped under the heading of *shruti* ("heard") do not claim the universal adherence of all Hindus.

What religious roles do the terms **guru, acharya**, and **pandit** refer to?

A *guru* is a religious teacher who represents a particular lineage or spiritual tradition and is authorized to initiate qualified students into the tradition. *Guru* comes from a root that means "heavy, grave" and suggests massive spiritual substance worthy of respect. *Gurus* have historically been distinguished according to certain specific tasks or offices. Those who perform the various rites of passage, and are particularly important in the rite of initiating young upper-caste boys into Vedic tradition, are called teaching (*shiksha*) gurus. A teacher who represents a particular sect and initiates members into it is called an initiatory (*diksha*) or *mantra guru*. This *guru* passes along to the disciple (*chela* or *shishya*) a sacred syllable or phrase intended only for that individual. *Gurus* may be either male or female, and disciples often consider them direct descendants of the deity, with a claim to virtually absolute authority over their students.

Many famous Hindu teachers throughout history have earned the title *acharya*. Often tacked on to a proper name as a suffix, as in Shankaracharya, the term identifies an individual who instructs others in right conduct. Many of those who have received the title have been famous philosophers and theologians.

Finally, anyone who watches news coverage around election time will invariably hear commentators referred to as "political pundits." In the history of Hinduism, a *pandit* is a person "learned" especially in a broad spectrum of oral tradition and practical lore. The scope of the *pandit's* learning was less specialized than that of the *guru*, who focused on a higher wisdom aimed at liberation of the soul. Nowadays *pandits* are generally from families of Brahmins dedicated to transmitting knowledge of the sources from memory, much the way the ancient rabbis preserved Judaism's oral Torah. In short, these three roles complement each other. *Pandits* have maintained the tradition as accurately as human memory allows. Acharyas further develop the tradition, reflecting on its deeper implications. And *gurus* help seekers to apply the tradition's wisdom to their personal spiritual lives.

What religious roles do the terms **sadhu, sannyasi**, and **yogi** refer to?

These three common terms refer to different specific religious roles or functions, any or all of which could be exemplified in a single person. They are often used synonymously, but there are important differences. A *sadhu* is "a person of unerring trajectory" or "one who has achieved a goal" by means of a regime of spiritual practices and disciplines called collectively *sadhana*. These methods encompass a whole range of external rituals, including fasting and other austerities, and forms of meditation, and often vary from one denomination or sect to another. *Sadhus* pursue a highly ascetic

A Hindu holy man (*sadhu*) at the Somnath temple in Gujarat, India. (Aleksandar Todorovic / Shutterstock.com.)

lifestyle, live on charitable donations, and are often entirely unconnected with specific social or religious institutions—apart from the fact that *sadhu*-hood has become virtually an institution in itself. Some *sadhus* are also *sannyasis,* renunciants officially initiated into this spiritual status by a *guru*. Individuals may formally enter into the state of *sannyasa* for various reasons according to tradition: a spontaneous quest for spiritual liberation; a quest resulting from more deliberate immersion in religious studies; withdrawal as a way to cope with great loss or sadness; or the realization that one's death is imminent. Formal initiation, also conferred on women in some orders, includes vows of poverty, chastity, and obedience for those who belong to monastic communities. *Sadhus* and *sannyasis* may also engage in the disciplines of *raja* and *hatha yoga,* but a *yogi* is not necessarily either a *sadhu* or a *sannyasi*.

What is a **swami**? Is that anything like a **maharishi**?

The term *swami* comes from the Sanskrit *svami,* meaning "owner, master." It was originally applied mostly to monastic *sannyasis* as an acknowledgment of their self-mastery. More recently the term has become a widely used title of reverence for a broader spectrum of religious scholars, teachers, and renunciants. One often hears Hindu religious leaders referred to as *"swamiji,"* a term of both respect and affection. The term *maharishi,* literally "great seer," is also an honorific title with roots deep in Hindu mythology. Great seers are individuals celebrated for their profound wisdom. Popular tradition designated as "great" a number of the ancient "seers" associated with the communication of primal religious insights. But several historical persons have likewise merited the title. Ramana Maharishi (1879–1950) attracted a great following in the south of India. Maharishi Mahesh Yogi (1914–2008), founder of the school of Transcendental Meditation, gained fame initially when he taught Indian spirituality to the Beatles.

Is there such a thing as a **Hindu saint**?

Certain features of the *sadhu* and *sannyasi* are quite consistent with concepts of sainthood in various religious traditions. But individuals called *sants* add still another dimension to the Hindu tradition's complex understanding of the human embodiment of holiness. *Sadhus* and *sannyasis* may seem at first to be socially liminal characters, but they are actually very much a part of the classical socio-religious system. The term *"sant"* is a vernacular version of the Sanskrit *sat*, meaning "real, authentic." Ironically perhaps, the *sants* are genuine because they stand apart from the system and have taken up the cause of the truly marginalized, the outcastes and untouchables. Associated with *bhakti* movements both Shaivite and Vaishnavite, *sants* have often spread their message as troubadours, gathering crowds by singing at important holy places. One of the most influential of them was Kabir (c. 1440–1518), whose songs were a major influence in Guru Nanak's (1469–1538) founding of the Sikh movement. Other important Hindu *sants* were Jñaneshwara (1275–96), Ekanatha (1533–98) and Tukaram (1608–49).

Have any **women** been considered **saints**?

Numerous saintly women (probably well into the hundreds) have been revered for their holiness, most with local or regional constituencies, but many also held in high regard across India. Here are some of the most famous, in more or less chronological order. In the fifth or sixth century, Karaikkal Ammaiyar was a legendary devotee of Shiva. The daughter of an affluent family, she was celebrated for her beauty before she lost it in a theophanic encounter with Shiva. Her first husband considered her a goddess after she made two mangoes appear by praying to Shiva. Lalleshvari was a fourteenth-century Shaivite poet-saint whose husband and mother-in-law abused and neglected her for twelve years. She left for the life of a wanderer, forsaking all worldly attachments even to the extreme of going naked until she died. Gauribai (1759–1809) was married and widowed around the age of five or six. In keeping with social norms, she fulfilled the expectation that all widows lead pious, devout, and extremely simple lives. She took up residence in a temple where for the rest of her life she studied, composed songs and poems, meditated, and performed works of charity. Her devotees believed she could predict the future and (like many Hindu saints) foretold the time of her own death. Aghormani Devi (1822–1908) was betrothed at age nine and widowed not long after. She became a close friend of Ramakrishna, and became famous for having frequent visions of Baby Gopala (Krishna), and came to be known because of her discipline and meditation as the "Mother of the Divine Child Krishna." Gaurimani Devi (1857–1938) was another disciple of Sri Ramakrishna; after years of travel and observation of the plight of women in India, she founded Saradeswari Asrama (spiritual retreat/foundation for women) as Sri Ramakrishna had requested before his death.

Performers from the Kalakshetra Dance Institute perform the folk dance "Shankara Sri Giri" at a festival in Chengdu, China. (Jack Q / Shutterstock.)

Who are some **other important women** in the history of **Hindu spirituality**?

Ancient tradition acknowledges that some anonymous women were among the authors of the Vedic hymns. Many other women whose names we know have made major contributions throughout the history of Hinduism. Here is a brief introduction to four of the better-known women from various denominations. Antal (725–755 C.E.) was one of the Alvars, poet-saints in the Vaishnava tradition. She was most famous for poetry in which she described her relationship with Vishnu in the language of "bridal mysticism." Seeing herself as the spouse of Vishnu she shares the spiritual longing of women mystics in other traditions who speak of total loving union with God. Devotees still sing hymns that set her poems to music. Mahadevi was a twelfth-century devotee of Shiva and a renowned poet in the Kannada language. In the temple of her village, the principal deity was a form of Shiva called Mallikarjuna, "Lord white as jasmine." Like Antal, she thought of herself as betrothed to God alone. She was apparently forced into an unhappy marriage, and much of her poetry alludes to the suffering she experienced and her longing to be liberated and live for God alone. A late medieval holy woman named Mirabai (1498–1550) was a devotee of Krishna. She thought of herself as a gopi who had been hopelessly enamored of the dark Lord. After extricating herself from an unsatisfactory marriage, she became a *sannyasi* and composed love songs in Hindi, a vernacular tongue in west-central India. Finally, a woman known by the honorific title Anandamayi Ma (Bliss-steeped Mother) lived in modern-day Bengal (now Bangladesh). Nirmala Sundari (1896–1982) lived a most colorful life, often flouting strict tradition in favor of sometimes highly symbolic or

221

Can women exercise religious leadership among Hindus?

Women's roles in Hindu tradition have varied enormously over its long history. During the Vedic period women apparently participated directly in many major rituals and exercised exclusive leadership in some. As the Brahmanic priesthood rose to prominence, women had fewer opportunities for official leadership. But women have continued to play major roles in many religious rituals outside the Brahmanic system. They often lead women's groups in communal prayer and song in gatherings connected with local observances. Some Brahmin women have functioned as itinerant preachers in rural areas. Others have become specialists, called *pandits,* in ritual and lore. Perhaps the best known are the women whose role as *gurus* has attracted seekers and devotees, often from great distances, to "take *darshan*" (that is, to be in their presence) and benefit from their counsel.

ecstatic behavior. In her later years she opted for a more settled life, founding an *ashram* and ministering to disciples who sought her out for spiritual guidance.

Have there been important **Hindu mystics**?

Many of the *sants* certainly rank among India's greatest mystics. Their poems and songs represent one of the two major strands of supranormal unitive experience often described as "mystical." For the *sants* and other exponents of the *bhakti* tradition, the divine–human relationship is above all intensely personal. It is precisely the infinite chasm separating God from the human devotee that gives their conviction of the transforming love of God its immense power. This type of mysticism is often called theistic or dualistic. A number of important devotional schools trace their origins to some of the most influential theistic mystics, such as Vallabha and Chaitanya. Another stream tributary to the great river of Hindu mysticism is often referred to as cosmic or monistic. Teachers like Shankara emphasize the need to arrive through disciplined meditation at the full realization that there is no divide between what most of us perceive as the "individual" and the Ultimate Reality. That realization of the simple unity of Brahman and atman (which conventional language might call "God" and the "soul") is the essence of the monistic mystical experience.

Are there any **organizations or institutions** that have their own **distinctive structures of leadership** within any of the branches of Hinduism? Anything like monks or nuns?

As in so many other traditions, monastic and other religious orders have played a major role in the history of greater Hinduism. Different styles of monastic life have evolved in connection with the last two of the four traditional "life stages," namely those of "forest-dweller" and "renunciant." Individual Hindu males who have arrived at the last stage, that of *sannyasi,* have been crisscrossing India on their solitary ways for millennia. Since perhaps twenty-five centuries ago, informal organizations developed as disciples gathered around renunciants renowned as spiritual teachers. These forerunners of stable monastic residences continued to welcome as occasional guests their unattached itinerant counterparts. Evidence of the earliest formal monastic organizations, from as long as eighteen hundred years ago, suggests that they followed a strictly ascetic regime. But Shankara (788–820) is the first individual credited with founding an order. The renowned philosopher and theologian organized monasteries in sacred cities marking the four cardinal directions across India. Four subsequent orders were founded by religious leaders associated with four of the five major Vaishnava denominations, Ramanuja, Nimbarka, Madhva, and Vallabha. Important orders have arisen in the nineteenth and twentieth centuries as well, such as those founded by Ramakrishna and Mahatma Gandhi. Most of the orders have offered various levels of commitment from temporary residency to long-term affiliation of men and women with families or lifelong celibacy.

Why was **Mahatma Gandhi** an important Hindu?

Mohandas Karmachand Gandhi (1869–1948) received the title Mahatma ("Great-Souled One") because of his towering example of personal integrity and commitment to social justice. He was a nationalist in the sense that he sought Indian independence from British rule. But he also taught tolerance for religious diversity at a time when strident voices cried out for vengeance against members of other communities of faith. His "experiments with truth" (*satyagraha,* "truth-grasping") led to his espousal of methods such as the quest for simple living and nonviolent resistance to oppression. On several occasions his willingness to fast nearly unto death called attention to the evils against which he fought. Gandhi spoke out often on behalf of the socially marginalized, the untouchables—the Lord's Children, he called them—and women. Human dignity and equality were the goals he pursued within the context of a vibrant religious faith. Gandhi's great-souled inclusiveness improved the lives of millions and eventually cost him his own. A militant Hindu, convinced that Gandhi was conceding far too much to the nation's Muslims, shot him on January 30, 1948.

Do Hindus have a system of **religious law**?

Surely the single most important Hindu religious concept is that of *dharma.* As a universal notion *dharma* is the cosmic "law" that binds all things together. Each individual person also has his or her *dharma,* the fundamental religious requirements and ethical expectations associated with each person's station in life. Classical Hindu sources also use the term *dharma* in reference to countless specific moral duties and ritual rubrics. Treatises called *shastras* are the principal repositories of the Hindu legal and ethical

223

materials. They belong to the larger category of sacred literature called *smriti* ("remembered"), revered as of divine origin, but subordinate in authority to *shruti* ("heard") scriptures. The *Dharma Shastras*, and related texts like the *Grihya Sutras* that include detailed information on every facet of "householder" life, derive ultimately from a text generally known as the *Laws of Manu* (dated variously from 600 B.C.E.–100 C.E.). The ancient law books have retained their authority well into modern times. Only recently have India's legislative bodies introduced serious and sweeping reforms. But the antiquity of tradition and inherent cultural resistance to change have kept many practices alive in spite of official attempts to adapt the classics to contemporary needs.

What is the **caste system**?

India's ancient Hindu social system combines several complex elements. Perhaps best known are the four principal *varnas* or "social classes." The term *varna* means "color or appearance." As early as the Vedic period, the Brahmin or priestly class rose to the top of the social ladder. They were responsible for maintaining the integrity of ritual practice and traditional teaching. Nowadays are by no means all connected with priestly activities as such. One rung below the Brahmins are the Kshatriyas, "those who govern," traditionally called the warrior or princely class. They have been the legislators as well as enforcers of the law. On the next lower rung are the more numerous merchants, financiers, agriculturalists, and industrialists who comprise the Vaishya class. As class designations the terms Kshatriya and Vaishya are now obsolete. Most numerous of all are the Shudras, the laborers and craftspersons who perform the basic services. *Varna* distinctions generally cut across language, occupational and geographical barriers.

A Indian Brahmin wears clothing indicating he is a member of the highest caste. (Paul Prescott / Shutterstock.com.)

In addition to the four varnas are the hundreds—perhaps even as many as four thousand—*jatis*. *Jati* means "birth or species" and refers to the countless local social groups defined by occupation and language. As many as twenty-five thousand additional groupings are called "sub-castes." Members of both *jatis* and sub-castes generally associate themselves with one of the *varnas*, and many Indians still observe strict rules of purity and separation. Finally, between one and two hundred million people are considered out-castes, untouchables, or "unscheduled" classes, those who don't fit in the great system. Since India gained independence the caste system has been officially illegal, but systems of such antiquity do not yield readily to legislation passed in capital cities.

How and where do members of local Hindu communities come together?

Local and regional temples are the major gathering places Hindus use religiously and socially and support financially. Individual temples in India are generally dedicated predominantly to a particular deity. Most center around some aspect or manifestation of Shiva or Vishnu, or one of their major female consorts or counterparts. A temple will typically also have subordinate shrines dedicated to other names and forms of the central deity. Some smaller local temples may also belong exclusively to sects worshipping deities largely unknown outside the area. Most temples draw sectarian clienteles.

In many regions outside India, however, greater diversity in the makeup of local communities often requires greater flexibility in the religious orientation of temples. For example, Indian immigrants around American cities such as Pittsburgh and St. Louis come from various places in India and represent a variety of sectarian backgrounds. As a result, the temples that serve the regions are sensitive to a wider spectrum of devotional needs than might be the case at a local temple in an area where Hindus are in the majority and where one sect predominates. Large temples in both Pittsburgh and St. Louis have been funded by Indian populations largely of immigrants from south India. Both temples are therefore dedicated to a popular south Indian manifestation of Vishnu called Shri Venkateshvara (Lord of the Sin-Forgiving Hill). But in order to serve the diverse local population, both temples include prominent devotional symbolism familiar both to Shaivites and to Vaishnavites.

HOLIDAYS AND REGULAR OBSERVANCES

What kind of religious calendar do Hindus observe?

Combining lunar months with seasons of the solar year, the Hindu calendar functions somewhat like the Jewish calendar. About every three years it inserts an extra month after a month with two new moons. Hindu lunar months vary from twenty-nine to thirty-two days. The names of the months, with the roughly corresponding Gregorian months in parentheses, are as follows: *Chaitra* (March/April), *Vaishakha* (April/May), *Jyaistha* (May/June), *Asadhe* (June/July), *Shravana* (July/August), *Bhadrapada* (August/September), *Ashvina* (September/October), *Karttika* (October/November), *Margasivsa* (November/December), *Pansa* (December/January), *Magha* (January/February), and *Phalguna* (February/March). Leap months take the name of the month preceding them.

For ritual purposes, each month is divided into its dark and light halves, with associated celebrations, and the moment of the full moon is a time of celebration each month. And some festivals and observances fall each year on the same solar date. Each year is likened to a day in the life of the deities, with the solar solstices symbolizing sunrise and sundown. In addition to the complexity introduced by the blending of solar and lunar reckonings, systems vary still further from region to region in India. Historically, the greater Hindu religious calendar has been so full that virtually every day some Hindu community has celebrated some feast somewhere in the subcontinent. Hinduism is not unlike Roman Catholic and Eastern Orthodox traditions in that respect, except that the majority of the Christian religious feasts are those of saints, rather than of the deity as such. All of this makes for an immensely rich sense of the intersection of sacred times and places. Every day is appropriate for religious observance, and no one day of the week is set aside as an especially sacred time.

What are some of the regular **monthly religious observances**?

The Hindu sense of sacred time presents an enormous array of possibilities, depending on various combinations of astrological phenomena, auspicious days of the week, and associations of times with particular deities. Different days in both dark and bright fortnights of each lunar month carry generic spiritual values. Most sacred is the eleventh day, while the first, fourth, ninth, and fourteenth are inauspicious. Some days are consecrated to different deities. More high occasions fall during the bright than during the dark half. During one half (both halves in some months and/or regions) the fourth day belongs to Ganesha, the eighth to Durga, the ninth and eleventh to Vishnu (a solar deity), and the thirteenth to Shiva (a lunar deity). New-moon days find some Hindus offering meals to placate the spirits of the dead. Many of these monthly or semimonthly occasions include a fast. Most Hindus observe only some of these special days, depending on their sectarian affiliation.

Are there other important **cyclical observances** based largely on **celestial signs**?

Every three years Hindus gather from all over India in one of four sacred cities (Hardvar, Prayaga, Ujjain, and Nasik, each on a different sacred river or confluence) for a huge religious fair called a *Kumbha-mela* ("grain-pot festival"). The mythological connection in the name is its reference to the *kumbha,* or vessel, from which drops of the nectar of immortality fell as the demons rested on their flight from the gods, making the four cities holy. Every twelve years, a series of astrological conjunctions make the gathering at Prayaga (known by Muslims as Allahabad) particularly auspicious. Since about the eighth century, travelers have made organized pilgrimages to the four cities to attain forgiveness of sins for themselves and eighty-eight generations of ancestors by bathing in their sacred waters. Four times each year, corresponding to the two solstices and two equinoxes, Hindus celebrate particularly important events in the solar calendar. The beginning of every solar month is auspicious because of the sun's move into a new sign of the Zodiac. But the winter solstice is the most important because it signals the lengthening of days and the beginning of the solar year.

Are any **feasts dedicated** especially to the **goddesses**?

Durga Puja, also called *Navaratri* ("nine nights"), occurs at the autumn equinox in honor of Shiva's consort Durga. As the slayer of the Buffalo demon (*Durgamahishasur-amardini*) Durga represents the power of good to quell all sources of evil. Devotees celebrate this deity's complete protection of her worshippers, but Durga's festival has room for other deities as well. The first day celebrates the goddess Sarasvati, patroness of learning and beauty. In some regions the fifth day belongs to a goddess called Lalita. Bengalis sometimes still sacrifice water buffalo in honor of Durga's cosmic victory over evil. Another festival, occurring at the end of winter to welcome spring, is called *Shri panchami* ("Goddess Fifth" day in the bright half of Magha). Devotees honor Sarasvati by piling up books and symbols of learning near local altars. Other days, such as several during the extended feast called *Divali*, also belong to the major goddesses.

What is **Holi**?

Originally a fertility festival, this late winter celebration of several days ending with the full moon of Phalguna is named after the demoness Holika. She was in the habit of eating a child each day until a holy widow summoned all the children to curse the demoness together. Amid great hubbub, participants today let out the kind of energy the children must have unleashed on Holika. They throw multicolored powders and liquids on each other, evidently a visual remnant of the children's curses. By a fascinating process of association, the celebration has also come to embrace the mythological downfall of evil female figures. For example, Krishna destroyed the demoness Putana, whom the evil King Kamsa had sent, disguised as a wet nurse, to kill the infant deity by poisoning him with her breast milk.

What is the celebration called **Divali**?

Divali is one of the most important and widely celebrated of all Hindu observances. Also called *Dipavali*, or "Row of Lights," this feast occurs in mid-autumn

Young Indians celebrate *Holi* in Jaipur, India. (Jeremy Richards / Shutterstock.com.)

(October or November—technically from the 13th of Ashvina's dark half to the 2nd of Karttika's bright half), composed of five distinct day-long festivities devoted to such mythic events as Krishna's conquest of two demons and Shiva's reconciliation with Parvati. Shaivites and Vaishnavites alike observe the occasion, marking it as theirs by dedicating the middle night of the five to either Kali's control of Shiva under control or Vishnu's consort Lakshmi, respectively. Socially speaking, the feast belongs to the merchant castes. *Divali*, strictly so-called, occurs on the fourth day, recalling Rama's return to his royal throne in Ayodhya to end his fourteen-year exile.

Do **Vaishnavites** observe unique **feasts** in honor of **Vishnu** or his avatars?

Rama Navami (Rama Ninth, during Chaitra in early spring) celebrates Rama's birthday. During a nine-day festival celebrants attend a lengthy retelling of the massive epic Ramayana. A related feast occurs on the fifteenth of Shravana, a full moon celebration of Rama's crossing over to Lanka to rescue Sita. Two major feasts focus on Krishna. *Krishna Janmashtami* ("Birthday Eighth" during the dark half of Shravana) in late summer, celebrates Krishna's birthday. For a full seven days devotees reenact events from Krishna's life. The festivities culminate with a fast and midnight worship on the seventh day, the eve of the birthday. *Naga Panchami* ("Serpent Fifth," so named because it occurs on the fifth day of Shravana's bright half) comes in late summer and recalls one of Krishna's many victories over embodiments of evil, his dispatching of the serpent demon Kaliya in the river Jumna. Although the evil demon in this case is a serpent, the fast and feast celebrate the grace represented by other cosmically beneficial serpents as well. Several feasts also recall other specific avatars. For example, on the full moon of Karttika some Vaishnavites celebrate Vishnu's descent as the savior-fish Matsya.

How do **Shaivites honor Shiva**?

Shivaratri, "Shiva's Night" is a monthly festivity occurring on the fourteenth night of the dark half of every lunar month, just before the appearance of the new moon. Once a year devotees observe *Mahashivaratri,* "Shiva's Great Night" either during the midwinter lunar month called Magha or during the following month, Phalguna, depending on regional custom. The feast celebrates Shiva's manifestation of his power and glory to Vishnu and Brahma in the icon called the *jyotirlinga* or "fiery *linga*." Girls who hope to marry soon often fast during the day and keep vigil all night. Festivities in parts of India generally last all night and often include massive street parties and processions featuring elaborate floats, ecstatic dancing, and sometimes extreme demonstrations of devotion in the form of self-mutilation. A full moon feast during Karttika, in the fall, is called *Tripuri-purnima.* It recalls how Shiva incinerated the demon Tripura's three cities, Tripuri, made of gold, silver, and iron. Meanwhile his consort Kali dispatched the demon himself, ending his partial dominion over Heaven, Earth, and Hell (the "three cities").

What are some of the **other religious days** Hindus observe?

Many of the lesser deities have feasts widely observed by Hindus across sectarian lines. The fourth day of the bright half of Bhadrapada in early autumn marks the birthday of Shiva's son Ganesha. This was originally a Dravidian fertility festival associated with early harvest. Another fertility feast celebrates the emergence of the Ganges from a sage's ear—one of a number of metaphors for the sacred origins of the river. Observed in early summer, the day marks a time during which devotees can cleanse themselves of ten specific evils. Some also celebrate a late summer festival called "tying the lucky threads." The day recalls how the wife of Vedic storm deity Indra saved her husband from a demon by slipping a magic string on his wrist. Sisters do the same for their brothers, and some celebrants use the occasion as a renewal of their investiture with the sacred thread of initiation.

CUSTOMS AND RITUALS

Are there **rituals** associated with **dedicating a new temple**?

Multiple festivities typically attend the formal consecration of a new temple and its sacred icons. It begins with the careful choice of a site on which the building can be aligned on an east-west axis with all interior shrines facing east. After the structure is completed, temple staff and devotees install permanent images of the deities in an elaborate three- or four-day ceremony named *Kumbhabhishekam* (sprinkling of water from pots filled at sacred rivers), after one specific moment in the lengthy ceremony.

Rituals begin with purification of the images with various substances (milk and clarified butter called *ghee*). Before fixing each image to its pedestal with ritually prepared adhesives, celebrants immerse it in water, grain, and flower petals. Vedic chants accompany an offering of *ghee* to a sacred fire to make up for any imperfection in the image. Then officiants pour water over the finial atop the womb chamber of each image and over the images themselves in the actual ritual called *kumbhabhishekam*. Since the images need eyes with which to "see" devotees, priests place eyes of semiprecious stones into the statues and pray that they be opened. To call the images to life they then perform a ritual that instills breath in them. Before engaging further in the ordinary forms of daily worship, officiants symbolize the great sanctity of the images so dedicated by turning their backs to the images and looking at their reflection in a mirror. Thereafter devotees may gaze directly on the images.

These festivities proceed all day long for as many as four days (perhaps more in some places), giving even devotees who live at a distance plenty of opportunity to participate. It is a most joyous occasion and a celebration of community to which (in most cases) any interested party is welcome. Many temples also celebrate the anniversary of their foundations or dedications.

What **rites** do Hindus practice in the **temple**?

Puja, meaning adoration or worship, is the generic name for a range of rituals in which devotees engage in the temple. Many temples are open early in the day until early afternoon, and again in early evening. Worshippers arrive at any time during a temple's regular hours, individually or in small groups. They always remove their shoes before entering. Temple priests serve each party in turn, helping them to make their offerings to the deity or deities of their choice. Devotees' choice of deities is based on various factors, including personal need, individual devotion, or sacred times associated with particular deities. While the priests conduct separate rituals, other parties wait their turn, sitting in the open areas of the temple and talking or praying quietly among themselves.

Ritual actions emphasize the spiritual symbolism of simple ordinary elements of life such as food, water, warmth, light, and beauty, all in the context of opening oneself inwardly to a closer relationship with the source of life. *Puja* takes the form of visiting a royal person and offering affectionate and awe-filled gestures. Worshippers "take care" of the deity by symbolically bathing its feet and offering food and drink. Circumambulation, always to the right, around the various womb-chamber shrines in a temple are a regular part of worship. At set times during the day, the temple staff engage in other worshipful acts apart from the ongoing *puja* of individuals and groups. They wake, bathe, and feed the deity, and take the sacred royalty out for a walk, so to speak.

What **rites** do Hindus practice at **home**?

In their homes many Hindus engage in a smaller-scale version of temple *puja,* morning, noon, and evening. Miniature shrines often occupy a special corner, where all the necessary materials and implements for worship are kept. *Puja* begins with entering

into the proper frame of mind and with invocations. Placing flower petals on the image, along with water and other elements (*ghee,* honey, milk), reminds devotees of the intimacy of their relationship with God. They symbolize that intimacy with actions and materials that communicate deep affection and warmth. Both in the home and in the temple, God is the guest whom the host and hostess strive to make perfectly welcome. Making the deity beautiful often means clothing the images in elaborate garments as well. People sometimes invite a priest to come to their homes to pray, but generally the head of the household leads the home *puja.*

Hindu ritual specialist performing a rite of passage or initiation for a young girl. (Photo courtesy of Beata Grant.)

Many Hindu householders regularly perform the individual morning prayer before sunrise. Facing east with the sacred thread over the left shoulder, worshippers take a sip of water, pronounce mantras over ashes, and place them on their foreheads, arms, ribs and knees. To be purified of sin, they pray the *gayatri mantra,* a lovely short hymn to the Light of the Sun. Several different forms of prayer might include facing the various cardinal directions while performing slightly different ritual actions. Other domestic rituals can include celebrations associated with building and entering a new home for the first time. Other occasions marked with religious rituals at home include especially the various rites of passage associated with birth and early infancy.

Is there a **standard Hindu group** or **individual liturgical worship**?

Ordinary daily *puja* is often communal in the sense that a number of people, such as an extended family, might make an offering together. But *puja* is not strictly speaking a congregational ritual. Some sub-communities, such as those living together in ashrams or members of other exclusive groups, engage in congregational ritual as a matter of course. In general, Hindus join in larger group rituals for special occasions. These may involve congregational singing or chanting of prayers or scriptural texts, practices called *kirtan(a)* or *bhajan(a)*.

Various forms of individual ritual prayer offer devotees opportunities to sanctify time alone wherever they may be. A form called *japa,* "muttering, recitation," is the most widespread. Devotees repeat a mantra, sacred syllable or phrase, and keep track of their repetitions with a string of beads (often 108 in number) called a *mala* ("garland"). Reciting names of the deity is the most popular type of personal prayer, as in the mantra "Hare Rama Hare Krishna" repeated by many devotees of Vishnu. Hindu texts distinguish fourteen kinds of *japa,* depending on variables such as purpose, physical posture, and method (whispered, voiced, or murmured). Processions are another important form of congregational worship. Occasionally the priestly staffs of local temples mount a processional image of one or more deities on shoulder-borne platforms to be paraded through the streets. Worshippers often join in, or stop and catch a glimpse of the passing icon.

Does **ritual sacrifice** play a role in Hindu ritual?

In Vedic times animal sacrifice was a major component in many rituals. Animals as large as horses and water buffalo were offered, sometimes in great numbers, along with smaller animals such as goats. Nowadays those large Vedic sacrifices are very rare, but wealthy patrons still occasionally bankroll them. Blood sacrifice does, however, survive as a regular component of *puja* in some temples in India, especially those dedicated to Shiva's terrifying consort Kali. Devotees regularly offer goats and chickens in places like the Kali temple called Kalighat, after which the city of Calcutta was named. The term *yaja,* meaning worship, homage, or sacrifice in a generic or symbolic sense, still describes many different kinds of ritual that involve offering or giving up symbolic or actual goods for the benefit of another. Offerings of oblations to the deities date from Vedic times, but many Hindus still perform personal deeds of sacrifice in which they connect spiritually with the ancient sages and ancestors, all the deities, and all of creation. Sacrifice for the benefit of living beings, human and animal, includes generosity with sustenance and charitable financial support.

What kinds of **ritual objects** figure in Hindu worship and prayer?

Since *puja* involves offerings and other uses of numerous symbolic physical substances, devotees employ quite a few ritual objects. Most are made of metals such as brass, bronze, silver, or silverplate. Objects owned by older temples may be ancient and precious works of art, but their purpose is to serve the larger ritual rather than to attract attention to themselves. Bells, sometimes with an image of the deity on the handle, summon devotees to attentiveness and announce their arrival to visit the deity. With a long-handled spoon they offer water or *ghee*, and in a smaller cup with no handle they offer a drink of water. In a small cuplike lamp with a handle they burn camphor and wave it before the deity, and a multiwicked oil lampstand provides sacred illumination. A ritual plate holds offerings of food. For some rituals a brass or bronze image of a closed lotus flower can be opened like a lotus at dawn, an image of divine disclosure. In some *puja* ceremonies the priest briefly places a small silver crown, like that worn by the deity, on the heads of devotees, symbolizing divine blessing.

Do Hindus consider **pilgrimage important**?

In a land with countless sacred places associated with numerous divine names and forms, pilgrimage (*yatra,* "going out") remains an essential expression of religious devotion for all who can afford it. For those whose modest means prevent them from traveling distances, a pilgrimage to closer sites is always a possibility. In ancient times Hindu pilgrimages may have been related to the increasing popularity of sites associated with sacred events in the life of the Buddha. Among the most important goals of pilgrimage are the sources and confluences of major rivers. With its many important temples of Shiva and Kali, as well as the bathing and cremation *ghats* that line its Ganges banks, Banaras tops the list of pilgrimage cities. A thirty-six-mile circuit around the city still attracts many travelers in search of blessing and forgiveness. Other important sites include those associated with events in the life of Krishna.

Are **music and dance important** in Hindu religious ritual?

Ordinary daily worship is generally conducted without instrumental or vocal music, apart from the priest's chanting of Sanskrit prayers of praise and supplication. Ceremonies, however, can include congregational chanting and singing of hymns. Many

Burning *ghats* of Manikarnika, where many families bring their dead for cremation, downstream from the bathing *ghats* on the River Ganges in Benares (Varanasi), city of Shiva. Note the stacks of firewood along the bank. (Photo courtesy of Beata Grant.)

temples, especially in India, employ temple musicians to accompany certain rituals and to walk ahead of portable icons of the deity during processions outside the temple. Playing traditional instruments such as oboe-like woodwinds, drums and other percussion pieces, the musicians fill the air with auspicious sound.

During medieval times troops of dancers, vocalists, and instrumentalists often performed works of classical religious poetry set to music on the steps of the great temples. Sacred dance reenacting mythic tales of the deities remains an important cultural treasure, but nowadays it takes the form of classical performance outside the context of religious ritual. Among the most popular dances are those that tell of the timeless romance of Krishna and his beloved Radha.

Hindu tradition includes a vast repertoire of devotional vocal music in dozens of major languages and regional styles. Singers pray to the various deities, often using classical poetry for their texts. Instrumental performers like the great sitar virtuoso Ravi Shankar have made classical Indian music known far beyond India in recent times. Working with the late violinist Yehudi Menuhin and the Beatles, to name only his most famous collaborators, Shankar popularized a tradition whose roots are deeply religious. Musical modes called *ragas* ("tints") play to the emotions, creating subtle "flavors" (*rasas*) with sounds and rhythms tailored to every season and time of day. God creates the world through sound, and dances creation into existence. Human beings need music and dance to connect with the divine.

233

Do Hindus have any special **dietary concerns**?

Food has always had powerful symbolic associations in Hindu tradition, beginning with the ancient Vedic sacrificial rites. Not until the rise of Jainism and Buddhism, with their emphasis on nonviolence, did vegetarianism become part of mainstream Hindu practice. Brahmins have generally been more careful to observe vegetarian practice than have members of other castes. Among the various denominations, Vaishnavites have paid greater attention to dietary issues. All foods have specific effects on one of the three psycho-spiritual qualities called *gunas*—light or purity, excitement or energy, darkness or inertia. A traditional Vaishnava diet avoids foods that stir the passions (garlic, red fruits and vegetables) or incline one to negative moods (flesh and intoxicants), while emphasizing those that have a positive effect (dairy products, grains, most fruits and vegetables). *Sannyasis* of all denominations are usually strict vegetarians. But the majority of Hindus nowadays tend to regard all foods, taken in moderation and as part of a balanced and healthful diet, as religiously acceptable. Most believe that strict vegetarianism is required only in ritual settings and in celebration of specifically religious observances. Some Hindus still refuse to take meals in the presence of members of other castes, whether lower or higher than their own, but this is a social rather than a dietary concern.

Do Hindus **pray** in any particular **language**?

Sanskrit remains the official sacred language of Hindu liturgical ritual. Ancestor of a number of modern Indian languages, Sanskrit is also linguistically connected with classical languages such as Latin and Greek and with modern languages such as Persian and a host of European tongues. Many Hindus still learn a little Sanskrit, not through formal language instruction, but through the use of ritual phrases and prayers. During temple rituals the priests typically recite sometimes lengthy texts from the Vedas in a chant using four or five tones. When families offer *puja* at home, the prayer leader often recites a number of short standard prayers in Sanskrit. Devotional hymns and prayers in a number of regional Indian vernacular languages, such as Telugu, Tamil, Kannada, and Bengali, as well as in India's "official" national language, Hindi, are standards in many ritual settings.

What are the **principal** Hindu **rites of passage**?

Hindu tradition includes important *samskaras,* "activators" or "impressions," for the various ages of life. Specific *samskaras* are associated with birth, childhood, adulthood, and older age. Connected with birth are rituals sanctifying conception, prayers for a male child, the husband's expression of love by grooming his wife between the fourth and seventh months of pregnancy, and welcoming the newborn with blessings that include placing a little *ghee* and honey on the child's tongue. Childhood sacraments include conferral of a name anywhere from eleven to forty-one days after birth;

making its first taste of solid food at around six months; piercing of the ears for gold earrings in either the first, third, or fifth year; and shaving the head any time from day thirty-one to the fourth year of life. One childhood ritual deserves notice. Initiation into religious studies is called *upanayana*, "bringing near," in which the youngster (girls were once included, but are generally not these days) is affiliated with a guru for formal tutelage in the Vedas. Another ritual marks the completion of formal studies, celebrating an official end to childhood and entry into adulthood.

Samskaras associated with adult life begin from puberty. The onset of menstruation and the shaving of a boy's beard for the first time occasion ceremonies in the home. When young adults are engaged their families exchange gifts. Marriage ceremonies can be quite grand, including great processions in which the groom makes his entry on a white steed. Some Hindus still acknowledge the passage into older adulthood at about age forty-eight, but more widely practiced still is the moment at which an older man puts ordinary social and family concerns behind him and becomes a renunciant or *sannyasi*. Last of all come the *samskaras* surrounding death, cremation, and mourning.

Are there **distinctive forms** of Hindu **initiation**?

Boys of the "twice-born" castes are initiated into the tradition in ceremonies called *upanayana*, which mark the beginning of formal instruction in sacred learning. The initiate receives a thread and wears it draped across the shoulder as a symbol of this "second birth." Women no longer receive the thread and only Brahmins nowadays wear it when not engaged in ritual ceremonies. Sacred threads are of white wool for Brahmins, of red hemp for Kshatriyas, and of yellow wool for Vaishyas. Tradition dictated that Brahmins be initiated at seven or eight years of age, Kshatriyas at eleven, and Vaishyas at twelve. But regardless of caste, most of those who still engage in the formal ceremony generally associate it with puberty.

How do Hindus **ritualize marriage**?

Traditional Hindu families continue the ancient practice of arranged marriage and generally do not countenance the kind of dating practices prevalent among non-Hindus in the United States. Marriage within one's caste remains a major concern for most Hindus, whether within India or abroad. An extended period of betrothal usually follows the initial arrangements between the families, and includes the exchange of gifts and chaperoned meetings of the betrothed.

Weddings typically occur in the early evening, after sunset, in a venue chosen by the families. In the temple, the home, or at a local hotel, one or more priests preside over the ceremony, reciting set ritual texts from the scriptures. In India one priest often appears as a representative for each family. Astrological consultation still often determines the specific auspicious timing of the ceremony. Wedding ceremonies begin

A young couple in a traditional Hindu marriage ceremony.

with the family of the bride symbolically "giving away" their daughter. After the community greets the new couple, the officiant chants prayers while the bride and groom sit before a fire holding hands. Concluding the formal ritual, the bride and groom express consent by taking the "seven steps" symbolizing energy, vitality, success, happiness, wealth (traditionally measured in livestock), auspicious turning of the seasons, and friendship. Extended receptions generally follow the ceremonies.

What is the practice known as **sati**?

The word *sati* originally referred to a "woman of virtue," a reference to a newly widowed individual who joined her husband in death by throwing herself on his funeral pyre. The name comes from Shiva's wife Sati, who committed suicide after her father insulted her new husband. Ritual suicide by widows spread through medieval times and continued well into the early modern era. Even after the practice was outlawed in 1829, it continued in many villages. Incidents of sati still occasionally make headlines, but increasing social action on behalf of women's rights continues to improve the situation all over India.

How do Hindus deal ritually with **death and mourning**?

Hindus generally prefer cremation to burial, and most hope that their loved ones will scatter their ashes over the waters of the Ganges or one of India's many other sacred rivers. Every year many thousands of Hindu families bring the bodies of their loved ones to Banaras for cremation at the "burning *ghats* (steps)" toward the downstream side of the holy city. There (or closer to home if they cannot travel easily), led by the eldest son or an older male relative, the family completes a set of ancient rituals. They bathe and dress the body and light the pyre. The ritual leader walks four times to the left around the pyre and pours *ghee* over the body while the family chant divine names.

For anywhere from eight days to a month the family observes a period of mourning and ritual impurity. To bring that period to a close, many families arrange a ritual meal called *shraddha*. Relatives must administer to and nourish the dead person's spirit, lest it continue to travel abroad as a restless and potentially troublesome demon. In the case of a famous Brahmin, an extended period of mourning might last a full year. Especially holy persons, such as noted *gurus*, are sometimes not cremated but buried, seated upright in the lotus posture. Some sects, such as the Lingayats or Virashaivas, prefer burial for all members—possibly the result of Islamic influence. Hindus in Europe and the United States generally cremate their dead within twenty-four hours of death. Mourners, wearing mostly white, gather at the home for a final viewing. Family members often arrange a memorial service in the local temple to observe the death anniversary.

BUDDHISM

HISTORY AND SOURCES

When and where did **Buddhism begin**?

Buddhism began in a region of northeast India, part of which is present-day Nepal. During the mid-sixth century B.C.E. the kingdom of Koshala ruled the area from its capital city of Shravasti (also known as Kapilavastu). One of the realm's leading factions was the Shakya clan, traditionally identified as belonging to the Kshatriya or warrior caste. India at that time was politically fragmented into well over a dozen major regional powers. The vast majority of the population practiced forms of Hindu tradition under the leadership of a strong Brahmin priesthood. Ritual and belief centered largely on this-worldly concerns, such as managing weather to insure good harvest and curing illness. But some who had inherited the ancient tradition were beginning to question its efficacy. The famed holy city of Benares was part of the Koshala realm. There and elsewhere in the kingdom individuals and small groups of religious seekers raised issues about possible life after death, including the notion of rebirth into other modes of existence. Within the Hindu tradition the new questioning gave rise to the scriptures called the Upanishads, with their deep reflection on the nature of the self and of greater spiritual realities. Some of these new seekers parted company with mainstream Hindu tradition altogether and eventually developed into whole new communities of belief and practice. One such community is now called the Jain tradition, named after the *jinas* or "spiritual conquerors" to whom tradition attributes its founding spirit.

The demanding ascetic discipline taught by Jainism's *tirthankaras* ("those who find crossing places in the river") formed one of the religious options available as early Buddhism developed. Buddhism itself would join Jainism as one of a number of splinter groups that, from a Hindu perspective, were unacceptable. These "heretics" got the name *nastika*, "those who deny" the fundamentals of Hindu belief as it was evolving

239

then. What we now call Buddhism thus grew out of an age of political and spiritual ferment, offering seekers one of a number of significant religious options.

Who was the Buddha and what does tradition say about his early life?

According to widely accepted tradition, a child called *Siddhartha* ("he who has achieved his goal") Gautama was born around 563 B.C.E. Recent scholarship has begun to offer various views as to the chronology of the Buddha's life, but this text will retain the more traditional account since it conveys an important sense of the "feel" of Buddhist lore. Siddhartha's father, Shuddhodana, was a wealthy member of the ruling elite, a prince of sorts. When the child was born, his father consulted religious specialists to see what portents the boy's body might communicate. They told him the child was destined to become either a world-renouncer or a "wheel-turner" (*chakra-vartin,* an expression roughly equivalent to "mover and shaker" and sometimes extended to mean "king of all India"). Shuddhodana resolved that his son would take the path of power and influence, so he contrived to shelter the boy from any experience that might incline him another way.

Gautama lived a life of ease and pleasure in his father's palace, surrounded by wealth and beauty and the trappings of authority. He married at sixteen and had a son. As it turned out, Gautama's father failed to insulate his son from contact with the harsher side of life. Eventually Gautama would leave the palace, as well as his own wife and child, and seek his own path. The traditional story is clearly meant to underscore certain dramatic elements in the Buddha's spiritual development. His son, Rahula, reappears later in the story as one of the early monks, and his wife is said to have become one of the first nuns.

What were the four passing sights?

On several occasions the young Gautama had to leave the confines of the palace. Although his father instructed his servants to clear the road of any unsightly reminders of human frailty, Gautama would nevertheless find himself asking the hardest questions of all. On one excursion, he saw someone bent and struggling to walk. Old age, his servants explained, a hardship many people must eventually face. Another time, Gautama spotted a leper lying by the way in pain. That was illness, his servants explained; it happened to many people. Then one day Gautama's entourage came across a funeral procession. Death, said his servants, and no one escapes that. Finally, according to the traditional account, Gautama saw by the road a young man who obviously possessed nothing and yet seemed content. That was the world-renouncer Shuddhodana so badly wanted his son not to become. The traditional account holds that all of the four experiences resulted from divine intervention, the gods assuming the roles of suffering human beings so that Gautama would be moved to take the next critical steps in ensuring the possibility of enlightenment for humankind. The clearly formu-

Three scenes from the life of the Buddha on wooden wall paintings, Jogye-sa Zen temple, Seoul, South Korea. They depict, from left to right, one of the "Four Passing Sights,' Siddhartha Gautama's departure over the palace walls, and his quest for Enlightenment in meditation beneath the Bodhi tree.

laic account admirably sums up the key issues that would eventually provide the foundations of Gautama's enlightenment and Buddhahood.

How did **Gautama** become the **Buddha**?

At the age of twenty-nine, tradition says, Gautama made the "great renunciation" of comfort and security. Borne aloft by his horse, he went over the palace walls to pursue a realistic understanding of the world and the human condition. Gautama went first to learn from two Hindu teachers, spiritual guides like those who tutor seekers in the Hindu scriptures called the Upanishads. Unsatisfied with that more philosophical approach, Gautama joined a group of ascetics in Benares, representatives of the Jain movement perhaps, and subjected himself to several years of dire austerity. When that, too, failed, he moved on and decided to meditate alone under a tree until he achieved enlightenment. During the course of seven weeks there Siddhartha went through four trancelike stages, arriving finally at the stark realization of what Buddhist tradition calls the most basic truths of human life. Siddhartha was now worthy of the name Buddha, the Enlightened One.

But tradition suggests that the Buddha experienced a terrible interior struggle with the temptation to keep his newfound wisdom to himself. Mara, the demon, summoned up all his might to prevent the truths of enlightenment from spreading abroad. Overcoming all inclination to selfishness, the thirty-five-year-old Buddha dedicated himself to teaching others the way to freedom from attachment that is the cause of all suffering. He returned to Benares, reunited with the five ascetics with whom he had parted company earlier, and preached the sermon called "Turning the Wheel of the Law." Now the Buddha was indeed a "wheel-turner," but not as his father had envisioned. For the next forty-five years, he would turn the greatest of all wheels, that of the *dharma*. He died in Kushinagara at the age of eighty, in about 483 B.C.E., of apparent food poisoning.

What were the **earliest Buddhist sacred texts**?

For several centuries the Buddhist community preserved the treasure of the Buddha's teachings orally. Monks and devout laypeople memorized increasingly formulaic versions of what the Buddha had said and the way he had behaved. As the community of monks became more stable, settling for longer periods in fixed residences, the practice of communal recitation of the sacred words became the primary mechanism for maintaining the teachings intact. Any error in recitation could be corrected immediately to ensure uniformity and, it was believed, perfect accuracy. Local communities recited the text in their own vernaculars, since no one sacred language had been decreed.

Earliest texts were organized into three major groupings or "baskets" (*pitaka*). One, called the Vinaya Pitaka, contained all the rules of monastic discipline. Another gathered the Buddha's speeches (the Sutra Pitaka), and a third, much later, text included seven lengthy theoretical interpretations of the Buddha's teaching (the Abhidharma Pitaka). At a gathering called the Third Council in 250 B.C.E., members agreed on the first official formulation of all three baskets as a single scripture called the Tripitaka in a northeastern Indian language called Pali. Monks continued to keep the texts alive almost exclusively through memory for perhaps another century or so. Finally, the sacred texts were systematically committed to writing and became the basis of what is now known as the Pali Canon.

What other **early schools** and **scriptures** are especially important in the history of Buddhism?

A number of early Buddhist schools or denominations arose in India during the five or six centuries after the Buddha's death. One cluster, known collectively as the *Hinayana* ("Small Vehicle") schools, developed as a result of differing interpretations of what manner of being the Buddha was. The most important of these schools is the *Theravada* ("Wisdom of the Elders"), the branch largely responsible for the Pali Canon. Theravada Buddhists taught that the Buddha was a historical human being who counseled others to pursue their own path to enlightenment. But some Buddhists inclined toward more expansive, spiritual interpretation.

The *Mahasanghikas* ("Proponents of the Great Assembly") taught that the Buddha's many previous lives as a Buddha-to-be, a *Bodhisattva*, prior to his birth as Siddhartha Gautama meant that the Buddha was more of a cosmic spiritual being than a mere mor-

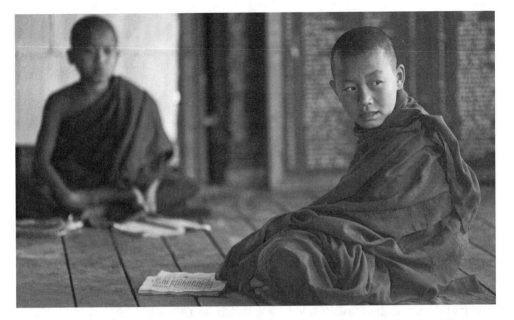

Boys studying the Theravada texts at the Shwe Yan Pyay monastery school in Nyaung Shwe, Myanmar. (Zzvet / Shutter-stock.com.)

tal. All but one volume of their sizeable Sanskrit (called Buddhist Hybrid) scriptures have been lost. Another school, the *Sarvastivadins* ("Proponents of the View that All Exists"), further emphasized the importance of the *Bodhisattva*'s spiritual evolution as a model of growth in virtue. They, too, produced a body of sacred writing, but the Sanskrit originals were lost and we know of them through Chinese and Tibetan translations.

Next to the Theravada school the most important of the early denominations was the *Mahayana* ("Great Vehicle"). So called because of its wider appeal, Mahayana teaching emphasized the larger-than-life qualities of the Buddha. More than a mere mortal, the Buddha was a saving figure whose compassion filled the universe and whose grace was available to all who asked. Mahayana scriptures in Sanskrit included sutras claiming to be the Buddha's own words, commentaries and treatises called *shastras,* and esoteric works called *Tantras* used by smaller sects.

Major Buddhist Scriptures

A. The Pali Canon (Tripitaka, "Three Baskets")

1. Vinaya-Pitaka (Basket of Order): contains material about the life of the Buddha and the origin of the monastic community, including the rules of discipline for monks.

2. Sutra-Pitaka (Basket of Instruction): contains teaching of the Buddha and his early disciples as well as the 547 *Jataka* (birth stories) tales of the Buddha's previous lives.

3. Abhidharma-Pitaka (Basket of Higher Teaching): contains seven sections of teaching designed for specialized instruction of advanced initiates, and it dates from the fourth century B.C.E.

1. The Mahavastu: Dating from around the first century B.C.E., this text was originally part of a much larger collection produced by the Mahasanghika school. It focuses on the various stages in the career of a Buddha-to-be (*Bodhisattva*) and details the various previous lives of the salvific being eventually embodied in the historical Buddha.

2. Questions of King Milinda (Milindapanha): Compiled in North India around the third century C.E., this text is a philosophical dialogue between a Buddhist sage named Nagasena and the Bactrian king Menander (Pali: Milinda). The discourses cover basic Buddhist themes such as self-lessness, suffering, and the attainment of nirvana.

3. The Lotus of the Good Law Sutra (Saddharmapundarika): Used especially by Tendai Buddhists of Japan, this text arose in its present form about 250 B.C.E. and is especially concerned with conveying the notion that all sentient beings possess the essential quality necessary for attainment of Buddhahood.

4. The Perfection of Wisdom (Prajñaparamita Sutra): With parts that date as far back as the first century C.E., this text is a collection of sayings of the Buddha that are in effect a comprehensive explanation of the attainment of Buddhahood.

Was **Buddhism** ever **identified** with any **political regimes**?

Buddhism enjoyed the patronage of two very influential Indian monarchs. A ruler of the Maurya dynasty named Ashoka (r. 270–230 B.C.E.) is credited with the first dramatic expansion of Buddhism across much of India. He declared Buddhism the state creed and sent missionaries westward through present-day Afghanistan and south to Sri Lanka. Not until nearly four centuries later did Buddhism again profit from formal political support. A king of the Kushan dynasty named Kanishka (r. 120–162 C.E.) picked up where Ashoka had left off. In fact, Kanishka may have learned of Buddhism in his native land to the northwest of India as a result of Ashoka's earlier missionary endeavors. Kanishka launched a new wave of missionary activity, dispatching monks to China, Tibet, and Burma. But it was the newer Mahayana teaching that Kanishka supported.

Only one other important Indian regime would give Buddhism the official seal of approval. From its capitol in Bengal to the northeast, the Pala dynasty (750–1150) supported a brand of Mahayana teaching that retained esoteric elements from Hinduism. Before the last of the Palas died, Buddhism would be nearly defunct in India. Outside of India, several Buddhist dynasties helped to establish the tradition in southeast Asia. On Indonesia's central island, Java, the Shailendras (778–864) professed a type of Mahayana teaching. Meanwhile, Buddhist monarchs helped the tradition take root in Tibet.

How was **Buddhism spread** through **Southeast Asia**?

Buddhists call the spread of the tradition through lineages of teachers and students "*dharma* transmission." Sri Lanka was one of the first regions outside of India to form a link in the "southern transmission." A lineage known as the Theravada ("Wisdom of the Elders") was introduced to Sri Lanka as early as the third century B.C.E. It spread into Burma and was well rooted there by about the fifth or sixth century C.E. There Buddhism benefitted from the patronage of King Anawratha (1044–77), under whose dynasty Burma became almost entirely Buddhist. According to tradition, Ashoka's own missionaries brought the faith to Thailand as early as the third century B.C.E. The earliest solid evidence of Buddhism in Thailand is indigenous Buddhist art from eight or nine centuries later. In Kampuchea (formerly called Cambodia) a blend of Mahayana and Hindu beliefs were dominant around the royal complexes of Angkor toward the end of the first millennium. Theravada teaching came to the fore after about 1200, but its institutions have just barely survived disastrous political upheavals of the late twentieth century. Vietnam seems to have participated in the Theravada transmission early on, but missionaries from China succeeded in establishing Mahayana teaching there between about 1000 and 1400.

How did Buddhism become **important** in **China, Korea**, and **Japan**?

Buddhism's spread across north and east Asia was an extended and complex process that was part of the "northern transmission" begun as early as the reign of Ashoka (r. 270-230 B.C.E.). Serious missionary efforts commenced in China sometime during the first century C.E. Within a century or so, a new wave of monk-translators from India was engaged in large-scale proselytizing among the Chinese. Buddhism spread rapidly and flourished in the form of several denominations and schools. Some estimate that over half the population had accepted the new tradition by around 450 C.E. A major persecution in 845 under a Daoist emperor did serious damage to all but the Pure Land and Ch'an (Zen) lineages.

A Chinese missionary monk introduced Buddhism to Korea around the late fourth century. By the mid-sixth century, Buddhism enjoyed royal patronage and spread throughout the Korean peninsula. In about 552 the Korean monarch sent the Japanese emperor, as a gift, an image of the Buddha and some sacred texts. The new faith soon found itself welcome, and adapted rapidly in the Land of the Rising Sun.

Monks from China and Korea continued to bring the teachings of various denominations to Japan during the seventh and eighth centuries. Those schools proved attractive to relatively small numbers of people. So during the early ninth century, three Japanese monks who had been studying in China brought back simpler teachings with greater popular appeal. Several schools based on Pure Land teach-

A Monk of the Son (Korean for Zen) Buddhist order in front of his cell at the To Son Sa temple in the hills overlooking Seoul, Korea.

ing enjoyed considerable success over the next three hundred years. Then a new wave of Buddhist growth and development washed over Japan in the late twelfth and early thirteenth centuries. Honen (1133–1212) established the Pure Land school as a distinct denomination, and two Japanese monks founded the main branches of Zen Buddhism.

How would you sum up the **history of Buddhism**?

For a quick overview, we can conveniently divide Buddhist history into four periods.

1. Foundations: A developmental period begins with the Buddha's enlightenment and early teaching and spans five centuries. During this period, Buddhists finalized their earliest scriptures in written form and spread their basic religious institutions across much of southern Asia. Several major schools of Buddhists articulated distinctive doctrinal and philosophical views and established themselves in India.

2. Spread: For about the next five or six centuries, up to around 550 C.E., Buddhist missionaries carried the message and scriptures of the various Indian branches of the tradition throughout central, southeast, and eastern Asia. As Buddhism's various schools traveled into new settings, still newer forms of Buddhist thought and practice evolved.

3. Inculturation and further development: From the sixth century to the eighteenth, Chinese, Korean, and Japanese cultures—as well as those in Tibet, Thailand, and Cambodia—all put their recognizable stamp on the Middle Way of the Buddha. Monks still traveled great distances and imported scriptures and artistic treasures from one culture to another. Buddhist kingdoms rose and fell in various parts of southeast Asia. During these centuries, sometimes referred to as Buddhism's medieval period, patterns of Buddhist institutional life that would endure into modern times took root all over Asia.

4. Colonialism and cultural readjustment: Sometimes called the modern period, the eighteenth through twentieth centuries have witnessed further dramatic changes, resulting from both political realignments and adaptation to accelerated intercultural communication. Buddhism is now a truly global tradition. Pilgrims have begun to return in great numbers to the sacred sites in India. Although Buddhism virtually disappeared from the land of its birth perhaps eight hundred of years ago, small Buddhist communities are again springing up on Indian soil.

Buddhism Timeline

Date	Event
c. 563–483 B.C.E.	Life of the Buddha
473 B.C.E.	First Buddhist Council
383 B.C.E.	Second Buddhist Council

Date	Event
273–236 B.C.E.	Reign of Emperor Ashoka
250 B.C.E.	Third Buddhist Council
c. 200 B.C.E.	Rise of Mahayana Buddhism; Theravada Buddhism
160 B.C.E.	Prajñaparamita Literature
120 B.C.E.	Synod of the Sarvastivadins
c. 100 C.E.	Lotus Sutra; Pali Canon
r. 120–162 C.E.	Reign of Emperor Kanishka
c. 150 C.E.	Fourth Buddhist Council
c. 200 C.E.	Nagarjuna, philosopher
220–552 C.E.	Missions to Vietnam, China, Korea, Burma, Java, Sumatra, Japan
fl. c. 430 C.E.	Career of Buddhaghosa, philosopher
594 C.E.	Buddhism proclaimed Japanese state religion
749 C.E.	First Buddhist monastery in Tibet
800 C.E.	Founding of Japanese Tendai (Saicho d. 822) and Shingon (Kukai d. 835) sects
845 C.E.	T'ang Dynasty persecutes Chinese Buddhists
1065 C.E.	Hindu Invasion of Sri Lanka
1133–1212 C.E.	Honen, founder of Japanese Pure Land tradition
1193–1227 C.E.	Rise of Japanese Zen sects
1203 C.E.	Destruction of Vikramasila, end of Buddhism in India
1222–1282 C.E.	Nichiren, philosopher
1260–1368 C.E.	Tibetan Buddhism influential in China
1360 C.E.	Buddhism becomes state religion in Thailand
1543–1588 C.E.	Final conversion of Mongols
1856–1857 C.E.	Fifth Buddhist Council
1868–1871 C.E.	Meiji Persecution of Buddhism in Japan
1954–1956 C.E.	Sixth Buddhist Council in Rangoon, Burma
1959 C.E.	Communist China represses Buddhism in Tibet

RELIGIOUS BELIEFS

Is the term **revelation** useful in understanding **Buddhist tradition?**

Revelation, as a number of traditions use the term, presupposes that the ultimate truths remain beyond the grasp of human beings until the source or custodian of those truths chooses to make them available. By "unveiling" the mystery, the giver of truth entrusts the ultimate realities to humankind, often through a mediating figure such as a prophet. Buddhist tradition considers ultimate truths within reach of any person willing to pay attention. The truth is not, as some have always believed, "out there." It is "right in front of you and within yourself." But dealing consistently with that kind of in-your-face truth is difficult and demanding—and often lonely. As a result, Buddhists over many centuries and in many places have developed their distinctive variations on the theme of revelation, with its suggestion of privileged access to hidden truths. Buddha told his followers to be lamps unto their own feet, but there have always been Buddhist teachers and preachers to remind people what the Buddha said. Buddha told his followers the truth was not wrapped in arcane mysteries, but there have always been special, sometimes very esoteric, teachings about the secret meanings of what the Buddha said. The major difference here between Buddhism and, say, the Abrahamic faiths, is that the concept of prophetic revelation is at the heart of the Jewish, Christian, and Islamic worldviews.

Are **doctrine and dogma** important to Buddhists?

The Buddha emphasized that all religious and ethical teaching, *dharma*, is like a raft. You use a raft to get across a body of water. Once on the far shore, you would hardly choose to strap the raft to your back and trudge on under its bulky burden. Doctrine is a tool, a temporary convenience, and not an end in itself. The problem with doctrine, he taught, is that it can easily distract people from their goal. Those who ask too many questions in search of doctrinal clarity and certainty are like a person who has been shot with an arrow. Friends approach to remove the arrow but the wounded person waves them off. Not until he knows who shot the arrow and what he looked like, of what kind of wood it was made, and what kind of bird provided the feathers, will he submit to having the arrow removed. Such speculation is simply a waste of time. Pay attention to the matter at hand, Buddha counseled.

Not long after the Teacher's death, followers of his *dharma* nevertheless developed many elaborate doctrinal frameworks with which to interpret the Buddha's teaching. Each of the various denominations has its preferred scripture and its own theoretical perspective, and some have emphasized correct belief as a criterion of membership. But no major Buddhist school has defined a large body of doctrine in the form of dogmatic pronouncements that require the explicit assent of all members. Buddhists often use the Sanskrit term *sasana* in reference to the whole package of belief and practice that the Buddha taught as a way of life.

How did the **Buddha reinterpret Hindu teaching**?

Key notions Siddhartha learned as a young Hindu included those of *karma* (action), *dharma* (law), *samsara* (cycles of rebirth), and *moksha* (final liberation). Most Hindus of his day understood the concept of *karma* as external ritual action performed in the hope of tapping into divine power. Some religious thinkers were beginning to suggest that, along with ancient Vedic ritual under the direction of the priestly class, the acts of individual people might also influence their spiritual as well as material prospects.

Others, like the Buddha, took their questioning of the old ways much further. They began to spiritualize the law of *karma,* explaining that choice and intent were more important than outward deeds. Along with their reinterpretation of *karma,* some contemporaries of the Buddha were also rethinking the Hindu concept of *dharma.* No longer merely the impersonal, inscrutable law of cosmic order, *dharma* now took on a personal ethical dimension. In the Buddha's view, *karma* included all the results of each individual's choices. He emphasized the need to purify one's intentions of all self-centeredness. Perform each act purely because it is your *"dharma,"* not because you hope to gain personally.

The Hindu notion of *samsara* meant that the souls of individuals who died unliberated from the negative effects of their past actions would return in another form. The Buddha understood *samsara* to mean not only the cycle of physical rebirths, but the whole series of interior or spiritual stages the individual went through on the way to enlightenment. Finally, the Hindu idea of *moksha* meant the release of the indestructible soul (*atman*) of each individual from the cycle of *samsara.*

The Buddha also taught the possibility of a final liberation, but he gave it an important twist. Genuine liberation meant the complete cessation of all craving—even of craving for liberation itself. He called that final freedom nirvana, "no wind," symbolizing the extinction of the flames of desire. Most radical of all, the Buddha rejected the Hindu concept of an immortal soul, teaching that there was in fact no permanent "self" at all.

How does the Buddhist tradition **describe existence** in general?

Buddhist teaching focuses on three fundamental qualities of all things—known as the "three marks of existence." Two are fairly obvious to anyone who cares to look, and are at the heart of the experience of enlightenment. The first is hardship or suffering (Pali *dukkha,* Sanskrit *duhka*), the second impermanence (*anicca/anitya*). Nobody is immune to sadness and disappointment. No one has a lock on success and genuine contentment. And everything comes to an end. Everything. The third quality is far from obvious even to the most careful observer, but an awareness of it does follow from the realities of suffering and impermanence. That is the notion that there is no permanent, indestructible core or "soul" at the center of any being (*anatta/anatman*). Hindu tradition taught Siddhartha Gautama that at the center of each individual being was a "self" or *atman* that survived physical death to be reincarnated in another life, assuming the person died still enslaved by the effects of self-centered choices. The Buddha's reinterpretation of Hindu tradition on this point was so radical that it cuts right to the psychological bone. Take away the "soul" and what remains?

Nothing, apparently. But the Buddha was not attempting to empty life of its meaning. He wanted people to change their minds about what matters most. Look hard at what motivates you, what can make you nearly desperate to achieve this good or avoid that evil. Look carefully, the Buddha argued, and you will see that the qualities that attract or repel you are deceptions. Probe deeply into your choices and you **249**

If there is no self that survives death, what is there to be reborn?

Buddhist tradition has devised various intricate ways of explaining the problem represented by the concept of nonself (*anatta*). One widely used image is that of a seal-ring. Take a pad of warm wax and press the seal-ring into it and you get a very clear impression, one that firms up as the wax cools. You've transferred "something" without actually leaving anything but an impression. The seal-ring is something like what remains when a human being dies still enslaved to inappropriate craving and desires. It represents the whole complex of psychic energies that make up a human "personality," energies so potent that most people are perfectly convinced of their individuality and separate personhood. In the cycle of death and rebirth, what transfers from one existence across the chasm of death into the "wax" of a new embodiment is precisely that incredibly powerful ego impulse. As the Buddha saw it, no one can be finally free so long as he or she clings to the notions of "I, me, mine."

will see that what you are really looking for you cannot get from this possession or that person. Each being is simply what it is and it is a serious mistake to treat your world as though it existed for you, as if what you value in each thing is its value. In a sense, the Buddha argued, all things are "empty," in that they simply do not possess the "soul" that a grasping, craving person invests them with. Pile all your expectations onto some person or object as though you truly hope it will deliver what you want, and you are making the fundamental mistake. The notion of nonsoul (*anatta*) is difficult to understand, but it is one of the Buddha's most provocative teachings.

What is **Enlightenment**?

In Buddhist tradition the term "enlightenment" means the simple, clear realization of the most basic truths about life. It presupposes the utmost attentiveness to whatever one is experiencing as one experiences it. And for that reason it sounds too simple and ordinary to be worth pursuing. But enlightenment begins and ends precisely with the simple and the ordinary. It is the realization that the headlong pursuit of pleasure (hedonism) and the dogged avoidance of pleasure (extreme asceticism) both yield the same results: suffering. Hope fuels the one, fear the other. Both are a flight from the real as it confronts every individual in the here and now.

Enlightenment means grasping the fundamental realities summed up in Buddhism's "Four Noble Truths." First, life is difficult. Look around. As the Four Passing Sights taught Siddhartha, the human condition includes some hard inescapable realities. This first truth is not as pessimistic as it might sound. It is the ultimate in realism. If human beings had the power to change the basic realities we experience, we would have done so long ago. But we can change the ways we respond to experience. Second, all that hardship and suffering comes from inappropriate attachment or grasping. Whatever I "must" either have or avoid will finally make me suffer. If I get what I want, it will soon disappoint. If I manage to avoid for a time what I fear most, something else will soon replace it. There is a solution in the third truth: to avoid suffering avoid inappropriate craving. Under ordinary circumstances no human being can stop craving altogether. The Buddha nearly killed himself with austerities before he realized the futility of such an approach. What is appropriate behavior? The fourth truth says simply, to stop inappropriate craving, and follow the Eightfold Noble Path.

What is the **Eightfold Noble Path**?

True to his hardheaded realism, the Buddha did not send his followers off on a wild goose chase. He suggested a method for achieving a balanced approach to everyday experience. Buddhists call his teaching the Middle Path because it aims at balance, propriety, and equanimity. Eat what you need and use whatever is necessary for a modest style of living. The eight elements in the classical formulation of the standards for such a life are divided into three larger categories: wisdom, ethics, and concentration. Achieving wisdom requires proper belief in the form of deep understanding of the Four Noble Truths, and proper intent, which means that one performs all acts out of compassion rather than out of selfish motives.

The next three steps on the Path involve ethics. Proper speech means avoiding all evils of the tongue. Proper action, expressed negatively, means refraining from inappropriate sexual relationships, killing, and stealing. And proper livelihood calls for the avoidance of occupations that cause harm, such as dealing in slavery or weapons.

Training in concentration also has a triple foundation. Proper effort means perfect balance in one's attitude toward work. Proper attentiveness flows from deep reflection on the Four Noble Truths. And proper absorption, a lofty goal, means the ability to be genuinely content in equilibrium between pursuing goals

Statue of the thousand-armed eleven-headed bodhisattva Guan Yin, in a religious goods store, Keelung, Taiwan, the port city of the Taiwanese capital of Taipei.

and running from fears. Everything depends on carefully measured responses. That does not necessarily mean the death of spontaneity. It means a habit of discipline and keen awareness of one's personal motivations.

Summary of Four Truths and Eightfold Noble Path

The Four Noble Truths

1) Life is suffering (*dukkha*)
2) Craving is the cause of suffering
3) In order to end suffering one must end craving
4) The means to end craving is the Noble Eightfold Path

The Noble Eightfold Path	Threefold Training
1) Right views 2) Right intention	Wisdom (*prajña*)
3) Right speech 4) Right action 5) Right livelihood	Morality (*shila*)
6) Right effort 7) Right mindfulness 8) Right absorption	Concentration (*samadhi*)

What are the **Three Jewels** and **Five Vows**?

Perhaps the closest thing to a summary of Buddhist beliefs is the brief creedal formula of the "Three Jewels." "I take refuge in the Buddha; I take refuge in the *dharma*; I take refuge in the *sangha*." Buddhists in various places and times have interpreted those Jewels rather differently.

For many the Buddha was a human teacher and an example, but no more. For many others, the Buddha represented the universal possibility of enlightenment. Still others regard the Buddha, along with countless Buddhas-to-be called *Bodhisattvas,* as a divine power and source of grace and salvation.

Buddhist tradition retained the important Hindu term *dharma* but reinterpreted it. For Buddhists, dharma means all that the Buddha taught. They know *dharma* as enshrined in the sacred texts and communicated by religious teachers.

The term *sangha* means "assembly" and refers to the Buddhist Order of monks and nuns and, by extension, to the whole community of believers. Along with the affirmation of the "Three Jewels," the believers take a secondary but very important affirmation of the "precepts" or vows. Members of the monastic *sangha* take ten vows, while devout laypeople take the first five.

Many Buddhists begin their day by reciting the "Three" (refuges) and then adding the "Five" (precepts). They promise to refrain from killing, theft, unchastity, deception, and intoxication. Reaffirming one's commitment to the precepts functions not unlike a creedal statement of assent to the core beliefs of a religious tradition.

Could you sum up the Buddha's **classical teaching** on how a **"good" life** might unfold?

Any person who wishes to make sense of life must begin by hearing the *dharma,* seeking to understand the teaching of the utterly trustworthy Buddha. Translating the teaching into action means abiding by the fundamental recommendations and rules of conduct for living a moral life. Moving a step beyond the "ethical minimum" requires a person to seek greater personal discipline by guarding the senses and doing whatever is necessary to avoid the subtle corrosion of evil influences. That in turn inevitably leads to a higher level of mindfulness and awareness of each moment. This may seem at first to suggest a bland, even incredibly boring, life. But Buddhist tradition insists, paradoxically perhaps, that this alone can offer genuine appreciation and enjoyment— true bliss. Only such enlarged awareness is really worth the name "living," for everything else is life on autopilot, a sure recipe for stress and frustration.

At some point the seeker will need to pursue serious training in meditation. Meditative discipline aims immediately to help the seeker identify and neutralize sources of anxiety and uncertainty. A kind of spiritual map for serious seekers is called the "Twelve-spoked Wheel of Conditioned Arising." It describes in schematic fashion the cycle by which ignorance gives rise to intent to act, which in turn gives rise to consciousness, awareness of name and body, capacity for sense contact, actual contact, sensation, craving, grasping, becoming, birth, old age, and death. The seeker must in effect work backward through the chain of conditions to eliminate the ignorance at the root. Those who persevere along this path hope to arrive at a genuinely contemplative approach to life and, ultimately, at spiritual liberation. This classical teaching clearly lays out a difficult and demanding path. Relatively few are able to follow it consistently. That is one of the reasons that more popular forms of Buddhist devotion and practice have had a broader appeal.

Is there a distinctively **Buddhist ethic**?

Compassion for all sentient beings is the overriding principle in Buddhist ethics. It was compassion (*karuna*) that urged the Buddha to share his message of enlightenment. Life's greatest challenge is to act out of genuine altruism, to be and do for others without hoping for reward. Compassion needs to be doubly disciplined. One needs to work toward the alleviation of suffering purely because that is humanity's highest calling. But it is also essential to know how best to put compassion into action. That calls for the practical wisdom that comes from a keen awareness of one's own spiritual history, including a recollection of one's previous lives. The ability to "recall one's former existences" is a mark of genuine enlightenment and a sign of profound awareness. Buddhist ethics combine the compassion of one who appreciates the pervasiveness of suffering with the practical wisdom that comes from a detailed experiential knowledge of what "works." The result is a virtue called "skill in means" (*upaya*). In other words, it is the motive for behaving ethically—compassion—the framework within which to choose a course of action—wisdom—and the resources with which to act.

What are the **Ten *Paramitas*** ("Great Virtues") of the Bodhisattva?

The following ten virtues are to be attained after continuing efforts in numerous past lives as Buddha-to-be:

- Charity
- Morality
- Renunciation
- Wisdom
- Effort
- Patience
- Truth
- Determination
- Universal love
- Equanimity

What do Buddhists believe about ultimate spiritual **reality or God**?

One of the many issues the Buddha refused to speculate on was the existence or significance of gods. As a Hindu he naturally learned the traditional stories of the divinities. As a man of his time, with all its religious and intellectual ferment, the Buddha questioned the wisdom of reliance on ritual sacrifice. He did not deny the existence of the gods. He merely insisted that whatever power the gods might possess, it could not solve the fundamental human dilemma. That remained the sole responsibility of the individual person. Many Buddhist sacred texts talk of the gods in mythic terms. It was, for example, the gods who made sure young Siddhartha Gautama encountered the Four Passing Sights that turned his life around. But classical Buddhist teaching does not refer to an Ultimate Reality in personal terms. That changed as popular devotional forms of Buddhism developed, especially in China, Korea, and Japan. Buddha himself assumed virtually divine proportions, and the concept of the universal Buddha-nature superseded that of the Buddha as historical human teacher. Gods of ancient Hindu myth retained a place in the Buddhist spiritual cosmos but remained very much in the background.

Do Buddhists believe in **miracles**?

Popular lore about the Buddha and numerous other holy personages is bursting with accounts of miracles. Buddhist tradition attributes far more miraculous deeds to the

Four stone cosmic Buddhas of the cardinal directions flank the central Buddha, Vairocana, in a grouping especially important in the more esoteric branches of Japanese Mahayana Buddhism, at Ninnaji, a temple of the Shingon sect, in Kyoto, Japan.

Buddha than almost any other tradition ascribes to a foundational figure. Scores of wonders occur at the moment of the Buddha's birth, all portents of the event's cosmic significance. Lamps all across the world lit themselves at that moment, the mute sang, the lame danced, and birds were suspended in their flight. The Buddha is said to have performed dozens of fabulous feats throughout his lifetime, traveling great distances instantly, ascending into the air, subduing wild animals, and walking on water. Several of the wonders have become part of a canonical list of eight "Great Events," each associated with one of the cardinal or intermediate directions.

Hardheaded realist that he was, the Buddha does not appear to have claimed miraculous powers of any sort. But within a short time of his death tales of his superhuman powers multiplied. Important tales include 547 Jatakas, stories of the Buddha's previous lives as the Buddha-to-be. Incarnated in myriad different forms, the Bodhisattva performs countless marvels on behalf of all suffering beings. Many other important Buddhist leaders have enjoyed similar notoriety. Founders of lineages, denominations and monasteries from Tibet to Japan are said to have performed deeds like those attributed to the Buddha himself.

Are there **mythic elements** in Buddhist tradition?

Mythic expression plays a far less central role in Buddhist teaching than in Hinduism. In fact, you might say one of the Buddha's main concerns was to "demythologize" Hindu tradition as he had received it. Hindu myth introduces believers to the impenetrable mystery of the divine while attempting to describe how the divine presence infuses the world of human experience. The Buddha cautioned against taking refuge in myth. However potent the divine presence may be, it does not relieve human beings of ultimate responsibility for their own choices.

As in so many religious traditions, the foundational figure himself soon became the focal point of a new mythology. Even the most hardcore Theravada tradition leaves room for the Buddha to expand into a being of supramundane qualities. Wondrous tales of the Buddha's previous lives, the Jatakas radiate mythic energy. Some of the Mahayana denominations and sects, those of the widely popular Pure Land variety in particular, evolved their own complex descriptions of a multilevel cosmos ruled by multiple Buddhas and populated by countless lesser spiritual powers as well. Vajrayana Buddhism, represented especially by various Tibetan lineages, retained much of ancient Hinduism's mythic spirit and cast of characters. But the Tibetans interiorized the myth, interpreting the many spiritual beings as projections of the inner powers with which one identifies through meditative practice. Even in popular Mahayana and the more esoteric Vajrayana teachings, mythic elements never attain quite the centrality they enjoy in Hindu tradition.

Do Buddhists believe in an **afterlife**?

Although the Buddha himself emphasized the need to focus on this-worldly concerns, his followers soon developed a complex understanding of the spiritual structure of the universe. According to both Theravada and Mahayana models, all of reality is divided into three realms. The Realm of Desire (*kama-dhatu*) encompasses everything from innumerable Hells through the dwelling places of animals, humans, lesser gods, and the various paradises in which good people can expect to enjoy the fruits of a good life. Each level of Hell is suited to a particular kind of selfishness and evil. The heavens are similarly graded for the enjoyment of the just. A certain sexist attitude is built into the notion of Paradise, since in order to gain entry into the highest Heaven women must first be reborn as men.

Those reborn into the next major level up, the Realm of Form (*rupa-dhatu*), leave behind the senses of taste, touch, and smell. Through hearing, sight, and mental impressions they continue the ongoing process of spiritual refinement and education. Denizens of this realm's multiple Heavens (from sixteen to eighteen) progress upward through various stages of contemplative discipline, arriving finally at the third cosmic realm, that of Non-Form (*arupa-dhatu*). Dispensing with sight and hearing, dwellers in this realm progress through four additional Heavens through meditation, arriving at last at *nirvana*.

Beyond that, according to some Mahayana schools, lie several Buddha-fields. Transcendent Buddhas, such as Amitabha in China (Amida in Japan), reign over their individual Buddha-fields. Amitabha's is the Western Paradise called the Pure Land. Popular belief suggests that devotees can bypass the lower intermediate steps and progress directly to this final abode merely by expressing perfect faith in the transcendent Buddha.

What is meaning of the concept **Three Bodies of the Buddha**?

Related to the grand cosmological conception of the "three realms," the concept of the "three bodies" (*trikaya*) of the Buddha evolved as a way of explaining how the spiritual entity called the Buddha-nature could transcend all earthly realities and at the same time manifest itself in the world. Pure Buddha-nature existed in the *Dharma*-Body and was personified as the Primal or Universal Buddha. Living in various heavenly abodes that made up the Bliss-Body were the five principal "meditational" Buddhas, one ruling the center and four ruling the paradises at the four cardinal points. Transcendent Bodhisattvas assisted the celestial Buddhas in the work of salvation through grace. Involved in earthly affairs were the Buddhas and Bodhisattvas who entered history in the Manifestation-Body, subjecting themselves to time and change out of compassion for all suffering beings.

Does **millennialism** have a place in Buddhist thinking?

Buddhist interpretations of history, like those of Hindu tradition generally, are relatively unconcerned with notions like beginnings, progress, and endings. Time is so much grander than any human mind can fathom. Unimaginably large cycles give way to more of the same. But just as Hindu explanations of cosmic cycles can include a sense of expectation, so Buddhist tradition also makes room for a kind of "adventist" thinking. Buddhists call the spiritual person or power whose future coming holds hope for all believers Maitreya, "the Benevolent One."

Five thousand years after the death of this age's Historical Buddha, the one originally called Siddhartha Gautama, Maitreya will enter the world of time and change. At present Maitreya lives as a Bodhisattva in the Heaven called *Tushita* ("contented ones," the celestial realm reserved for future Buddhas). Both Theravada and Mahayana traditions give Maitreya an important role, but devotion to this Bodhisattva is much more developed in several Mahayana denominations. Classical Chinese teachings regarded Maitreya as a savior figure, but the cult of Amitabha gradually displaced that of Maitreya. Tibetan tradition holds that Maitreya will arrive in thirty thousand years to teach all people.

This Bodhisattva has a long history of popular devotion in Korea and Japan under the name Miruk or Miroku. Colossal statues of Miruk stand on Korean hillsides and in temple compounds, some visible for several miles. And in Japan, Kyoto's ancient Koryuji temple enshrines an exquisite sixth-century statue of Miroku. Gazing down on all who enter, the beautiful and very feminine-looking Miroku radiates compassion. Moving from the sublime to the deliberately ridiculous, a comical figure called Mi-lo in China and Hotei in Japan represents another facet of Maitreya altogether. Hotei is depicted as a fat, jovial, scantily clad character. He is actually a Chinese Zen monk named P'u-t'ai who claimed to be a manifestation of Maitreya.

Do Buddhists believe in **angels**?

Buddhist popular belief inherited and retained many of the different types of celestial and semi-divine beings that populated Hindu myth. Nearly all Hindu deities have their personal attendants. In addition, a variety of other spiritual presences fill the heavenly and earthly realms. Artists often depict these characters as floating gracefully, but they generally lack the wings most people associate with angels. A class of being called *apsaras* (Sanskrit for "moving in water") are the most numerous of these denizens of the intermediate realm. Early Buddhist artists sometimes depicted *apsaras* as devotees worshipping the Buddha's footprints or gathered around the tree of enlightenment. Another group, called the *gandharvas,* were Hindu demigods who entertained the deities as musicians and dancers. Buddhist tradition retained them in that capacity.

The classic angelic function of guardianship and protection resides in other classes of beings regarded as gods in some sects. *Lokapalas* ("World Guardians") are those who stand watch over the four quarters of the universe. Many Buddhist temples depict them as muscular, heavily armed gatekeepers. The *dharmapalas* ("Guardians of the Teaching") are a band of fearsome deities whose task is to guard believers (especially in Vajrayana). As a kind of personal deity assigned to each individual, these protectors can take on either benevolent or angry form, depending on whether they are dealing with a believer or with an enemy of the faith.

Do Buddhists believe in **devils**?

Perhaps the closest thing in Buddhism to what many readers think of when they hear the word "devil" is the archdemon Mara. As the Buddha achieved enlightenment, Mara assailed him in hopes of preventing him from sharing his newfound wisdom. Mara summoned up his own three seductive daughters as well as his hateful host of demons. Various troublesome beings, from the mildly mischievous to the viciously malevolent, haunt the Buddhist universe at every level. Unhappy spirits of the deceased pester the living. A class of characters called "Earth demons" personify various powers and riches of the earth itself. Human beings who die after a particularly unethical life may be reborn as one of a class of evil beings, inherited from Hindu tradition, called *asuras*. Just as the Buddha insisted that none of the gods could rescue anyone from the human condition, so he taught that no demonic power was great enough to destroy anyone. Still, mainstream Buddhism has allowed room for the ranks of devilish characters that are part of indigenous popular belief systems throughout Asia.

Are **dreams and visions** important to Buddhist tradition?

Important figures in Buddhist tradition are said to have learned essential truths through dreams and visions. Queen Maya dreamed that she would give birth under unusual circumstances to a child who would become the Buddha. In dreams famous people learn of the proper course of action. Buddhist sources tell, for example, of how a dream persuaded the Chinese Emperor Ming Di to send for Buddhist missionaries and scriptures. Stories of this sort are told about many holy persons throughout Buddhist history, usually as a vehicle for underscoring the individual's personal authority.

Accounts of dreams and visions are by no means uniquely Buddhist, of course, and tell us more about the tone and feel of popular Buddhist lore than about the tradition's central teachings. Visionary meditative techniques, a different matter altogether, are of great importance in some Mahayana schools. Esoteric schools, such as those of Tibetan Vajrayana Buddhism, use *mandalas* as visual aids in complicated techniques for

Sand-painted *mandala* executed by Tibetan monks of the Gelug-pa (Yellow Caps) to which the Dalai Lama belongs. (Photo courtesy of David Oughton.)

creating mental images. The meditator generates a visionary world patterned on the *mandala,* in which the divine and the human interact and all distinctions vanish. Simpler visualization techniques are used in the more popular Pure Land tradition as well. Facing west, the meditator visualizes the sun setting, and water turning into ice. Gradually, the mind fills with images of a golden land with crystalline streams, lotus-filled lakes with golden bottoms, and shores of diamond sand. As the Pure Land, with its myriad jewelled palaces, takes shape in the mind's eye, the meditator sees the Buddha Amitabha and his attendant Bodhisattvas. At length the meditator visualizes himself being reborn into that happy land enfolded in a lotus flower.

What does Buddhist tradition teach about **religious justification of violence**?

Though the Buddha himself grew up in a Kshatriya (warrior caste) family, he was also steeped in the tradition of *ahimsa,* noninjury, that was an increasingly important theme in religious groups emerging in his day, especially the Jain tradition. Classical Buddhist sources analyze the human tendency to violence as arising from a deep-seated pattern of consciousness. The fundamental problem is that the "three poisons" (hatred or anger, lust or craving, and ignorance or delusion) can easily control one's choices. People crave something and become insecure when they fear losing the object of their desire. Hatred and anger arise with the fear that an enemy will take what one prizes most, and one can then be easily deluded into thinking that violence is the only solution. Gradually the power of this delusion can become the dominant conviction of whole societies, leading to wholesale identification of large segments of humanity as "the enemy."

Over the centuries, schools of Buddhist thought in effect conceded that there were nonetheless certain circumstances in which violence might indeed be the solu-

259

tion of last resort. As so often happens in religious traditions of all kinds, Buddhist scholars sought specific justification in ancient sources. The example of the Buddha himself provided such legitimation. In one of the Jataka (stories of previous lives of the Buddha), the Teacher actually killed some Hindu "heretics" in order to preserve the dharma from degradation. A general principle arose that it was acceptable to kill one person to prevent the deaths of many others, though the killer would still be condemned to suffer a stint in Hell. By extension, a secondary principle allowed that it was preferable to kill another who is himself about to kill, on the grounds that the actual killer is acting altruistically, taking on himself the suffering that his victim would otherwise have had to undergo once he had carried out his crime. On a theoretical level, some have argued that since there is no individual "self," killing in any case results only in the illusion of ending "someone's" existence.

In practice, even Buddhist monastic organizations have been involved in systematic violence on the grounds that liberating others from the snares of delusion is actually a form of compassion. Buddhist elements infiltrated even the Samurai code, and during the mid-twentiethth century, some Japanese Buddhists argued that America must be vanquished lest its values destroy the possibility of peace altogether.

Buddhism Glossary

(Sanskrit/Pali terms unless otherwise indicated)

anatman/anatta—nonself, the teaching that there is no individual personality or soul to "be saved" or transmigrate; one of the three marks of existence.

anitya/anicca—impermanence, nothing survives, all things pass away; one of the three marks of existence.

ar(a)hat—Theravada ideal of enlightened follower of Buddha.

bodhisattva/bodhisatta—"being of enlightenment," one who forgoes entry into nirvana out of compassion for all sentient beings, preferring to stay and assist them.

dharma/dhamma—Buddhist teaching, fundamental truth; the second of the "three jewels" in which Buddhists take refuge.

duhkha/dukkha—sorrow or suffering; one of the three marks of existence.

dhyana/jhana—meditation, concentration.

karma/kamma—action, deeds whose results determine the quality of one's future existence.

karuna—compassion, regard for the deepest needs of other suffering beings.

mandala—symbolic sacred circle, visual metaphor for the spiritual cosmos and the self used for meditational purposes.

mudra—gesture, symbolic hand symbol, or posture, an essential iconographic key to reading all Buddhist sacred sculpture and painting.

nirvana/nibbana—"no-wind/breath," unperturbed state that is the essence of liberation.

parinirvana/parinibbana—perfect nirvana, especially referring to the Buddha's passing into full liberation from earthly life.

prajñapañña—pure intuitive wisdom.

samadhi—absorption en route to final liberation.

samsara—flux, flow, the ever-changing state of things from which Buddhist seekers desire to be liberated.

Sangha—the assembly of monks and nuns, generally, but also referring to all Buddhists in Mahayana communities.

satori (Jap.)—Zen synonym for enlightenment, realization of the emptiness of all things.

shunyata—emptiness, the realization of which is synonymous with nirvana.

skandhas—the so-called "aggregates" that together constitute the illusion of a "self."

tanha/trishna—desire, craving, the thirst that leads human beings to cling to all the causes of rebirth.

upaya—skillful means, the ability to enact compassionate knowledge for the good of others.

SIGNS AND SYMBOLS

Are there any **signs or symbols** that might **identify an individual as a Buddhist?**

In most parts of the world in which Buddhism remains an important presence, it is a safe bet that many people on the street have had some direct contact with Buddhist tradition, but it is usually difficult to tell Buddhists from non-Buddhists merely by looking at their clothing or other personal effects. Occasionally you will spot an item of jewelry whose symbolism is more or less explicitly Buddhist. The eight-spoked Wheel of Dharma is a common symbol easily reproduced on small-scale items. Buddhist pilgrims, however, often stand out because of the traditional garb and variety of symbols they wear. In Japan, for example, some pilgrims wear a large, round, pointed or bowl-like straw hat, carry pilgrim staffs, and wear around their necks a small cloth wallet in which to collect the souvenir stamps they receive from each temple they visit.

Monks, nuns, and priests bear the most obvious examples of distinctive signs. Nearly everywhere in the world, monks and nuns shave their heads. They typically wear a distinctive habit or garb, consisting of two or three wraps—two for novices, three for senior monks and nuns. One wrap covers the lower body, another the upper. For religious rituals, monks wear a long cloth of twelve folds, sometimes called the stole, over the left shoulder. Colors vary according to region and institutional affiliation, from one branch of the monastic order or Buddhist lineage

A group of Japanese Buddhist pilgrims visiting Kyoto's Kiyomizudera on their round of sacred sites. They wear the characteristic pilgrim hats and wallets (worn over the neck) for collecting souvenir seals at each stop on the circuit.

A collection of miniature images of the Bodhisattva Jizo, patron of unborn children. Women who have had abortions often purchase the small statues as votive offerings and leave them at certain temples, sometimes adorning them with knit red caps or bibs, along with pinwheels and other toys.

to another. Saffron is the most common color for monastic garb, but, for example, Tibetan monks often wear a dark burgundy, Japanese monks typically don darker shades of gray, brown, and violet, and Chinese nuns often wear a simple gray robe.

What signs or symbols distinguish Buddhist **ritual specialists**?

Priests who officiate in Buddhist temples that serve the public wear a variety of colors and use various implements. Priests often wear a robe called a *kashaya* (*kesa* in Japan). The vestment is unusual in that it is typically a patchwork of many colors and textures, recalling the simplicity and poverty of the Buddha's earliest disciples. An abbreviated form of the *kesa* is the *wagesa,* a simple swatch of cloth worn over the shoulders. Some monastic priests in Japan carry a staff called a *shakujo.* Six metal rings near the top make a jangling sound, alerting small defenseless creatures to remove themselves from harm's way. The Bodhisattva Jizo, usually dressed as a monk or priest, typically carries the staff. Within private or monastic settings, ritual specialists have an even greater diversity of signs and symbols, since their rituals are often more esoteric and complex. Tibetan monks, for example, don very colorful headgear distinctive of their various lineages. Tibetans and members of other esoteric sects also use a wider variety of ritual objects than are used in popular denominations, most notably the bell and the *vajra,* a metal object with several spokes on each end closed into a lotus shape and a symbol of the indestructible reality of the *dharma.*

Do Buddhists mark their **sacred spaces** with any distinctive signs and symbols?

Though Buddhist ritual spaces vary a great deal architecturally and decoratively from one region to another, a number of commonly used signs and symbols appear. Perhaps the single most important is the eight-spoked Wheel of *Dharma*, reminder of the Four Noble Truths and the Eightfold Noble Path. Tibetan temples identify themselves with a characteristic form of the classical Indian *stupa* called a *chorten*, a five-level architectural form crowned with a conical shape. Chinese Buddhist temples borrowed their ground plans from the traditional royal residence, a walled enclosure with one or more interior courtyards surrounding the main sacred structures. The principal inner structures face south and are lined up on an axis with the main gate. A multistoried polygonal *pagoda* may be part of the complex. Japan largely borrowed the classical Chinese ground

A classic five-story Japanese pagoda at Kofukuji temple, Nara, Japan.

plan, varying the placement of the inner buildings somewhat. Always found at the back of the walled enclosure is the main image hall where central rituals occur. Three-, five-, or seven-story square pagodas are a regular feature in the main courtyard of many Japanese temples. Thai temples feature a very distinctive roofline and post very imposing guardian figures before the main door, but do not generally have separate pagoda structures.

What's the difference between a **stupa** and a **pagoda**?

A *stupa* is an ancient Indian burial or reliquary monument. Its fundamental unit is a solid hemispherical earthen mound called the "egg" (*anda*) or "womb" (*garbha*). Atop the mound sits a solid square or rectangular shape, originally surrounded by a four-sided railing, called the *harmika,* which may be a remnant of the days when the village altar stood inside a fenced enclosure. Growing treelike from that is a pillar that pierces several circular discs of decreasing diameter, usually an odd number from three to eleven. The result looks like a multitiered parasol. The Buddha's cremated remains are said to have been originally enshrined in a large number of *stupas* built all over India. Mahayana teaching developed the notion that the Buddha was a cosmic spiritual being, rather than a mere human teacher, and the architecture of the *stupa* evolved to reflect those changes. *Stupa* designers began to raise the mound off the ground by using several square bases, meanwhile stretching the mound itself upward much the way a potter turns a round lump of clay into a tall graceful vase. The "parasol" is also stretched heavenward, becoming more streamlined and adding disks.

When Mahayana Buddhism moved into China, architects transformed the upper portion of the *stupa* into an independent structure, turning the multiple discs into roofs. The earth-hugging funerary mound was replaced by the *pagoda*. The new structure was derived from the *stupa* and still contained relics, but the *pagoda* symbolized transcendence rather than earthly existence. *Pagodas* soon added their own sets of multiple discs, leaving the *stupa,* so to speak, in the dust. In the Theravada lands of southeast Asia, reminders of the *stupa* remain in the gently tapered monuments of Burma and Thailand. Mahayana Buddhist establishments all over East Asia identify themselves with their graceful, multiroofed *pagodas*. Unlike the typical *stupa,* the *pagoda* actually has interior space, sometimes on several levels.

What will I see if I visit a **Buddhist temple**?

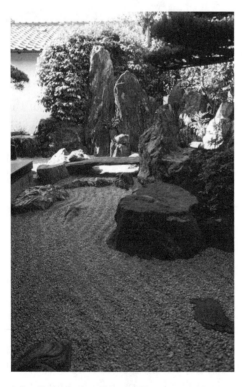

A Zen dry meditation garden in Daisen-in, one of twenty-three subtemples of Kyoto's Daitoku-ji.

A lot depends on where you are and the size of the temple. Local or neighborhood temples are generally of simpler design than those that function like "cathedral" temples or are closely associated with the main institution of a monastic community. Larger foundations throughout Asia are often visible from a distance, punctuating the skyline with their *stupa* spires or lofty *pagodas*. Walled enclosures entered through monumental gateways surround the more important foundations. Before entering any temple, however grand or humble, you will see a rack in which to deposit your footwear. Interior appointments vary somewhat according to culture and denomination.

Most traditional temples are divided into two main areas. The congregational space usually has no furniture. When worshippers pause for meditation or recitation, they ordinarily either stand or sit on the floor. Some temples have individual meditation pillows stacked along the walls. But some Buddhist temples in Europe and the United States have adopted the Protestant Christian use of pews or benches without kneelers. Many such temples actually belong to denominations that call themselves "churches." Look at the back of a bench and you are likely to find hymn books in a rack. Many temples separate the sanctuary area from the body of the building with a railing or columns. A large image of the Buddha or a major Bodhisattva stands or sits atop an altar, sometimes in the company of several smaller images. Before the altar is a place for the priest or prayer leader to sit. Side altars dedicated to Bodhisattvas or holy persons, such as founders of the various lineages, are not uncommon. Some temples have meditative gardens adjacent to the formal worship space.

What are some helpful **clues** for understanding **Buddhist iconography**?

Most important of all are images of the Buddhas and Bodhisattvas. Buddhist sculpture and painting have evolved in many different styles. Each lineage or denomination has a number of symbols and signs to which it attaches distinctive meanings. But it is possible to suggest some general features to look for when you visit a museum's Asian galleries. As with Hindu iconography, start by noting posture, gesture, garb and other implements. Buddha images are usually seated in the lotus posture, legs crossed so that the soles of the feet face upward. Some images depict the Buddha standing or walking, but these are less numerous. Principal gestures include those that indicate blessing, teaching, or meditation. One of the most important has the left hand resting palm up in the lap and the right touching the ground just in front of the right knee, symbolizing the Buddha's conquest of Mara's temptation. Buddha images are typically clad in simple monk's garb and do not hold any specific tools or implements. Bodhisattvas sometimes appear seated in a relaxed posture called "royal ease," but standing images are more common. They ordinarily wear crowns and royal finery as symbols of the life of the Buddha-to-be prior to his renunciation. Seated Bodhisattvas often recline graciously forward and offer a gesture of kindly welcome or attentiveness. Some Bodhisattvas have multiple arms and heads to symbolize their infinite power and ability to respond to every human need. In their many hands these potent images can carry as many as several dozen separate items, including weapons, musical instruments, and symbols of healing. Guardian figures are the most numerous subordinate images. Distant cousins of beings with similar functions in Hindu tradition, these characters glower menacingly on beings of evil intent and brandish weaponry sufficient to dispatch all undesirable elements daring to approach the holy place.

What is a **mandala**? Is it the same as a **thanka**?

Mandala is a Sanskrit word for "circle." As a two-dimensional design, a mandala is equivalent to the plan of a *stupa*. Viewed directly from above, a *stupa* reveals a series of alternating concentric square and circular shapes. From the outside in, you see the square foundation, the circular earth mound, the square "altar" inside its square railing, and finally the circular discs mounted on the shaft of the spire. Some *mandalas* depict four gates on the sides of the foundation square and add yet another outer circle symbolizing the "eight cemeteries" through which a meditator must first pass, becoming oblivious to the senses and all other distractions before entering the sacred space. Vajrayana and other esoteric Buddhist sects adapted this bird's eye perspective on the *stupa* and interpreted it as an image of both the macrocosm (the whole spiritual cosmos) and the microcosm (the individual meditator). Devotees meditate on the sacred design of the spiritual "city" as they move symbolically inward from the gates toward the center and enlightenment. Various "deities" and forms of Buddhas and Bodhisattvas are depicted in the different spaces of the *mandala,* each symbolizing some aspect of spiritual power. Tibetan monks sometimes create large *mandalas* using grains of colored sand. After many hours of work, they conduct rituals around it and then discard it in a river as a reminder of impermanence and nonattachment.

Thanka is a more generic term for a Tibetan wall hanging depicting a religious theme. Some *thankas* depict *mandalas,* and some display sacred imagery of other kinds. Multiple scenes illustrating Jataka tales offer material designed for meditation on essential virtues modeled by the Buddha-to-be.

Do Buddhists use **symbols** when they engage in **personal or private rituals**?

A number of prayer aids and other ritual accoutrements are common in many Buddhist households. Prayer wheels and prayer flags, used especially in the Himalayan nations but elsewhere as well, symbolize the belief in the ideal of continual prayer. Prayer wheels contain bits of sacred text inside a small drum fitted with an axle-like handle. A short weighted chain attached to the drum makes it easier to spin it steadily. Prayer flags are strips of cloth containing sacred text and petitions, prayers sped aloft by the winds. Many Japanese households have a small altar, called the *butsudan,* in which families keep tablets with the names of deceased relatives as well as images of the Buddha. In general, private rituals employ a scaled-down set of the same principal symbols used for temple worship.

Have Buddhists always **depicted** the **Buddha** in **painting and sculpture**?

For generations after the Buddha's death his followers hesitated to depict the Teacher in human form. Perhaps they avoided direct visual representation out of respect for the Buddha, one too sacred to be so portrayed. Whatever the motivation, early Buddhist artists chose a variety of symbols to represent the Buddha. Early Christian artists likewise refrained from depicting Christ in human form, opting for symbols like the fish and the empty cross. The most important symbols for the Buddha included the riderless horse, the parasol, the tree, the empty throne, footprints, the eight-spoked wheel, and the *stupa*. A riderless horse recalled the Buddha's renunciation and departure from his father's palace. Parasols were symbols of royalty and represented the great honor due to an Enlightened One. Buddha reached enlightenment beneath the

Bo tree, and artists often left a space before the tree to suggest the presence of the Buddha. Some scenes place an empty throne beneath the tree. Artists sometimes choose to show a pair of footprints just in front of the throne. Footprints also appear by themselves somewhere in a scene to indicate where the Buddha would have been. A wheel of eight spokes was a reminder of the Eightfold Noble Path and the Four Noble Truths. Depictions of a *stupa,* resting place of the Buddha's remains, frequently served as a reminder of his spiritual presence. Several other items especially popular in China among the "Eight Auspicious Signs" include a pair of fish, symbol of universal Indian monarchy; the lotus blossom of purity; and the conch shell of victory. Chinese Buddhist altars often held clay or carved wooden images of these symbols.

What has the **swastika** got to do with Buddhism?

A revolving cross with bent cross-beams, the *swastika* has been a symbol of longevity and success throughout eastern Asia for millennia. Buddhists inherited the symbol from Hindu tradition, in which it referred to different forms of cosmic energy, depending on whether the symbol rotated to the right or to the left. The symbol appears often in Chinese sculpture on the upper chest of the Buddha. There it is a reminder of the eternal validity of his teaching, a meaning attached to the Chinese use of the swastika as the number ten thousand. In some Japanese temples (such as the Asakusa Kannon temple in Tokyo) the *swastika* even functions as the central icon on the main altar, replacing the image of the Buddha. Zen tradition sees the *swastika* as a symbol of the "buddhamind" handed down from teacher to disciple. It may have become associated with the Buddha as a result of his identification with solar imagery and power. Some suggest that the *swastika* symbolizes the Buddha's teaching as an abstract stylized version of the Wheel of *Dharma*.

Have **relics** been important in Buddhist practice?

Practically since the Buddha's final entry into *nirvana,* which coincided with his physical death, Buddhists have placed great importance on sacred relics. Numer-

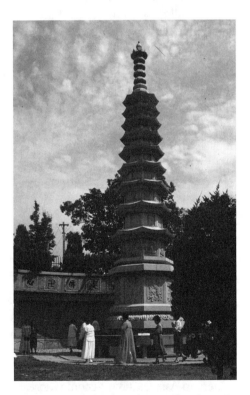

Worshippers circumambulate large stone *pagoda* near Po Mun Sa temple, Seoul, Korea. Worshippers walk in a clockwise direction, past the *swastika* on the wall beyond the *pagoda*.

ous early accounts tell of the distribution of Buddha's cremated remains to political rulers so that they could enshrine them as sacred markers. One account says the great King Ashoka built 84,000 *stupas* as reliquaries for the Buddha's ashes. Some sources report that Buddha's followers discovered among the ashes a tooth, still intact. In Kandy, Sri Lanka, the Shrine of the Tooth claims to possess the only authentic dental relic, said to have been brought there ten days after Buddha's death. But as recently as the late 1990s, a tooth kept in Beijing made news when it was flown to Hong Kong after the Chinese takeover there, in time for a celebration of the Buddha's birthday. Meanwhile a tooth in the possession of a Tibetan monk was installed in Taipei, Taiwan, amid mainland Chinese denunciations of its authenticity. Other relics of the Buddha included his staff, begging bowl, and robe.

Buddha's footprint does not belong to the sacred relics of the first-class (actual bodily remains) or the second-class relics (personal effects of the sacred person), yet it is still important throughout the Buddhist world. Many temples claim to possess an "actual" print, but most are highly stylized stone or metal images that devotees bathe with various liquids and adorn with flower petals. Prints frequently have various symbols of the Buddha on the sole. Most common are the Wheel of the Law and sets of either 32, 108, or 132 hallmarks of the Enlightened One. Footprints belong to a third category of relic, items that directly remind one of the Buddha. All images of the Buddha, as well as physical copies of the sacred texts, are therefore considered a type of relic.

In addition to relics of the Buddha himself, symbolic reminders of numerous other holy persons have become prominent. First- and second-class relics of Bodhisattvas, patriarchs, and eminent monastic founders and teachers are enshrined in *stupas* and *pagodas* throughout Asia. Miniature *stupas* and *pagodas*, made of wood, stone or metal, have often provided the visual and devotional focus in temples, monasteries, and even private dwellings.

MEMBERSHIP, COMMUNITY, DIVERSITY

Where do **Buddhists live today**? Are any estimates of **numbers** available?

Buddhism enjoyed much greater success in other parts of Asia than in India, the land of its birth. Estimates of the global population of Buddhists vary from about a third to half a billion. Political circumstances make statistics particularly hard to get for China and Tibet, but it is clear that Buddhists have suffered terribly in both areas during the past half-century. Meanwhile, the tradition has been enjoying modest revival elsewhere in Asia, and has become increasingly popular in Europe (up to twenty-four million) and North America (from three to five million) as a result of both immigration and conversion. Nations with the highest percentage of Buddhists among the general population are Thailand (94% of national population), Cambodia (90%), Myanmar (formerly Burma, 88%), Japan (78%), and Korea (45%). Many millions of Buddhists once lived in China, but their number dwindled dramatically with the advent of the Communist system. Buddhism has been making a comeback in China in recent years, and there are now an estimated 13,000 temples and two hundred thousand monks and nuns. Tibet's population was, until recently at least, almost entirely Buddhist. Between six hundred thousand and a million Buddhists, representing all major denominations, live in the United States.

Have Buddhists traditionally sent out **missionaries** to convert others?

Buddhism's vigorous missionary heritage is traditionally traced to two kings: Ashoka (270–230 B.C.E.) and Kanishka (r. c. 120–160 C.E.). The first is said to have converted to Buddhism after repenting of his bloody conquests. Ashoka declared that the Buddha's teaching would be the official creed of the realm. Tradition credits Kanishka with supplying a major impetus to Buddhism's spread into central and eastern Asia. Monks (and, to a lesser extent, nuns) have historically been the most important and effective missionaries. Wherever they traveled they carried sacred texts and art as their prime teaching tools. Buddhist missionary work continues in the form of various contemporary adaptations of traditional methods of evangelization. They call their missionary workers *dhammadutas,* (those who spread the *dharma*), convinced of the universal relevance of the teaching. In much of Theravada southeast Asia, missionaries continue to bring the message of Buddhism to rural areas. In Thailand, for example, teams of five travel about from March to June, then return to monasteries for the rainy season retreat. They begin by setting up a monastery and training young boys in the temple compound. Eventually they start to visit homes and ask about people's general well-being. The next step is to start elementary schools and encourage youngsters to enter the monastic life.

Are there any Buddhist **holy sites** or cities?

Important to Buddhists universally are the places associated with central events in the life of the Buddha. Sites identified with his birth (the Lumbini Grove), enlightenment (Bodhgaya), first sermon (the Deer Park near Benares), and entering into nirvana (Kushinagara) are at the top of the list. Pilgrims from all over the world now travel to India on pilgrimage to these and dozens of other locations of slightly lesser importance. No one city in India functions for Buddhists quite the way Mecca, Jerusalem, and Rome do for Muslims, Jews, and many Christians. Various cities have become associated with important Buddhist temples and monasteries, but they have rarely if ever attracted pilgrims precisely as cities. Instead, pilgrims head for specific sites and temples.

Outside India, dozens of places are sacred to members of the various Buddhist denominations. Many are associated with mountains. Ancient pre-Buddhist traditions in both China and Japan, for example, attributed supreme sanctity to the high places that, according to some spiritual maps, marked the outer limits of the cosmos at the

269

Mountains are considered spiritual places to Buddhists, who lend them cosmological importance.

cardinal points. Different sects and lineages often chose mountains for their spiritual centers because of the centrality of Mt. Meru in ancient Hindu myth. Mountains symbolize a point of interconnection among the several levels of the cosmos. They also can be readily imagined as huge *mandalas* around which spiritual seekers circumambulate en route to the center.

Who are **Theravada Buddhists**?

Theravada Buddhists are members of a more or less homogenous community of faith and worship built around the notion that the Buddha was a human being who taught by example. The historical Buddha, Siddhartha Gautama, was the last of many nonhuman and human reincarnations of the Buddha-to-be. A separate school from the second council on in the fourth century B.C.E., their main scriptures are called collectively the Pali Canon.

Theravadins seek deliverance from rebirth by eliminating craving and ignorance through self-discipline. The ideal and model of the enlightened life is the *arhat*. *Arhats* benefit others chiefly by their example, and they possess no saving power as such. They embody primarily the virtue of wisdom. Their ultimate goal, *nirvana*, is a state beyond this world of *samsara* in which the liberated person experiences neither desire nor impressions of any kind. Theravada sources describe nirvana as a permanent pleasant state of knowledge, freedom, and peace that is largely the result of a process of personal effort. When Theravadins pray, their primary intent is more to honor the Buddha than to worship him. All good acts, including religious ritual, done with proper intent can help one gain merit toward the eradication of negative *karma*. For most Theravada Buddhists, the concepts of merit making and merit transfer are more basic and accessible than the kind of lofty ethical and spiritual discipline embodied in an *arhat*. There are, of course, some regional and cultural variations in Theravada expression and practice, but considerably less so than in the other main branches of Buddhist tradition.

Who are **Mahayana Buddhists**?

By contrast, Mahayana Buddhists belong to a wide variety of sub-communities for whom the historical Buddha called Siddhartha Gautama was one of many manifestations of enlightenment capable of saving those who ask for help. Mahayana scriptures evolved in some half-dozen languages over many centuries as the tradition moved through Asia. Mahayana teaching universalized a number of classical Buddhist concepts, broadening their popular appeal and expanding the religious options available to ordinary folk. For example, Mahayana teaching regarded the historical Buddha of this age, Siddhartha Gautama, as only one of many embodiments of enlightenment. Not merely an ethical model, the Buddha was actually a world-filling spiritual presence and power. The compassionate Bodhisattva supplanted the more self-contained arhat as a religious ideal. Bodhisattvas represented saving grace as well as a lofty goal to which any person might aspire. Mahayana teachings expanded still further by personifying wisdom as a feminine principle, attractive and accessible.

At the same time, somewhat paradoxically, Mahayana tradition was also a great deal more open to the sort of speculative thinking most Theravadins considered fruitless. Mahayana philosophers developed the concept of "emptiness" (*shunyata*), for example, as a way of emphasizing the futility of clinging to anything at all, even to neat doctrinal distinctions. Of the dozen or so Mahayana schools and denominations that arose in India, China, and Japan, two deserve mention here. First and most popular are the Pure Land communities. Amitabha (Amida in Japan), one of the five transcendent or "meditational" Buddhas, rules the western paradise called the Pure Land. Devotees seek rebirth in that heavenly realm through various spiritual means, including the simple repetition of phrases such as "Glory to Amida Buddha." In addition, several major Chan (Zen in Japan, Son in Korea) lineages have been extraordinarily influential in eastern Asia. The Soto school emphasizes quiet, methodical meditation, while the Rinzai school uses, in addition, the mind-stopping device called the *koan*—questions, puzzles, or parables with no clear answer or meaning—to hasten the seeker's experience of enlightenment.

Different Emphases in Theravada and Mahayana Buddhism

	Theravada	Mahayana
Person:	individual seeking enlightenment	individual involved in society
Key virtue:	wisdom	compassion, skill-in-means
Buddha:	human ethical model	suprahuman savior
Shakyamuni:	historical Buddha	one of innumerable Buddhas
Bodhisattva:	Buddha-to-be (prior lives of Shakyamuni/Jatakas)	intermediary saving figure
Spiritual ideal:	*Arhat,* seeks own enlightenment	*Bodhisattva,* seeks to save others
Goal of Life:	*Nirvana*	rebirth in Buddha-land
Means to Goal:	meditation, self-discipline	grace of Buddhas/Bodhisattvas
Prayer:	emphasis on meditation	includes petition/supplication

Who are **Vajrayana Buddhists**?

Vajrayana Buddhism consists of a number of schools and lineages that blended Mahayana concepts with the esoteric interpretations of Hinduism's Tantric schools. Local pre-Buddhist elements of shamanism and folk religion gave further distinctiveness to the different schools. In some places, Vajrayana (also called Tantrayana, "eso-teric vehicle") has blended with popular traditions. In the monasteries the monks and mystical adepts engage in arcane rituals open only to initiates, but the monks also minister to the public through more accessible teaching and worship. Monastic institutions have dominated much of everyday life in the Himalayan nations and, until recently, to a greater degree than elsewhere in Asia. Many of the largest and most powerful monasteries are perched high above cities and villages so that their physical setting is itself an unmistakable symbol of their centrality. Before the Chinese takeover of Tibet, as many as one out of five Tibetans were monks or nuns. Some half a dozen major monastic orders developed, of which the Dalai Lama's Gelug-pa Order is now the best known. Vajrayana Buddhists developed their own extensive sacred scriptures, largely by way of translation of Indian Sanskrit and Chinese texts. In 108 volumes the *Kanjur* ("Translation of the Word") includes monastic regulations along with philosophy. The 225-volume *Tanjur* ("Translation of Treatises") includes Sutras, Tantras, and commentaries on them. Perhaps most distinctive of the various Vajrayana schools is the use of ritual symbolism and meditative techniques to achieve their spiritual objectives. Visualization techniques and highly developed forms of chanting assist the meditator toward union with the divine center. Outside Tibet and the other Himalayan nations, Vajrayana tradition exercised considerable influence on the increasingly esoteric Japanese Shingon school.

What **gender-related issues** are important for Buddhists?

Tradition has it that the Buddha rejected various forms of social discrimination deeply embedded in the Indian culture of his day. He is said to have repudiated caste distinctions altogether. The Buddha's attitudes toward the place of women in religion and society also represented a step forward in some respects, but many problems remained. When the Buddha's aunt, who had raised him after his mother died, asked to be allowed into the *Sangha*, the Buddha balked. Only after a prominent monk named Ananda took up the woman's cause did the Buddha relent. So began the Buddhist order of nuns, but female members of the Order have never achieved the status of their male counterparts. There has been a

A Buddhist nun in Bangkok, Thailand asks for offerings. (Charlie Edward / Shutterstock.com.)

breakdown in the lineage of the nuns' *Sangha*—a complete rupture, according to some historians. Some women continue to live in community and call themselves nuns, but they lack official sanction. A sore point for many women has been that classical Buddhist teaching says that women must be reborn as men before having a chance at *nirvana*.

Still, it appears that early Buddhist tradition did introduce significant improvements in the lot of many women in India. No longer merely the possessions of their men, women had a larger purpose than childbearing, had personal psychic lives and could seek their own spiritual goals. So much of the gender bias that persists everywhere in our world has a great deal more to do with culture than with any one religious tradition as such. Interaction of religious tradition and culture often makes it impossible to distinguish between the two. And it is not uncommon for people in any given culture to claim religious sanction for time-honored values and practices even when the religious tradition's sources offer little support for them.

What are some of the main features of Buddhism's **relationships to other traditions**?

Buddhism's most important connections historically have been with Hinduism, out of which it grew, and the major indigenous traditions of the Asian lands to which it spread. Over the centuries Buddhists have therefore interacted primarily with Hindus, Daoists, Confucians, and adherents of Shinto. An earlier question outlined crucial features of Buddhism's relationship to Hinduism. Here are some features of Buddhism's conceptual connections with the other traditions.

China's ancient Daoist tradition made room for the Buddha among the swelling ranks of its deities, even claiming that foundational figure Lao Zi had himself become a Buddha. Dharma, some scholars argued, was the Buddhist analogy to the concept of the Way or Dao. They suggested further parallels between the Buddhist *Arhat* and the Daoist Immortal, and between *nirvana* and the concept of non-action. Confucian tradition also found ways of accommodating to the newcomer. Some scholars saw in Buddhist ethics a parallel to Confucian filial piety, even though Buddhist elevation of celibate monasticism seemed quite irreconcilable with the Confucian emphasis on family life. To Buddhism's "Five Precepts" some likened Confucianism's "Five Constant Virtues." When Buddhist missionaries brought the new teaching to Japan, the Buddha met the *kami* ("high beings") of the indigenous tradition called Shinto.

As was so often the case in China and elsewhere, Buddhism's ability to survive and grow in its new environment depended a great deal on royal patronage. Imperial support gave impetus to various Buddhist-Shinto accommodations. Shinto's Sun Goddess, Amaterasu, became a counterpart to the Buddha of Infinite Light, Vairochana. Hachiman, Shinto deity of war, dressed as a Buddhist monk and became the guardian of the great Buddha. And in Mahayana teaching's multiple Buddhas and Bodhisattvas some saw parallels to Shinto's countless *kami*. Representatives of various Buddhist denominations have continued active dialogue with other traditions, especially through the monastic connection.

Major Buddhist Lineages

Early Indian Schools

The Sthaviravadins: Although not formal lineages these early followers of the Buddha should be clasified as Theravadins and found their philosophical point of departure in the teaching that the self or ego is merely a loose grouping of impermanent and everchanging aggregates. The end of such teaching was to assert that everything is transient and that one should not become attached to selves or other objects.

The Saravastivadins: This group contended that "everything exists", including all past, present, and future happenings in spite of there being no existent self or ego. The combination of all things according to one's karma brings about one's state of consciousness. The group was declared heretical by most other Buddhist lineages.

China
Mahayana Schools imported from India

San Lun or Madhyamika: Based on the Chinese translation of Nagarjuna's (2nd century) *Madhyamika Karika* and two other works of uncertain authorship, this lineage emphasized the notions of *shunyata* (emptiness) and *wu* (non-being). So rigorous was the teaching of this lineage that it declared that the elements constituting perceived objects, when examined, are really no more than mental phenomena and have no true existence.

Yogacara: Founded in the third century by Maitreyanatha and made famous by Asanga and Vasubandhu in the fourth or fifth century, this school held that the source of all ideas is *vijñana* ("consciousness"), which is seen as the fundamental basis of experience. Ultimate reality is therefore only perceived but has no real existence.

Indigenous Mahayana Lineages

T'ien T'ai: Named after the mountain on which its founder Zhi Yi (538-597) resided, this lineage is based on a scheme of classification intended to integrate and harmonize the vast array of Buddhist scriptures and doctrines. This scheme of classification is based on the Buddhist doctrine of *upaya* ("skill in means"). The most important form of Buddhism for this lineage is the Mahayana devotionalism found in the Lotus Sutra.

Hua Yen or Avatamsaka: This lineage takes its name from the Avatamsaka Sutra, its central sacred text, and like the T'ien T'ai school is oriented toward a classification of sutras and doctrine based. Basic to this lineage is the assertion that all particulars are merely manifestations of the absolute mind and are therefore fundamentally the same.

Ching T'u or Pure Land: Based on the Sukhavati Vyuha ("Pure Land Sutra"), this lineage was founded in 402 by Hui Yuan. The Pure Land lineage held that the spiritual quality of the world had been in decline since its height during the lifetime of the Buddha and taught followers to cultivate through prayer and devotion a sincere intent to be reborn in the heavenly paradise of the Buddha Amitabha.

Ch'an: Its name derived from the Sanskrit term *dhyana* ("meditation"), this lineage emphasized meditation as the only means to a spiritual awakening beyond words or thought, dispensing almost entirely with the teachings and practices of traditional Buddhism. Ch'an Buddhism is thought to have been brought to China by the enigmatic Indian monk Bodhidharma around the year 500. Salvation is primarily a personal experience, although emphasis is also laid on the master–disciple relationship in attaining an insight into one's own true nature and thus attaining Buddhahood. Two of the most important Ch'an schools are the Ts'aotung ("Five Baskets"), founded by Ihsuan (d. 867), which emphasized the attainment of enlightenment through a program of meditation that can last many years; and the Linchi ("Shouting and Striking") school founded by Liangchieh (807-869), which held that one could attain more immediate results through the use of arresting methods designed to shock the aspirant out of dependence on linear thinking.

Japan

Tendai: (Chinese T'ien T'ai) Founded in Japan by Saicho (767-822), this lineage quickly rose to prominence as the most important lineage of Japanese Buddhism. The basic doctrines of this lineage and the Chinese T'ien T'ai are the same, as is their reverence for the Lotus Sutra, but Tendai differs in its emphasis on the mystical and esoteric aspects of Buddhism. The four primary categories of this lineage are 1) morality, 2) monastic discipline, 3) esoteric practices, and 4) meditation.

Shingon: Founded by Kukai (774-835), this lineage grew to rival the Tendai lineage as early as the late ninth century. The Shingon belief system was tantric and taught that through *mantras* (short, repetitive incantations or prayers), meditation, and the performance of hand gestures, one can gain access to the power of the Buddhas and Bodhisattvas.

Jodo or Pure Land: Begun around the time of the publication of the treatise by Honen (1133-1212) entitled *Senchakushu*, this lineage traces its scriptural heritage to the Pure Land Sutra (Sukhavati Vyuha) which prescribes loving devotion to the Buddha Amida as a means to be reborn in the Pure Land, or paradise over which he presides. Pure Land prayer centers on the repetition of the phrase *namu amida butsu* ("Homage to Amida Buddha") and became one of the most popular forms of Buddhism in Japan.

Joho Shinshu or True Pure Land: Founded by Shinran (1173-1262), this lineage takes Pure Land teaching one step further claiming that humility and faith in Amida's love are in themselves true signs that the

Great bronze Amida Buddha, twelfth century, Kamakura, Japan. The statue is nearly forty feet tall and was once housed in a wooden temple structure. Visitors can ascend stairs inside and look out.

redeeming grace of the Buddha has already been bestowed. Amida Buddha seeks and saves without first requiring faith and good works. These spring up spontaneously from Amida's spiritual presence in the heart.

Nichiren-shu: Named after its founder Nichiren (1222-1282), this lineage was founded on the Lotus Sutra and taught that mere repetition of the title of that sutra *Nammyohorengekyo* ("Homage to the Lotus Sutra") was sufficient to gain one access to Paradise.

Zen: The monk Eisai (1141-1215) is usually considered the first proponent of Zen in Japan, although Ch'an had existed since the early sixth century and probably existed also in Japan before Eisai's time. The earliest forms of Zen generally avoided intellectualism and deemphasized scriptures, doctrine, and ceremonial. Eisai, whose form of Zen took on the name *Rinzai* (*Linchi*, Ch.), affirmed the authority of the traditional Buddhist scriptures and used the *koan* or meditational riddle as a means of transcending linear thinking. *Soto Zen* (*Ts'aotung*, Ch.), tracing its roots back to Dogen (1200-1253), also affirmed the validity of the Buddhist scriptures but rejected the use of *koans* and focused solely on extended, silent meditation.

Tibet

Nyingmapa: Tracing its origins to the legendary Padmasambhava, an eighth-century Tantric magician, this lineage of Buddhism is uniquely Tibetan in that many aspects of traditional Bon religion are mixed together with more properly Buddhist beliefs and practices to form a unique expression of Buddhist piety. This lineage emphasizes the move toward more advanced stages of enlightenment through "preliminary practices" comprising the beliefs and practices of Buddhism before the advent of Tantra, and through "higher practices" which involve the attainment of enlightment through the chanting of magical spells, special hand gestures, mystical diagrams, and ritualized sexual intercourse.

Gelugpa: Founded by Tsongkhapa (1357-1419) as a reform movement within Tibetan Buddhism, followers acclaimed the lineage's third teacher as an incarnation of the Bodhisattva Avalokiteshvara, thus inaugurating the line of Dalai Lamas. The fourteenth and most recent of whom was born in 1935. Emphasis in this lineage is on a strict monastic discipline and on the conviction that the Bodhisattva, a Buddha who has foregone final nirvana out of compassion for all sentient beings, is continually present.

LEADERSHIP, AUTHORITY, AND RELIGIOUS ROLES

What are some of the main varieties of Buddhist **religious officials or specialists**?

Each of the many distinct denominations and their constituent religious institutions has its characteristic division of labor. One way to keep it all straight is to think in terms of the four functional categories of administration, instruction, pastoral care, and spiritual example. There is naturally some overlapping, but the four categories offer an idea of the kinds of responsibilities and duties Buddhists consider most important. Denominations, monastic institutions, and local temples all have adminis-

Buddhist priest performing prayer ritual for worshippers in a small temple in Kyoto, Japan. (Photo courtesy of David Oughton.)

trative structures and offices. Buddhists use terms roughly equivalent to bishop, abbot, and chief priest or pastor in this regard. Teachers or preceptors are charged with instructing both monastic and lay Buddhists, especially in the meditative disciplines. At the local level, priests and monks who serve the public in monastery temples and chapels fulfill the pastoral care function, offering such services as counseling and visiting the sick, as well as leadership in worship. A final category that is in many ways distinctively Buddhist and yet difficult to define is that of spiritual exemplar. Here are located all the various ranks of revered patriarchs, founders, incarnations of previous holy persons, and individuals celebrated for teaching by example. Tibetan Buddhists, for example, call such people by various titles including *lama, rinpoche,* and *tulku.*

What is a **lama**? Is it anything like a **rinpoche** or a **tulku**?

A *lama* (Tibetan term meaning "none higher") is a teacher or guru in the tradition of Vajrayana Buddhism associated especially with Tibet. Many *lamas* are monks, but membership in the monastic *Sangha* is not a prerequisite. Whether monk or layman, a *lama* is one who represents the Buddha's teaching best of all. A *lama*'s role is somewhat broader than that of the traditional Hindu guru in that *lamas* lead religious rituals as well as offering instruction about them. Extensive study and meditation includes a three-year period of seclusion. Some *lamas,* distinguished for their learning and spiritual attainment, receive the honorific title of *rinpoche,* "precious being." Some *rinpoches* have the further distinction of being considered reincarnations of some earlier figure. A *tulku* ("transformation body") can reincarnate the spirit of former leaders of a

277

religious order or even be manifestations of a Buddha or Bodhisattva. In every case the individual *tulku* deliberately chooses to be reincarnated in a particular time and place, whereas the average person does not exercise such discretion. When certain signs appear, religious officials must investigate carefully to determine whether a possible *tulku* meets all the criteria. The three *lamas* currently most visible and influential are: the Dalai Lama, symbolic leader of the Tibetan people; the Panchen Lama, generally considered the Dalai Lama's spiritual representative and associated with the Buddha Amitabha; and the Bogdo Lama, who leads Mongolia's Buddhist community.

Is there a **central teaching authority** for Buddhists?

No single individual or institutional center claims central authority to all Buddhists. Not long after the Buddha's death various interpretations of his teaching gave rise to distinct schools of thought, and eventually, of practice. Perhaps the closest approximation to centralized authority in the history of Buddhism is the various councils convened over many centuries. Most Buddhists concur on the authority of the first three monastic convocations, convened about a century apart, with the first only months after the Buddha's death. Members took up a range of issues, from the particulars of

monastic discipline, to the shape of the canonical scriptures, to doctrinal differences. But Buddhists disagree on the number of authentic councils, and even the universally acknowledged councils have exercised limited authority. Today, many non-Buddhists think immediately of the Dalai Lama as a major Buddhist leader and authority figure. Even though the Dalai Lama has enormous moral authority and commands the respect of Buddhists in many communities, his role remains quite different from that of the pope or the College of Cardinals in Roman Catholicism.

Who is the **Dalai Lama** and why is he important to so many Buddhists?

The man known the world over as the Dalai Lama is the fourteenth in a series of sacred figures believed to be reincarnations of the Bodhisattva Avalokiteshvara as well as of the preceding Dalai Lama. The original Dalai Lama was head of the

The current Dalai Lama is considered by Buddhists to be the fourteenth reincarnation of the Bodhisattva Avalokiteshvara. (vipflash / Shutterstock.com.)

Gelug-pa order on whom a Mongol leader bestowed the title, which means "teacher of ocean-wide wisdom," in 1578. Tenzin Gyatso is the current Dalai Lama and a monk of the Tibetan Gelug-pa order. When the thirteenth Dalai Lama died in 1933, officials of the order began investigations in search of his successor. They found three likely candidates, baby boys who manifested certain signs. They chose Tenzin, born in 1935, and in 1940 brought him to the Potala Palace in Lhasa to begin his monastic life. His extensive training included studies in philosophy and the arcane scriptures of the Vajrayana tradition, as well as meditative disciplines. He learned the difficult skill of Tibetan ritual chanting, with its strikingly deep pitch and haunting overtones. Outsiders often find it difficult to understand why the monks would take a baby away from his family to sequester him for a life of spiritual discipline. Tibetans see it all as part of a much larger picture. A family could scarcely hope for a greater blessing. But the Dalai Lama's traditional role in Tibetan history has not always found him enjoying the serenity of monastic meditation. Dalai Lamas have traditionally been important political leaders in Tibet. When the Chinese invaded Tibet in 1950, they put increasing pressure on the Dalai Lama. He went into exile in India in 1959. From his headquarters in Dharmsala, His Holiness has continued to represent the cause of the oppressed Tibetan people. He has written several books that explain beautifully the genuinely open and universally tolerant teaching he espouses.

What is a **Roshi**?

The Japanese term *roshi* means "old (i.e., venerable) teacher." It is the title of the spiritual master in Zen monasteries. Monks admitted to the Zen life must submit themselves entirely to the direction of the Roshi, however harsh and unrelenting his discipline may seem. Regular activities in which Roshi and monks encounter each other include the master's instructions to the group and monks' individual sessions in the Roshi's room. A Roshi's instructions (*teisho, koza*) take place in a lecture hall. Accompanied by two assistant monks, the Roshi burns incense before the Buddha image. After the monks recite sacred texts, the Roshi assumes his teaching chair and teaches for about an hour, using short narratives and parables and concluding with a specific case of the issue he has been discussing. The monks are left to ponder the matter in depth. During the week-long retreats called *Dai-sesshin* ([the great] "collecting thoughts") that occur monthly during the traditional rainy season seclusion, the Roshi gives instructions daily. Ordinarily, individual monks will have the opportunity for voluntary individual sessions with the Roshi at regular intervals during the course of daily order. But during the *Dai-sesshin* they will each see him briefly four times daily to discuss their *koan* or their progress in meditation. These sessions, called *sanzen,* are not a simple chat. There is no small talk with the Roshi. In a few choice words, the monk signals to the teacher whether he is making genuine progress. If he talks nonsense, the Roshi will toss him out unceremoniously with an admonition to get serious. One of Zen's greatest teachers, Dogen (1200–53), described the ideal *roshi*   **279** as able to transmit the *dharma*, warm but able to be harsh when necessary, standing in the Buddha's place in educating, humble enough to ask for his monks' forgiveness, uninterested in fame or prestige, and concerned above all with simplicity. When it seems appropriate the monk and the Roshi might even share a hearty laugh.

Are there **religious hierarchical structures** in any branch of Buddhism?

Early Buddhist teaching replaced the caste system's dramatic social and religious stratification with an egalitarian ideal. "Be a lamp unto your own feet," the Buddha counseled his followers. His rejection of a mediating priesthood made the Buddha a sort of "protestant reformer." He wanted the life of the *Sangha* to represent a perfectly level playing field. In practice, the elevation of the monastic life over that of the laity introduced a kind of stratification into Buddhist life. Within the early monastic community seniority alone distinguished one member from another. As the *Sangha* expanded and the itinerant mendicants began to settle into fixed residences, monastic life became more complex and required a division of labor. Though many decisions were taken by a monastic council, a de facto hierarchy developed. At the top was the abbot, assisted by spiritual guides and preceptors chosen from among the senior monks. The majority of the community was made up of senior monks and nuns and novices. In addition, many of the denominations eventually took on a semblance of hierarchical organization.

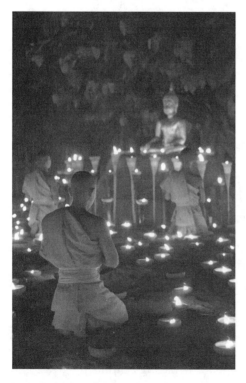

But there is a major difference between the function of such organizational structures in Buddhist institutions and parallels in traditions like Roman Catholicism and Shi'a Islam. Buddhist hierarchies seem to evolve as a result of internal structural needs rather than as a result of doctrine. Traditions that teach the need for mediators between ordinary people and the ultimate sources of truth and spiritual power develop hierarchical structures for theoretical as well as practical reasons.

What is a **monk** and how are Buddhist **monasteries organized**?

In its wider sense, "monk" refers to any male Buddhist who enters a monastic institution, whether permanently or for a

Monks pray in a Buddhist monastery in Chiangmai, Thailand.

Why was the monk Eisai an important figure?

The Japanese Buddhist monk Eisai (1141–1215) introduced the Zen Buddhist Rinzai sect to Japan, and under him Zen first became acknowledged as an independent school of Buddhism. He is also responsible for popularizing the cultivation of tea in Japan. Also known by his honorific title of Zenko Kokushi (national teacher), Eisai came from a family of Shinto priests in the district of Okayama. Like many famous priests in his period, he studied at the great Tendai center on Mt. Hiei. In 1168 he made his first trip to China, where he visited Zen centers, especially those flourishing on Mt. Tian Tai. He was much impressed by what he saw and felt with growing conviction that Zen could contribute greatly to a reawakening of Buddhist faith in Japan. In 1187 he undertook a second trip to the continent for the purpose of tracing the origins of Buddhism to India. The authorities, however, refused him permission to go beyond Chinese borders. He studied on Mt. Tian Tai until 1191, where he was ordained in the Rinzai (Chinese, Lin Chi) sect and returned to Japan. He constructed the first Rinzai temple, the Shofukuji, at Hakata in Kyushu. Eisai proclaimed the superiority of Zen mediation over other Buddhist disciplines, thus provoking the ire of the Tendai monks who sought to outlaw the new sect. However, Eisai enjoyed the protection of the shogun Minamoto Yoriie, and in 1202 he was given the direction of the Kenninji in Kyoto. Like Saicho, and particularly Nichiren, Eisai associated his type of Buddhism with national welfare and promoted Zen by publishing a tract entitled *Kozen Gokoku Ron* (The Propagation of Zen for the Protection of the Country).

short time, receiving at least the lower ordination to the status of novice (*shramanera*). Strictly speaking, a monk is a male at least twenty years old who has been in the monastery at least five years and received the higher ordination to the status of *bhikshu* ("mendicant"). Monasteries are generally independent and autonomous foundations. Rather like Benedictine monasteries in Roman Catholicism (a very loose analogy), Buddhist monasteries of the same lineage or "order" are administered separately. Each monastery's internal structure combines offices—positions assigned by a monastic council or other governing body—and ranks—distinctions often based on seniority or spiritual acumen. Offices in a Japanese Zen monastery include, for example, chief abbot (in a complex with many sub-monasteries and temples), abbot (*kancho*), Zen master (*roshi*), meditation leader and disciplinarian (*jikijitsu*) in the Zendo or meditation hall, administrator of the Zendo (*jisha*), and head cook. An important rank is that of head monk (*jushoku*), who might also hold the office of abbot in a sub-temple. Similarly, in Thai Theravada monasteries offices include abbots and meditation masters, and recognize various ranks, such as those of elder (*thera,* ten years' seniority), and great elder (*mahathera,* with twenty years' seniority).

What is a **Buddhist nun**?

The Buddha himself decided, not without hesitation, to institute a female counterpart to male membership in the monastic *Sangha*. Nuns, called *bhikshunis* or "female mendicants," had from the start to defer to monks and were required to abide by over a hundred additional disciplinary regulations. Many scholars note that the formal lineage of the order of Buddhist nuns has long since been disrupted. Still, groups of women throughout Asia live in communities and consider themselves members of the *Sangha*. Most shave their heads, wear monastic garb, and live according to traditional norms and engage in practices such as scriptural recitation. Representatives of several Chinese lineages are perhaps the most numerous. Like their male counterparts, nuns also undergo a period of training as novices before they can be considered for higher ordination to full monastic membership. Once presented by her sponsor, the candidate submits to an in-depth questioning as to her suitability. If she passes, a senior nun proposes acceptance. Then the candidate is questioned again by a panel of monks. Passing that, the candidate is sent back to her sisters for further training and acceptance into the higher initiation.

How do **monasteries function** in Buddhist life?

During the early centuries of Buddhism monks and nuns lived as itinerant beggars with no fixed abode. The practice of staying put during the monsoon season gave rise to permanent monastic institutions. Monks and nuns lived either in *viharas,* separate structures, or dwellings carved like caves into hillsides (*guhas*). Many early monasteries functioned somewhat like parishes, offering spiritual services to the local population. These smaller, more pastorally oriented monasteries were eventually replaced by larger monastic complexes with a focus on learning. Many monasteries, especially in Theravada lands, still offer educational services to the people of the area. In general, Theravada monasteries throughout southeast Asia maintain somewhat more active links with the outside community than do Mahayana monasteries. Japanese Zen monasteries, for example, still focus on a life of seclusion and solitude. Tibetan institutions have until recently been the virtual backbone of community life on the "Roof of the World" and were home to an extraordinarily large percentage of the male population. Some monasteries are now part of what one might call consortiums, with as many as two dozen individual "temple monasteries" of the same denomination clustered within one larger institution. Most classic monasteries are walled enclosures divided into private and public areas. Monks' residences and private ritual spaces are separated from the ritual and educational facilities that serve visitors.

Do Buddhists have a **system of religious law**?

A great deal of the Hindu tradition of religious law that affected the young Siddhartha's life concerned ritual stipulations and social restrictions. By fundamentally

Have there been important Buddhist mystics?

If transforming encounter with mystery and the cultivation of mental and spiritual states beyond everyday awareness counts as mysticism, then Buddhist tradition can certainly claim its mystics. But there are important differences between Buddhist mysticism and those of traditions such as Hinduism, Islam, and Christianity. All three of those traditions talk of at least two large categories of extraordinary spiritual experience. In "theistic" or "dualistic" mystical experience, the human person meets the divine "other" but retains his or her individuality. In "monistic" or "cosmic" mysticism, the human person becomes one with (or realizes the oneness that already exists in) an ultimate reality, with no trace of individuality surviving. Buddhist teaching insists that there is no "self" to begin with, so neither of those two models quite fits. True, some Buddhist schools use the language and symbolism of deity and union, but they understand those symbols as meditative aids rather than representations of metaphysical realities.

rejecting Vedic ritual practice as ineffectual and the caste system as discriminatory, the Buddha virtually wiped out at a stroke any need for much of the kind of legislation that is so central to religious systems such as Hinduism, Judaism, and Islam. Buddhist tradition does, however, have its own distinctive regulatory concerns. They have to do mostly with individual conduct. The eight-spoked Wheel of the Law symbolizes Buddhist ethical teaching in general.

What about more **specific directives**?

One of the earliest scriptures in the Pali Canon is the Vinaya Pitaka, the Basket of Discipline. Buddhist law generally emphasizes the "Thou shalt nots" over the "Thou shalts." On the negative side, the Vinaya lists several hundred actions considered offensive and unacceptable behavior for monks and nuns. Of those, some 250 apply to monks and 348 to nuns. Topping the list for all monks and nuns is a group of ten precepts that forbid lying, intoxicating substances, adultery, theft, killing, eating after noon, elegant beds, cosmetics, frivolous entertainment, and possession of luxuries. The first five also apply to laypeople, who might also choose to observe the next three on the four monthly "duty days" or sabbaths. Monks and nuns are automatically expelled from the monastic community for killing a human being or an animal, grand larceny, or sexual misconduct. Other important categories in monastic law include offenses that require a community consultation, those that call for restitution of some kind (return of goods improperly received), and issues of due process in resolving problems. Apart from these specific regulations, Buddhist teaching offers a number of more general guidelines for laypeople. It recommends, for example, seeking adequate income, acquiring a professional skill, frugality, freedom from debt, and giving generously to good causes. So what "happens" in Buddhist mysticism? Some sources talk of realizing the "emptiness" of all things. Profound experience of the meaning of the Four Noble Truths transcends all ordinary levels of awareness. It is possible to attain *nirvana* in this life—"*nirvana* with a remainder," they call it—and that means full insight into the way things are. One who arrives at such a state of "objectless contemplation" might justifiably be called a Buddhist mystic.

Is there such a thing as a **Buddhist saint**?

Nearly all of the Mahayana denominations look to embodiments of holiness for guidance, inspiration, and even the occasional miracle. Japanese Buddhists call some of these figures *shonin,* an honorific designation bestowed especially on patriarchs and founders of lineages and denominations. A group called the "Eighteen *Lohans*" (*lohan* is derived from the Sanskrit term *arhat*) are set apart from the Buddha's earliest disciples as uniquely sacred because of their unselfish commitment to spreading the *Dharma* rather than retiring into peaceful solitude. Theravada tradition still uses the term *arhat* ("worthy one") to refer to a living embodiment of sanctity and wisdom. But the *arhat* remains an ethical model only, and a rather distant ideal at that. Mahayana teaching sees the *Bodhisattva* as the ultimate in human potential. Some even confer the title on living individuals, such as the Dalai Lama. Bodhisattvas not only model spiritual perfection, but function as mediators as well. As emissaries of the various Buddhas, they exercise saving power and make comforting grace available to all who ask.

Have there been any important **Buddhist religious reformers**?

Many of the various Buddhist denominations and sects are the result of attempts at reform. Some people even regard the Buddha himself as one who sought to reform Hinduism. Among the best examples of religious reformers are those who aimed to rescue Buddhist teaching from complex formulas and make it accessible to real people. Tradition calls Bodhidharma (d. 532) the first patriarch of Chinese Zen. Apparently quite a colorful character, Bodhidharma criticized several schools for getting lost in their own long-winded treatises. Toss all the superfluous verbiage, he advised, and focus on direct dharma transmission from master to student.

About three centuries later in Japan, two other reformers set out to develop spiritual methods that would appeal to a broader public than some of the schools that had arrived in Japan during the previous several centuries. Kukai (744–835) and Saicho (762–822) founded the Tendai and Shingon lineages, respectively. But eventually Tendai turned more speculative and Shingon more mystical and esoteric.

Further reform developments eventually grew out of Tendai in the twelfth and thirteenth centuries. A Tendai monk, Honen (1133–1212), started a Japanese branch

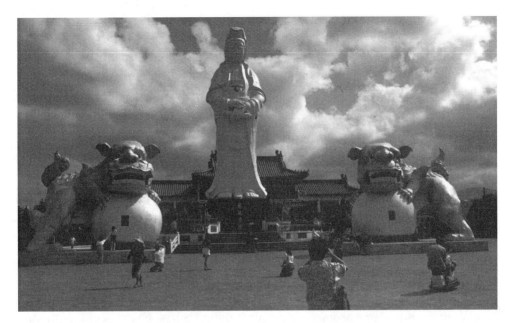

The giant statue of the Bodhisattva Guan Yin, popularly known in China as the Goddess of Mercy, is flanked by a pair of protective doglike lions at a temple on a hill overlooking the harbor of Keelung, Taiwan.

of Pure Land in hope of attracting people with its reliance on Amida Buddha. A successor named Nichiren (1222–1282) took Honen's insights a step further, insisting that a devotee approaching in good faith had only to repeat the name of the scripture called the Lotus of the Good Law Sutra—a mantra popular singer Tina Turner recommends—to be assured of salvation.

Who is the **Bodhisattva Guan Yin**?

Next to the various Buddhas, Guan Yin is certainly one of the most important and popular sacred figures in Buddhist tradition. This Bodhisattva began life, mythically speaking, as a male guardian figure named Avalokiteshvara, the "Lord Who Looks Down." Known in China as Guan Yin and in Japan as Kannon, he was originally one of Vairochana's (the central figure among the Five Transcendent Buddhas) attendants, presiding over the cosmic northwest. Avalokiteshvara came to be particularly associated with compassion when paired with the Bodhisattva Manjushri, who represented wisdom. Boundless in his care for all, the compassionate one has appeared with multiple heads and arms—one of the few Bodhisattvas to be commonly so depicted.

As Mahayana communities grew in China, Guan Yin's perfect compassion gradually transformed him into a female Bodhisattva. With a thousand arms and eleven heads, Guan Yin often has a decidedly feminine countenance. But she appears more often as a kindly woman smiling gently and inclined slightly toward her devotees. In

285

more recent times people have begun to call her more ordinary human manifestation the "Goddess of Mercy," a convenient but misleading epithet that resulted from Buddhism's interaction with Chinese popular religious lore. In Japan, the thousand-armed, eleven-headed Kannon often appears in multiple images within the same temple, sometimes even as a life-sized sculpture. Popular lore claims that each Kannon has a different face to symbolize this Bodhisattva's undivided attention to every single person on Earth.

HOLIDAYS AND REGULAR OBSERVANCES

What kind of **religious calendar** do Buddhists observe?

Since Buddhism has long been identified with so many different cultural settings, there is some variation in the ways Buddhists keep track of sacred times. The basic religious calendar remains tied, at least nominally, to the ancient Hindu combination of lunar and solar reckoning, but many Buddhists now observe some festivities on fixed dates. The earliest Buddhists apparently did not concern themselves with marking special occurrences on their calendar. But within a generation or so, India's growing and spreading Buddhist communities began to incorporate religious social occasions into ordinary life. As Buddhist communities arose outside of India they naturally tended to blend religious observances imported by Buddhist missionaries with the indigenous festivities of the land. In most places where Buddhism is an important presence today, the reckoning of years begins with the date of the Buddha's entry into *nirvana* (which coincided with his death). In any given year, Buddhists observe various festal occasions. Some commemorate major events in the life of the Buddha, others celebrate different institutional features of the tradition, others are tied to seasonal festivities, and still others are linked to events only in certain countries.

Calendar of Major Buddhist Festal Days

Precise dates of the following major Buddhist observances vary somewhat by sub-community and region, as well as from one solar year to another. They are listed here according to solar calendar months in which they most often occur. Many communities also observe seasonal festivities associated with the vernal and autumnal equinoxes, and some mark special times each month for heightened devotion, marked by the new, full, and quarter moons.

February

Magha Puja: Also called *Sangha* or Fourfold Assembly Day, recalls the Buddha's speaking to a gathering of 1250 *arahats*.

Parinirvana Day: Theravada Buddhists observe the Buddha's final entry into Nirvana. Mahayana Buddhists call it Nirvana Day and recall the Buddha's death on the occasion.

April

New Year (Theravada): Three-day celebration beginning with April's first full moon, featuring a symbolic cleansing of monasteries and Buddha images, paralleling a spiritual purification of all bad karma and renewal of Buddhist values.

May

Buddha Day: Occurs during the full-moon, known variously as Wesak, Visak, or Vaishakha, is Buddhism's principal and most widely celebrated festal day. For virtually all Buddhists the day mark's the Buddha's birth, but some also recall his attainment of enlightenment and his death on the day.

June to September (Rainy Season)

Varying "retreat" activities find increasing visits to temples, young men entering monasteries for brief experience of the monk's life.

July

Asala: Also known as Dharma Day because of its association with the Buddha's preaching his "first sermon," in which he set in motion the "wheel of Dharma" just after achieving enlightenment.

August

Some Buddhists (especially in Sri Lanka) celebrate the Festival of the Tooth at full moon, with special reverence for one of the Buddha's most important "relics."

October/November

Kathina : Theravada Buddhists observe Kathina month to end the rainy season, with increased pilgrimage visits and merit offerings, including presentation of new robes to monks.

December

Bodhi ("Enlightenment") Day: Some Buddhists commemorate Gautama's becoming the "Buddha" as a result of his enlightenment in meditation beneath the Bodhi tree.

Buddhists in various places commemorate three important events in the Buddha's life: his birth, his enlightenment, and his entry into *nirvana*. Theravada Buddhists celebrate them all on the same day, called simply Buddha Day, on the full moon day of Vaishakha (April/May). Some Mahayana groups hold separate festivities on fixed dates, with Buddha's birth observed on April 8 (called Hanamatsuri in Japan), his enlightenment (called Bodhi Day) on December 8, and his final entry into *nirvana* on February 15. Religious activities on these occasions include special gatherings in monastery temples. Devotees bathe images of the Buddha, listen to narratives of the Buddha's life, circumambulate his relics enshrined either in large structures called *chaityas* or small *stupa-* or *pagoda*-shaped reliquaries, and water small bodhi trees. Theravadins combine the festivities because tradition says that all three events occurred on the same day in different years. In Theravada southeast Asia, Buddha Day remains associated with the onset of the monsoon rains and the planting of the rice crop.

Are there **cyclical observances** or **feasts** that occur regularly but not just once a year?

During each lunar month, many Buddhists observe four "moon" days called *uposatha*. These are the full moon days, new moon days, and days midway between them, or the 1st, 8th, 15th, and 23rd of the month. Originally important as fast days in ancient Hindu practice, Buddhists now attach ceremonies to them somewhat the way Christians do to Sundays, Jews to Saturdays, and Muslims to Fridays. Lay Buddhists in some countries still regularly congregate in the local temple for a time of heightened religious discipline. Rituals include listening to a monk preach, meditating, and praying as monks chant the scriptures. Some devotees seek to gain spiritual merit by observing eight, rather than the usual five, precepts during that day. Monastic life singles out the new and full moon days. Monks assemble then to recite the rules of monastic discipline from a text called the *Pratimoksha*. They also engage in a communal confession of faults not unlike the traditional practice known as the "Chapter of Faults" in some Christian religious orders and monastic communities. After the monks recite each prohibition in the *Pratimoksha*, they pause to allow individuals to admit any transgression. Some Buddhists engage in fasting on new and full moon days, emulating the monastic practice of taking no food between noon and breakfast the following day.

Are there **days devoted** to other **aspects** of Buddhist **teaching**?

On the full moon day of the third lunar month of Magha, some Buddhists commemorate Buddha's teaching of the monastic disciplinary code called the Vinaya. Thais celebrate by circumambulating the *chaitya* and listening to a sermon in the temple. Theravada Buddhists celebrate the Buddha's first sermon on the full moon day of Asadha (eighth lunar month) by revering the scriptural text. Some schools celebrate days dedicated to their central scriptures. For example, the denomination named after the Japanese reformer Nichiren (1222–1282) honors the Lotus of the Good Law Sutra, as do other groups in China and Japan. Monasteries typically celebrate anniversaries of their founding and in some countries a festive day marks the anniversary of Buddhism's arrival with the first missionaries. Members of the Jodo Shinshu (True Pure Land) sect remember their founder Shinran (1173–1262) on the 16th of each month, and with a week-long memorial every year in either January or November.

What **observances** are **linked** with **seasonal cycles**?

The so-called Rain Retreat (*Vassa*) begins on the day after the full moon day of the eighth lunar month, Asadha (July/August), and continues until the full moon day of the eleventh lunar month Ashvina (September/October). Monks spend more time in meditation and study and are expected to remain in the monastery. Lay Buddhists visit temples and monasteries more frequently than usual to receive instruction, and marriages are generally not performed. Theravada Buddhists begin the season with monastic ordinations and end it with merit-rituals said to be in memory of Buddha's emergence from Heaven. Also at the end of the retreat comes the festival called *Kathina* ("cloth"). During this joyous month-long festivity, laypeople give the monks new robes and other useful gifts. This is a favored time for pilgrimages to southeast Asian sites such as Rangoon's Shwe Dagon temple and Thailand's shrine of the Buddha's Footprint. In connection with the rice harvest in February or March, Theravada devotees make merit by celebrating the story of how the Buddha-to-be entered the world as Prince Vessantara in a previous incarnation.

What about **observances related** to the **locality or indigenous practice**?

In many parts of the world Buddhists celebrate New Year's Day on January 1. The observance is not a specifically Buddhist tradition but has become associated with it through a process of syncretism. Japanese Buddhists observe the spring and autumn equinoxes on March 21 and September 21 respectively. A festival honoring the dead, called Obon Matsuri, occurs between July 13 and 15. Chinese All Souls' Day, a parallel festivity, celebrated during the seventh lunar month, features offerings thought to assist seven generations of deceased relatives. A good example of an observance linked specifically to a single region is the celebration of Buddhist Churches of America Founding Day on September 1.

Do Buddhists celebrate **feast days** of any **other important religious figures**?

In China, Japan and Tibet especially, Buddhists hold feasts in honor of various Bodhisattvas and holy persons. The death anniversary of Bodhidharma, traditionally believed to be the founding patriarch of Chinese Zen, occurs on the 5th day of the tenth lunar month, Bhadrapada (August/September). Events in the life of Tibetan Buddhism's important patriarch Padmasambhava provide a kind of narrative sacred structure for the entire year with observances occurring on the tenth day of each lunar month. Devotees celebrate his flight from the world in the first month, his taking of religious vows in the second, and his miraculous transformation of fire into water during the third, for example. One of the most widely celebrated sacred persons is the Bodhisattva Guan Yin (called Kannon in Japan). Her day is the 19th of a given lunar month, with her birthday occurring during the second month, her enlightenment during the sixth, and her entry into *nirvana* during the ninth.

Worshippers at Tokyo's Asakusa Kannon temple bless themselves by wafting incense smoke from the large courtyard burner toward themselves and rubbing in on their faces and bodies.

CUSTOMS AND RITUALS

What **rites** do Buddhists practice in the **temple**?

Some of the ordinary ritual activity that occurs in most Buddhist temples is communal. Congregational chanting of mantras or singing of hymns occasionally plays an important role. But a great deal of Buddhist temple ritual remains relatively unscheduled and highly individualized. Worshippers in Theravada temples sit or bow before the Buddha image and recite traditional prayers in praise of the historical Buddha. Devotees often hold as an offering a candle, flower, food, or a small parasol, symbols of respect for royalty. Offerings of flowers are particularly helpful reminders of impermanence, since they invariably wither and fade. Worshippers generally regard sacred images as aids to prayer and often also as possessing certain magical powers, but the image is not itself the Buddha. Theravada ritual aims to overcome the suffering born of inappropriate craving. Some temples have wall murals depicting scenes from the Jataka tales, each one exemplifying one essential virtue. Worshippers can meditate on these scenes in succession and ponder the ethical implications. Since the Buddha was like an extinct fire that needs no more fuel, people do not worship him as such. Theravada temple ritual is meant to dispose the devotee for greater spiritual development. Popular Mahayana rituals are similar in some outward respects, but they focus on the Buddha and Bodhisattvas as repositories of saving grace and power. Worship is a means to assure rebirth in one of the Buddha-lands. Rituals emphasize the need to surrender entirely to saving grace and boundless compassion. Ritual helps overcome ignorance of the ultimate sources of transforming spiritual power. Mahayana temples often display multiple images, sometimes having several walls lined with statues. Devotees can pay their respects to each, waving an incense wand clasped between folded hands as a gesture of veneration.

What **rites** do Buddhists practice at **home**?

Many devout Buddhists pray daily at home before their domestic shrine, a miniature version of the temple or monastic oratory. They show reverence to

A small Buddhist house-sized shrine. Kyoto, Japan. (Photo courtesy of David Oughton.)

the image of the Buddha with incense, flower offerings, and a lighted candle. All three of these simple symbols bring home the central realization of impermanence. They give pleasure to the worshipper, who should enjoy them while they last. Unburned incense is analogous to a person who does not use his or her talents. A lotus flower is a reminder of the Buddha's being rooted in the muck of real life but blossoming above it and in spite of it. These symbols also represent homage to the Buddha, not because the Buddha needs or enjoys that, but because it focuses the mind on his message. Rituals also include reciting the "Three Refuges" and reaffirming the commitment to the "Five Precepts." Prayers of petition include the same sorts of things people of many traditions ask for—happiness, success, longevity, and salvation. Mahayana devotees might wear a small rosary around a wrist, as they often do when worshipping in the temple.

What is the **Buddhist Rosary**?

Buddhists in many places have used a number of variations on the string of beads for devotional purposes. In ancient India, Buddhists used a string of 108 beads (very similar to the ancient Hindu rosary) as a symbol of the Bodhisattva Avalokiteshvara. This compassionate being, whose name means, roughly, "Lord Looking Down on the World," took on 108 human characteristics in his saving descent to assume the human condition, using the beads while doing so. Chinese and Japanese images of the Buddha, as well as of various patriarchs and monastic founders, sometimes show them holding rosaries. For ritual purposes, the rosary has been particularly important in the more esoteric sects of Tibet and Japan. Tibetan rosaries have three larger beads at the end as symbols of the Three Jewels. Devotees in those sects use the beads to count repetitions of their mantras. In some more popular sects, devotees count repetitions of names of the Buddha or phrases like "Glory to Amida Buddha."

Is there a standard Buddhist **liturgical worship**?

Buddhist denominations that emphasize communal worship exhibit considerable variation in their services. Recitation of sacred texts is the single most common element. One Japanese Pure Land denomination uses the following "order of service." After a call to worship expressing prayerful intent, worshippers pronounce the "Three Refuges," invoke the presence of the Buddha, praise him, make a symbolic confession of sins, and recite the name of Amida Buddha ten times. Then follows a segment of scriptural chanting, explicitly dedicated to rebirth in the Pure Land. Again invoking the name of Amida Buddha ten times, worshippers reflect on its deeper meaning. Between two further invocations of the name, they recite from the teachings of founder Honen. After a recitation of the vows of the Bodhisattva the ritual concludes with the "Three Refuges" and a final prayer to send the Buddha back to his heavenly abode.

Do Buddhists engage in **ritual sacrifice**?

Sacrifice has never been part of mainstream Buddhist ritual. The Buddha himself rejected the ancient Hindu sacrificial heritage as spiritually bankrupt, as did many others among his contemporaries. Some later popular devotional Hindu sects retained animal sacrifice as an essential feature of ritual. But Theravada and Mahayana popular devotion have, in effect, spiritualized the concept of sacrifice. Traditional forms of sacrifice typically aim to appease a divine power. Buddhist tradition virtually does away with the concept. When worshippers make offerings of flowers, incense, and other symbols, they are not giving gifts to a spiritual power but offering signs of reverence and providing reminders for themselves of life's impermanence.

What is the **connection** between **ritual** and the **Theravada notion** of **making merit**?

Some actions and attitudes take on a ritual dimension because they are associated with the two essential spiritual activities of making and transferring merit. Actions that make merit for the individual store up positive energy needed to overcome the inappropriate craving that can prevent one from achieving liberation. These actions prominently include a group of ten: proper beliefs, reverence and service of one's elders, giving generously to monks, observing the five (or eight) precepts, various forms of meditation including recitation of scriptural verses, respect for others, preaching, hearing a sermon, empathizing with merit, and transfer of merit. When lay Buddhists commit themselves temporarily to the Eight Precepts they add the monastic practices of avoiding food after the noon meal, certain forms of entertainment, and the use of cosmetics. Some lists of merit-making deeds also include building a monastery, becoming a monk or having a son do so, donating funds for the repair of a temple, and observing every *uposatha* ("sabbath"). Transfer of merit is a doubly meritorious form of altruism, since in the very intention to share, one receives back. In fact, Buddhists characteristically see a reciprocity in all ritual deeds. Devotees give generously to monks, for example, and the monks give spiritual encouragement, good example, and teaching in return.

What is the meaning of Buddhist "ordination"?

Ordination in the Buddhist tradition does not imply the same kind of conferral of spiritual power or authority that it does in many Christian denominations. A closer parallel would be the taking of religious vows. Young men and boys in many Buddhist denominations submit themselves for ordination to the monastic *sangha* under a variety of circumstances. In some cultures boys as young as seven can enter the monastery and receive the "lower ordination" (*parivraja*) to the rank of novice in the order. Those who choose to stay and commit themselves to the monastic life permanently can receive the "higher ordination" (*upasampada*) to full status of monk or *bhikshu*. Ordinations are often held at the start of the Rain Retreat, and it is not unusual for young ordinands to remain in the monastery only for one rainy season. Thai men sometimes still enter the monastery for a week or less after the death of a family member. In some areas ordinations occur after rice harvest, since increased revenue makes for better celebrations, but the rituals can occur anytime outside of the Rain Retreat itself. Prospective ordinands petition the abbot of a local monastery, who might then allow them in directly if they intend only a short stay. Those who propose to remain and take the full monastic ordination eventually go through a more elaborate ritual. They kneel before ten monks and the abbot, ask permission to enter, and receive the two-piece robe of the novice. After donning the garb, the candidates recite the Three Refuges and Ten Precepts. Ordination to full membership in the monastic order repeats the novitiate ritual and adds a further examination of the candidates. Each novice receives a begging bowl and a three-piece garment.

What is a day in the life of a Buddhist monastery like?

Daily monastic rituals vary somewhat according to place and denomination. Theravada monasteries revolve around the chanting of scriptures from the first two "baskets," the Vinaya and Sutra Pitakas. After waking at around three a.m., members lie prostrate together in the oratory to recite the Three Refuges and chant sutras. They spend several hours in study and meditation before heading out to beg. Breakfast precedes more communal chanting and a class on the rules of discipline. Supper is scheduled before noon, after which members spend the afternoon studying scripture and resting. More chanting, study, and prayer, along with a chance to once again examine the conscience and confess faults, bring the day to a close by ten. Theravada monks in many areas engage in considerable social service activity, assisting villagers in various kinds of practical projects and in community organization. In places like Japan, monks leave the monastery on a quest for alms that is more a symbolic reminder of their dependence than a substantial necessity.

Daily order is strictly regulated with relatively little time for individual activities. Certain days are designated for shaving and bathing. Zen monks engage in periods of manual labor around the monastery, such as gardening, gathering fuel, and general maintenance, and place greater emphasis on silent meditation than on recitation of scriptural texts. Each month a whole week is dedicated to virtually round-the-clock *zazen,* or sitting meditation, together in the same hall where the monks sleep. Monastic life generally allows sufficient sleep and nutritious food to maintain good health, but nothing superfluous in either case. It is a physically and psychologically demanding life. In most cases, individuals can join a monastery for a time, with the understanding that they do not intend to make a lifelong commitment to it.

What kinds of **ritual objects** figure in Buddhist worship and prayer?

Among the most common implements used in regular ritual are acoustic devices such as bells, gongs, and hollow wooden blocks. Prayer leaders will occasionally strike a large bronze bowl-shaped bell set on a pillow. As its vibrant, mellow ring decays into silence, devotees recall the universal characteristic of impermanence. When ritual leaders, sometimes accompanied by the congregation, chant sacred texts, they generally strike a hollow block of wood rhythmically to keep chanters together in their recitation. Incense burners and containers of sand into which devotees can insert their lighted incense wands are part of nearly every ritual setting. Sometimes devotees will approach a temple's large incense cauldron, waft the smoke toward themselves with their hands, and then rub it on various parts of their bodies for healing and general well-being. Esoteric sects typically employ a larger variety of objects. Tibetans use a small scepter symbolizing the indestructibility of the thunderbolt in one hand. The other holds a small bell whose vanishing sound represents impermanence. Some groups use weapons associated with Hindu deities who became part of the Buddhist pantheon. Some also use a begging

bowl, as the Buddha did, or a fly whisk, symbol of adherence to the *dharma*. Most basic among the ritual objects in both home and temple are the candle holder (one for the home, two in temple), flower vase (one at home, two in temple), and small censer. Other common objects include tablets or scrolls containing sacred names or mantras, either in Sanskrit or the vernacular.

Is **meditation** important for Buddhists?

Buddhist tradition has refined a number of meditative practices. Two important aspects taught by an ancient Theravada

A gong and ritual drum at a Japanese Buddhist temple.

fifth-century authority named Buddhaghosa are called "dwelling in tranquility" (*shamatha*) and "insight" (*vipashyana/vipassana*). In order to catch the "fish" of intuitive knowledge, one has first to get to the calm, clear lake. Attaining a measure of tranquility is a process of disciplined concentration in which the meditator gradually withdraws from sensory input through nineteen successive stages of attentiveness and reflection. Insight meditation involves the discipline of observing sensory input with perfect mindfulness in order to arrive at genuine wisdom. Traditional explanations typically recommend *shamatha* before *vipashyana,* but they go together and the process may actually be circular—tranquility leading to insight leading to deeper tranquility. Buddhaghosa suggests forty objects for contemplation to eliminate distraction and lead to contemplative states. Each person is characterized by tendencies to one of the three "qualities" of lust, hatred, and delusion, and must focus on counteracting that major cause of distraction.

To transform lust into faith, first meditate on physical impermanence and then on the virtues of the Buddha. Transform hatred into understanding by meditating first on love, compassion, and joy, and proceed to an awareness of mortality and physical dissolution. Turn delusion to deliberation by focusing on breathing as a means to calming.

As for the achievement of Insight, Buddhaghosa recommends the "Seven Purities." Here the meditator focuses on the purity of virtue, of mind, of belief, of overcoming doubt, of the knowledge of right and wrong action, of insight into spiritual progress, and of knowledge and insight themselves. Mahayana tradition adapted Buddhaghosa's classical methods to its teaching about the Bodhisattva's saving role. Each dedicated seeker progresses spiritually by meditating on the "Ten Stages" of the Bodhisattva career. This is the steepest of paths, beginning with the accumulation of merit and knowledge and proceeding through multiple levels of meditative discipline.

Is **pilgrimage** important for Buddhists?

Just as meditators pursue an inward path to liberation, pilgrims seek the ultimate goal using external symbolism. Sites associated with the principal events in the life of the Buddha very soon became pilgrim goals. Some texts even suggest that the Buddha directed his followers to visit the places of his birth, enlightenment, first sermon, and entry into *nirvana*. But Buddhists have beaten paths to hallowed places in China and Japan as well. Chinese devotees have mapped out a sacred landscape for pilgrim itineraries centered on four sacred mountains. Individual temples have also taken on a special aura, perhaps as a result of an apparition or miracle, or by association with some famous holy person. Pilgrims head for those places both on special occasions and whenever the mood strikes them. Hoped-for spiritual benefits range from grace to get through a difficult time to healing serious illnesses. Japanese Buddhists also continue to follow a pilgrim road to numerous holy places. One of the most popular circuits is that of the eighty-eight Temples on the island of Shikoku. There pilgrims retrace the steps of the venerable monk Kukai, founder of the Shingon denomination, from temple to temple, gathering spiritual souvenirs as they travel.

Do Buddhists practice rituals of exorcism?

Since the Buddha emphasized that the individual was the only power of ultimate significance in the quest for liberation, he saw no need for formal ritual designed to do away with negative forces. Keen awareness of one's own motives and intentions would take care of all problems. Still, Buddhist practice has absorbed various indigenous forms of exorcism from virtually every culture in which the tradition has taken root. Many of the practices still in use in Japan originated in China and were brought to Japan by founders of Japan's Tendai and Shingon sects in the early ninth century. Japan's Nichiren school, a development of Tendai tradition, acknowledges four types of demonic possession. Phenomena range from pain caused by an angry spirit to hallucinations to possession by some animal spirit as signaled by personality changes to severe disorders manifested in multiple personalities and voices. Priests of the Nichiren school undergo strict ascetical preparation before performing an exorcism. Someone close to the possessed person serves as a medium to the spirit world, speaking for the possessed person and delivering answers on behalf of the forces of good. In other cases, the exorcist deals directly with the possessed person. Wearing white, the exorcist recites from the principal Nichiren scripture, The Lotus Sutra, makes sharp noises using a set of wooden castanets, and interrogates the one possessed. Some Buddhists prefer exorcism as an alternative to psychotherapy.

Are **music and dance** important in Buddhist religious ritual?

Formal Buddhist rituals generally do not incorporate music as such, with the exception of more recent denominations that have absorbed practices from Protestant Christianity. Chanting and rhythmic recitation use tones other than those of normal speech but are not usually done to musical accompaniment. Buddhist rituals do, however, make extensive use of a wide variety of sounds and percussive devices. Bells, gongs, drums, hollow blocks, and clappers of many sizes are standard equipment in different areas of temples and monasteries. Large and medium-sized bells signal the beginning of worship services, and Zen masters use smaller bells to signal the end of sessions with individual monks. Large drums announce the time for certain exercises and gatherings. The most common ritual use of sound devices is that of keeping time during recitation and chanting or scriptural texts. Hollow blocks make a hypnotic "klop" to focus the attention and heavy bronze bowls emit a rich lingering note that reminds worshippers of the impermanence of all things. The combination of sustained warm bell-like tones punctuated by stark wooden percussion is very effective and surprisingly easy to listen to. Buddhists in various parts of the world sometimes use music and dance para-liturgically—that is, outside of their primary ritual settings. Zen meditative mood, for example, is often associated with the haunting sound of the bamboo flute called the *shakuhachi,* and Tibetans have traditionally used vigorous dancing in ceremonies such as exorcism and other protective rituals.

How do Buddhists **celebrate birth** or **initiation** or **other rites** of passage?

Buddhist tradition generally marks fewer of life's passages than, say, Hindu tradition, and ceremonies are typically much simpler. Rites of passage also vary considerably from one region to another. Here are a couple of representative ceremonies observed by some Japanese Buddhists of one of the Pure Land groups. A celebration marks the child's seventh day of life. On the one hundredth day, the family gathers at the temple to symbolize the baby's taking refuge in the Three Jewels and becoming a spiritual child of the Buddha. Some Pure Land Buddhists also acknowledge a variation on the theme of "coming of age" or puberty rite. The young man or woman stands before the altar and reaffirms the desire to adhere to Buddhist values. One symbol of the young person's attainment of adulthood is a white cloth inscribed "Amida Buddha." There is no set day for these ceremonies, but they sometimes occur on anniversaries or when the Chief Abbot can be present. Rituals of death and mourning are the most important rites of passage for Buddhists generally, with nuptials perhaps second in importance.

Are there Buddhist rituals of **marriage**?

Marriage has generally not been an important religious rite of passage in Buddhist tradition. Perhaps that is because of the great emphasis on the centrality of monastic life. In various regions of Asia, other religious traditions supply the devotional settings associated with new beginnings. In Japan, for example, people generally either associate marriage with Shinto or consider it a purely civil ceremony. Some do use Buddhist symbolism in their wedding ceremonies. That might include, for example, offering incense, and receiving the rosary as a reminder of a union witnessed before the Buddha. In the United States and some other regions where Buddhist missionaries have more recently introduced the tradition, Buddhists often use a modified Protestant ceremony. Held either outdoors or in a temple, the service may include brief readings from scriptures on the theme of compassion, a period of silent meditation, and a short sermon from the officiating priest or minister. An officiating monk or priest might also chant prayers from a scripture.

How do Buddhists deal ritually with **death and mourning**?

Practice varies according to denomination and cultural setting, but there are a number of common elements. These include: prayer at the deathbed and preparation of the body; a wake that includes final viewing; funeral service typically in a mortuary or funeral home; interment, usually of cremated remains but with full burial in some circumstances; and a series of memorial services at intervals beginning immediately after death and then in anniversary years calculated in various different ways. Viewing

A Buddhist cremation in Laos.

the body at the wake is a powerful reminder of the universal fact of impermanence. Funeral ceremonies center on recitation or chanting of appropriate sacred texts chosen to help mourners to see the event in the context of the full sweep of human existence. An officiating priest, monk, or minister may offer a eulogy, and participants make offerings of incense. In some places, like Japan, families inter the cremated remains either in a columbarium connected to a temple or in a cemetery on temple grounds.

Memorial services are important in virtually all Buddhist denominations, especially when Buddhism intersects with ancient traditions of ancestor veneration. Many Mahayana Buddhists observe memorials seven, thirty-five, forty-nine and one hundred days after death, and after one, three, seven, thirteen, seventeen, thirty-three, fifty, and one hundred years. Some consider the forty-ninth day especially important, since at that point the soul ceases its wandering. Theravada practice often includes memorial services two days after death at the home, two or three days after that at the funeral establishment, and again seven days after interment. The object of the last ceremony is to transfer merit from the living to the dead to ensure a good rebirth. Many Buddhists also offer a meal in the home or elsewhere for mourners after funeral services or interment.

HISTORY AND SOURCES

What is **religious Daoism** and what are its **origins**?

"Daoism" (or Taoism) refers to a wide range of philosophical, religious, and magical traditions dating from perhaps the fourth century B.C.E. in China. Here the focus will be on the specifically religious aspects of these complex and ancient developments. The most ancient roots of the tradition were in shamanistic cults dating back perhaps several millennia to prehistoric China. Legendary imperial figures of that age, Yu, Shun, and Yao, are still revered as great sages. According to legend, Daoism formally began with Lao Zi's writing of the Dao De Jing, the Classic of the Way and Its Power, in the sixth century B.C.E. Scholars now believe the Dao De Jing actually dates from between 300 and 250 B.C.E. Teachings of the Dao De Jing came together with those of thinkers like Yang Zhu (340–266 B.C.E.) and Zhuang Zi (369–286 B.C.E.) to form the broad conceptual basis of a wider "Daoist" tradition that had become largely philosophical (*Dao Jia*) by the fourth century B.C.E. But religious Daoism (*Dao Jiao*) was still a long way off.

Solid scholarly research suggests that Daoism as a religious tradition began in the mid-second century C.E. It seems a teacher named Zhang Dao Ling (34–156 C.E.) claimed that Lao Zi himself commissioned him to spread the teaching of the Dao. Zhang inaugurated the "Five Bushels of Rice" movement (a reference to the suggested offering for would-be members) and built a religious polity in Szechuan province. According to legend, Zhang Dao Ling's emphasis on acquiring immortality culminated in his ascension into the heavens. Out of that movement grew the first and one of the most influential branches of religious Daoism, the Celestial Masters school. Religious Daoism has since developed numerous sects and schools, each with its distinctive emphasis on various spiritual teachings and ritual practices.

What is meant by the term "**Chinese Community Traditions**" (CCT)?

Much more ancient than religious or even earlier philosophical Daoism are the various currents of popular religious belief and practice that together comprise what will be referred to as Chinese Community Traditions or CCT. Historians of religion suggest that most Chinese who engage in public expression of religious beliefs actually belong to this broad popular stream. Many of their beliefs have Daoist connections, but, unlike Daoism as such, CCT has not been associated with formal religious institutions such as priesthood and monastic orders, and does not possess a scriptural canon. Many beliefs and practices now widespread in popular tradition also have roots in ancient Confucian and Imperial cultic institutions, and in Buddhism as well.

Countless CCT temples began to appear in towns and villages several centuries ago. Since they do not have their own resident ritual specialists, these temples often enlist the services of Daoist priests, but their day-to-day services are often handled by dedicated laypeople. Many such temples are associated with families, who maintain them as a public service and a family tradition. Some elements of CCT also appear in temples ostensibly identified as Buddhist. A Guan Yin temple in Honolulu, for example, combines Buddhist rituals with a host of other popular practices. Though the main image is that of the Buddha, numerous other icons are prominently displayed.

That particular temple is run by a group of Chinese Buddhist nuns who are especially concerned with preserving the image that theirs is a purely Buddhist temple, in spite of the obvious diversity within it. Recently, when a visitor asked permission to snap a few photos inside, the nun in charge agreed. But whenever she thought his camera lens was wandering toward Confucius or another icon, she tugged his sleeve and waved a disapproving finger at him. "Only Buddha," she insisted. Just a few blocks away, above a small upholstery shop, is the Lum family temple. There, all the deities are clearly of the CCT variety, even though some are often inaccurately identified as Daoist.

Who was **Lao Zi**? Do people think of him as a religious founder?

Lao Zi was likely an altogether legendary figure whose "name" simply means "old teacher or master." Tradition says he was

A life-sized statue of the Yellow Emperor in a glass case in Bao An Gong temple, Taipei, Taiwan.

born around 604 B.C.E., making him a much older contemporary of Confucius (Kong Fu Zi, 551–479 B.C.E.), who was in turn an almost exact contemporary of the Buddha. The legend says Lao Zi was a clerk in the archives of the Zhou dynasty who practiced the "Way and its power" and emphasized self-effacement and anonymity. When he became convinced that social disintegration and political corruption in the Zhou dynasty were irreversible, he decided to withdraw from society. Riding his water buffalo, the old man came to the frontier. There a customs officer besought him to write down his lofty teachings before departing. Lao Zi wrote the Dao De Jing, roughly translated as The Classic of the Way and Its Power, and disappeared, leaving a legacy of mystery.

Much later stories, perhaps from a time when Daoists and Confucians were in competition for followers, tell of a meeting between Lao Zi and a youthful Confucius. No use wasting so much time studying your history, Lao Zi counseled the newcomer. Observe nature and you will see that love for the Dao is all that one needs. Popular tradition tends to identify Lao Zi as the one who first taught that ordinary folk could seek and attain immortality. Some scholars suggest that Lao Zi's legendary stature may have been enhanced as a result of his mistaken identification with the legendary Huang Di—known as the Yellow Emperor—who ruled in the middle of the third millennium B.C.E. Lao Zi was officially declared a god around 666 C.E. and eventually became part of a much-expanded Daoist pantheon.

Another man sometimes identified as the founder of Daoism was Lao Lai Zi, who also came from Chu. He is designated as a contemporary of Confucius and is credited with a fifteen-chapter book expounding on the teachings of the Daoist school. Nothing more is known about him. According to a third account, the original Lao Zi lived 129 years after the death of Confucius. This man went by the name of Tan, the historian of Chou.

What is the main source of information on Lao Zi's life?

The main source of information on Lao Zi's life is a biography written by the historian Si Ma Chen (145–86 B.C.E.) in his *Records of the Historian*. By this time a number of beliefs about the founder of Chinese Daoism were circulating, and Si Ma Chen himself was unsure of their authenticity. The biography, in fact, contains an account of not one, but three, men called Lao Zi. The first Lao Zi was a man named Li Er or Lao Dan who came from the village of Chu Ren in the Southern Chinese state of Chu. Li Er served as historian in charge of the official archives in the Chinese imperial capital of Loyang. He was a contemporary of Confucius and is reported to have granted an interview to the Confucian master when he came to Loyang seeking information on the Zhou dynasty ritual.

How did Lao Zi become deified?

There seem to have been a number of stages in that process. First, the legendary figure began as a teacher and writer, whose image eventually blended with that of the

301

Yellow Emperor when Lao Zi came to be identified as a confidant of royalty. Traditional accounts, such as the life story summarized above, transformed him into a cultural hero whose mother had conceived him virginally. By the mid-second century C.E., Lao Zi had become the deity who delivered to Zhang Dao Ling the revelation of a new religious faith, giving rise to the Celestial Masters school. But his image was still not complete. Next, perhaps also around the second or third century C.E., Lao Zi seems to have been identified as a creator god who also enters the world to rescue humanity from tribulation. Lao Zi was now capable of incarnating himself, almost like a Buddhist Bodhisattva. Not long thereafter he joined the triad of the Three Pure Ones, and finally Lao Zi emerged as the chief divine person. We have here one of the more interesting examples of apotheosis, or deification, in the history of religion.

What was the **earliest Daoist sacred text**?

First and most influential of the Daoist sacred texts is the Dao De Jing, which translates into English roughly as Classic of the Way and Its Power. Traditionally attributed to Lao Zi, the text actually dates from between 300 and 250 B.C.E. Authorship and immediate historical context remain uncertain. Its attribution to the "Old Master" may have arisen out of a desire to lend the text greater legitimacy and credibility. The Dao De Jing's eighty-one tantalizing short poems brim with paradox as they try to describe the indescribable by saying what it is not. Just as the value of a cup is the emptiness within, so the Way progresses by (apparently) going backward. As all of nature acts without conscious effort, so the person who strives in hope of gain loses all.

The curiously attractive teaching of the Dao De Jing emphasizes the Way of utter simplicity. Divided into two parts, poems one to thirty-seven focus on the Way, poems thirty-eight to eighty-one on its Power. Some describe the Way as the passive principle and its Power as primal spiritual energy. Anyone who tries to define the Way must know that it remains indefinable. Dao is the source of all energy but eludes discovery. Imperceptible yet irresistible, impersonal yet ever-present, the Dao's power is like that of water: the softest of all elements inevitably dissolves the hardest. Although the text may sometimes give the impression that it favors the more mysterious female *Yin* over the male *Yang,* that is perhaps a result of its need to counter prevalent social biases. In the end, life can proceed only with a perfect balance of *Yin* and *Yang,* mountain and valley, light and dark, dry and moist, evident and hidden.

Yin and *Yang* symbols on a pair of Zen balls.

What other **early sacred texts** are especially important for Daoists?

A text known as the Zhuang Zi, named after the man whose disciples may have authored it, dates from about the fourth century B.C.E. The work is also known as the *Divine Classic of Nan Hua*, the town to which Zhuang Zi was believed to have retired. Zhuang Zi the Daoist philosopher (c. 389–286 B.C.E.) remains a relatively little-known figure. But the work that bears his name stands out as a foundational document in philosophical Daoism, whose interpretation of basic concepts also influenced many religious Daoists.

In addition to its bold attacks on the inadequacy of Confucian teaching, the Zhuang Zi presents essentially the same worldview as the Dao De Jing, especially the importance of non-effort (*wu wei*) or "unmotivated action" and its political implications. Zhuang Zi emphasizes the concepts of longevity and immortality that would later take on great significance for many religious Daoists. Perhaps more important is the concept of mental purification called "fasting of the heart."

Zhuang Zi's teaching has become an important element in Daoist mysticism, speaking often of a kind of oneness with the Dao. A Daoist philosopher named Lie Zi is likewise said to have penned a work that bears his name. That book, also known as *The True Classic of the Expanding Emptiness*, however, was almost certainly of a later time, and Lie Zi is probably a legendary figure. Containing materials of many different literary types, especially narrative forms such as anecdotes and parables, the book was probably compiled around 300 C.E. Its eight chapters arrange their literarily disparate materials thematically, addressing such topics as fate and human freedom, problems in establishing ethical standards, and the challenge of following the Dao. Here for the first time we hear of the Isles of the Blest, home of the Immortals. Like the Zhuang Zi, the later work speaks at length about the complete freedom experienced in becoming one with the Dao.

Is there an **official canon** of Daoist scripture?

Around 471 Lu Xiu Jing (406–477 C.E.) compiled the earliest formal attempt at a Daoist canon. He only catalogued important works, but there would eventually be seven major edited collections of Daoist sacred texts. Between about 1000 and 1250 C.E., five enormous collections would appear. The final product was a large anthology of separate texts organized in three sections and published in its present form in 1444 C.E.

The triple division of the canonical collection, called the *Dao Zang*, may have been associated with, or perhaps a response to, the Buddhist scriptural canon known as the "Three Baskets." Each is named after one of the three heavens that were the abodes of the Three Pure Ones and begins with a major text said to have been revealed by one of the Pure Ones. *The Dao Zang (jing)*'s three parts include 1,476 disparate works in over 5,000 scroll-volumes. Every imaginable variety of text is available in the modern sixty-volume reprint of the canon. Twelve subdivisions arrange the material as follows: primal revelations, talismans, scriptural interpretation (or exegesis), sacred diagrams, historical texts, ethical texts, ritual texts, practical techniques, biographical

Daoist deity (no further identification available), bronze with gilding, sixteenth century (Ming Dynasty). (The Saint Louis Art Museum.)

information, sacred songs, and memorials. Most of the various sects and schools of Daoism focus on one or a select few of the many possibilities the canon offers. As we shall see later, recitation or chanting of sacred texts forms an important part of some ritual observances.

Are there any important **mythic elements** in Daoist **traditions**?

Daoist stories of how the world came to be are full of mythic features similar to those of other cosmogonies. They tell how order overcame chaos, how the heavens and Earth came to be separated, and how the innumerable deities—thirty-six thousand, according to one reckoning—fit into the grand picture. What is unique and most interesting about Daoist myth is that the gods do not necessarily take an active role in cosmic affairs. They do not intervene in the unfolding cosmos, nor even nudge the process along, for that matter. Instead they allow the fundamental laws of creation itself to operate unimpeded. Indeed the gods themselves come into being as part of this whole unfolding set in motion by an impersonal power called Heaven.

What good are the deities then?

They, along with the spiritually accomplished ones called sages and immortals, instruct humankind in the ways to achieve salvation. A clue to the place of many of these celestial beings in the grand scheme of things is their connection with the stars. Dozens of the members of the Daoist and popular Chinese pantheons are or have been associated with specific heavenly bodies or constellations. They are thus both visible and impossibly distant.

Has Daoism ever been identified with any political regimes?

During several periods of Chinese history, Daoism has enjoyed the considerable benefits of imperial patronage. One Daoist emperor in particular, during the mid-ninth century, launched a devastating persecution of Buddhism that did serious damage to many of that tradition's institutions. There is a certain irony in that, given the classical Daoist teaching about law and government. According to the Dao De Jing and Zhuang Zi, the best hope for society is unobtrusive leadership that does not need to rely on law and force to lead. Governmental institutions are considered meddlesome and oppressive. According to early Daoist authorities, the ideal social setting is the small village in which no one carries weapons. Very unlike classical Confucian tradition in this respect, the ideal Daoist society does away with social stratification of all kinds. Where all are equal, ruling and military classes are unnecessary. Throughout Chinese history, however, Daoists and Confucians have competed with one another for imperial support and patronage. Confucianism generally has been far more closely identified with government than has Daoism. Despite classical Daoist aversion to formal structures of government, both the official and popular pantheons have retained a good deal of the imagery of imperial bureaucracy, as in the names of such deities as the Jade Emperor.

What is **Neo-Daoism**?

Neo-Daoism is a name commonly given to various developments around the third and fourth centuries C.E. Some scholars suggest that there were two recognizable schools. One was called *Secret Mystical Teaching* (*Xuan xue*). According to some interpreters, an important theme was its emphasis on the quest for physical immortality. Earlier Daoist sources had spoken of immortality, but generally of the spiritual rather than the bodily sort. Neo-Daoism recommended exercises in breathing, diet, use of potions, elixirs, and talismans, and sexual activity reminiscent of Hindu and Buddhist Tantric practices. But perhaps more fundamental in this alchemy were intense meditative practices intended to reveal the Dao within the individual. Some scholars interpret *Xuan xue* as developing out of Confucian rather than Daoist thought. A major feature of the second school, known as Pure Conversation (*Qing tan*), is its attempts to blend aspects of Daoist, Confucian, and Buddhist thought. Among its proponents were the so-called Seven Sages of the Bamboo Grove, whose penchant for detached philosophical discourse and the cultivation of a Daoist aesthetic were among their hallmarks. On the basis of their reading of the Zhuang Zi and Dao De Jing, they developed a Neo-Daoist interpretation of the so-called Confucian classics. After the fifth century, Buddhist concepts infiltrated the movement to such a degree that Neo-Daoism gradually lost its distinctiveness and identity.

Did **Daoist tradition spread** beyond China?

Daoism has exerted some influence at various times all over east and southeast Asia. Wherever Chinese have traveled, Daoism has gone and left its mark, but it rarely has made its presence felt dramatically outside of China and territories under Chinese control. Daoist teachings, however, have had a significant impact on Chinese Buddhism over the centuries. Buddhism in turn has transported those usually well-hidden contri-

305

butions on its missionary road throughout Asia. In relatively recent times Daoism, and teachings that claim to be Daoist, have begun to enjoy increasing popularity in Europe and the Americas, but on a much smaller scale than other traditions of Asian origin.

In brief, what is the **history** of **religious Daoism**?

Religious Daoism emerged as a recognizable tradition in its own right during the latter decades of the Han dynasty (202 B.C.E.–221 C.E.). Confucianism enjoyed imperial favor as the official creed of the state. But when the Han dynasty disintegrated, both Daoism and Buddhism found room to grow. The early Celestial Masters school dominated the Daoist scene for the most part. Various schools teaching forms of alchemical Daoism developed early on and have continued throughout the past two thousand years. In addition, new revelations claimed by various teachers gave rise to several new schools between the third and sixth centuries, times of political fragmentation (see below for discussion of individual schools and denominations).

With political reunification during the Sui (581–618) dynasty, Daoism's various schools managed to survive in spite of meager imperial support. Many monasteries flourished but remained apart from the general populace. Things improved under the Tang dynasty (618–906), when Daoists once again had friends in high places. Under the Song dynasty (960–1279), Neo-Confucianism proved a powerful rival for Daoists at court. But Daoists fared well anyway, since many Neo-Confucians gladly exchanged ideas with Daoism's leading lights. During the Southern Song dynasty (1127–1279), in spite of an almost complete lack of public imperial patronage, several new Daoist schools sprang up. Things took a turn for the worse under the Yuan dynasty (1260–1368). Daoists invited to participate in court debates suffered serious setbacks and paid dearly with the loss of monasteries and precious libraries. During the late medieval Ming dynasty (1368–1644), Daoist fortunes improved again dramatically and many Daoist masters enjoyed prominent official positions. But under the last of the imperial regimes, the Ching (or Manchu) dynasty (1644–1911), the pendulum swung the other way and religious Daoism struggled to survive the early modern period.

Through the periods of the first Chinese Republic (1912–1949) and the People's Republic (1949–present), Daoism has held on largely thanks to the establishment of several organizations designed to provide a public presence for the various orders and schools. After disastrous losses as a result of the Cultural Revolution (1966–1976), Daoist religious groups are again struggling to pull themselves back together.

Daoism/CCT Timeline

Date	Event
2697–2597 B.C.E.	Huang Di, Yellow Emperor, one of the "culture heroes" in Chinese lore; was patron of ancient *fang shi* or shamans

Date	Event
2637 B.C.E.	Reckoning of Chinese lunar calendar of twelve months of twenty-nine or thirty days
604 B.C.E.	Traditional date of Lao Zi's birth
389–286 B.C.E.	Zhuang Zi, Daoist philosopher
c. 350–300 B.C.E.	Dao De Jing composed
34–156 C.E.	Zhang Dao Ling, cited as the founder of the first Daoist religious movement, the Celestial Masters school
166 C.E.	Han Chinese Emperor sacrifices to Lao Zi and Buddha
184 C.E.	Rebellion of Yellow Turbans behind a military force
202–220 C.E.	Religious Daoism emerges
220–280 C.E.	Three Kingdoms period: Wei (220–266); Shu Han (221–263); Wu (222–280)
251–334 C.E.	Wei Huacun, famous woman Libationer
c. 300 C.E.	Lie Zi composes *The True Classic of Expanding Emptiness*
c. 300 C.E.	Daoist sect Sacred Jewel introduces influential rituals
364–370 C.E.	Highest Purity (Mao Shan) sect emphasizes meditation
c. 406–477 C.E.	Li Xiujing compiles earliest Doaist canon
618–906 C.E.	Tang dynasty; Daoism enjoys favor in high places
650–750 C.E.	Life of Zhang Guolao, patron of pharmacists
666 C.E.	Lao Zi is officially declared a god in the Daoist pantheon
675 C.E.	Religious Daoism makes significant impact on imperial Chinese court
700 C.E.	He Xian'gu, patron of musicians, is noted for her asceticism and kindness
739 C.E.	Monastic Daoism flourishes during the Tang period
748 C.E.	Celestial Master recognized
c. 1000–1200 C.E.	Five enormous collections of the Daoist Canon appear
c. 1016 C.E.	Initial printing of Daoist Canon
1119–1182 C.E.	Sun Buer, female ritualist in the Perfect Realization order
1123–1170 C.E.	Life of Wang Zhe, founded the "Perfect Realization School," or Chuan Zhen
1281 C.E.	Emperor Kublai Khan burns Daoist Canon
1368–1644 C.E.	Ming dynasty; late Medieval Daoism gains strength; Roman Catholic missionaries in China
1444 C.E.	Anthology of separate Five Daoist texts published
1594 C.E.	General Guandi/Wudi is deified by imperial decree
1644–1912 C.E.	Ching (Manchu) dynasty in China; religious Daoism struggles to survive
1850–1864 C.E.	Tai Ping "Highest Peace" rebellion
1948 C.E.	Maoist Revolution; Daoism wanes
1966–1976 C.E.	Chinese Cultural Revolution; disastrous losses for Daoism
1976 C.E.	Chairman Mao Zedong dies, Daoist fortunes in China begin to improve
1980s C.E.	Daoism doing better in China, monasteries reopen

RELIGIOUS BELIEFS

Is the term "**revelation**" useful in understanding Daoism or CCT?

Most Daoist sects and schools, and CCT generally, teach that religious truths are embedded in virtually all levels and facets of reality. Access to those truths is available largely through the mediation of ritual specialists and spiritual masters. Their task is not so much to disclose the mysteries as to facilitate the passage of power from the realm of gods and spirits to that of human beings. When ordinary people find themselves in the neighborhood of these spiritual powers the truth behind them remains mysterious and cloaked in ambiguity. There are, however, accounts in which famous masters and sages claim to have received explicit revelations or missions directly from a deity. When Daoists speak of the language of revelation in these relatively rare instances, they suggest that they are pointing only to the tip of the iceberg, so to speak. The whole truth remains hidden from view and available only to a select few. This contrasts markedly with the general thrust of the Abrahamic traditions, for example, where revelation implies the disclosure of the full truth insofar as human beings can fathom it. Finally, an experience called "divination writing" deserves mention here since it is occasionally described as a revelatory medium. The Shang Qing school claims to be based on a series of nocturnal revelations. Founder Yang Xi reported that heavenly beings came to him in a vision and caused his hand to write the sacred texts.

Are **doctrine and dogma** important to Daoism or CCT?

Most of the various schools and sects of Daoism can point to at least one source or compendium of their central teachings. In that sense, there is such a thing as Daoist "doctrine." A body of doctrine does, in effect, define the boundaries of some of the schools, especially the more esoteric ones, and sets them apart from one another. But even in those instances, the doctrinal core is largely subordinate to a given school's central rituals and practices. CCT, on the other hand, does not define itself according to any clearly articulated doctrinal system. Children learn from their parents and extended family of elders a host of convictions and practices of the sort often called "folk beliefs." Where there is no formally defined doctrine, there can be no dogma in the sense of a minimum required for membership. Of those Daoist schools and sects that have developed distinctive doctrinal tenets, only the most esoteric have even approached the kind of "official" dogmatic pronouncement one finds, for example, in Roman Catholicism.

What do Daoists believe about **ultimate spiritual reality** or **God**?

Daoists call the ultimate spiritual reality "Dao," the Way. Long before the formal beginnings of Daoism's various movements and school, Chinese tradition used the term

"Dao" as a general ethical notion implying the appropriate and moral way of acting. As so often happens when a religious tradition enters a new cultural setting, Buddhism's arrival in China led some thinkers to talk of a Buddhist "Way" in contrast with which they began to define an indigenous Chinese "Way" in the sense of religious beliefs and values. Daoist philosophers emphasized the unfathomable mystery of the Dao, but they viewed it as non-personal power rather than a personal divine entity. The religious equivalent seems to have been a deity called the Supreme Oneness (*Tai Yi*).

The Dao De Jing's description of how the transcendent Dao became manifest suggests a type of emanation: Dao gave rise to the One, which produced the Two, and so on. That grand and uplifting description of the ultimate mystery still remained a bit too abstract for most people. As a result, when the first schools of religious Daoism began to formulate their beliefs they naturally gravitated toward more concrete imagery. That included the deification of the individual long believed to represent the Way as an accessible teaching—namely, Lao Zi. The process also led to personification of certain essential features of the mysterious Dao in the form of the heavenly triad called the Three Pure Ones. Developments of this sort multiplied, and the deities took on life stories and personalities that invited devotional interaction. In practice, the many personifications of divinity are arrayed according to an administrative structure parallel to that of the imperial bureaucracy. Religiously speaking, of course, the reality is just the other way around: the imperial institutions imitated the heavenly order of things.

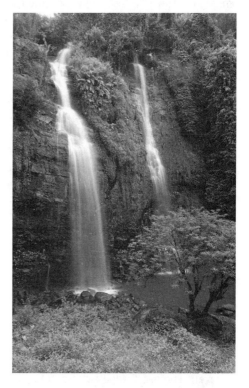

The Taad-Dao Waterfall in Sri Satchanalai National Park, Sukhothai, Thailand. In the Daoist tradition, problems arise in life when humans attempt to control nature rather than living in harmony with it.

What is the essential Daoist **approach to Nature**?

According to Daoist tradition, all things naturally exist in a primordial harmony. When things go wrong, whether in nature or in human society, the cause is invariably an imbalance in the equilibrium of *Yin* and *Yang* that results in a blockage of the flow of natural energies, *qi* or *chi*. Part of the problem is the human tendency to seek control. When that desire leads to ill-conceived attempts to dominate nature, the outcome can only be disastrous. Nature yields its abundance easily and graciously to all among the "ten thousand things" (creatures) that are willing to receive without grabbing or hoarding. When human beings develop a warped notion of their place in the larger scheme of things, attempting to force their will, all of nature may suffer temporary setbacks. But in the end, nature's balance will return. Traditional Chinese landscape paintings say it much better than words can. Massive mountains loom in the upper part of a hanging scroll, their craggy peaks bathed in sunlight. From the heights a waterfall cascades into the valley below, forming a lake as the stream emerges into the plain. Tucked away in a mountain scene, a tiny human figure sits meditatively in a picturesque pavilion. Further below, an unobtrusive figure shoulders a load across a small bridge. A solitary fisherman drops a line from his slender craft. Between valley and peaks, or perhaps where the peak imperceptibly becomes valley, hangs a misty cloud of that cosmic force known as *qi*. Landscape paintings, called "mountain-water pictures," thus suggest the perfect balance between *Yang* and *Yin*.

Who are some of the **chief Daoist deities**?

Bearing in mind that it is not always possible to draw neat distinctions between Daoist divinities and those of CCT, here are some of the figures that appear to have at least originated in Daoist circles. They are called the Earlier Heaven Deities. At the top of the pantheon are the Three Pure Ones (*San Qing*). They seem to have been Daoism's theological rejoinder to the Buddhist groupings in which Bodhisattvas flank Amitabha Buddha to form a celestial triad. The Three Pure Ones (or Sacred Beings) are named after the heavens in which they dwell: the heavens of the Jade, Higher, and Great Purity, respectively.

This triad evidently developed out of a trio of deified human beings of history or legend. Lao Zi, known as Tian Shang Lao Jun (Lord of the Daoist Teaching), was the first so elevated. Later a deity called "Heavenly Venerable of the Original Beginning" (Yuan Shi Tian Zun) was named as chief deity. And still later a third deity, Grand Lord of the Dao (Tai Shang Dao Jun), leap-frogged the two others to the top of the triad. These three, often depicted as enthroned elders, came to be identified with the more transcendent and abstract Pure Ones. Many consider the deified Lao Zi still a separate deity who ranks above the Three Pure Ones. The Jade Emperor, Yu Huang Da Di, was eventually identified either as the chief deity's younger brother or as an incarnation of the Lord of the heaven of Great Purity, and became the prominent deity in some CCT cults. According to one theological model, the Three Pure Ones are manifestations of the primordial cosmic energy, *qi*.

Are there any other important **Daoist sacred figures**?

One important subordinate deity is Xuan Tian Shang Di, Supreme Emperor of Dark Heaven. The Jade Emperor dispatched him to Earth to battle a band of renegade demon-kings. His iconography shows him enthroned and using a serpent and a turtle—leaders of the demons—as a footstool. A legendary woman named Xi Wang Mu, also known as the Queen Mother of the West, figures prominently in some Daoist writings. She is a

An altar dedicated to Guan Di, whose red-faced image it enshrines. Note the scaly dragon painted behind the icon. Bao An Gong temple, Taipei.

patroness of immortality, often depicted in the company of Jade Maidens, one carrying a fan and the other a bushel of the peaches of longevity. Ruling the East is her divine consort, Dung Wang Gong, who lives in the remote magical fastness of the Kun Lun mountains. In a reversal of the more usual dynamic, a "God of walls and moats," also known as the City God, began as a popular deity and made his way into the Daoist pantheon. During certain periods in history, the Heavenly Master appointed a given city's tutelary deity. City God has the assistance of several other figures, called "spirit secretaries," in the idiom of public administration. They help the City God deliver his reports on the conduct of citizens to the authorities in Hell. A goddess named Dou Mu (Mother of the Bushel of Stars, or Northern Dipper) functions in Daoism much the way Guan Yin does in Buddhism, offering limitless compassion for the suffering. Some other potent beings are clustered in groups. The *Sen Nin* are a group of sacred figures who dwell in Heaven or in the distant misty mountains. Among the *Sen Nin* the most important are the Eight Immortals. Originally persons either historical (three) or legendary (five), they function as guardian figures of Daoism. Although they are not officially divine, popular lore sometimes attributes divine powers to them. They are called Later Heaven Deities, as are all human figures who eventually achieved immortality.

Who are some of the **principal gods** of CCT?

Many of the popular deities play multiple roles and sometimes resemble each other enough that one has to look carefully to identify them correctly. One of the most pop-

311

ular and frequently depicted deities is Guan Di (d. 220 C.E.), often inaccurately characterized as the "war god" under the name Wu Di. He was a third-century military leader named Guan Yu who gained a kind of martyr status after he was executed. By imperial decree in 1594, the deceased general was deified and the word for deity or emperor (*di*) added to his name. By a peculiar twist, he also acquired the status of secondary God of Literature. Kui Xing is the other secondary god of literature, distinguishable by his dragon-fish, writing brush and official seal, small stature, unpleasant countenance, and awkward one-legged stance. Many pray to him as they prepare for examinations. In popular belief, Kui elbowed out the principal deity of literature, Wen Chang Di Jun, who had actually begun his mythic life as a star deity who was then born as Chang Ya, a famous literary figure. Wen is generally depicted wearing a flowing robe and a large hat and either enthroned or astride a mule. Kui Xing usually stands on his left while on his right stands a red-coated figure. A widely popular goddess in CCT is sometimes called "Holy Heavenly Mother" (Ma Zu). She actually lived during the tenth century and was formally deified by several emperors during the twelfth and thirteenth centuries. Originally the patroness of sailors and rescuer from storms, she soon became famous for a wider range of powers. Taiwan alone has several hundred Ma Zu temples, where she sits enthroned wearing a royal diadem.

What about **lesser or subordinate** popular **deities**?

Associated with Ma Zu is the Great Emperor Protecting Life (Bao Sheng Da Di). A physician during medieval (Song Dynasty) times, he remains a popular healing power. Legend says that he suffered from unrequited love for Ma Zu. Shou Lao, god of longevity, appears often in Chinese art and in temple decorations. He holds a peach and a staff, walks with a crane or a deer or both, and has an exceptionally high forehead and a long white beard. Another god of longevity, Shou Xing, has the responsibility of appointing each person's time of death. Like Shou Lao, he holds a peach, but Shou Xing's companions are the stag and bat. He is sometimes depicted as one of a trinity of star gods of happiness. Dozens of other lesser gods fill out the popular pantheon. Dung Fang Shuo is the divine patron of metalsmiths, connected with the planet Venus and depicted standing on gold and silver ingots. Bian Ho is the patron deity of jewelers. Si Ming, a deity of Daoist origin, became the Kitchen God, or Director of Destinies, who oversees the fates of family members and submits reports annually to the Jade Emperor on how each person is progressing. Depicted as an elderly Mandarin, this household deity rules from his place above the family hearth.

Do Daoists and practitioners of CCT believe in **miracles**?

Devout Chinese, whether associated with Daoism or with some form of CCT, consider asking for favors an ordinary part of being religious. In general, however, what many readers mean by the term "miraculous" would not quite describe even apparently spectacular results of supplicatory prayer and ritual in this context. A fundamental

A ritual specialist assists a worshipper in her prayer offering at an elaborately decorated altar in a CCT temple, Taipei, Taiwan.

consequence of the *Yin/Yang* view of life is the conviction that there is an identifiable cause of everything, whether positive or negative. All evil, illness, and suffering is a result of disharmony and imbalance. It is true that ordinary people cannot always put their finger on the direct cause, but ritual specialists know about these things. More importantly, the gods and those spiritual beings who have found the secret of immortality can assist suffering humankind by bringing about needed balance and harmony of forces. A "miracle" in this context, therefore, might be a divine intervention not for the purpose of doing the impossible, but for helping the possible to happen more quickly and easily.

What do Daoists believe about the **goal of human life**?

Although the principal early sacred texts do not discuss prospects of life after death explicitly, the question of immortality turned into an important issue for Daoists. Archaeological evidence from well over three thousand years ago suggests that many people believed in some sort of survival after death, but that apparently meant a kind of extended earthly existence. Religious Daoism does not always make the distinction some traditions make between life here and life hereafter. Some Daoists have held views not unlike those of many Christians, believing that at death, "Life is changed, not taken away." But many have argued that if indeed life is a seamless reality, it may be possible to go on indefinitely without crossing that great divide called death. Whatever specific imagery Daoists have used to describe the nature of human life, the underlying point is

313

that the tradition has been keenly interested in promoting a sense of vitality and in helping adherents to develop a positive attitude toward the human condition generally.

Is **salvation** an important concept for Daoists?

Some elements in Daoist tradition discuss at length a type of salvation from mortality itself. That is quite different from the kind of salvation Muslims and Christians look forward to, which is something closer to salvation in spite of mortality. For Daoists, the most spiritually accomplished individuals are capable of so purifying themselves that they can actually live on eternally in the Paradise of Immortals. They might appear to die and be buried, but only because they allowed that to happen as a concession to widespread belief and socially acceptable convention. In fact, they are able to substitute something else for their body and to slip away to Paradise unnoticed.

What about ordinary people incapable of such lofty feats? They can still hope to receive an immortal body after resurrection, a belief with some similarity to classic Christian notions of bodily resurrection. Another important distinction between Daoist notions of salvation and, for example, Christian beliefs, is that there is no single savior figure in Daoist thought.

Do Daoists and practitioners of CCT believe in **Heaven and Hell**?

Since long before the beginnings of religious Daoism, the notion of "Heaven" (*tian*) as an impersonal transcendent reality has been very important to the Chinese. Some Daoists have identified "Heaven" as the first materialization, or a kind of emanation, of the Dao's spiritual power. In this sense, Heaven becomes an intermediary between the unmanifest Dao and all of creation, for Heaven is the source of all good things. Along with Earth and Humanity, Heaven is one of the "three powers" that bring about life as we know it. However, Daoists do not generally talk of Heaven as the eternal abode of those who lived virtuously on earth. One region beyond ordinary earthly experience is the Isles of the Blest (*Peng Lai Shan*), in the far reaches of the Eastern Sea, where the Eight Immortals dwell amid an idyllic landscape. Many Chinese express the hope of finally reaching the Isles and attaining immortality there.

Belief in retribution after death for a less-than-praiseworthy life has given rise to a wealth of imagery. But Daoism and CCT call Hell a multistoried "earthly prison." There are ten levels of Hell—some prefer to talk of ten separate hells—each with its ruling deity. They function rather like the circles of Hell in Dante's *Inferno*, each designated for those who commit specific sins and crimes. Presiding over the first level is a sort of chief judge who wields authority over the other nine judge-kings. Some souls never make it to their assigned Hell, a difficult passageway to the hope of better things beyond that. They spend eternity wandering aimlessly and forever hungry, dependent on the kindness of the living to attend to their needs. Some sources talk of

Hell much as many Christians describe Purgatory as temporary suffering with long-range benefits.

What does **alchemy** have to do with Daoism?

A complex system of practices known as inner alchemy (*nei dan*) and outer alchemy (*wai dan*) alchemy developed for the purpose of allowing practitioners to achieve earthly longevity and perhaps complete immortality. While the outer form works with chemicals and other substances, the inner form focuses on cultivation of the divine within each person by a variety of techniques. The goal

Daoist alchemy consists of countless intricate formulas and recipes involving jade and gold, like in this ornamental barrette, as well as cinnabar.

is to transform all three of the individual vital forces into the pure spirit called *shen*. Daoist alchemy consists of countless intricate formulas and recipes involving cinnabar, jade, and gold. Initiates must virtually soak enough of these elements into their systems to render the body indestructible. A method called Gold Cinnabar Daoism spells out the details of a technique shared by various schools of alchemy. A regimen of physical exercises called *qi gong,* now even more popular than *tai ji chuan,* is historically related to classical Daoist inner alchemy. Requirements such as the consumption of specific numbers of potions and pills on devilishly difficult schedules make the goal all but impossible to reach.

But if the pharmaceutical demands were not enough, there is an even more elusive ethical component. For example, a person who desires immortality must perform an uninterrupted chain of charitable acts (1,200 according to one ancient source). One stumble invalidates the process and requires a fresh start. Descriptions of Daoist alchemy too often leave out this ethical component, a feature that says more about the underlying spirit of the quest than any mere list of chemicals can begin to suggest. Although it is easy enough to see how an alchemical search for immortality could easily deteriorate into a crassly magical pursuit, the classical sources still have the power to remind one that beneath it all is serious insight into the human condition.

Has Daoism ever been associated with **millennialism or messianic movements**?

Several major movements of a millenarian and messianic cast have been associated with Daoism. One occurred during the late second century C.E. under the leadership of the three Zhang brothers who claimed authority in the domains of Heaven, Earth and Humanity. They espoused a type of Daoism called Huang Lao (possibly a combination of the first parts of the names of Huang Di, the Yellow Emperor, and Lao Zi) and claimed divine origins for their eschatologically charged sacred text, the Highest Peace Scripture. The brothers Zhang established a theocracy, complete with elaborate hierarchies. Toward the end of the second century the movement swelled into full-scale rebellion led by a military force called the Yellow Turbans. The rebellion fizzled even though its leaders considered 184 C.E. an ideal time, beginning as it did a fresh sixty-year cycle.

Shortly after that ill-fated rebellion in the east, another Zhang from an unrelated family organized a theocratic state that lasted from 186–216 C.E. This Zhang Lu claimed the authority of his grandfather Zhang Dao Ling (34–156 C.E.), traditionally cited as the founder of the first Daoist religious movement, the Celestial Masters school. Both theocracies hoped to reestablish the utopian regimes they believed had existed in the past. After the fourth century, new and more powerful movements emerged, with various leaders claiming to be incarnations of a divinized Lao Zi (called Li Hung). All taught the expectation of a messiah and a final battle which only the elect would survive to live on in their religious utopia. None had long-term repercussions. Loosely related by symbolism to the Yellow Turban rebellion of 184 was the Taiping (Highest Peace) rebellion of 1850–1864. It was a syncretistic movement that borrowed heavily from Christian millennialist imagery.

Do Daoists and practitioners of CCT believe in **angels**?

Spirits of all kinds inhabit the ordinary world of countless adherents of Daoism and CCT. But none quite fit the precise description most readers would identify as angelic. Angels are generally understood as pure immortal spirits made that way from the start. Chinese Daoist and popular beliefs include countless immortal beings, but, apart from the highest gods, most of those began as human beings and achieved immortality later. In addition, angels in other traditions typically function as messengers or guardians. A variety of spirits play those roles in Daoist and CCT lore. Perhaps the closest thing to angels in the Chinese repertoire of religious symbolism are the *apsaras,* imported into China with Buddhism.

Do Daoists and practitioners of CCT believe in **demons or devils**?

Demonic forces abound in the spiritual universe of millions of Chinese. Many demons are the unsettled spirits of the dead who roam the world in search of an elusive contentment. Some demons can herald good tidings, but most are disgruntled and thirsty for vengeance. Evil spirits, or *gui,* belong to a large category distinguished from an equally large category of generally benevolent beings called *shen,* a category that includes both deities and ancestral spirits. One of the essential features of Chinese thought on these matters is the notion that there are several different kinds of soul or spirit. The heavenly "*Yang* soul" (called *hun*) rises at death to become a *shen* and abides from then on in Heaven and in the ancestral tablets that have a prominent place on every home altar. The earthly *"Yin* soul" (called *po*) returns to the grave with the body. Under certain circumstances, the *po* takes a negative turn and becomes an evil spirit, a *gui,* destined to create havoc for the living. Some of these evil spirits can be particularly dangerous, but unlike the "devils" of some other traditions, the *gui* are not particularly noted for their role in tempting humans to sin.

Are **dreams and visions** significant in Daoism or CCT?

An ability to interpret the dreams of ordinary people has long been part of the ritual menu of Chinese religious specialists, beginning with the shamans of old. In ancient times, specialists called *zhan ren* interpreted dreams using divination and astrology as their tools. Powerful and famous people, too, report having revelatory dreams that move them toward a new course of action. Dream accounts therefore frequently function as an instrument of divine or spiritual legitimation. There is often a very fine line between dream and vision, except that one can experience a vision while awake. Religiously important visions or dreams frequently feature major deities, such as Lao Zi or the Jade Emperor, who deliver instructions or revelations to the dreamer or visionary. In addition, visualization techniques figure prominently in the meditative practice of some Daoist schools. The Shang Qing school, for example, recommends that the meditator focus imaginatively on his or her indwelling deities, a technique similar to that used by several Tibetan Buddhist schools. By conjuring up intricate detail as described in the school's sacred texts, the meditator makes the presence of the god real and can thus unite with the divine presence.

Is there a **distinctively Daoist ethic**?

Daoism's version of the Golden Rule is this: If a person treats me well, I do so in return. If that person treats me unjustly, I nevertheless respond with goodness, like the ever-constant Dao. The central ethical principle is the enigmatic concept of *wu wei.* The term translates literally as "non-action" or "non-effort," but it means something like "acting naturally or "creative inactivity." *Wu wei* is the ultimate in "natural law." All things behave according to their inherent makeup. Human beings alone have a tendency to get it wrong by trying to take control where we have no business doing so—and where there is ultimately no good reason for doing so. Only by observing the Way of nature can people hope to grasp this elusive principle of uncontrived accomplishment.

Wu wei is not to be confused with laziness or indifference. Observe how nature brings about whatever is needed without stratagem or artifice. Nature does act, of course, and there is no lack of struggle in its doings, but it always returns to equilibrium. The key, then, is to act spontaneously, but that is not a recommendation to act impulsively. Behind the Daoist principle is the conviction that human beings will act for the greater good so long as they are not merely reacting to unreasonable social or

What does Daoist tradition teach about religiously sanctioned use of violence?

Daoism's classic text Dao De Jing, along with many other important religious sources, emphasizes the centrality of harmony in all aspects of life. That harmony presupposes the perfect blend of *Yin* (the female principle) and *Yang* (the male principle). Disharmony results, at the most fundamental level, from an imbalance of the primal forces. A certain level of violence in nature is virtually presupposed, but human beings who seek to imitate the Dao's principle of "creative inaction" (*wu wei*) can at least hope for a peaceful society. However, as often happens when religious organizations become entwined with political institutions, Daoism has become associated on occasion with large-scale violence. Especially during historical periods in which Daoism has been favored as the more or less "official" religious ideology of a political regime, Daoism has been implicated in large-scale systematic violence. For example, during the mid-ninth century, Daoists enjoyed imperial support of the Tang dynasty at the expense of Buddhism, which suffered widespread persecution in the year 845.

In practical terms, Daoists acknowledge that there may be times when self-defense is necessary. One must then struggle to engage in violence only in the effort to restore harmony and must seek always to defend oneself without rancor or bitterness. On balance, Daoist tradition seems to emphasize the responsibility of each practitioner to avoid the inward violence that can corrupt one's outward action. If one must engage in outward violence, one must regard even victory not as a cause for jubilation, but act as one would when attending a funeral.

governmental restraints. Genuine moral leadership requires authentic altruism, the desire to lead by serving—the diametric opposite of demagoguery. Concern for effective government in a time of social and institutional disintegration seems to have given rise to the notion of *wu wei*. But Daoism's sages embodied the principle in a way that recommended it as a fundamental religious and philosophical value.

Glossary of Daoist Terms

Bagua—the eight trigrams symbolizing various primal elements composed of varying combinations of *Yang* (unbroken line) and *Yin* (line broken in the middle).

Dao—the "Way," unnameable source of all things, immutable eternal principle both transcendent and immanent.

Dao De Jing—Treatise of the Way and its Power, principal Daoist sacred text.

feng shui—"wind-water," a form of geomantic divination designed to harmonize all conditions of life to the underlying forces of nature.

Lao Zi—Old Master, name of the man traditionally associated with the origins of Daoism.

Qi—(pronounced chee), vital energy that flows freest where *Yin* and *Yang* are in appropriate balance.

Shen—celestial spirits associated with *Yang* forces, including various deities and ancestors.

Tai Ji—the "great ultimate," symbolized by the circle divided by an S-shaped curve, with dark *Yin* interlocking with light *Yang*.

Tian—sky or Heaven, an impersonal divine presence through which mortals connect with eternal forces.

Wu wei—principle of non-active accomplishment by which the Dao operates in all things.

Xian—Daoist immortals, historical figures who achieved immortality and dwell in the Isles of the Blest.

Yang—natural principle identified as male, active, dry, warm, bright, associated with mountain peaks.

Yin—natural principle identified as female, passive, moist, cool, dark, associated with valleys and streams.

SIGNS AND SYMBOLS

What **signs or symbols** might **identify someone** as a Daoist or practitioner of CCT?

Symbols associated with religious beliefs and folk practices abound in societies heavily influenced by Chinese culture. Over the centuries, the major Chinese religious traditions—Daoist, Confucian, Buddhist, and popular—have shared many of those symbols and signs. Overlapping of symbols of various traditions makes it difficult, if not impossible, to know at a glance to which tradition the owner and user of the symbols belongs.

Signs and symbols generally associated with CCT include a vast range of protective and magical devices, amulets and talismans. Perhaps the most widely used symbol is that of the perfect harmony of *Yin* and *Yang*. Appearing on all sorts of personal items such as rings and pendants, the so-called *tai ji* (Supreme Ultimate) is a circle in which two equal but opposite curving tear-shapes embrace. In other words, an S-curve line divides the circle in two equal parts. The darker half symbolizes *Yin*, the brighter half *Yang*, but the commingling of the two is symbolized by a dark dot in the larger end of the *Yang* shape and a corresponding bright dot in the *Yin* shape. Sometimes, as on the national flag of South Korea, that symbol is surrounded by the eight Trigrams (*ba gua*). The Trigrams are made up of combinations of solid *Yang* lines and broken *Yin* lines.

Charm-like devices are extremely popular in Chinese societies. Textiles and other decorative items, like ceramic wares, invariably display a range of symbolic features. Symbols can include any of dozens of animal, plant, or inanimate objects associated with aspects of the greatest mysteries of life, of those things that human beings most hope for or fear. For example, the tortoise and crane mean long life, the dragon means protection, the phoenix warmth. The heron and countless other birds of good omen betoken happiness, while creatures of ill omen, such as the owl, portend death and bad fortune.

What signs or symbols distinguish Daoist **ritual specialists**?

Daoist "priests" or "masters" make extensive use of symbolic vestments in ritual settings. Apparently in imitation of the garments emperors once wore for religious rituals, Daoist specialists today wear three types of vestments in various colors, depending on sectarian affiliation. For the most sacred occasions a high priest wears a square red silk poncho-like vestment called the "garment of descent" that symbolizes Earth. For regular major rituals the celebrants might wear a red or yellow silk over-garment called the "Dao Gown" with the character for "*tai ji*" or the Eight Trigrams on the front and back. Other common decorative motifs include images of the Eight Immortals, often depicted on the hems of broad, flowing sleeves. Abstract cloud designs often stand for *Yin* while cranes and male versions of the mythical creature called the *qi lin* (sometimes associated with the unicorn, but very different from the European unicorn) represent *Yang*. For penitential rites the assistants might wear the "sea-blue" vestment whose darker color accords with a darker ritual purpose. Under these garments specialists wear a square silk apron. Officiants also wear distinctive headgear, including a black skullcap under a metal five-pointed crown (recalling the five elements) bestowed in the ordination ceremony. Ritual shoes like those once worn in the imperial court bear cloud symbolism that suggests the ability to walk the very heavens as the priest delivers the prayers of the people to the deities.

What would a visitor see in a **Daoist or CCT temple**?

Larger traditional Chinese temples, of whatever affiliation, are generally laid out according to the ground plan of ancient imperial residences. Like the palace, the temple enclosure and its main interior structures generally face south. Approaching the temple, the visitor first sees a monumental gateway that offers entry through the temple's surrounding outer wall. Gracefully curved roofs decorated with numerous small multicolored glass or ceramic figures crown the gate as well as the main interior buildings. In some of the more elaborate temples, the main gateway opens into a covered forecourt, or a vestibule in which the worshipper can begin to experience the change of mind and calming of the spirit necessary for efficacious devotion. Around the perimeter of the main courtyard one might find small separate halls that function like chapels for devotion to subordinate sacred figures, as well as features like bell towers. But the focal point of the temple, whether Daoist or CCT, is typically a freestanding structure in the middle or toward the rear of the main courtyard. A large cauldron or kettle filled with sand—into which devotees insert their offerings of incense sticks—stands ten or fifteen feet away from the main entry to the shrine.

Central courtyard of a popular Chinese temple in Taipei. Worshippers place their incense stick offerings in the main kettle and then approach the outer doors of the central building. On the roofline are decorative symbols and a tiny pagoda at the center of the ridge beam.

At either end of the main building's roofline (and often on the rooflines of other structures in the temple as well) the visitor probably will encounter sculptures of a curious hybrid aquatic creature, dragon-headed and fish-tailed, called the *ji wen*. Popular lore says the exuberant creature protects the building from destruction by fire. Pillars or columns decorated with deeply carved stone dragons spiraling from bottom to top often flank the entry to the main shrine. Smaller pillars, similarly decorated, sometimes protrude from the two ends of the roof peaks; they represent columns that support the firmament. Chinese temples typically created a covered space in a portico surrounding the main courtyard and an open space in the courtyard itself. The main shrine may be a fairly large structure, but ordinary worshippers usually make their offerings standing in front of the building, while temple staff perform associated ritual actions closer to the altars within the shrine. Smaller neighborhood or family temples naturally lack the grand architectural layout: many are tucked away unobtrusively over small business storefronts; others are separate single-room structures with folding doors that open the entire width across the front.

Are Daoist and CCT **sacred spaces** marked with any **distinctive signs and symbols**?

It is not always possible to determine from a Chinese sacred space's exterior design and decor to which of the religious traditions it belongs. Mosques (including those in

321

Chinese settings) have their distinctive minarets, churches have their spires and crosses, and Hindu temples have their monumental facades and towers marking inner shrines. Some Chinese Buddhist temples announce their identity with pagodas or *stupas*, but that is not always the case. Chinese temple rooflines often display colorful small figures that appear to be engaged in vigorous action, but even these are not a reliable indicator of the holy place's specific religious affiliation. The animated figures on the rooflines are sometimes scenes taken from Chinese opera or classical novels, chosen here because they allude to certain important moral virtues.

Inside the temple more specific clues are available, but even there one has to look carefully to distinguish the sacred symbols of Daoism from those of CCT. For example, a statue of the Bodhisattva Guan Yin (originally Buddhist) may appear on a small altar under the covered area toward the front of the inner courtyard, but that does not mean that this is a Buddhist temple. It does, however, indicate that this is not a Daoist temple and probably belongs to CCT, which has "borrowed" Guan Yin from Buddhism and made her an important deity.

A Daoist temple's most distinctive symbol is its main altar. Although the overall setting varies from one sect to another, there are several important common features. Before the central deity on the altar stands a perpetually lit lamp symbolizing wisdom and the light of the Dao. Two candles symbolizing sun and moon flank the lamp a few inches further toward the front of the altar. Cups of water (*Yang*), tea (*Yin*), and uncooked rice (*Yang* and *Yin* united) stand before the candles. Further toward the front of the altar stand five plates of fruit, each of a different color, symbolizing the five elements in perfect proportion. Centered near the front stands an incense burner, a reminder of the heat that purifies the three vital energies, which are symbolized by three sticks of incense. Some temporary sacred spaces are constructed of bamboo for specific seasonal Daoist rituals.

Are **statues** and other **visual imagery** important in Daoist and CCT **temples**?

With the notable exception of major Confucian and Imperial temples, Chinese ritual spaces are almost always filled with images of deities and other sacred figures. Principal deities occupy main altar spaces, but they often share the central spot with smaller images of other sacred figures arranged below the main image and toward the front of the altar. For many centuries Daoists and practitioners of CCT evidently felt no need for anthropomorphic depictions of their deities. The advent of Buddhism, with its growing iconographic repertoire, seems to have been an important factor in the development of Chinese religious representational imagery. Images of Daoist deities, and of those that originated outside Daoist circles but are often identified as Daoist by association, run a wide gamut. Some of the deities are of divine origin. Others began as human beings, either historical or legendary, and achieved divine status either in life or after death. In addition to statues, colorful banners, low relief carvings in stone and other media, and mural paintings depict mythological and other scenes meant to keep the worshipper in the proper frame of mind. Even temples that began as Buddhist institutions and which still display distinctively Buddhist imagery in their main shrines and altars have often become transformed into CCT temples by accretion over the centuries. Whatever the individual deity's life story, anthropomorphic images abound.

What are **trigrams** and **hexagrams**?

Trigrams are sets of three vertically stacked horizontal lines made up of every possible combination of broken (— —) and solid (———) line. Solid lines stand for the solar male *Yang*, high, bright, active, and dry. Broken lines stand for the earthy and lunar female *Yin*, which is dark, moist, mysterious, and associated with valleys. Combinations of *Yin* and *Yang* in varying proportions give rise to the eight essential elements in creation. Traditional presentations usually arrange the eight trigrams as an octagon at whose center stands the *tai ji* symbol for perfect *Yin–Yang* harmony. Each trigram is arrayed so as to face its opposite in the set. So for example, if you held a compass before you with north pointing up, Heaven's three solid lines would stand across from Earth's three broken lines at what would be north and south. At due east stands Water, with a solid line between a pair of broken lines, across from Fire, with its broken line sandwiched between solids in the west. At northwest, Lake's broken-solid-solid (reading from top to bottom) stands across from Mountain's solid-broken-broken. And in the northeast, Wind's solid-solid-broken balances off Thunder's broken-broken-solid.

Take the eight trigrams and arrange them in all possible permutations by stacking one trigram atop another and you get sixty-four hexagrams. Pile Heaven upon Heaven and the result is called the "creative principle." Add Earth to Earth and you get the "passive principle." Earth over Heaven yields "peace," while Heaven over Earth means "stagnation." The single most important source for interpreting these arcane indicators is the *Yi Jing*, The Classic of Change. Tossing and rearranging a set of fifty sticks and then reading them as hexagrams with the help of that text remains a widely popular form of divination.

What are some **clues** to understanding Daoist and CCT **iconography**?

By far the majority of Daoist and CCT images of sacred figures are portrayed with identifiably human bodies. They rarely have multiple heads or limbs, but they do have various features. Deities are more often than not somber, sometimes of downright forbidding countenance,

Images of Guan Yin and a barrel of joss sticks used for divination rituals in a CCT temple in Keelung, Taiwan.

and typically depicted in such a way that the viewer is not likely to think of them as ordinary human beings. Bright red or yellow skin, flaring nostrils, riveted gaze, and the occasional menacing gesture discourage a too casual approach. Exceptions are some of the CCT deities who appear as gently smiling "family members," kindly aunts or grandparents, for example. But even they often have unusual skin tones, suggesting that these are not mere mortals. Some deities are recognizable, at least by association, because of the groupings in which they appear. Most important in this respect is the triad formation, generally depicting a main central figure flanked by two slightly smaller figures. Depending on the temple, these may depict any of several of the triadic variations mentioned above. Many temples install subordinate deities and semidivine powers on side altars or in small rooms of their own along the inner perimeter of the main courtyard.

Each deity has his or her distinguishing characteristics, but one generally finds fewer clear iconographic clues here than in Hindu or Buddhist art. For example, several deities may sport the same skin tones and facial expression and even carry very similar symbols. It is therefore sometimes impossible to discern individual identities of the characters without knowing in advance to whom a given temple is dedicated.

Apart from the trigrams and *tai ji,* what are some other common traditional symbols?

Ancient lore associates fundamental features of Chinese cosmology with specific symbols. It all goes back to the "Chinese Adam," Pan Gu. In his task of imposing order on primal chaos, Pan Gu enlisted the help of five cosmic assistants: Azure Dragon, White Tiger, Phoenix, Tortoise, and Unicorn. Pan Gu assigned to each of the first four a quarter of the universe. Azure Dragon governed the East, associated with spring, new life, benevolence, and protection. White Tiger ruled the autumnal West, symbol of maturity and a life well spent, all made possible by good government and courage. Phoenix, the ultimate solar bird, presided over the summery South with the kindly warmth and joy that arises in a world at peace. Hard-shelled and indomitable, the ageless Tortoise faced the unforgiving, wintry North. Wandering freely among them all, the rare and delicate Unicorn was commissioned to appear wherever and whenever benevolence and justice reigned on Earth. It is not surprising that all five of these wondrous beings retain their appeal to the popular imagination and remain essentials of the religious symbolic repertoire.

A cluster of items associated loosely with Daoism are called the "Eight Daoist Emblems." Each represents one of the Eight Immortals, a group of human beings who became immortal in various ways. They appear often as decorative motifs on all kinds of objects. The emblems are a fan, a sword, a gourd, castanets, a flower basket, a bamboo drum, a flute, and a lotus flower. This is one of several sets of eight motifs popular in Chinese art and, along with the Eight Buddhist Emblems, one that still carries specifically religious resonances.

What does **feng shui** have to do with Daoism?

Feng shui, a term meaning "wind and water," is a type of terrestrial divination designed to help practitioners make practical decisions about living arrangements that will be in harmony with natural energies and forces. This symbolic system coordinates critical elements of time and space to allow for maximum harmony in every conceivable human interaction with nature. All natural features, including trees, rivers, mountains, and valleys, for example, have their distinctive influences on the flow of energy. Failure to take of these forces into account can make life much more difficult than it need be.

In practical terms, *feng shui* assists people most of all in choosing the orientation and design of the "built environment"—in other words, architecture and urban planning. A geomantic compass allows people to arrange the spaces in which they live and work in accordance with the principle of the "Nine Palaces." The compass indicates where *Yin* and *Yang* energies flow. A grid of nine squares, each of which contains three numbers from one to nine, can be used in connection with building plans to indicate optimum placement of particular kinds of spaces within a home or office (e.g. storage, study, eating, or sleeping spaces). This ancient environmentalist system has grown from careful observation of the consequences of human interaction with the greater cosmos. Chinese tradition emphasizes the need to conform to the "way" of nature rather than attempting to dominate it. Daoism's sensitivities to the natural world in general and its quest for harmony through seeking nature's inherent balances make *feng shui* a critical ingredient in popular Daoism.

Are **number, color, or nature symbolism** important in Daoist tradition and CCT?

Astrological calculation and cosmological imagery have long been an integral part of Chinese religious views. Hundreds of symbolic elements make up this vast system of correspondences. Zodiacal animals are associated with the twelve months. Each of the four quadrants of the universe has its seven constellations in addition to its connection with specific trigrams, all related to particular aspects of good fortune or difficulty. Each of these elements is further coordinated with one of the five symbolic colors (black, white, red, green, yellow), elements (wood, water, earth, metal, fire), and organs of the human body.

Here are some examples of popular animal symbolism. The crow, surprisingly perhaps, symbolizes the sun. The crane, guide of the Immortals, means long life, as do the dove and the hare. Fish are reminders of renewal of life and abundance. By association with plowing new fields, the ox means spring and vitality. The sharp-eyed, quick-tongued parrot looks after faithfulness in marriage. Flowers, trees, and fruits almost always have some symbolic resonance. The springtime peony means tenderness and womanly beauty, as does the jasmine. The plum means winter and is a reminder of

Lao Zi, who was born beneath a plum tree. Bamboo betokens endurance, the orange benevolence. A complete listing would fill several books. Of course, not everyone thinks consciously of specific symbolic meanings upon seeing any of the hundreds of visual decorative motifs in the full catalogue. But most Chinese still grow up surrounded by countless symbolic associations of this kind.

MEMBERSHIP, COMMUNITY, DIVERSITY

Where do **Daoists live** today? Are any estimates of **numbers** available? How about CCT?

Until fairly recently, Daoism has been an almost exclusively Chinese phenomenon. Since the Maoist revolution of 1949, practice of Daoism in the People's Republic of China has diminished dramatically. Buddhism had the advantage of being an international tradition and thus of at least limited political utility. In addition, Buddhism qualified officially as a "religion" while Daoism was defined as mere superstition. Daoist temples and monasteries were shut down or destroyed and thousands of Daoist ritual specialists had to seek other means of livelihood.

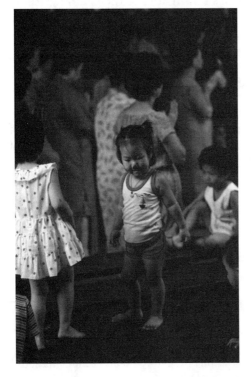

Things have taken a turn for the better since the 1980s. Monasteries have reopened, and as of 1995 counts, Daoist temples number over 600, with about ten times that number of nuns and priests. Some institutions have even managed to revive formal seminary training for ritual specialists. The Celestial Masters school and the monastic order of Chuan Zhen (Complete Realization school) are the liveliest Daoist organizations in the People's Republic now. Many hundreds of temples are active in Hong Kong and Taiwan, many more belonging to CCT than to specifically Daoist groups.

Elsewhere in Asia, wherever significant populations of Chinese have gathered, such as Malaysia and Singapore, Daoism and CCT are growing but are still relatively small. Estimates of active Daoists vary wildly from 2.7 to 225 million, while some demographers number

Children play, parents pray, at Taipei's Xing Tian temple.

adherents of CCT or "Chinese Folk Religion" between one hundred and four hundred million. These numbers seem relatively small next to counts of other major traditions, but they do not include the many millions of people whose days are full of ancient symbols and small rituals even if they are not formally identified with the institutional trappings of Daoism or CCT.

What is the **Daoist Celestial Masters** school and why is it important?

Daoism's Celestial Masters school (*Tian Shi Dao,* also called *Zheng Yi,* "Correct One") stands out as the original institutional expression of religious Daoism and one of several early attempts to establish theocratic communities. It was originally known as the Five Bushels of Rice school, the "dues" expected of members, the Celestial Masters school. Founded by Zhang Dao Ling (34–156 C.E.) in about 142, the sect focused initially on physical, moral, and spiritual healing through ritual confession of faults and exorcism. Regular rituals included recitation from the *Dao De Jing* and communal meals, with feasts three times annually to acknowledge the three celestial bureaucracies overseeing Heaven, Earth, and water. Over the centuries the Celestial Masters school has worked to prevent the popularization of religious rituals by attempting to maintain standards in the training of ritual specialists. Two main divisions, the southern and northern schools, developed more or less independently and then merged around the fourteenth century. After losing ground to various other schools for many centuries, the school has risen to prominence in modern times and now generally dominates the formal practice of Daoism and its rituals. The school is represented officially by the sixty-third Master, who lives in exile in Taiwan.

What is the **Perfect Realization** school of Daoism?

Founded by Wang Zhe (c. 1123–70, also called Wang Chong Yang), the Perfect Realization (*Chuan Zhen*) school is among the most important Daoist monastic orders. According to legend, Wang Zhe received new revelations from one of the Eight Immortals, Lu Dong Bin. Ascetic self-denial was a central feature in the order's discipline, including meditative practices designed to maximize *Yang* energy and minimize *Yin*. The founder evidently insisted on the importance of studying the teachings of Buddhism and Confucianism along with those of Daoism, but focused on the characteristically Daoist spiritual goal of immortality. Of its several branches, the *Lung Men* ("Dragon Gate") is perhaps the most influential. Like religious orders in some other major traditions, the Perfect Realization order historically has been socially active and responsible for preserving much traditional Chinese religious culture in times of turmoil. For example, they have done extensive refugee relief work and published a major edition of the Daoist scriptural canon in 1192. From the White Cloud monastery in Beijing, the *Lung Men* branch of the order continues its work today.

Have there been any other **sub-communities** or **denominations** within Daoism?

Dozens of other schools and sects have arisen over the long history of religious Daoism. The Great Purity School (*Shang Qing*), also known as Mount Mao (*Mao Shan*) Daoism, arose during the late fourth century. The *Shang Qing* claims as its central revelation a set of scriptural texts in over thirty volumes. Almost contemporary in origin with that school is another called the *Ling Bao*. It also claims a distinctive scriptural revelation, based in part on the *Shang Qing* scripture. Heavenly Mind (*Tian Xin*) Daoism, emphasizing the importance of exorcism and based also on its own scriptural revelation, began in the late tenth century. The Divine Highest Heaven (*Shen Xiao*) school, dating from the twelfth century, is best known for its talismans of legendary potency and its elucidation of correspondences between the microcosm of the body and the macrocosm of the universe. Great Oneness (*Tai Yi*) Daoism, also from the twelfth century, was a celibate monastic school important for its integration of Confucian and Buddhist elements. Though none of these schools remains active today, all have made significant historical contributions to the large and complex reality called Daoism.

How do Daoists view their tradition's **relationships to other traditions**?

By the beginning of the first millennium, philosophically minded Daoists had rubbed elbows for several centuries with proponents of a cultural and ethical system often identified as Confucian. Together the Confucians and the Daoists were increasingly important elements of a larger cultural matrix. "Religion," for which they had as yet no specific term, was a blend of ancient divinatory rites, ancestor veneration, exorcism, and offerings meant to secure blessings and protection from "Heaven" and several other fairly generic and non-personal divine powers. Religious Daoism evolved during the period when Buddhism was taking root in China. It was not until Chinese Buddhism was several centuries old that Chinese thinkers began to talk of "three ways" of being both Chinese and religious. It is as though the Chinese people had not thought of their ancient traditions as anything but "the way things are," rather like the air they breathed, until an imported form of thinking and acting called "the Way of the Buddha" entered the scene.

Buddhist-Daoist relations have had a checkered history. At first many Daoists regarded Buddhism as a new Daoist school or sect, thanks to Buddhist efforts at translating key concepts into terms Daoists would understand. Before long, full-scale hostility developed when Daoists began to think of the missionary-minded Buddhists as a threat. Confucians often sided with Daoists in condemning Buddhism as "un-Chinese." Periods of persecution of Buddhists alternated with rich interchange and mutual influence. Since the 1800s Daoist-Buddhist relations have been much more stable and peaceful, so that many Chinese now perceive few or no important distinctions or barriers between the two traditions. CCT has been a kind of meeting ground.

Are there any Daoist holy places?

Mountains are the most prominent of Daoism's sacred sites, but they were sacred to the Chinese long before Daoism. Four mountains marked the cardinal directions of ancient Chinese symbolic geography, and a fifth was eventually added at the center, perhaps in connection with the notion of five elements (earth, air, water, fire, and metal). Each mountain has its chief deity who discharges his own distinctive duties. A number of individual mountains in addition to the main five also possess special properties and are connected with particular deities or Daoist sects and schools. Mount He Ming (Szechuan province) is famed as the place where Zhang Dao Ling inaugurated religious Daoism. Daoists share Mount Zhong Nan (Shensi province) with Buddhists as a sacred site. The Celestial Masters school established its center on Mount Long Hu (Kiangsi province). Hundreds of Daoist and Buddhist temples have stood on dozens of such sacred peaks. Two related features of Daoist sacred geography are the system of ten great and thirty-six lesser Grotto-Heavens and seventy-two Blessed Spots, some of which are located on famed mountains. These sites, mostly caves, are so designated because they are foci of sacred energy. They are often associated with religious figures believed to have found meditative solitude there and are likened to heavenly dwellings.

As for Daoist-Confucian relations, there has been intermittent rivalry for imperial patronage. The two traditions share a great deal in the way of broad doctrinal and cultural themes, such as the so-called *Yin/Yang* worldview and ancestor veneration. During the Confucian revival of the twelfth and thirteenth centuries, in a development often dubbed Neo-Confucianism, there was renewed positive interaction and mutual exchange of ideas. Nowadays, relations remain generally cordial, but without much substantial discussion of core belief.

Daoist Organizations, Schools, and Sub-communities

Black Hats—non-monastic priests as well as lay ritual specialists responsible for a wide variety of rituals.

Celestial Masters school—*Tian Shi Dao,* second century C.E., arose out of the Five Bushels of Rice movement; one of the oldest religious organizations.

Dao Jia—common term referring to philosophical Daoism.

Dao Jiao—common term referring to religious Daoism.

Fa Shi—known as the Red Turbans who specialized in occult rituals.

Fang Shi—ancient term for popular religious specialists called shamans.

Five Bushels of Rice school—early religious Daoism movement of the second century C.E., associated with Zhang Dao Ling.

Great Oneness school—*Tai Yi,* twelfth century, integrated Confucian and Buddhist teachings.

329

Great Purity school—Shang Qing, also called *Mao Shan,* late fourth century, claiming a thirty-volume revealed scripture.

Heavenly Mind school—Tian Xin, late tenth century C.E., emphasized importance of exorcism.

Huang Lao school—an early religious movement from around the third century B.C.E., named after two important sacred figures, Huang Di (the "Yellow Emperor") and Lao Zi.

Ling Bao school—based partly on Great Purity scriptures, and roughly contemporary with that school.

Neo-Daoism—general name for several movements that developed around the third and fourth centuries C.E.

Perfect Realization order—Chuan Zhen, monastic order founded in the twelfth century by Wang Zhe, emphasized meditation and asceticism as means to immortality.

Pure Conversation school—Qing Tan, a Neo-Daoist school that blended elements of Buddhism, Confucianism, and Daoism.

Secret Mystical Teaching—Xuan Xue, third- to fourth-century C.E. Neo-Daoist movement emphasizing (according to some scholars) the quest for physical immortality.

Shi Gong—"lay masters," non-priestly ritual specialists.

LEADERSHIP, AUTHORITY, AND RELIGIOUS ROLES

How are Daoist **leaders chosen** and given authority?

Traditional Daoist priesthood has long been a hereditary occupation, though that appears to be changing in recent times. This feature obviously applied consistently only to non-celibate branches of the priesthood. Individuals who successfully completed requisite initial training are ordained, following general patterns similar to those of Buddhist monastic practice. Ordination requires a quorum of ordained priests, and the ordinand takes "refuge" in the Dao, the canon of scripture, and the tradition's spiritual teachers, much as the Buddhist monk takes refuge in the Buddha, the *Dharma,* and the *Sangha.*

Lay specialists, whether Black Hats or Red Turbans, apprentice to an authoritative master called a *dao jang*—perhaps the equivalent of "high priest." His task is to lead novices through several levels of ritual assistantship. Students begin with basic musical accompaniment, learn to watch over the incense burners, and lead group prayers. More difficult training includes learning to chant and memorizing often intricate rubrics (ritual movements). After learning to copy sacred texts and write talismans calligraphically, aspirants are ready to lead ritual. In the People's Republic of China some seminaries still provide formal doctrinal instruction, but that is generally not the case in Taiwan. Formal ordination focuses on the symbolism of the master conferring the seal of priesthood and the texts the specialist will follow. Some scholars suggest the training of Black Hats is more rigorous and literate than that of the Red Turbans, who tend to serve less official, more "popular" functions and have much in common with the shamans of old.

What are some of the main **varieties** of Daoist **officials or specialists**?

Since about the fourth century C.E., religious specialists called *dao shi,* "masters of the Dao," have led Daoist communities at prayer. These leaders can be celibate monks (there are also nuns called *dao gu*) who live almost exclusively in monastic communities. Monastic priests—mostly members of the Complete Realization school—occasionally perform public rituals, but, not unlike cloistered monks in some other traditions, their principal focus is on their more private spiritual pursuits. Some ritual specialists are married family men who live near a monastery. These so-called "lay masters" (*shi gong*) make up the majority of Daoist ritual specialists. Individuals generally specialize in certain types of ritual, such as exorcism and faith-healing.

Among the non-monastic, those ritualists whose functions most closely resemble those of priests in various other traditions are called the Black Hats. Many of them belong to the Celestial Masters school, perhaps the oldest of all Daoist organizations. In addition to the Black Hats—the "official" and intricately trained priests—there are the Red Turbans known as *fa shi,* specialists in the occult. Black Hats, so called because of their small mandarin cap with a gold knob on top, are authorized to perform both the greater festivals and the more ordinary ceremonies to which the Red Turbans are restricted. (The two groups are alternatively known as Blackheads and Redheads.) Specialists of earlier times called "libationers" in the Celestial Masters school had the triple duty of religious instruction, local administration, and ritual leadership, not unlike the typical parish pastor in many Christian denominations.

What has been the **shaman's role** in Daoism?

Remnants of ancient shamanism continue to color much Daoist religious thought and practice. In pre-Daoist times, shamans were tribal leaders possessed of extraordinary powers. Reports from around the third century B.C.E. describe how these *fang shi* or "masters of prescriptions" worked their magic. They could tap natural energies, exercise control over life and death, and assume the form of various powerful creatures. Shamanic specialists included many women as well as men. With the dawn of empire and agricultural economy, shamans became part of the governmental structure. Their duties included: drawing spiritual powers to themselves as they entered into trance, exorcism, explaining omens and dreams, influencing the weather for favorable harvest, curing the sick, and divining heavenly portents at the behest of the emperor.

A transformed shamanism lives on in various Daoist practices that are generally divided among the Black Hat priests, Red Turban masters, and spirit mediums. Daoist ritual specialists still fend off evil spirits and perform a vestige of the ancient ceremonies symbolizing the shaman's journey to the upper and lower worlds. That spiritual journey of ascent and descent remains perhaps the most distinctive survival of shamanistic lore. It appears in various traditions in surprising forms, including, for example, Muhammad's famous Night Journey and Ascension. Daoist ritual symbolism of the journey occurs in the master's "pacing the clouds" as he prepares the sacred space for the great religious observances.

Are there Daoist **hierarchical structures**?

Since there are many different sects and schools, there are no official and universally acknowledged hierarchical structures that unite all Daoists. But there are de facto hierarchies both religious, within individual Daoist organizations, and social, based on a broader kind of class consciousness. For example, in the Celestial Masters school, the living Heavenly Master functions as a sort of archbishop, overseeing the running of the school's temples in the region. Within the administration of the school, ranks are named after those of the imperial bureaucracy, such as libationer, recorder, and director of ceremonies. The Celestial Masters school has retained much of its ancient hierarchical structure today. In addition, each of the various monastic orders is internally structured according to authority and leadership roles, with the equivalent of an abbot at the head.

Hierarchical structures have also been very much a part of the several short-lived attempts to create theocratic states, but their claims to authority were naturally limited. Within their everyday lives, most Daoists would likely be aware only of the functional hierarchy inherent in the more elaborate ritual celebrations. There, a high priest presides, while subordinate priests perform much of the ceremonial action and musical accompaniment. Other non-ordained assistants busy themselves with the overall mechanics of the ritual, keeping the action moving by making sure necessary supplies are plentiful and other practical matters are in order.

Have **women exercised leadership** among Daoists?

One of the most famous libationers was a woman named Wei Hua Cun (251–334 C.E.). Her rank as libationer apparently indicates that she originally belonged to the Celestial Masters school. Some regard her as a foundational figure in the *Shang Qing* sect. She is perhaps most famous for having appeared posthumously on many nights over a six-year period to reveal to a certain Yang Xi the sacred texts of the *Shang Qing* sect. Those texts consist mainly of liturgical ritual. Throughout its long history, the Celestial Masters school has allowed women into the lower rungs of its ritual hierarchy, up to but not including that of Celestial Master itself. Another school, called "Pure Rarity" (*qing wei*), is said to have been founded by a woman named Zu Shu in the early tenth century. Centered on a thunder deity, the sect blended elements from the *Ling Bao, Shang Qing,* and Celestial Masters schools. There have

Is there a central teaching authority for Daoists? For CCT?

Individual Daoist sects, orders, and schools have regarded—and in some cases still do regard—their teaching office as a solemn and demanding role. But on the whole, Daoists do not think of themselves as following any particular teaching or adhering to a particular orthodoxy. Even when important patriarchs, such as the living leader of the Celestial Masters school, have delivered formal pronouncements, relatively few Daoists take notice. What is true of Daoism in this respect is even truer of the much more amorphous CCT. In neither case is any specific articulation of doctrine of any particular importance. Doctrinal standards are replaced here by pure tradition—"the way we've always done things."

been many priestesses over the centuries, and a celibate community of women maintain a temple in Kaoshung, Taiwan.

Hagiographical sources are extant on a number of holy women of ancient times. They make it clear that women who preferred to pursue the spiritual life rather than devote themselves to family risked almost certain disapproval. Even so, it seems that some women were associated with religious orders. Sun Bu Er (1119–1182) and her husband were both ritual specialists in the Perfect Realization order, and she founded a new division of the school dedicated to the religious education of women. A selection of her writings in translation is available in Thomas Cleary's *Immortal Sisters: Secret Teachings of Taoist Women*. A sect associated especially with the Red Turbans is popularly called San Nai, "Three Ladies," evidently so named to honor a trio of priestesses about whom little else is known. As has often been the case in other religious traditions, many Chinese women have found possibilities for active leadership and ministry more often outside the institutional structures than within.

Is there a system of Daoist **religious law**?

Apart from the charters or disciplinary codes of Daoist organizations such as monastic orders, there is no such thing as formal Daoist religious law. The very idea goes against the grain of the concept of natural balance and harmony that is so central to Daoist thought. That is not to say that there aren't countless standard practices and expectations as to behavior. The difference between Daoism and, say, Islam or Christianity, in this respect is that the Muslim and Christian traditions have systematically codified those expectations while the Daoist has not. Every cultural and religious system has its standards and sanctions. But in the cases of both Islam and Christianity, independent legal systems became necessary largely because the religious traditions expanded into new cultural settings very different from those in which the traditions arose. In the case of Daoism, religion and culture have been much more closely and consistently identified, making a separate system of religious law largely unnecessary. **333**

Where do **members** of local Daoist communities and members of CCT **come together**?

By far the most important Daoist and CCT gathering places are local temples and shrines, as well as the elaborate but temporary altars set up in open spaces for the larger religious ceremonies. Temples vary in size and wealth and, naturally, the smaller the temple the more likely it is to serve a purely ritual purpose and not to have room for other activities. Community temples at the center of towns and villages often serve as multipurpose facilities. There might be any number of functions going on at one time—classes for children, play during recess, community meetings—while worshippers attend to their devotional needs. In larger towns and cities, other organizations, such as various Daoist (and Buddhist) associations, apparently fill some of those communal functions as well. Most people still think of Daoist and CCT temples primarily as ritual facilities that also serve as centers of parish life. Temples typically govern their ordinary affairs through an elected committee entrusted with all major decisions about ritual calendar, maintenance, and finance.

Are there any **organizations** that have their **own distinctive structures** within Daoism?

Monastic institutions have been of great importance in the history of Daoism. Celibate monks adhere to demanding disciplinary codes. The five basic rules of Daoist monastic life are not unlike some of the essential regulations of Buddhist laity. Monks are forbidden to take life, to eat meat or drink alcohol, to lie or steal, or to engage in sexual activity including, of course, marriage. But like their Buddhist counterparts, Daoist monks face far greater demands as well. Fasting is a large element in monastic life, including ten fast days each month plus dozens of others scattered throughout the year. Historically, different orders required adherence to additional regulations varying in number from ten to several dozen. Some orders structured their membership according to levels of spiritual attainment. For example, the Realization of Truth School had three grades among its monks. "Noble transformation" characterized the "Master of Excellent Conduct," who successfully managed the first set of challenges. Abiding by a set of three hundred specific regulations brought a monk to the level of "Master of Noble Virtue." To achieve the level of "Nobility in the Dao," aspirants had to match the Immortals themselves in virtue.

Is there such a thing as a Daoist **saint**?

Perhaps the closest thing in Daoism to what many people mean by "saint" is the ideal of human development called the sage (*zhen ren*). Unlike ordinary people, the sage keeps his knowledge hidden, because there is no need to impress or persuade others. A sage is thus like the silent, unobtrusive Dao. Neither does the sage labor over the right course of action, for love is squandered when spent on specific deeds rather than lav-

Who is the Jade Emperor?

One of the more intriguing personalities in the Daoist and CCT pantheons is the Jade Emperor, Yu Huang Da Di. His emergence as a power to be reckoned with in popular worship offers important insight into the dynamics of Chinese religion generally. During the fifth and sixth centuries Yu Huang Da Di was but one among many relatively minor deities. During the Tang dynasty of the seventh through ninth centuries he gained prominence as a result of the appearance of a new text called the Jade Emperor Scripture (*Yu Huang Jing*). It tells how centuries earlier a queen had dreamed that Tai Shang Dao Jun, second of the Three Pure Ones, handed her an infant. She awoke and bore a child, who after a short time as a young prince, withdrew to mountain solitude. Lengthy spiritual discipline transformed the youth into the Jade Emperor. In the tenth century, a Song dynasty emperor named Jen Zung (r. 998–1022) chose Yu Huang Da Di as his patron deity and spread word of an expected revelation. That came in 1008 in the form of sacred scriptures, thus bolstering the weak emperor's position. Thereafter the Jade Emperor rose to the top of the popular pantheon, thus becoming the CEO of a divine bureaucracy. Stories like that of the Jade Emperor help to explain why enumerations of the Daoist and CCT pantheons are sometimes a bit confusing.

ished equally on all. The sage understands that failing to yield is not to be confused with courage. The sage knows how to give without being emptied, how to take in without being filled. Completely in harmony with nature, the sage acts without intent, learns without studying intently. Chinese religious traditions often have elevated otherwise ordinary human beings to a status above the merely human. But there is no standard formal process by which this elevation takes place. In this respect Daoism is closer to Islam than to Christianity, for example, where sainthood requires elaborate and lengthy investigation and verification. Emperors and others in authority have sometimes announced honors of this kind by decree, but sages are generally acknowledged as such as a result of grassroots movements rather than by pronouncement from on high. There is at least one other distinctive feature of the making of a Daoist sage. Whereas saints in some other traditions arrive at a level of spiritual perfection as a result of divine grace, the Daoist sage is a product of self-help.

Who is **Guan Di** and why is he so important?

Like the Jade Emperor, Guan Di (also known as Guan Gong) claims a place in both Daoist and CCT pantheons. He has the additional distinction of ranking high in the upper echelons of the imperial cult, and through that channel connects with Confucian tradition as well. Guan Di was originally a military man of the third century,

Various deities available in a popular religious goods store, Keeling, Taiwan. Here you can find everyone in the several pantheons, from the red-faced Guan Di and other Daoist figures to Guan Yin and the jolly Buddhist figure on the right called Pu Tai.

named Guan Yu, who was executed after enemies of the Han dynasty captured him in battle. The court funded temples in his honor and publicized his cause. Meanwhile, the newly deified Guan Di was gaining popularity among practitioners of CCT as a refuge from problems as diverse as illness, bad weather, and failing business. The ever-ready all-purpose deity thus rose to such prominence that his popular cult situated him above even the Jade Emperor. In the seventeenth century a Ming dynasty emperor conferred on Guan Di the title of Grand Emperor.

During the following regime, that of the Ching or Manchu, Guan Di received the title under which he is perhaps most widely known, Military Emperor or Wu Di, thus making him the official guardian of the empire. Guan Di's celebrity represents a relatively recent development. Unlike many of the older deities, whose imagery and entourage were typically patterned on those of the imperial bureaucracy, Guan Di is reminiscent of the Buddhist Bodhisattva. In fact, some scholars suggest, Guan Di also was absorbed into certain Buddhist groups after the seventh century. It seems likely that, as in the case of other indigenous Chinese deities, Guan Di was first depicted under the general influence of Buddhism's use of sculpture. He appears as a very tall man with a very long beard and a red face, sometimes accompanied by his son. Variant versions of his story give somewhat different details, as in the popular classic Chinese novel *Romance of the Three Kingdoms,* of which Guan Di is the hero. Many popular theatrical presentations based on the novel have become a major vehicle for the spread of Guan Di's popularity.

Who is the **Yellow Emperor**?

Ancient Chinese lore tells of Five August Emperors whose reigns date back to before 2500 B.C.E. They are sometimes called "culture heroes," in that tradition credits them with providing humankind with a host of skills and essential practical wisdom. As guardians of the five sacred mountains, the divine quintet ruled the cardinal directions and the center. Each was associated with a color: green with the east, red with the south, white with the west, black (or "dark") with the north, and yellow with the center. By far the most famous and popular of them is Huang Di, the Yellow Emperor, giver of such arts as medicine, agriculture, weaving, pottery, silkworm culture, and domestic architecture, to name only a few.

Huang Di began his life in legend as a ruler and a shaman whose magical powers allowed him to confront all manner of evil. Dated either 2697–2597 or 2674–2575 B.C.E., he was evidently a patron of the ancient *fang shi,* or shamans. But the Yellow Emperor went on to become one of the two patrons of an early Daoist school called Huang Lao, perhaps a combination of the first names of Huang Di and Lao Zi. Huang Lao Daoism may have begun as a religious movement as early as third century B.C.E. In any case, though the figure of Lao Zi seems to have upstaged that of Huang Di for some centuries, the Yellow Emperor made a comeback in popularity. In any number of Daoist and popular temples a visitor may encounter a statue of Huang Di prominently displayed, perhaps in his own glass case. Standing erect, the sovereign, of solemn countenance, wears elaborately embroidered robes whose main color is, of course, yellow.

Daoist female immortal He Xian'gu holding her bamboo vessel and a long-stemmed lotus, ivory with polychrome and gilt decoration, Dao Guang period, 1821–1850. (The Saint Louis Art Museum.)

Who are the **Eight Immortals**?

Three historical and five legendary persons believed to have achieved immortality figure prominently in Chinese religious lore. Daoist sources tell of many other mortals who have achieved immortality, but these eight are especially important. Chinese religious lore contains many sets of eight (trigrams, precious objects, and cosmic directions, for example). The Immortals (*xian*) are in some ways analogous to Christianity's saints and Islam's Friends of God.

Lu Dong Bin, originally a patriarch of the Complete Realization school during the eighth century, generally leads the group. He usually dresses as a scholar and carries a fly whisk. Some images show him with his magical sword, one of the Eight Daoist Emblems. Lu is patron of barbers and is celebrated for his healing powers. Li Tie Guai, a purely legendary figure whose emblems are the gourd and crutch, appears as an old crippled beggar. He champions the weak and marginalized and is a patron of pharmacists. Zhang Guo Lao lived sometime between 650 and 750 C.E. Capable of making himself invisible, Zhang appears riding (often backward!) on a white mule which he could roll up and tuck into his sleeve. His emblem is the percussion instrument made of a bamboo tube and two sticks and he is the patron of elderly men. He Xian'gu, the lone female of the group, holds a bamboo ladle, a lotus or basket of flowers, and sometimes the peach of immortality. She is said to have lived around 700 C.E. and is noted for her asceticism and kindness. Han Xiang Zi is the patron of musicians. He carries a flute and is known for his spendthrift ways and delight in mountain solitude. Zhong Li Chuan is supposed to have been a soldier of old who failed in battle and became an alchemist. Apparently once a historical figure, the aging and portly fellow eventually ascended to Heaven on a stork and now carries a fan. Lan Cai is a strange figure among strange figures. With one foot bare and one shod, sometimes appearing as a woman, sometimes as a boy, he carries a basket of flowers and is patron of florists. Cao Guo Jiu, patron of actors, carries a pair of castanets or, alternatively, a jade court tablet that was his entry pass and from which the image of castanets may have developed. Tradition makes this eighth Immortal the brother of a Song Dynasty empress and dresses him in royal finery. The whole octet are still widely popular and sought out for their magical powers.

Have there been any **Daoist mystics**?

Traditional accounts of many famous Daoists describe their inner experiences in terms consistent with those often associated with mysticism. A mystic, in general terms, is a human being who, through a variety of ritual or devotional practices, experiences spiritual transcendence. Moving out of and beyond him or herself, the mystic abides at least temporarily in a dimension very different from what most people experience most of the time. Some refer to the great Daoist figures as "nature mystics" since they enter into that different dimension by contemplating nature. They experience oneness with the cosmos intuitively rather than by reasoning their way to an intellectual conclusion. In a trance-like state, the mystic loses all sense of selfhood and individuality, becoming one with the Dao. Some have referred to the experience as the "fast of the mind" in which one listens with the ears of the spirit. What exactly the experience feels like, Daoist sources are reluctant to say, but they readily offer advice about how to cultivate the experience. By way of exception, some Daoist sources also hint that the occasional mystic has experienced a somewhat more personal form of union with the divine akin to what Hindu and other traditions call "theistic mysticism."

HOLIDAYS AND REGULAR OBSERVANCES

What kind of **calendar** do Daoists and practitioners of CCT observe?

Firmly anchored in traditional astrological calculations, the Chinese lunar calendar consists of twelve months of twenty-nine or thirty days, since the time between new moons is about twenty-nine and a half days. The lunar year dovetails with the solar with the intercalation of extra months at certain intervals. Reckoning began around 2637 B.C.E., so that the year 2000 marks the year 4637. Each of the twelve animals of the zodiac is associated with a particular quality or event and gives its name to every twelfth year, beginning with the Rat (industry and prosperity) and proceeding in order through Ox (spring planting), Tiger (valor), Hare (longevity), Dragon (power and good fortune), Snake (cunning), Horse (perseverance), Sheep or Goat (filial piety), Monkey (health), Rooster (protection), Dog (fidelity) and Pig (home and family). The year 2000 is the Year of the Dragon, 2001 that of the Snake, 2002 that of the Horse, and so on. Five full cycles, each named after one of the five elements (wood, fire, earth, metal and water) equals sixty years, an important interval for ritual purposes. Major annual markers are the winter (maximum *Yin*) and summer (maximum *Yang*) solstices and vernal and autumnal equinoxes.

During each month, the most important times are the moments of new and full moon. Each month is divided into ten-day periods, six of those in turn considered a special time period, and six of those in turn equaling a full year. In addition, each year is divided into twenty-four climatic periods called breaths or nodes, described by such phrases as "full of snow" or "clear and bright." Every year, month, day, and hour is further identified by a combination of ten heavenly "stems" and twelve earthly "branches" (the monthly or zodiacal symbols). Branches and stems are primarily numerical designators, but each also bears important symbolic connotations. If you match one stem with one branch for succeeding years and only match odd-numbered stems with odd-numbered branches and even-numbered stems with even-numbered branches (S1/B1, S2/B2 … S1/B11, S2/B12, S3/B1, and so on), you end up back at the beginning after sixty years. The result is an extremely detailed system of pinpointing certain times according to a host of definitive characteristics. Each event occurring on Earth has its heavenly parallel. For every conceivable type of human behavior there is an auspicious moment. Thus, the calendar has been not merely a way of keeping track of times for religious observances, but a kind of temporal map for negotiating the cosmos as well.

What are the major types of Daoist **religious observance**?

Daoist sources talk about three levels of ceremony: "Great Services" called *jiao*, which occur relatively infrequently; "Ritual Gatherings" called *fan hui*; and "Feast Days" called *tan*. Two essential features of every religious celebration are the preparation and the actual event. *Zhai* refers to several types of purifying fasts. Strictly speaking the *zhai* is preparatory to the main ceremonial event, the offering or *jiao*, but certain dis-

339

Why is the Chinese New Year so important?

Chinese New Year festivities are associated, not surprisingly, with renewal and with powers that hold the promise of protection for the coming year. During these celebrations, religious Chinese add to their regular roster of symbolism extra images of important figures like the Eight Immortals and the deities of happiness, success and longevity. New Year is not a specifically Daoist observance, but rather a more generic occasion on which people are moved to intensify their awareness of essential values. Festivities begin about ten days before the actual day. It starts when families send Cao Jun, deity of the Stove, to give an account of the family's deeds over the previous year to the Jade Emperor. On New Year's Day, Cao Jun returns to his kitchen throne, where the family welcomes him with a fresh picture for the wall. Most families observe a series of private rituals, including elaborate meals and reverence to the ancestors. During the following two weeks or so, people pay homage to the god of wealth. Festivities end with the Lantern Festival at the New Year's first full moon.

tinct actions set the purification apart. Both celebrants and their sacred space need to be prepared ritually. To purify both mind and body, participants meditate in solitude, eat vegetarian meals, fast for a time, and refrain from sex. Preparation may commence as much as three days ahead, for the major feasts, and continue through the main event itself. Celebrants prepare the sacred space through a combination of actions, including chanting and burning incense. A category of events called *jiao* includes various kinds of festivities. In ancient times the principal *jiao* were associated with planting and harvest. Eventually, various Daoist sects incorporated elements of the time-honored traditions into their liturgies, but the agricultural element became secondary. Different groups compiled extensive collections of liturgical rites in massive tomes, with specific ceremonies for a wide range of occasions.

Does Daoism have any **annual celebrations**?

For virtually every temple community, the principal deity's birthday provides the occasion for a major yearly festivity. Celebrants focus on the temple and the main icon, sprucing up the building and decking out the deity in new finery. In addition there are dozens of other festal days. The New Year emphasizes a fresh start, with Lao Zi's feast on the first day and prayers to the Jade Pure One on the eighth and the Jade Emperor on the ninth day of the first month. The latter is a lengthy festivity that culminates on the fifteenth with the Lantern Festival. "Clear and Bright" falls on the first day of the third month. (In mainland China this is not lunar but occurs always on April 5.) Its main thrust is to remember the dead, maintain burial places, and offer ritual meals at the graves. Dragon Boat races on the fifth day of the fifth month commemorate the drowning of a poet of old. More important, however, is the association of that month with the need to ward off spirits of disease at a time when, with the summer solstice approaching, *Yin* energy begins to replace *Yang* as the dominant energy. CCT devotees celebrate Guan Yin's ascension to Heaven on the nineteenth of the sixth month, during which people also mark the midpoint in the year.

On the seventh day of the seventh month, people observe the only night when the Weaving Maid and the Cowherd, a celestial couple, can be together. And the fifteenth marks the birthday of a Daoist deity called the Earth Controller, known in CCT as the emperor-sage Shun. Numerous rituals acknowledging the need to placate the wandering dead occupy many during the seventh month. Most prominent is the Ghost Festival on the fifteenth day, when people seek to propitiate the spirits by leaving food out for them. Daoist masters now officiate at the occasion, which was formerly a Buddhist

Statue of Choi Bak Sing Gwan, a deity of wealth, in a family-run CCT temple, Honolulu. Thanks to Mrs. Au for allowing the author to take photos in the temple.

observance. A mid-autumn celebration of the moon goddess' birthday, once a harvest festival, occurs on the fifteenth of the eighth month. On the ninth day of the ninth month, called Double-*Yang* because of the auspicious nature of the number nine, people once sought protection in amulets and fled lowland evil by taking to the hills. Nowadays, most people simply go for walks in the cool fresh autumn air. On the fifteenth of month ten, worshippers mark the birthday of a Daoist deity called the Controller of the Waters, known in CCT as the sage Yu. A winter festivity marks the solstice during the eleventh month. Before the twelfth month is even half spent, planning begins for the New Year.

What is the **most important Daoist observance**?

A grand affair called the ritual of Cosmic Renewal occurs at varying intervals in different places. It was once on a sixty-year cycle, according to the ancient calendar reckoning calculated with the "branches and stems." Some temples celebrate this way as often as every ten years now. Whenever a community erects a new temple it is time for a renewal ritual. This major festival belongs to a larger category called *jiao*. Ritual specialists from the so-called Black Hat group have exclusive rights to officiate in these events. A standard feature is recitation from the Jade Emperor Scripture, and the focus of prayer is on seeking blessings of all kinds for the future. Massive organizational efforts precede the larger celebrations. They include interviewing prospective high priests from whom the committee can choose a leader, who will then arrange for a full staff of ritual specialists. Full-scale festivities require extensive construction of temporary altars or shrines. Celebrations nowadays typically go on for from three to five days, though they formerly lasted as long as nearly two months.

Do Daoists and practitioners of CCT **celebrate** the **birthdays** of any **religious figures**?

Deities both great and small are generally thought to have birthdays because the vast majority of them were once human beings. CCT has transformed numerous figures originally Daoist, Buddhist, and Confucian into more comfortable characters—members of everybody's family, in effect. Other deities remain in their more exalted original Daoist forms. The following are only a few of the literally hundreds of divine birthday dates.

Among the earliest in the year is the Jade Emperor, celebrated on the ninth of the first month. On the third day of the second month, CCT acknowledges Wen Chang Di Jun, the god of literature and learning. Guan Yin's birthday occurs on the nineteenth of the second month. Xuan Tian Shang Di, the Supreme Emperor of Dark Heaven, was born on the third of the third month and is celebrated in some four hundred Taiwanese temples. A quasi-Daoist deity called the Great Emperor Who Protects Life, Bao Sheng Da Di, is celebrated on the fifteenth of the third month. Ma Zu, often referred to as the Great Aunt or Grandma, has her celebration on the twenty-third of the third month. On the thirteenth day of month five the general-become-deity Guan Di gets his due. The fifteenth of the sixth month is dedicated to an anonymous figure called a City God. Devotees of CCT observe the birthdays of Cao Jun on the third day of the eighth month, and that of Tu Di Gong on the fifteenth. Also on the third of that month Daoists celebrate the birthday of Si Ming, the Director of Destiny, known in CCT as the Kitchen God or Hearth Deity.

What are some **other important celebrations** for Daoism and CCT?

Daoists dedicate days to the Three Officials (or Officers or Rulers), whom CCT call Shun, Yao, and Yu, on the fifteenth days of the first, seventh, and tenth lunar months. Their days are associated respectively with Heaven, Earth, and water. The Heavenly Official, Shun, ranks highest and remains very popular in Taiwan, for example. The Water Official, Yu, is celebrated for having saved the world from uncontrolled flooding. Three Daoist deities considered at the pinnacle of the pantheon are known as the Three Primordials. Their festival days coincide with those of the Three Officials, respectively, the first two of which also coincide with the CCT Lantern Festival and Ghost Festival.

CUSTOMS AND RITUALS

What **rites** do worshippers practice in Daoist and CCT **temples**?

One of the most important and easily observable temple rituals involves the offering of incense. Worshippers buy three slender sticks of incense at a small temple shop that supplies a variety of materials for different sorts of offerings. Devotees can make their offerings either at the main altar or at any of a number of side or subordinate altars, depending on the size of the temple and which deity they choose to address. Those who wish to worship at the main shrine may first approach the large incense kettle that normally stands in the central courtyard. Igniting their incense sticks, they hold them upright between folded hands, wave them before the deity, and bow from the waist toward the object of their devotion. After prayer they insert the handles of the burning incense wands into the sand and ashes in the kettle. On some occasions a devotee might have his or her sticks placed in a holder on an altar. Some worshippers take incense ash home for use as a curative medicine.

Equally important is a more ritually generic type of devotional prayer in which devotees supplicate the various deities for favors. Worshippers generally kneel to address the chosen deity, praying either aloud or in silence, either bowing humbly or looking at the image. Offerings other than incense include a variety of foods, most commonly fruits, rice, vegetables, wine, and sweets. When worshippers make such offerings, they often have a temple staff member light a candle for them on the altar. Toward the end of a typical episode of temple worship, devotees will burn symbolic imitation paper money as an offering. All temples provide one or more small furnaces in which worshippers offer gold paper to the deities and silver to ancestors. These burnt offerings symbolize personal sacrifice in hope of blessing and commitment to the ongoing well-being of departed family members.

Is there a **standard** Daoist **group liturgical worship**?

Most of the ritual activity one can observe at temples throughout the day consists of individual or family worship. At various times during the day, members of pious organizations may gather for group chanting of liturgical prayers. The priest may address a sermon to such gatherings as well. Major Daoist sects have devised their own communal rituals, and some have survived intact into our time and are still practiced, especially in rural areas and more traditional villages. Many of these involve group chanting of sacred texts, in imitation of the chanting of the assembled gods themselves when they created the universe. One important communal ritual is that based on the teachings of the Ling Bao sect. Elaborate theatrical liturgies address issues and powers in three levels or "registers"—the celestial, the terrestrial, and the human. The Golden Register of rituals honors the family of the emperor at the celestial level. A terrestrial level called the Yellow Register is aimed at peaceful rest for the deceased. The now-discontinued Jade Register once focused on securing salvation for all people. Using ritual implements, the officiants mediate between the divine and human participants. Rites once dedicated to the emperor and his court are now undertaken on behalf of local or family groups known to uphold religious standards.

Observances begin with an evening or vespers prayer to announce the start of the rituals and symbolically reconstruct a sacred realm in which to enact the rites. Great attention goes into setting the ritual scene, a miniature of the cosmos with gates at the four cardinal directions. Action resumes the next morning with a fast and an offering. Imitating a creative divine act, the officiant recreates the sacred space by pacing out creation and journeys symbolically to the heavens to bring down heavenly powers. As part of the ritual the master (or priest) meditates silently, focusing on visual imagery as a way of bringing health to the assembled people. The entire ritual ends on the next day with the master facing the assembly as one now returned to Earth. He then dismantles the altar, burns the sacred texts, and sends the deities back to their heavenly abodes.

Main altar in a family temple in Honolulu, Hawaii, dedicated to the Empress of the West, known also as Mazu and by a variety of other names. Many such altars hold more than one image of the central deity (note the two with the fringed "mortar board" headdress) as well as images of other sacred figures. Thanks to Mrs. Au for showing the author around the temple

Is **meditation** important in Daoism or CCT?

Dominant forms of devotional expression in CCT tend to be associated with more extroverted ritual and supplicatory prayer. Classical and later Daoist sources, on the other hand, describe various meditative methods designed to help the practitioner turn inward. In fact, Chan Buddhism, the Chinese precursor to the more famous Japanese Zen, seems to have borrowed much from Daoism in this respect. The meditator "sits and forgets" in the presence of nature, engaging in the "fast of the mind." Principal stages in Daoist meditative technique are the following: First the meditator calms the body by adopting a fixed posture and slow, regular breathing. As the meditator becomes one with his or her breathing, distractions begin to dissolve. To develop greater concentration, the meditator chooses a specific symbolic focus for detailed visualization. In the next stage, the meditator moves beyond this discursive intellectualizing into the "fast of the mind." Leaving behind all symbols and ideas, the meditator enters a realm where images are irrelevant. Finally, the meditator loses all sense of self and attains union with the Dao.

How do Daoists **worship at home** and throughout the day when they are not in temples?

Worshippers perform at home many of the same rituals they perform in the temple. Home shrines or family altars are miniature versions of the temple's sacred objects. Smaller images of the various deities enjoy places of honor. Before the image family members place a few apples or oranges, for example, and small incense pots hold small burning sticks just as the kettle in the temple courtyard does. Many devout Chinese begin their day by offering incense to the terrestrial deity of the home, who is sometimes depicted as five separate figures recalling the five elements. This Earth deity is at the bottom of an administrative "flow chart," reporting to the district deity, who in turn reports to the city god, and he to the country god. Offerings to family ancestors and consultation with an almanac as to the spiritual qualities of the particular day are other regular rituals. Many private individuals still practice *tai ji chuan,* a set of rhythmic movements designed to balance *Yin* and *Yang* and maximize energy.

What kinds of **ritual objects** figure in Daoist worship and prayer?

Specific lists of objects vary somewhat among the different schools and sects. Here are the most important ritual devices of the Celestial Masters school. First and foremost are the ubiquitous talismans that consist of a written magical formula or mantra symbolizing a contract between the deities and human beings engaging in a ritual exchange. Only a qualified ritual specialist may execute a talisman, which usually includes a specially drawn Chinese character as well as other visual symbols appropriate to a particular spiritual purpose. Possessors of talismans generally think of them as guarantees of divine aid. People wear them or hang them in home or office to attract positive energies. The "Precious Sword of the Seven Stars," symbolizing the Big Dipper, appears often in blessings and exorcisms, whether for individuals or as part of Cosmic Renewal observances. As a symbolic purification to the cardinal directions, ritualists sip from a copper bowl and blow a spray through closed lips. Stone seals of various kinds

Symbol standards used in Daoist and popular Chinese rituals, Bao An Gong temple, Taipei, Taiwan.

345

allow the specialist to make official documents such as talismans. Priests hold a stiff tablet, as if reading from a book. In exorcism rituals, Black Hats use the sword along with handbells, while Red Turbans use a horn and a whip.

Is **exorcism** important in Daoist practice?

Many Daoist rituals are designed to expel, control, or pacify troublesome spirits, or, by extension, to banish drought, famine, or outlaws who might have been plaguing the local citizenry. Daoists rarely identify individual problems as personal cases of demonic (*gui*) possession. Much more common are instances in which a specialist's skills are required to liberate temples, homes, and business establishments from evil influences. Until some thirty years ago, Roman Catholic tradition included a specific ritual to ordain young candidates for the priesthood to the Order of Exorcist, one of four so-called "minor orders." Ordination to the Daoist priesthood still includes an emphasis on the ability to perform exorcism as one of its essential features. Rare descriptions of demonic possession suggest some elements similar to those described in Roman Catholic archival accounts of exorcism, including the need to have several stout attendants restrain the possessed person occasionally. After performing a variety of ritual actions, such as lighting candles and incense and burning the appropriate charm, the exorcist enjoins the spirit to depart and a contest of wills ensures. More common—indeed regularly scheduled—rites of temple purification may include dramatization of an encounter between the offending demon and the deity called Chung Kuei, dispatcher of demons. After the demon (sometimes played by a member of the temple staff or a professional actor) steals an incense burner, the priest/deity subdues the evil one and returns the stolen item to the temple gods. Only through the dominance of *Yang* over *Yin* can a successful exorcism be carried out. A high moment occurs as the high priest drives the evil spirit out to the accompaniment of intense sound from percussion instruments. Another method for ridding a building of an evil presence is to create billows of holy smoke by boiling oil and adding water to it.

Women and children drop and retrieve crescent shaped divining blocks in Taipei's Xing Tian temple.

Is **divination** important to Daoists and practitioners of CCT?

Divinatory rites are more critical to Daoism and CCT than to many other major traditions. Long before Daoism came into being as a distinct set of traditions, the Chinese practiced divination through the stars, yarrow sticks, oracle bones, and tortoise shells. Important types of divination are the celestial, the terrestrial, interpretations of events and omens, and the forecasting of individual destinies. Celestial divination, a variety of astrological interpretation, plots the locations of stars according to one of the twelve "palaces" associated with the lunar month of one's birth. This is done in order to understand a host of factors including sickness and health, luck, family issues, and personality. Terrestrial divination uses an elaborate geomantic compass to assist practitioners in aligning their lives most effectively with the forces of nature. All ordinary events in the life of each person have their hidden meanings, and divinatory skills allow one to interpret the nature of the energy played out in all events in relation to the specific time of day or year. Some events clearly have ominous qualities and require specialized interpretative skills. Thunder or lightning and other natural events suggest forces that set them aside from more mundane happenings. Perhaps the most important and widespread forms of divination are those that help people divine their personal destinies. Some focus on reading physical features, such as facial characteristics or palm lines. Here we are moving away from strictly Daoist teaching and into popular practice.

How do Daoists and practitioners of CCT **today determine** their **destinies with divination**?

Most common of the methods are those that involve the use of bamboo sticks and crescent-shaped blocks. In CCT temples, devotees approach a barrel crammed full of long sticks containing combinations of trigrams called hexagrams, or, alternatively, numbers from one to sixty-four (the total number of combinations of the eight trigrams). Grabbing a handful of sticks, they shake them and then let them fall back into the barrel. Invariably one stick will protrude above the rest, and it provides the critical symbol for that individual to interpret. When sticks are numbered, devotees request a corresponding slip of paper from the temple staff. On the paper they then read an often enigmatic or poetic interpretation of the corresponding hexagram. Devotees can also drop a pair of crescent-shaped blocks with one smooth side symbolizing *Yang* and one convex side symbolizing *Yin*. Devotees pose questions as they drop the blocks. One *Yang* and one *Yin* side up means "yes," while the other combinations mean "no." Worshippers unsatisfied with a particular answer may simply continue dropping blocks until they receive the desired response.

Do Daoists and practitioners of CCT make **pilgrimages**?

Pilgrimage has long been integral to most of the major Chinese religious traditions. The Chinese term typically translated as "making pilgrimage" (*chao shan jin xiang*) actually means "paying respects to a mountain by presenting incense." Beginning in at least the fourth century C.E. and growing dramatically from the eighth to twelfth centuries, pilgrimage practices of the various traditions came to be identified with certain specific mountains, with some mountains claimed by more than one tradition.

347

Once identified as a particularly sacred place, a mountain became the site of one or more temples. Eventually Daoists and others developed elaborate sacred geographies mapped out with reference to the major sacred peaks or ranges. Pilgrimage to the sacred mountains thus became a symbolic journey through the universe. On some mountains, such as Wu Dang Shan, Daoists have constructed miniature versions of the macrocosm, identifying its subdivisions with such enchanting names as Jade Void, Primordial Harmony, Purple Empyrean, and Perfect Felicity. Mountains are the dwelling places of the gods and immortals and as such naturally became favorite places of retreat for Daoist scholars and masters. Mountain settings have other, more primal, symbolism for Daoists as well. They embody the perfect harmony of male *Yang* and female *Yin*. Deep within mountain caves spiritual seekers could contact the eternal feminine energies.

Popular pilgrimage has generally revolved around visits to the mountain temples rather than around extended spiritual retreat. A deity called generically the Old Man of the Mountain, often depicted with his pet tiger, appears in many temples all over Asia, including Buddhist sites, making a symbolic pilgrimage possible even for those who cannot manage the actual journey. Today, various organizations arrange pilgrimage tours to any of several dozen sacred sites in the People's Republic and in Taiwan.

Do **acupuncture and acupressure** have any Daoist connections?

Neither acupuncture nor acupressure is a specifically religious practice. They are associated with healing, but both draw on ancient Chinese principles that have found their way to the center of Daoist teaching. Illness indicates a lack of *qi,* the vital force, which courses through the body along an intricate system of meridians. Blockage of vital energy causes an imbalance of *Yin* and *Yang*. Traditional Daoist-influenced maps of the body associate particular nodes with specific symptoms and internal organs. The whole system is based on a carefully observed network of correspondences. Not only is every part of the human body connected to every other part and to the spirit, but the human microcosm parallels in every detail the macrocosm of the universe. Proper placement of acupuncture needles, or appropriate application of pressure, to the malfunctioning energy juncture along any of the meridians seeks to restore the flow and balance, and hence promotes the rise of vital energies that are the essence of health and well-being.

Is **music** important in Daoist and CCT ritual? What about **dance**?

Music has been an essential ingredient in virtually all indigenous Chinese religious ritual for millennia. Students of Daoist masters are expected to begin their formal training by becoming accomplished in the use of a full range of string, wind, and percussion instruments. These ancient devices include not only the mysterious booming gongs and bowed or plucked strings many readers may already associate with Asian music, but the less well-known woodwinds whose high reedy voices produce an almost eerie effect. Daoist ritual music has been related to imperial court music and, somewhat more recently, Chinese opera. Ritual music aims at stirring feelings uniquely appropriate to the occasion. In these last several respects, Daoist ritual music has much in common with the music that is an essential ingredient in many Shinto ceremonies in Japan. Two percussion instruments used to keep time for chanting and recitation of scripture are virtually identical to those used for the same purpose in Buddhist ritual all over Asia. Large-scale chanting on especially solemn occasions is accompanied by an ensemble of four or more instruments of various types. Percussion instruments along with other wind and string instruments back up the lead played on oboe-like woodwinds, lutes, and bowed strings. When a single master recites a sacred text, a solo instrument is generally the only accompaniment.

Liturgical dance is just as important as music. During the festival of Cosmic Renewal, for example, the principal ritual specialist performs a dance of shamanic origin called the Steps of Yu. The dancer traces the outline of the Big Dipper to commune with the god of the Pole Star. He ascends symbolically into the heavens to visit the Three Pure Ones. Some dances engage the assembled community of worshippers, as when all gathered celebrate the new light by circumambulating the altar. Another dance functions as an offertory procession in which worshippers bring offerings to the ritual leaders who in turn present them to the gods.

What is the **connection** between **Daoism** and the **martial arts**?

Early each morning, nearly everywhere in China, people gather in public places both large and small to practice a slow graceful routine of physical movements called *tai ji chuan*. People of all ages can engage in this activity. Though it is not strenuous the way higher-speed exercises can be, *tai ji* (also commonly spelled *t'ai chi*) nevertheless puts noticeable demands on an astonishingly wide range of muscles all over the body. The idea is not simple physical toning, however, even though that is an obvious benefit. Its purpose is to maintain or restore one's overall sense of health and well-being through relaxed concentration. Proper practice relieves

A woman practices tai ji, a form of martial arts designed to enhance health and well-being. It also has physical benefits and improves one's mental concentration.

349

blockages of vital energy and returns the whole person to balance and harmony both physically and spiritually. *Tai ji* routines and styles are varied, with three methods called Chen, Wu, and Yang most common nowadays.

Many of the underlying principles in the practice are of Daoist origin and remain a regular part of the regimen in many Daoist monasteries. But it seems more reasonable on the whole to identify *tai ji* as a more generically Chinese phenomenon, since for centuries non-Daoists have made use of it with no apparent direct connection with Daoist beliefs. As for its relationship to actual martial arts, *tai ji* movement is based on the notion that nonaggressiveness, what is called "being weak like water," is ultimately more effective than trying to overwhelm one's opponent with brute force. Hence, for example, the Japanese term *ju-do* derives from a Chinese term (*rou dao*) that means "the way of yielding."

Are there any other important Daoist **ritual settings apart from public temple** and private **home**?

Perhaps the most common Daoist sacred space is the spectacular yet temporary structure unobtrusively called an altar (*tan*). Usually set up in large open fields or vacant lots, multilevel facades made of bamboo and covered with colorfully decorated paper simulate grand architectural spaces. These altars are the scene of the major festivals (*jiao*) that extend over several days. They enshrine such popular deities as the Jade Emperor and Zhang Dao Ling. Afterwards, the altars are taken down and the decorations burned. Several other ritual venues have been important as well, though not all intended for larger gatherings. Organizations within the various sectarian movements that have come and gone throughout the history of Daoism have typically practiced their own unique and often esoteric rituals. Always preceded by elaborate purification, these specialized rituals could take place either in natural settings, such as remote mountain retreats, or in enclosed meditative venues called "purity chambers." There initiates would closet themselves for lengthy periods of disciplined mental focusing.

How do Daoism and CCT commemorate **death and mourning** ritually?

Specific rites are designed for those approaching death, for burial day and for subsequent memorials. For the elderly and terminally ill, ceremonies can include rituals related to aging and specific illnesses. Prayers for longevity might include, for example, recitation from the scripture called The Northern Dipper's Extension of Life. Traditional funerals conducted under Daoist auspices can be very elaborate. At many funerals, a central feature is the recitation of scripture often performed, curiously, by Buddhist monks or nuns. Many Chinese, both in China and in places like Malaysia where there are sizable Chinese communities, still choose to bury their dead in distinctive graves. A horseshoe-shaped stone or concrete enclosure is set into a gentle slope with the open side to the south and the arms of the "horseshoe" inclining

Traditional Chinese grave site with horseshoe shape sloping and opening toward the south, and memorial spirit tablet over the grave, near Malacca, Malaysia.

toward the south. Following the principles of *feng shui,* the enclosure helps to contain the maximum positive *qi* while allowing necessary drainage. Burial ceremonies typically conclude with placing a memorial or name tablet atop the coffin during final prayers. The coffin is then buried, head to the south, within the semicircular enclosure. Family members take the tablet home for installation on the domestic altar.

Weekly rituals held from the seventh to the forty-ninth day after death may be even more complex than that of the actual burial. Salvation rituals are especially important in cases of violent or premature death. In order to liberate such unfortunate souls, a ritual of "crossing over" is designed to shatter the very portals of the underworld. The so-called Ghost Festival, held either at the end of a Cosmic Renewal or on the fifteenth day of the seventh month, placates the "hungry spirits" with often elaborate offerings and animal sacrifice presided over by seven officiants. For those who died before being able to marry, posthumous "spirit marriages" engage a living proxy to marry the deceased person symbolically, while allowing the proxy to proceed with his or her marriage plans in due course.

What is **ancestor veneration** and what is its connection with Daoism or CCT?

Concern over maintaining the integrity of one's connections with family lineage is one of the hallmarks of Chinese religious and social life. Members of each family line— male descendants from a shared ancestor, with wives attached to their husband's line—

351

acknowledge both the continued spiritual presence and the sacredness of their forebears. Their reasons are many: expression of grief, assistance of the deceased in his or her struggles beyond the grave, the desire for blessings, feeling a sense of family cohesiveness, and showing continued affection for the dead. Long after the funeral and an extended period of official mourning, families pay homage to the dead both at the cemetery and at the ancestral shrine in the home. There, on the altar table, the family preserves a set of tablets, each with the name of one deceased relative inscribed on it. In very wealthy families of times past the oldest son would dedicate his life to looking after the proper performance of the rites, foregoing virtually all other activities.

For most families today, ongoing activities include chiefly the regular visits to the cemetery, annual refurbishment of the grave for the feast called "Clear and Bright" (*ching ming*), and daily prayers at the home shrine. At home, family members make the same kinds of symbolic offerings to the ancestors as to the deities enshrined on the domestic altar. Very wealthy families have often built special ancestral temples as major monuments to the spiritual power of the dead. Few if any of these practices or specific concerns are uniquely Daoist. It is all part of the broadly Chinese religious patrimony, with some elements perhaps more closely linked to CCT than to any specific major tradition.

CONFUCIANISM, THE LITERATI, AND CHINESE IMPERIAL TRADITIONS

HISTORY AND SOURCES

Who was Confucius and what do we know about his life?

According to traditional accounts, Confucius was born around 551 B.C.E. and died in 479 B.C.E., making him an almost exact contemporary of the Buddha. The name by which he is most commonly known, Confucius, is a Latinized form of Kong Fu Zi, Venerable Master Kong. According to tradition, his mother, Yan Zheng Zai, had prayed on Mount Ni that she would have a child. Confucius' father, Shu Liang He, died when the child was three years old, and his mother raised him under difficult circumstances. At nineteen, Confucius married and had a son and a daughter. His marriage, which was not very happy, would end with the death of his wife, and his son died during Confucius' life.

At twenty-two, he began the first of several jobs for the state of Lu. At twenty-six (some say thirty-three), Confucius went to the Zhou dynasty's imperial capital of Lu to study royal ceremony and seek a government position. There he is said to have met the aged Lao Zi. Traditional accounts of that meeting (with a decidedly Daoist slant) report that Lao Zi took Confucius to task for wasting effort on formal study and reliance on ethical absolutes. He would do far better to observe how nature accomplishes all good things without contrivance, effortlessly. Still Confucius pursued his effortful path. He spent many years teaching privately and sought to win converts to his ethical and political views. At about fifty, he won a minor governmental post. But he failed to gain the public recognition he craved. Hoping to find a willing political patron, he went into a thirteen-year self-imposed exile, wandering in and out of nine provinces. Confucius returned home at the age of sixty-eight, there to spend his last five years studying and editing the Classics. The Master had a passion for fostering the kind of order in society that he felt sure could offer genuine happiness. He sought to

Confucius in stone, Tokyo Confucius temple.

articulate a view of the individual who could contribute to society through self-mastery and personal responsibility.

How did **tradition treat Confucius** after he was gone?

Very soon after after his death, the followers of Confucius initiated what would become a centuries-long process of elevating their teacher above the ranks of ordinary people. They revered him as a special ancestral figure, the pinnacle of wisdom. They built a temple in his honor in Qufu in 478 B.C.E. and, not long after that, began to enshrine statues and paintings of the Teacher and his major disciples there. Official imperial exaltation of Confucius did not begin until nearly five centuries after his death. After Han emperor Ping proclaimed Confucius the "Exalted Mt. Ni Duke of Highest Perfection" in the year 1 C.E., a dozen other sovereigns followed, bestowing similar accolades until at least the sixteenth century. In keeping with the hierarchy of royal titles, the emperors decreed that Confucius would be known by such titles as Duke, First Teacher, First Sage, High King of Learning, and Ultimate Sage. Around 1530 C.E., emperors stopped using the language of royalty and switched to a set of titles designed to reflect wisdom rather than temporal power. As early as the mid-fifth century C.E., the imperial authority dedicated a temple to Confucius, and within a century or two decreed state-sponsored offerings in the Master's honor. Though Confucians have never considered Confucius divine, he has clearly ranked at the very zenith of human perfection.

What is **Chinese Imperial Tradition** (CIT) and what are its **historical roots**?

Long before the time of Confucius, a system of beliefs and practices had developed around the role of the emperor in cosmic affairs. The Chinese had come to regard the emperor as the Son of Heaven. He bore the awesome responsibility of securing the welfare of all his subjects by discerning and executing faithfully the Will (or Mandate) of Heaven. Though the emperor was called Son of Heaven, he was not considered a deity. He was rather one who had the ultimate sanction for exercising authority on Earth, so long as he maintained contact with the heavenly mandate. Whenever a ruler failed to see that his people enjoyed universal justice, the people could justifiably conclude that Heaven's mandate had passed to a more worthy leader. Revolution was the solution. Chinese Imperial Tradition had its pantheon of deities arranged in several hierarchical levels, so that the earthly royal administration appeared to mirror the heavenly. CIT did not revolve around a sacred scripture, nor did it have a separate "ecclesiastical" structure or ordained priesthood. It did, however, have its own equivalent of religious doctrine, elaborate rituals comparable in form and content to those of many major religious traditions, and a hierarchical organization complete with ritual specialists. CIT is an integral part of the religious history of China, since it formed the broad backdrop against which nearly the whole of that history has been played out.

What is **Confucianism** and who were the **Literati**?

"Confucianism" refers to the system of social, ethical, and religious beliefs and practices associated with Confucius. The term does not imply the worship of Confucius as a supreme or central deity, but it does acknowledge his foundational and pivotal role in the cultivation of beliefs and practices that have remained important in many Asian societies for centuries. Some scholars suggest that we replace "Confucianism" with "Literati Tradition" to indicate that the complex of beliefs and practices now generally attributed to Confucius is actually part of a broader cultural phenomenon. "Literati" (the Latin for "the lettered, educated") is a name coined by non-Chinese scholars to describe the cultural elite most influential in promoting and preserving the Chinese imperial system. The Literati were the highly educated, professionally specialized bureaucrats who maintained the far-flung governmental structures of the empire. They also functioned as the ritual specialists in the many religious ceremonies performed under imperial auspices for sponsorship.

How have **Confucianism** and **Literati** traditions **intersected**?

Confucius was one of the Literati, but he and the movement that bears his name have also had a life of their own. The Literati were the social class most responsible for maintaining all the mechanisms of the imperial administration. One of their chief tools was an elaborate system of training that culminated in "civil service" examinations (the grandfather of all civil service systems) and the awarding of degrees. When the imperial examination system was abolished in 1905 in favor of more modern educational methods, the Literati began to disappear as a social class. In 1911, the last emperor was deposed, ending three millennia of Chinese imperial rule. But Confucius did not die with the Literati and the Empire, for over the centuries he had become an integral part of Chinese culture. He was both a symbol of the best in Chinese tradition and a man revered religiously. There is some overlapping, therefore, among these three developments—Confucianism, the Literati tradition, and the CIT—but they are not identical. Think of them as a railway that has sometimes run along a single track and sometimes branched off into two or three parallel tracks along the same broad right-of-way. In short, all Literati were Confucians, and since CIT in general incorporated the Confucian philosophy, the Literati became the official "staff" of CIT. But not all those who consider themselves Confucians are Literati. And with the end of the empire came the end of the Literati as a cultural/religious elite.

What was **Meng Zi's role** in the development of Confucian thought?

Meng Zi (also Mencius; 371–289 B.C.E.) was a Chinese philosopher and one of the most important early Confucian thinkers. His philosophy is characterized by its idealism and the assertion that human nature is basically good. Meng Zi was born in Tsou, a small state south of Lu, the home state of Confucius. Almost nothing is known about his early life. Like Confucius, Meng Zi apparently lost his father at an early age, and was raised by his mother. Meng Zi may have studied in one of the Confucian schools established in the Lu area, perhaps the school created by Confucius's grandson Zu Ssu. Meng Zi was trained as a scholar and teacher and received instruction in the standard Confucian texts such as the Book of Odes (Shi Jing) and the Book of Documents (Shu Jing). Meng Zi's teachings are preserved in a book titled Meng Zi, a seven-chapter work of anecdotes most likely collected by his disciples. Most of the anecdotes consist of conversations between Meng Zi and his disciples or, occasionally, a ruler. His basic philosophy is an extreme idealism that views human nature as basically good and views evil as only an obfuscation of one's innate goodness. He placed great emphasis on the necessity that one try to recover his or her original goodness and, through learning, to seek what he called the "lost mind" of benevolence. Meng Zi also believed that if the government fails to maintain benevolent rule and abuses the people, then the people have a right to launch a revolution.

What were the **earliest Confucian sacred texts**?

A set of works called the Five Classics (Wu Jing) became a formal collection sometime during the Han dynasty (202 B.C.E.–220 C.E.). The Yi Jing, or Classic of Change, is a manual of divination dating from the early Zhou dynasty (c. 1030–256 B.C.E.). Based on the sixty-four hexagrams formed by combinations of the eight trigrams (described on page 323 in the chapter on Daoism), the Yi Jing assists practitioners in the interpretation of fundamental life choices. Although it was originally designed as a descriptive device, popular usage over the centuries has bestowed on the book powers of prognostication. The Classic of History (Shu Jing) assembles historical documents from as early as 600 B.C.E. to as late as 200 C.E. The Classic of Poetry (Shi Jing) is an anthology of over three hundred poems, some from as early as 800 to 600 B.C.E. Ancient tradition that Confucius himself had compiled the material from a larger collection of over three thousand pieces is probably inaccurate. But it does appear that Confucius and his disciples used the poems as sources of ethical example. Completed around 100 C.E. of material from much earlier times, the Classic of Rites (Li Ji) preserves ceremonial records that offer essential insights into ritual life. Along with the Ceremonial and Ritual (or Yi Li) and the Officials of the Zhou [dynasty] (or Zhou Li), it eventually became one of

Inside the main memorial hall of Taipei Confucius temple is the central altar dedicated to Confucius himself, with his spirit tablet behind the table holding ritual vessels and beyond the curtained arch.

three texts on "rites" known collectively as the Li Ching. Finally, the Annals of Spring and Autumn (Chun Qiu) chronicles events in Confucius' home province of Lu from 722–481 B.C.E. (called the Period of Spring and Autumn), and the tradition that Confucius edited the text seems to be accurate. Confucius may also have authored part of an extensive commentary on the Yi Jing. A now lost Classic of Music (Yue Jing) would have constituted the sixth "Classic." Confucius probably did not edit the last four classics as ancient tradition claims, though he certainly knew the material intimately.

What **other canonical texts** are especially important in **Confucian tradition**?

A second collection called the Four Books (Ssu Shu) consists of very ancient texts eventually brought together during the Song dynasty (960–1279 C.E.). Most famous of the four is a work commonly called the Analects (Lun Yu), a compilation of Confucius' sayings and dialogues edited by second-generation disciples around 400 B.C.E. The Great Learning (Da Xue) is a chapter excerpted from the Classic of Rites, singled out now as a separate book because of its centrality to Confucian thought. Dating to about 350 B.C.E., this work is probably the single most important statement of Confucian views on the cultivation of the ideal human being, or "superior person," essential to a harmonious society. Another excerpt from the Classic of Rites is now regarded as a separate book called the Doctrine of the Mean (Zhong Yong), traditionally attributed to Confucius' grandson Zu Ssu. Its theme is the harmonious development of human nature by means of right action and the principle of reciprocity as manifest in the five

357

fundamental relationships. Finally the Meng Zi includes the largely ethical and political teachings of Meng Zi (c. 372–289 B.C.E.), commonly known as Mencius. He was one of the foundational figures in the interpretation of the classic Literati themes expounded by Confucius. The book's seven sections emphasize the need for vigilance in cultivating virtue with the ultimate goal of living in harmony with the Will (or Mandate) of Heaven. By about 1200 C.E., the complete Literati "canon" of texts included not only the Five Classics and the Four Books, but four other works considered to contain the essentials of Confucian and Literati views on all things under heaven.

Excerpts from Book II of the Analects

1. The Master said, "He who exercises government by means of his virtue may be compared to the north polar star, which keeps its place and all the stars turn toward it."

3. The Master said, "If the people be led by the laws, and uniformity sought to be given them by punishments, they will try to avoid the punishment, but they have no sense of shame. If they be led by virtue, and uniformity sought to be given them by the rules of propriety, they will have the sense of shame, and moreover will become good."

4. The Master said, "At fifteen, I had my mind bent on learning. At thirty, I stood firm. At forty, I had no doubts. At fifty, I knew the decrees of Heaven. At sixty, my ear was an obedient organ for the reception of truth. At seventy, I could follow what my heart desired, without transgressing what was right."

5. Mang-I [Tzu] asked what filial piety was. The Master said, "It is not being disobedient."

   Soon after, as Fan Ch'ih was driving him, the Master told him, saying, "Mang-I asked me what filial piety was, and I answered him: 'Not being disobedient.'"

   Fan Ch'ih said, "What did you mean?"

   The Master replied, "That parents, when alive, should be served according to propriety; that, when dead, they should be buried according to propriety; and that they should be sacrificed to according to propriety."

10. The Master said, "See what a man does. Mark his motives. Examine in what things he rests. How can a man conceal his character?"

20. Chi K'ang [Tzu] asked how to cause the people to reverence their ruler, to be faithful to him, and to go on to nerve themselves to virtue. The Master said, "Let him preside over them with gravity—then they will reverence to him. Let him be filial and kind to all—then they will be faithful to him. Let him advance the good and teach the incompetent—then they will eagerly seek to be virtuous."

Who was **Wang Bi** and what was the **Mysterious Learning**?

Wang Bi (226–249 C.E.) and his patron, Ho Yen, are credited with founding the movement known in the West as "Neo-Daoism." This name is misleading, however, since the movement grew principally out of Confucianism. It began with studies of the Confucian classic the Yi Jing, was enthusiastically discussed with reference to the Daoist Dao De Jing and Zhuang Zi in the later third century, and in the fourth century merged into Mahayana Buddhism. The movement is probably most accurately known by its Chinese name: *xuan xue* (mysterious learning).

Wang has been accused of trying to interpret the Yi Jing in Daoist terms and of praising Confucius as the supreme Daoist because he refrained from saying anything about the ineffable Dao. The truth is that Wang rejected labels such as Confucian and Daoist, and instead strove to unearth the ultimate truths concealed in each. During the waning years of the Han dynasty (207 B.C.E.–220 C.E.), various thinkers, notably the great Wang Chung (c. 27–100 C.E.), had become disillusioned with standard Confucian metaphysics, which had emphasized elaborate systems of correspondences between Heaven, Earth, and Man—cycles of the so-called Five Elements—and attempts to predict the future based on these. The desire to understand the basic principles of the universe was not lost, nor were the basic ideas entirely rejected, but the simplistic excesses—the teleology and the easy belief that Heaven was regular, purposeful, and concerned with humankind—were shaved away.

At the same time, the so-called "New Text" versions of the Confucian classics lost their standing and were replaced by versions of the texts purporting to be older. These "Old Texts" did not fit neatly into vast cosmological systems and left a cosmological void in Confucian thought. By the end of the Han, the great pattern of the universe had seemingly dissolved into chaos. In the third century, *xuan xue* emerged to fill this metaphysical vacuum. *Xuan xue* is predicated on the belief that the infinite phenomena of this universe are random, transitory, and without any meaningful pattern. Yet they all must, it was reasoned, be generated by one single, eternal verity. That was the original nothingness (*ben wu*), or nonbeing (*wu*), the origin of all being.

Did **Confucian tradition** ever come into **conflict** with the wishes of an **emperor**?

In 213 B.C.E., Emperor Qin Shi Huang Di accepted the recommendation of his prime minister, Li Si, that all books—except the history books about Qin—be burned. Li made this recommendation to strengthen Qin's authority and to give him greater control over the scholarly class. All the books of lyrics and the writings of the various schools of thought were to be brought to governors of prefectures for burning; those who had these books and would not burn them within thirty days were to have their faces branded, then be sent to labor for four years on the Great Wall. Those who dared to talk about these books were to be executed. Those who quoted the past to criticize the present were to be killed together with their entire families. Those who knew of and did not report violations were to suffer the same punishment. The only books that were not to be burned (apart from histories of Qin) were books on medicine, divination, and tree planting.

During the next year, 212 B.C.E., some Confucian scholars and magicians talked among themselves, accusing the emperor of being power hungry, prone to kill and punish, and neglectful of intellectuals. When Qin Shi Huang Di learned of their dissent, he ordered a thorough investigation, during which the scholars blamed each other, rather than admitting to the criticisms. Finally, it was discovered that more than 460 scholars were involved. Qin Shi Huang Di ordered them all buried alive in the capital.

Pavilion of the Absolute built during Tang dynasty.

How was the **Tang Dynasty important** in the history of **Confucianism/CIT**?

The Tang (617–907 C.E.) was the sixth-to-last Chinese dynasty. It is well known because the period saw great achievements in government and business as well as in letters and the arts. Considered a golden age of Chinese civilization, the Tang was also an age of great expansion. At its height, the empire stretched from Turkmenistan in the west to Korea (which was a vassal state) in the east, and from Manchuria to northern India. One historian called the Tang "the consummate Chinese dynasty ... formidable, influential, and innovative." One of the Tang's innovations was the balance of administrative power. Government was separated into three main branches: the Imperial Secretariat (which organized the emperor's directives into policies), the Imperial Chancellery (which reviewed the policies and monitored the bureaucracy), and the Department of States and Affairs (which carried out the policies through the administration of six ministries). One of the most forward-thinking developments of the Tang dynasty was the growth of a civil service. Candidates for public service were trained in the Confucian principles before they took an examination that would qualify them for official duty.

What is **Neo-Confucianism**?

During the Song dynasty (960–1279 C.E.), Confucian tradition underwent a kind of renaissance. Buddhism and Daoism had both developed into powerful influences at all levels of Chinese life and culture. A host of talented Confucian scholars reinterpreted their tradition in light of, and in "dialogue" with, Buddhist and Daoist concepts. Three tenth- and eleventh-century scholars pioneered what has come to be known in China as "Learning of Principle" (*li xue*) and beyond Asia as Neo-Confucianism. Sun Fu (922–1057), Shi Qia (1005–1045) and Hu Yuan (933–1059) transformed and revitalized the Confucian curriculum, thus paving the way for later teachers in their movement. Zhou Dun Yi (1017–1073) continued the dramatic changes by developing *li* as a spiritual or metaphysical principle rather than as simply a term for propriety in relationships and ritual. He and his successors expanded Confucian teaching into a full-scale cosmological system. Zhu Xi (1130–1200) is the "Thomas Aquinas" of the school in the sense that he synthesized the teachings of his predecessors into his own carefully coordinated system. Zhu Xi became a sort of lightning rod for subsequent generations of scholars, all of whom had to account for his pioneering thought one way or another.

Did **Confucian tradition spread** beyond China?

Confucian themes pervade the cultures of both Korea and Japan. Temples dedicated to Confucius have never been nearly as numerous in either country as Buddhist temples or Shinto shrines, for example, and today very few active ones remain. But the influence of the Master is still discernible everywhere. Much of that influence is due to a long history of cultural and diplomatic relations between China and Korea. As early as the seventh century, Korean rulers welcomed Confucian thought as a master plan for political administration. Under the Koryo dynasty (918–1392 C.E.), Confucianism took its place alongside divination and Buddhism as the third in a triad of essential traditional teachings. Korean Confucianism reached its zenith during the long-lived Yi dynasty (1392–1910). There was a time, Koreans occasionally point out, when even the Chinese confessed that their Korean neighbors had outdone them in devotion to Confucius. In Seoul, a Confucian university called Sungkyunkwan remains an important symbol of the tradition's impact on Korea. Confucian tradition came to Japan via Korea around 400 C.E., a century and a half before Buddhism. Early Confucian scholars brought Chinese ideas to the Japanese imperial court, diffusing concepts that would go on to become an integral part of Japanese culture. Today the once-elegant Confucian temple in downtown Tokyo has few visitors and is badly in need of repair. But Confucian ideals of family and social relationships are still part of the cultural air the Japanese people breathe.

Has Confucianism ever been intimately **identified with** specific political **regimes**?

Confucian teaching offers a great deal of reflection on the nature of an orderly society and methods of governing. It is therefore not surprising that a number of political regimes have chosen the Confucian system as their official ideology. Emperor Wu Di (r. 140–87 B.C.E.) of the Han dynasty (202 B.C.E.–220 C.E.) was the first to do so, paving the way for a long and complex association between Confucian teaching and Chinese government. In Korea, Confucianism became the official religion of Korea by decree of the Yi (1392–1910) dynasty in 1392, to Buddhism's detriment. Leaders condemned

Buddhism's view of this world as illusory and argued for the more humanistic approach of Confucian tradition. Perhaps the most far-reaching result was that education toppled from its elite pedestal and became available to a wide public. Confucianism took somewhat longer to forge its links to the Japanese imperial government. During the Tokugawa period (1600–1868), after the capital had moved to Tokyo, Confucian tradition enjoyed its closest association with Japanese imperial rule. Particularly in the realm of international relations, the legacy of Confucian political thought stood out. Confucians played an important role in the Meiji Restoration of 1868, which involved a restructuring of imperial administration. As the Japanese grew to regard Confucianism as an unwelcome import, the tradition's official influence in governmental circles diminished steadily.

What was especially important about the **Ming dynasty**?

The focus on Chinese culture that was the hallmark of the Ming dynasty (1368–1644 C.E.) was both its strength and its weakness. After the foreign Mongols (whose dynasty had been established by Kublai Khan in 1260) were overthrown as rulers of China in 1368, the Ming emperors returned their—and their subjects'—attention to those things that are distinctively Chinese. The focus on Chinese culture produced a brilliant flowering in the arts, as evidenced by the name "Ming" itself—meaning "bright" or "brilliant." It was architects working during this period who produced the splendor of Beijing's Forbidden City. And though the Ming rulers promoted this artistic renaissance and reinstated Confucianism and the program of civil service suspended by the Mongols, the rulers' myopia prevented them from seeing the threat of the nomadic Manchu people. In 1644, the Manchus invaded from the north and conquered China, setting up the last dynastic period in Chinese history, which lasted until 1912.

What is the **Forbidden City** and why is it important?

A sprawling complex of over half a mile square in the heart of Beijing has been known for centuries as the Forbidden City. Some fourteen hundred royal rooms, all in single-story buildings, cover one hundred and eighty acres. Yong Le (1403–24 C.E.), third emperor of the Ming dynasty (1368–1644), founded the Forbidden City as his seat of government when he moved his capital from Nanjing to Beijing. From this heart of imperial Beijing radiates a network of sacred sites toward the four directions. Aligned along the City's main north-south axis are the principal residential and ritual structures, the palaces of the inner court to the north and the halls of public ceremony forming the outer court further south. To the east and west are the dozens of subordinate residential and administrative buildings. In a massive plaza before the southernmost ritual space, the Hall of Supreme Harmony, an artificial river runs east to west. Five small bridges, symbolizing the five Confucian virtues, span it. In the various halls along the main axis all the great rituals celebrating the empire took place. In overall symbolism, the Forbidden City reproduced on Earth the court from which the Heavenly emperor, Shang Di,

A decorative and symbolic river, crossed by five bridges representing the main Confucian virtues, runs east to west in the courtyard before the Hall of Supreme Harmony in Beijing's Forbidden City.

ruled the universe. Beijing was the last of a series of walled royal capitals. Beginning as far back as 1700 B.C.E., cities such as Anyang, Changan, and Hangzhou all had their sacred centers. Beijing saw the abdication of its last emperor in 1912.

What is the historical and religious significance of **Tian An Men Square**?

In June of 1989, media coverage of the so-called Tian An Men Square massacre—in which many (mostly young) pro-democracy protestors were killed by army forces—brought world prominence to one of China's most important public spaces. The huge plaza stands directly south of the Forbidden City and is named after the City's massive southern outer gate, the Gate of Heavenly Peace (Tian An Men, literally "Heaven Peace Gate"). In a matter of days the space had become a globally recognized symbol for a younger China's struggle for democracy. But Tian An Men Square had been a powerful symbol for the Chinese people for some years before 1989. Early revolutionary publications spoke of the place as "the people's guiding star," the emblem of the new China.

Situated just south of the ancient seat of empire, the square was created as a clear revolutionary response to imperial repression. The open "people's" square was an obvious counterpoint to the exclusivity and mystery of the Forbidden City. Its placement to the south of the palace also meant that the square overpowered the palace by virtue of its greater access to *Yang* energy—a symbolism surely not lost on countless traditional Chinese. Mao Zedong and his communist colleagues preferred to play off their new symbols of power against the old. They could have chosen simply to destroy

363

the trappings of the decadent regime, but they might thereby have risked investing the former symbols with even greater power in the popular imagination. Better to reduce them to the status of mere museums.

In the square now stand Communist Beijing's Great Hall of the People and the Museum of Chinese History and of the Chinese Revolution, contemporary replacements for the old imperial symbolism. Between them and to the south stands the mausoleum of Chairman Mao (d. 1976), but facing north rather than south as the imperial centers had done for over three thousand years. The goal of countless "pilgrims" today, Mao's Memorial Hall functions as a quasi-religious monument, even in its rejection of China's imperial religious tradition.

How would you sum up the **history of Confucianism**?

During the first couple of centuries after the time of Confucius, two major thinkers developed the beginnings of what we now call Confucianism. Mencius, or Meng Zi (371–289 B.C.E.), and Xun Zi (d. 215 B.C.E.) codified the teachings of the Master into the foundations of a political philosophy. Emperor Qin Shi Huang Di (221–210 B.C.E.), displeased with the emerging movement, tried to suppress it by burning all the Confucian texts. Before that emperor died, in 210 B.C.E., he had succeeded in transforming feudal China into a centralized bureaucracy, but Confucianism survived. Under the new Han dynasty (206 B.C.E.–220 C.E.), the state espoused Confucianism as its core ideology. Confucianism took institutional shape as a system for training the empire's bureaucrats and officials, thereby strengthening the cultural elite known as the Literati.

For the next several centuries, Confucianism's prestige dwindled as Buddhism's star rose with increasing imperial patronage. During the Southern and Northern (265–581 C.E.), Sui (581–618), and Tang dynasties (618–906), Confucian ritual and Literati authority held on, criticizing Buddhism as an insidious import and enjoying sporadic periods of notoriety. Confucianism returned to prominence during the Song dynasty (960–1279) as a result of the Neo-Confucian revival. Scholars finalized the Canon of the Five Classics and Four Books, plus several subsidiary works. Official Neo-Confucian philosophies drifted away from traditional beliefs in a transcendent divine Heaven, emphasizing ethics and social responsibility. But a cult centered around Confucius survived. During the last of the Chinese dynasties, the Qing or Manchu (1644–1911), a generally strong

Chinese Communist leader Mao Zedong tried to eliminate Confucianism. (Hung Chung Chih / Shutterstock.com.)

Literati class continued to promote an increasingly static and dogmatic form of Confucian "orthodoxy." The last emperor fell with the arrival of Sun Yat Sen's new Republic and the Literati became functionally obsolete. Still, the leaders of the Republic held Confucius up as the epitome of Chinese culture. When Mao Zedong's Communist movement began its rise in the 1930s, the Chairman declared himself fed up with Confucius and the old ways. In response, the Republican-Nationalist movement insisted that Confucianism represented all genuinely Chinese values. As the Nationalists fled the mainland and established themselves in Taiwan under Zhang Gai Shek in 1949, overt acknowledgment of Confucian tradition went with them.

Confucianism/CIT Timeline

2637 B.C.E.	Reckoning of Chinese lunar calendar of twelve months of twenty-nine or thirty days.
1994–1525 B.C.E.	Xia dynasty instituts the principle of hereditary succession.
1525–1028 B.C.E.	Shang dynasty overthrows the last Xia tyrant.
1028–222 B.C.E.	Zhou dynasty: Yi Jing, (Classic of Change), manual of divination.
c. 800–600 B.C.E.	Shu Jing (Classic of History).
722–481 B.C.E.	Chun Qiu (Annals of Spring and Autumn).
551–479 B.C.E.	Lifetime of Kong Zi (Confucius).
400 B.C.E.	Confucius' sayings edited.
c. 372–289 B.C.E.	Meng Zi (or Mencius) and Xun Zi codified the teachings of Confucius into the foundations of a political philosophy.
221–210 B.C.E.	Emperor Qin Shi Huang Di tries to suppress Confucian texts, and transforms feudal China into centralized bureaucracy.
1 C.E.	Emperor Ping proclaims Confucius the "Exalted Mt. Ni Duke of the Highest Perfection."
c. 100 C.E.	Li Ji (Classic of Rites).
c. 140–187 C.E.	Emperor Wu Di of Han dynasty makes Confucian system his official ideology.
195 C.E.	Early Imperial sacrifice at Confucius' tomb.
c. 206–221 C.E.	Han dynasty; Confucianism official state philosophy.
220–280 C.E.	Three Kingdoms period: Wei (220–266); Shu Han (221–263); Wu (222–280).
c. 400 C.E.	Confucianism is introduced to Japan from Korea.
710–784 C.E.	Confucianism introduced to Japan in first permanent Japanese capital at Nara.
918–1392 C.E.	Confucianism important during Koryo dynasty in Korea.
c. 960–1279 C.E.	Song dynasty; Neo-Confucian revival; Canon of the Five Classics and Four Books finalized by scholars.
1033–1107 C.E.	Cheng Yi, his brother Cheng Hao (1032–1085), and Zhu Xi (1130–1200), establish "Cheng Zhu School," the School of Principle (li xue).
1392–1910 C.E.	During Yi dynasty, Korean Confucianism reaches its zenith.
1403–1424 C.E.	Yong Le, third emperor of Ming dynasty (1368–1644), founds the Forbidden City in Beijing.
1472–1529 C.E.	Life of Wang Yang Ming, leader of School of Mind (xin xie).

1516–1555 C.E.	Yang Jishang, Confucian Literati; dies as a martyr.
1530 C.E.	CIT hierarchical structure is replaced with titles.
1552–1610 C.E.	Matteo Ricci, Jesuit missionary to China.
1600–1868 C.E.	Confucianism gains influence in the Japanese Imperial government during Tokugawa period.
1622–1685 C.E.	Yamaga Soko, Japanese Confucian scholar and military theorist, originator of the way of the warrior, *bushi-do*.
1852–1932 C.E.	Liao Ping, who considers himself Confucius' prophet.
1868–1945 C.E.	Confucians play important role in the Japanese Meiji Reform, with restoration of the emperor's divine status.
1911 C.E.	Foundation of Chinese Republic; Confucius and sages held in the highest reverence.
1912 C.E.	Abdication of the last Chinese emperor.
1948 C.E.	Maoist Revolution; destruction of Confucian institutions.
1949 C.E.	The Republican Nationalist movement (origin of Taiwanese government) insists that Confucianism represents all genuine Chinese values.

RELIGIOUS BELIEFS

Are Confucianism or CIT appropriately called **religious traditions**?

Some scholars argue that the teachings customarily identified as Confucianism constitute a system of ethics or political philosophy rather than a system of religious beliefs. Imperial ritual, on the other hand, might qualify as an authentically religious phenomenon because it pays homage to deities called Heaven and Earth. Neither, however, has a distinct "ecclesiastical" structure, official ordained priesthood, or scriptures that claim the authority of divine revelation. Nevertheless, Confucian tradition has many important features that might identify it as a religious tradition, partly because it has been historically so intertwined with the Chinese imperial cult and partly because of its strong sense of the sacred in ordinary human experience. Those features include an acknowledgment of transcendent power called the Dao, manifest in Heaven and Earth, and the long-standing reverence of Confucius as a Holy One on a par with Heaven and Earth.

Is there a **Confucian or CIT creed**?

Neither Confucianism as such nor CIT have ever formulated a specific creedal statement to which all members are expected to confess their allegiance. If asked to summarize his or her religious beliefs, a devout and well-informed Chinese man or woman of a century or two ago would likely have included a number of basic elements relating to Confucian-

What is the Mandate of Heaven?

Confucians have interpreted the concept of Mandate or Will of Heaven in various ways over the centuries. As an ingredient in Confucian political thought, the concept has functioned both as a means of legitimation of the regime in power and a justification for overthrowing an unjust regime. The notion derives from a traditional Chinese belief in an elaborate network of correspondences among all levels of existence—the heavenly, the earthly, and the human. Human beings are not the independent source of authority. They can hope for harmony only through sensitivity to the ways of Heaven above and of nature below. Order in society depends on the good faith effort of a single human being, the emperor as "Son of Heaven," to rule unselfishly by always consulting the Will of Heaven.

A theory of immanent retribution holds that there is a direct connection between natural and moral evil in the world and Heaven's displeasure with any emperor who arrogantly forgets the source of his authority. When the people prosper, one can conclude with certainty that affairs of state are in order, all as a direct result of the emperor's keeping his priorities straight. Many of the great Confucian thinkers have taught that the tradition's most consistent contribution to society has been that of fearlessly holding the ruler responsible to his people. If the one on the throne presides over an unjust regime, that person is no longer worthy of the name emperor. According to Meng Zi, for example, the people have the right to remove such a fraudulent leader. Meng Zi argued that violent overthrow of an unjust ruler was not regicide but tyrannicide. The greatest sovereign, therefore, is the one who governs only after first submitting to a higher authority.

ism and CIT. Divine Heaven rules all things through a "mandate" made known to a "Son of Heaven" called the emperor. The emperor in turn governs all earthly affairs by enacting that mandate, whose hallmark is justice and equity. It is the emperor's duty to make timely and appropriate offerings to Heaven and Earth to insure the felicitous coordination of all cosmic events for the benefit of humankind. Confucius, as one of the Sages, represents a revered tradition of practical wisdom to which a sincere emperor subscribes. All good subjects, too, will acknowledge the Sage and those of his stature and will venerate them along with their own ancestors. All of this, they might add, fits into the larger picture of the ultimate harmony represented by the balance of all things under the power of the Dao, which is manifest in Heaven and Earth.

Are there **mythic elements** in Confucian tradition or CIT?

Confucius looked to history for lessons about life. The stories he found to have the greatest educative value were those about human beings, the truly great and the mean-spirited alike, who had shaped life in the Middle Kingdom for good or ill. The high examplars were themselves people, the rulers and sages of old. Like his Indian contemporary the Buddha, Confucius preferred not to commit his time and energy to discrediting the stories of the gods and superhuman heroes of his culture. He was simply convinced that, whatever their powers and prerogatives, the subjects of China's myths could not relieve human beings of their most fundamental responsibilities. The ultimate divine favor, Confucius believed, was a climate in which people could turn their full attention to the everyday realities of family, livelihood, and the betterment of society. Still, under pressure from Daoism and Buddhism, later Confucians cloaked the birth and life of the Master in wondrous tales. A unicorn presaged Confucius' birth by presenting his mother with a tablet of announcement, a pair of dragons and five ancient men symbolizing the five directions appeared in the heavens on the day he was born, and a celestial musical ensemble provided accompaniment for his birth. CIT likewise did not revolve around mythic narratives as such. Divinely sanctioned representatives of the people under Heaven had more pressing concerns. But the emperor had the power to elevate individual heroes and gods from local to universal stature. As a result he was, ironically perhaps, China's most important myth-maker.

Do Confucians believe in **miracles**?

Some have described Confucian teaching as philosophical in content and religious in function. As such, Confucian tradition focuses on the role of humanity in the greater scheme of things. It does not deny the existence a divine realm or the power of beings who inhabit that realm. Instead it emphasizes the importance of each human being's full acceptance of his or her responsibility. About the rest we cannot know in detail. What we have to work with are the myriad small realities we confront every day. Countless wonders await anyone willing to observe carefully each detail of ordinary life. Confucius would not have approved of any approach to life that amounted to waiting for the gods to do what human beings alone are responsible for. As such, Confucian teaching is highly realistic. It does not deny the possibility of miracles, events beyond the ordinary. It merely suggests that people who are genuinely attentive to life as it unfolds already have more than enough to occupy them. Many devoutly religious people think of miracles as the ultimate cause for gratitude.

What do Confucians believe about **ultimate spiritual reality**?

Two of the most important concepts that define what Confucius and his followers thought about ultimate spiritual reality are the Dao and Heaven (*tian*). Confucian texts do not always make clear how the two differ, and at times it seems they are virtually interchangeable. In Confucian teaching, the Dao and Heaven are generally non-personal realities that are equivalent, respectively, to a primordial or eternal cosmic law (*Dao*) and the source of that law (Heaven). Early Confucian texts emphasize the immanent, rather than the transcendent, aspect of the Dao. For example, Confucius is

Main memorial hall of Taipei Confucius temple. Note the dragon columns on the porch and dragon design on the front pedestal.

reported to have observed that the Dao is very close to human beings. Dao is therefore accessible and knowable, but that does not mean the Dao is not also mysterious. Confucius did not simply deny the existence of transcendent realities. He preferred to interpret ultimate reality from the ground up, so to speak.

Many of history's great theologians have constructed their systems of thought by beginning with the existence of some divine reality and working their way down. Not Confucius. He was interested primarily in the ethical implications of traditional teachings that he had inherited. He apparently thought of Heaven as the ultimate moral authority or principle. Heaven makes its "will" known to, and through, an upright sovereign. What Heaven discloses is, in turn, the Dao. Confucius reportedly described "his" Dao as consisting of two fundamental ethical components, responsibility or loyalty (*jung*) and reciprocity (*shu*). His interpretation of Dao and Heaven is therefore quite different from the traditional Daoist interpretation. In much of Daoist thought, Dao has priority and gives rise to Heaven, which in turn manifests the "ten thousand things" that many people call creation or the universe.

What would Confucius have considered a **cause for gratitude to Heaven**?

First and foremost, propriety in all of the important human relationships. In addition, he would have been grateful for the predictable workings of nature. As essential as they both are to life, neither is a sure thing. When relationships and the cosmos are as they ought to be, these are the great wonders. As for Confucius himself, though he

369

healed no one and raised no one from the dead, he did something equally marvelous: he taught without discrimination.

Who are the **principal deities** in **CIT**?

CIT's formal recognition of members of its pantheon went through many changes over the course of more than three thousand years. Here are some of the principal features of this vast and rather fluid phenomenon. Deities and heavenly powers generally fit into a three-level system. At the top were the powers deemed most necessary to cosmic survival. Ancient tradition includes belief in a mysterious celestial power called Shang Di. Eventually the word di came to be the standard term now translated as "emperor." But Shang Di was still the "supreme emperor." Standard Chinese religious usage also referred to Tian, Heaven, as a generic term for the region in which Shang Di lived. Neither Shang Di nor Tian was a personal deity actively involved in human affairs. They were rather the generic source of all things manifest in the universe. But there was yet another power behind Shang Di and Tian. That was the Dao, whose eternal energies of Yang and Yin are manifest in the universe and made known to humanity as the Will of Heaven. Also on the top level were the royal ancestors, the spirits of earth and grain, and the Earth, sometimes referred to as "empress" to Heaven's "emperor."

A notch lower came the principal heavenly bodies, Sun and Moon, and Jupiter, whose revolutions of the sun determine the ritual calendar. Rulers of earlier dynasties, patrons of farming and silk cultivation, and the spirits of Heaven and Earth round out the second level. Confucius was once a member of the second rank, but was elevated to the first in 1907. At the third level CIT begins to overlap somewhat with Daoism and CCT, with their more specialized and local deities. Here are gathered the deities of fire, literature, war, artillery, soil, mechanical arts, the hearth, the granary, and the home threshold. Along with the patron deity of Beijing are three dragon deities associated with the city. Finally, several historical heroes fit here as well. A deity called Guan Di or Guan Gong deserves mention as a crossover figure important in more than one pantheon listing. Guan Di is known by a wide variety of names, depending on the constituency of worshippers. Many people identify him as the God of War, though the red-faced, full-bearded deity is chiefly a paragon of civic virtue. The emperor had the authority to rearrange, shrink or expand the pantheon. He could simply decree a spirit worthy of a particular rank and eventually even declare worship of that being the practice of the realm by instituting temples in his or her honor.

Do Confucians believe in **angels**? What about **devils**?

Confucius and his disciples preferred not to speculate about the existence of the countless beings which in popular belief animated the spirit world. If there is good in the world, human beings can take some of the credit. When evil gets the upper hand, human beings must acknowledge their responsibility and set about reestablishing a

Carved and painted scenes depicting the principal Confucian virtues on the roof beams of the inner gate of the Confucius temple in Taipei, Taiwan.

just order. Confucian tradition does not explicitly deny that spirits, both satisfied and malevolent, regularly pass unseen and generally undetected through the lives of ordinary people. In fact, its insistence on the centrality of ancestor veneration is a clear, if implicit, acknowledgment of the spirit world. But apart from that, the tradition emphasizes the need for human beings to focus on the more immediate facts of life. Follow the example of the virtuous, strive to establish justice every day, and build all relationships on honesty. There will always be events human beings cannot explain simply, and circumstances beyond human control. Some of them may be attributable to spirits, but the important thing is not to become distracted from the ongoing demands of the call to personal virtue and responsibility.

What is the **nature of the human person** in Confucian tradition?

Chinese tradition uses the word *xing* to describe human nature in its most fundamental form. The term combines the concepts of "life/progeny" with "heart/mind," the two basic constituents of the person. Confucius further described the fully developed person using the term *ren,* a Chinese word that combines the characters for "human being" and "two." A full person, therefore, is one who exists in society, in communication with others. Human beings are always works in progress, ever shaping themselves in pursuit of an elusive goal of perfection. *Ren,* sometimes translated as goodness, human-heartedness, or even love, is that which activates the other four of the so-called five great virtues—devotion, justice, wisdom, and propriety. Only in light of

371

ren does law function properly, as a guide rather than as a straitjacket. *Ren's* two components, *jung* (individual) and *shu* (the virtue of reciprocity) allow human beings to enact the principles known as the "mean," the ability to hold feelings in abeyance, and the "measure" by which one can express emotions in balance.

How does the notion of **Superior Person** function as a **human ideal**?

Confucian teaching describes the epitome of the ideal society as the "superior person" (*jun zi*). That means an individual who arrives at a high level of personal development through self-discipline and inquiry. The superior person values justice more highly than profit, and prefers to be quiet and serene rather than vulgar and uncongenial. Cultivating a dignified manner, the superior person nevertheless avoids arrogance. Such a person looks first to his or her personal shortcomings rather than blaming others for their lack of understanding or appreciation. It is said that the way of the superior person is a lengthy journey that begins from "right here." Five "constant virtues" characterize the superior person: self-respect, generosity, sincerity, responsibility, and openness to others. Expanding on the earlier teaching of Confucius, Meng Zi taught that fully developed human life begins with four principles. Compassion leads to true humanity, shame leads to righteousness, reverence and respect to propriety, and a sense of moral value to wisdom. Behind the notion of the superior person lies a deep-seated conviction of human potential for almost unlimited moral growth.

Is there a **distinctively Confucian ethic**?

A Confucian formulation of the universal Golden Rule at first strikes the ear as rather negative and passive: "Do not do to others what you do not want done to you." But the Confucian ethic turns out to be overwhelmingly active and positive because of its emphasis on cultivating the natural human capacity for virtue.

The Master's positive approach revolves around several key concepts. First and foremost is *li,* principle or propriety, consisting of a whole range of directives for human behavior. Much of *li* arises from the customs that embody the spirit of community. When people can rely on propriety in all relationships, as enshrined in time-honored practice, they experience assurance and freedom in their relationships. Confucius gathered a huge catalogue of social rituals, not out of antiquarian curiosity, but as a way of preserving what he considered the best of tradition. Ritual propriety is not meant to confine, but to give a sense of lightness and freedom. Without *li,* he thought, there can be no justice, no morality, for a society without propriety has no foundation in respect.

Of equal importance is the notion of *shu,* reciprocity in interpersonal relationships. Reciprocity is essential to putting *li* into action, for it governs the "five principal human relationships and the ten associated virtues." In the father–son relationship, the father must cultivate kindness, the son reverence. The elder brother must deal gently with his younger brother, who responds with respect. A mutuality of faithfulness and obedience should characterize husband–wife relationships. Let all elders be considerate of those younger, and expect deference in return. Finally, a ruler must strive to treat subjects with benevolence and benefit from their loyalty as a result.

What is the **principal Confucian virtue**?

Behind all the other virtues, what makes a good Confucian tick is "filial devotion" or *xiao*. The Chinese term is composed of "son" with "old" placed above it. Confucius taught that all other moral virtue, and indeed civilization itself, flows from filial devotion. As a bare minimum, one should do no harm to one's parents. Filial devotion culminates in doing one's family proud. Traditional texts go into great detail about how one ought to treat parents, summarizing ideal behavior in five duties: reverence always, joyful service, solicitude for ailing parents, sincere grief at a parent's death, and proper ritual veneration thereafter. Lack of filial devotion was a most serious offense. Individuals could be put to death for cursing their elders. Filial devotion was the very bedrock of social order, a fundamental acknowledgment of authority on the family level, without which there could be no exercise of authority in society at large. Chinese tradition regards society as built on the family. Sons and daughters do not "go out" into the world as they reach maturity. Rather than "leaving the nest," they invest themselves in the family, knowing that their children will do the same. Only in that way can the foundations of society as a whole remain firm.

What does Confucian tradition teach about the **use of violent means**?

Confucius grew up in a time of feudal disintegration during which the Zhou dynasty's imperial capital, Lo Yang, functioned chiefly as a religious center. He shared the fundamental Daoist teaching that natural harmony based on the perfect blend of Yin and Yang was the ideal to be cultivated. His personal experience of political unrest, however, made his view of the human exercise of power somewhat less idealistic than the classic Daoist teaching.

In Confucius' view, soldiers comprised a high ranking social class—the Superior Person was originally described as a member of the military class, and education included training in warfare. Indeed, he insisted that no one should be allowed to carry weapons without seven years of education in agriculture, ethics, and military tactics. Confucius did not disapprove of military campaigns in principle, but he regarded war as a solution of last resort. He taught that since the emperor's ability to communicate with Heaven was essential to good order, loss of the Mandate of Heaven was grounds for violent overthrow of an incompetent ruler.

Later Confucian thinkers held various views on the use of violence. Mo Zi (480–390 B.C.E.) was schooled in Confucian teaching but took more utilitarian approach: He generally opposed war but not to the point of pacifism, and emphasized strong defense. Meng Zi (372–298 B.C.E.) reaffirmed Confucian emphasis on virtue as curb to violence. The so-called Legalists (fourth century B.C.E.) reacted to earlier trends toward pacifism by glorifying the role of militarism and emphasized conquest as the sole guarantee for maintaining political power.

What is meant by the term "**rectification of names**"?

If Confucius were here today he would surely be aghast at the way inflated language seems to have taken over ordinary conversation. "I was so tired I was literally dead on my feet." No, you weren't, he might say. Drop the "literally" and your expression will have far more impact, even though your surrounding culture insists that more is better. He would be amazed to hear restaurant staff introduce themselves as "your food and beverage counselor" or hear store cashiers and stockers identified as "sales associates" and "inventory specialists." But Confucius would worry less about such trivial matters than about the very same deep social issues he agonized over in his own time. When a man fails to show respect to his parents, do not call him a son. If he fails to guide his children, he is unworthy to be called a father. If a woman does not attend to her family faithfully, one can hardly call her a wife or mother. If a man is unfaithful to his wife, do not call him a husband. Of greatest political import is his insistence that no unjust ruler deserves the name "emperor."

Beneath this apparently nit-picking criticism Confucius was getting at a profound truth: Over the long haul, imprecise speech allows injustice to go unnoticed because it can be hidden behind acceptable names. Euphemism can erode one's sense of right and wrong and desensitize a person to violence. Eventually we persuade ourselves that "misspeaking" is not a lie, or that stealing is nothing more than the redistribution of wealth. Confucius believed that language matters because it not only reflects, but can even change, the way we think.

Confucius envisioned a society shaped by ethical education and the moral example of just rulers, and he saw recourse to military institutions as a symptom of a society in decline.

What is the basic Confucian concept of **appropriate moral leadership**?

Confucius believed that order was essential for bringing out the best in human beings. He and his disciples rejected the early Daoist notions that all things work for the best if only people learn the ways of nature and that there is no need for government or military force or oppressive laws. In Confucius' view government was essential, and that almost always required bureaucratic structures. But he believed the external trappings had to be supported by a foundation of example rather than coercion. No one can bring about the good society by force of will. One can only foster appropriate government by creating an environment of propriety, reciprocity, and good music—yes, good music. Law, he believed, can erode moral values because people often prefer to act a certain way merely to escape punishment. The example of a great leader is preferable, for it instills a sense of healthy shame that leads people to seek improvement.

Confucius was a realist, however, and conceded that law was often a practical necessity. What he wanted for the people most of all was the sense of confidence that can grow when people feel prosperous and educated. A good leader knows how to bring out the best in his people and how to wield authority deftly. But as a concession to the vast differences among human beings, government needs levels of power—some can lead, some can support a leader, some can follow but may not understand why they ought to do so. A leader knows how to cultivate conditions conducive to the betterment of society by tapping the roots of human resources rather than waiting until the plant is fully grown and incapable of nurturance.

Is there a distinctively **Confucian interpretation of history**?

Confucius refused to think of himself as an innovator. Any individual bent on inventing his own system of thought was doomed to failure, so interdependent are we humans. His task, he believed, was what he called the "renewal of antiquity." His first step was to translate his knowledge of tradition into clearly articulated principles so that he could intelligently sort out the best of the past. Confucius discerned in the drift of history a serious problem of societal entropy—the tendency to let things unravel.

Looking back to the legendary founders of Chinese society, Confucius believed the first major problem set in when the Xia dynasty (1994–1525 B.C.E.) instituted the principle of hereditary succession. When decline in the quality of the rulers reached a disastrous low, the Shang dynasty (1525–1028 B.C.E.) overthrew the last Xia tyrant. Unfortunately, the Shang rulers retained the hereditary throne, thus virtually sealing their own eventual demise. Sure enough, the Zhou dynasty (1028–222 B.C.E.) was destined to be the instrument of renewal. By the Master's own time, the Zhou, too, showed signs of serious decay. The Master wondered what power under Heaven might again correct the course of history. Confucius was convinced that it was possible to imitate the eternally true in history, to avoid reliving all of the past by distinguishing the good from the evil in it. True authority arose out of the ability to blend the ancient with the new. And only through learning could a leader assimilate the eternally true to changing needs. Beginning with politics and ethics, Confucius set out to contribute to the renewal of antiquity.

Do **millennialism or messianism** have a place in Confucian thinking?

Confucius was far more concerned about the present and its relation to the past than about possible but distant futures. He was keenly interested in offering people hope

Do Confucians believe in an afterlife?

Confucius did not focus on life after death as though it were the ultimate standard against which to measure the success of a life on Earth. With the majority of his fellow Chinese, the Teacher shared the conviction that biological death did not signal a definitive end to life. Death did not mean annihilation and loss in some great void beyond the grave. Confucius clearly believed in some form of spiritual survival, and in the ongoing presence of those who have departed this life. Hence the importance of ancestor veneration. But like the Buddha, Confucius and his disciples chose not to speculate about possible celestial or infernal postmortem scenarios. Daoism and CCT would offer ample options in that regard. He neither denied nor affirmed any particular views. Confucius was convinced that human beings understood far too little of life here and now to waste it planning for a hereafter they understood even less. When classical Confucian sources talk about Heaven, therefore, they do not have in mind anything like a realm of eternal reward for those who die in a state of righteousness. Heaven is merely a name for the highest spiritual presence of which human beings are aware.

through the cultivation of a balanced society. Some have suggested that Confucius was very much a utopian, in that the society he sought to foster was destined to remain an unattainable ideal. In any case, Confucius did not envision any kind of inevitable cataclysm, an end of time at which the world of history would implode in a cosmic conflagration. Confucian thought has been intimately associated with a traditional Chinese reckoning of time that includes cycles of sixty years, but those cycles do not carry apocalyptic implications. There have been millennialist and messianic movements in Chinese history, but none of importance has arisen out of Confucian or Literati circles. However, some scholars detect in Confucian history elements that have a messianic tone. According to that view, Confucius himself may have fulfilled expectations of a messianic ruler nurtured as far back as the legendary Shang dynasty.

Is there such a thing as **Confucian fundamentalism**?

Confucian scholars have devised a wide range of methods for interpreting the classical sources. Many of the central concepts in Confucian thought are simply too large and subtle to interpret literally. Take the notion of the Mandate of Heaven, for example. Dynasties have come and gone frequently in China's long history, and many have interpreted dynastic decay as a sure indication that the emperor had lost his contact with Heaven's Will. That is an easy enough judgment to make in retrospect. But using the Mandate theory as a criterion for deciding whether the people are justified in bringing down this regime now is a much more complicated matter. Some interpreters have chosen to apply the criteria of the classical sources directly to current events. They have their Christian counterparts, for example, in those who have discerned portents of the Apocalypse in the world around them at various times in history. Some Confucian texts have lent themselves more readily to literal interpretation, so much so that their prescriptions have become the very fabric of life for countless Chinese who have never set foot in a Confucian temple. Those are books like the Li Ji, with its detailed descriptions of ritualized relationships across the full spectrum of human activity.

Glossary of Key Confucian Terms

Bagua—the eight trigrams symbolizing various primal elements composed of varying combinations of Yang (unbroken line) and Yin (line broken in the middle).

Dao—the "Way," unnameable source of all things, immutable eternal principle both transcendent and immanent.

Jun Zi—Superior Person, ethical ideal fostered by Confucian tradition.

Kong Fu Zi—Master Kong, latinized as Confucius.

Li—propriety as cultivated especially in Confucian tradition through scrupulous attention to detail in all relationships, as embodied in ritual.

Qi (pronounced chee)—vital energy that flows freest where Yin and Yang are in appropriate balance.

Ren—true humanity characterized by the virtue of benevolence, as cultivated especially in Confucian tradition.

Shen—celestial spirits associated with *Yang* forces, including various deities and ancestors.

Shu—reciprocity and other-mindedness such as characterize the Superior Person.

Tian—sky or Heaven, an impersonal divine presence through which mortals connect with eternal forces.

Wen—"things that beautify life," that is, the arts of peace (literature, music, dance).

Xiao—filial piety, central Confucian virtue manifest in all proper relationships.

Xin—made up of characters for "human being" (ren) and "word" (yen), meaning "good faith, genuineness."

Yang—natural principle identified as male, active, dry, warm, bright, associated with mountain peaks.

Yin—natural principle identified as female, passive, moist, cool, dark, associated with valleys and streams.

Zhen ren—the Confucian sage, rough parallel to a saint.

SIGNS AND SYMBOLS

Are there any **signs or symbols** that might **identify an individual** as a Confucian?

Confucian tradition consists far more of actions and the preservation of proper relationships than on the expression of specific doctrines. The tradition so pervades Chinese and other Asian cultures that it is like the air one breathes, rather than a distinct set of beliefs. As a result, it is virtually impossible to tell who among Chinese, Japanese, or Koreans think of themselves as Confucians. There are still some people who identify themselves as disciples of the Master, but they are relatively few in number. Since so many rituals that Chinese and other east Asians perform are common to members of various religious traditions, the fact that an individual practiced ancestor veneration, for example, offers no clues in this regard. There are, however, a number of symbols connected with daily life originally associated with Confucius that still appear in popular arts of Asia. The so-called "Four Treasures of the Literary Apartment," for example, include an ink stick, ink block, brush, and paper.

What signs or **symbols** distinguish Confucian and CIT **ritual specialists**?

Even today, leaders of Confucian rituals are typically also government officials. When they function as ritual specialists, they don the garments once worn by representatives of the imperial household and administration. As for CIT, since there is no longer any official imperial religious worship, there are no longer CIT ritual specialists. Prior to 1911, however, CIT ritualists, from the emperor on down to the humblest assistant, simply wore the garments that signified their respective bureaucratic ranks and offices. In this case, the Literati did double duty as custodians of both civil and religious ritual.

For especially important events, officials wore various garments known generically as "dragon robes," each decorated with emblems of the wearer's administrative rank. Imperial robes worn by the ruler during rituals were once festooned with an array of symbolic decorative motifs known collectively as "The Twelve Ornaments (or Symbols)." Symbolizing Heaven and its wisdom were the sun, shown with a three-legged raven inside its red disc; the blue or green moon surrounding a hare grinding the elixir of immortality with mortar and pestle; and the constellations. Images of mountains symbolized Earth and strength. Standing for all living things, the dragon symbolized resilience; the pheasant, culture and literary accomplishment. In images of bronze ritual vessels celebrants saw filial devotion, in cereal grains abundant harvest, in flame illumination, and in the water plant purity. Along with the mountains, the latter four also corresponded with the five elements. Finally, the "fu," a geometric form meaning good fortune, and the axe, referred respectively to the imperial prerogatives of judgment and punishment. When displayed together, the twelve were done in combinations of the five symbolic colors associated with the five directions. None but the emperor's ritual vestments could depict all twelve ornaments, since they constituted a symbolic summary of the whole cosmos.

Is there such a thing as **Confucian art**?

A number of Confucian Literati have been credited with some of China's finest landscape paintings. They were particularly attracted to this artistic theme and medium because both were consistent with deep-rooted Confucian values. Images of mystic mountain settings shared scroll space with equally haunting poems that reflected on human life and the grandeur of nature. These visual and literary images were sometimes autobiographical in tone, offering insight into the creator's personal spiritual convictions. Paintings often depicted solitary scholars lost in contemplation of natural beauty, meditating on moon-rise or creating calligraphy in a mountain pavilion. Here Confucian tradition crosses paths with classic Daoist views of nature and with the spontaneous and abstract landscapes painted by Chan Buddhist monks. Painting and poetry became forms of meditation for the Literati, expressions of their holistic view of the balance and harmony of nature. Literati painting is a didactic art with ethical impact, for ideally it expresses the feelings of the superior person. Confucian theory accords visual art the ability to communicate ideas too delicate or too forceful for words. The mind of the artist takes precedence over the content of the work, for the ultimate benefit of a great work is that it offers a connection with a person who represents the highest moral values. Great art can arise only out of genuine virtue.

An example of a Literati landscape, this meditative hanging scroll painting called "Pavilion in a Landscape" (dated 1757) shows the classic "mountain-water" imagery influenced by a Daoist worldview, with nature dominating and signs of human life and habitation blending in. (The Saint Louis Art Museum.)

Are there **symbolic dimensions** in CIT **sacred spaces**?

Imperial temples and altars have been highly symbolic down to the smallest detail. First, their placement in relation to each other and to the royal residence was critical. In imperial Beijing, for example, the Forbidden City stood at the center of the center of empire, which in turn was the center of the universe. Within the palace, arranged along its central north-south axis, is a succession of ceremonial halls. Beginning in the north and moving southward are the Palace of Earthly Peace, the Palace of Heavenly Brightness, the Hall of Protecting Harmony, the Hall of Middle Harmony, and the Hall of Supreme Harmony. On north-south and west-east axes stood pairs of sacred spaces balancing *Yin* and *Yang* forces. North of the Forbidden City was the Altar of Earth (*Yin*), square in shape. Its counterpart due south of that below the palace was the complex centered on the round Altar of Heaven (*Yang*) and its various related temple and other ritual buildings. West of the Forbidden City stood the Altar of the Moon (*Yin*) in its square enclosure, and to the east, the Altar of the Sun (*Yang*) in its round-edged enclosure. These four spaces are considerable distances (about two miles) from

The circular, three-tiered Altar of Heaven in the Temple of Heaven compound, Beijing.

the palace. But immediately south of the palace, on either side of the north-south axis that leads out of the Forbidden City and into today's Tian An Men Square, the Altar of Land and Grain stood to the west across from the imperial ancestral temple.

A good example of structural symbolism is the Altar of Land and Grain's division into five sections, recalling both the directions and the five elements. Different-colored earth, brought from the corners and center of the empire, filled each section: yellow in the center, black in the north, red in the south, azure or green in the east, and white in the west. That structure and its companion ancestral temple were located between the Meridian Gate, which marks the southern extremity of the Forbidden City, and Tian An Men, the Gate of Heavenly Peace, which marks the northern perimeter of the square that bears its name.

What would I see if I visited one of the surviving **CIT sacred places**?

Beijing's Temple of Heaven (*Tian Tan*) is perhaps the best example of such a site. The Chinese long ago mastered the art of creating monumental public spaces, as the Temple demonstrates admirably. From its southern gate to the northern wall the complex stretches half a mile along its main ceremonial axis. The compound covers an area larger than that of the Forbidden City about two miles to the north, and it is some four times the area of its original northern Yin counterpart, the Temple of Earth. Whereas the temple compounds devoted to the feminine Earth and moon are square in plan, those of Heaven and sun are round-shouldered at their rear perimeters and squared off (like a large U-shape) at the opposite ends where their entry gates are located. Confucian-Literati concepts of hierarchy in authority structures and in family lineage are based on a patriarchal model, and are evident in these as well as most other traditional Chinese structures.

As you enter the main southern gate of the Temple of Heaven and walk north, you come first to the Altar of Heaven. It is a square enclosure surrounding a circular terrace of three concentric tiers—round Heaven surrounded by square Earth, as in the overall plan of the site. The Altar's symbolism includes its use of nine courses of pavement on each of its three levels—nine being the maximum level of Yang energy. The posts in its surrounding railings, numbered in multiples of nine on each level, total three hundred

The Temple of Heaven, Beijing, is also set on a circular, three-tiered platform.

and sixty, recalling the totality of degrees in Heaven's circle. The circular Hall of Harvest Prayer at the northern perimeter of the compound also stands within a square enclosure. Symbolizing the firmament, the triple-roofed structure stands on two concentric circles of twelve columns apiece, reminders of the months of the year and the Chinese reckoning of twelve units of time per day. Four larger central columns inside the circle symbolize the seasons. Like the Altar, the Hall sits atop a triple-tiered circular platform. Geometric and numerical symbolism abound.

If I visited a **Confucian temple**, what would I see?

Major Confucian temples are arranged along the same general lines as traditional Buddhist and many CCT temples, all influenced by the plan of the imperial residence. Simple but elegant formality sets the Confucian temples apart from the others. Most Confucian temples greet the outside world through a main gate on the south side of the surrounding outer walls.

Here is what you would see if you visited the Confucian temple in Taipei, Taiwan, whose plan is unique by reason of local tradition. Through either the eastern or western portals, you enter a garden with a pond. The high walls recall the Master's parable comparing great teachings to unscalable ramparts that preserve the building's secrecy, so that one must work to gain entry through the door. From there you pass through doors on either side of the main gate into a forecourt that offers further opportunity to shift mental gears before approaching the heart of the temple. Local tradition has it that there the main south gate must remain closed to all but those scoring highest on imperial exams. Since no one from the region ever achieved that rank, the south gate remains closed except for special occasions. Walking northward you pass through the Gate of Rites into the main courtyard, surrounded by rooms built into the outer walls.

Immediately inside the inner gate you find yourself in one or another of the temple's study rooms.

What is the symbolism of **Dragon and Phoenix**?

One of the most important symbolic pairs is that of the dragon and the phoenix. Often depicted as though they are engaging in a heavenly ballet, they symbolize the harmonious relationship between the emperor (dragon) and empress (phoenix). The intertwined pair of celestial beings appears regularly on the interior oculus (center peak) of domes in Confucian and imperial temples especially. Dragon and phoenix also appear often on the rounded ends of roof tiles. Such symbols were not allowed as decoration on any but imperial structures. Since the emperor was considered the Son of Heaven (*Tian Zi*), you might expect various types of imagery associated with the firmament, and abstract cloud forms are among the favorites.

What is at the **heart** of the **Confucian temple**?

Looking into the courtyard you would see the main structure, the free-standing central memorial hall on a raised platform. Until the fourteenth century, most if not all Confucian temples would have had a full complement of statues of Confucius and the other major Sages. As a result of an imperial decree in 1530 (some date the change to 1382), pictures and statues of the great Teacher and his spiritual comrades were replaced by memorial "spirit-tablets" bearing the names of the sages and scholars. The main hall's (*da zheng*) central altar houses the tablets of Confucius (named "The Most Holy Former Master, the Wise Kong") and his four most important followers, Yen Hui, Zu Si, Zeng Zi and Meng Zi. Over the central altar is a panel that reads "Teach without discrimination"; in other words, accept all sincere comers as potential students. Along the right and left walls of the main hall are side altars, each bearing six tablets commemorating the twelve Sages—eleven students of Confucius and one of the founders of the medieval development called Neo-Confucianism, Zhu Xi (1130–1200 C.E.). In the rooms along the right and left sides of the main courtyard you would see several more altars on which are enshrined a hundred and fifty-four more name tablets, forty Sages and thirty-seven Scholars on the east, thirty-nine Sages and thirty-eight Scholars on the west. These major historical figures represent the cream of the Literati over many centuries. Finally, behind the main memorial hall, along the north wall of the courtyard, stands a room (the *jung zheng*) enshrining tablets of five generations of Confucius' ancestors.

Do **Confucians** mark their **sacred spaces** with any other distinctive **signs and symbols**?

Although they are usually less flamboyant in their decor than other Chinese temples, Confucian temples typically sport a variety of intriguing iconographic details. When

Roofline of the Taipei Confucius temple. Frolicking dragon and Ji Wen figures protect the holy site.

you enter the outer garden courtyard of the Taipei Confucian temple, you notice on its outer wall several traditional Chinese symbols: a pair of dragon-fish called *ji wen* (of which a total of fourteen protect the temple from fire—dragons bring rain, and the fish symbolizes water as well) and a pair of exuberant green dragons. On the north face of the garden's south wall is a large tile image of the *Qi Lin* (unicorn). Writhing dragons are the principal motif on the main hall, both on the roofline and two main front columns and around the main altar, where nine of the creatures guard the spirit tablet of the Master. A pair of carved "sky pillars" appear to protrude at either end of the main hall's central ridge beam. Some say they symbolize both Confucian ethics, which alone can support the firmament, and the chimneys in which many scholars hid their books during Qin emperor Qin Shi Huang Di's attempt to burn all the texts of the Literati. In the center of that same roof beam, a small seven-roofed pagoda may symbolize the axis of the universe, standing as it does directly over the altar dedicated to Confucius himself. In rows along the beams of the sloping eaves stand birds of prey, for according to tradition, even the fiercest raptors alighted and paused to listen when Confucius taught. Beneath the eaves of the main hall are numerous small carved figures of popular Chinese characters, such as Shou Lao, deity of longevity. Even smaller carved friezes around the upper walls of the main hall depict scenes of high virtue from popular Chinese stories. In front of the door to the Master's altar, at the base of the platform supporting the memorial hall, stands a stone carving of the dragon that symbolizes the emperor. Inside, the octagonal cupola over the main altar shows the eight trigrams arrayed around the circular symbol of Yin and Yang, the *tai ji*.

383

What is a **tao tie mask**?

Shou Lao, deity of longevity, holding the peach of immortality, is depicted here on a roof beam of the main hall of Taipei, Taiwan's main Confucius temple.

One of the most common and important visual motifs in the arts associated with Confucian and CIT ritual objects is the mask known as the "*tao tie* mask." Visit your local museum's Asian galleries and head for the cases that display the Chinese bronzes. Around the main part of the body of the object you will probably see what appear to be eyes and mouth arranged along a vertical that could very well be a nose. Look more closely and a face, like that of a large cat, will begin to emerge from the patterns of the rich design. Look again, this time examining the design on each side of the central vertical, and you may see what appear to be a pair of dragons rearing up toward each other. These mesmerizing designs have long fascinated art historians. The name *tao tie* means "ogre" or "glutton," a name given to the motif perhaps because it suggests the visage of bottomless hunger capable of devouring all in its path. This terrifying apparition probably represents a deity from the ancient Shang dynasty pantheon. Its presence on the sacred ritual vessels is a protective device to safeguard the contents of the vessel. The *tao tie* disappeared from the Chinese decorative repertoire around 1000 B.C.E., but its early prominence and striking visual power make it a superb example of deep-rooted religious symbolism.

MEMBERSHIP, COMMUNITY, DIVERSITY

Where do **Confucians live** today? Are any estimates of **numbers** available?

Compared to the hundreds of millions whose cultures and ways of thinking have been profoundly influenced by Confucian teaching, people who identify themselves exclusively as Confucians are relatively few in number—six to seven million according to some estimates. In China, the ancestral home of Confucianism, very few people today think of themselves as Confucians. Many Confucian temples survived the demise of imperial rule, and the founders of the original Chinese Republic in 1911 continued to hold Confucius and the sages in the highest reverence. As a result of the Maoist revo-

Where does academic regalia come from?

Nearly every student who graduates from high school or college makes a passing connection with Confucian tradition. Academic robes with their wide flowing sleeves are at least vaguely similar to those worn by Confucian ritual leaders even today in places like Taiwan and Korea when they celebrate the Master's birthday or honor royal ancestors. But one look at the headgear and the viewer knows instantly where the so-called "mortar board" came from. Principal participants in important Confucian rituals sport large flat rectangular boards worn with flat sides (rather than corners, as in common graduation practice now) facing the wearer's front, back, and sides. Confucian mortar boards outdid modern ones in ornamentation, with rows of tassels all along the front and back edges.

lution in 1948, however, hundreds of institutions associated with Confucian tradition were destroyed, damaged severely, or shut down. Since the Cultural Revolution, which ended with Mao's death in 1976, some of those institutions have enjoyed a revival. Countless citizens of the People's Republic of China revere Confucius but are not likely to call themselves Confucians. This is also true of Koreans and Japanese, a very small minority of whom will identify Confucian tradition as their principal ethico-religious affiliation.

Are there any contemporary **remnants of CIT**?

A full century has passed since the last emperor stepped down from the dragon throne, and CIT as an institution is little more than a fading memory. For many Chinese, CIT remains a historical curiosity. A large tourism industry has grown up around the preservation of major monuments such as the Forbidden City and the Temple of Heaven in Beijing. Chinese tourists flock to these great repositories of their ancient heritage. Mao Zedong and his political heirs considered the remnants of feudal and imperial society as reminders of a thoroughly discredited way of life. They are mere museum pieces to many, and relics of an oppressive past to others, but they remain important evidence in reconstructing the story of Chinese religion.

What **gender-related issues** have been important in Confucianism and CIT?

Confucian tradition emphasized social order, and that called for clearly delineated gender functions. Given the conviction that only a patriarchal structure could guarantee social order, what many people today call "social equality" was simply not included in the Confucian lexicon. Confucian teaching envisioned male–female relationships according to a political model. First and foremost among questions of gender are those relating to family structure and roles. But whether within the family or in soci-

The entrance gate to the Confucius Grave Yard Qufu, Shandong Province, China.

ety at large, women and younger people generally shared the expectation of dutiful obedience. Women remained in the home to serve the family, which sometimes brought as many as four generations together in one household. Widows were typically expected not to remarry. When a wife produced no son, a husband could marry one or more secondary wives in the hope of securing a male heir. A telling fact is that no women are numbered among the great sages and scholars memorialized in Confucius temples. In the imperial household, there were sometimes several empresses and many royal concubines. An empress remained out of view for the most part, participating in a few affairs of state annually. Eunuchs looked after the harem, strictly organizing the lives of all women in the imperial household.

Are there any Confucian or CIT **holy sites** (other than temples) or **cities**?

Confucian tradition spotlights a number of places associated with the lives of Confucius and other major sages and scholars. Only a year after Confucius' death the Duke of Lu dedicated a temple to him in Qufu (478 B.C.E.). Within a few years, his tomb and temple in Qufu had become widely known holy places. As early as 195 B.C.E., an imperial sacrifice at the tomb further broadened Qufu's fame as a sacred site. Confucian tradition did not elevate any one city to prominence as a center of authoritative teaching, but certain cities were home to the great Confucian universities. The most important cities were always associated with the seat of imperial government, and that changed often through Chinese history, even during the tenure of a single dynasty. Beijing has been perhaps the most important Confucian city. It was the capital uninterruptedly for nearly five hundred years, and Confucianism was highly favored and influential through virtually that whole period.

Have there been any **sub-communities** or **denominations** within Confucianism?

An early historian of Confucian tradition, Liu Xiang (77–6 B.C.E.), claimed that by his time the Confucians had divided into 103 schools of thought, each defined by its distinctive manner of interpreting the essential texts. Whether that was literally the case or not, it is clear that during the Song and later dynasties, several important schools developed within the larger phenomenon called Neo-Confucianism. The two main branches became known as the School of Principle and the School of Mind, according to their respective theoretical points of departure.

The School of Principle (*li xue*) was also called the Cheng-Zhu school, combining the first names of the men it claims as its founders, Cheng Yi (1033–1107), his brother Cheng Hao (1032–85), and the later Zhu Xi (1130–1200). The brothers Cheng developed a sophisticated theory in which "principle" (*li*) meant not the classical Confucian rites and canons of social propriety, but an unchanging universal law inherent in all nature. Zhu Xi further refined that concept of principle, defining it as the Great Ultimate from which all forces in nature emerge. In what one might call a variety of "process theology," Zhu Xi argued that the path to ethical development was "the investigation of things."

The other major branch of Neo-Confucian thinking was known as the School of Mind (*xin xue*). Wang Yang Ming (1472–1529) was one of the school's leading lights. Principle, he argued, was not merely a transcendent and inaccessible cosmic force, but was one with the human mind. He taught that one could cultivate good conduct through "reverent seriousness," a type of meditative discipline through which one could realize the unity of mind and principle.

Were any **other related schools of thought** important in understanding Confucianism?

Mo Zi (468–390 B.C.E.) started out as a Confucian but went his own way, opting for a less stratified, more egalitarian model of society. Some have characterized Mo Zi as a pragmatist because he insisted that observable improvement in the welfare of the populace was the ultimate criterion of good public policy. Confucius, he argued, put too much emphasis on ritual and filial devotion and too little on measurably advancing civilization. Mo Zi taught the importance of striving for a society united by a kind of mutual love that amounted to a form of enlightened self-interest. His school flourished for just over a century, but it offers a glimpse at one of several credible critiques of the classical Confucian approach. Another dissenting voice of Mo Zi's era were the Legalists (*fa jia*). They took Mo Zi's critique several steps further from Confucius' global confidence that the mere example of virtuous leadership could bring about a moral conversion in society. Governance, they argued, required clear and comprehensive legislation that capitalized on people's fear of punishment and hope of reward. Confucius and Mo Zi clearly had greater faith in human perfectibility and in a reservoir of good will at the heart of humankind.

How would you sum up Confucianism's historical **relationships to other traditions**?

Confucianism's most important and enduring inter-religious relations have been with Buddhism and Daoism. There have been periods during which Confucians have had more or less cordial dealings with representatives of the other two "ways" of China. But since so much has often been at stake, especially in terms of imperial patronage, Confucian scholars have frequently leveled serious criticisms at Daoist and Buddhist views. For example, Confucians have sometimes faulted Buddhism for being too otherworldly, too disconnected from the ordinary problems and needs of regular people. Confucians generally interpreted the Buddhist ideal of celibate monastic life as an abdication of filial devotion and the responsibility to perpetuate the family lineage. Daoists, on the other hand, have characteristically struck Confucians as naive in their conviction that, if left to themselves, people will naturally follow an exemplary leader. Daoism's emphasis on doing things nature's way leaves society too vulnerable to simple lawlessness. In addition, the Confucian tradition's strong emphasis on education seemed to many to be irreconcilable with Daoism's more "organic" and seemingly anti-intellectual approach to learning. When Confucian tradition began to come into prominence during Japan's Tokugawa era, it found an increasingly hostile official response from representatives of Shinto. Confucianism, Shinto authorities argued, was a non-Japanese influence and therefore undesirable. By that time, however, Confucius had already made an indelible impression on Japanese society.

What role did **Matteo Ricci** play in Christian-Confucian Relations?

Matteo Ricci (1552–1610) was an Italian missionary who opened China to Roman Catholic evangelization. He was the best-known Jesuit and European in China prior to the twentieth century. Born at Macerata in 1552, Ricci went to Rome in 1568 to study law. In 1571 he entered the Society of Jesus (Jesuit). After studying mathematics and geography at a Roman college, he set out for Goa in 1577 and was ordained there in 1580. In 1582 he was dispatched to Macao and started to learn Chinese. In 1601, Ricci made his way to Beijing and received a warm welcome from the Emperor. This imperial favor provided Ricci with an opportunity to meet the leading officials and Literati in Beijing, some of whom later became Christian converts. Ricci obtained a settlement with an allowance for subsistence in Beijing, after which his reputation among the Chinese increased. Besides the missionary and scientific work, from 1596 on he was also superior of the missions, which in 1605 numbered seventeen. When he died in 1610, he was granted a burial place in Beijing. Some of the outstanding Chinese Literati with whom Ricci had contact later became his converts, including the famous scholar-officials Hsu Kuang-ch'i, Li Chih-ts'ao, and Yang T'ing-yun. Ricci's writings include about twenty titles, mostly in Chinese, ranging from religious and scientific works to treatises on friendship and local memory. The most famous of these are the Mappamondo and the True Idea of God.

Major Confucian Organizations, Schools, and Sub-communities

Fa Jia—The Legalist school, fifth to fourth century B.C.E., argued that Confucian thought needed to be bolstered by more specific legal mechanisms, rather than relying on virtuous example to motivate the people.

Kong Jia—term used to refer specifically to the "teachings of Kong (Confucius)," as distinct from the teachings of earlier scholars (*Ru Jia*).

Literati—a class of scholar-bureaucrats associated with the promulgation of Confucian values and intimately associated with imperial court affairs. Many people have used the term Mandarin as a synonym for a member of the Literati class.

Neo-Confucianism—a general term that includes several schools that developed from the tenth through the fifteenth centuries.

School of Principle (*Li Xue*)—a Neo-Confucian school, also called Cheng-Zhu after two founders' names, begun during the tenth to eleventh centuries and further elaborated during the later eleventh and twelfth. Its hallmark was the elaboration of a metaphysical theory in which *li,* formerly understood as a term referring to ritual and propriety in relationships, becomes a cosmic spiritual principle.

School of Mind (*Xin Xue*)—a fifteenth-century Neo-Confucian school associated with the reformer Wang Yangming, known for its idealist tendencies.

LEADERSHIP, AUTHORITY, AND RELIGIOUS ROLES

How are Confucian or CIT **leaders chosen** and given authority?

Priestly orders or classes in many traditions derive their authority from either hereditary lineage or from a perceived ability to manage spiritual power, or both of these. The case of the Literati as a distinct class is quite different in many respects. Their role in imperial religious affairs may have originated with the office of royal astrologer, a person possessed of a type of arcane knowledge. They had to understand all there was to know about how to plan imperial matters in perfect coordination with the rhythms of the cosmos. But the Literati's continued prestige rested on their identification with a broader range of knowledge—that of literature, history, and writing. Their privileged access to the canonical texts, the Classics and Books of Confucian tradition, gave them

The throne room in the Forbidden City's Hall of Protecting Harmony, where the emperor performed important rituals.

unquestioned authority. The Literati oversaw virtually every detail of imperial ritual and administration (so much of which was highly ritualized) and were responsible for propriety and auspiciousness in all affairs of the state under heaven. They were, in effect, a kind of lay priesthood whose patron and model was Confucius.

Prospective members of the Literati underwent extensive education designed to imbue them with the classical texts, an exquisite sensitivity to the nuances of ritual, and an appreciation of the social and political implications of the relationships implied in the great rituals. Literati achieved their various ranks within the hierarchical structure on the basis of their achievement in the imperial examinations. From about the seventh century C.E. on, an elaborate system of examinations could give access to any of three degrees or ranks, each requiring as many as ten different kinds of examination. The Board of Rites oversaw the examinations, and the Board of Civil Office made the final appointments. An important feature of this system was that, at least in theory, it bestowed authority on the basis of personal achievement rather than heredity or social status. The higher the rank of a local government's main official, the greater the prestige of its ancestral temple.

Who are some of the **principal** Confucian and CIT **officials** or **ritual specialists**?

Strictly speaking, Confucians have no separate structure of ritual officials. Bureaucrats of the imperial administration were responsible for offerings performed in Confucian memorial halls. The Emperor himself was the supreme ritual specialist in the sense that he exercised sole rights to perform certain ceremonies judged essential to the good order of life under Heaven. All subordinate, regional, and local ceremonies were delegated to the various ranks of the Literati. Today, even in the absence of imperial structures, government officials still play that role. In imperial times, the emperor's administration was divided into nine departments. Most important in this context was the Imperial Academy, whose chief officer was the Minister of Ceremonies. His function was similar to that of Chief Priest, since he was responsible for rituals performed in all imperial temples. A common ritual at local imperial altars required that a newly appointed local magistrate stay overnight, before his official installation, in the temple of the "spirit magistrate," a deity who was the earthly magistrate's celestial model.

Are there Confucian or CIT **hierarchical structures**?

Confucian thought discerns an essential need for hierarchies in all aspects of human society. It is a question of order. Human beings may be identical in essence, but they clearly differ in personal attributes, talents, knowledge, and age, to name only a few distinguishing characteristics. Confucius believed that realism required taking account of those differences. Take the challenge of living an ethical life, for example. Each stage in life has its unique problems. Young people need to conquer sensuality, adults combativeness, and the elderly greed. As for the variety of human capabilities, Confucius saw four levels: those who possess knowledge from birth, those capable of becoming Superior Persons by acquiring knowledge, those who learn only with great effort, and those not at all disposed to learning. Confucian thinking has often been very class conscious. The Master believed that society needed stratification in order to function smoothly. At the top was the scholar, supported by the farmer who produce life's basic needs, artisans who make practical items, merchants who buy and sell what others produce, and soldiers who, unfortunately, often wreck what others make.

Within the highest echelons of the Confucian hierarchy there were still further distinctions. Until around 1530, those enshrined in Confucian memorial halls were ranked according to titles taken from imperial administration. Confucian greats were honored as king, duke, marquis, or earl, for example. After 1530, Confucians replaced those royal honorifics with the titles sage, correlate, especially learned one, worthy one, and scholar. Over the course of history, some individuals within the Confucian hierarchy have been promoted, others demoted in rank, and still others restored after being demoted. Such hierarchical adjustments have depended a great deal on ideological leanings within various imperial regimes, the last major rearrangement occurring around 1724. CIT was, of course, hierarchical, but with the emperor at the top and a much higher place allotted to the military.

Have **women exercised leadership** in Confucianism or CIT?

Confucian tradition is staunchly patriarchal. Long-standing practice all over Asia, as a result of Confucian influence, has until only recently expected women to obey father **391** before marriage, husband during marriage, and oldest son when her husband dies. Education under classical Confucian direction was limited to males. That is no longer the case in societies that still acknowledge, however indirectly, their Confucian heritage. As for CIT, a number of empresses and princesses came to prominence over the centuries, but here too the leadership was male. Empresses were generally in charge of the so-called inner court. Empress-mothers frequently had duties in matters of state and thus were often more active in the outside world. Women were never allowed in the main halls of the Forbidden City's outer court, except on the day a new empress married her emperor.

What have been the **principal ritual venues** for Confucian communities and CIT?

Three main kinds of sacred spaces have been at the center of activities. Several kinds of venues called "memorial halls" enshrined the spiritual presence of great Literati, beginning with Confucius himself and his ancestors. These facilities go by the generic name *wen miao,* "temple of literature/culture," while those specifically dedicated to Confucius are often called *Kong* (or *Kong Zi*) *miao*. Until at least the middle of this century, Confucian temples enjoyed prestigious locations in nearly every Chinese city—as well as many Korean and some Japanese cities.

In most Confucian temples one of the more important community functions has been that of a place of study. These temples tend to draw clientele from a wider area than do CCT temples, which function more like local parishes. Unlike Buddhist and CCT temples, Confucianus temples do not hum with the ritual devotions of a steady stream of worshippers. There the ritual is more likely to be quiet academic work in the side rooms provided for that purpose. Once dedicated to the reading of the Confucian classics, these rooms now provide students whose homes are crowded and noisy a chance to concentrate on any academic subject. Second in importance and number are three different types of altars for the worship of agricultural deities, natural powers of mountain and river, and ancestral spirits. Generally set in a shared compound were the first two kinds of altar, twenty-foot square platforms, walled in and facing west. Temples of the imperial cult, finally, could be either of grand scale, as in Beijing's Temple of Heaven, or relatively humble, as in a local temple to the earth deity. All three venues provided a variety of circumstances under which communities have come together.

Is there a **central teaching authority** for Confucians or CIT?

One could argue that the social institution of the Literati functioned as a central teaching authority. There is no doubt that they set up the system to which any person of talent and ambition who wished to advance would have to conform. Complete with its regimen of demanding examinations, degrees, and apprenticeships, the Literati

A *wen miao*, or memorial hall, in Shanghai.

system of public service also had its religious implications, given the overall context in which traditional Chinese saw the role of the emperor. And there is no doubt that the system offered little or no flexibility—make the grade or wash out. The Literati system was, therefore, a central teaching authority for a limited segment of society. Even the ordinary people in towns and villages came under at least indirect influence of the system. But the system did not make its demands on regular people the way it did on those who aspired to rise within its ranks.

Is there a system of Confucian or CIT **religious law**?

Confucian tradition's closest analogy to the kind of religious regulation important to Jews and Muslims, for example, are the canons of ritual. It may sound at first as though Confucian law is limited to what are sometimes called "rubrics." Rubrics are instructions on how to perform a ceremony, that take their name from the Latin for "red" because the directions are printed in red ink to set them off from the liturgical text. But what Confucians mean by the canons of ritual actually includes an enormous range of human behavior. Here the Confucian scholars have codified ways of acting for every age and station in life, from members of the ordinary household, to the servant who prepares fruit for the emperor, to the emperor himself. These often elaborate and even somewhat theatrical stipulations might strike the outsider as extreme or downright compulsive. But the traditional interpretation is that a person of cultivated virtue will always act in such as way as to express precisely his or her relationship to

393

those with whom he is dealing. In this way Confucian tradition preserved a definite social hierarchy still very much reflected in the formal language usage of Korea and Japan, as well as of China. Because of its unique relationship to the civil authority represented by the emperor, Confucianism as such, with its Five Classics and Four Books, did not develop a specific code of penal law. That was still largely the province of the Literati as royal administrators, but it emanated from the imperial household and developed over many centuries.

Is **education** especially important in Confucianism?

No major religious tradition has placed greater emphasis on education than Confucianism. That is not to suggest that Confucian teaching reduces the truth to mere intellectual development. For Confucians, education goes far beyond developing mental skills and acquiring information. It means the cultivation of the whole person within the broadest possible perspective—humanism under Heaven. A number of very important Confucian institutions of higher learning have made major contributions throughout Asia over the centuries. Perhaps even more pervasive has been the Confucian influence in the development and maintenance of China's imperial civil service system, the educational system that produced and regulated the social class called the Literati.

Are there any **organizations or institutions** that have their own **distinctive structures of leadership** within Confucianism?

Throughout history, various Confucian societies of laypeople have come and gone. Few of those have been more than local or regional. But since the Confucian community is composed exclusively of laity, there has been no Confucian priesthood, no religious orders, and no monastic life. The single most important organizational structure has been that of the Literati class with its elaborate hierarchy and system of advancement determined by examinations. Apart from that, Chinese authorities have often regarded as subversive all attempts to form separate groups within society as a whole. There have been times in Chinese history when prominent Literati have withdrawn from society, opting for the eremitical life. These reclusive types borrowed a page from the Buddhist phenomenon of the solitary monk, but the Confucian hermits were by definition loners and not at all inclined to band together.

Is there such a thing as a Confucian **saint**?

Confucius revered the ancient kings as sages (*sheng*), figures of towering intellect and virtue who represented an ideal never again to be attained by mere mortals. Their inimitability prevented the ancients from functioning as exemplars and restricted them to the role of venerable ancestors to whom all owed a debt of gratitude. Meng Zi began to modify the role of the sage. He suggested that the sage appears in every age, not only in the distant past. And he emphasized the sage's humanity and imitability.

Individuals could aspire to and cultivate the qualities of the sage through education. With the Song dynasty came Neo-Confucianism and a further expansion of the sage's role. Building on the classic text called The Great Learning (*Da Xue*), medieval scholars spoke of a series of stages through which an aspirant could advance toward the lofty goal of sagehood. Neo-Confucians identified the sage as the individual who had fully actualized all moral and intellectual potential and arrived at a state of oneness with the universe.

Like the Daoist sage, as described in the Dao De Jing, the Confucian sage embodies perfect harmony with the cosmos. Unlike the Daoist sage, the Confucian puts wisdom's insights to work by active involvement in the ordinary affairs of society. A Confucian sage is like the Buddhist Bodhisattva in that both are committed to the betterment of the human condition. The ten-stage "Bodhisattva career" offers a general parallel to the Neo-Confucian system of steps toward sagehood. But whereas the Bodhisattva has the power to reach down and change the plight of those who ask for help, the sage offers the hope of transformation through determination and effort. Sages model the best in Confucianism's spirituality of public service.

How do the **Sage, Correlate, Worthy One, Scholar**, and **Superior** person differ?

The first four are all stages or levels in the Confucian hierarchy of human striving and perfectibility. They are the ranks of extraordinary individuals judged suitable for inclusion in the Confucian temples' various memorial halls. All four are, by definition, superior persons. At the pinnacle of the pyramid stands the sage, the Confucian analogy to the saint. Confucian tradition devised the various other terms, such as "worthy one" and "correlate" to describe the historical and "spiritual" proximity of famous scholars and sages to Confucius himself. In most Confucian temples the ranks or levels in the tradition's memorial hierarchy are indicated by the relative placement of name tablets. Those closest to the Master's tablet rank highest, and are generally called "sages" or "correlates." Those in the rooms along the side of the temple compound are the far more numerous "worthies and scholars." Scholars of sufficient prestige to have their names in the temple qualify as "superior persons," but that designation is not used in the memorial rankings.

What is a **Mandarin**?

"Mandarin" comes from the Sanskrit term *mantri,* meaning "minister or counsellor." It became common especially after the sixteenth century, when Europeans came into more regular contact with Chinese culture. Europeans used the term to refer to China's social elite, so that "Mandarin" was in effect a synonym for "Literati." Technically, that meant all the bureaucrats who belonged to the nine administrative ranks of imperial government or "civil service." When the Italian Jesuit missionary Matteo Ricci

Matteo Ricci (1552–1610) was an Italian Jesuit missionary who studied Confucianism and became so learned that he was considered a kind of honorary Mandarin.

(1552–1610) determined to dedicate himself to working in China, he set out to steep himself in classical Confucian learning. An important feature of his reputation is that he was so successful that he virtually became a Mandarin. In popular usage, the term Mandarin has come to refer to Asian social and cultural elites and governmental administrators in general. Mandarin is also the name given to one of the most important and widely spoken of the many Chinese dialects.

Have **martyrs** ever been important in Confucian history?

Several Confucian Literati have come to be known as martyrs. They died because those in power would not countenance their calls for greater justice in the imperial regime. One such figure was Yang Ji Sheng (1516–55C.E.). So strong was his conviction that the imperial system would respond to good-faith Confucian criticism that he risked all to denounce a corrupt official at court. Yang meticulously crafted his case against Yen Sung and his son, fasting for three days before presenting his charges. Yen Sung managed to poison the emperor's mind against Yang, implicating him falsely in a conspiracy. Yang languished in prison for three years while fellow Literati attempted to defend him at court. All appeals lost, the heroic Yang refused to take a sedative before being tortured in prison. Before he was executed, he composed a short poem, in true Literati style. In it he expressed the hope that he would live on in spirit, still loyal to the emperor and grateful for his life of service. What is essential to note here is this martyr's dedication to advancing society through selfless commitment to justice in public administration, an outstanding feature of the Confucian spirituality of service.

Have there been any important **Confucian reformers**?

Wang Yang Ming (1472–1529 C.E.) was an outspoken government official of the Ming dynasty. He was perhaps the most influential teacher of the Neo-Confucian "School of Mind," also known as the Idealists (*xin xue*). Wang believed that the teaching of his predecessors in the Neo-Confucian movement had lost all credibility when Yuan dynasty bureaucrats made it the official curriculum for civil service examinations.

Reduced to a fixed set of questions and answers, Neo-Confucian ideas no longer required people to think independently. Wang's major work, *Investigation into the "Great Learning"*, commented on the ancient Confucian text, underscoring the need for active engagement with ideas. He condemned slavish adherence to rigid canons of ritual propriety. Wang argued for an understanding of *li* as a living universal principle rather than a list of prescribed procedures and policies. He borrowed from Daoist and Buddhist teachings, as earlier Neo-Confucians had done, attempting to reinvigorate the tradition as a way of interpreting the whole of life. And Wang reintroduced a metaphysical element by speaking of a "true self" and a "heavenly principle." Above all, he insisted, one must not lose sight of the underlying challenge of human development and the struggle for moral improvement. Institutionalize what is meant to be a living tradition, Wang warned, and you create a giant fossil.

Have there been any Confucian **mystics**?

Scholars of the history of religion rarely describe the Confucian tradition as a wellspring of mystical spirituality. But several important figures, particularly among the Neo-Confucians, spoke a language reminiscent of some of the great monistic mystics of other traditions. Zhu Xi (1130-1200 C.E.), a leading light in the Neo-Confucian School of Principle, saw in the practice of meditation a way of becoming one with cosmic harmony. One could draw instructive parallels between traditional descriptions of this type of meditation, and of certain qualities of the sage, and characteristics of "nature mystics" in other traditions. In Zhu Xi's view, "silent sitting" promised the realistic possibility of experiencing unity with all things and all people. Wang Yang Ming (1472-1529 C.E.), a later exponent of the Neo-Confucian School of Mind, spoke of realizing one's "true self" in a meditative quest for enlightenment. He identified cosmic principle (*li*) with the mind, so that discovery of the true self meant discovering the ultimate reality. Some discern parallels between Wang's mysticism and that of the German mystic Meister Eckhart (c. 1260–1327 C.E.).

Does the **shaman** have a place in Confucianism and CIT?

Shamans played an important role in Chinese religious history long before the time of Confucius. They have retained a place in Daoism and CCT, functioning as guides to the spirit world. But since Confucian teaching is far more concerned with how things are going in the "outer" world of ordinary human affairs, there have never been Confucian shamans as such. Shamans have generally been associated with folk and popular beliefs. As an important ingredient in CIT, Confucianism has often had a more aristocratic tone. However, some functions anciently connected with shamanism have had continuous importance throughout much of Chinese history for CIT as well as popular religion. Confucian Literati and their imperial patrons alike have regularly consulted diviners, specialists in *feng shui* and astrology, for help in determining auspicious times and places for momentous events and structures.

HOLIDAYS AND REGULAR OBSERVANCES

What kind of **calendar** do Confucians and CIT observe?

Whether Daoist, CCT, Buddhist, or Confucian, all Chinese have historically acknowledged the same overall reckoning of time. Official Confucian and CIT events were traditionally set by a Board of Astrology and promulgated by a Ministry of Rites. In overall structure, the Chinese lunar calendar consists of twelve months of twenty-nine or thirty days, since the time between new moons is about twenty-nine and a half days. The lunar year dovetails with the solar, with the intercalation of an extra month approximately every six years or when five additional days per year total thirty. Reckoning began around 2637 B.C.E., so that the year 2000 marked the year 4637. Each of the twelve animals of the Chinese zodiac is associated with a particular quality or event and gives its name to every twelfth year, beginning with the Rat (industry and prosperity) and proceeding in order through Ox (spring planting), Tiger (valor), Hare (longevity), Dragon (power and good fortune), Snake (cunning), Horse (perseverance), Sheep (filial piety) or Goat, Monkey (health), Rooster (protection), Dog (fidelity), and Pig (home and family). The year 2000 was the Year of the Dragon, 2001 that of the Snake, 2002 that of the Horse, and so on. Five full cycles, each named after one of the five elements (wood, fire, earth, metal, and water) equals sixty years, an important interval for ritual purposes. Major annual markers are the winter (maximum *Yin*) and summer (maximum *Yang*) solstices and vernal and autumnal equinoxes when *Yin* and *Yang* are in balance. During each month, the most important times are the moments of new and full moon.

Is there any **further symbolism** attached to the structure of the **calendar**?

十二生肖
CHINESE ZODIAC

Dragon   Rat   Ox   Tiger
Rabbit   Snake   Horse   Goat
Monkey   Rooster   Dog   Pig

Each of the twelve animals of the Chinese zodiac is associated with a particular quality or event and gives its name to every twelfth year.

Each month is divided into ten-day periods, six of those in turn considered a special time period, and six of those equaling a full year. In addition, each year is divided into twenty-four climatic periods called breaths or nodes, described by such phrases as "full of snow" or "clear and bright." Every year, month, day, and hour are further identified by a combination of ten heavenly "stems" and twelve earthly "branches" (the monthly or zodiacal symbols). The ten heavenly stems are associated with colors, two stems with each of the five symbolic colors (azure, red, yellow, white, black), which are in turn linked to the four directions and center as well as to the five elements. Branches and stems are both primarily numerical designators, but each also bears important symbolic connotations. If you match one stem with one branch for succeeding years (S1/B1, S2/B2 … S1/B11, S2/B12, S3/B1, and so on), you end up back at the beginning after sixty years. In this system, only odd-numbered stems combine with odd-numbered branches, even-numbered stems with even-numbered branches. We are currently in the sixty-year cycle that began in 1984.

The result of all this calculation is an extremely detailed system of pinpointing ritual times according to a host of definitive characteristics. Each event occurring on earth has its heavenly parallel. For every conceivable type of human behavior there is an auspicious moment. The calendar has thus been not merely a way of keeping track of times for religious observances, but a kind of temporal map for negotiating the cosmos as well. Each year, during the ninth lunar month, imperial officials set up the liturgical calendar for the year to come.

What regular or **annual observances** have been part of Confucian tradition?

For many centuries Confucians celebrated with large feasts in the Master's honor at both the vernal and autumnal equinoxes, corresponding with the second and eighth lunar months. During the fourth of the night's five watches, celebrants paid homage to Confucius' ancestors and then moved to the central memorial hall at sunrise. Arrayed carefully across the entire main courtyard were row upon row of participants, arranged according to rank, with imperial bureaucrats along the sides and six groupings of students in the center. Before and within the memorial hall the offerings and sacrificial animals were arranged. These offerings included a roll of silk; vessels full of wine, soup and various foods; and a ritually slaughtered ox flanked by a pig and a lamb. A lengthy order of ceremony included specific offerings of each item, first to Confucius and then to the other sages enshrined in the main hall. This was accompanied by profound bowing and prostration and songs of praise. A full classical Chinese orchestra punctuated by booming drum beats marked changes in the action. In addition to those semiannual festivities, smaller semimonthly observances included offerings to the spirit of Confucius at each new and full moon. In Korea, at the spring and autumn equinoxes, Confucians honor both Korean and Chinese sages at the Confucian University's shrine.

What are the **major festivities** historically associated with CIT?

Each year on the day before the winter solstice, the emperor and his retinue visited the Temple of Heaven for an elaborate event. When paying homage to Heaven and Earth, the emperor would perform gestures of humility by kneeling three times and prostrating himself nine times. When he sacrificed to other powers, such as the sun, the moon, and the gods with power over the forces of nature, the emperor did not perform those rituals of self-abasement. At the Forbidden City's Hall of Supreme Harmony, major sacred events included the enthronement of a new emperor, royal weddings, an event held every ten years called the Great Anniversary, announcement of results of civil service examinations, and celebrations of the winter solstice and new year. In the Hall of Middle Harmony, the emperor formulated decrees to be made public in royal temples at all the various seasonal festivities. Imperial officials designated by the emperor, or local administrators in the case of smaller events, took care of the regular agriculturally significant occasions throughout the country.

What were some of the **other formerly regular festivals** once associated with CIT?

Many of the religiously significant times acknowledged with rituals in sacred sites affiliated with CIT overlap with popular Daoist and CCT practices. The Literati, who functioned as ritual specialists in service of the imperial house, generally looked down on Daoist and CCT devotionalism and often made fun of their beliefs. But as servants of the emperor, they could hardly afford to snub the very deities to whom the general populace prayed for success in mundane but important matters such as timely rain and abundant harvest. When the emperor's far-flung political administrators entered into their roles as religious ritualists, they often found themselves crossing an imaginary line from the elite to the everyday life of the locals. Celebrating days associated with deities of purely local or regional origin and importance remained the task of Daoists and practitioners of CCT. But when they paid homage to local or regional deities whom the emperor had elevated to the CIT pantheon, the Literati were providing implicit legitimation for popular beliefs and practices. In addition to the birthday of Confucius on the twenty-seventh day of the eighth lunar month, CIT also celebrated new and full moon occasions, some of which coincided with feasts like that of Lao Zi (second month, day fifteen) and the Hungry Ghosts (seventh month, day fifteen).

Could you describe an **example** of an **annual CIT ritual** occasion in greater detail?

At the Temple of Heaven in Beijing, a major event occurred at the winter solstice. Preparations commenced two months in advance. With five days to go, authorities inspected the animals to be offered. The next day they prepared the hall in which the emperor would spend a day in spiritual preparation, and the day after that the emperor began his abstinence. A procession made its way from the Forbidden City to the Temple, commoners taking care not to look at the royal person as he passed by. The emperor spent that day and night in the so-called Hall of Abstinence, a large complex to the west of the main north-south axis and about halfway between the Altar of Heaven to the south and the Hall of Harvest Prayer at the north of the compound. He bathed ritually and fasted for a day. (Later emperors often prepared in the Forbidden City itself.) Two days before the solstice, ritualists made final preparation of all ceremonial objects for the emperor's review. The day before the solstice, the emperor left the Hall of Absti-

Interior of the dome of the Temple of Heaven's Hall of Harvest Prayer in Beijing, showing two of the four large floor-to-dome columns (extreme right and left) representing the seasons, and several of the inner circle of twelve shorter columns symbolizing the months. At the oculus are the dragon and phoenix intertwined.

nence and proceeded to the Altar of Heaven to honor Shang Di and his own royal forebears with incense and bowing, and then returned the Hall of Abstinence.

Early the next day, he began a nine-part ceremony. At the round Altar of Heaven, where his ancestors' spirit tablets were arrayed, animals were sacrificed and he paid obeisance to the ancestors. Offerings included silk and jade as well as the sacrificial meats. To music and dancing, he presented wine to Shang Di and the spirits in the first of three such offerings. After the emperor bade the sacred presences farewell he withdrew to an observation dais, while officials consigned the offerings to a furnace. The ceremonies ended with the emperor exiting by the south gate and returning to the Forbidden City.

Do Confucians **celebrate** the **birthdays** of any **religious figures**?

September 28 of each year marks the birthday of Confucius in Taiwan, for example, and there it has also been declared Teachers' Day. In the People's Republic of China, celebrations of the day have been forbidden since the Maoist revolution of 1948, largely because of Confucianism's long-standing association with imperial rule. Taiwanese celebrations, however, are still elaborate and traditional, beginning at six in the morning according to ancient practice. Ceremonies commence with ritual drumming, followed by a procession in which participants dressed in ancient regalia carry in symbols to welcome the spirit of Confucius. Processional symbols include a royal canopy and fan, as well as ritual long-handled axes. In the capital city, Taipei, the celebration is modeled on the ancient pattern in which Literati bureaucrats performed the main rituals. There, the mayor presides over the various ranks of governmental employees and educational administrators, joined by ranks of students of different ages. Birthdays of particular deities or immortals do not play a role in Confucianism or CIT as they do in Daoism and CCT.

CUSTOMS AND RITUALS

How important is **ritual** in Confucianism and CIT?

There is perhaps no more fundamental notion in Chinese religious thought than that of *li,* proper ritual. The Chinese term is composed of two characters meaning sacrifice and spirit—more precisely, "contact with the upper world"—combined with a character that once depicted a sacred vessel. It applies to all religious ceremony, from the most "popular" to the most official imperial cultic worship. Historically overseen by a Ministry of Rites, state rituals have generally been the most formal and precise. Pre-modern ritual practice distinguished several levels of ceremony. Supreme Offerings, performed mostly by the emperor himself, addressed Heaven, Earth, the forebears of the emperor and empress, and the deities of earth and seed. Middle Offerings propitiated sun and moon, ancestors of previous reigns, the god of agriculture called Emperor Shen Nung, and the goddess of silk production, Lei Zu. Lower Offerings occurred in local or regional state temples and revered Guan Di as deity of war, Wen Zhang as deity of literature, and Sage Emperor Fu Xi, among others. When Confucius spoke of *li,* he had in mind all of these, plus the entire range of ceremonies enacted on a smaller scale or in private. But more than that, he conceived of *li* as informing all proper human relationships.

What were some of the principal CIT **sacred times**?

Ritual responsibilities of the emperor and his official delegates included ceremonies at various major state sacred sites: the Altar of the Spirits of Land and Grain, the Imperial Ancestral Temple, the temples of Heaven and Earth, of Sun and Moon, and within the audience halls of the Forbidden City. At the Altar of the Spirits of Land and Grain (*she ji tan*) the emperor performed sacrifices in spring for fertile fields and in the fall for plentiful harvest. At the Imperial Ancestral Temple (*tai miao*), he led ceremonies associated with the anniversaries of his own ancestors back through the history of the dynasty. There, the ancestors were said to grant audiences with their royal public much as the emperor himself did from his own audience halls. At the Temple of Heaven, the imperial officials offered harvest prayers on New Year's Day, rain prayers at the onset of summer, and announced royal events, such as the designation of the heir to the throne. Within the Forbidden City, various important rituals occurred at the new year, the winter solstice, and the emperor's birthday. Subjects acknowledged the emperor's lofty authority in the various audience halls of the City's outer court, located just south of the more private palaces of the inner court.

The ceremony began early in the morning outside the Meridian Gate, the southern entrance to the Forbidden City. At the sound of two drum beats, three thousand officials in nine ranks processed into the courtyard before the Hall of Supreme Harmony. Once they were arranged, three drum beats announced that the emperor would enter from the Hall of Middle Harmony, just to the north, and take his seat on the throne. Music accompanied his entry and continued as the officials paid homage. Military leaders lined up on the west and civil authorities on the east, both groups facing the central axis of the courtyard. Bird and animal symbolism was arranged on the robes so that the birds and animals of both groups were facing north, honoring the emperor as he sat on the dragon throne within the hall. All of creation was thus symbolically ordered toward the emperor, who represented Heaven. After the announcement of the specific occasion for the ritual, music resumed for another round of obeisance to the emperor. Once the emperor had departed, the ceremony ended with an exit procession of all present.

How did CIT **structure** its **main ritual activities**?

CIT rituals were arranged in a symbolic hierarchical order that coordinated the authority of those performing the rituals with the various ranks of the CIT pantheon. To symbolize universal dominion, the emperor would make offerings to the powers controlling all four cardinal directions, to all mountains and rivers, and to the "five domestic sacrifices." On lower levels, ritual responsibilities reflected a division of labor and authority. Imperial princes made offerings only to the power ruling their own quarters of the universe and the associated mountains and rivers, and to the five domestic sacrifices. These took place at regional sacred sites. In turn the princes' chief officers were to perform only the domestic offerings, and their subordinates only the offerings to their own ancestors. These last rituals occurred in home settings and in cemeteries.

Specific rituals include many of the same kinds of actions Daoists or practitioners of CCT engage in. Ritual specialists generally purified themselves for the ceremonies by fasting and ablutions. Before making offerings to divine powers of the top level in the pantheon, specialists fasted for three days, and for second-level deities, two days. During times of fasting, ritualists were especially careful to avoid certain strong foods (garlic and onions) and fermented beverages. An essential ingredient in the preparatory period was avoidance of contact with death and disease. Festivities and music were put aside. Central to the actual worship ceremonies was the offering of food, wine, and incense, along with prayers of petition and physical prostration before the deities.

Have Confucians or CIT ordinarily engaged in **ritual sacrifice**?

Sacrifice of certain animals has long been part of Confucian observances, both of the Master's birthday and of certain types of ancestor memorial. Two kinds of ritual sacrifice have also been historically associated with CIT. The *Feng* (high altar mound) and *Shan* (level ground) sacrifices were those offered to Heaven and Earth, respectively. Some emperors used the public performance of these rituals as a way of declaring and expressing gratitude for their possession of the Mandate of Heaven. History records that a number of emperors, even down to the last dynasty, engaged in the sacrifices atop or at the foot of sacred mountains. Animals sacrificed ritually most commonly included sheep and pigs, but occasionally wild game animals like deer were also sacrificed. Larger and more expensive ceremonies might feature oxen splayed across a rack after slaughtering, or the burnt offering of a whole young red bull—red is the color of *Yang*, the energy needed to return warmth to the earth so that spring will renew all living things. In the Temple of Heaven complex, for example, a large slaughterhouse and "spirit kitchen" accommodated extensive sacrificial needs. Eighty butchers and two hundred eighty cooks processed vast quantities of material. A year's worth of sacrifices, according to one record, included nearly a thousand pigs, over eight hundred sheep, over two hundred each of deer, cows, and rabbits, and over a hundred goats.

What kinds of **ritual objects** figure in Confucian and CIT worship?

When Confucius was young he was particularly intrigued by the classic bronze vessels his ancestors had used for centuries in honoring Heaven. Most of these vessels held materials to be offered. The principal forms developed in connection with the particular types of material. A vase (*yu*) was to hold sacrificial wine; a jug (*zhue*) poured libations; and a beaker (*gu*) may have been used for sharing a communion-like drink. The *ding* was a bowl for ritual foods such as cereal grains or fruit. Some of these objects apparently were designed in particularly symbolic shapes, such as the "hill-shaped" censer, whose form recalled the Five Sacred Mountains. Some bronzes bear abstract

representations of the four directional creatures: the black tortoise of the wintry north, the green dragon of the vernal east, the scarlet bird of the summery south, and the white tiger of the autumnal west. Inscriptions dedicating an object to a father, for example, or expressing the hope that sons and grandsons will use the vessel for "ten thousand years," suggest that they were commonly used in ancestor veneration rituals. Even today, copies of those antique objects adorn the altars in Confucian temples and are part of the relatively infrequent offerings held there. Many of the sacred vessels were buried in tombs or even thrown into river beds during invasions to prevent them

Stone Sage or ancestor figure on the grounds of the National Palace Museum in Seoul, South Korea.

from falling into the hands of barbarians. Nearly every large museum has good examples in its Asian collections, and they are well worth a visit.

Do Confucianism and CIT consider the **practice of divination** essential?

Two types of divination have been important ingredients in the ritual life of both Confucianism and CIT. As in Daoism and CCT, the practice of geomancy (Earth-prognostication) called *feng shui* has always been a necessary prerequisite for the siting and planning of all structures, from the humblest home to the grandest temple or palace. Those contemplating any building project would enlist a specialist in *feng shui* for a thorough reading of the natural characteristics of the proposed site. For more detail on the practice, see the section on Daoism, page 325. In addition, people from the emperor on down regularly consulted specialists in interpreting the oracles of the Yi Jing, the Classic of Change, before undertaking any significant course of action. The imperial staff included experts in divination who could be consulted on short notice. Such specialists were not specifically members of the Literati or Confucian hierarchies, but their services were generally regarded as indispensable.

What **attitudes toward pilgrimage** are important in Confucianism and CIT?

Confucian teaching generally did not promote the popular practice of pilgrimage, associated as it was with Daoism and Buddhism. A larger concern had to do with the social and political implications of devotional travel. Many Confucians considered pilgrimage a potential threat to the stability of society. Anthropologists talk about the experience of "liminality" as an essential part of pilgrimage. Pilgrims step out of their accustomed social roles, leaving behind the rules, duties, and responsibilities of ordinary daily life. They become "liminal" in that they step across a threshold (*limen* in Latin) into another way of being and thinking, if only temporarily. For people who regard their function as maintaining social order, the prospect of throngs of pilgrims heading out across the countryside in hope of miracles or magic naturally poses a threat. Enthusiastic crowds are prey to demagogues and can turn into unruly mobs. Still, a parallel to devotional pilgrimage developed among Confucians on a smaller scale.

Confucius himself became a model of the itinerant scholar, traveling from one province to another in search of disciples and patrons. Later Confucians often followed his example. Eventually the places in which these Confucian exemplars had lived and taught began to attract visitors. Not surprisingly, the tomb of Confucius in Shandong became a goal for Confucian pilgrims, who were generally in search not of miracles, but of inspiration in the struggle to live a good life. In general, it appears that the tradition of family members caring for ancestral graves may have been significant in preventing burial places from becoming pilgrimage goals. Mountains were also important destinations for China's Literati. There, one could contemplate most abundantly nature's sacred beauty. There, too, was the incomparable source of poetic inspiration. **405**

How important is **music** in Confucian and CIT ritual?

Celebrations like that of the Master's birthday are filled with the sound of music. Confucius had always insisted that training in both music appreciation and instrumental proficiency were essential ingredients in a proper education. Many Confucian temples keep the principal musical instruments on display in the main memorial hall flanking the tablet of Confucius. Important stringed instruments include plucked cousins of the Japanese *koto* called the *jin* and *se,* which are not typically found in Daoist instrumental repertoires. Percussion pieces include a variety of bells, both individual large ones and sets of tuned smaller ones, and similar sets of metal chimes. Wind instruments include multitube flutes, similar to European panpipes, as well as wooden transverse flutes. A category of decorative motifs called the "Eight Musical Instruments" appear on all sorts of fine wares, suggesting the importance of music in Chinese tradition. The eight include the musical stone, a large bell, a lute, a flute, a metal percussion instrument, a drum, a reed organ, and an ocarina. CIT rituals always included large musical ensembles that played during lengthy segments of the ceremonies, especially for the entrance and exit of the emperor and while the royal subjects were paying homage to him.

Is **dance** also a significant ingredient in Confucian and CIT ritual?

Once a central feature of many rituals in China, Confucian dance has been preserved as an art form only in Korea. During the semiannual gathering to honor the spirits of Confucius and the sages at the Confucian University, and at the annual gathering to honor the kings of the Yi dynasty at the Royal Ancestral Shrine, dancers perform elaborate routines. Originally, Confucian dance was limited to male performers. Both military and nonmilitary forms of dance make up the repertoire. Dancers gesture with the long pheasant feathers and small flutes they carry. Complex ritual movement was formerly integral to virtually all the major ceremonies of CIT. Whether in the courtyards of the Forbidden City or around the altars of the Temple of Heaven and other sacred imperial sites, intricately choreographed scripts called for dance on a grand scale.

What are the principal Confucian and CIT **rites of passage**?

Confucian tradition prescribes a full range of very detailed ritual procedures to be observed for various family, as well as a few public, occasions. They differ from rites of passage in many other traditions in that they generally do not assume an overtly religious form. Confucian teaching places enormous emphasis on ritualized attentiveness to every detail of daily family life. All of that occurs within the larger, presumed context of life under Heaven and in a society that is at least potentially just and harmonious. In pre-modern times, many Chinese practiced rites of initiation for young women and men alike. Families conferred on young men a hat and a name symbolizing maturity. Young women received some new clothes and had their hair done specially. More recently, Chinese social custom has linked these rituals to marriage, now considered the primary sign of adulthood.

Has **meditation** been an important ritual activity for Confucians?

Confucian tradition has generally emphasized the need for a calm, contemplative approach to life. Few individuals can develop the habit of reflection without engaging deliberately in practices designed to facilitate that habit. Meditation has not occupied as prominent a position in Confucian spirituality as it has in Chinese Buddhism, but it is important nevertheless. Confucians who engage in solitary or group meditation usually sit on small stools, rather than on the floor in the lotus posture, as many Buddhists do. When Confucians meditate, they reflect on the underlying propriety and order of the universe. Cultivation of the ethical self for the purpose of contributing more conscientiously to society is the goal. Classical Confucian and Neo-Confucian writers describe meditation as "quiet-sitting" and "abiding in reverence."

Unlike Zen meditation, Confucian meditation has a distinctly ethical emphasis. Some authors say the goal of meditation is to make a place in one's mind for the human beings who constitute one's own community—family, friends, associates. Not unlike a process of free association, this form of meditation gathers whatever comes to mind and allows it all to sift and settle naturally. "Settled nature" is the goal, a state in which the meditator is free from the agitation that arises from disordered relationships. Confucian meditation may sound quite unstructured, but it requires constant mental and emotional discipline. A meditator must be alert to abstract notions that distract from concrete ethical concerns, for it is often much easier to drift off into speculation than to confront life as one is actually living it.

Are there Confucian rituals or beliefs around **marriage and family life**?

Confucian tradition—Chinese tradition in general, really—teaches that marriage is meant to perpetuate the extended family rather than to create new small social units, all going their separate ways. Marriages arranged by matchmakers have long been the rule, complete with elaborate astrological calculations to assure cosmic compatibility. The equivalent of a dowry from the groom's parents means the bride has been bought from her family of origin. When young Chinese marry in the traditional way, the new couple virtually fuse with the husband's family of origin. As long as an older male survives in the groom's family, the groom and his wife own no property. Most striking of all, perhaps, is that the bride no longer makes ritual offerings to her own family, but only to her husband's ancestors. Young married couples have historically felt enormous pressure to produce a male heir for the family. Traditional Chinese marriage rituals have not generally been considered "sacramental" as in some other traditions. Nor is marriage a purely civil matter, for the family is the custodian of the sacred in Chinese tradition. **407**

Though much of the imagery here is largely Buddhist in origin, the practice of memorial services for deceased loved ones (note the photographs on the altar) testifies to the pervasive influence of Confucian tradition throughout Asia: Judgment Hall in a popular Buddhist temple, Pong Won Sa in Seoul, South Korea. The *bodhisattava* Chi Jang (not visible here, known as Jizo in Japan) rules over the realms of the next life, along with the Ten Kings of the Underworld whose images are arranged around the right and left sides of the room and who function as judges.

How do Confucians deal ritually with **death and mourning**?

Confucian practices associated with funerals and ancestor veneration are of a piece with those of Daoism and CCT, in that the basic elements are common to most segments of traditional Chinese societies. Confucius and his disciples did have some specific thoughts on the matter, though. Disciple Xun Zi wrote that the feelings of loss and longing for a deceased person, and the ritual expression of those feelings, represented the height of human civilization and culture. In a way, one knows the humanity of others through the attachment they express for lost loved ones.

Although Confucius himself declined to speculate about the experience of death or the condition of one who has died, he seems to have felt strongly that there were appropriate ritual and emotional responses. When asked whether he recommended the full three-year period of mourning, Confucius responded that if Literati who lose loved ones were to dispense with the practice, they would risk the irrevocable loss of some of society's most important rituals. He added that if the questioner felt comfortable performing only a year's grieving, he might do so. After the questioner had left, however, the Teacher commented how heartless such a person must be. Parents attend to their infants unceasingly for three years; the least their children can do is return the favor symbolically.

One specific issue that has historically been very important for Confucianism and CIT is the question of monumental funereal architecture and memorials for the great and powerful. Confucius and several of the tradition's later teachers have been remembered with fairly modest grave markers. Tombs of emperors, on the other hand, have often been grand, even extravagant, architectural works. At least one ruler even commissioned a virtual reconstruction of the royal residence underground, complete with thousands of life-sized terra cotta soldiers to protect the imperial remains.

What is the Confucian and Literati view of **ancestor veneration**?

Confucius did not invent ancestor veneration, but his teaching placed great emphasis on the practice. Already a millennium old by Confucius' time, ancestor veneration had much to do with the rather utilitarian belief that malcontent spirits of the deceased could cause great trouble. Better to attend to their needs before they became disgruntled. But Confucius stressed a more positive note of reverence for those who have gone before and of maintaining connections with one's sacred past. So much of what we are is our history. In Korea, descendants of the Yi dynasty still gather annually to perform memorial rites with full traditional costume and music. This Yi Dynasty Association maintains dynastic memorial tablets in an ancestral shrine in Seoul called Chongmyo. To each of the eighteen major Yi rulers enshrined there the worshippers offer three cups of wine and choice food. Scholars often credit Confucian influence in Japan with the continued prevalence of ancestor veneration there.

SHINTO

HISTORY AND SOURCES

What is Shinto and what are its origins?

"Shinto" derives from two Chinese words—*shen,* meaning "deity," and *dao,* meaning "way." The Japanese reading of the Chinese expression comes out *kami no michi,* the "Path of the *Kami.*" Since at least several centuries B.C.E., the Japanese have acknowledged the sacred presence and power of numinous entities called *kami,* "high or superior beings." Until about the middle of the sixth century C.E., the Japanese people evidently did not think of their ancient religious traditions as a separate system. So organically integrated were those traditions with their entire culture and heritage that worship of the *kami* was largely assumed as the Japanese way. Only with the arrival of Buddhism, called in Japanese "the Way of the Buddha" (*butsu-do*), did it become necessary to give the indigenous beliefs and practices a name to distinguish them from this imported tradition.

Unlike many other major traditions, Shinto had neither a founder nor a single foundational figure who represents concrete historical origins. In a sense, Shinto is as old as Japan itself, somewhat the way Hinduism is as old as India. At its core, the Way of the Kami enshrines profound insights into the sacred character of all created nature. Shinto calls people to a deep awareness of the divine presence suffusing all things, to the challenge of personal and corporate responsibility for the stewardship of the world that is home, to unending gratitude for all that is good, and to a willingness to seek purification and forgiveness for humanly inevitable but avoidable lapses. Observe worshippers at a Shinto shrine—as Buddhism has temples, Shinto has shrines—and there can be little doubt of the sincere devotion that moves so many people to prayer and ritual expression of their beliefs.

A solitary worshipper pays respects to the *kami* at a small local wayside shrine, Kyoto, Japan.

What were the **earliest Shinto sacred texts**?

Two eighth-century documents are Shinto's foundational texts. These are among the youngest of the major religious tradition's primary works. Unlike many other sacred texts, they are not considered to have been divinely written even though their subject matter is of divine origin. In other words, these scriptures are not considered divine communication as such, but communication about things divine. The Records of Ancient Matters, or Kojiki, dates to 712 C.E. Composed by a courtier named Yasumaro, its three volumes deal with events beginning with the creation of the Japanese islands and people and continuing down to 628 C.E. Exegetes have authored scores of major commentaries (called *kojikiden*) in relatively recent times. The thirty-volume Chronicles of Japan, called Nihongi as well as Nihon Shoki, was completed in 720 C.E. About three times the length of the Kojiki, the Chronicles also recount the ancient cosmogonic myth, though in a less detailed fashion. Greater detail about subsequent imperial history includes events up to 697 C.E. These two texts enjoyed prominence after the seventeenth century, when a school of Shinto studies called "National Learning" (*kokugaku*) set out to probe the sources for the essence of being Japanese that they communicate. These primary texts are so important because they record the history of the imperial family and legitimate its authority by establishing its divine lineage.

What **other early scriptures** are especially important for Shinto practitioners? Is there a Shinto scriptural canon?

Scholars refer to the various sacred texts collectively as *shinten,* "texts of the deities." But although they generally agree on the importance of a certain set of works, there has never been an official process of "canonization" by which representatives of the tradition have formally declared certain texts as definitive.

Here are the most important of the classical documents: From the early eighth century, the Fudoki ("Records of Wind and Earth") provided data about very early religious rituals from major shrines. The early ninth century Kogo-shui (807), or "Gleaning of Ancient Words," commented on previous documents in an attempt to legitimate the Imbe family against their enemies, the Nakatomi clan. The Manyoshu, "Collection of Countless Leaves," anthologizes a large selection of seventh- and eighth-century Japanese poetry of various genres. Some Shinto scholars have insisted that these poems represent the purest form of Japanese literary expression. First published in

927, the Engi-shiki includes a collection of more than two dozen prayer texts. A work called the Kujiki (also Sendai Kuji Hongi), or "Records of Ancient Happenings") bears the date 620 but was probably contrived as late as the ninth century to compete with the similar-sounding Kojiki in antiquity and authority. It amounts to what some traditions might call an "apocryphal" work—not what it claims to be, but still full of valuable material. Finally, a group of thirteenth-century texts called the Five Shinto Scriptures (Shinto gobusho) emphasize the antiquity of Japan's Shinto heritage. Seventeenth-century scholars who studied these texts as prime examples of Japanese culture and values went on to spearhead the National Learning school of thought.

What does the term **Dual Shinto** mean?

Dual (or *Ryobu,* "Two-sided") Shinto arose out of the early interaction between Shinto theology and Buddhist thinking newly imported from China. Some use the term *ryobu shugo,* "dual compromise," to describe the resulting syncretism. Some accounts describe the developments this way: In 715 C.E. a Shinto shrine annexed a Buddhist temple. Twenty years later a smallpox epidemic created a crisis, to which the emperor responded by commissioning the colossal forty-eight-foot-tall bronze Great Buddha (*daibutsu*) at Nara's Todaiji temple. At the same time, the ruler dispatched the Buddhist patriarch Gyogi to Ise shrine to seek the blessing of Amaterasu, the Shinto sun goddess. Gyogi secured a favorable oracle, and the next night the emperor had a dream in which Amaterasu identified herself as the Mahayana Buddha of Infinite Light, Vairocana. This laid the groundwork for further identification of the various *kami* (high beings) as alter egos of various Buddhas and Bodhisattvas.

In 750, an image of the Shinto war *kami*, Hachiman, was transported from its shrine at Usa on the island of Kyushu (just south of the main Japanese island, Honshu) to Todaiji in Nara so that the *kami* might pay respects to the Daibutsu. Hachiman thereafter remained in a shrine at Todaiji, where he became the guardian *kami* of Todaiji temple. Thus did a Shinto *kami* come to protect the teachings of the Buddha. This account reflects an interpretation formulated during the ninth century by teachers of a new esoteric school of Buddhism called Shingon. As always, this theological accommodation had its political implications and set the stage for many years of Buddhist growth and royal patronage. From then on until the Meiji Restoration in 1868, Dual Shinto was the dominant form of Shinto. With the Meiji Restoration of imperial power came increasing pressure from Shinto scholars to purge the tradition of all Chinese influences, including of course Buddhism and Confucianism, both of which had by turns exerted considerable pull at court for many years.

How important was the **school of National Learning**?

"National Learning," or *Kokugaku,* had perhaps more to do with the modern understanding of Shinto than has any other movement within the tradition. Kada no Azu-

Was Shinto associated with the Samurai code?

Japan's fabled tradition of *Samurai* warriors did have important connections with Shinto, but it did not arise out of Shinto alone or even primarily. Some credit a seventeenth-century Japanese Confucian scholar and military theorist named Yamaga Soko (1622–85) as the originator of the "way of the warrior" (*bushi-do*). Yamaga emphasized the importance of sincerity and utter devotion to the ancestral *kami* as a sure road to experiencing the divine presence. Along with other thinkers of his time, he focused on the concept of Amaterasu as the ancestral *kami* of the imperial family. Total devotion to the ancestral *kami* therefore implied perfect allegiance to the person of the emperor, the *shogun,* and the territorial feudal lords called *daimyo*. Feudal society depended on the loyalty of its *samurai*, the knightly or military class. Even after the shogunate and the feudal system gave way to a rejuvenated imperial government under the Meiji Restoration (1868), military supporters of the emperor turned the code of unquestioning dedication to good effect by underscoring the necessity of unstinting affection for the royal person and his household.

mamaro (1669–1736) is generally considered the founder of the school, insisting on the need to return to the earliest genuinely and purely Japanese sources. Among those he included the Kujiki, but emphasized the Kojiki and Nihongi especially. Kamo no Mabuchi (1697–1769) continued what Kada had begun by applying philological methods to classical Japanese prayer and poetry. He considered spontaneity the native Japanese gift, without which nothing could be truly Japanese. Motoori Norinaga (1730–1801) continued the scholarly dynasty, and is still regarded by some as Shinto's best theological mind. His forty-four-volume commentary on the Kojiki remains a monument of scholarship. Hirata Atsutane (1763–1843) was the latest and perhaps most influential exponent of the school, in that he implemented the thought of his predecessor Motoori. Together these four men were largely responsible for the articulation of modern Shinto's highly nationalistic and ethnocentric tone.

Has Shinto ever been identified with any **political regimes**?

What came to be known in 1945 as State (*kokka*) Shinto began as a formal development after the Meiji Restoration in 1868. The term "State Shinto" was coined in the "Shinto Directive" of 1945 to distinguish formal Japanese government involvement in religious affairs from the religious concerns of Japanese generally, which were called Sect (*shuha*) Shinto. After 1868, the Japanese government imposed a system of devotion to the emperor as a kind of state creed. Most Christians and Buddhists, as well as adherents of other traditions, considered themselves part of that system. "Shrine Shinto" was another term used to refer to the system, since the government had insti-

A group of *Samurai* aficionados from Nagoya visit Los Angeles during Nisei Week in 2009. (Jose Gil / Shutterstock.com).

tuted in 1868 an elaborate structure of ranks for administering the nation's shrines. Government directives regulated everything in shrine life, including specific rituals to be performed and how records were to be kept. Underlying all this was the principle of "Worship–government unity" (*saisei itchi*). Directives also set up an elaborate hierarchy of the Shinto priesthood.

One of the principal results of this extensive government control was the doctrine of absolute loyalty to the emperor and the expression of that loyalty in religious practice. A major symbol of the new way was the founding in 1869 of Tokyo's Yasukuni Shrine as a memorial to all war dead. As a way of controlling powerful symbolic expressions long connected with Shinto, the government decreed in 1884 that the *torii* gate could be used only for state shrines. In 1900, the government further ordered that Shrine Shinto was no longer to be considered a religion as such, but a universally binding attitude of reverence for the emperor, complete with appropriate rituals.

Another aspect of Shinto's relationship to the Japanese government is that long before the Meiji era, imperial palaces in the various capitals had maintained a system of three shrines within the compounds for exclusive use by the royal family. In the center, the *kashiko-dokoro* enshrined the symbols of the emperor's divinity. The *koreiden,* on the left, was dedicated to spirits of past emperors and their wives, and to the right the *shinden* enshrined all the *kami* of Heaven and Earth. These shrines remain integral to imperial ritual today. State Shinto consisted of the approximately one hundred thousand shrines held under central control between 1868 and 1945, and the

Shinto rites unique to the Imperial Household. Japan's post-World War II Constitution guarantees freedom of religion and mandates strict separation of state and religious affairs.

How did the **Emperor express commitment** to his ruling responsibilities?

The following oath is taken from the 1889 Constitution of the Empire of Japan. It was spoken by the emperor in the sanctuary of the Imperial Palace:

> We, the Successor to the prosperous Throne of Our Predecessors, do humbly and solemnly swear to the Imperial Founder of Our House and to Our other Imperial Ancestors that, in pursuance of a great policy co-extensive with the Heavens and with the Earth, We shall maintain and secure from decline the ancient form of government. In consideration of the progressive tendency of the course of human affairs and in parallel with the advance of civilization, We deem it expedient, in order to give clearness and distinctness to the instructions bequeathed by the Imperial Founder of Our House and by Our other Imperial Ancestors, to establish fundamental laws formulated into express provisions of law, so that, on the one hand, Our Imperial posterity may possess an express guide for the course they are to follow, and that, on the other, Our subjects shall thereby be enabled to enjoy a wider range of action in giving Us their support, and that the observance of Our laws shall continue to the remotest ages of time. We will thereby give greater firmness to the stability of Our country and promote the welfare of all the people within the boundaries of Our dominions; and We now establish the Imperial House Law and the Constitution. These Laws come to only an exposition of grand precepts for the conduct of the government, bequeathed by the Imperial Founder of Our House and by Our other Imperial Ancestors. That we have been so fortunate in Our reign, in keeping with the tendency of the times, as to accomplish this work, We owe to the glorious Spirits of the Imperial Founder of Our House and of Our other Imperial Ancestors. We now reverently make Our prayer to Them and to Our Illustrious Father, and implore the help of Their Sacred Spirits, and make to Them solemn oath never at this time nor in the future to fail to be an example to Our subjects in the observance of the Laws hereby established. May the heavenly Spirits witness this Our solemn Oath.

What effect did the **Japanese loss of World War II** have on Shinto?

In 1868, after the emperor Meiji restored imperial power when the last of the great Shoguns asked to be relieved of the burden of authority, loyalty to the emperor became a central theme. Prior to 1945, the vast majority of Japanese regarded the emperor, Hirohito, as infallible. Dedication to the imperial person and rule was perhaps the most important element in national unity. Admission of defeat in 1945 naturally struck at the heart of this central cultural institution. Since most people associated the emperor's divine descent with ancient Shinto tradition, the disastrous defeat called into question the viability of Shinto as a way of understanding the world and the place of the Japanese people within it.

On December 15, 1945, the Supreme Commander of Allied Powers, General Douglas MacArthur, issued the Shinto Directive, dramatically altering the shape of Japan's indigenous religious tradition. Acknowledging the tremendous symbolic connection between Shinto and Japanese nationalism, the decree disestablished all shrines and declared them private institutions. Priests were no longer officials of the government. The Directive replaced three earlier national structures—the National Association of Shrine Priests, Research Institute for Japanese Classics, and Supporters of the Grand Shrine (of Ise)—with the Association of Shinto Shrines. It attempted to bring as many shrines as possible into a voluntary organization whose purpose was to redefine Shinto as non-nationalistic religious tradition. Most shrines agreed to join, and most remain under local administration, entirely responsible for their own fundraising and upkeep. Long-standing tradition, however, does not yield so easily to the decrees of conquering foreigners. A number of major shrines, such as Yasukuni in Tokyo and others dedicated to Japan's war dead, still have the power to stir nationalist sentiment. Even now, politicians who want to play that card occasionally make highly publicized visits to Yasukuni.

How would you sum up the **history of Shinto**?

Beliefs now associated with the religious tradition called Shinto originated long before anyone ever referred to them as "the Way of the Kami." Archaeological evidence points to various forms of nature worship, ancestor veneration, shamanistic rituals, and animistic beliefs in an agricultural society during the neolithic (7000–250 B.C.E.) and bronze-iron (250 B.C.E.–100 C.E.) ages. Primitive shrines dedicated to the community or clan deities called *ujigami* appeared between 100 and 552 C.E. Sometime in the later sixth century C.E., after the arrival of *Butsu-do* or "the Way of the Buddha," Japanese distinguished indigenous beliefs from the imported tradition by inventing a name for it. During the Nara period (710–794), the Nakatomi clan served as priests of a nascent imperial Shinto whose earliest major shrines were those of Ise and Izumo. By 737 Shinto shrines numbered over three thousand, one in four enjoying direct government support.

The Fujiwara clan founded the important Kasuga shrine in Nara, the first capital. Kasuga was destined to play a critical role in the development of a hybrid of Buddhism and Shinto through its relationship with the nearby Buddhist temple of Todaiji. Throughout the Heian period (794–1185), with the capital newly established at Kyoto, Shinto's fortunes were intimately bound up with developments in Buddhism. Theologians on both sides devised theories designed to fit the two belief systems together, thereby inventing "Dual Shinto," a blend of both.

The remains of the Hiroshima Genbaku Dome, where the Americans dropped the first of two atomic bombs that ended the war, is now a memorial for the tens of thousands who died. The end of World War II also marked the end of the days when the Japanese revered the emperor as an infalable, divine leader.

The Kamakura period (1185–1333) witnessed the rise of feudal lords (*daimyo*) and a *samurai* warrior caste under a *shogun* ("throne field marshal") of the Minamoto family, which had toppled the Fujiwara clan. The *Samurai* code, *bushido,* was a blend of Confucian aristocratic conservatism, Buddhist mental discipline, and Shinto patriotism. Under the Minamoto the two chief *kami* were Sugawara Michizane, patron of literary and social concerns, and Hachiman, *kami* of war. Shinto grew as a popular religious tradition during the Muromachi/Ashikaga period (1333–1568, the first name referring to the capital outside Kyoto and the second to the clan in power) with imperial patronage of pilgrimage to Ise shrine.

Pre- and early modern developments during the Momoyama/Azuchi (1568–1615) and Edo/Tokugawa periods (1615–1867) included Shinto's steady ascendancy over Buddhism and identification with the political power of dictatorial *shoguns*. Eighteenth- and nineteenth-century Japanese isolationism went hand in hand with attempts to rid Shinto of foreign elements. That culminated in the Meiji Reform, ushering in the modern period (1868–1945) and restoring the emperor to divine status. World War II called Shinto's imperial theology into question and saw a return of popular sectarian movements.

Shinto Timeline

Date	Event
660 B.C.E.	Jimmu Tenno, first human emperor, divine son of Sun goddess Amaterasu.
c. 100–552 C.E.	Primitive Shinto shrines dedicated to clan deities (*Ujigami*) appear and spread.
c. 620	*Kojiki,* Records of Ancient Matters.
710–784	First permanent capital established at Nara; introduction of Confucianism, religious Daoism, and Buddhism; Shinto formally organized as all religions interact.
715	Buddhist temple annexed to a Shinto shrine.
720	*Nihongi* or *Nihon Shoki,* Chronicles of Japan, Shinto's main "scriptures."
737	Shinto shrines number three thousand.
750	An image of the Shinto war *kami* Hachiman is transported from the Shrine at Usa to Todaiji, in Nara.

Date	Event
794–1185	Heian period in Japan: Shinto's fortunes intimately bound up with the developments in Buddhism; foundation of Shingon and Tendai sects of Buddhism.
845–903	Sugawara Michizane, poet-calligrapher, becomes a *kami*.
901–923	*Engi-shiki,* or *Institutes of the Engi Era* promulgated by Heian emperor.
1185–1333	Japanese Buddhist and Shinto theologians devise theories designed to blend the two belief systems, thus inventing "Dual (*ryobu*) Shinto."
1333–1568	Muromachi period in Japan; Shinto grows as popular religion.
1600–1868	Tokugawa period in Japan; Confucianism gains influence in the Japanese Imperial government.
1622–1685	Yamaga Soko, Japanese Confucian scholar and military theorist, originator of the way of the warrior, *bushi-do,* blending Shinto and Buddhist themes.
1669–1736	Life of Kada no Azumamaro, considered the founder of the school of National Learning or *Kokugaku.*
1697–1769	Life of Kamo no Mabuchi, applies philological methods to classical Japanese prayer.
1730–1801	Life of Motoori Morinaga, regarded Shinto's best scholarly mind.
1763–1843	Life of Hirata Atsutane, influential exponent of *Kokugaku.*
1868	Dual Shinto becomes dominant form of Shinto.
1868	Japanese impose a system of devotion to the emperor, a kind of State Creed.
1868–1871	Japanese persecution of Buddhists by Meiji emperor.
1868–1945	Confucians play important role in the Meiji Reform; restoration of the emperor's divine status.
1869	Founding of Tokyo's Yasukuni Shrine as memorial to war dead.
1900	Shrine Shinto no longer considered a religion, but a universally binding attitude of reverence for the emperor.
1945	Supreme Commander of Allied Powers, General Douglas McArthur, issues the Shinto Directive; emperor no longer considered divine.
1989	Death of last "divine" Japanese emperor, Hirohito, ending the Showa era.
2012	Shinto remains dominant "cultural" code of Japan, blending residual Confucian values, symbolizing much of Japanese heritage.

RELIGIOUS BELIEFS

Is it appropriate to call **Shinto** a **religious tradition?**

Religious studies scholars have increasingly come to appreciate the genuinely religious qualities of Shinto. Every now and then criticism still surfaces that Shinto is so much a part of ordinary Japanese life that it is really a set of cultural beliefs and practices rather than a religious tradition. Some critics base their conclusion on polls of the Japanese public that seem to suggest widespread apathy about religious issues. Decreasing numbers of people are willing to identify themselves as adherents of any religious tradition, including Shinto. Other critics note that that even Japanese who do consider themselves active participants in a Shinto-based community are likely to claim that they are Buddhist as well. Doesn't that suggest that Shinto is less than authentically religious? If it were, some argue, it hardly would tolerate multiple religious allegiances, would it? Some point to Shinto's concern with the ordinary, the everyday, the natural world that surrounds us, and its lack of interest in transcendent mystery. Shouldn't a religious tradition be more invested in turning people's attention to a world beyond this one?

In fact, these and other distinctive aspects of Shinto are among its strengths and the basis for its unique contributions to our world. Shinto offers arresting insights into the inherent divine quality of the simplest things, of the beauty hidden away in life's nooks and crannies. Shinto tradition discerns innumerable causes for profound gratitude to the powers beyond the merely human that make life itself possible. Shinto may not be celebrated for producing sophisticated schools of theological speculation, but it undoubtedly possesses many characteristics that identify it as a religious tradition.

Is there a **Shinto creed**?

Shinto beliefs, like those of Daoism and the Chinese Community Traditions, have never been reduced to a concise formal summary statement. If one were to produce a brief Shinto creedal affirmation it might go something like this: I believe that sacredness surrounds me, that it pervades all things including my very self, and that the all-suffusing divine presence is ultimately benevolent and meant to assure well-being and happiness for all who acknowledge it and strive to live in harmony with it. Shortly after the Meiji Restoration in 1868, the imperial authorities formulated the rough equivalent of a brief creedal statement, called the Three Great Teachings, in an attempt to enhance the emperor's status. The three teachings included patriotism and respect for the *kami*, the establishment of heavenly principles in relation to human culture, and dedication to the emperor and his pronouncements. Authorities interpreted the creed in the context of worship of the sun goddess, Amaterasu, and the other chief deities in the creation myth. Although it approximated a creed in some ways, this statement was more like an acknowledgment of the importance of underlying religious conviction for the good order of Japanese society.

Are there **creation stories** or other **mythic elements** in Shinto tradition?

Two of the earliest of Shinto's foundational documents recount the story of the divine origins of Japan and its people. In variant accounts, the Kojiki and Nihon Shoki tell of how Japan came into existence, but the myth is not so much a narrative of creation as it is of Japan's unique sacred history. The basic myth goes like this: In the beginning, Heaven and Earth were as one, positive and negative unseparated. In a primal egglike mass dwelt the principles of all life. Eventually the purer, lighter element rose and became Heaven, while the heavier descended to form Earth. A reed shoot grew between Earth and Heaven and became the "One who established the Eternal Land." After some aeons, two *kami* formed by spontaneous generation. Descending to Earth on the Floating Bridge of Heaven, Izanagi (the Male Who Invites) and Izanami (the Female Who Invites) came into the world. In an image of sexual procreation, Izanagi stirred the ocean depths with his spear and created the first lands. On the eight Japanese islands the union of the Male and Female produced the mountains and rivers, and thirty-five other *kami*. Last to be born was Fire, the *kami* of heat, who burned his mother fatally during his birth. Izanagi slew Fire with his sword, creating numerous additional *kami* in the process.

The Female fled to the underworld, the Land of Darkness, desperate to prevent her husband from seeing her corrupted state. When the Male followed and lit a fire so that he could see, she chased him out and blocked the entry to the underworld. Returning to the surface, the Male immediately purified himself ritually, ridding himself of the underworld's pollution. Corruption from his left eye formed the sun goddess Amaterasu, who rules the High Plain of Heavens, and from his right, Tsukiyomi, the moon, whose province is the oceans. From his nostrils he created the storm *kami*, Susanowo, Withering Wind of Summer and ruler of the Earth. Susanowo soon made trouble for his sister, the Sun, who took refuge in a rock cave. Needing the sun to return, the eight hundred thousand *kami* discussed how they might entice her from her cave. At length they resorted to enlisting the Terrible Female of Heaven to dance and shout obscenities to rouse Amaterasu's curiosity. They then offered her blue and white soft offerings, a mirror, and a bejeweled Sakaki tree. She finally came out and dispatched her grandson Ninigi to rule the world. In turn, his son Jimmu Tenno became the first human emperor at age 45, on February 11, 660 B.C.E.

What do Shinto practitioners believe about **ultimate spiritual reality** or **God**?

Kami is the most important term in Shinto theology. Its general meaning is "high or superior being," and it can be applied to a host of spiritual presences and powers. Every *kami* is said to emanate its own distinctive divine energy or force. Among the various specific designations are the following: Nature *kami* include the deities of mountain, and agriculture, and bestowers of sustenance, vegetation such as sacred ancient trees, and the heavenly lights. Some deities have manifested themselves as animals, such as a white bird, a deer, or a monkey. Ancestral or tutelary deities (*ujigami*) include patrons of the clans, but they can also be nature *kami*. These are associated especially with shrines in regions once under the political control of the powerful families. As has often happened in Chinese traditions, some of Japan's *kami* also originated as historical figures who became deities by dint of their leadership in a clan. Large numbers of major shrines are dedicated to such figures. Other important historical *kami* include literary figures as well.

Zoomorphic *kami* form another significant category, as represented, for example, by Inari's fox. A classification of *kami* connected with ancestor veneration and exorcism are wrathful deities and malcontent spirits called *goryo* or *onryo*. They reflect the moral ambivalence Japanese discern in the spirit world. Popular belief holds such evil spirits responsible for disasters from earthquake and famine to war and political failure. Many of the great sacred sites enshrine tragic heroes who suffered political downfall. Some *kami* function as scapegoats in that they become the focus of popular blame for all manner of unhappy events. Japanese tradition sometimes identifies *kami* as either *ara*, wild and natural, or *niki*, placid and cultivated. In some cases separate shrines dedicated to these aspects of the same *kami* are located some distance apart. Another distinction is that between celestial deities (*amatsukami*) and the *kami* anciently associated with particular localities. Tradition portrays some *kami* as guests or visitors from a mysterious and faraway land called *tokoyo*, perhaps an acknowledgment of their origin in Buddhism and other imported traditions.

Who are some of the **principal Shinto male deities**, apart from those mentioned in the primal myth?

Stone statue of Daikoku-ten, one of the seven *kami* of good fortune. A length of *shimenawa* girds his pedestal, where he kneels on two bales of rice, holds a sack over his left shoulder, and wields his wish-granting mallet in his right hand.

Hachiman, generally identified as the *kami* of war, is near the top of the pantheon. It is no surprise that he often appears in painting and sculpture as armed and dangerous. But some of the most famous images portray Hachiman as a meditating monk or a solicitous Bodhisattva. Almost half of all officially listed Shinto shrines—some fifty thousand or more—honor Hachiman.

A curious grouping called the "Seven Gods of Good Luck" (*shichi-fuku-jin*) brings together figures of mixed background. Daikoku (sometimes called Daikoku-ten) hails from India, mythologically speaking, and probably traveled to Japan with an early influential Buddhist founder named Saicho. Daikoku is associated with accomplishment of one's goals and with wealth. Stone statues show a jovial bruiser with a sack over one shoulder, sitting on bales of rice and wielding a mallet with which he grants wishes. Also a god of prosperity, Ebisu is popular especially in fishing villages, rice farms, and local marketplaces. Ebisu is deaf and fails to hear deities being called together for his own October celebration! Like Daikoku, Bishamon (also Bishamon-ten) is of Indian origin. In the Hindu pantheon he was one of the four heavenly guardians, presiding over the north. In Buddhist as well as Shinto iconography, Bishamon is heavily armed and holds a miniature *pagoda* in his left hand as a symbol of his authority. Fuku-roku-ju, who originated in Daoism, stands for happiness, fortune, and long life, as his name indicates. When depicted in the arts he looks very much like his Chinese counterpart, Shou Lao, generally accompanied by a crane or deer. Like the *next* God of Good Luck, Jurojin, he also has a walking stick to which he has attached a sacred text. Jurojin is another patron of longevity of Daoist origin. Hotei, likewise drawn from the Daoist pantheon, stands for happiness and wealth. Benzaiten, also known as Benten, is the lone female of the bunch.

The septet of good fortune *kami* have been a favorite subject for popular and charming miniature carvings called *Netsuke*. A large number of *kami* are associated with forces of nature. Fujin, *kami* of wind, carries a large bag, and his companion *kami* of thunder, the menacing red-faced Raijin (or Raiden), holds a massive drum. A generic group of minor deities called *dosojin* protect travelers ever since Izanagi brought them into being upon his return from the underworld. A *kami* called Koshin is one protector of travelers, but some also identify him with farming. His three monkey partners have become popular as "See no evil, hear no evil, do no evil." *Kami* keep watch over every conceivable feature of ordinary life. Suijin, a god of water, guards wells and other water sources, for water is the principal means of purification and an essential of life.

Who are some **important female deities**?

Amaterasu, the sun goddess, is the most important of the goddesses. Hundreds of shrines throughout Japan are dedicated to her. One of the most colorful goddesses is Ama no Uzume, the "terrible female of Heaven," widely popular because of her identification with frivolity and dance. A *kami* described as both masculine and feminine is Inari. Because of her association with rice harvest, Inari is among the most important deities. Her messenger is the fox, and popular custom often refers to the fox itself as Inari. Bright reddish-orange or red *torii* gates, sometimes in great numbers, usually mark shrines dedicated to Inari. A pair of goddesses associated with the war *kami* Hachiman appear in a sculptural triad with him. One is called Nakatsu-hime, but the other remains to be identified. Seiryu Gongen was one of several goddesses adopted by Shinto in their role as protectors of Buddhist temples.

Two other "imported" goddesses with Buddhist connections are Zenmyo Nyoshin and Byakuko-shin. Stories tell of how a Korean monk fell in love with Zenmyo while he was studying in China. Byakuko was once an Indian Earth deity who became a Shinto *kami* through her associations with powers of nature. Goddesses like Kumano Fusumi Okami are often depicted round and full to suggest abundance. Goddess Tamayori-hime appears in a triad, flanked by two other goddesses, once worshipped as

423

A Shinto shrine side altar, showing the Fox, messengers of the *kami* Inari. Kyoto, Japan. (Photo courtesy of David Oughton.)

the "three protectresses of children." Tamayori was the daughter of Watatsumi no Kami, *kami* of the oceans, and Japan's first emperor's mother. Benten (also called Benzaiten) is a goddess of Indian origin. Hindus know her as Sarasvati, consort of the god Brahma and patroness of culture. She plays the Japanese lute (called the *biwa*), as Sarasvati plays the stringed instrument known as the *veena*, and devotees beseech her for protection and for gifts of eloquence and knowledge. Numerous female *kami* have played important roles in Shinto life over the centuries, and some were frequently depicted in human form, but only a few remain significant in contemporary devotion.

Have the **Japanese** ever **worshipped the emperor**? And is the emperor still a religiously important figure?

In early modern times, especially since the Meiji Restoration of 1868, Japanese governmental policy included the veneration of the divine Emperor as a central element. Major institutions enshrine twenty of the total number of one hundred and twenty-four emperors, as well as eleven princes, and focus on their worship. Seven of the imperial shrines are dedicated to honoring the spirits of rulers who died unfortunate deaths. Since the end of World War II, the role of Japan's imperial family has undergone dramatic changes from its former centrality to culture and religion. People still revere the emperor and his household as noble people who continue to represent and uphold ancient Japanese tradition. Many venerable and arcane Shinto rituals still occur only behind the walls of the imperial palace. But fewer and fewer Japanese have much interest in those ceremonies, and the emperor no longer has the national priestly status he once enjoyed. Still, many hope a royal son will continue the imperial line long into the future, and some even dream nostalgically of an eventual return to the days when the emperor wielded considerable political power. On the whole, though, it is safe to say that most Japanese no longer regard the emperor as divine and do not think of him or his family as significant religious symbols.

What role do views of the **material world** play in Shinto tradition?

Shinto is one of the world's most ecologically attuned religious traditions. Divine energy suffuses all of creation and is thus cause for reverence and wonder. Very optimistic in its outlook about life in this world, Shinto teaches that when human beings are in harmony with nature, all persons and things flourish. There is therefore no serious distinction or incompatibility between the physical and the spiritual, the human and the divine. Shinto is very much what some call a world-affirming tradition. When devotees worship at a shrine the mood is generally solemn and reverent. But a sense of joy and exuberance pervades festivals. Such celebrations, which can go on for days, leave little doubt that at the heart of Shinto tradition there is a delight in the everyday world and a conviction of the inherent goodness of creation.

What is the **nature** of the **human person** in Shinto tradition?

Shinto tradition has not given great attention to speculation about the metaphysical aspects of the human person. Conceptions of soul or spirit at the core of human nature tend to be rather fluid, not unlike popular Chinese ideas about these things. Reflecting the various aspects of both human and divine action, soul or spirit (*tama*) can manifest itself as either rich in blessings, granting harmony and union, full of mysterious power, or "rough." Individuals take second place to the needs of society as a whole; as a result traditional Shinto thought does not reflect in depth about the self apart from the collective. Above all, human beings are children of the *kami* whose natural birthright is to benefit from nature's gifts. Society and family, as well as nature, are the wellsprings of life. Acknowledging and venerating one's ancestors keeps healthy the link between individual and society because it keeps alive the continuity of heritage.

Do adherents of Shinto believe in **angels**?

Perhaps the closest formal analogy to the angel in Shinto tradition are the *tennin*, the Japanese version of Buddhism's celestial nymphs called *apsaras*. They are spirits, but other than that, they do not function quite the way angels do in other traditions. Lovely celestial beings have sometimes been said to descend and dance in response to divinely beautiful music. If we focus on the functional parallels—on angels as messengers of the divine world—Shinto offers a number of analogies. But they don't "look" at all like angels. These messengers are, for example, Inari's fox and the monkey assistant of Sanno, "the mountain king." Another functional aspect of angels is that of protection and generally mediating peace and blessing. Shinto psychology divides "soul" or "spirit" into two main types—positive and negative. *Nigimitama* are the benign spirits that either bestow blessing on or effect spiritual changes in people or natural objects. In that sense, they function somewhat like angelic spirits, but they were not necessarily created as spirits as angels are. They can be the spirits of the deceased that continue to roam the cosmos. A post-war sect called Byakko Shinko-kai, however, focused on a modified version of the "guardian angel" as an essential spiritual power.

What about **devils or demons**?

Numerous demons (*oni*) inhabit the cosmos of popular Shinto belief, but their particular province is the north. They are associated with negative forces generally and bad luck. "Rough spirits" (*aramitama*) are among the larger category of generic spirits or souls. A category of beings called *onryo* consists of angry spirits. Other beings called *goryo,* or "august spirits," are also generally troublesome but deserving of respect for their power. Some of Shinto's most important shrines are known as *goryo* shrines, because the *kami* dwelling there was once a human being who died under inauspicious circumstances. Another large category of evil spirits is that of *bakemono,* a term that refers to several specific groups of beings especially prevalent in folklore.

Have **dreams and visions** or other spirit manifestations been important in Shinto tradition?

Shinto legends are full of famous figures who have enjoyed—or barely survived—encounters with the spirit world. Many religiously prominent individuals have claimed to receive divine visitations and privileged communications in dreams. Various spirits, even evil ones (*goryo),* are capable of making their presence known for the purpose of delivering a message. These spirits, also called "living human *kami*" (*arahitogami*), can return in their human form to make things both positive and negative happen in the land of the living. Certain famous people, like Prince Shotoku Taishi (574–622) and poet-calligrapher Sugawara Michizane (845–903), who died untimely or violent deaths and later became *kami*, could also exert an unhappy influence if not dealt with properly. This is a striking amalgam of positive and negative powers in one spirit. Such a spirit can manifest itself in frightening apparitions or in blessings.

Is there a **distinctively Shinto ethic**?

Some have characterized Shinto as a type of naturalistic humanism that begins with the conviction of innate human goodness. When evil gains the ascendancy, it is not because of some inherent or inherited human tendency. Evil advances whenever human beings lose their concentration on life at its simplest, most basic level. As an ethical ideal, the concept of *makoto* means something like genuineness or authentici-

> ## How does one know when he or she has crossed the moral divide?
>
> **S**hame is a very powerful index of morality in Shinto tradition. What members of some traditions identify as moral guilt incurred objectively as a result of some specific act, Shinto tradition regards a breach of social contract for which the individual ought to be ashamed and seek forgiveness through purification.

ty. An ethical person is one who characteristically makes choices unspoiled by ulterior motives. Purity of intention thus takes precedence over adherence to any specific set of commands and prohibitions. Scholars refer to an ethic of this kind as "contextual" or "situational." All acts derive their moral value from the overall setting in which people perform them. A virtuous person is one who enjoys maximum harmony with the totality of the powers of nature.

How does one **assess** the quality of **virtue**?

The ethical barometer is a faculty called *kokoro,* a term that suggests a union of mind and heart. What some traditions call purity of heart, Shinto tradition calls brightness (*seimei*). Purified of all ill intent, the mind and heart are illumined through intimacy with the divine. Individuals do not evaluate their actions in terms of whether they will reap reward or suffer punishment as a consequence. Rather, they think of how their actions might affect the life of the community here and now.

How does Shinto tradition relate to the **use of violence**?

Many readers will be most familiar with three violence-related themes popularly associated with Shinto tradition. First, the *Samurai* tradition based on a code called *Bushido* (way of the warrior) is actually a blend of elements from three religious traditions: Confucian conservatism that tended to favor the aristocracy, Buddhist serene focus allowing one to submit to the inevitable, and Shinto patriotism and unquestioning loyalty. The Samurai code became especially important in Feudal Japan under the Minamoto Shogunate during a time of diminished centralized imperial emperor authority.

Second, the *kami-kaze* tradition, whose name means "Divine Storm Blast", a term that so many World War II films brought into relatively common English usage. The Japanese began to use the term during the Middle Ages in reference to how the *kami* fended off the Mongol invaders led by Kublai Khan in 1280, a descendant of Ghengis Khan. During World War II, the Japanese air force resorted to a desperate tactic when the tide began to turn against Japan. Pilots willing to commit suicide for their nation's honor aimed their explosive-laden dive bombers at enemy warships and went down with them. Ever since then, popular usage has referred to any self-immolating tactic or maneuver born of desperation as a "*kamikaze* mission."

Third, a form of ritual suicide called *hara-kiri* or *seppuku* has sometimes been associated with Shinto by way of the Samurai code of honor. The principle behind taking one's life has been that one can be cleansed of shame incurred through bad judgment or ill will by means of suicide. *Hara-kiri* means literally "belly cutting," a grim ritual in which the subject disembowels himself with a short blade while kneeling. His "second" then dispatches the subject by decapitating him with the longer samurai sword. There have been few publicized instances of the ritual, also called by the preferred and more polite term *seppuku*, in recent times. Surely the most famous such act was that of celebrated novelist Yukio Mishima in 1970. Most people no longer consider ritual suicide in any way laudable or virtuous and certainly do not think of it as part of Shinto religious belief.

All three themes do indeed have undeniable links to Shinto, but they do not by any means fully represent the ethical core of the tradition. To identify Shinto narrowly with a warrior code, desperate acts such as those associated with *kamikaze* pilots, or ritual suicide, is to miss out entirely on an overwhelmingly peaceful and beautiful tradition at whose core is the celebration of life and the sacred riches of creation.

Do adherents of Shinto believe in **salvation** or an **afterlife**?

Salvation is not a question of deliverance from the present human condition into a realm beyond. Shinto tradition teaches that the solution to the human predicament is just the reverse: sincere worshippers welcome the *kami* into the world of everyday concerns. Salvation therefore means making the ordinary sacred so that life here and now becomes the best it can be. Ancient traditions tell of another world, a realm beyond this one, called the High Plain of Heaven (*takama-no-hara*). It is a happy state, Heaven (*ame*), a spiritual land connected to Earth by a wondrous bridge. That mythic realm overflows with life and fecundity (*tokoyo-no-kuni*). Devout worshippers invoke the *kami* down, recalling how they descended before time began to bring the sacred land and its people into existence. There is also a netherworld, a most unpleasant state called the Land of Darkness (*yomi-no-kuni*). Ruled by death, that land is filled with wretched pollution and impurity. To that land worshippers dispatch troublesome spirits and hope their prayers and attentiveness to the rites of ancestor veneration will keep the negative forces at bay. Most people today do not believe that the dead end up in one or other of the realms beyond this world. Nevertheless, certain fundamental criteria determine whether an individual spirit will be content or disgruntled after death. Those include the ethical quality of one's life and one's attentiveness to avoiding the impurity attached to taboo behavior. Some speak simply of a "world beyond view" (*kakuriyo*), an otherwise nondescript state of being after this life.

Do **millennialism or messianism** have a place in Shinto thinking?

Mainstream Shinto thought has not developed millennialist or messianic themes of any significance. Some recent sectarian movements, however, have centered around such notions. Events surrounding and in the aftermath of World War II not surprisingly raised questions of Japan's historical destiny for many Japanese. So-called "new religions" of Japan, many with roots deep in Shinto tradition, have been fertile soil for messianic expectations. One such organization is Ananai-kyo, which teaches open relationships with and among the "five" (*nai*) religious traditions—Christianity, Islam, Buddhism, Daoism, and Confucianism. Various relatively recent Shinto-related cults and sects have centered around charismatic leaders whose teachings focus on preparation for an apocalyptic end of this world. For much of the 1990s, for example, members of a group called Aum Shinri Kyo attempted to implement the doomsday doctrine of their leader, Shoko Asahara. Conspiring to plant biological and chemical agents in Tokyo subways, they planned the final act of human history.

What is **Shinto** like **compared** to **Buddhism** and **Christianity**?

The overview below suggests some of the major similarities and differences.

Shinto: numerous *kami* associated with both nature and culture

Buddhism: spectrum from nontheistic to belief in multiple divine manifestations of the Buddha-nature

Christianity: one true God—no others

Shinto: purification from all symbolic outward pollution

Buddhism: enlightenment offers an end to earthly suffering

Christianity: provides for forgiveness of sins

Shinto: followers may participate in different religious traditions at the same time

Buddhism: also allows for simultaneous participation in other religious traditions

Christianity: permits participation in just one religious tradition

Glossary of Key Shinto Terms

Amaterasu—Shinto goddess of the sun, from whom the Imperial household descended.

Bushido—"Warrior Way," blending Buddhist discipline, Confucian loyalty, and Shinto purity.

Dosojin—wayside guardian deities to whom people pray for protection and fertility.

Jingju—shrines of top rank under imperial auspices.

Jinja—"dwelling of the *kami*" (*kami* = *jin*, related to Chinese *shen* above), most common name of basic Shinto shrine.

Kami—"high being," generic name for deity or divine spirit, including some humans who have been thus elevated.

Kamidana—"deity shelf," where a miniature Shinto shrine is kept in the home, business, or mode of conveyance (such as a ship, for example).

Kami no michi—"Gods' Way," Japanese reading of the Chinese characters *shen dao* (Shinto).

Ko—local association organizing devotees for worshipping particular *kami* or making pilgrimage.

Kojiki—sacred text, primary repository of Shinto mythic narratives.

Makoto—Shinto virtue of sincerity and moral purity.

Matsuri—common name for festival; communal celebration often with ancient Shinto roots.

Nihongi or *Nihon shoki*—ancient sacred text in Chinese, chronicling early Japanese history.

Ryobu shinto—"Dual" Shinto, so called because of its syncretistic amalgam of Buddhist and Shinto elements.

Taisha—"great shrine," major Shinto religious and ritual center.

Torii—stylized gateway with two uprights and two crossbeams marking entry to Shinto shrine.

SIGNS AND SYMBOLS

What **signs or symbols** distinguish Shinto **ritual specialists**?

Shinto priests wear distinctive garb (called *shozoku*) modeled on courtly fashions from the Heian period, the days when Japan's capital was in Kyoto. Ritual robes are of several types. They wear a kimono and a pair of very full-cut pants underneath. Outer garments originally indicated courtly rank with various colors (robin's-egg blue, red, purple, yellow, and light green), but now a priest's rank is indicated by either pale blue, black, or red. Outer garments have very wide flowing sleeves and extend down to the feet. For ordinary ceremonies priests wear a white silk vestment called a *karinigu* ("hunting cloak," a name from medieval times). With the simpler garments for ordinary duties, priests wear a plain roundish hat called *eboshi,* reserving a taller and more elegant version called *kanmuri* for high ritual occasions. High-ranking priests wear polished wooden shoes for rituals, and their subordinates wear thong sandals of wood. During all ceremonies, officiants carry a slender, tapered slab of wood called the *shaku* in the right hand, similar to the one seen in images of Chinese ancestor figures. Since even a layperson sometimes leads rituals and wears these same garments, they do not function like a "habit" to distinguish priests from laity. When not performing their shrine duties, Shinto priests wear ordinary street clothes. Shrine maidens (*miko*) wear a white kimono top and a vermillion or scarlet split skirt, only when they are performing shrine duties. Musicians, whether priests or not, also wear similar versions of Heian court fashion during ceremonies.

A Shinto priest, wearing the less formal headgear called the *eboshi*, receives and arranges offerings in preparation for a shrine festival. The lanterns are decorative and symbolic items found in great numbers around most larger shrines.

Do Shinto practitioners **mark sacred spaces** with any distinctive signs and symbols?

Easily the most important symbol of Shinto sacred spaces is the *torii* gate. Marking the entry and pathways to every shrine, torii typically consist of a pair of unadorned upright columns and a pair of crossbeams (or lintels) at the top. The upper crossbeam generally sits directly atop the column and protrudes on both sides, while the lower beam either ends at the columns or goes through and protrudes. Some *torii* have more elaborate uprights and crossbeams, depending on local and regional architectural styles. Devotees give *torii* as votive offerings to some shrines, lining pathways with hundreds of them inches apart, so that the entry to the shrine feels almost like a covered walkway. According to legend, the *torii* recalls the perch from which birds sang to entice the sun goddess from her cave.

Most Shinto shrines use the simplest and most natural materials available, imitating nature as much as possible. Natural wood grains and the lovely green forest patina that eventually accents thatch or wood-shingled roofs give them a rustic character and charm. Many shrine roofs still display remnants of primitive architectural elements as a reminder of antiquity. Although newer building methods no longer require them, many shrines retain a row of logs called *katsuogi* set along the ridge beam of the roof. Older structures needed the *katsuogi* to hold the thatch roof down. Another bit of architectural nostalgia are the vertical extensions of the eave beams above the roofline. As you view a shrine from either front or rear, you notice that the roofline forms an X. Horizontally trimmed upper ends of these beams, known as *chigi,* mark the shrines of female *kami*, and vertically trimmed ends those of male *kami*. Several rather mysterious symbols adorn holy places, whether or not the site has a structure on it. Thick straw ropes called *shimenawa* mark sacred places such as trees and rocks. Outer portals of shrines, whether actual buildings or miniature models used on home altars, also suspend *shimenawa* across their facades. Attached to the rope are pieces of white paper cut in zigzag fashion symbolizing offerings to

A tunnel of *torii* gates, votive offerings of worshippers, lines the path up from street level to the hill on which the Hie Jinja shrine rises above the bustle of Tokyo's Akasaka Mitsuke business district. The Hie Jinja is one of the shrines associated with a *kami* known as the Mountain King (*Sanno*).

the *kami*. The same bits of paper are attached to a ritual wand called the *gohei*. Legend has it that the rope originated as a way of restraining the sun goddess from escaping back into her cave.

If I visited a **Shinto shrine**, what would I see?

Walk down almost any street in almost any Japanese city or town and not many blocks along you will notice a simple, unobtrusive *torii* gate at street side. Turning to your right to look through the gate, you will be surprised to see a small grove of trees in the midst of storefronts and houses. You know from the *torii* that a Shinto shrine is nearby, but no structure is immediately evident. You walk through the gate and perhaps up a small hill, and as the shrine comes into view amid the trees you will pass through another *torii* gate. At the end of the path stands a neighborhood shrine, consisting perhaps of only a single wooden structure. Standing several feet off the ground and too small for a person to enter is the residence of one of the local *kami*. On the "front porch" of the shrine, or perhaps alongside the tiny steps that lead up to the porch,

A small side shrine at Kamakura's Zeni Arai Benten, dedicated to the one female *kami* among the seven gods of good fortune, shows the *shimenawa* above, the five-colored rope attached to the small bell, the offering box, and the symbolic mirror inside the doors that are usually closed in most shrines.

there are several small white ceramic foxes, messengers of the deity Inari. Also on the porch just outside the shrine door are small offerings of various kinds, including a little wooden box for donations. Uncounted thousands of these unassuming shrines are quiet testimony to the presence of the divine powers.

Larger shrines are naturally fewer in numbers but still abundant. Preserving often relatively extensive tracts of forested land in burgs like Tokyo and Kyoto, the great shrines are all the more remarkable. Even in the heart of bustling Tokyo, for example, the Hie Shrine still sits atop a surprisingly high and densely wooded knoll. As you pass under one and another monumental *torii* along the pathway to the center of shrines like Tokyo's splendid Meiji Jingu, you will find yourself slowing down and marveling at the beauty of ancient trees. The sheer power of place here is almost overwhelming, enveloping you with a profound sense of the sacred. At the heart of the place are worshippers, perhaps in large numbers depending on the day, approaching the outer building of the sanctuary to pray and make their offerings. If your timing is right, you might witness formal ceremonies of blessing or priestly offering.

Shinto shrines do not present the kind of public face that Japan's numerous Buddhist temples show. Shinto's miniature—and not so miniature—holy forests are vivid reminders of the need to acknowledge the sanctity of nature, especially when the hunger for expediency and immediate gratification compromises reflection.

What are the main **architectural and ritual elements** of a major Shinto **shrine**?

At the heart of a major shrine is a complex of three units called the *hongu* (for a *jingu,* *honsha* for a *jinja*). This central area, all oriented to the south as in Chinese sacred structures, houses the shrine's principal deity. Within the *hongu* are the *haiden, heiden,* and *honden* arranged front to rear along the south-north central axis. The outer and most public of the spaces is called the *haiden,* or worship hall, where devotees gather individually or in small groups for blessings and other rituals. Most people who come to the shrine without prior arrangements for ceremonial ministrations from the priestly staff perform their brief prayers in front of the *haiden*. But if the staff are performing rituals inside, those outside are welcome to observe. From that hall, worshippers can look across an interior courtyard to the central structure, the *heiden* or offering hall, where only the priestly staff perform more sacred rituals. From there, in turn, the celebrants can see (sometimes across yet another courtyard) the *honden,* the Shinto equivalent of the "holy of holies." There, behind closed doors and visible to no one, the *kami* reside. Also on the grounds of many large shrines one may find subordinate shrines called *bekku,* which house related major deities. *Massha* house lesser deities. Some shrines also have small Buddhist temples (called *jingu-ji,* "shrine-temples") on the property, remnants of the ancient connections between the two traditions.

Is there such a thing as **Shinto art** or **aesthetic**?

Every twenty years, priests and specially skilled carpenters gather at the Grand Shrine at Ise for a ritual that says a lot about Shinto artistic sensibilities. They construct a new inner shrine on a plot left vacant for the previous twenty years. Then they dismantle the older shrine separated by only a small partition and leave its space empty until it is time to rebuild there. The carpenters use only the finest cypress, fashioned with the simplest of tools, and use no nails, adhesives, or artificially produced material of any kind. Each stroke of the plane or hammer is part of an ancient ritual that blends religious reverence and awe with the practical demands of sacred architecture. Each structure, however small and humble, is a work of sacred craftsmanship.

During the Middle Ages, Shinto sculptors created anthropomorphic images of various *kami,* largely under the influence of Buddhism's rich iconography. Some sculptures remain important symbols in a few individual devotional cults within Shinto (such as Sanno Ichijitsu, with its images of the *kami*'s monkey messengers). But on **433**

A Shinto religious goods store in Tokyo displays miniature shrines for home use, as well as miniature *torii* gates and other ritual objects used for making offerings.

the whole, modern Shinto worship is aniconic, focusing on the presence of symbolic objects, such as the mirror and sword, within the holy of holies. A unique and historically important art form is the so-called shrine *mandala*. Stylized depictions of individual shrines depict the sacred site as a meditative device on a hanging scroll. Members of certain sects have used these *mandalas* as devotional focuses of esoteric contemplative rituals. Above all, shrines and their settings remain the most important visual expression of Shinto beliefs and values. Simple, natural beauty is the key.

Do Shinto practitioners use **symbolism** in personal or **private rituals**?

Many Japanese households have a corner dedicated to the *kami*. A miniature shrine building (*kamidana*) at which worshippers pray daily is placed on a shelf or table. For special occasions they will go to the actual shrine, but everyday reverence to the *kami* happens at home. People can purchase these charming miniature shrines, some done up in exquisitely fine architectural detail, at religious goods stores in any Japanese city or at some of the larger shrines. Worshippers who get them from shrine shops often prefer to purchase them at shrines to which their families have ancestral connections. Priests often visit parishioners to dedicate their new home shrines and sometimes make annual house visits for brief renewal ceremonies. People with more ample homes and yards might afford larger outdoor miniature shrines called *yashikigami* (*kami* of the home). Miniature shrines range from simple and affordable to finely wrought and costly. Business establishments, restaurants, police stations, and bridges

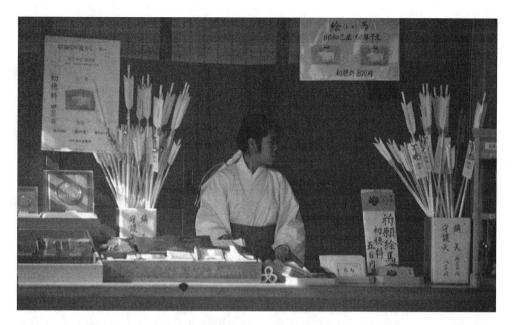

A shrine maiden called a *miko* attends to the shrine shop at Tokyo's Meiji Jingu, selling various devotional materials such as the protective arrows and cards on which worshippers can write their petitions to leave on special racks at the shrine.

on oceangoing ships, for example, might also have a *kamidana* to which the staff make daily offerings. Many miniature shrines have their own tiny *torii* gates and *shimenawa*. In addition, worshippers often bring small votive offerings when they visit local shrines. A popular offering is the miniature *torii* gate on which devotees write names and prayers of petition before hanging it on a rack along with hundreds of others like it at the shrine.

Have **relics** been important in the Shinto tradition?

Sacred objects play a very important role in Shinto ritual. Every shrine houses some small token of the deity who graciously calls this humble place home for the benefit of worshippers who come to pay their respects. These objects, called *go-shintai* or "revered *kami* body," are said to include such unremarkable items as a mirror, sword, comb, ball of iron, paintings, pebbles, or pieces of carefully cut paper. Worshippers generally do not get even a passing glimpse of the objects, for they remain always behind the innermost shrine's closed doors. People visit a shrine not so much because the sacred objects are there, as because the presence of the *kami* makes the place holy. When Christians or Buddhists, for example, make pilgrimage to a church or *stupa*, they frequently do so because certain objects associated with a particular sacred person are enshrined there. They may not believe that the objects themselves contain miraculous powers, but it is the presence of the objects that makes the place worth visiting. Shinto's sacred objects play a very different role. Many worshippers may not

435

even be aware of exactly what items a given shrine holds. In other words, the symbols of the *kami* are of secondary importance from the perspective of Shinto worshippers.

MEMBERSHIP, COMMUNITY, DIVERSITY

Where do Shinto practitioners **live today**? Any estimates of **numbers** available?

By far the majority of people who identify themselves with Shinto tradition still live in Japan. Some eight in ten Japanese practice a religious syncretism of Buddhism and Shinto. There are also Shinto shrines in many areas of Asia (and a few elsewhere as well) in which significant Japanese communities have developed. Honolulu's Shinto shrine, for example, is a highly visible sign of a large and prosperous Japanese community there. Accurate statistics as to membership are hard to come by, largely because an increasing number of Japanese do not identify themselves as religious at all—even if they continue to engage in some traditional Shinto practices. We do, however, have fairly reliable information about numbers of shrines and active priests from which we have some idea of the tradition's vitality today. Some twenty thousand priests serve between eighty thousand and a hundred thousand shrines.

Are there any especially important Shinto **holy places**?

One of the most striking features of Shinto tradition is the intuition of the world's pervasive sacredness. Wherever the *kami* are, there is holiness—and that means just about everywhere people are willing to look carefully. Places where the *kami* dwell are called *otabisho,* "stages on a journey," and are not necessarily identified with shrine buildings. Certain natural settings stand out as particularly potent. Mountains, waterfalls, caves, and trees have attracted Japan's spiritual athletes (ascetics) and pilgrims over the centuries. Mount Fuji remains a revered symbol of natural perfection and beauty, and pilgrims still consider a hike to the volcano's summit spiritually uplifting. On a clear winter's day you can occasionally glimpse Fuji's symmetrical slopes and snowy cap from taller buildings in Tokyo, sixty miles away, and it is easy to see how the mountain has assumed such symbolic importance.

In addition to countless holy places left as close to their natural states as possible, sacred architecture marks many others as sacred. "Founding stories" (*engi*) record how Shinto communities have chosen certain sites. These mythic tales tell how, for example, a deity went looking for a suitable dwelling and decided at last on one perfect spot. Amaterasu is said to have revealed in a dream to an imperial princess of old that she wanted her shrine built at Ise. Even into relatively recent times, Shinto tradition has considered such hierophanies (sacred manifestations) important explanations as to why certain places are high on the ladder of sanctity and power. But Shinto has not been

Two young men seek a blessing on a new business venture at Tokyo's Meiji Jingu. At left is the principal priest, while at right the assistant priest and the *miko* (deaconess) bow.

associated with holy cities as have traditions like Hinduism and Islam, for example. Shinto tradition has not associated the *kami* so much with urban settings as with pristine nature. Some major shrines, like Kyoto's Heian Jingu, have arisen conspicuously in the midst of bustling urban areas, showing a surprisingly public face. But most represent the cultivation of holy serenity in an increasingly disquieted world. Major publications list shrines according to their popularity and reputation for spiritual success stories, rating shrines according to particular categories of greatest interest, such as healing, help on examinations, good starts in new businesses, and fertility.

Are there any **sub-communities** or **denominations** within Shinto?

Numerous varieties and schools of Shinto have come and gone over the past thirteen hundred years. Here briefly are a few of the more important: An ascetical "mountain" sect called Shugendo began as early as the Nara period (710–94), and small groups remain active today. Beginning during the Middle Ages, several schools have arisen under the patronage of important members of powerful clans. Now identified by the names of those families or of the schools' individual founders, the larger groups are Urabe (also known by the later family name of Yoshida, and Yui-itsu—"unification"— Shinto), Watarai (also called Ise Shinto), the Confucian-oriented school of Yoshikawa, and Kurozumi-kyo, named after its nineteenth-century founder. Several other schools are identified by terms that suggest their principal teaching or emphases. For example, a seventeenth-century school called Suiga ("Bestowal of Blessings") Shinto laid groundwork for the growth of National Learning. Sanno-ichijitsu blended Shinto themes with esoteric teachings of Tendai Buddhism in the seventeenth century, focusing on the divine manifestation of a "mountain king." Finally, Minkan Shinko is a general designation for a host of developments called "folk" religious beliefs and practices, incorporating elements of Shinto as well as other traditions. Japanese governments have promulgated various types of legislation, especially since the late nineteenth century, aimed at keeping track of the many religious groups that have occasionally leveled severe criticism at the imperial form of governance.

What is **sectarian** Shinto?

Thirteen principal sects comprise what is generally referred to as "sectarian" or "sect" (*kyoha*) Shinto. Arising over the centuries and officially recognized in the early twentieth century, the thirteen cluster around five themes or emphases. First, two groups that emphasize purification are known as Misogi-kyo and Shinshu-kyo (-*kyo* means teaching or school). Fuso-kyo, Jikko-kyo, and Ontake-kyo are called "mountain sects" because they centered around cults of two sacred mountains, Fuji and Ontake. They restructured along distinctively Shinto lines the teachings of several earlier ascetically oriented groups called Shugendo. Three more recent sects have focused on faith healing. They are Kurozumi-kyo, Tenri-kyo, and Konko-kyo, and they all trace their origins to a founding figure. Two sects called Shinto Shusei-ha and Shinto Taisei-kyo have emphasized Confucian elements and have blended features of the purification and mountain sects as well. Finally among the "thirteen" are the most recent groups, whose mission has been to renew Shinto tradition. These are Izumo Oyashiro-kyo, Shinri-kyo, and Shinto Tai-kyo. The latter is an umbrella organization that was largely responsible for the official recognition of the thirteen. From these sects dozens of smaller movements have arisen in recent times.

What **gender-related issues** are important for Shinto practitioners?

Shinto priests (and priestesses) have almost always been married people with families. Ongoing social taboo still prohibits menstruating women from participating as official ministers in ritual activities. Contemporary custom, however, has in all likelihood loosened such restrictions. It is safe to say that in general women have historically had greater direct participation in many Shinto shrine rituals than they do presently. Only unmarried young women are eligible for the office of *miko* in shrines, and typically have access to the positions hereditarily, as a result of their families' priestly traditions.

Did Shinto **tradition spread** beyond Japan?

Shinto has gone as far as Japanese emigration and military expansion have carried that ancient tradition. You'll see the occasional Shinto shrine in various parts of the Pacific basin even now, reminders of a time when Japan projected its imperial presence beyond its shores. Where Japanese communities have taken root and continue to grow, especially during the last fifty years or so, older people especially take comfort in celebrating at the nearest shrine for festivals. But on the whole, Shinto has remained about as purely Japanese a phenomenon as one can imagine. Even in parts of the United States, for example, where now sizeable communities of Japanese descent make their homes, traditional Shinto priests are exceedingly rare. Some suggest that Shinto anywhere but in Japan is a contradiction in terms. Shinto remains, ideally, a tradition inseparable from the very soil of Japan and its sacred streams, groves, and mountains.

Are joining or leaving the Shinto community significant **membership issues**?

Membership in traditions so closely identified with ethnicity as Shinto has a great deal to do with trends in society generally. That is of course true of most religious traditions, but here there are several features about Shinto worth noting. Japanese ethnicity does not imply adherence to Shinto beliefs and practices any more than Jewish ancestry implies that an individual actively participates in Judaic religious traditions. Shinto is integral to the fabric of Japanese life, yet large numbers of Japan's present population do not engage in regular Shinto rituals at all, and many others are very selective as to their involvement. But that does not imply a deliberate choice to reject the ancient traditions as such. It does, however, underscore the impact of cultural and social change on all things traditional. Shinto tradition calls people to unhurried, careful attentiveness to the mysterious details of life. In a fast-paced, often tumultuous world, the drum-beat of change can easily drown out the sound of the drums that announce the beginning of a sacred ritual.

Since Shinto is so intimately identified with being Japanese, the concept of conversion is largely irrelevant. That does not mean that no non-Japanese has ever deliberately chosen to become a practitioner of Shinto, but such instances are very rare. The case of Judaism offers a rough parallel. Many consider membership in Judaism a matter of ethnicity, but some Jewish congregations nevertheless welcome converts into their community. Some have developed formal initiatory rites for ethnically non-Jewish individuals, but Shinto tradition does not have such a rite for non-Japanese who wish to practice and profess Shinto tradition. The difference here is that membership in Judaism presupposes assent to certain basic creedal affirmations, whereas Shinto does not.

What issues have characterized Shinto's **relationships to other traditions**?

Shinto has important connections primarily to Buddhism and Confucianism, and secondarily to the Christianity that missionaries brought to Japan in the early modern period. During much of medieval and early modern times, Shinto and Buddhist leaders and teachers worked together at articulating points of theological cooperation between various schools of thought in the two traditions. That ongoing interaction resulted in the various types of Ryobu (Dual or Two-sided) Shinto as well as other syncretistic

The focus of *Fuso*, one of the thirteen *kyo* of sectarian Shinto, is the deity of Mt. Fuji, Sengen Daishin.

denominations and sects. Such cooperation continued until the thirteenth and fourteenth centuries, when some Shinto thinkers developed belief systems in which Shinto stood at the top of a theological mountain. By the seventeenth century, the "National Learning" movement began to offer a fully articulated interpretation of Buddhist-Shinto relations. Scholars suggested that the major figures of the Buddhist pantheon were nothing more than local forms of the *kami*, and that the emperor descended directly from the Sun goddess, Amaterasu.

Confucianism had by that time made its presence felt more vigorously than ever through its impact on courtly life and administration of the Tokugawa shogunate (1600–1867). Confucian scholars and bureaucrats also contributed significantly to the Meiji Restoration in 1868. But the more closely Shinto theology came to be identified with the Japanese throne, the more it developed into a national ideology with little room for systems of belief considered non-Japanese—Buddhism and Confucianism, first and foremost, but now missionary Christianity as well. Contemporary Shinto has once again become more open to interaction with other traditions, and Shinto leaders take it for granted that many who worship at shrines also maintain other religious affiliations. For many Japanese, the Kami Way is not a separate system of religious beliefs. It is simply what all religious persons believe underneath all their otherwise distinctive doctrines. Shinto is therefore nothing less than the very essence of acknowledging the divine in the world.

Shinto Organizations, Schools, and Sub-Communities

Fuso—inspired by teachings of Kakugyo Hasegawa (1541–1646), one of the thirteen *kyo* of sectarian Shinto whose focus is the deity of Mt. Fuji, Sengen Daishin.

Jikko—"practice teaching," one of the thirteen *kyo* of sectarian Shinto, founded in early eighteenth century but based on teachings of a seventeenth-century devotee of the Buddhist Bodhisattva Miroku.

Kurozumi—one of the thirteen *kyo* of sectarian Shinto named after founder Munetada Kurozumi (1780–1850).

Minkan Shinko—general term used to refer to a large number of folk beliefs and practices.

National Learning—*Kokugaku* was an early modern (seventeenth–early nineteenth-century) development that called for a return to ancient Japanese sources, emphasizing a quest for the purest expressions of the Japanese spirit.

Ontake—"Great Mountain Sect," a *kyo* of sectarian Shinto originating in the early nineteenth century.

Sanno-ichijitsu—"Sole Reality of the Mountain King," one of the thirteen *kyo* of sectarian Shinto, also known as Tendai Shinto, one of a number of sects focused on worship of various *gongen* (manifestations) of sacred mountain-based deities often linked to Buddhist figures believed to parallel Amaterasu, the sun goddess.

Sect(arian) Shinto—*shuha* or *kyoha* Shinto, refers to a variety of sub-communities that arose over many centuries. Traditionally numbered at thirteen *kyo*, teachings or schools.

Shinshu—one of the thirteen *kyo* of sectarian Shinto, officially recognized in 1880, emphasizing ascetical practices.

Shinto Tai—"Great Teaching of Shinto," began 1873; one of the thirteen *kyo* of sectarian Shinto.

Shinto Taisei—nineteenth-century "Fulfillment of the Way of the *Kami*," one of the thirteen *kyo* of sectarian Shinto.

Shugendo—early ascetical "mountain sect," from as early as the eighth century.

State/Shrine Shinto—*kokka* Shinto developed out of changes arising out of the Meiji Restoration in 1868. Also known as Shrine Shinto, it came into clearest focus as a distinctive aspect of Shinto after the Shinto Directive of 1945 coined the term "State Shinto" as a way of describing official Japanese sponsorship of certain shrines associated with the spirits of those who died in war. It is especially distinguished from Sectarian Shinto.

Suiga—"Descent of Divine Blessing," a *kyo* of sectarian Shinto founded in the seventeenth century.

Tenrikyo—"Divine Wisdom," one of the thirteen *kyo* of sectarian Shinto, mission-oriented, founded in 1838, and increasingly identifying itself as universal and independent of Shinto.

LEADERSHIP, AUTHORITY, AND RELIGIOUS ROLES

How are Shinto **leaders chosen** and given authority?

Shinto priesthood has historically been a hereditary occupation. Even after the government officially took over the appointment of chief priests after 1868, hereditary succession continued in many localities. Perhaps the most important ingredients in maintaining standards among Shinto officials are the two educational institutions now solely responsible for the training of priests. Tokyo's Kokugakuin ("national learning") University is a relatively recent development, a private university that offers general education as well as the equivalent of Shinto seminary curriculum. It supplies research for the present centralized shrine authority, the Jinja Honcho. The Kogakkan ("Imperial hall of learning") University near Ise was originally a public institution that closed after World War II and then reopened in 1952 as a private university. Priests-to-be study Japanese history and literature, but focus on Shinto studies, especially ritual and theology. Shinto priests are not ordained clergy, strictly speaking. They are laypeople granted certification or licensure upon satisfactory completion of the seminary curriculum and its qualifying exams.

Have **women exercised leadership** among Shinto practitioners?

In ancient times, women played an indispensable role as shamans in countless Shinto shrines. Even after imperial decrees reduced women's roles in shrine life, giving precedence to a male priesthood, women continued to fill some key positions. Well into the sixteenth century, for example, women functioned as priestesses in some shrines. The last of the priestesses was a young woman serving the Suwa Shrine in Nagasaki. Women have long acted as spirit mediums consulted by many a priest over the centuries, as well as by individual worshippers. Restrictive legislation arising from the Meiji Restoration in 1868 dramatically curtailed women's official participation in shrine staff ministries. Only at the Ise Grand Shrine, sacred to the sun goddess Amaterasu, does a woman currently hold the position of high priestess. During the Second World War, many women took over priestly functions when their husbands departed for military service.

Is there a central Shinto **teaching authority**?

Shinto's close identification over the centuries with Japanese culture and imperial rule has sometimes made it appear that the royal administration functioned as a central religious authority. Certain regimes have made concerted efforts to encourage uniformity of traditional thinking among the Japanese people, and that has sometimes involved "official" statements about Shinto beliefs as well as attempts to centralize the organization of large numbers of shrines. In addition, training for Shinto ritual specialists in recent times has devolved on only a select few educational institutions very much associated with "national" identity. Those academic–religious organizations have set themselves the task of clarifying and, in some cases, restructuring the countless elements of ancient Shinto tradition into a coherent system. Theirs has been an increasingly "theological" enterprise in modern times. Even so, Shinto tradition has remained quite fluid and inclusive, and far less identified with definitive teaching authority than, say, Roman Catholicism. Over the centuries various centralized institutions have come and gone. The "Institute of the Great Teaching" (*daikyo-in*), for example, was motivated largely by the desire to root out Buddhist and Christian influences in nineteenth-century Japan. The "Bureau of Divinity" (*Jingikan*) sought to unify the administration of shrines and the appointment of priests. It is perhaps best to think of the centralized authority as regulating matters of practice rather than of belief, setting out detailed instructions for rituals (*jinja shaishiki*) and for coordinating observances nationally.

Is there a Shinto system of **religious law**?

There have been numerous bodies of legislation concerning the structure and administration of the Shinto shrine system, and about governmental controls over the spread of religious organizations in Japan generally. Laws have decreed relationships between imperial rule and religion, and between Shinto and Buddhism, and others have stipulated conditions for religious liberty. But there has never been the kind of comprehensive codification of religious law that one finds in Islam's Shari'a, Judaism's rabbinical law, or Roman Catholicism's Canon Law. Virtually everything related to the regulation of conduct in Shinto tradition has been integrated into an all-encompassing and very demanding, but mostly unwritten, code of ethics. People learn what is expected of them religiously through family and local community tradition.

Are there Shinto **hierarchical structures**?

Like so many other religious traditions, Shinto community structures often reflect the belief that human life mirrors divine life. Just as there is at least an implicit hierarchy among divine beings, human society needs a certain degree of structure. Long-standing Japanese tradition, much influenced and reinforced by Confucian teaching over the centuries, lays great emphasis on knowing one's place in society. Each individual stands in a relationship of higher-to-lower, or vice versa, with his or her fellow human beings, and basic etiquette requires that one be aware of social subordination in every context. Everyday Japanese speech, with its various levels of polite address, reflects that awareness. Although contemporary Japan is a democratic society, with all the political institutions needed to support a democracy, hierarchy runs deep in the culture and so too in Shinto belief and practice. Everything, from ranks within the network of shrines to division of labor among ritual specialists, mirrors that awareness of multilevel structure in society at large. For several centuries in the early history of Shinto, four groups were responsible for most Shinto rituals. The Nakatomi family oversaw rituals generally, the Imbe family were concerned with maintaining ritual purity, the Urabe family focused on divinatory rituals so as to know the divine intentions in all matters, and shrine musicians performed the "divine entertainments." Other powerful clans or families held and relinquished positions of power and influence over subsequent centuries.

How and where do members of local Shinto communities **come together**?

Larger shrines provide the principal venue for Shinto community gatherings. The more elaborate shrines might have a dozen or more separate structures, each designed for a specific function. The ritual

A senior priest serves his fellow priests a symbolic communion sip of sake at the conclusion of a new moon ceremony at Itsukushima Jinja, on an island near Hiroshima. He kneels before each in turn until all have been served, then they file out and return to the priests' quarters. The priest on the far left holds a symbol of ancient courtly authority called the *shaku*.

Children dressed in *happi* coats play during neighborhood Shinto street procession in which the *mikoshi*, a portable minia-ture shrine, is paraded about on men's shoulders (in background).

center includes facilities along the entry path for purification by water, as well as the var-ious halls of worship and the sanctuary itself. There is often a separate facility in which the shrine ritual specialists purify themselves. Secondary shrine functions include a wide range of activities. Smaller buildings provide facilities for weddings (*gishiki-den*), sacred dance and performance of plays (*kagura-den*), and storage of the portable proces-sional shrines called *mikoshi*. There is usually a sacred kitchen for preparing offerings and a small shop where worshippers can purchase mementos and items such as cards on which to write petitions to be hung on boards outside the main worship hall. Officials administer the whole operation from a shrine office, looking after all the more mundane concerns of any institution. That includes everything from scheduling of events and staff to arranging for supplies and paying bills. Smaller shrines naturally have fewer of these separate facilities, and the smallest often do not have resident priests.

Shrines are organized in a variety of ways. Some are directly managed by heredi-tary priestly families still connected with powerful clans of old. Committees of local elders oversee many village shrines that lack permanent priests. Trade guilds, called *za,* still worship together and manage their own shrines. Wealthy families sometimes even own and administer shrines just for their private use. Finally, some historic Bud-dhist temples have set up and maintained shrines in hopes of securing the protection of the *kami* for the temple. Some larger shrines attract worshippers from all over Japan, while most local shrines have relatively stable memberships of parishioners. But parishioners often have family or devotional ties to more than one local shrine.

How does the **hierarchy** among Shinto **shrines** work?

Over the centuries Shinto authorities have devised a number of structures and classifications by which to distinguish various levels and functions of shrines. The most important is called the "shrine-rank system" (*shakaku seido*) that has been in place since shortly after the Meiji Restoration of 1868. Jingu designates shrines of top rank under imperial auspices, such as Meiji *Jingu*, in Tokyo, which enshrines royal ancestors, and Ise Jingu, which is at the top of the hierarchy and is called the *Daijingu*, Grand Imperial Shrine. Next in rank are the approximately one hundred thousand *jinja*, a generic term including virtually all shrines larger than little wayside structures. About two hundred and fifty are included on a list of highest ranking ones. Of these some two hundred were designated prior to World War II as "governmental shrines" (*kansha*). Many larger *jinja* have spawned affiliated or branch shrines called *bunsha*. Multiple shrines dedicated to a single *kami* generally constitute distinct families, with one shrine usually acknowledged as the original foundation from which branch shrines developed.

Some very important *jinja*, such as Kasuga in Nara and about a dozen others, have the honorific title *taisha*, "grand shrine," roughly equivalent to "cathedral basilica." They are also part of a cluster of twenty-two (*ni-ju-ni sha*) institutions elevated to privileged status, but even they are divided into three levels: seven high, seven middle ranking, and eight lower. That grouping arose out of the practice of ranking shrines within a given region according to their order of priority on pilgrimage routes, or to guide devotees intent on visiting a sequence of holy places. In various prefectures, a further ranking of area shrines simply lists them as "first, second, or third" shrine, acknowledging the three regional shrines that draw the largest crowds of worshippers. A number of *jinja* (some count 138) have been specially designated as "nation-protecting shrines" (*gokoku jinja*) because of their dedication to the souls of those who died in battle. Twenty-seven shrines within that category, also called "deceased spirit-invoking shrines" (*shokonsha*), have been accorded a high rank because of the importance of the heroes from all periods of Japanese history that they commemorate. Tokyo's Yasukuni Jinja ranks at the top of that category. Before 1945, countless smaller local memorials represented the bottom of this hierarchical category. The main central administration for the rating of shrines is called the Association of Shinto Shrines (*jinja honcho*), which has branches (called *jinja cho*) in each Japanese prefecture.

What are some of the main **varieties** of Shinto **officials or ritual specialists**?

Shinto tradition refers to the priesthood in general as either *shinshoku* or *kannushi*. Larger shrines with full priestly staffs distinguish among a number of ranks. The chief priest is called the *Guji*, generally the highest ranking local official. *Guji* might have oversight of up to thirty subordinate shrines. The *Gon-guji* is second-in-command and

Shrine deaconesses (*miko*) dance together on a stage at Tokyo's downtown Hie Jinja shrine.

oversees a staff of several lower ranks as well, including junior assistant chief priests (*shin-gon-guji*). Senior priests are called *negi,* assistant senior priests *gon-negi,* and regular priests (*shuten* or *kujo*) fill out the ranks of male staff. A national ranking system also distinguishes among priests by acknowledging their levels of learning with the equivalent of academic degrees, named "purity" (*jokai*), "brightness" (*meikai*), "righteousness" (*seikai*), and "uprightness" (*chokkai*).

Young unmarried women, called shrine maidens (*miko*), function rather like deaconesses. Dressed in striking vermillion skirts and white blouses, they assist in blessing rituals, run the shrine shop, and perform sacred dance. *Miko* traditionally begin their association with the shrine and training for service as "sacred children." Highest in rank is the unique position called *saishu,* found only at the Ise shrine and held by a woman. She is an imperial princess with the symbolic title "master of the *matsuri* (festivals)." Assisting her is a priest with the rank of *dai-guji,* "great chief priest," a function unique to Ise. In the imperial household, ritual specialists have either of two ranks. The *shoten* parallels the shrine rank of senior priest, the *shotenho* that of assistant senior priest. But the emperor himself or a personal delegate presides, much as the Chinese sovereign once did, at over two dozen annual ceremonies.

Do Shinto practitioners run **private schools** for their **children**?

Private schools equivalent to parochial educational systems in some other traditions have not been institutionally significant in the history of Shinto. Perhaps the closest thing to structured education in Shinto beliefs and values have been occasional government attempts to insert components of Shinto—i.e., traditional or national Japanese—ethics into school curricula. In 1937, for example, the Ministry of Education incorporated themes from an 1890 imperial document on education into a new ethics curriculum called "Principles of the National Entity" (*Kokutai no hongi*). Meant to implement the concept of "State Shinto," the document emphasizes the historicity of the classic mythical narratives concerning the emperor's divine descent. It praises unquestioning dedication to the corporate good of the Japanese people under the virtuous rule of the emperor. These pre-war governmental actions, however, are entirely different from the grassroots impulses that gave rise to private religious schools in traditions such as Islam and Christianity. There is really no Shinto parallel. In fact, the Meiji and subsequent regimes' attempt to teach ethics from on high, so to speak, explicitly forbade religious education on the local or shrine level. Since World War II, however, numerous shrines throughout Japan have developed programs for children and young people, including nursery schools and kindergartens. But these are exclusively social and cultural, rather than religiously educational, developments.

Are there any **organizations or institutions** that have their own **distinctive structures of leadership** within Shinto?

An important organization in Shinto is the shrine guild (*miya-za*), composed of village elders who share responsibility for their local clan or parish shrine. Each man agrees to oversee shrine affairs for a full year. Other organizations called *kosha* have occasionally sought to raise funds to send members on pilgrimage or to galvanize public support for a particular project such as shrine renovation. Some of those groups eventually grew into the various Shinto sects of modern times. Various groups known as *sodai-kai, ujiko-kai,* and *ujiko-sodai* (loose synonyms for "associations of parishioners/worshippers") have sprung up all over Japan for the purpose of gathering donations and sponsoring festivals. Unlike some other traditions, Shinto is not famous for developing major internal organizations such as religious or monastic orders. That may connect to the fact that the Shinto priesthood itself is historically associated with heredity and clan and has never been an ordained clergy as such. There are, however, exceptions, such as the monastic order that grew out of a sectarian lineage called Yui-itsu Shinto.

Have there been any Shinto **mystics**?

Mainstream Shinto tradition has not been particularly noted for producing important mystical figures. That is not to say that there have been no Shinto mystics. But talk of mystical union with the divine has come more from various syncretistic schools and sects, especially those heavily influenced by non-Japanese schools of religious thought. Kurozumi Munetada (1780-1850), founder of the Kurozumi sect with a distinctively Neo-Confucian tilt, taught the importance of the deliberate quest to become a *kami*. He himself is said to have experienced oneness with the sun goddess Amaterasu when she suffused his body.

Have **martyrs** occupied an important position in Shinto tradition?

Shinto tradition reveres many religious heroes who died defending their emperor and homeland. They are martyrs in the broadest sense of the term. They died not for a religious creed narrowly defined, but out of allegiance to the larger complex of beliefs that has been integral to Japanese history and culture. People like the cultural icon Sugawara Michizane (845-903), who is said to have perished as a result of his convictions, take their place alongside the royal heroes, the princes who died in defense of the imperial house. Shrines designated as "nation-protecting" shrines are dedicated to the memory of war dead. They enshrine as *kami* the souls of all who gave their lives out of conviction. Yasukuni Jinja in Tokyo is a fine example of such a martyr memorial.

Do Shinto practitioners **revere** any persons as especially gifted with **wisdom**?

Japanese tradition generally has held teachers in high regard. But, in the words of one famous Japanese scholar, Shinto is "caught" rather than "taught." As a result, sages, scholars, and teachers do not occupy the place of honor in Shinto tradition to which, for example, Confucianism has elevated them. Human beings are made to worship the divine in all things and to respond in gratitude for countless gifts. Thanksgiving is the wisdom of Shinto. One can encourage it, but most of all it is a gift in itself. Shinto tradition emphasizes firsthand experience of the world and of one's place in it.

Is there such a thing as a Shinto **saint**?

Many exemplary human beings have been identified and revered as *kami* after their deaths. Since the category of *kami* is an all-inclusive grouping of forces and persons considered "above" the merely human, Shinto tradition has no need of an intermediary category such as that of "saint." Most traditions that discuss sainthood in one form or another do so out of one of two convictions. In some traditions the deity is so exalted and transcendent that ordinary human beings can scarcely imagine approaching it directly. Saints function as intermediaries because they share the humanity of devotees and are thus more approachable. Other traditions, however, elevate certain persons not as intermediaries or intercessors, but as examples of lofty yet attainable perfection. Shinto stands alone here in the sense that the *kami* are everywhere and thus perfectly accessible, and that certain human beings are themselves *kami*.

HOLIDAYS AND REGULAR OBSERVANCES

What kind of **calendar** do Shinto practitioners observe?

Shinto reckoning of ritual time has been much influenced by Chinese traditions. As early as 675 C.E., religious Daoism had made a significant impact on the Japanese imperial court, which formally adopted many Daoist practices. Most importantly, the court set up a bureau of divination, called the Onmyoryo ("Office of *Yin-Yang*"), based on Daoist principles. One of the Onmyoryo's chief functions was to establish a liturgical calendar that patterned earthly life on the rhythms of the cosmos. This lunar calendar retains all the main features of its Chinese model, including the cycles of sixty years based on the combinations of twelve "branches" and ten "stems" (see the sections on Daoism and Confucianism). The Japanese call their Chinese version of the lunar calendar *Kyureki,* as distinct from the modern solar calendar adopted in 1872, the *Shinreki.* An early formal cycle of annual observance, called the *nenchu gyoji,* literally "year-round-discipline-rituals," developed as early as the tenth century C.E. Imperial authorities promulgated it in a vast historical record called the *Engi-shiki* ("Institutes of the Engi Era," 901–923 C.E.), an essential source of information about Shinto ritual in general. Japan's lunar calendar needs to tuck in an extra month every three years or so.

Prior to the nineteenth century, many Shinto shrines maintained their own calendars of events, including uniquely regional and local festivities. Today some major events still take place according to various ways of adapting the lunar calendar to fit the solar. For example, some festivals now occur on the same numbered day within the same numbered month, but transferred to the solar reckoning. In other words, a festival that fell on the seventh day of the seventh lunar month now falls on July 7. Some festivals are now dated by keeping the day date but adding a solar month, so that a celebration once held on the seventh day of the seventh month now occurs on August 7. Finally, and more rarely, a few days retain their lunar dating completely, so that they rotate backward against the solar year. From the solar point of view, therefore, these are moveable feasts. Since the late nineteenth century, the timing of the major festivals has been coordinated so that all the larger shrines observe them at the same time. But there are still many distinctive local and regional festivities attached to individual shrines, such as the rituals dedicated to the patron deities of particular places. In addition to the liturgical calendar, an important related feature is the Japanese custom of dividing history according to imperial reigns or epochs. Emperor Hirohito died in 1989, ending the Showa era, and his son Akihito's accession inaugurated the Heisei epoch.

How does the Shinto tradition **determine** specific **days for festivities**?

Carrying on the Chinese custom, Shinto tradition has designated certain days each month auspicious and certain others inauspicious for religious celebrations. The days most favored include the four each lunar month that correspond with the new and full moons (the first and fifteenth) and waxing and waning half-moons (around the seventh/eighth and twenty-second/third). Since solar months are longer than lunar months, festivals that retain the same day- and month-numbers they once had in the lunar calendar (e.g. seventh of the seventh) do not always correspond perfectly with the lunar event that originally made certain days auspicious and others not. Calculation of the beginning of a festival day begins with the eve of the feast (*yoi-matsuri*). Festal days begin at sunset on the eve and last through sunset of the actual festival day (*hon-matsuri*). Japanese call the actual day of a feast *saijitsu*. Large-scale annual *matsuri* associated with a particular shrine, such as observance of the anniversary of the shrine's founding, are called *reisai*, "regular festivals." These are distinguished from lesser festivals or national occasions such as those associated with the imperial household.

How does the **agricultural cycle** affect Shinto-related **ritual celebrations**?

Many festivities are still tied to various agricultural occasions. Spring and autumn festivals correspond with planting and harvesting. A large cluster of so-called spring festivals (*haru-matsuri*) covers events that run generally from January to May, though some areas stretch the season into July. In late March or April people celebrate the Cherry Blossom festival, one of nature's sublime but fleeting glories. On May 5 (fifth of the fifth in some places, other days elsewhere) many people observe a Rice Planting day. Two of Kyoto's larger shrines, Kamigamo and Shimogamo in the north of the city, celebrate a prayer for good harvest called Hollyhock Festival (*aoi-matsuri*), complete with elaborate processions and reenactments of ancient imperial events. With countless regional variations, the planting (or transplanting) rites occur generally during May, June, and July, stretching well into the summer season. This seasonal overlap is a result of using more than one system for converting ritual occasions from the lunar to the solar calendar. Some shrines host enormous gatherings centered around processions and contests of various kinds.

Autumn festivals (*aki-matsuri*) include a similar grouping of celebrations that begin even before the summer festival season has ended and extend into October. At the beginning of each imperial era, the new emperor performs an autumn celebration called the "Great Feast of New Food" (*daijosai*), offering rice to the Sun Goddess and imperial forebears. Whether in the imperial palace or at local shrines, these are all occasions for gratitude to the *kami* for bountiful harvest. Between planting and harvest are a host of generally smaller summer festivals (*natsu-matsuri*), during which people pray for a healthy crop. Some shrines, however, still host major celebrations during July, August, and September. Many of these are occasions for teams (made up primarily of younger men and boys) to engage in spirited competition, vying to get their *mikoshi* along the procession route faster and arrive at the shrine first.

Winter festivals (*fuyu-no-matsuri*) revolve largely around preparations for the end of the year and New Year's celebrations (*shogatsu*). Calculated on the solar calendar, the winter solstice heralds the new year, so many people begin these rites with ceremonial cleaning and wrap up the old year by laying old sewing needles to rest at a local shrine. Honor for all things that contribute to human civilization—not for human beings alone—that have come to the end of their lives is essential. Seven days during a period called the "great cold" (*daikan*, generally between January sixth and twenty-first) retain some of their ancient associations. People gather at shrines to enjoy the return of the sun in lengthening days that portend spring, and to pray for good fortune in general.

What **annual festivities** do Shinto practitioners celebrate?

"Five seasonal days" (*gosekku*) celebrate simple but essential blessings. Timing of the five seasonal days is still based on the lunar calendar, but transferred to the solar months. For example, the days were originally observed on the third day of the third lunar month, the fifth of the fifth, the seventh of the seventh, and the ninth of the ninth. The days now retain the same position, but in solar months of the same numbers. Seven Herbs Day now falls on January 7, when people greet the spring with a specially seasoned soup. For *Hina-matsuri*, or Doll Festival (nowadays called Girls' Day) on March 3, many people reenact the ancient practice of floating clay or paper dolls on a river or the sea to ensure the health of their daughters. Boys' Day (*kodomo-no-hi*) falls on May 5, when little boys receive dolls of heroic figures who model valor and loyalty. On July 7, *Tanabata*, or "Seventh Night," recalls the Chinese story of the celestial cowboy and the weaver maid, condemned to be distant stars forever because their romance caused them to slacken their labors. On this night the two reunite briefly on the bridge of the Milky Way. Farmers and textile workers take the opportunity to pray for success in their occupations. Finally, Chrysanthemum Day (*kiku-no-sekku*) falls on the ninth of September. Many still go to local shrines to appreciate the beautifully cultivated flower, which became the official symbol of the emperor during the Meiji era in the mid-nineteenth century. One curious period calculated by the lunar calendar (equivalent to October usually) sees all shrines sending off their *kami* to the Izumo Taisha, where they stay together for a spell before moving for similar brief visits to two other shrines. At their home shrines, worshippers observe "a month without *kami*" (*kami-na-zuki*).

Are there **cyclical Shinto observances**, such as feasts that happen regularly but not annually?

Some gatherings still take place on set days in certain odd-numbered months, but not monthly. For example, a practice called Waiting for the Sun (*himachi*) finds people gathered in private residences on the fifteenth day of the first, fifth, and ninth lunar months to keep vigil until dawn. A Shinto priest is often among the celebrants. During the same

At Kyoto's Kitano Tenjin shrine, worshippers revere a large marble effigy of a sacred bull that is the symbol of the *kami* Sugawara Michizane.

months, but on the odd-numbered nights of the third week, people come together in "Groups Awaiting the Moon" (*tsukimachi*). September's full moon is especially beautiful, for it falls in the ninth month and is known as the harvest moon. Participants celebrate the lunar beauty with songs and food. These gatherings occur only in homes. Some people still make arrangements to observe their "unlucky year"—age forty-two for men and thirty-three for women—with rites at a shrine to ward off misfortune. They may take precautions by means of extra rituals of purification on that day. Some regard certain days each month as "fortuitous connection days" because they associate them with particular *kami*, and such days often occasion shrine visitation.

Do Shinto practitioners celebrate **sacred birthdays** or honor particular figures?

Many shrines hold festivities in connection with dates important in the lives of enshrined *kami* who were historical figures prior to their deification. For example, the Akama Jingu enshrines the child Emperor Antoku (1178–85) who reigned for the final five years of his very brief life. From April 23 to 25, celebrants recall his untimely death and the reign of his predecessor, Emperor Gotoba. *Tenjin Matsuri*, from July 24 to 25, celebrates the deified scholar and court minister Sugawara Michizane (845–903). Over ten thousand branch shrines ritualize the deity who is mythically associated with oxen and cattle. According to tradition, Sugawara was born and came of age in the year of the ox and was saved from his enemy by a bull who miraculously appeared to kill his would-be assassins. Ironically, it was members of that same enemy clan, the Fujiwara, who had

Sugawara enshrined some fifty years after his death. He received the name Tenjin ("celestial *kami*") and has remained popular as the *kami* of learning. Large numbers of worshippers still go to his shrines on the twenty-fifth (both his birth and death day) of each month to reverence statues of reclining bulls, rubbing them and then rubbing the blessing onto themselves or their children. Birthdays are not as important on the whole as are death anniversaries and seasonal associations with the deified figures.

What are some of the **other festal days** Shinto practitioners celebrate?

O-Bon matsuri is one of those feasts whose timing is determined by adding a solar month to the lunar reckoning. Hence a feast formerly celebrated during the middle (i.e., full moon) of the seventh month now occurs during the middle of August, the eighth. On November 23 and 24 falls the "New Food" festival (*nii-name-sai*). Acting as high priest, the emperor himself leads the ceremonies. When a newly enthroned emperor presides, the feast is called "Great Food" festival (*daijosai*), and the ritual seals and formalizes the new ruler's accession. This is one of some thirty regular imperial ceremonies (*koshitsu saishi*) that occur through the year, most conducted privately within the palace. The Autumnal Equinox still calls for quite elaborate observances in some places. The Suwa shrine in Nagasaki, for example, holds its annual *Okunchi* for three full rousing days and nights. Involving a full range of activities, from raucous processions to solemn predawn purifications conducted in almost total silence, the festival engages large numbers of worshippers actively. Festivities begin and end with more private rituals designed to bring the *kami* into the ceremony and see them back to their places of repose.

Some ceremonies occur often but on a more ad hoc basis than the regularly scheduled festivals. Nearly every new architectural venture occasions religiously inspired observances. "Earth Sanctification" (*Jichin-sai*) is a ritual of Daoist origin conducted by a Shinto priest to prepare the ground for new construction. Participants call on the *kami* of the place for protection. These ceremonies are roughly analogous to the American practice of hoisting a small evergreen to the top of a newly completed structure—perhaps religious in origin, but now purely customary. A rite called *senza-sai* or *sengu* can occur on any number of occasions. In this ritual, a *kami* is relocated—either permanently to a new shrine or temporarily in the case of repairs or, for a *matsuri*, for a time or repose—in one of several of the deity's regular abodes. In the case of Ise shrine, for example, the ceremony happens every twenty years, when a new shrine is constructed on the grounds.

CUSTOMS AND RITUALS

What does the term *matsuri* mean?

Matsuri is the inclusive word for virtually all Shinto-inspired communal celebrations. The term derives from a root that can mean "to deify or enshrine." These festivities generally celebrate manifestations of the *kami* who have a special relationship to a region or town, though some celebrate *kami* of more widespread significance as well. They acknowledge the inseparable link among the *kami*, the land, and the community of people living there. Since it emphasizes the seamless interrelationships among these three elements, Shinto tradition makes no distinction between sacred and profane time. All of creation, time and space, is sacred. *Matsuri* mark those times and places that are more than ordinarily sacred. Just when divine energy appears on the wane, a *matsuri* occurs and renews that spiritual potency. Festivities periodically restore the ancient cosmic order of nature.

Japanese often celebrate *matsuri* with an enormous vigor, an almost uncontrolled energy. Bands of young men undertake strenuous feats of lifting and hauling enormous loads, competing with other groups to deliver their sacred burdens to the shrine or another ritual destination. That feeling of wild unpredictability offers an important insight into the Shinto sense of the divine as both benevolent and dangerous. Some *matsuri* are explicitly identified as non-religious civic events, but even today the majority are of religious origin and reflect classical Shinto or folk beliefs, or both. Most also retain their ancient associations with seasonal and agricultural concerns. *Matsuri* typically include both processions and activities within a shrine compound. Special offerings and prayers, plays and dancing and other entertainments, and communal meals are features of all the great festivities.

What place does **purification** occupy in Shinto ritual?

Few traditions place greater emphasis on the need to purify both participants in ceremonies and the place designated for the rites. Just as the primordial deity, Izanagi, purified himself upon exiting from the underworld, so must all worshippers cleanse before engaging in sacred rituals. The contrasting states of pollution or spiritual alienation (*kegare*) and ritual–moral purity (*harae*) encompass a great deal of what Shinto tradition considers important. Purification with water is a prerequisite to even the simplest acts of worship. As an ordinary part of rituals performed by priests and shrine staff, purification requires waving a wand over the individuals or their offerings, and sometimes involves sprinkling saltwater or salt. Watch a Sumo wrestling match and you will see the behemoth contestants liberally scattering fistfuls of salt across the ring as they enter to confront each other—a clue to the ancient religious associations of the sport.

Japanese boy prepares to offer the author a ladle of water for purification at a small Shinto shrine in Tokyo.

More elaborate purification involves ceremonial bathing to cleanse the individual of pollution and sin. Priests sometimes purify by immersion before major rites. Some adepts seek out sacred mountain waterfalls and stand beneath their frigid cataracts in winter as an especially potent form of purification. Most important is the ceremony called "great purification," in which priests of the imperial household, and those throughout the country, symbolically purify the whole nation—the whole world, according to some interpretations. Reciting prayers, they mark the middle and end of the year with cleansing. Before a major festival, shrine priests put considerable time and effort into preparing themselves and the site. Officiants enter seclusion the day before the festival, bathe several times, and follow strict rules with respect to clothing, food, and abstinence from sexual activity.

What are the basic **features** of the more elaborate **shrine rituals**?

Larger rituals typically include four features. Before beginning any sacred act, including the simplest ones, celebrants purify themselves with water or salt. Welcoming the *kami* (*kami-mukae*) is among the first acts of the presiding priest. The invocation is necessary because many *matsuri* begin away from the shrine in places where the *kami* does not ordinarily reside. Next is the offering to the *kami* (and that includes ancestors, as in Chinese traditions). In addition to responding to the obvious requirement of funds to maintain the thousands of shrines great and small all over the country, people make symbolic offerings and the priests in turn formally present them to the deities. Flowers, food and drink, beautiful textiles or jewelry, and even the performance of traditional art forms or sport can be included among offerings. Entertainment arranged in connection with a religious festival is known as "divine amusement" (*kan-nigiwai*).

When the priestly staff perform elaborate offerings, the chief priest opens the doors of the innermost sanctuary. The priests pass the offerings among themselves and finally the assistant chief priest places the offerings before the sanctuary doors. Ritual specialists then recite prayers—many of ancient origin and some more recently composed—of praise, thanksgiving, historical recollection about the meaning of the particular occasion, all concluded with appropriately humble leave-taking of the *kami* with a gesture called "sending the *kami* away" (*kami-okuri*). Ceremonies conclude with a kind of communion rite in which the chief priest serves the other members of the ritual staff a symbolic sip of sake. The priests walk in procession from the inner worship hall to the outer hall for this rite, which is usually brief, depending on the number of officiants participating. When large crowds are in attendance for a particularly festive occasion, the closing meal can be quite elaborate, and include a share in some of the food just offered to the *kami*. One ritual element notably lacking in Shinto worship is preaching. Since worship is entirely focused on relating ritually to the deities, Shinto tradition does not regard persuasive religious rhetoric a necessary tool.

What **rites** do Shinto practitioners perform in their **shrines**?

When worshippers go to their local or larger regional shrines, they may engage in several types of rituals called "worship gestures" (*omairi*), depending on the occasion. A simple list of "Four P's" sums up the essential ingredients of Shinto ritual: purification, presentation (of offerings), petition (or prayers for blessing), and participation (of the assembled worshippers). For ordinary, everyday prayers, in which they express a whole range of needs and concerns, worshippers typically perform a simple offering before the sacred presence. Alone or in small groups, they enter the shrine precinct and proceed along the path, passing beneath perhaps several *torii* gates, to the purification font. There they take some water to cleanse the mouth and hands as necessary preparation (a ritual action called *misogi*) for approaching the holy place. Moving to the front of the shrine, worshippers announce their arrival by ringing a bell that hangs over the threshold of many shrines. Ringing the bell may be either for quieting the mind or summoning the *kami*. With or without the bell, all toss a coin in the offering box, then bow and clap their hands twice to summon the deity. After making a brief prayer, they bow twice (one deep and one slight bow) and then depart.

For some occasions, individuals or small groups can arrange for the services of the priestly staff. Rites that last from ten to fifteen minutes take place inside the front worship hall (*haiden*). Various spiritual purposes of the rituals include divine blessing and protection, the opportunity to communicate with the *kami* about countless daily happenings and concerns, and expressions of personal dedication to the divine beings. These services are available most days in shrines with larger staffs, for the tradition has set aside no one day of the week as a canonical day of worship. In larger shrines, the priestly staff also make daily morning and evening offerings to the *kami*. In addition to the various daily rites, shrines host numerous events throughout the year for special occasions,called *matsuri*.

Is there a **regular, standard** Shinto **group liturgical worship**?

Communal worship is not a regular feature of Shinto liturgical practice. People may arrive at a shrine in large numbers, but they generally do not gather to worship as a large congregation. Individual and small group worship is the norm, whether for brief impromptu visits made outside the shrine or for more elaborate priestly rituals in the worship hall. A distinctive feature of Shinto architecture is the absence of worship spaces large enough to accommodate sizeable congregations. By contrast, the bigger Japanese Buddhist temples accomodate sizable groups in a single worship space. Even in larger Shinto shrines, the parts of the worship facility open to the public are in any case not fully enclosed. Being very much at the mercy of cold weather is the price of wanting a sacred space to be as much in tune with nature as possible. This also reflects the underlying sense that people build community through other activities, but perform their most intimate spiritual duties as individuals or families.

What does Shinto **home worship** entail?

Religiously committed Japanese families still maintain regular daily home rituals centered around the *kamidana,* and perhaps also around the *butsudan* or miniature Buddhist temple. Home shrines are dedicated and put into service when family members invite a priest over to install a talisman from the local shrine on which is written the name of the *kami* to be honored in the home. Worshippers perform a brief purification ritual and then do before the miniature shrine much the same thing they would do at an actual shrine. These rituals, often observed morning and evening, are generally very brief, lasting perhaps three to five minutes. Some families still ritually incorporate in the evening meal food offered to the *kami.*

What kinds of **ritual objects** figure in Shinto worship and prayer?

Shinto tradition refers to all of its "ritual furniture and utensils" with the term *saikigu.* It includes several items used on every altar during offering ceremonies. The priest carries the offerings (*heihaku*) and gifts of food (*shinsen*) on a tray (*sambo*), which he sets upon an eight-legged table (*hassoku-an*) made of a reddish cypress wood (*hinoki,* "fire tree"). Priestly staff remove these objects after worship ends. Objects used regularly in nearly all rituals include several items that ritual specialists wave over those to whom they are ministering. Branches of the *sakaki* (combining characters for "tree" and "*kami*") provide a splash of greenery and association with living nature. A wand used for purification, either in place of or in conjunction with the *sakaki* branch, is called *haraigushi*—a thick cluster of white paper streamers attached to a long stick. Another stick with a set of zigzag-cut white paper (and sometimes of other colors) symbolizes the *kami*'s presence in the holy place. All three objects are mounted on stands and displayed when not in use by one of the priests or a *miko.* *Miko* also use a set of five bells (*suzu*) for their sacred dances.

Several larger implements play a central role in the great public festivals called *matsuri.* Most important is the portable shrine called the *mikoshi.* Celebrants carry this miniature, but still often very heavy, four-sided model of a shrine sanctuary in procession, shouldering long beams that hold the shrine aloft. Larger *mikoshi* can weigh up to several tons and require a large crew of strong bearers. In some places large wagons called *yatai* and *dashi* rumble through the streets on massive wheels, carrying groups of musicians and revelers. Built like mobile shrines, the hefty wooden wagons range in height from just over thirty feet to about sixty-five feet.

Are there any Shinto **divination rituals**?

Bokusen is the Japanese term for the complex process of divining auspicious times for agriculturalists. Divination encompasses a variety of specific devices. As in Chinese Community Traditions, people often draw lots—the Chinese shake bundles of numbered sticks and pull the one left protruding, and Shinto worshippers draw numbered bits of paper. Sometimes they will read the angle at which an arrow sticks in its target, or read the designs on a turtle shell, or hold a deer's shoulder blade in a flame and observe how it cracks. (A similar ritual uses arrows for slightly different purposes. People purchase white arrows at shrine shops, especially around the New Year, and use them as amulets, protective devices, at home throughout the year.) Divination is required for setting the dates for many major festivals. Ritual leaders invite certain divinatory *kami* to be in attendance as the diviner kindles a sacred fire on which to heat a turtle shell. Specialists then read the relationship of the cracks to lines and characters predrawn on the shell.

A couple consult the divining arrows they have purchased at the Shinto Shrine shop, Meiji Jingu, Tokyo.

A ritual cousin of Chinese *feng shui* is called *kaso*. It involves a set of geomantic calculations to establish optimal conditions for all sorts of human habitations. Another type of divination has worshippers write on small pieces of paper their various options as they prepare to make a major decision. In what may be a variation on a contemporary popular Chinese practice, people typically pull a stick from a bundle, read its number, and take a piece of pre-written advice from a correspondingly numbered drawer. Numerous Shinto shrines provide racks where people who find the advice unpalatable can tie their paper to be rid of the effects of the bad news.

Is **exorcism** important in Shinto practice?

Demons and assorted evil influences miss no opportunity to make nuisances of themselves, especially at times when human beings and natural processes are most vulnerable. Beginnings, such as planting time or the birth of an infant, can be particularly difficult in this respect. Shinto tradition includes various understandings of how evil forces work and several methods for contending with them. Most undesirable forces are associated with impurity and pollution. Some evil spirits will depart in a ritual that designates as a scapegoat any animal or object capable of taking on the negative forces. Emperors of old rubbed a human effigy over their bodies, leaving all personal impurity on the image, which officials of the "Bureau of *Yin* and *Yang*" then ritually consigned to a river. Other rituals use a weapon such as a sword to attack the evil power as though it were a physical presence. Some rituals assume the evil forces have taken on demonic bodies and must be pursued and expelled from a locality. In one rite, people throw soybeans in unlucky directions and command the demons to depart, an important part of the spring *Setsubun* ("season change") *Matsuri*.

The festival of *Gion Matsuri* is over a thousand years old and is the most famous festival held in Kyoto. (Chiharu / Shutterstock.com.)

Some large festivals are entirely dedicated to a type of communal exorcism. An originally Buddhist rite called *Goryo-e* ("meeting with august spirits") has been associated with Kyoto's famous *Gion Matsuri,* for example. That festival arose out of a need to banish the spirits of disease, and eventually grew into a full-scale Shinto celebration. Another important interpretation of spirit possession has been traditionally associated with the belief that the fox is capable of changing shapes. Extraordinary spiritual states were therefore sometimes explained as a type of "fox-possession." Some popular traditions identify various psychosomatic illnesses as forms of possession. "Soul pacification" (*Tama-shizume*) is a kind of reverse exorcism in which ritualists seek to make a spirit content to remain in the body of a person suffering from illness.

How is **music** important in Shinto ritual?

Gagaku, "refined music," is ancient courtly music originating in China as early as the Han dynasty and cultivated by the Japanese in Heian imperial circles. Often associated with dance, the fourteen-member instrumental ensemble consists of percussion and reeds. But it also includes the stringed instrument similar to the Hawaiian guitar called the *so,* cousin of the larger *koto,* identifiable by its frequent use of the technique of note-bending. A plucked string called the *biwa* is also part of the ensemble. Woodwinds are the "three reeds" (*sankan*): short, piccolo-like, six- and nine-hole flutes; a primitive oboe-like woodwind that produces a sharp, edgy sound; and a cluster of seventeen bamboo pipes called the *sho* that is in fact a tiny pipe organ for the

459

mouth. Slow stately rhythms beat out by the percussion underlie the haunting, almost plaintive sounds of the high-pitched reeds. Few sounds are a more apt musical communication of the solemnity and perfect "otherness" of the deities the music addresses in Shinto shrines. Most non-Japanese who encounter music identified as Japanese are likely to associate that musical tradition with the sound of plucked strings, such as the *koto* and *shamisen*. In Shinto shrine ritual, however, stringed instruments do not play the major role they play in Chinese ritual. Percussion and woodwinds make up the bulk of the typical ceremonial ensemble. Percussion instruments include the massive *taiko,* a large barrel with two skin heads that sits sideways on an elevated stand just inside the outer ritual hall of larger shrines. A shrine ritualist, often one of the *miko* ("deaconesses"), announces the beginning of ceremonies by a pulse-pounding crescendo-decrescendo on the great drum. Various smaller drums keep time for dances.

Are **dance and drama** equally important?

Bugaku, "refined dance" in 160 different styles, is often performed to the accompaniment of a *gagaku* ensemble and sometimes occurs in Buddhist temples as well as Shinto shrines. It is somewhat more formal and classical than *Kagura,* a uniquely

Shinto form of liturgical dance with musical accompaniment. The name apparently derives from a term that means "temporary abode of the *kami*," a place on Earth to which worshippers summon the deities. *Kagura* has its mythic roots in the dance of the Terrible Female of Heaven that lured the sun goddess to emerge from her cave. Unlike the more staid classical version danced for the emperor on December's full moon night, the shrine (or village) *kagura* now reenacts often raucous scenes from mythological narratives. Several of the great shrines—such as those of Izumo, Kasuga, and Ise—are especially known for their longstanding traditions of kagu-

Though not a religious ritual in itself, Sumo wrestling is associated with many Shinto traditions.

ra performance. Some shrines have structures dedicated to *kagura*, but many still stage the dance in the large open space in front of the worship hall. *Bon odori* is a popular form of folk dancing performed at festivals on shrine grounds. Celebrants dance around a large, raised, scaffoldlike platform on which drummers and other musicians perch to play their popular *hayashi*-style music. Perhaps the best known of Shinto-related dances is the Dragon dance often associated with festival parades. In shrine dances, the dragon begins by bowing to the *kami* and the chief priest before writhing its way across the sacred precincts. The ancient Japanese theater form called *No* also has roots in the reenactment of Shinto myths.

How do **trials or ordeals** function in Shinto ritual?

Remnants of ancient practices reminiscent of "trial by fire" survive in several Shinto ceremonies, most of which are still practiced, in relatively few locations. Unique to the Suwa shrine in Nagasaki is a frightening ritual called *yutate-sai*. At the end of the purification and exorcism rituals, the chief priest of the shrine thrusts his hand into a kettle of boiling water. This rite dates back to the Shugendo sect of late medieval times. Now it represents not the ascetic or magical power of ancient practitioners, or the power to banish spirits possessing an unfortunate soul, but the need for radical purification. Some sects use a variation on this ritual, with a priest scattering scalding water on the main participant with a bamboo stick. A related ritual of trial involves walking over burning coals. Called *chinka shiki* ("taming the fire"), the ceremony involves circumambulating the bed of embers before walking across it. Anyone present may participate after the principal ritualists complete the ordeal. Again the purpose is purification, and prayers may include petitioning the *kami* of the moon to exert his influence on the fire *kami*.

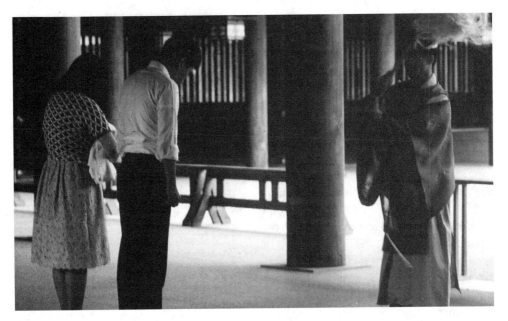

A young couple bring their new baby for a special blessing at Tokyo's Meiji Jingu. The officiating priest waves over them the purifying wand called the *haraigushi*. In the background is the courtyard that separates the Hall of Worship (*haiden*) from the Hall of Offerings (*heiden*), where the priestly staff perform more exclusive rituals. Yet another, smaller courtyard stands between that and the holy of holies (*honden*).

How do Shinto practitioners **celebrate birth**?

Not long after a couple have a baby—traditionally about thirty days—they take the child to the shrine for a natal blessing. This is consistent with the belief that all new ventures and beginnings will fare better if brought before the *kami*. In addition, the symbolism includes the belief that the infant thus becomes a child of the family's protector *kami*. Parents arrange with shrine staff for a standard ceremony that takes place inside the *haiden,* or outer worship hall. At larger shrines a senior priest, assistant priest, and *miko* typically perform the ceremony. Pronouncing solemn prayers in an archaic Japanese, the priests then perform blessings over the young family by waving the *haraigushi*. The *miko* may also participate by blessing the worshippers with a green *sakaki* branch. Ancient Shinto tradition retains a class of divine beings called "*kami* of birth or beginnings" (*musubi no kami*). They include *kami* of fire, youth, plenty, and the creator divinities who brought all things to birth.

Are there other distinctive Shinto rites of **passage or initiation**?

Several types of ceremony and celebration are associated with various stages in life. Tradition recommends that parents (formerly the grandmother, since mothers remained impure for a time after childbirth) bring thirty-two-day-old boys or thirty-three-day-old girls to the shrine for a blessing. This "first shrine visit" (*hatsu-miya-mairi*) functioned

Young Japanese women walking along the main path of one of Tokyo's major Shinto shrines after celebrating the annual Coming of Age Day (*seijin no hi*) for which they are decked out in their fanciest traditional dress.

as the infant's initiation into the Shinto shrine community. Older children also have their days. Each November 15, a festival called *Shichi-go-san* ("Seven-five-three") marks a rite of passage for both boys and girls. Three- and seven-year-old girls and five-year-old boys don their fanciest dress-up outfits for a shrine visit to pray for a safe and happy future. Putting on celebratory clothes is a major ingredient in rites of initiation. Young people reach the age of adulthood at twenty. On "Coming of Age Day" (*seijin-no-hi*)—January 15 each year—young adults, especially women, visit shrines in formal attire for a blessing. Other coming-of-age observances identify manhood with age seventeen and womanhood with nineteen, acknowledging the difficulty of life's changes with the bestowal of protective talismans. Many older Japanese still observe rites of passage that acknowledge the challenges of aging. They may visit shrines when they reach the ages of 61, 70, 77, 88, and 99, to ask for protection and blessings.

Does Shinto tradition include **ritual pilgrimage**?

Pilgrimages of various kinds have long been important to Japanese in connection with both Buddhism and Shinto. Sacred natural objects and shrines are of course the most common goals of Shinto pilgrims, but people do not always make neat distinctions between Buddhist and Shinto sacred sites. What is most significant is that the place has been hallowed by some event or person of great influence in Japanese history, or by natural qualities that betoken beauty and perfection. A distinctive aspect of Japanese pilgrimage is the formation of pilgrimage circuits (*junpai*) that encompass multiple stops at sacred groves, mountains, caves, waterfalls, shrines or temples, in all imaginable combinations. Most common are circuits of either thirty-three or eighty-eight sites set up in relatively recent times by railway and other transportation companies. In medieval times there was even talk of "thousand-shrine pilgrimages" (*senja mairi*), with multiple visits motivated by desire for greater spiritual merit. Some pilgrims undertake their journeys as acts of asceticism or spiritual discipline, but most seem to regard pilgrimage as an opportunity for reflection and spiritual renewal. A type of pilgrimage to Shinto's most sacred site, the Ise shrine, has come to be known as the "blessing visit" (*okage-mairi*). Another popular pilgrimage circuit leaves by rail from Osaka and takes in sites associated with the "seven gods of good luck," including both Shinto shrines and Buddhist temples. Over four hundred traditional pilgrimage routes still attract Japanese Buddhist and Shinto devotees.

Are there Shinto rituals of **marriage**?

Weddings in Japan have traditionally followed Shinto ritual, and the vast majority still include Shinto elements even when performed in connection with other traditions, such as Christianity. Until recent times, however, weddings occurred in homes and were performed by laypeople only. Since the mid-nineteenth century, shrine nuptials performed by Shinto priests have been more common. A ceremony called *shinzen-kekkon* (nuptials in the presence of *kami*) may take place in a wedding hall, on shrine grounds, or in other public spaces. According to some, a marriage deity called *musubi no kami* ("the god who ties the knot") is a Japanese counterpart to the moon-dwelling Daoist, Yue Lao, who bound together the feet of marriage partners. Many Japanese continue the ancient practice of arranged marriage, and some young couples still live with the groom's family, following Confucian traditions. At the heart of the wedding ceremony is a shared drink of *sake* (rice wine). Many Japanese families still value elaborate ritual as a form of social communication, and some will even have two ceremonies, one Shinto and one Christian, for example. Daoist-influenced traditions still recommend that couples be wed only on days determined to be auspicious.

What occurs at a traditional Japanese **wedding**?

Contemporary Japanese weddings are celebrated in many ways, often combining traditional Japanese and Western elements side by side. Typically, a religious wedding ceremony is performed in Shinto style at a shrine located inside the hotel where the wedding celebration occurs. A Shinto priest conducts a ceremony attended only by the couple's closest family members. After rites of purification, the couple drink *sake*, and the groom reads a statement of commitment. Symbolic offerings to the *kami* conclude the ritual. Wearing traditional Japanese garb, the couple host a reception after the ceremony, welcoming anywhere from 15 to 250 guests: relatives, friends, and co-workers. After the bride and groom are introduced, a meal is served and brief speeches are delivered. At the end of the party, the couple thank their guests for joining them on this important day.

In recent years, many Japanese couples have incorporated traditionally Western elements into their weddings—for example, brides wearing white, Christian-style dresses. Sometimes the entire ceremony takes place in a Christian church and according to a Christian-like ritual, even when the couple is not Christian. Many couples also perform other Western-style rituals, including cake-cutting, an exchange of rings, and elaborate honeymoons.

How do Shinto practitioners deal ritually with **death and mourning**?

According to a saying, "Shinto marries, Buddhism buries." During the Tokugawa era (1600–1868) an imperial decree stipulated that only Buddhist priests should conduct funeral rites. Most cemeteries in Japan are connected to Buddhist temples rather than Shinto shrines. But there are exceptions to that general rule, and practitioners of Shinto have important beliefs and rituals concerning death and mourning. A major difference between Buddhist and Shinto practices is that Shinto rites never occur in shrines, for shrines are strictly dedicated to the *kami*.

Shinto tradition regards death as a form of evil and a serious source of pollution. Shinto belief and practice has been profoundly influenced by certain Confucian attitudes toward departed ancestors, and large numbers of Japanese still perform rites of ancestor veneration. Some Japanese families still follow the practice of enshrining a deceased person's symbols in a "spirit house" (*tama-ya*), placed beneath the home's (*kamidana*), seven weeks after a funeral. Some of Japan's largest shrines are dedicated to memorializing the spirits of great human beings elevated to the status of *kami*. Grief (*kibuku*) is associated with a prescribed period during which the experience of death renders family members impure. The bereaved family should stay away from shrines and refrain from Shinto ritual generally during that interval. In pre-Buddhist times, the Japanese sometimes constructed monumental memorials to the dead. Historically, laypeople performed Shinto funeral rituals, with main participants wearing white. Today, Shinto rites, led by priests, occur in homes or funeral establishments. Some shrines continue to perform memorial rites for those who have died in battle.

MAPS

Spread of Islam
622 to 750 C.E.

Kabul

Afghanistan

Baluchistan

Oman

Persia

Baghdad

Arabia

Yemen

Syria

Armenia

Damascus

Madina

Mecca

Constantinople

Byzantine Empire

Cairo

Egypt

Tripoli

Fezzan

Maghreb

Kingdom of the Franks

Tours

Spain

☐ Islamic world during Muhammad 622 to 632 CE

☐ Territory added by first four Caliphs, 632 to 651 CE

☐ Territory added by Umayyad Caliphs, 651 to 750 CE

→ Military campaigns

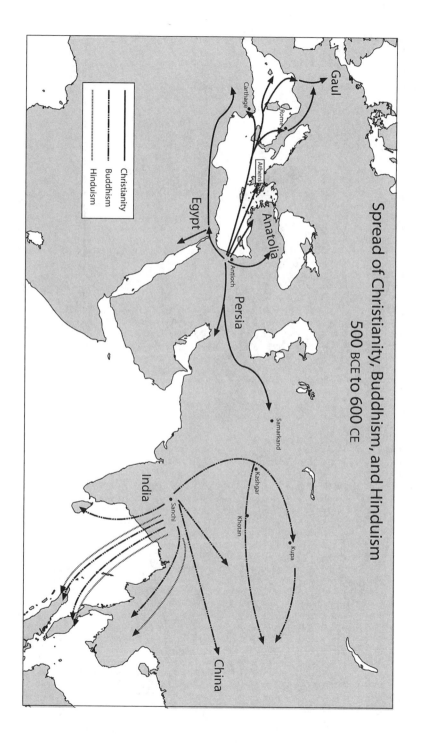

Spread of Christianity, Buddhism, and Hinduism
500 BCE to 600 CE

Christianity
Buddhism
Hinduism

Gaul
Carthage
Rome
Athens
Egypt
Anatolia
Antioch
Persia
Samarkand
India
Kashgar
Sanchi
Khotan
Kupa
China

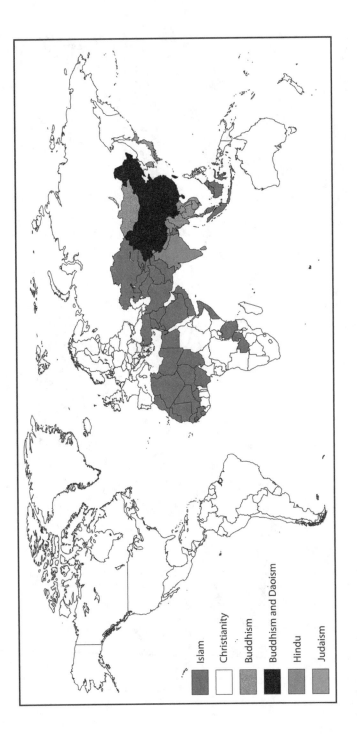

Islam

Christianity

Buddhism

Buddhism and Daoism

Hindu

Judaism

The indicated religions by region are those faiths that are *predominant* but not *exclusive* to those regions.

470

Global Religion Timeline

B.C.E.

4000   The Vedic period begins; earliest Vedic hymns (Hinduism).

3500   Roots of the Semitic tradition.

2700–1500   Indus civilization flourishes as evidenced by archeological data from Harrapa and Mohenjo (Hinduism).

2697–2597   Huang Di, Yellow Emperor, one of the "culture heroes" in Chinese lore, was patron of ancient *fang shi* or shamans (Daoism).

2637   Reckoning of Chinese lunar calendar of twelve months of twenty-nine or thirty days.

c. 2000–1400   Patriarchal Age; Abraham, revered in Hebrew Bible as father of the Hebrew people, Isaac, Jacob and Joseph; Ishmael, son of Abraham by Hagar; Muhammad considers Ishmael and Abraham as ancestors of Arabs, and associates them with the construction of the Ka'ba at Mecca.

1900   Age of *Ramayana* epic (Hinduism).

1994–1525   Xia dynasty instituted the principle of hereditary succession (Confucianism).

c. 1700   God's covenant with Abraham (Judaism).

1500–1200   Traditional dating for Aryan invasion of Indus Valley; now disputed (Hinduism).

1500–500   Major Upanishads composed (Hinduism).

1525–1028   Shang dynasty overthrows the last Xia tyrant (Confucianism).

c. 1400   Age of Krishna; Great Bharata War; early version of *Mahabharata* (Hinduism).

c. 1250–1050   Moses leads Exodus out of Egypt; development of Jewish community; conquest and subsequent settlement of Canaan; period of the Judges.

c. 1200–1000   Composition of the hymns of the Rigveda (Hinduism).

1028–222   Zhou dynasty: Yi Jing, Classic of Change, manual of divination (Confucianism).

c. 1020–1000   Kingship of Saul (Judaism).

c. 1000–973   Kingship of David over Israel (Judaism).

c. 970   Solomon, son of David, builds the First Temple in Jerusalem (Judaism).

922–722/1   Northern Kingdom of Israel (Judaism).

922–587/6   Southern Kingdom of Judah (Judaism).

835–765	Prophet Amos from Tekoa is the earliest of the biblical prophets (Judaism).
c. 800–600	Shu Jing, *The Classic of History* (Confucianism).
c. 740–700	Isaiah prophesizes (Judaism).
c. 732–725	Prophet Hosea (Judaism).
722–481	Chun Qiu, *Annals of Spring and Autumn* (Confucianism).
722/1	Assyrians conquer Samaria; exile of ten northern tribes (Judaism).
660	Jimmu Tenno, first human emperor (Shinto).
c. 627–587	Prophet Jeremiah (Judaism).
604	Traditional date of Lao Zi's birth (Daoism).
c. 593–571	Ezekiel, priest of Jerusalem, prophesizes (Judaism).
587–6	Babylonians destroy Jerusalem Temple and exile Judeans to Babylon (Judaism).
563–483	Siddhartha Gautama, the Buddha.
551–479	Kong Zi (Confucianism).
539	Beginning of return from Babylonian Exile to Zion (Judaism).
515	Jewish Temple rebuilt; emergence of classical Judaism.
c. 500–200	Bhagavad Gita composed (Hinduism).
468	Traditional death date of Vardhamana Mahavira, the twenty-fourth and last great "Ford-finder" of Jainism.
400	Confucius' sayings edited.
400–400 C.E.	Mahabharata epic composed (Hinduism).
400–200	Soferim class of scholars, forerunner of early rabbinical Judaism.
389–286	Zhuang Zi, Daoist philosopher.
383	Second Buddhist Council.
c. 372–289	Meng Zi or Mencius and Xun Zi codified the teachings of Confucius into the foundations of a political philosophy.
c. 350–300	Dao De Jing composed (Daoism).
327–325	Alexander the Great invades northwest India.
322–185	Mauryan dynasty; Buddhism spreads throughout northern India.
300 B.C.E. –600 C.E.	Buddhist missions expand beyond India to central, eastern and southeastern Asia.
c. 274–236	Maurya dynasty; Emperor Ashoka (c. 273–237), a convert to Buddhism, sends missionaries.
250	Third Council, official formulation of Tripitaka (Buddhism).
221–210	Emperor Qin Shi Huang Di tries to suppress Confucian texts and transforms feudal China into centralized bureaucracy.
c. 206–221 C.E.	Han dynasty; Confucianism official state philosophy.
c. 200	Rise of Mahayana Buddhism, distinction from Hinayana schools.
202–220 C.E.	Religious Daoism emerges.
220–280 C.E.	Three Kingdoms period: Wei (220–266); Shu Han (221–263); Wu (222–280).
200–200 C.E.	Rise of Mahayana; Buddhism spreads to central Asia and China.

200–200 C.E.	Ramayana epic composed; period of increased Buddhist and Jain influence (Hinduism).
c. 200	Population shifts from northwest India to the Ganges plain (Hinduism).
200–30 C.E.	Class of Judaic scholars called Five Pairs of Teachers.
195	Early Imperial sacrifice at Confucius' tomb.
168	Maccabees revolt (Judaism).
165	Temple restored and purified (Judaism).
150–75 CE	Essenes live ascetical life at Qumran at northern end of Dead Sea (Judaism).
c. 140–87	Emperor Wu Di of Han dynasty makes Confucian system his official ideology.
135–104	John Hyracanus attempts to secure both religious and civil authority (Judaism).
100	Lotus Sutra (Buddhism)
103–76	Alexander Yannai restores the Pharisees to position of influence (Judaism).
100–100 C.E.	Rise of Hindu literature of bhakti (devotion).
63	Rise of Roman rule; conquest of Palestine (Judaism).
c. 50–30 C.E.	Hillel the Elder, influential Jewish teacher.
37–4 C.E.	Herod the Great, Idumaean king of Judea.

C.E.

1	Emperor Ping proclaims Confucius the "Exalted Mt. Ni Duke of the Highest Perfection."
4 B.C.E.–29	Jesus of Nazareth; ministry (26–29); Crucifixion (29) (Christianity).
30–200	Tanna'im School lays foundation of the Mishna (Judaism).
34–156	Zhang Dao Ling, cited as the founder of the first Daoist religious movement, the Celestial Masters School.
c. 50–135	Martyr Rabbi Akiva (Judaism).
c. 65	Death of Apostle Paul (Christianity).
66	Massacre of Jews at Alexandria.
70	Fall of second Temple to Romans (Judaism).
70	Rabbi Yochanan ben Zakkai founds center for legal study and administrative rule in Yavneh; canonization of biblical literature at Yavneh (Judaism).
c. 100	Li Ji, Classic of Rites (Confucianism).
c. 100–552	Primitive Shinto shrines dedicated to clan deities Ujigami appeared.
c. 100–165	Justin Martyr (Christianity).
110	Martyrdom of Ignatius of Antioch (Christianity).
c. 120–162	King Kanishka of Kushan dynasty continues spread of Buddhism.
c. 120–220	Apologetic writing (Christianity).
c. 150	Fourth Buddhist Council.
c. 150–250	Nagarjuna, Buddhist thinker.
c. 160–220	Tertullian, Christian apologist.
166	Han Chinese Emperor sacrifices to Lao Zi and Buddha.

473

184	Rebellion of Yellow Turbans behind a military force (Daoism).
c. 185–254	Origen, Greek Father (Christianity).
200–500	Jewish class of rabbi-scholars called Amoraim (Speakers) in Babylonian academies.
203	Martyrdom of Perpetua and Felicitas (Christianity).
220–552	Buddhist missionaries to Vietnam, Burma, China, Korea, Japan, Indonesia
249–51	Decian Persecution of Christians.
c. 250–356	Anthony of Egypt, "father of monasticism" (Christianity).
c. 250–336	Arius, propagator of Arian heresy (Christianity).
251–334	Wei Hua Cun, famous woman Libationer (Daoism).
284–305	Emperor Diocletian's persecution of Christians.
290–347	Pachomius of Egypt, founder of first monastic community (Christianity).
c. 296–373	Athanasius of Alexandria, Church Father (Christianity).
300–500	Early Puranas: Markandeya, Matsya, Vaya, Narashimha, Vishnu, Devi (Hinduism).
c. 300	Lie Zi composes *The True Classic of Expanding Emptiness* (Daoism).
c. 300	Daoist sect Sacred Jewel introduces influential rituals.
305–311	Emperor Galerius persecutes Christians in the eastern empire.
306–373	Ephrem of Syria, church father (Christianity).
312	Constantine, patron of Christianity, assumes control of Roman Empire.
c. 320–550	Gupta dynasty; India's Golden Age (Hinduism).
325	Council of Nicea (Christianity).
327–379	Macrina, sister of Basil and Gregory of Nyssa (Christianity).
c. 329–389	Greek Father, Gregory of Nazianzus (Christianity).
c. 330–379	Greek Father, Basil (Christianity).
c. 330–395	Greek Father, Gregory of Nyssa (Christianity).
354–430	Augustine of Hippo (Christianity).
364–370	Highest Purity (Mao Shan) Sect emphasizes meditation (Daoism).
c. 390	Jerusalem Talmud is completed (Judaism).
c. 390	Simeon, Syrian ascetic (Christianity).
399	Buddhism is introduced to Korea from China.
c. 400	Confucianism is introduced to Japan from Korea.
fl. c. 430	Buddhist philosopher Buddhaghosa
c. 406–477	Li Xiu Jing compiles earliest Daoist canon.
450	The Northern Transmission: Buddhism enters northern and eastern Asia.
451	Council of Chalcedon (Christianity).
c. 480–547	Benedict of Nursia, founder of western monasticism (Christianity).
c. 499	Completion of Babylonian Talmud (Judaism).
c. 500–1000	Geonim ("Eminences") dominate Jewish scholarship in Babylonian academies.
500–1800	Medieval period, devotional theism develops through the narrative theology of the Puranas (Hinduism).
c. 552	Korean monarch sends an image of Buddha as a gift to the Japanese emperor.

570–632	Muhammad; marriage to Khadija (595) (Islam).
594	Buddhism proclaimed state creed in Japan.
610–622	Muhammad prophesizes; Meccan Suras of the Qur'an are composed (Islam).
618–906	Tang dynasty; Daoism enjoys favor in high places.
c. 620	Kujiki, Records of Ancient Happenings (Shinto).
622	Hijra, "emigration," of Muhammad and his followers from Mecca to Medina (Islam).
622–32	Medinan Suras of the Qur'an revealed (Islam)
630	Muslim community regains access to Mecca (Islam).
634–44	Umar, the Second Caliph, mobilizes a tribal force against Syria and Mesopotamia, Egypt, and Persia (Islam).
638	Muslim conquests of Jerusalem and surrounding area.
644–656	Uthman and Ali compass the downfall of the last Sasanian Emperor (Islam).
650–750	Zhang Guo Lao, patron of pharmacists (Daoism).
661	Mu'awiyah, Ummayad caliph, moves capital to Damascus (Islam).
666	Lao Zi is officially declared a god in the Daoist pantheon.
675–754	Boniface of England, missionary to continental Europe (Christianity).
675	Religious Daoism makes significant impact on imperial Chinese court.
680	Massacre of Husayn and his Shi'ite followers at Karbala, Iraq (Islam).
680	Flourishing of Tamil Bhakti movement (Hinduism).
700–1000	Jewish Khazar kingdom in the Caucasus.
700	He Xian Gu, patron of musicians, is noted for her asceticism and kindness (Daoism).
710–784	First permanent capital established at Nara; introduction of Confucianism, religious Daoism, and Buddhism; Shinto formally organized as all religions interact (Shinto).
711	Muslim armies cross North Africa into Spain.
715	Shinto shrine annexes a Buddhist temple to itself.
720	Nihongi and Nihon Shoki, Chronicles of Japan, Shinto's main "scriptures."
725–755	Antal, poet-saint of the Alvars (Hinduism).
726–843	Iconoclast controversy (Christianity).
732	King Charles Martel defeats Muslims at Poitiers.
737	Shinto shrines number three thousand.
739	Monastic Daoism flourishes during the Tang period.
740–747	Reform of Frankish Church under Boniface (Christianity).
742–814	Charlemagne first "Holy Roman Emperor" (Christianity).
748	Celestial Master recognized (Daoism).
749	First Buddhist monastery in Tibet.
750	Fall of Umayyads; rise of Abbasid dynasty; flowering of classical Islamic civilization at new capital Baghdad.

750	An image of the Shinto war *kami* Hachiman is transported from the Shrine at Usa to Todaiji, in Nara.
760–1142	The Pala dynasty in Bengal supports a brand of Mahayana Buddhism that retains esoteric elements from Hinduism.
762–767	Anan ben David, Karaite leader, elected counter-exilarch of the Jewish communities in Iraq.
778–820	Major Hindu theologian Shankara.
778–864	The Shailendra dynasty in Java profess a type of Mahayana Buddhism.
794–1185	Heian period in Japan, Shinto's fortunes intimately bound up with the developments in Buddhism; foundation of Shingon and Tendai sects of Buddhism.
800	Charlemagne is crowned Holy Roman Emperor.
801	Rabi'a dies, a woman from Baghdad, first Muslim mystic.
845	Buddhists persecuted by a Daoist Chinese emperor.
845–903	Sugawara Michizane, poet-calligrapher, becomes a *kami* (Shinto).
850	Benjamin of Nehavand develops Karaite School of Thought (Judaism).
882–942	Saadia, Gaon of the Iraqi communities who led counter attack against the Karaites (Judaism).
c. 900	Daniel ben Moshe systematizes Karaites, leads proto-Zionist movement in Jerusalem (Judaism).
900	According to the Sunni tradition, the "door of independent investigation" closed for Islamic religious law.
901–923	Engi-shiki, or Institutes of the Engi Era, promulgated (Shinto).
916–1234	Northern Conquest dynasties; reunification of China; Chan is major form of monastic Buddhism.
918–1392	Koryo dynasty in Korea (Confucianism).
d. 922	Mystic Hallaj condemned and executed for blasphemy (Islam).
c. 950	Shaiva Siddhanta School blends theism and monism whereby all individual things are eventually reabsorbed into Shiva (Hinduism).
c. 960–1279	Song dynasty; Neo-Confucian revival; Canon of the Five Classics and Fours Books finalized by scholars.
960–1040	Gershom ben Judah, Jewish scripture scholar.
c. 1000–1200	Five enormous collections of the Daoist Canon appear.
c. 1016	Initial printing of Daoist Canon.
1033–1107	Cheng Yi, his brother Cheng Hao (1032–1085), and Zhu Xi (1130–1200) establish "Cheng Zhu School," the School of Principle (li xue) (Confucianism).
1038	Death of Ibn Sina (Avicenna), the Muslim philosopher.
1040–1077	King Anawartha makes Burma entirely Buddhist.
1049–1054	Pope Leo IX excommunicates the Eastern Patriarch of Constantinople (Christianity).
1050	Christian persecution and massacre of the Jews in the Rhineland.
1054	Schism between East and West Christendom.

1055	Saljuqid Turks conquer Baghdad, institute Sultanate and diminish power of Caliphate (Islam)
1056–1137	Traditional dates for Ramanuja, Vaishnava theologian (Hinduism).
1071	Seljuk Turkish victory over Byzantines at Manzikert (Islam).
1090–1153	Bernard of Clairvaux, mystic (Christianity).
1095–1099	First Christian crusade to regain control of Jerusalem.
1096–1141	Hugh of St. Victor, leader of Victorine School in Paris (Christianity).
1098–1179	Hildegard of Bingen, woman visionary (Christianity).
1099	First Crusade results in beginning of the Latin Kingdom of Jerusalem (Christianity).
1105–1167	Basavanna, poet and influential source of qualified dualistic theism (Hinduism).
1111	Death of Ghazali, Muslim theologian and philosopher.
1119–1182	Sun Bu Er, female ritualist in the Perfect Realization order (Daoism).
1123–1170	Wang Zhe, founded the "Perfect Realization School," or Chuan Zhen (Daoism).
1133–1212	Tendai monk Honen establishes the Pure Land School in Japan (Buddhism).
1133–1568	The Muromachi/Ashikaga period in Japan; Shinto grows as a popular religion.
1134–1204	Moses Maimonides, Jewish theologian.
1138–1193	Saladin, the Kurdish Muslim leader of the anti-Crusade.
1141–1215	Eisai, founder of Rinzai Zen sect (Buddhism).
1147	Second Crusade undertaken (Christianity).
1170–1221	Dominic, founder of the Dominican Order (Christianity).
1179	Third Lateran Council restricts Jewish residences, origins of Jewish ghettoes (Christianity).
1181–1226	Francis of Assisi, founder of Franciscan Order (Christianity).
1185–1333	Buddhist and Shinto theologians devise theories designed to blend the two belief systems, thus inventing "dual Shinto."
1187	Saladin reconquers Jerusalem at Battle of Hattin (Islam), ending Latin Kingdom of first Crusade.
1190	Persecution and massacre of Jews at York, England.
1192	Richard I "Lionhearted" makes truce with Saladin (Christianity).
c. 1197–1276	Madhvacarya, Hindui bhakti theologian.
1198	Death of Ibn Rushd (aka Averroes), Muslim theologian and philosopher.
1250–1517	Mamluk dynasty in Egypt rules much of central Middle East (Islam).
1200–1253	Dogen, founder of Soto Zen lineage in Japan (Buddhism).
1207–1273	Jalal ad-Din Rumi, Muslim mystic and original "whirling dervish."
1210–1526	Delhi Sultanates, powerful Muslim presence in India.
1215	Fourth Lateran Council (Christianity), discriminatory laws against Jews.
1222–82	Nichiren, Japanese reformer, honors Lotus of the Good Law Sutra (Buddhism).
1224–1274	Thomas Aquinas (Christianity).
1228	Eliezer ben Judah and Samuel the Pius foster Hasidic spirituality at Worms and Speyer respectively (Judaism).

1229–1244	Crusaders establish brief Christian control over Jerusalem.
1240–1292	Abraham ben Samuel Abulafia in Sarragossa, Spain, advocates spiritual freedom (Judaism).
1240–1305	Moses ben Shem Tov of Leon composes the Zohar, the Book of Splendor (Judaism).
1244	Ritual burning of the Talmud by Christians in Paris (Judaism).
1256–1302	Gertrude, Christian mystic.
1258	The Mongols destroy Baghdad (Islam).
1260–1327	Meister Eckhart, German Dominican and mystic (Christianity).
1260–1368	Yuan or Mongol dynasty in China favors Tibetan style Buddhism, Daoists lose monasteries and libraries in court debates.
1281	Mongol Emperor Kublai Khan burns Daoist Canon.
1290	Jews expelled from England, series of pogroms.
1293–1381	Jan van Ruysbroeck, mystic (Christianity).
1300–1921	The Ottoman Turkish dynasty (Islam) rules much of Middle East.
1305	Jews expelled from France.
1328	Persecution and massacre of the Jews at Navarre; death of Ibn Taymiyya, major Muslim theologian.
c. 1329–1384	John Wycliffe, Christian reformer.
1333–1568	Muromachi period in Japan; Shinto grows as popular religion.
1336–1565	Vijayanagara kingdom, major Hindu empire in India.
c. 1340–1380	Catherine of Sienna, mystic (Christianity).
c. 1342–1423	Julian of Norwich, English mystic (Christianity).
1360	Buddhism becomes state religion in Thailand.
1368–1644	Ming dynasty; late Medieval Daoism gains strength; Roman Catholic missionaries in China.
c. 1369–1415	John Hus, Christian reformer.
1391	The first Dalai Lama is born in central Tibet (Buddhism).
1391	Persecution of Jews in Spain as Christian Reconquista proceeds.
1392–1910	Yi dynasty; Korean Confucianism reaches its zenith.
1403–1424	Yong Le, third emperor of Ming dynasty (1368–1644), founds the Forbidden City in Beijing (Confucianism).
c. 1440–1518	Kabir, a Hindu saint, influences Guru Nanak (1469–1539) and the founding of the Shikh movement.
1444	Anthology of separate Five Daoist texts is published.
1450–1547	Mirabai, Hindu holy woman and ardent devotee of Krishna.
1453	Ottoman Turks conquer Constantinople (Islam).
1469–1538	Guru Nanak, founder of Sikhism.
1472–1529	Wang Yang Ming leads School of Mind (xin xie) (Confucianism).
c. 1475–1531	Vallabha, bhakti theologian (Hinduism).
1479	Ferdinand and Isabella establish Spanish Inquisition (Christianity).
1483–1546	Martin Luther, leader of German Reformation (Christianity).

1484–1531	Ulrich Zwingli, Swiss Protestant Reformer (Christianity).
1485–1533	Chaitanya, Bengali mystic and devotee of Krishna (Hinduism).
1491–1547	King Henry VIII of England (Christianity).
1491–1556	Ignatius of Loyola, founder of the Society of Jesus (Christianity).
1492	Ferdinand and Isabella take Alhambra in Granada; expel Jews and Muslims from Spain; Columbus reaches West Indian islands (Christianity).
1501–1722	The Safavid dynasty replaces descendants of Genghis Khan in Iran, and establishes Shi'ite Islam as state creed.
1502–1757	Mughal dynasty establishes Islamic rule in much of South Asia.
1509–1564	John Calvin, Christian reformer in Geneva.
1513–1572	John Knox, Scottish reformer (Christianity).
1515–1582	Teresa of Avila, Christian mystic.
1516	First Jewish "ghetto" opens in Venice.
1516–1555	Yang Ji Shang, Confucian Literati, martyred.
1517	Luther's *Ninety-five Theses* are published in Wittenberg (Christianity).
1520–1523	Printed edition of the Talmud produced in Venice (Judaism).
c. 1526–1757	Moghul rule in India; destruction of Hindu temples in North and Central India.
1530	CIT hierarchical structure is replaced with titles (Confucianism).
1540	The Society of Jesus is founded by Ignatius of Loyola (Christianity).
c. 1542	Francis Xavier, Jesuit missionary, lands in Goa (Christianity).
1542–1591	John of the Cross, Spanish mystic (Christianity).
1545–1563	Council of Trent (Christianity), beginnings of "Catholic Reformation."
1552–1610	Matteo Ricci, Jesuit missionary to China, steeps himself in classical Confucian learning (Christianity).
1580	Religious discussions take place between Mughal Emperor Akbar and Jesuit missionaries in India (Islam and Christianity).
1582	Pope Gregory XIII shortens the Julian Calendar.
1594	General Guan Di/Wu Di is deified by imperial decree (Daoism).
1600–1868	Tokugawa period in Japan; Confucianism gains influence in the Japanese imperial government.
1619	First Black African Muslim slaves sold in Americas.
1622–1685	Yamaga Soko, Japanese Confucian scholar and military theorist, originator of the way of the warrior, *bushi-do* (Shinto).
1632–1677	Baruch Spinoza, Jewish philosopher.
1644–1912	Ching (Manchu) dynasty in China; religious Daoism struggles to survive.
1649–1660	Puritan Revolution in England (Christianity).
1666–1708	Gobind Singh, the tenth and final Sikh Guru.
1669–1736	Kada no Azumamaro, considered the founder of the school of National Learning or Kokugaku (Shinto).
1697–1769	Kamo no Mabuchi applies philological methods to classical Japanese prayer (Shinto).

1700	Last of the major Hindu Puranas composed.
1700–1760	Baal Shem Tov, master of the Good Name Movement organized by Israel ben Eliezer in Eastern Europe (Judaism).
1703–1791	John Wesley, founder of Methodism (Christianity).
1728–1786	Moses Mendelsohn; Enlightenment ideas promoted, movement called *Haskalah* (Judaism).
1730–1801	Motoori Morinaga, regarded Shinto's best scholarly mind.
c. 1740–1760	First Great Awakening in America (Christianity).
1756–1834	David Friedlander replaces Hebrew prayers with German.
1763–1843	Hirata Atsutane, influential exponent of Kokugaku (Shinto).
1772–1833	Ram Mohan Roy founds Brahmo Samaj (1828) (Hinduism).
1780–1842	William Ellery Channing, Unitarian reformer (Christianity).
1791	Death of Muhammad ibn Abd al-Wahhab, founder of Wahhabi movement in Arabian Peninsula (Islam).
1803–1882	Ralph Waldo Emerson, American transcendentalist (Christianity), popularizes Bhagavad Gita and Upanishads in America.
1805–1844	Joseph Smith, Jr., founder of Church of Jesus Christ of Latter-day Saints (Christianity).
1806–1860	Samuel Holdheim, initiated liturgical reforms in Berlin (Judaism).
1810–1874	Abraham Geiger; dramatic liturgical changes; leads a gathering of rabbis and argues for a reduced authority for both Bible and Talmud (1837) (Judaism).
1817–1892	Lifetime of Baha'ullah, founder of Baha'i faith, developing out of Shi'ite Islam.
1823–1897	Sabato Morais, founded Jewish Theological Seminary of America.
1830	Church of Jesus Christ of Latter-day Saints founded by Joseph Smith.
1834–1886	Ramakrishna Paramahamsa, Bengali mystic (Hinduism).
1835–1908	Mirza Ghulam Ahmad claims to be both the Mahdi and Jesus' Second Coming (Islam).
1849–1905	Muhammad Abduh promotes reason as source of knowledge (Islam).
1850	Rig Veda first translated into English (Hinduism).
1850–1864	Tai Ping "Highest Peace" rebellion (Daoism).
1852–1916	Charles Taze Russell, founder of Jehovah Witnesses in the United States (Christianity).
1852–1932	Liao Ping considers himself Confucius' prophet.
1856–57	Fifth Buddhist monastic council.
1863–1902	Vivekananda founds Ramakrishna Mission (Hinduism).
1865–1935	Rashid Rida, founder of Egyptian Salafi movement calling for revival of pristine days of the Prophet (Islam).
1868	Dual Shinto becomes dominant form of Shinto.
1868	Japanese impose a system of devotion to the emperor, a kind of State Creed (Shinto).
1868–1871	Japanese persecution of Buddhists by Meiji emperor.

1868–1945	Confucians play important role in the Meiji Reform: restoration of the emperor's divine status (Shinto).
1869–1948	Mohandas Karmachand Gandhi, received the title Mahatma "Great-Souled One" (Hinduism).
1869	Founding of Tokyo's Yasukuni Shrine (Shinto).
1873	Union of American Hebrew Congregations founded (Judaism).
1874–1952	Chain Weitzmann, influential Zionist leader (Judaism).
1875	Arya Samaj founded by Swami Dayananda Sarasvati (Hinduism).
1879	Church of Christ, Scientist founded by Mary Baker Eddy.
1881–1983	Mordecai Kaplan leads a movement and teacher that Jews were a civilization in process.
1881–present	Revival of Jewish nationalism, called Zionism.
1885	Pittsburgh Reform Platform (Judaism).
1890	Nathan Birnbaum coins the word "Zionism."
1892	Death of Baha'Allah, who claimed to be a prophet (Baha'i faith).
1896	Theodore Herzl organized Zionist political movement (Judaism).
1896–1977	A. C. Bhaktivedanta became a *sannyasi* in 1959 (Hinduism), leading figure of International Society of Krishna Consciousness.
1896–1982	Nirmala Sundari (Hinduism).
1897	Theodore Herzl convened first Zionist Congress at Basle.
1900	Shrine Shinto no longer considered a religion, but a universally binding attitude of reverence for the emperor.
1900s	British Mandate Rule over the Holy Land of Palestine.
1911	Foundation of Chinese Republic. Confucius and sages held in the highest reverence.
1912	Abdication of the last Chinese emperor.
1917	Balfour Declaration (Judaism), early development leading to state of Israel.
1917	Bolshevik Revolution.
1924	Rabbinical Assembly of America became Conservative Judaism's Institutional anchor.
1924–29	Buddhist scriptural canon published in Tokyo.
1927	Founding of Muslim Brotherhood by Hasan al-Banna (1906–1949, Islam)
1933	The Shoah Holocaust begins (Judaism).
1933	The thirteenth Dalai Lama dies (Buddhism).
1942	Jews begin to return in large numbers to Israel from Europe.
1945	Supreme Commander of Allied Powers, General Douglas McArthur, issues the Shinto Directive; Japanese Emperor no longer considered divine.
1947	The State of Israel is formed.
1947	The partition of India and the creation of the Indian Union and Pakistan as independent and separatist Hindu and Muslim nations.
1948	Maoist Revolution; destruction of Confucian institutions; Daoism diminishes.

1949	Discovery of the Dead Sea Scrolls by a Bedouin shepherd near the Dead Sea (Judaism).
1949	The Republican Nationalist movement insists that Confucianism represent all genuine Chinese values.
1949	Indian constitution outlaws caste system's social discrimination.
1950	China invades Tibet; Dalai Lama flees to India in 1959.
1954–1956	Sixth Buddhist Council in Rangoon, Burma (now called Myanmar).
1956	Buddhism celebrates twenty-five hundred years of existence; B. R. Ambedkar leads revival in India.
1960s	Maharishi Mahesh Yogi and other popular teachers spread Hinduism beyond India and into Europe and Americas.
1962–1965	Second Vatican Council (Christianity).
1966–1976	Chinese Cultural Revolution; disastrous losses for Daoism.
1966	Death of Sayyid Qutb, ideologue of Muslim Brotherhood.
1967	Six Days War is fought between Israel and Egypt.
1971	Pakistan is divided into Pakistan and Bangladesh.
1976	Chairman Mao Zi Dong dies; fortunes of Buddhists and Daoists in China begin to improve.
1979	In Mecca, a claimant to status of Mahdi seeks to grab political power, trying to seize control of Muslim central shrine, the Ka'ba.
1979	Shi'ite Iranian students take over the United State's embassy in Tehran, Islamic Republic of Iran proclaimed.
1980s	Daoism doing better in China, monasteries reopen.
1989	Tian An Men Square massacre: symbol of young Chinese struggle for democracy.
1989	Emperor Hirohito of Japan dies, ending the Showa era (Shinto).
1992	Li Hongzi founds Fa Lun Gong (Daoism).
1992	Destruction of Babri-Masjid and rioting in many Indian cities due to Hindu agitation concerning Rama's presumed birthplace in Ayodhya.
1993	Parliament of World Religions, Chicago, marks centenary of original Parliament called by Vivekananda.
1999	Chinese authorities attempt to suppress the sect called Fa Lun Gong (Daoism).
2010	World population surges past seven billion, with India and China comprising over one third of the human race.
2011	"Arab Spring" witnesses political reform movement across central Middle East.

Glossary

Amulet A symbolic object, usually of popular beliefs, that protects the owner from negative or malevolent forces, as in the common "folk-religious" symbol of a large "eye" designed to protect the bearer from the "evil eye."

Anchorite From the Greek *ana-chorein* ("to withdraw"), refers to those who choose a monastic life but live alone or as a hermit rather than in a community.

Angels From the Greek *Angelos* ("messenger"), they are supernatural beings who do the bidding of God, prominent in Christian, Islamic and Jewish traditions with multiple functions, from delivering divine communication to protecting and guiding. Similar beings inhabit the cosmic realms in other traditions as well, such the *amesha spentas* in Zoroastrianism, and the *apsaras* in Buddhism.

Anthropology, Religious Interpretations in different religious traditions about what it means to be a human being, including such important themes as the origin and the makeup of the human person, and the divine-human relationship, grace, moral freedom and responsibility.

Anthropomorphism Use of human analogies to describe the divine reality, such as references to God as seeing or sitting on a throne; having features such as face, eyes, or hands; or manifesting emotional responses such as anger or disappointment.

Apocalyptic From the Greek for un-veiling or revealing (*apo* + *kalyptein*), referring in general to a view of history in which time moves inexorably toward a cosmic cataclysm to be heralded by a variety of otherwise unimaginable events, and specifically to a type of literature developing that theme.

Apocrypha "Hidden," as used largely in reference to secondary religious texts not judged worthy of inclusion in a faith community's "canonical" scriptures.

Apostasy From the Greek *apo-stasis* ("standing away or apart from," "rebellion"), a blanket rejection of one's faith tradition, manifested typically in a return to former views or to another tradition.

Apostles From the Greek *apo-stellein* ("one who is sent out"), those special prophets who are given a scripture and a mission to all people. They are not unique to Christianity (known as "the twelve"). In Islam, they are called *mursalun*, often in reference to "prophets."

Archaeology The study of material evidence of past cultures and civilizations, which reconstructs at least tentatively, institutions, social systems and beliefs of previous forms of religious communities.

Ascetic A person who engages in demanding "exercise" (from the Greek *askesis*) in the interest of spiritual progress, resulting in freedom from the encumbrances of material existence, self-denial, and attentiveness to inner movements of spirit.

Assimilation The issue of "assimilation" and "distinctiveness" signifies the struggle of religious groups to balance between maintaining their faith and identity and adapting themselves to societies in which they are the minorities (e.g., Jewish communities and new Muslim communities in the United States).

Authority The cohesive, powerful guidance and moral compass in religious communities, developing a wide variety of structures within different traditions. Some are more centralized (e.g., Roman Catholicism, Mormons and Shi'i Islam); some are entirely local (tribal traditions, village Hinduism); others fall somewhere in between, forming conventions or conferences to which the local communities are affiliated.

Belief As a religious concept, assent to the *content* of a tradition's central teaching, as distinct from "faith," the personal commitment to the meaning of a creed, or more generally, a set of universal claims that a person or a school holds.

Calendar, Lunar Calendars that are based on cycles of lunar phase that drift "backwards" in relation to the solar year by 11 to 12 days. Some religions use a purely lunar calendar (e.g., Islam), while others use "lunisolar" calendars by adding days or a month each calendar year in order to keep the festivals connected to seasonal cycle and agricultural needs (e.g., Chinese calendar).

Calendar, Solar Calendars that are based on the revolution of earth around the sun, in which the festivals are more associated with planting and harvest with more emphases on winter/summer solstices and vernal/autumnal equinoxes (e.g., Gregorian Calendar and the modern calendar).

Canon An authoritative collection of central sacred texts.

Canonization The ritual for officially announcing a person as a "saint," most known in the Roman Catholic Church.

Celestial Hierarchy Many religious traditions have populated every level of their universes with spiritual powers assigned in different task, and typically, in hierarchical orders (such as the Nine Choirs of Angels).

Cenobites From the Greek *koinos* and *bios* ("common life"), the members of a monastic group who live together in community at all times.

Church and State The complex issue of the struggle between religious power and civil/political power. While the term "church" seems to indicate only the struggle between Christianity and civil powers, religions all over the world face issues on their relations with civil or secular powers.

Contemplation A prayerful focus on inner spiritual realities whose immediate goal is to enter imaginatively into a spiritual reality, and ultimately to be united with that reality as the Latin root (*cum,* "with"; *templum,* "temple") suggests.

Conversion From the Latin *convertere* ("to turn about"), a process of dramatic change on one's religious commitment, oftentimes a transfer of allegiance or membership from one religious tradition to another. It can also mean a soul-shaking experience that leads to a new direction of spiritual searching, as described variously by many great religious teachers.

Communities, Established Sometimes identified by the term *ecclesia* (Latin "assembly"), communities that enjoy some degree of official sanction or approval within a modern nation-state; for example, the Church of England, or Buddhism in Thailand.

Communities, Parent Communities from which a new or different religious belief or community derives. Nonetheless, the relationship is never unilateral, and there are complicated interactions between the "parent" and the "children."

Communities, Universal Those communities well established in many national and cultural contexts; for example, Sunni Islam and Roman Catholicism.

Cosmology, Religious Interpretation of how the world came to be (or "cosmogony"), the structure or order of the cosmos and what it means spiritually. The most common models for describing time and change are the *linear* views of the Abrahamic faiths and the *cyclical* models represented, for example, in Hinduism and Buddhism. As for the beginning of the world, there is a wide spectrum of explanations, most notably creation from nothing and variations on the theme of "emanation" theory.

Creed The totality of what members of a religious tradition believe; technically, a formal statement that sums up the key points in a belief system.

Cult Can refer either to a given faith's practices of worship and ritual, or to new religious movements, typically small groups revolving around a charismatic leader in a very localized community more isolated from the society than "sects"; some cults seem to be oriented toward an "end-time" scenario.

Custom Activities that people in a particular time and cultural setting are used to doing, ranging widely from social expectations and etiquette to "Common Law" (practices that have assumed legal status and authority). Anthropology assists religious studies here by distinguishing between beliefs and practices that are explicitly religious and those inherited from earlier local and regional cultures.

Dance, Sacred Dance used in religious rituals, in which central mythic narratives are preserved and reenacted, from which many liturgical traditions develop. The use of dance may represent various levels of sacrality according to different occasions.

Demons Any spiritual beings (in a broad sense), but now typically identified as hostile; in Abrahamic traditions, they are generally lesser evil forces who act as Satan's minions. In traditions such as Hinduism, demons (*asuras*) were mythically distinguished from deities (*devas*) in that demons lacked necessary cleverness to prevail.

Denomination The various Christian "churches" that came into being during the Protestant Reformation; a term that can also refer to developments of subcommunities in other traditions. Usually these groups differ more in organization than in doctrine, but there are also many exceptions.

Devils In contrast to angels, these are supernatural beings representing evil forces; when used in the singular "devil," it typically refers to a single malevolent being of sufficient power that may they even compete with the supreme being. In Islam, the Devil is called *Shaytan* ("Satan," "the Adversary") and *Iblis* (from the Greek *diabolos*).

Disciples Those who learn from a master; followers of religious or charismatic leaders.

Divination A host of specific ritual practices to give practitioners a sense of control in the face of life's uncertainty or mystery. Oracles of ancient Greco-Roman culture, some astrological beliefs, reading signs from the stars, palms, or tea leaves fall into this category.

Doctrine "Teaching" or "instruction" (Latin *doctrina*), referring to body of specific beliefs or principles; a measure of the role of authority in a religious tradition and a framework for passing

along the content of faith and protecting practices of ritual and worship from losing their distinctive character.

Dogma Belief or opinion (Greek *dokein, doxa*) in general, but specifically referring to the clarification and prescriptive form of a *particular doctrine* that is decided by a teaching body (or authority) when necessary under certain historical circumstances.

Dreams Across traditions, dreams are one means of communication between God and human beings. Important religious figures receive special teachings or revelation in their dreams, which can combine both visual and auditory input.

Ecumenism All the ways in which members of many Christian churches and denominations have sought to come together in dialogue of mutual understanding (from the Greek *oikoumene*, the "inhabited earth").

Education, Religious The process of passing the religious tradition's beliefs and related institutional developments. While this kind of tutelage may remain private within a particular community, it can at times also connect with the social/civil educational system (e.g., Confucianism).

Eschatology "Study of the last things" (Greek *logos* = study; *eschata* = last things—death, judgment, heaven, and hell); used mostly in the Abrahamic traditions in keeping with the beginning-middle-end structure of their "linear" concepts of time and history; that is, religious teachings concerning how history and the world as we know it will come to an end.

Ethnic Issues SEE Racial Issues

Excommunication The process of banishing or shunning individuals or groups from participation in their religious communities, usually associated with the Roman Catholic Church, but also practiced by Jewish and other Christian communities and sects.

Exegesis "To draw out" (Greek *ex* = out; *hegeomai* = to lead or draw); processes of reflection and study focused on the interpretation of a text, especially sacred scripture, often resulting in extensive commentarial traditions. Among the many principal "styles" of exegesis are the literal, historical, legal, and mystical.

485

Faith The act or process of relying on or assenting to realities that one might not be able to prove (in contrast to *belief*); a kind of fundamental trust or a "leap" into the unknown.

Fakir Originally from the Arabic *faqir* ("poor person," "beggar"), someone who chooses spiritual and sometimes also material poverty. Can also refer to a class of individuals, especially in western and southern Asia, who engage in shocking and apparently painful physical actions (e.g., lying on beds of nails) without suffering disastrous consequences.

Fasting A common religious practice of limited eating and drinking, whose regulations vary among different traditions; it is also very common among ascetics, sometimes in an extreme way.

Fundamentalism An approach to religious teachings and values that emphasizes strict and direct reliance on a tradition's most ancient sources with relatively literal interpretation, rather than appealing to the intervening history of interpretation (exegesis) that comprises the community's repository of tradition.

Gender Gender roles are often "constructed" out of a blend of social custom and religious justification. Both social and religious gender roles are intimately related to the exercise of power; religious rhetoric invariably canonizes the social status quo, arguing that time-honored gender-based divisions of labor are divinely ordained. Particularly in recent times, women's roles in different religious traditions are gradually rewriting the history.

Hagiography From the Greek *hagie graphe* ("sacred writing"), accounts of the lives of the holy persons (or "saints"), underscoring the amazing and often downright miraculous elements, such as the special signs at their birth, extraordinary events in their childhood, or a dramatic conversion.

Heresy From the Greek *haireo* ("to seize, choose, decide"; in other words, "to take a position" [*hairesis*]), in general the deliberate holding a set of beliefs in direct opposition to a religious tradition's established and widely accepted authority.

Hermeneutics "Principles or theories of interpretation" (Greek *hermeneutike*); the study of human interpretation of texts (religious or non-religious) based on a wide variety of particular points of view (e.g., gender, denomination, philosophy).

Heterodoxy From the Greek for "variant opinion" (*hetere doxa*), a term used to characterize doctrinal views at odds with mainstream thinking in a tradition. In the early stage of a religious tradition, diverse views are commonly seen until some views become so extreme that the majority of believers start to define the limits and decide some views as "heretical."

Holy City A geographical focal point that typically begins as a sacred spot because of divine manifestation or the sacred people's residence and gradually develops as *the* place where virtually everything of religious significance has happened. Thus it becomes "a microcosm" of history, the center of all times and all spaces, as one religious tradition (or even more than one) recognizes.

Inspiration From the Latin "to breathe into" (*inspirare*), a common way of describing a divine intervention in the process of composing the sacred texts.

Interreligious Dialogue Direct attempts made by members and administrations of the larger faith traditions to come together in hopes of deeper appreciation of their common interests as well as of the issues that divide them.

Law, Religious Strictures and sanctions required by a tradition's sacred texts; with respect to issues not explicitly or unambiguously mentioned in sacred texts, some communities develop the equivalent of charters, constitutions or by-laws and thus a rather elaborate system of religious law comes about. "Custom," or the long-standing practice of local communities, though not specifically mentioned in the sacred texts, may sometimes be "sanctified" by religious law. Major examples are Roman Catholic "Canon" law, Jewish Rabbinical law, and Islamic *sharia* and *fiqh*.

Lay, Laity Ordinary believers in a religious tradition as in contrast to the religious specialists, "ordained" clergy, or monastics (monks, nuns).

Literature, Apocalyptic A particular style of religious literatures, especially referring to the literatures in Judeo-Christian tradition that involves figurative languages, the revealing of things hidden, and the end of the world.

Literature, Historical Accounts that preserve the history of the community or the biography of a foundational figure.

Literature, Prophetic Accounts of the deeds and words of the "prophets," who "speak on behalf of" an ultimate spiritual power and focus on the need for change.

Literature, Wisdom Sayings or moral exhortations in the form of easy-to-remember proverbs that exist almost in every religious/cultural tradition.

Liturgy From the Greek *leitourgia* ("a public duty or service"), a term first appearing in the early Christian context with religious connotation, now generally indicating any system of rituals mandated for public reenactment by members of a religious tradition.

Mantra A word or phrase repeated slowly and deliberately as the focal object of meditation.

Marriage, Interfaith Marriage between members of two religious traditions. In some traditions (e.g. Muslims and Catholics) interfaith marriage is either not allowed or frowned upon and fraught with restrictions (e.g. the agreement to raise children in its own tradition).

Martyrs From a Greek word that means "witness," those who are so committed to their faith that they have been willing to die, either in the active spread and defense of faith or as a way of protesting forced conversion or apostasy.

Meditation A prayerful focus on inner spiritual realities. In general, meditation involves a nondiscursive concentration on some object (either verbal or visual). By targeting the focal object exclusively, the meditator frees up the mind and spirit to achieve a deeper level of simple awareness. SEE also *Contemplation*.

Millennialism Derived from "millennium" ("a thousand-year period"); the general expectation of a certain point in human history that will undergo a dramatic turnabout, marking the end of time itself and the beginning of another age.

Miracle An apparent breach in the laws of nature that so defies rational explanation as to suggest the possibility of divine intervention, as broadly defined; religiously perceived, either as a witness of divine power and mercy, or as a gift from divine source to establish spiritual credentials.

Mission/Missionary From the Latin *missio* ("sending out"), the organized propagation of a religion outside of its local context and geographical boundary. Christianity ("evangelization"), Islam ("da'wa" or "invitation"), and Buddhism are the three great missionary traditions, though the effort varies between groups within each tradition.

Monasticism A term narrowly used to refer to early Eastern Christianity, the ascetic lifestyle that some Christians chose to live, seeking God through penance and prayer. Broadly speaking, monasticism indicates lifestyle that is dedicated to spiritual pursuit, either individually or collectively, which can be observed in Buddhism, Hinduism, and Christianity. Monastic communities of monks and/or nuns sometimes develop elaborate systems of leadership and training new members.

Music Some traditions favor arcane music in religious rituals to establish a mood of solemnity and to mark the occasion out of the ordinary. Others use music to encourage maximum participation of the believers and thus develop extensive hymnographies.

Mysticism From the Greek *myein* ("to close one's [eyes/lips]") and *mystes* ("initiated person"), the teachings, belief and knowledge of the immediate personal encounter or experience with the sacred; in the first-hand account of these experiences, there are some apparent similarities across traditions: one type is called "theistic" or "dualistic" mysticism, in which the personal encounter does not indicate the loss of individuality; another type is called "monistic" mysticism, implying total absorption of the individual in a greater totality or impersonal cosmic reality.

Myth Accounts of the deeds of the spiritual powers that brought the (religious) community into being; poetic expression of profound reflection on the human condition; a type of "narrative theology."

Novice (Aspirant) The first stage of training in being a monk or a nun, or member of, e.g. a Sufi order (Islam).

Offering, Votive Ritual gift associated with the making of vows (from the Latin *votum*, "something promised") in connection with requests for special vows. Believers may vow to perform certain devotional or charitable acts if the deity will grant their request.

487

Oral Tradition Teachings preserved in oral forms or in ritual performance, such as the Native American and African traditions.

Ordination A special ritual for dedicating individuals to priesthood or monkhood.

Orthodoxy From the Greek *orthe doxe* ("correct opinion"), a term indicating right beliefs accepted by the religious community, in contrast to the diverging views (*heterodoxy*) or the opposing views (*heresy*) of these beliefs.

Priesthood A socio-religious class that functions as the chief ritual specialist and is often considered as a mediator of spiritual power, an indispensible connection between the divine and the human; special training or education for priests is usually needed.

Prophet An intermediary in the divine communication to the humankind who sometimes also functions as a critic of the ethical and religious status quo, especially important in the traditions of Middle Eastern origin.

Pseudepigrapha "Works written under assumed names"; religious literatures of secondary value (in contrast to *canon*).

Racial Issues As one formative element in the history of religion, race, as gender, causes some complicated issues. While the religious tradition expands beyond the original racial context, one might find a kind of "religious colonialism" prevailing because of the cultural hegemony, relegating members of "outside" racial groups to secondary status (e.g., Islam's expansion to non-Arab cultures).

Redemption Concept in which a savior figure spends him or herself as a kind of ransom, identifying profoundly with the plight of humanity, though very familiar to Christians, less commonly seen in other religious traditions.

Reformers Religious people who try to awaken the awareness that it is time to change, to renew, or to recapture the original spirit that give birth to the tradition, not always but sometimes involving returning to the sources.

Relic A physical reminder of the ongoing spiritual presence of some important religious figure. There are two main types: the bodily remains of a holy person, and objects that once belonged to, or were touched by, a holy person.

Religion Adherence to a set beliefs or teachings about the deepest and most elusive of life's mysteries (Latin root *religo*, "to bind" or "to obligate"); commitment to the quest for ultimate answers that transcend the appearances of things, usually involving a complex process of assessment from three critical sources: culture, tradition, and personal experience.

Religion, Comparative Studies of parallels between one tradition and another (or others); studies of religious traditions by comparison that enhance the knowledge of how they develop and how their teachings differ or reinforce one other.

Religion, Philosophy of Attempts to give a rational justification for religious beliefs, with subcategories involving the analysis of religious expressions (religious language, rituals, statements of belief).

Religious Officials/Specialists Distinctive roles in religious traditions specializing in the practice and preservation of ritual, interpretation and implementation of rules, works of teaching and pastoral guidance, and internal services and social outreach.

Religious Tolerance/Diversity A political and theological concept forms in the modern era but with its root in Judeo-Christian history. The principle holds the tolerance to different religions, or religious freedom of each individual.

Religious Tradition Various systems of belief and values around which communities of religious believers have formed throughout history and across the globe, including Judaism, Christianity, Islam, Hinduism, Buddhism, Confucianism, Taoism, and Shinto.

Revelation A divine self-disclosure; "drawing back the veil" that covers the deepest mysteries of life, thus disclosing their inner meaning; a supernatural intervention to reveal the saving realities which human beings are incapable to attain by themselves, especially true to Abrahamic traditions—Judaism, Christianity, and Islam. Some traditions distinguish between "general" and "special" revelation, denoting respectively broader and more restricted access to divine truth.

Rites of Passage Religious rituals that acknowledge, celebrate, and help people to cope with the critical moments in life, such as birth, puberty, the assumption of a new state in life (marriage), and death.

Ritual Practices that belong to the larger category of custom but tend to follow rigid and symbolic rules and to repeat in the same pattern in the interest of insuring the appropriateness and effectiveness of the action. Religious rituals help the believers establish relationship of presence, imagination, or memory with the spiritual, some of which effect or mediate a connection between participants and a divine presence. In some religious settings, precise instructions of the performance, or "rubrics" (from the Latin *ruber,* "red" since the instructions were written in red to set them off from the "text") are applied.

Ritual Object (or Implement) Essential devices of religious practices, with practical functions and/or symbolic meanings, including offerings and their utensils (practical), images or icons, books or scrolls of sacred texts (symbolic), and so on.

Sacred Geography (or Sacred Places) The spiritual mapping of each tradition, designating several physical spots that are significant to its own; for example, places associated with events in the life of some sacred person, or places where a natural feature (such as a tree, or mountain, or spring) possesses unusual spiritual power.

Sacred Space Locations dedicated to the proper and effective performance of religious rituals. Yet the degree to which the primary ritual sites are dedicated and restricted to specific ritual actions varies, and the restrictions on what space is suitable for which ritual also varies across traditions.

Sacred Time The special meanings of history, the specific moments that are pointed out in the individuals' lives and in the ordinary cycles of days, months, and years. Also moments of ritual/revelatory encounter with the divine, time to hallow the decisive life experiences with rites of passage.

Sacrifice From the Latin root *sacrum* ("holy") and *facere* ("to make"), including both performances of actual slaughtering of a living being and symbolic "offering up" of something dear to the one making the sacrifice in order to sanctify, petition, or expiate.

Sage A religious figure who is celebrated as a living repository of wisdom, especially important in Judaism, Hinduism, and Confucianism; this figure is respected not only because s/he preserves the ancient ways but also because he injects new meanings into the old as a way of adapting to changing times.

Saints Individuals who embody to the highest degree a religious tradition's spiritual ideals; the ability to perform miracles (oftentimes in the form of healing) is one of the major features to be a "saint" in many traditions. Some traditions include "cults of devotion" to these saints and some of these figures are considered "patron saints" of specific activities or places.

Satan From a Hebrew root meaning "accused" or "adversary," equivalent of "the Devil."

Savior Figures Figures in religious traditions who deliver solutions to human difficulties and bring an end to human suffering; some traditions do not include such figures but emphasize the importance of self-effort (by following the religious exemplar) or self-surrender (to the divine).

Schism From the Greek *schismos* ("rupture, break or tear"), a phenomenon mostly referring to events in Christianity, but may also occur in other traditions; it occurs when a faction within a larger religious community decides to break away and assert its independence, in matters ranging from doctrine and theology, to social, political and ethnic issues.

Scripture Sacred literatures (literally "writings"), whether composed over a relatively short period of time and perhaps associated with only a single person (e.g., Islam's Qur'an) or over centuries and bound together into a single volume (e.g., the Hebrew scriptures) or even whole libraries of sacred texts gathered through more than two millennia (e.g., Hindu and Buddhist scriptures).

Scripture, Inerrancy of The teaching that the divine communication must surely be perfect in every detail since it comes from a perfect sources; some insist on the perfection of literal meanings, while others insist the inerrancy in regard to its religious or moral implications.

Sect From the Latin *sequi* ("to follow"), generally denoting any group that acknowledges a common leadership and shares a common set of beliefs; historically used by larger traditions to refer to nonconformist groups.

489

Semantics Study of meanings of words and phrases; in particular, study of how signs or symbols draw upon different "fields" for their contents, including sacred scripture, theological formulation, allusion to a widely known cultural symbol, or nature. Especially relevant to *exegesis.*

Semiotics From the Greek *semeion* ("sign"), the study of signs and symbols; a branch of logic that examines how we put together all the various elements of thought so that they communicate complex ideas; can include interpretation of signs and symbols, such as inscriptions (text in any language), aniconic imagery (visual but nonrepresentational form referring to a sacred personage), and iconic imagery (representations of a sacred person or object).

Shamans In some traditions shamans are also called medicine men (or women). They belong to a general category of priest/religious specialist, but with greater emphasis on esoteric and arcane practices. Shamanistic rites often involve trances or loss of control and include exorcism to expel undesirable spiritual forces, as seen in many indigenous or tribal traditions.

Sign Any verbal or visual indicator that conveys some basic message (in general); an object or an action that communicates a specific religious meaning. In contrast to "symbol," sign has a more direct relationship with the referent. Some traditions, such as Christianity and Islam, use the term to refer to "miraculous" events.

Social Works Major religious traditions, including Islam, Hinduism, Buddhism, and Christianity, are very concerned about reaching out to the society, and many communities within these traditions devote themselves to social works such as health care, disaster relief, feeding the hungry, and sheltering the homeless.

Spirituality The experiential dimension of a religious tradition; how believers as individuals and members of a religious community perceive their relationship with all things and what the source and final goal of human existence are. It may be expressed in many aspects of one religion, from literature and rituals to institutions and structures of authority.

Symbol An object or act that represents some reality other than itself; oftentimes a compacted set of meanings.

Syncretism From a Greek root meaning "mixing together"; in general the blending of doctrinal and ritual elements from two or more religious traditions to form a new tradition or sub-tradition.

Talisman A symbolic object, usually of popular beliefs, that promises good fortune. Nonreligious examples: four-leaf clovers or rabbit's feet.

Theology "Talk or thinking about God" (Greek *logos* = talk, *theos* = god). In traditions that have a more developed discipline of theology, it involves three things: a systematic reflection on the scriptures and teachings of the tradition, the formulation of a distinctive way to talk about tradition's central teachings, and the articulation of the distinctive symbols.

Theology, Natural The study of divine justice (or "theodicy") as a branch of philosophy of religion; using reason rather than revelation or divine communication as the source of its truth claims; exploring aspects of human souls such as ethical freedom and immortality.

Vision Like dreams, visionary experiences are considered to be the privileged occasion to encounter some important spiritual presence or special revelation. While dreams tend to be private, sometimes visions become the rallying point for large numbers of believers.

Further Reading

(Selections of works published since the first edition of this volume)

Judaism

Collins, John J. and Daniel C. Harlow, eds. *The Eerdmans dictionary of early Judaism*. Grand Rapids, MI: William B. Eerdmans, 2010.

De Lange, Nicholas R. M. *An introduction to Judaism*. Cambridge, UK; New York: Cambridge University, 2010.

Donaldson, Terence L. *Jews and anti-Judaism in the New Testament: decision points and divergent interpretations*. London; Waco, TX: Baylor University, 2010.

Donaldson, Terence L. *Judaism and the Gentiles: Jewish patterns of universalism (to 135 CE)*. Waco, TX: Baylor University, 2007.

Drucker, Malka ed. *Women and Judaism*. Westport, CT: Praeger, 2009.

Eisen, Robert, *The peace and violence of Judaism: from the Bible to modern Zionism*. New York: Oxford University, 2011.

Feldman, Louis H. *Judaism and Hellenism reconsidered*. Leiden; Boston: Brill, 2006.

Gelernter, David Hillel. *Judaism: a way of being*. New Haven: Yale University, 2009.

Greenspahn, Frederick E., ed. *Women and Judaism: new insights and scholarship*. New York: New York University, 2009.

Hayes, Christine E. *The emergence of Judaism: classical traditions in contemporary perspective*. Minneapolis: Fortress, 2011.

Hughes, Aaron W., ed. *Defining Judaism: a reader*. London; Oakville, CT: Equinox, 2010.

Jaffé, Dan, ed. *Studies in rabbinic Judaism and early Christianity*. Leiden; Boston: Brill, 2010.

Kessler, Herbert L., and David Nirenberg, eds. *Judaism and Christian art: aesthetic anxieties from the catacombs to colonialism*. Philadelphia: University of Pennsylvania, 2011.

Lupovitch, Howard N. *Jews and Judaism in world history*. London; New York: Routledge, 2010.

Popovic, Mladen, ed. *Authoritative scriptures in ancient Judaism*. Leiden; Boston: Brill, 2010.

Raphael, Marc Lee, ed. *The Columbia history of Jews and Judaism in America*. New York; Chichester: Columbia University, 2009.

Raphael, Melissa. *Judaism and the visual image: a Jewish theology of art*. London; New York: Continuum, 2009.

Solomon, Norman. *The A to Z of Judaism*. Lanham: Scarecrow, 2009.

Stone, Michael E. *Ancient Judaism: new visions and views*. Grand Rapids, MI: W. B. Eerdmans, 2011.

Christianity

Bahr, Ann Marie B., chief consultant. *Christianity: the illustrated guide to 2,000 years of the Christian faith*. Elanora Heights, NSW (Australia): Millennium House, 2009.

Baker, Gregory A., and Stephen E. Gregg, eds. *Jesus beyond Christianity: the classic texts*. Oxford: Oxford University, 2010.

Bradshaw, Paul F. *The origins of feasts, fasts, and seasons in early Christianity*. Collegeville, MN: Liturgical, 2011.

Dacy, Marianne. *The separation of early Christianity from Judaism*. Amherst, NY: Cambria, 2010.

Freeman, Charles. *A new history of early Christianity*. New Haven: Yale University, 2009.

González, Justo L. *The story of Christianity*. 2 vols. New York: HarperCollins, 2010.

Johnson, Todd M., Kenneth R. Ross, and Sandra S. K. Lee, eds. *Atlas of global Christianity 1910–2010*. Edinburgh: Edinburgh University, 2009.

Kennedy, Philip. *Christianity: an introduction*. London; New York: I. B. Tauris, 2011.

Kirk-Duggan, Cheryl A., and Karen Jo Torjesen, eds. *Women and Christianity*. Santa Barbara, CA: Praeger/ABC-CLIO, 2010.

Lynch, Joseph H. *Early Christianity: a brief history*. New York: Oxford University, 2010.

Koepping, Elizabeth, ed. *World Christianity: critical concepts in religious studies*. London; New York: Routledge, 2011.

O'Mahony, Anthony, and Emma Loosley, eds. *Eastern Christianity in the modern Middle East*. London; New York: Routledge, 2010.

Porterfield, Amanda. *Healing in the history of Christianity*. Oxford; New York: Oxford University, [2009], 2005.

Rubin, Miri, ed. *Medieval Christianity in practice*. Princeton: Princeton University, 2009.

Standaert, Nicolas, ed. *Handbook of Christianity in China*. Leiden; Boston: Brill, 2001–2010.

Witte, John Jr., and Frank S. Alexander, eds. *Christianity and human rights: an introduction*. Cambridge, UK; New York: Cambridge University, 2010.

Islam

Ahmed, Akbar. *Journey into America: the Challenge of Islam*. Washington, DC: Brookings Institution 2001–05.

Berg, Herbert. *Elijah Muhammad and Islam*. New York: New York University, 2009.

Bonner, Michael. *Jihad in Islamic history: doctrines and practice*. Princeton: Princeton University, 2008.

Campo, Juan Eduardo. *Encyclopedia of Islam*. New York, NY: Facts On File, 2009.

Cook, Michael, ed. *The new Cambridge history of Islam*. Cambridge; NY: Cambridge University, 2010.

Dallal, Ahmad S. *Islam, science, and the challenge of history*. New Haven, CT: Yale University, 2010.

Denny, Frederick Mathewson. *An introduction to Islam*. Upper Saddle River, NJ: Pearson Prentice Hall, 2011.

Elias, Jamal, ed. *Key themes for the study of Islam*. Oxford: Oneworld, 2010.

Esposito, John L. *Islam: the straight path*. New York: Oxford University, 2011.

Hafez, Sherine. *An Islam of her own: reconsidering religion and secularism in women's Islamic movements*. New York and London: New York University, 2011.

Halverson, Jeffry R. *Theology and creed in Sunni Islam: the Muslim Brotherhood, Ash'arism, and political Sunnism*. New York: Palgrave Macmillan, 2010.

Hirji, Zulfikar, ed. *Diversity and pluralism in Islam: historical and contemporary discourses amongst Muslims*. London; New York: I. B. Tauris Publishers; London: In association with the Institute of Ismaili Studies; New York: Distributed in the U.S. and Canada exclusively by Palgrave Macmillan, 2010.

Michel, Thomas F. *A Christian view of Islam: essays on dialogue*. Maryknoll, NY: Orbis Books, 2010.

Renard, John. *Friends of God: Islamic images of piety, commitment and servanthood*. Berkeley: University of California Press, 2008.

Renard, John. *Islam and Christianity: theological themes in comparative perspective*. Berkeley: University of California, 2011.

Renard, John, ed. and trans. *Tales of God's friends: Islamic hagiography in translation*. Berkeley: University of California Press, 2009.

Sachedina, Abdulaziz A. *Islam and the challenge of human rights*. Oxford; New York: Oxford University, 2009.

Shepard, William E. *Introducing Islam*. London; New York: Routledge, 2009.

Smith, Jane I. *Islam in America*. New York, NY: Columbia University, 2010.

Sonn, Tamara. *Islam: a brief history*. Chichester, West Sussex, UK; Maldon, MA: Wiley-Blackwell, 2010.

Volpi, Frédéric. *Political Islam observed: disciplinary perspectives*. New York: Columbia University, 2010.

Woodward, Mark R. *Java, Indonesia and Islam*. Dordrecht; New York: Springer, 2011.

Yilmaz, Hakan, and Çagla E. Aykaç, eds. *Perceptions of Islam in Europe: culture, identity and the Muslim "other."* London: Tauris Academic Studies, 2010.

Hinduism

Bhaskarananda, Swami. *The essentials of Hinduism: a comprehensive overview of the world's oldest religion*. 2nd ed. Seattle: Viveka, 2002.

Copley, Antony, ed. *Hinduism in public and private: reform, Hindutva, gender, and Sampraday*. New Delhi; New York: Oxford University, 2003.

Cush, Denise, Catherine Robinson, and Michael York. *Encyclopedia of Hinduism*. New York: Routledge, 2008.

Denton, Lynn Teskey. *Female ascetics in Hinduism*. ed, Steven Collins. Albany: State University of New York, 2004.

Hawley, John Stratton, and Vasudha Narayanan, eds. *The life of Hinduism*. Berkeley: University of California, 2006.

Jacobsen, Knut A., Helene Basu, Angelika Malinar, and Vasudha Narayanan, eds. *Brill's encyclopedia of Hinduism*. Leiden; Boston: Brill, 2009.

Johnson, W. J. *A dictionary of Hinduism*. 1st ed. New York: Oxford University, 2010.

Klostermaier, Klaus K. *A survey of Hinduism*. 3rd ed. Albany: State University of New York, 2007.

Klostermaier, Klaus K. *Hinduism: a beginner's guide*. Oxford: Oneworld, 2008.

Llewellyn , J. E., ed. *Defining Hinduism: a reader*. New York: Routledge, 2005.

Long, Jeffery D. *A vision for Hinduism: beyond Hindu nationalism*. London; New York: I.B. Tauris; New York: In the United States and Canada distributed by Palgrave Macmillan, 2007.

Michaels, Axel. *Hinduism: past and present*. Princeton: Princeton University, 2004.

Narayanan, Vasudha. *Hinduism: origins, beliefs, practices, holy texts, sacred places*. New York: Oxford University, 2004.

Nicholson, Andrew J. *Unifying Hinduism: philosophy and identity in Indian intellectual history*. New York: Columbia University, 2010.

Olson, Carl. *The many colors of Hinduism: a thematic-historical introduction.* New Brunswick, NJ: Rutgers University, 2007.

Rodrigues, Hillary. *Introducing Hinduism.* New York; London: Routledge, 2006.

Sharma, Arvind. *Hinduism and human rights: a conceptual approach.* New Delhi; New York: Oxford University, 2004.

Sharma, Arvind. *Hinduism and its sense of history.* New Delhi; New York: Oxford University, 2003.

Sharma, Arvind. *Hinduism as a missionary religion.* Albany: State University of New York, 2011.

Stoddart, William. *Hinduism and its spiritual masters.* Louisville, KY: Fons Vitae, 2006.

Sugirtharajah, Sharada. *Imagining Hinduism: a postcolonial perspective.* London; New York: Routledge, 2003.

Whaling, Frank. *Understanding Hinduism.* Edinburgh: Dunedin Academic, 2010.

Williams, Raymond Brady. *An introduction to Swaminarayan Hinduism.* Cambridge, UK; New York: Cambridge University, 2001.

Buddhism

Borup, Jørn. *Japanese Rinzai Zen Buddhism: Myoshinji, a living religion.* Leiden; Boston: Brill, 2008.

Burnouf, Eugène. *Introduction to the history of Indian Buddhism.* trans. Katia Buffetrille and Donald S. Lopez Jr. Chicago: University of Chicago, 2010.

Gregory, Peter N., and Susanne Mrozik, eds. *Women practicing Buddhism: American experience.* Boston: Wisdom Publications, 2008.

Harris, Ian Charles. *Cambodian Buddhism: history and practice.* Honolulu: University of Hawaii, 2005.

Hershock, Peter D. *Chan Buddhism.* Honolulu: University of Hawaii, 2005.

Keown, Damien, and contributors Stephen Hodge, Charles Jones, Paola Tinti. *A dictionary of Buddhism.* Oxford: Oxford University, 2004.

Kinnard, Jacob N. *The emergence of Buddhism: classical traditions in contemporary perspective.* Minneapolis: Fortress, 2011.

Leidy, Denise Patry. *The art of Buddhism: an introduction to its history and meaning.* Boston: Shambhala; Enfield: Publishers Group UK [distributor], 2009.

LeVine, Sarah, and David N. Gellner. *Rebuilding Buddhism: the Theravada movement in twentieth-century Nepal.* Cambridge: Harvard University, 2005.

Mitchell, Donald W. *Buddhism: introducing the Buddhist experience.* 2nd ed. New York: Oxford University, 2008.

Mollier, Christine. *Buddhism and Taoism face to face: scripture, ritual, and iconographic exchange in medieval China.* Honolulu: University of Hawaii, 2008.

Olson, Carl. *Historical dictionary of Buddhism.* Lanham, MD: Scarecrow, 2009.

Porcu, Elisabetta. *Pure Land Buddhism in modern Japanese culture.* Leiden; Boston: Brill, 2008.

Prebish, Charles S., and Damien Keown. *Introducing Buddhism.* 2nd ed. London: Routledge, 2010.

Puri, Bharati. *Engaged Buddhism: the Dalai Lama's worldview.* New Delhi: Oxford University, 2006.

Reischauer, August Karl. *Studies in Japanese Buddhism.* Charleston, SC: BiblioLife, 2010.

Shah-Kazemi, Reza. *Common ground between Islam and Buddhism,* with an essay by Shaykh Hamza Yusuf; introduced by H. H. the Fourteenth Dalai Lama, H. R. H. Prince Ghazi bin Muhammad, Mohammad Hashim Kamali. Louisville, KY: Fons Vitae, 2010.

Stone, Jacqueline I., and Mariko Namba Walter, eds. *Death and the afterlife in Japanese Buddhism.* Honolulu: University of Hawaii, 2008.

Tarocco, Francesca. *The cultural practices of modern Chinese Buddhism: attuning the dharma.* London; New York: Routledge, 2007.

Tsomo, Karma Lekshe. *Buddhism through American women's eyes.* Ithaca, NY: Snow Lion Publications, 2010.

Williams, Paul. *Mahayana Buddhism: the doctrinal foundations.* 2nd ed. London; New York: Routledge, 2009.

Daoism

Bokenkamp, Stephen R. *Ancestors and anxiety: Daoism and the birth of rebirth in China.* Berkeley: University of California, 2007.

Despeux, Catherine, and Livia Kohn. *Women in Daoism.* 1st ed. Dunedin, FL: Three Pines, 2005.

Girardot, N. J., James Miller, and Liu Xiaogan. *Daoism and ecology: ways within a cosmic landscape.* Cambridge, MA: Center for the Study of World Religions, Harvard Divinity School: Distributed by Harvard University, 2001.

Kohn, Livia. *Cosmos and community: the ethical dimension of Daoism.* Cambridge, MA: Three Pines, 2004.

Kohn, Livia. *Daoism and Chinese culture.* Cambridge, MA: Three Pines, 2001.

Kohn, Livia, ed. *Daoism handbook.* Leiden; Boston: Brill, 2000.

Kohn, Livia. *Introducing Daoism.* London; New York: Routledge, 2009.

Komjathy, Louis. *Cultivating perfection: mysticism and self-transformation in early Quanzhen Daoism.* Leiden; Boston: Brill, 2007.

Littlejohn, Ronnie. *Daoism: an introduction.* London; New York: I. B. Tauris & Co.; New York: Distributed in the United States and Canada exclusively by Palgrave Macmillan, 2009.

Miller, James. *Daoism: a short introduction.* Oxford: Oneworld, 2003.

Moeller, Hans-Georg. *Daoism explained: from the dream of the butterfly to the fishnet allegory.* Chicago, IL: Open Court, 2004.

Pregadio, Fabrizio. *Great clarity: Daoism and alchemy in early medieval China.* Stanford, CA: Stanford University, 2006.

Raz, Gil. *The emergence of Daoism: creation of tradition.* London: Routledge, 2009.

Wang, Yi'e. *Daoism in China: an introduction.* Trans. Zeng Chuanhui; ed. Adam Chanzit. Warren, CT: Floating World, 2006.

Zhuangzi. *The wisdom of Zhuang Zi on Daoism.* Trans. with annotations and commentaries Chung Wu. New York: Peter Lang, 2008.

Confucianism

Bell, Daniel A. *China's new Confucianism: politics and everyday life in a changing society.* Princeton; Woodstock: Princeton University, 2010.

Berthrong, John H. *Confucianism: a short introduction.* Oxford: Oneworld, 2000.

Bol, Peter Kees. *Neo-Confucianism in history.* Cambridge, MA: Harvard University Asia Center: Distributed by Harvard University, 2008.

DeBary, William Theodore, and Tu Wei Ming, eds. *Confucianism and human rights.* New York: Columbia University, 1998.

Elman, Benjamin A., John B.Duncan and Herman Ooms, eds. *Rethinking Confucianism: past and present in China, Japan, Korea, and Vietnam.* Los Angeles: UCLA Asian Pacific Monograph Series, 2002.

Goldin, Paul Rakita. *Confucianism.* Berkeley: University of California, 2011.

Huang, Siu-chi. *Essentials of Neo-Confucianism: eight major philosophers of the Song and Ming periods.* Westport, CT: Greenwood, 1999.

Littlejohn, Ronnie. *Confucianism: an introduction = Ru.* London; New York: I. B. Tauris, 2011.

Makeham, John, ed. *New Confucianism: a critical examination.* New York; Houndmills, England: Palgrave Macmillan, 2003.

Ng, On Cho. *Cheng-Zhu Confucianism in the early Qing: Li Guangdi (1642–1718) and Qing learning.* Albany: State University of New York, 2001.

Oldstone-Moore, Jennifer. *Confucianism: origins, beliefs, practices, holy texts, sacred places.* New York: Oxford University, 2002.

Rosenlee, Li-Hsiang Lisa. *Confucianism and women: a philosophical interpretation.* Albany: SUNY, 2006.

Taylor, Rodney Leon. *The illustrated encyclopedia of Confucianism.* New York: The Rosen Publishing Group, 2005.

Van de Weyer, Robert, ed. *366 readings from Taoism and Confucianism.* Cleveland, OH: Pilgrim; New Alresford, UK: A. James, 2000.

Yao, Xinzhong. *An introduction to Confucianism.* New York: Cambridge University, 2000.

Yao, Xinzhong, ed. *RoutledgeCurzon encyclopedia of Confucianism.* London; New York: RoutledgeCurzon, 2003.

Zhao, Yanxia. *Father and son in Confucianism and Christianity: a comparative study of Xunzi and Paul.* Brighton, UK; Portland, OR: Sussex Academic, 2007.

Shinto

Breen, John. *A new history of Shinto.* Chichester; Malden, MA: Wiley-Blackwell, 2010.

Breen, John and Mark Teeuwen, eds. *Shinto in history: ways of the kami.* Honolulu: University of Hawaii, 2000.

Harris, Victor, ed. *Shinto: the sacred art of ancient Japan.* London: British Museum, 2001.

Hay, Jeff, ed. *Shinto.* Farmington Hills, MI: Greenhaven, 2006.

Kasulis, Thomas P. *Shinto: the way home.* Honolulu: University of Hawaii, 2004.

Kato, Genchi. *A study of Shinto: the religion of the Japanese nation.* London: Routledge, 2011.

Littleton, C. Scott. *Shinto: origins, rituals, festivals, spirits, sacred places.* Oxford; New York: Oxford University, 2002.

Llewellyn, Ann. *Shinto Norito: A book of prayers.* Bloomington, IN: Trafford, 2006.

Nobutaka, Inoue, Itô Satoshi, Endo Jun, and Mori Mizue, eds. *Shinto, a short history.* Trans. and adapted by Mark Teeuwen and John Breen. London: New York: RoutledgeCurzon, 2004.

Picken, Stuart D. B. *Historical dictionary of Shinto.* 2nd ed. Lanham, MD: Scarecrow, 2011.

Picken, Stuart D. B. *Shinto meditations for revering the earth.* Foreword by Yukitaka Yamamoto. Berkeley, CA: Stone Bridge, 2002.

Rankin, Aidan. *Shinto: a celebration of life.* Brooklyn, NY: O Books 2011.

Reader, Ian. *Simple guides: Shinto.* London: Kuperard, 2008.

Yamakage, Motohisa. *The essence of Shinto: Japan's spiritual heart.* Translators Mineko S. Gillespie, Gerald L. Gillespie, Yoshitsugu Komuro; eds. Paul de Leeuw, Aidan Rankin. Tokyo; New York: Kodansha International, 2007.

Index

Note: (ill.) indicates photos and illustrations

N

Naga Panchami, 228
Nagarjuna, 247, 274
Nagasena, 244
Nakatomi clan, 412, 417, 443
Nakatsu-hime, 423
Nakir, 139
"Nakrathundi," 188 (ill.)
namarupa, 205
names, rectification of, 374
Nanak, 220
Nanda dynasty, 189
Nandi, 209–10
Nara period, 417, 437
Nara-simha, 193, 195
Nasrids, 132
nastika, 239
Nathan, 17, 19
Nation of Islam, 155–56
National Association of
    Shrine Priests, 417
National Learning Shinto
    (kokugaku), 412–14, 419,
    438, 440
nature, Daoist/CCT approach
    to, 309 (ill.), 309–10,
    325–26
Nature of the Gods (Cicero),
    70
Nazism, 11, 25, 32, 211
Nebuchadnezzar, King, 50
negi, 446
Nehemia, 3, 37
nei dan, 315
nenchu gyoji, 449
Neo-Confucianism
    about, 360–61
    founder of as sage, 382
    history of, 306, 364–65
    Kurozumi-kyo Shinto's
        relation to, 447
    meditation, 407
    movement, 396–97
    positive interaction with
        Daoism, 329
    sainthood, 395
    sects of, 387, 389
Neo-Daoism, 305, 330,
    358–59
Neoplatonism, 70
Nero, 68
Nestorians, 96
Netsuke, 423
New Food Festival, 453

New Testament
    beatitudes in the, 85
    beginnings of Christianity,
        59
    books of the, 61–62, 67
    as Christian exegesis of
        Hebrew scriptures, 64
    creedal statements in the,
        73
    dreams in the, 78
    end of times in the, 82
    exorcism, 116
    Islamic prophet in the,
        126
    Jesus as Messiah, 18
    Jesus' resurrection, 110
    Paul's letters in the, 66
    saints in the, 105
    same length as the Qur'an,
        124
    teaching peace, 84
    theology missing from the,
        71
    women in the, 97
New Year, Chinese, 340
Ni, Mount, 353
Nicene Creed, 73–74, 96, 133
Nichiren, 247, 276, 281, 285,
    288
Nichiren-shu Buddhism, 276,
    296
Nicholas V, Pope, 84
Nicodemus, 68
Night Journey and Ascension,
    123, 170, 172, 332
Night of Forgiveness, 173
Night of Power, 170–71
nigimitama, 426
Nihon Shoki. See *Nihongi
    (Chronicles of Japan)*
*Nihongi (Chronicles of
    Japan)*, 412, 414, 418, 420,
    430
niki, 422
Nimbarka, 214
Nimbarka Hinduism, 223
Nimrod, 138
Nine Palaces, 325
Ninigi, 421
Nirmala Sundari, 221
nirvana
    attaining in this life, 244,
        284
    Buddha's entry into, 267,
        295

calendar starts with
    Buddha's entry into,
    286–87
comparison to non-action,
    273
definition of, 260
as final freedom, 249
and gender roles, 273
Guan Yin's entry into, 289
in afterlife, 256
in Buddhism, 196
site of Buddha's entry into
    as holy, 269
as ultimate goal, 270
Nirvana Day, 286
No, 461
Noah, 18, 20, 136, 174
non-action, 273, 317
Non-Form, 256
nonself, Buddhist belief in,
    250, 260, 283
Northern Dipper's Extension
    of Life, 350
number symbolism in reli-
    gion
    Daoism/CCT, 325
    Judaism, 27–28
nuns, Buddhist, 272 (ill.), 282
Nyingmapa Buddhism, 276

O

objects used in prayer, ritual
    Buddhism, 266, 294, 294
        (ill.)
    Christianity, 112–13
    Confucianism/CIT, 404
        (ill.), 404–5
    Daoism/CCT, 323 (ill.), 345
        (ill.), 345–46
    Hinduism, 203 (ill.), 232
    Islam, 178 (ill.), 178–79
    Judaism, 28 (ill.)
    Shinto, 434 (ill.), 435 (ill.),
        457
Obon Matsuri, 289, 453
observances, regular reli-
    gious. See holidays and reg-
    ular observances, religious
officials, religious. See spe-
    cialists, religious ritual
Okunchi, 453
Old Man of the Mountain, 348